Global Strategy

Mike W. Peng

Provost's Distinguished Professor of Global Strategy
University of Texas at Dallas

THOMSON
™
SOUTH-WESTERN

Australia · Canada · Mexico · Singapore · Spain · United Kingdom · United States

Global Strategy

Mike W. Peng

Vice President/Editorial Director:
Jack W. Calhoun

Vice President/Editor-in-Chief:
Dave Shaut

Senior Publisher:
Melissa S. Acuña

Executive Editor:
John Szilagyi

Sr. Developmental Editor:
Mardell Toomey

Marketing Manager:
Jacquelyn Carrillo

Manager of Technology, Editorial:
Vicky True

Technology Project Editor:
Kristen Meere

Media Editor:
Karen L. Schaffer

Production Editors:
Daniel C. Plofchan, Lora Arduser

Manufacturing Coordinator:
Doug Wilke

Art Director:
Chris A. Miller

Production House:
Interactive Composition Corporation

Cover and Internal Designer:
Lou Ann Thesing

Cover Illustration:
©Getty Images

Printer:
QuebecorWorld—Taunton
Taunton, MA

Preface

My goal in writing *Global Strategy* has been to set a new standard for strategic management and international business textbooks in general and global strategy textbooks in particular. This book endeavors to satisfy the needs of three types of undergraduate or MBA courses: (1) global or international strategy courses, (2) strategic management courses (especially those taught by internationally oriented professors), and (3) international business courses (especially those taught by strategically oriented instructors).

At present, the limited number of global or international strategy textbooks almost exclusively focus on how to manage larger, multinational enterprises (MNEs), which primarily come from and compete in developed economies. While MNEs are important, such a focus ignores the facts (1) that many smaller, entrepreneurial firms have also aggressively internationalized recently and (2) that MNEs often have to compete in emerging economies, which increasingly nurture strong local competitors. Most "mainstream" strategic management textbooks, despite often paying lip service to the hot theme of globalization, contain only one chapter on "international strategy." The implication is that other chapters in strategy textbooks do not need to deal with international topics. This, of course, is not realistic in today's global economy. Most international business textbooks do have a section (containing several chapters) on international strategy. However, they always carry a wider coverage of major business functions such as marketing, operations, finance, and accounting. Many international business professors, who often have some background in strategy, have neither the time nor the necessary expertise to cover such a wide variety of topics. Consequently, their efforts to make their international business courses more strategic are often frustrated.

In response, *Global Strategy* is written to offer a number of new perspectives. These include (1) a broadened definition of "global strategy," (2) a comprehensive and innovative coverage, (3) an in-depth and consistent explanation of cutting-edge research, and (4) an interesting and accessible way to engage students.

A BROADENED DEFINITION OF "GLOBAL STRATEGY"

In this book, "global strategy" is defined not as MNE strategy only, but as "strategy around the globe." While emphasizing international strategy, we do not focus on it exclusively. Just like "international business" is about "business" (in addition to being "international"), "global strategy" is most fundamentally about "strategy" before being "global." Most global strategy and international business textbooks take the foreign entrant's (typically the MNE's) perspective, often dealing with issues such as how to enter foreign markets and how to select alliance partners. Important as these issues are, they only cover one side of international business, namely, the foreign side. The other side, naturally, is how domestic firms compete against each other and against foreign entrants. Failing to understand the "other side," at best, captures only one side of the coin.

A COMPREHENSIVE AND INNOVATIVE COVERAGE

With a broadened definition of "global strategy," this book covers the strategies of both large MNEs and small entrepreneurial firms, both foreign entrants and domestic firms, and firms from both developed economies and emerging economies. As a result, this text offers the most comprehensive and innovative coverage of global strategy topics available in the market. In short, this is the world's first *global*, global-strategy book. Unique features include:

- A chapter on institutions, cultures, and ethics (Chapter 4) and a focus on the emerging institution-based view of strategy (in addition to the traditional industry- and resource-based views) throughout the book
- A chapter on entrepreneurship (Chapter 5), especially its internationalization aspects
- A chapter on global competitive dynamics (Chapter 8), including substantial discussions on cartel, antitrust, and antidumping issues ignored by other textbooks
- A chapter on both product and geographic diversification (Chapter 9), which is the first time these crucial aspects of corporate strategies appear in the same textbook chapter
- A chapter on corporate governance around the world (Chapter 11), which is the first time both the principal-agent and principal-principal conflicts are given equal "air time"
- A chapter on corporate social responsibility (Chapter 12), an increasingly important area of interest around the world
- A geographically comprehensive coverage, not only covering firms from the developed economies of the Triad (North America, Western Europe, and Japan), but also those from emerging economies of the world (including Africa, Asia, and Latin America)
- A consistent theme on ethics, which is not only highlighted in Chapters 4 and 12 but also throughout all chapters in the form of ethics-based critical discussion questions

AN IN-DEPTH AND CONSISTENT EXPLANATION

The breadth of the field poses a challenge to textbook authors. My respect and admiration for the diversity and insights of the field has increased tremendously as research for this book progressed. To provide an in-depth explanation, I have systematically drawn on the full range of the latest research. Specifically, *every* article in each issue published in the past fifteen years in leading scholarly journals such as the *Academy of Management Journal, Academy of Management Review, Journal of International Business Studies,* and *Strategic Management Journal* has been systematically read and coded. Many forthcoming publications, working papers, and doctoral dissertations have also been consulted and cited. Consequently, the endnotes after each chapter are lengthy and comprehensive. While not every article in the literature is cited, I am confident that I have left no major streams of research untouched. Feel free to check the Author Index to verify this claim.

Given the breadth of the field, it is easy to lose focus. To combat this tendency, I have endeavored to provide a consistent set of frameworks in *all* chapters. This is done in three ways. First, I focus on the four most fundamental questions in strategic management raised by Richard Rumelt, David Teece, and Dan Schendel.[1] These are (1) Why do firms differ? (2) How do firms behave? (3) What determines the scope of the firm? and (4) What determines the international success and failure of firms? These four questions are first discussed in Chapter 1 and then revisited in every chapter throughout the book. A particular emphasis is on the fourth question on firms' international performance, which has been argued to be the leading question guiding international business practice and research.[2]

Another way to combat the tendency to lose sight of the "forest" while scrutinizing various "trees" is to consistently draw on the three leading perspectives on strategy, namely, industry-, resource-, and institution-based views. In *every* chapter on business-level and corporate-level strategies, a comprehensive model based on these perspectives is developed and discussed at length.

Finally, I have written a "Debates and Extensions" section for *every* chapter except Chapter 1 (which is a debate in itself). Virtually all textbooks uncritically present knowledge "as is" and ignore the fact that the field is alive with a number of debates. Because students are often told "there are no right or wrong answers" and the debates drive practice and research ahead, it is imperative that students be exposed to various cutting-edge debates and be encouraged to form their own views when engaging in these debates.

---

[1] R. Rumelt, D. Teece, & D. Schendel (eds.), 1994, *Fundamental Issues in Strategy: A Research Agenda,* Boston: Harvard Business School Press.

[2] M. W. Peng, 2004, Identifying the big question in international business research, *Journal of International Business Studies,* 35 (2): 99–108.

AN INTERESTING AND ACCESSIBLE WAY TO ENGAGE STUDENTS

Students often find theories dry and boring. However, they usually enjoy stories. Learning is easier, better, and more fun if the subject matter is communicated in an interesting and accessible way. It is the author's responsibility to highlight the theories behind the stories. I have developed a number of tactics to engage students:

- Every chapter starts with an **Opening Case** that draws students into the plot. The Web sites for all companies mentioned in the Opening and Closing Cases as well as Strategy in Action boxes are available for additional research.

- After the Opening Case, every chapter starts with a series of questions.

- I have woven a large number of interesting anecdotes as examples into the text. In addition to business anecdotes, "non-traditional" examples range from ancient Chinese military writings to Roman empire's import quotas, from quotes from *Anna Karenina* to mutually assured destruction (MAD) strategy during the Cold War. Popular movies such as *007: The World is Not Enough, Lion King, Star Wars, The Full Monty, The Hunt for Red October,* and *The Rising Sun* are also discussed——I believe the first time they are introduced in a business textbook. Overall, in over 90% of the main substantive paragraphs, there is at least one example in the paragraph.

- Every chapter contains a number of **Strategy in Action** boxes (with company Web sites), which single out interesting examples as "mini-cases" to enhance learning.

- Every chapter ends with a **Closing Case** (with company Web sites) with discussion questions.

- Every chapter also contains a number of critical discussion questions to facilitate open-ended discussions. At least one and sometimes two or three of these questions in *every* chapter focus on ethics, driving home the point that ethics is a theme that cuts across all chapters and is not necessarily limited to Chapters 4 and 12.

- After each of the three main sections, there are a number of shorter **Video Cases** (drawn from CNN) and longer **Integrative Cases.**

SUPPORT MATERIALS

A full set of support materials is available for adopting instructors. The **IRCD (ISBN: 0-324-30610-5)** includes the instructor's manual, prepared by Jude Rathburn of University of Wisconsin–River Falls. The instructor's manual represents one of the most helpful instructor's aids available. Comprehensive teaching materials, including chapter overviews, chapter outlines, instructor's notes, and suggested answers to end-of-chapter questions, are provided for every chapter. Additional instructor support includes case notes and suggested research topics along with an integrative case guide prepared by myself. A PowerPoint slide presentation by David Ahlstrom of The Chinese University of Hong Kong covers all the main concepts and terms, including questions to help generate classroom discussion.

CNN Global Strategy Video (ISBN: 0-324-30611-3) features segments from current CNN news clips highlighting many of the companies discussed in the text. I have written a video guide to accompany the videos to help instructors better integrate exciting video content in the classroom. Video cases are presented at the end of each part in the text.

ACKNOWLEDGMENTS

Undertaking a project of this magnitude makes me owe a great deal of debt—intellectual, professional, and personal—to many people, whose contributions I would like to acknowledge. Intellectually, I have been greatly influenced by Charles Hill (University of Washington), my former Ph.D. advisor. Charles' market-leading textbooks in strategic management and international business have inspired me to write this text at the intersection of these two fields. I am also indebted to other leading textbook authors such as Jay Barney (Ohio State University), Michael Hitt (Texas A&M University), Bob Hoskisson (Arizona State University), Mike Pustay (Texas A&M University), and Oded Shenkar (Ohio State University), whose scholarship and friendship often provide much needed guiding light for my own journey to complete this book. At Ohio State, I thank my colleagues Sharon Alvarez, Jay Barney, Venkat Bendapudi, Jay Dial, Jill Ellingson, Jeff Ford, Rob Heneman, Steve Hills, Roy Lewicki, Mona Makhija, Michael Leiblein, Ray Noe, Arnon Reichers, Jeff Reuer, Marc Sandver, Oded Shenkar, Judy Tansky, John Wanous, and the leadership team—David Greenberger (department chair), Joseph Alutto (dean), and Steve Mangum (senior associate dean)—for creating a supportive intellectual environment. In addition, this research has also been supported, in part, by a National Science Foundation Faculty Career Grant (CAREER-SES-0238820).

At Thomson South-Western, I thank John Szilagyi, executive editor, for proactively singling me out as someone who could potentially master the art of textbook writing even *before* I had tenure. I really appreciate such a vote of confidence. I also thank Mardell Toomey, senior developmental editor, for skillfully managing the process of writing, reviewing, revising, and solving a number of problems along the way. Dan Pflofchan, senior production editor, was also very diligent in his work on the text. I also appreciate Lora Arduser, production editor, for seeing the project through to completion. Finally, I want to acknowledge the heroic efforts of Karyn Morrison, freelance permissions specialist, and Jennifer Crotteau, project manager, Interactive Composition Corporation (and her team of unsung heroes in India) for helping turn this manuscript into a book.

In the academic community, I am fortunate to be able to count on a number of friends, who informally read and critiqued my proposal and/or certain chapters: David Ahlstrom (Chinese University of Hong Kong), Trevor Buck (Loughborough

University), Jonathan Doh (Villanova University), Igor Filatotchev (King's College London), Seung-Hyun Lee (University of Texas at Dallas), Klaus Meyer (Copenhagen Business School), Bill Wan (Thunderbird), and Michael Young (Chinese University of Hong Kong). Three practitioner friends, Charles Cao (Alcatel Paris), Ken Chee (State Teachers Retirement System of Ohio), and John Cullivan (Cardinal Health), also kindly read and commented on certain chapters and cases.

Most of my ideas in this book have been classroom tested in Beijing, Columbus, Hanoi, Hong Kong, Honolulu, Memphis, and Seattle, involving not only under-graduate and MBA students, but also executives and faculty training participants. Greg Gregoriades and Bakshi Mamta (Ohio State MBA 2003) critiqued the book proposal. In addition, a number of research assistants have worked on the book and made it better. They are Yi Jiang, Daniel Sangcheol Song, Tara Wedwaldt, Qi Zhou, and David Zhu. I really appreciate their help.

A total of 24 colleagues from Australia, Denmark, Hong Kong (China), Israel, and the United States have kindly contributed case materials. Many of them are experts who are located in or come from the countries in which these cases take place. They are:

- David Ahlstrom, *Chinese University of Hong Kong, Hong Kong, China*
- Uri Ben-Zio, *Ben-Gurion University, Israel*
- Garry Bruton, *Texas Christian University, USA*
- Asda Chintakananda, *University of North Carolina at Chapel Hill, USA*
- Mauro Guillén, *The Wharton School, University of Pennsylvania, USA*
- Gdaliahu Harel, *Technion Institute of Technology, Israel*
- Yi Jiang, *Fisher College of Business, The Ohio State University, USA*
- Aldas Pranas Krianciunas, *Purdue University, USA*
- Peter Liesch, *University of Queensland, Australia*
- Yuan Lu, *Chinese University of Hong Kong, Hong Kong, China*
- Mona Makhija, *Fisher College of Business, The Ohio State University, USA*
- Daniel McCarthy, *Northeastern University, USA*
- Sara McGaughey, *Copenhagen Business School, Denmark*
- Klaus Meyer, *Copenhagen Business School, Denmark*
- Duncan Poulson, *University of Tasmania, Australia*
- Sheila Puffer, *Northeastern University, USA*
- Charles Stevens, *Fisher College of Business, The Ohio State University, USA*
- Qingjiu (Tom) Tao, *Lehigh University, USA*
- Tony W. Tong, *State University of New York at Buffalo, USA*
- Adrian Tschoegel, *The Wharton School, University of Pennsylvania, USA*
- Tara Wedwaldt, *Fisher College of Business, The Ohio State University, USA*

- Anne York, *University of Nebraska at Omaha, USA*
- Michael Young, *Chinese University of Hong Kong, Hong Kong, China*
- David H. Zhu, *University of Michigan, USA*

My thanks also go to the 15 reviewers, who provided excellent and timely feedback and helped shape this book into a better product. They are

- David Ahlstrom, *Chinese University of Hong Kong*
- Jeff Belsky, *Pittsburgh Technical Institute*
- Darla Domke Damonte, *Coastal University*
- M. D. Giambattista, *University of Washington*
- Michael Hergert, *San Diego State University*
- Andrew Inkpen, *Thunderbird Graduate School of International Management*
- John A. Kilpatrick, *Idaho State University*
- Klaus Meyer, *Copenhagen Business School*
- Mark Milstein, *University of North Carolina at Chapel Hill*
- Ed Murphy, *Nova Southeastern University*
- Laura Poppo, *University of Vermont*
- Jude Rathburn, *University of Wisconsin–River Falls*
- William Ritchie, *Florida Gulf Coast University*
- William D. Roering, *Michigan State University*
- Carol Sanchez, *Grand Valley State University*

Last, but by no means least, I thank my wife Agnes, my daughter Grace, and my son James—to whom this book is dedicated. When the editor first contacted me in November 2002, Grace was only two months old and there was no James. Now the book is finished, James is four months young , and Grace is a two-year-old. Both are very healthy, happy, and quiet babies, each crying for no more than 5-10 minutes everyday and being very cooperative. Grace now knows when "Daddy write book," she is not supposed to come to hug daddy (although she can hardly resist the temptation) and James now smiles back. As a third-generation professor in my family, I can't help but wonder whether one (or both) of them will become a fourth-generation professor someday. A great deal of thanks also go to my two in-laws, who came to help when Grace was born, and my mother (a retired professor), who rose to the challenge when James showed up. Without such instrumental help, the writing of this book would have been significantly delayed. To all of you, my thanks and my love.

MWP

October 10, 2004

To Agnes, Grace, and James

About the Author

Mike W. Peng is the Provost's Distinguished Professor of Global Strategy at the University of Texas at Dallas, which specifically created this chair position to attract him to join its faculty in 2005. He holds a PhD from the University of Washington, Seattle, where he started his teaching career. Prior to joining UTD, Professor Peng had been on the faculty at the Ohio State University, Chinese University of Hong Kong, and University of Hawaii. In addition, he has held visiting or courtesy appointments in China (Xian Jiaotong University, Sun Yat-sen University, and Cheung Kong Graduate School of Business), Denmark (Copenhagen Business School), Great Britain (University of Nottingham), Hong Kong (Hong Kong Polytechnic University), Vietnam (Foreign Trade University), as well as the United States (University of Memphis, University of Michigan, and Seattle Pacific University). On a worldwide basis, Professor Peng has taught students at all levels—undergraduate, MBA, PhD, EMBA, executive, and faculty training programs.

Professor Peng is widely regarded as one of the most prolific and most influential scholars in global strategy. Truly global in scope, his research focuses on firm strategies in regions such as Asia, Central and Eastern Europe, and North America, covering countries such as China, Hong Kong, Japan, Russia, South Korea, Thailand, and the United States. He has published over 40 articles in leading academic journals and authored three books—the first two are *Behind the Success and Failure of US Export Intermediaries* (1998) and *Business Strategies in Transition Economies* (2000). *Global Strategy* is his third book, which is being translated into Chinese in 2006. He is currently writing his fourth book, *Global Business* (Thomson, scheduled for 2008 release).

Professor Peng is active in leadership positions in his field. At the Strategic Management Society, he is the first elected Program Chair of the Global Strategy Interest Group (2005-07). At the Academy of Management, he is in charge of the Junior Faculty Consortium for the International Management Division at the Atlanta meetings (2006). At the Academy of International Business, he is a Co-Program Chair for the Research Frontiers Conference in San Diego (2006). Professor Peng has served on the editorial boards of the *Academy of Management Journal, Academy of Management Review, Journal of International Business Studies,* and *Strategic Management Journal.* He has also guest edited the *Journal of International Business Studies* and *Journal of Management Studies.* At present, he is the editor-in-chief of the *Asia Pacific Journal of Management.*

Professor Peng is also an active faculty trainer and consultant. He has provided on the-job-training to over 70 professors. He has consulted for organizations such as BankOne, Berlitz International, Chinese Chamber of Commerce, Hong Kong Research Grants Council, National Science Foundation, Nationwide Insurance, Ohio Polymer Association, US-China Business Council, and The World Bank. His practitioner oriented research has been published in the *Harvard Business Review, Academy of Management Executive,* and *China Business Review.*

Professor Peng has received numerous awards and recognitions. He has been recognized as a Foreign Expert by the Chinese government. One of his *Academy of Management Review* papers has been found to be a "new hot paper" (based on citations) representing the *entire* field of Economics and Business by the Institute for Scientific Information (ISI), which publishes the Social Sciences Citation Index (SSCI). He is a recipient of the Scholarly Contribution Award from the International Association for Chinese Management Research (IACMR). He has also been quoted in *Newsweek, The Exporter Magazine, Business Times* (Singapore), *Voice of America,* and *The World Bank.*

In addition, Professor Peng's high-impact, high-visibility research has also attracted significant external funding, totaling more than half a million dollars from sources such as the (US) National Science Foundation, Hong Kong Research Grants Council, and Taiwan National Science Council. At present, his research is funded by a five-year, prestigious National Science Foundation CAREER Grant (formerly known as the Young Investigator Award). At $423,000, this is the largest grant the NSF has awarded to a business school faculty member.

Brief Contents

Contents

chapter 4 **Emphasizing institutions, cultures, and ethics 106**

part III   **Integrative cases**

part I

Foundations of Global Strategy

chapter I

Strategizing Around the Globe

Outline

- A *global* global-strategy book
- Why study global strategy?
- What is strategy?
- Fundamental issues in strategy
- What is global strategy?
- What is globalization?
- Global strategy and globalization at a crossroads
- Organization of the book

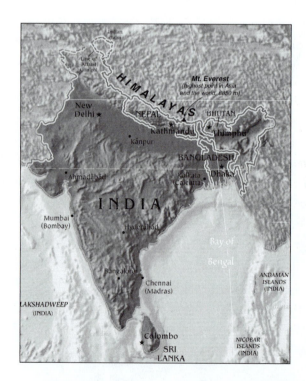

Opening Case: Competing In and Out of India

India's recent rise as a leading global player in information technology (IT) and related services has been phenomenal. The revenues of Indian IT firms reached $6.2 billion in 2003, up from $500 million in the mid-1990s. Their future growth is estimated at a compound annual rate of 34 percent until 2008, by which time they may total $77 billion. Having started with two basic functions, software programming and call centers, the range of work being performed by Indian firms now includes medical record transcribing (and in some cases providing diagnoses as well), desktop publishing, tax return filing, insurance claims processing, presentation preparing, and the like. As boundaries between software, IT services, and business processes become blurred, the term "IT" seems too limiting. A new jargon, "business process outsourcing" (BPO), is emerging.

Such growth is all the more remarkable considering that India did not initiate major market-opening reforms until 1991, and unlike China, which has become a manufacturing powerhouse, India missed the boat in attracting significant foreign direct investment (FDI). Instead of the usual progression from low-skill manufacturing to higher, value-added products and services (as exemplified by Singapore and South Korea), India is the first major emerging economy that has directly built its international competitiveness in services.

Why has the Indian IT (or BPO) industry emerged as a global powerhouse (second only to the United States)? The nature of the industry, the capabilities of the Indian firms, and the larger institutional environment governing competition in and out of India combine to provide some compelling explanations. First, the nature of this industry—meeting the IT-related service needs of multinational enterprises (MNEs) such as Boeing (http://www.boeing.com), DaimlerChrysler (http://www.daimlerchrysler.com), and Lehman Brothers (http://www.lehman.com)—dictates an intense rivalry among service providers. The usual crowd, which includes Accenture (http://www.accenture.com), PricewaterhouseCoopers (http://www.pwcglobal.com), IBM (http://www.ibm.com), and EDS (http://www.eds.com), has been joined by a number of Indian firms. For example, Tata Consultancy Services (TCS, http://www.tcs.com), Infosys (http://www.infosys.com), Wipro (http://www.wipro.com), Satyam (http://www.satyam.com), and HCL (http://www.hclinfosystems.com) provide excellent quality combined with significantly lower costs—often on the magnitude of 25 to 50 percent lower than Western rivals. For some, although not all, projects, a $10,000-a-year programmer in Bangalore can perform the same, or sometimes better, work as a $60,000-a-year programmer in Silicon Valley. Many Indian firms first entered the industry as subcontractors to overloaded Western firms during the Y2K software crisis at the turn of the millennium. Since then, they have expanded their responsibilities to include core IT support. For example, Indian engineers at Wipro have two screens on their desks—one is of their own system while the other mirrors another professional's at Lehman Brothers. Consequently, any glitches are monitored and fixed from India. Now, some of the leading Indian firms aspire to become higher value-added and better paid "full service providers."

Indian firms possess a number of valuable, unique, and hard-to-imitate capabilities. The ten-hour time difference between the United States and India allows US clients to offer twenty-four-hour service by switching to Indian workers during the American night. The fact that they have an English-speaking staff makes it more difficult for non-English-speaking competitors from Brazil, China, and Poland to win service contracts from Western MNEs. Scrambling to stem the onslaught of Indian firms, some American companies, including Accenture, PricewaterhouseCoopers, IBM, and EDS, have fought back by setting up their own subsidiaries in India. During 2004, for instance, Accenture and IBM each hired 4,000 people in India. To combat this, a number of Indian firms have invested heavily in Western countries, particularly the United States, in an effort to be more responsive to current customers and gain face time with future clients. In the process, these Indian firms, which have become a new breed of MNEs, aspire to be "less Indian." For instance, Wipro plans to increase the proportion of non-Indian staff, from 3 percent of a total of 13,000 now, to 15 percent in the next five years. It recently set up its second corporate headquarters in Santa Clara, California, the heart of Silicon Valley.

Institutionally, India's post-1991 economic reforms have made an open, competitive, and entrepreneurial environment possible. Beyond India, the larger, global environment in favor of globalization has helped. However, as the winds change, the phenomenal success of Indian firms has more recently been under attack in the West, both formally and informally. Formally, in order to protect jobs, a number of American states have recently passed laws that ban Indian firms from being awarded official contracts. Informally, the backlash is more widespread. Facing the prospects of significant job losses, numerous politicians, journalists, union activists, and displaced employees in developed economies are discontented (see, for example, stories posted at http://www.yourjobisgoingtoindia.com) and demand that protectionist action be taken. In addition to such political backlash, the Indian IT (BPO) firms are also facing significant international competition. In the short term, the Philippines, with its large supply of low-wage, English-speaking professionals, seems determined to eat some of India's lunch. Longer term, Bulgaria, China, and Romania are emerging as potential global contenders. For executives at Indian IT (BPO) firms and their (current and would-be) client firms, learning how to strategize in a cost efficient, quality satisfactory, and politically correct manner is job number one.

Sources: Based on (1) S. Baker & M. Kripalani, 2004, Will outsourcing hurt America's supremacy? Business Week, March 1: 85–94; (2) Economist, 2003, America's pain, India's gain, January 11: 57; (3) Economist, 2003, An American in Bangalore, February 8: 64; (4) Economist, 2003, Backroom deals, February 22: 70–71; (5) Economist, 2004, The remote future, February 21: 14–15; (6) Y. Huang & T. Khanna, 2003, Can India overtake China? Foreign Policy, July-August: 74–81; (7) D. Kapur & R. Ramamurti, 2001, India's emerging competitive advantage in services, Academy of Management Executive, 15 (2): 20–32; (8) M. Kripalani, 2004, Scrambling to stem India's onslaught, Business Week, January 26: 81–82.

A "GLOBAL" GLOBAL-STRATEGY BOOK

How do companies compete around the globe? In the IT (or BPO) industry in India, how do various local firms and foreign entrants interact, compete, and/or sometimes collaborate? What strategies do Indian firms, aspiring to join the top ranks in the world, use? How do their Western multinational rivals react? What determines their success and failure? Because strategy is about competing and winning, this book on global strategy helps current and would-be strategists answer these and other important questions.

However, this book does *not* focus on a particular form of international (cross-border) strategy, as characterized by the production and distribution of standardized products and services on a worldwide basis. Commonly referred to as **global strategy** for lack of a better word, this strategy has often been advocated in traditional global strategy books for more then two decades.[1] However, there is now a great deal of rumbling and soul-searching among managers who are frustrated by the inability of their "world car," "world drink," or "world commercial" to conquer the world.[2] In truth, **multinational enterprises (MNEs),** defined as firms that engage in **foreign direct investment (FDI)** by directly controlling and managing value-adding activities in other countries,[3] often have to adapt their strategies, products, and services for local markets. For example, the very foundation behind Indian IT firms' success is customization. The automobile industry has no "world car." Cars popular in one region are often rejected by customers elsewhere. The Toyota Camry is America's best-selling car, but a poor seller in Japan. The Volkswagen Golf and the Ford Mondeo (marketed as the Contour in the United States) that have dominated Europe have little visibility in the streets of Asia and North America.[4]

The so-called "world drink," Coke Classic, actually tastes differently around the world (with varying sugar content). The Coca-Cola Company's effort to push for a set of "world commercials," centered on the polar bear's presumable appeal to some worldwide values and interests, has been undermined by uncooperative TV viewers around the world. In response, Coca-Cola has switched to more costly, but more effective, country-specific advertisements. For instance, the Indian subsidiary has launched an advertising campaign that equated Coke with "thanda," the Hindi word for "cold." The Chinese subsidiary airs New Year's greetings on behalf of the company on the eve of the *Chinese* new year (usually in February). The German subsidiary has developed a series of commercials that show a "hidden" kind of eroticism (!).[5]

It is evident that the narrow notion of "global strategy"—in other words, the "one-size-fits-all" strategy—in vogue over the past two decades, while useful in certain industries for some firms, is often incomplete and unbalanced. This is reflected in at least three manifestations:

- Too often, the quest for worldwide cost reduction, consolidation, and restructuring in the name of global strategy has sacrificed local responsiveness and global learning. The results have been unsatisfactory in many cases and disastrous in others. Many MNEs have now decided to pull back from such a strategy. For example, MTV switched from standardized (American) English-language programming to a variety of programming in local languages. Mitsubishi Motors recently scrapped its plan to make its Montero Sport a "world car." Interestingly, this Japanese company has endeavored to make the car more "American." With more than 5,000 branches in 79 countries and territories, the Hong Kong and Shanghai Banking Corporation (HSBC) was the world's largest bank prior to the merger of Citigroup and Travelers in 1998. Yet, instead of highlighting its "global" power, HSBC brags about being "the world's local bank" (Figure 1.1).

■ Almost by definition, the narrow notion of global strategy focuses on how to compete internationally, targeting how global rivals, such as Coca Cola versus Pepsi, Toyota versus Honda, and Reuters versus Bloomberg, challenge each other in one country after another. As a result, how domestic companies compete, both with each other and with foreign entrants, seems to be ignored. Does anyone know the nationalities and industries of the following three companies: Hutchison Whampoa, Singtel, and Cemex? Based in Hong Kong, Singapore, and Mexico, these three firms are major competitors in the diversified industries, telecommunications industries, and construction materials industries, respectively. They are also the top three MNEs from emerging economies ranked by assets *outside* their home countries.[6] If such companies are outside the radar screen of global strategists, then perhaps the radar has too many blind spots.

■ The current brand of global strategy seems relevant only for MNEs from developed economies, primarily from North America, Europe, and Japan—commonly referred to as the **Triad**[7]—to compete in other developed economies, where income levels and consumer preferences may be similar. In 2002, China replaced the United States as *the* largest FDI recipient in the world. The rise of China is followed by the rise of other emerging economies such as those in Brazil, India, Mexico, and South Africa—each of which is attracting an increasingly global percentage of FDI. **Emerging economies,** a term referring to the fastest-growing developing economies since the 1990s, now command a full one-third share of the worldwide flow of FDI. As emerging economies increasingly become the new global battleground, many local firms are rising to the challenge.[8] India's TCS, Infosys, and Wipro, for example, have now emerged as serious challengers to Western MNEs such as IBM and EDS (see Opening Case). Companies from emerging economies that increasingly compete both inside and outside of their home markets are creating serious ramifications for Triad-based MNEs—thus necessitating our attention.[9]

As a result, more and more managers and scholars are entertaining the idea of modifying (or even abandoning) the traditional global strategy approach.[10] Strategy in Action 1.1 (p. 8) illustrates how to strategically focus on the bottom of the global economic pyramid, namely, the four to five billion people around the world living in poverty who have been ignored by traditional global strategy, and who may provide strong growth engines for future development. Overall, this book can be considered as part of the broad movement in search of a better understanding of *how to effectively strategize and compete around the globe,* not merely "global strategy" per se.

FIGURE 1.1   **HSBC: The World's Local Bank**

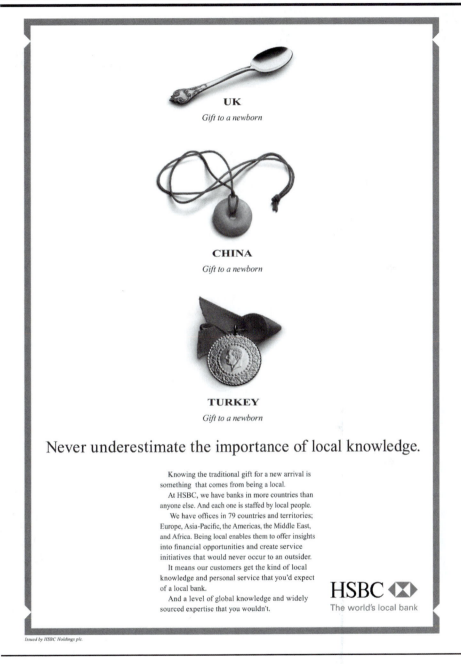

This book differentiates itself from existing global strategy books by providing a more balanced coverage, not only in terms of the traditional global strategy and non-global strategy, but also in terms of both MNEs' perspectives and local firms' viewpoints. Moreover, this book has substantially gone beyond examining competition in developed economies, by devoting extensive space to competitive

STRATEGY IN ACTION 1.1. *Strategy for the Bottom of the Pyramid*

For Triad-based MNEs, even their traditional "global strategy" is not very global as it often focuses on affluent customers in North America, Europe, and Japan. Even when they enter emerging economies, the Triad-based MNEs often concentrate on high-income customers. Consequently, this strategy deals only with the one billion people at the top of the global economic pyramid and virtually ignores the vast bottom. The second tier of the pyramid consists of more than one billion people making $2,000 to $20,000 each year. Four billion people in the world at the bottom of the pyramid earn less than $2,000 each per year.

The MNEs' strategy is easy to understand. They assume that the poor have no money and that no profitable opportunities exist. However, despite low individual income, the poor's collective buying power is substantial. The poor in Rio de Janeiro, for instance, have a total purchasing power of $1.2 billion. While existing business models on how to serve affluent customers would indeed have a hard time at the bottom of the pyramid, entrepreneurial opportunities exist and are being exploited, mostly by local firms and a small number of far sighted MNEs. In India, for example, Arvind Mills (*http://www.arvindmills.com*) introduced Ruf and Tuf jeans, a ready-to-make kit priced at $6, which is now the market leader in India beating global brands such as Levi's (*http://www.levi.com*), which sell for $20 to $40 a pair. In China, Li Ning (*http://www.lining.com.cn*) fights off Nike (*http://www.nike.com*) and Reebok (*http://www.reebok.com*) by tapping into the rural market, about which MNEs are clueless. Li Ning now leads with a 50 percent market share in China (see Closing Case in Chapter 5). In rural Bangladesh where the per capita income was only $300, few

could afford cellular phones. Grameen Telecom (*http://www.gtctelecom.com*) innovatively provided a $175 "micro loan" with a cellular phone to entrepreneurs, who would then sell phone usage on a per-call basis to locals and make $300 a year.

Given that developed markets are well saturated, the bottom of the pyramid may provide strong growth engines, not only for emerging economies, but also for developed markets. For example, Unilever (*http://www.unilever.com*), based on the success in rural India of its Indian subsidiary Hindustan Lever (*http://www.hll.com*), has now focused on the bottom of the pyramid as a strategic priority at the *corporate* level. At present, a number of automakers such as GM (*http://www.gm.com*) and Honda (*http://www. honda.com*) are racing to develop $5,000 car models for the emerging Chinese middle class. Given their inability to profitably produce such models in the United States and Japan, imagine the profit potential these developed-in-China models may have back home where entry-level cars now sell for close to $10,000. Overall, discovering creative ways to configure products and services to tackle the bottom of the pyramid has great ethical and moral values because they improve the standards of living for many people and facilitate economic development. However, firms do not have to do this for charitable purposes. There is money to be made by such a strategy of the *great leap downward*. The million-dollar question is: How?

Sources: Based on (1) S. Hart & C. Christensen, 2002, The great leap: Driving innovation from the base of the pyramid, MIT Sloan Management Review, Fall: 51–56; (2) S. Hart & M. Milstein, 1999, Global sustainability and the creative destruction of industries, MIT Sloan Management Review, Fall: 23–33; (3) C. K. Prahalad & A. Hammond, 2002, Serving the world's poor, profitably, Harvard Business Review, September: 48–57.

battles waged in emerging economies. In a nutshell, this is truly a *global* global-strategy book.

WHY STUDY GLOBAL STRATEGY?

Global strategy is one of the most exciting and challenging subjects offered by business schools. There are at least three compelling reasons why you should study global strategy. First, the most sought-after and highest-paid business school graduates (both MBAs and undergraduates) are typically management consultants with expertise in global strategy. You can be one of them. Outside of the consulting industry, if you aspire to join the top ranks of many large firms, expertise in global strategy is often a prerequisite. Eventually, international experience, not merely knowledge, may be required.[11] However, mastering the knowledge of and demonstrating interest in global strategy during your education will make you a more ideal candidate for an expatriate managerial position, which will allow you to gain that important international experience.[12]

Second, even as graduates at large companies with no interest in working for the consulting industry and no aspiration to compete for the top job, or as individuals working at small firms or self-employed, you may find yourself dealing with foreign-owned suppliers and buyers, competing with foreign-invested firms in your home market, and perhaps even selling and investing overseas. Alternatively, you may find yourself working for a foreign-owned corporation, working for a previously domestic employer that was acquired by a foreign player, or unemployed because your unit was ordered to shut down for global consolidation. Each of these is a likely scenario. Foreign-owned corporations directly employ approximately 80 million people worldwide, including 5.2 million Americans, nearly 1 million British, and 18 million Chinese. Subsidiaries of US corporations, on the other hand, employ approximately 8 million Africans, Asians, Australians, Canadians, Europeans, and Latin Americans.[13] Understanding how strategic decisions are made may facilitate your own career in such organizations.[14] If there is a strategic rationale to downsize your unit, you would want to be able to figure this out and be the first one to post your resume on Monster.com as opposed to being the first one to receive the pink slip. Given that an estimated 11 percent of US jobs, both blue-collar and white-collar, may be vulnerable to global competition,[15] this is a very realistic scenario. In other words, you want to be more *strategic*. After all, your career is at stake. Don't be the last in the know!

Finally, even for non-business school students and general readers, having knowledge about global strategy can help you stay abreast of what is going on in the global economy. You do not have to be a business major or manager to appreciate the impact of globalization on your life. A cursory examination of which countries made your shirts, computers, and cars (or bicycles) should drive home this point. As a well-educated and informed citizen, you need to understand this important factor of our contemporary world. To do that, you first need to understand what strategy is, which is discussed next.

WHAT IS STRATEGY?

This section introduces the origin of strategy, highlights the two main schools of thought in modern discussions of strategy, and spells out our definition of strategy used throughout this book

Origin

Derived from the ancient Greek word *strategos*, "strategy" originally referred to the "art of the general." Strategy has strong military roots, dating back to the work of

TABLE 1.1   What Is Strategy?

STRATEGY AS PLAN
■ "Concerned with drafting the plan of war and shaping the individual campaigns and, within these, deciding on the individual engagements" (Von Clausewitz, 1976)[1]
■ "A set of concrete plans to help the organization accomplish its goal" (Oster, 1994)[2]

STRATEGY AS ACTION
■ "The art of distributing and applying military means to fulfill the ends of policy" (Liddel Hart, 1967)[3]
■ "A pattern in a stream of actions or decisions" (Mintzberg, 1978)[4]
■ "The creation of a unique and valuable position, involving a different set of activities . . . making trade-offs in competing . . . creating fit among a company's activities" (Porter, 1996)[5]

STRATEGY AS INTEGRATION
■ "The determination of the basic long-term goals and objectives of an enterprise, and the adoption of courses of action and the allocation of resources necessary for carrying out these goals" (Chandler, 1962)[6]
■ "An integrated and coordinated set of commitments and actions designed to exploit core competencies and gain a competitive advantage" (Hitt, Ireland, and Hoskisson, 2003)[7]

Sources: Based on (1) K. Von Clausewitz, 1976, On War, vol. 1 (p. 177), London: Kegan Paul; (2) S. Oster, 1994, Modern Competitive Analysis, 2nd ed. (p. 4), New York: Oxford University Press; (3) B. Liddell Hart, 1967, Strategy, 2nd rev. ed. (p. 321), New York: Meridian; (4) H. Mintzberg, 1978, Patterns in strategy formulation (p. 934), Management Science, 24: 934–948; (5) M. Porter, 1996, What is strategy? (pp. 68, 70, and 75), Harvard Business Review, 74(6): 61–78; (6) A. Chandler, 1962, Strategy and Structure (p. 13), Cambridge, MA: MIT Press; (7) M. Hitt, D. Ireland, & R. Hoskisson, 2003, Strategic Management, 5th ed. (p. 9), Cincinnati: Thomson South-Western.

Chinese military strategist, Sun Tzu, who wrote in approximately 500 BC.[16] His most famous teaching is "Know yourself, know your opponents; encounter a hundred battles, win a hundred victories." Applying the principles of military strategy to business competition, known as **strategic management** or **strategy** in short, is a more recent phenomenon beginning in the 1960s.[17]

Plan versus Action

Because business strategy is a relatively young field (despite the ancient roots of military strategy), what defines strategy has been a subject of intense debate. Shown in Table 1.1, three schools of thought have emerged. The first school, **strategy as plan,** is the oldest. Drawing on the work of Von Clausewitz, a Prussian (German) military strategist of the nineteenth century,[18] this school suggests that strategy is embodied in explicit, rigorous formal planning as in the military. The most extreme example of long-range planning can probably be found in Matsushita's 250-year plan (see Strategy in Action 1.2).

However, the planning school, even within the field of military strategy, has been challenged by the likes of Liddell Hart, a British military strategist of the early twentieth century, who argued that the key to strategy is a set of flexible, goal-oriented actions.[19] Hart favored an indirect approach seeking rapid, flexible actions to avoid clashing with opponents head-on. Within the field of business strategy, this **strategy as action** school's most vigorous advocate is Henry Mintzberg, a Canadian scholar. Mintzberg posits that in addition to the **intended strategy** that the planning school emphasizes, there can be **emergent strategy** that is not the result of "top-down" planning, but is the outcome of a stream of smaller decisions from the "bottom up."[20]

STRATEGY IN ACTION 1.2. *A 250-Year Plan at Matsushita*

Konosuke Matsushita is universally referred to as KM at Matsushita *(http://www.panasonic.co.jp),* the company he established in Japan. On May 5, 1932, the fourteenth anniversary of the company's founding, KM announced his business philosophy and a 250-year plan for the company, broken up into ten 25-year segments. The business philosophy, which has become institutionalized through training programs worldwide, defines fundamental goals of the company and the primary means of achieving them. The philosophy proposes that "the purpose of an enterprise is to contribute to society by supplying goods of high quality at low prices in ample quantity," and that "profit comes in compensation for contribution to society." It is encapsulated in the Seven Spirits of Matsushita: (1) service through industry, (2) fairness, (3) harmony and cooperation, (4) struggle for progress, (5) courtesy and humility, (6) adjustment and assimilation, and (7) gratitude. Within Matsushita, managers still refer to these obviously flexible principles constantly and use them to guide strategic thinking long after the death of KM.

Source: Based on (1) C. Bartlett & S. Ghoshal, 1989, Managing Across Borders: The Transnational Solution (p. 41), Boston: Harvard Business School Press; (2) http://www.panasonic.co.jp (accessed July 26, 2004).

Strategy as Theory

Although the debate between the planning school and the action school is difficult to resolve, many scholars and managers have realized that in reality, the essence of strategy is likely to be a *combination* of both planned deliberate actions and unplanned emergent activities, thereby leading to a **strategy as integration** school.[21] First advocated by Alfred Chandler,[22] an American business historian, this more balanced, strategy as integration school of thought has been adopted in many strategy texts,[23] and is the perspective embraced in this book. Specifically, we extend the strategy as integration school by defining **strategy** as *a firm's theory about how to compete successfully.*[24]

Four advantages are associated with our strategy as theory definition. First, it capitalizes on the insights of both the planning and the action schools. This is because a firm's theory of how to compete remains an idea until it has been translated into action. In other words, **formulating** a theory—advocated by the planning school—is merely a first step; **implementing** it through a series of actions—noted by the action school—is a necessary second part. Graphically, Figure 1.2 shows how a strategy entails a firm's assessment at point A of *both* its own strengths (S) and weaknesses (W), its desired performance levels at point B, and the opportunities (O) and threats (T) in the environment. Such a **SWOT analysis** resonates very well with Sun Tzu's teachings on the importance of knowing yourself and your opponents. After such an assessment, the firm formulates its theory on how to best connect

FIGURE 1.2   **The Essence of Strategy**

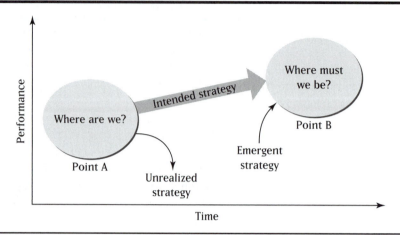

points A and B. In other words, the broad arrow becomes its intended strategy. However, given so many uncertainties, not all intended strategies may prove successful, and some may become unrealized strategies. On the other hand, other unintended actions may become emergent strategies with a thrust toward point B. Overall, this definition of strategy enables us to retain the planning school's elegance with its more orthodox, logical approach and to entertain the action school's flexibility with its more dynamic, experimental character.

Second, this new definition rests on a simple, but powerful, idea: The concept of a theory. Even though the word "theory" often frightens students and managers because it implies something abstract and impractical,[25] it shouldn't. A theory is merely a statement that describes relationships between a set of phenomena. A theory, at its core, serves two powerful purposes: to *explain* the past and to *predict* the future. If a theory is too complicated, no one can understand, test, or use it. Einstein's theory of relativity, expressed by a deceptively simple formula, $E = MC^2$, is perhaps one of the most striking examples of a theory that has changed the world. While strategy is not rocket science, the same principle applies. For example, Wal-Mart's "every day low prices" strategy clearly indicates its theory about how to compete successfully. Similarly, Komatsu's strategy, "Encircling Caterpillar," serves both explanatory and predictive purposes when communicating the essence of its numerous activities worldwide.

Third, that a theory is proven successful in one context, during one time period, does not necessarily mean it will prove successful elsewhere. As a result, a hallmark of theory-driven research is **replication,** that is, the repeated testing of theory under a variety of conditions. This seems to be the essence of business strategy.[26] Firms that are successful in one product or country market—having proven the merit of their theory once—constantly seek to expand to newer markets. In other words, they attempt to replicate the previous success. Sometimes they succeed, other times they fail. As a result, firms are able to gradually establish the *limits* of their particular theory about how to compete successfully.

Finally, the strategy as theory perspective helps explain why it is often difficult to change strategy.[27] Imagine how hard it is to change an established theory. Certain theories are widely accepted because of their past success. However, past success does not guarantee future success. In scientific research, although scientists are supposed to be objective, they are also human, and many of them may be unwilling to concede the failure of their favorite theories even in the face of repeatedly failed tests. Think about how much resistance from the scientific community Galileo, Copernicus, and Einstein had to face initially. The same holds true for strategists. National heritage, organizational politics, and personal career considerations may prevent many strategists from admitting the evident failure of an existing strategy. Yet, the history of scientific progress suggests that although difficult, it is possible to change established theories. If enough failures in testing are reported and enough researchers raise doubts about certain theories, their views, which may be initially marginal, may gradually drive out failed theories, thus introducing better ones to the field. The painful process of strategic change in many companies is similar. Usually a group of managers, backed by performance data, challenge the current strategy. They propose a new theory on how to best compete, which initially is often marginalized by top management. Eventually, however, the momentum of the new theory may outweigh the resistance of the old strategy, thus leading to some strategic change.

Overall, strategy is not a rulebook, a blueprint, or a set of programmed instructions. Rather, strategy is a firm's theory about how to compete successfully, a unifying theme that gives coherence to its various actions. Because every firm—just like every individual—is different, one firm's successful theory (strategy) does not necessarily work for other firms.

Just as military strategies and generals have to be studied simultaneously, understanding business strategies around the globe would be incomplete without an appreciation of the role top managers play as strategists. Although mid- and lower-level managers need to understand strategy, they typically lack the perspective and confidence to craft and execute a *firm-level* strategy. Top management must exercise leadership by making strategic choices.[28] Since the directions and operations of a firm typically are a reflection of its top managers, their personal choices and preferences, based on their own culture, background, and experience, may affect firm strategies.[29] Therefore, although this book focuses on firm strategies, it is also about strategists who lead their firms.

FUNDAMENTAL ISSUES IN STRATEGY

Although strategy around the globe is a vast subject, this book focuses only on the *most fundamental* issues, which define a field and orient the attention of students, practitioners, and scholars in a certain direction. Specifically, we will address the following four fundamental questions:

- Why do firms differ?
- How do firms behave?

- What determines the scope of the firm?
- What determines the international success and failure of firms?[30]

Why Do Firms Differ?

In every modern economy, firms, just like individuals, differ. This question thus seems obvious and hardly generates any debate. However, much of our knowledge about the firm is from research on firms in the United States and to a lesser extent the United Kingdom, which are embedded in what is known as Anglo-American capitalism. A smaller knowledge base deals with other Western countries such as Germany, France, and Italy—collectively known as continental European capitalism.[31] Although some differences between Anglo-American and continental European firms have been reported (such as a shorter and a longer investment horizon, respectively), the contrast between these Western firms (collectively) and their Japanese counterparts is more striking.[32] For example, instead of using costly vertical integration and acquisitions typically found in the West, Japanese firms extensively employ a network form of supplier management, giving rise to the term *keiretsu* (interfirm network), which is now frequently used in English-language publications without explanation—an educated reader of *Business Week, Economist,* or the *Wall Street Journal* is supposed to understand the term.[33]

More recently, as the strategy radar starts to scan the business landscape in emerging economies, more puzzles emerge. For example, it is long established that economic growth could hardly occur in poorly regulated economies. Yet, given China's recent strong economic growth and its underdeveloped formal institutional structures (such as the lack of effective courts), how has China been able to achieve rapid rates of economic growth?[34] Among the many answers to this intriguing question, one suggests that interpersonal networks (*guanxi*) cultivated by managers may serve as informal substitutes for formal institutional support. In other words, interpersonal relationships among managers are translated into an interfirm strategy that relies on networks and alliances to grow the firm, which, in the aggregate, contributes to the growth of the economy.[35] As a result, the word *guanxi* has now become the most famous Chinese business word that frequently appears in English-language media (again it is often without explanation).[36] Similarly, the Korean word *chaebol* (large business group) and the Russian word *blat* (relationships) have also entered the English vocabulary.[37] Behind each of these deceptively simple words lie some fundamental differences on how to compete around the world. For current and would-be strategists, knowing what drives firm differences helps you size up competitors and partners in different countries and prevents you from being caught off guard by competitor's actions.[38]

How Do Firms Behave?

This question focuses on what determines firms' theory about how to compete. Figure 1.3 identifies three leading perspectives. The first, **industry-based view,** suggests that the strategic task is mainly to examine the five competitive forces affecting an industry (interfirm rivalry, bargaining power of buyers, bargaining

FIGURE 1.3   **Three Leading Perspectives on Strategy**

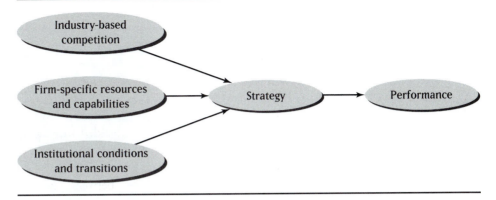

power of suppliers, threat of new entrants, and threat of substitutes), and stake out a position that is less vulnerable relative to these five forces.[39] While the industry-based view primarily focuses on the *external* opportunities and threats (the O and T in a SWOT analysis), the second, **resource-based view,** largely concentrates on the *internal* strengths and weaknesses (S and W) of the firm.[40] This view posits that the firm-specific resources and capabilities largely differentiate successful firms from failing ones.

Recently, an **institution-based view** has emerged to account for differences in firm strategy. This view argues that in addition to industry- and firm-level conditions, firms also need to take into account wider influences from sources such as the state and society when crafting strategy.[41] Firms in emerging economies (such as the Indian IT firms in the Opening Case) may be especially susceptible to institutional influences, such as domestic market reforms and foreign political backlash.[42] Overall, these three views form the backbone of the first part of this book, "Foundations of Global Strategy" (Chapters 2, 3, and 4). They shed considerable light on the "How do firms behave?" question.

What Determines the Scope of the Firm?

This question first focuses on the growth of the firm. Except for some family-owned firms that choose to remain small, most companies in the world seem to have a lingering love affair with growth. In this regard, the strategy of a large, successful, and publicly listed corporation, such as Limited Brands, to stick to its home market is rather unusual (see Strategy in Action 1.3). The motivation to grow is fueled by top management's desire to provide more complete and better products to more geographical markets (such as cities and countries), as well as the excitement of being associated with a growing organization. For publicly listed firms, without growth, the share price will not grow. However, there is a limit beyond which further growth can backfire. As a result, downsizing, downscoping, and withdrawing are often necessary. In other words, answers to the question, "What determines the scope of the firm?" pertain not only to the growth of the firm, but also to the contraction of the firm.

STRATEGY IN ACTION 1.3. *Limited to America?*

Starting with one women's apparel store in Columbus, Ohio in 1963, The Limited (*http://www.limitedbrands. com*) has grown into a successful retail empire of more than 4,000 stores and seven brands (The Limited, Express, Victoria's Secret, Bath & Body Works, The White Barn Candle Co., Aura Science, and Henri Bendel) throughout the United States. By renaming itself Limited Brands in 2002, the firm committed to "building a family of the world's best fashion brands." In 2003, *Fortune* magazine named Limited Brands the world's most admired specialty retailer. Interestingly, although it purchases merchandise from approximately 2,900 suppliers and factories located throughout the world, Limited Brands does not intend to expand its core retail operations internationally. Limited Brands' theory about how to compete successfully seems to be limited to its home country. Confronting the wave of globalization, Chairman and CEO Leslie Wexner argued in a recent annual report that "We didn't go 'international' and I believe some of those that have will live to regret it," and that "We will continue our strategy of conservatism and discipline." Whether Limited Brands will continue its US-only strategy remains to be seen, as it faces competition from leading fashion retailers from Europe, such as Italy's United Colors of

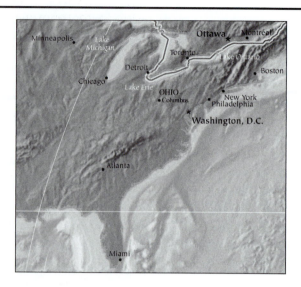

Benetton (*http://www.benetton.com*) and Sweden's Hennes & Mauritz (H&M, *http://www.hm.com*), which entered the US market.

Sources: Based on (1) Business Week, 2003, Stefan Persson, January 13: 63; (2) http://www.limitedbrands.com (accessed January 14, 2003); (3) S. Alvarenga, C. Owona, & P. Szelle, 2002, Limited Brands: Pursuing Growth and International Expansion, case study, Fisher College of Business, The Ohio State University.

In developed economies, a conglomeration strategy in vogue during the 1960s and 1970s featured unrelated product diversification, but this was found to destroy value and was largely discredited by the 1980s and 1990s (witness how many firms are still trying to divest and downsize in the West). However, this strategy still seems to be alive and well in many emerging economies. Although puzzled Western media and consultants often suggest that conglomerates destroy value and should be dismantled in emerging economies, empirical evidence suggests otherwise. Recent research in China, India, Indonesia, Israel, Peru, South Africa, South Korea, and Taiwan reports that some (but not all) units affiliated with conglomerates may enjoy higher profitability than independent firms, suggesting some discernible performance *benefits* associated with conglomeration in emerging economies.[43] One reason behind such a contrast lies in the institutional differences between developed and emerging economies. Viewed through an institutional lens, conglomeration makes sense, at least to some extent, in emerging economies, because this strategy, and its relatively positive link to performance, may be a function of the level of institutional (under) development in these countries.[44]

In addition to product scope, careful deliberation of the geographic scope is important. On one hand, a strong position in *each* of the three Triad markets is often necessary for companies aspiring to become global leaders. Expanding market position in key emerging economies, such as Brazil, China, and India, may also be desirable. On the other hand, however, not all companies can or should forge a narrowly defined global strategy. Given the recent hype to "go global," many companies may have entered too many countries too quickly and are being forced to withdraw.

What Determines the International Success and Failure of Firms?

This focus on performance, more than anything else, defines the field of strategic management and international business.[45] We are not only interested in *acquiring and leveraging* competitive advantage, but also in *sustaining* such an advantage over time and across regions.[46] All three major perspectives ultimately seek to answer this question. The industry-based view posits that the degree of competitiveness in an industry largely determines a firm's performance. For example, this view explains that the unique attributes of the IT industry—knowledge-intensive and not bound by location—allow a number of Indian firms to provide off-site, remote services to Western MNEs. The resource-based view believes that firm-specific differences in capabilities drive the performance differences. Even within the same Indian IT industry, while some firms are winning, others are struggling and failing. Winning firms tend to have valuable, unique, and hard-to-imitate capabilities that their rivals have a hard time matching. The institution-based view argues that institutional forces also provide an explanation for differences in firm performance. While India's pro-market reforms have opened many doors for its IT firms, legislation in certain American states bans these firms from being awarded official contracts, which obviously curtails their global reach and profits. Although different schools of thought often debate the true determinants of firm performance, firm performance is probably driven by a three-pronged *combination* of these forces (see Figure 1.3).[47]

While these three views present relatively straightforward answers, the reality of global competition often makes these answers more complex and murky. If you ask ten managers from ten countries to define performance, you are likely to get ten different answers. Long-term or short-term performance? Financial returns or market shares? Profits maximized for shareholders or benefits maximized for stakeholders—ranging from employees to fishermen downstream from your polluting plant? Finding an easy, uncontroversial answer is difficult, and generalizations based on stereotypes may not hold. For example, it is widely believed that relative to Western firms, Asian firms tend to be more willing to sacrifice short-term financial performance for long-term market gains.[48] Yet, when actually working side-by-side with Asian counterparts in joint ventures, many Western managers are surprised that some of their Asian colleagues actually have a much *shorter* horizon, and are eager to "harvest" for a quick buck (or yen, yuan, or won).[49] The reasons behind such myths and realities around the world remain to be explored.

In summary, these four questions represent some of the most fundamental puzzles in strategy. While other questions can be raised, they all relate in one way or another to these four. Therefore, the primary focus of this book is to answer these four strategic questions embedded in the context of global competition. *Every* chapter addresses these questions in detail.

WHAT IS GLOBAL STRATEGY?

Because the word "global" is so broad and ambiguous, it is important to set its two derivative terms—*global strategy* and *globalization*—straight. First, at least two meanings can be identified for "global strategy." As noted earlier, a traditional, narrowly defined notion of global strategy refers to a particular theory on how to compete that is centered on offering standardized products and services on a worldwide basis.[50] This strategy obviously is only relevant for large, Triad-based MNEs active in a variety of countries. Smaller companies in developed economies and most firms in emerging economies that are operating in only one or a few countries may find little use for this definition.

Global strategy also refers to any strategy outside one's home country. Americans seem more likely to use the word "global" this way, which essentially means "international." For example, Wal-Mart's first foray outside the United States in 1991 was widely hailed as evidence that Wal-Mart had "gone global," even though Wal-Mart only went to Mexico at that time. While an admirable first step for Wal-Mart, this action is similar to Hong Kong firms doing business in mainland China or German companies investing in Austria. To many Asians and Europeans familiar with international business, nothing is significantly global about these activities in neighboring countries. So, why the hype about the word "global," especially among Americans? This is because historically, the vast US domestic markets made it unnecessary for many firms to seek overseas markets. As a result, when many US companies venture abroad, even in countries as close as Mexico, they are likely to be fascinated about their "discovery of global markets." Partially due to such traditional US-centric mentality, calling non-US (or non-domestic) markets global markets has become a cliché.[51] Because everyone seems to want a more exciting global strategy rather than a plain-vanilla international one, we may lose the ability to differentiate types of cross-border strategy (such as the traditional global strategy previously discussed).[52]

So what do we mean by global strategy in this book? It is *neither* of these definitions. For the purposes of this book, **global strategy** is defined as *strategy of firms around the globe,* which is about firms' theory about how to compete successfully. Breaking out of the typical US-centric straightjacket, this book deals with both the strategy of MNEs, some of which may fit in the traditional, narrow global strategy definition, and the strategy of smaller firms, some of which may have an international presence while others may remain purely domestic. These firms are based and operate in both developed and emerging economies. Unlike the traditional global strategy books, while we focus on the international aspects, we do *not* exclusively concentrate on firms doing business abroad. To the extent that international business involves two sides—domestic firms and foreign entrants—an exclusive focus on foreign entrants only covers one side. The strategy of domestic firms is equally important. Because this book is a truly *global* global-strategy book, it provides balanced coverage.

WHAT IS GLOBALIZATION?

The rather abstract five-syllable word, "globalization," is now frequently heard, debated, and abused.[53] Those who approve of globalization count among its contributions higher economic growth, better standards of living, increased technology sharing, and more extensive cultural integration. Critics argue that globalization undermines wages in rich countries, exploits workers in poor countries, devastates the environment, compromises human rights, diminishes national sovereignty, and gives large MNEs too much power. So what exactly is globalization? More importantly, how should current and would-be strategists view globalization?

Depending on the sources you read, globalization could be (1) a new force sweeping through the world in recent time, (2) a long-run historical evolution since the dawn of human history, or (3) a pendulum that swings from one extreme to another. An understanding of these views helps put things in perspective. First, a critical view suggests that globalization is a new phenomenon since the late twentieth century, driven by both the recent technological innovations in transportation and communication and the notion of an alleged Western hypocrisy by MNEs to exploit and dominate the world. While presenting few clearly worked-out alternatives to the present economic order—other than an ideal world free of environmental stress, social injustice, and branded sportswear (allegedly made by "sweatshops")—pundits of this view nevertheless often argue that globalization needs to be slowed down if not stopped.[54] Most antiglobalization protesters seem to share this view.

A second view contends that globalization has always been part and parcel of human history.[55] MNEs, for example, existed for more than two millennia, with their earliest traces discovered in the Assyrian, Phoenician, and Roman empires.[56] International competition from low-cost countries is nothing new. In the first century AD, the Roman emperor Tiberius was so concerned about the massive quantities of Chinese silk imports that he imposed the world's first known import quota on textiles.[57] Today's most successful MNEs do not come close to wielding the clout of some historical MNEs, such as Britain's East India Company during colonial times.[58] Just as our generation must confront "hypercompetition" or rapid "paradigm-changing" technological advances, previous generations also had to put up with waves of innovations (ranging from printing to the internal combustion engine).[59] In a nutshell, globalization is nothing new and will always march on.

A third view suggests that globalization is the "closer integration of the countries and peoples of the world, which has been brought about by the enormous reduction of transportation and communication costs, and the breaking down of artificial barriers affecting the flows of goods, services, capital, knowledge, and (to a lesser extent) people across borders."[60] Globalization is neither recent nor one-directional. It is, more accurately, a *process* similar to the swing of a pendulum. The world at the dawn of the twenty-first century bears some resemblances to the world of the late nineteenth century. The late nineteenth century saw barriers to trade and travel diminish, with the United States becoming the world's leading "emerging economy" of the day. That era was abruptly ended by World Wars I and II.

The current era of globalization originated in the aftermath of World War II, when major Western nations committed to global trade and investment. However, between the 1950s and 1970s, most developing and communist countries did not share this view. Communist countries, such as China, Poland, and the (former) Soviet Union, sought to develop self-sufficiency. Noncommunist developing countries such as Argentina, Brazil, Egypt, India, and Mexico focused on fostering and protecting domestic industries. However, refusing to participate in global trade and investment ended up breeding uncompetitive industries. In contrast, four developing countries in Asia, namely, Hong Kong, Singapore, South Korea, and Taiwan, earned their stripes as the "Four Tigers" by participating in the global economy. They are the *only* countries once recognized as less developed (low-income) by the World Bank to have subsequently achieved developed (high-income) status. Inspired by these examples, more and more countries and regions, such as China in the late 1970s, Latin America in the mid-1980s, Central and Eastern Europe in the late 1980s, and India in the 1990s, realized that joining the world economy was a must. As these countries started to emerge as new players in the world economy, they become collectively known as "emerging economies."[61] As a result, for the first time since World War I, the world economy became more integrated and international business blossomed. Between 1990 and 2000, global trade grew by 80 percent, and the total flow of FDI increased fivefold compared with the world output growth of 23 percent during the same period.[62]

However, like a pendulum, globalization is unable to keep going in only one direction. The 1990s, a period of very rapid globalization, saw some significant backlash against globalization.[63] First, globalization's rapidity gave birth to the historically inaccurate view that it is new. Second, it created fear among many people in developed economies, because not only does it appear that low-cost emerging economies are taking away many low-end, manufacturing jobs through competition, but that they are also threatening some high-end, high-tech jobs (see Opening Case). Finally, some factions in emerging economies complain against the onslaught of MNEs, which allegedly not only destroy local companies, but also local cultures and values as well as the environment. For instance, many people in Indonesia, South Korea, and Thailand that were devastated by the 1997 Asian economic crisis bitterly resent the pre-1997 policies of rapid capital market liberalization. These policies allegedly subjected these countries to both the rational and irrational exuberance and pessimism of the global (read: Triad-based) investment community. They further resent the "rescue" policies of the International Monetary Fund (IMF), a leading globalization institution, which they felt might have exacerbated the downturns.[64] While small-scale acts of vandalizing corporate symbols, such as McDonald's restaurants, are reported in a variety of countries, the December 1999 antiglobalization protests in Seattle and the September 2001 terrorist attacks in New York and Washington were undoubtedly the most visible and most extreme acts of antiglobalization forces at work. As a result, international business travel has been severely curtailed, and global trade and investment flows have slowed.[65] In contrast to the 1990s, globalization in the 2000s, with a worldwide recession, is in slow gear. Worldwide FDI shrank to $650 billion in 2002, approximately 43 percent of the peak $1.5 trillion level achieved in 2000 and at its the lowest since 1998.[66] Nevertheless, globalization is not likely to go away.

In summary, like the proverbial elephant, globalization is seen by everyone and rarely understood. Our task is more challenging than the blind men who studied a standing animal, because we try to live with and even profit from a rapidly moving (back and forth) beast called globalization. Overall, viewing globalization as a pendulum seems to be a more balanced and realistic perspective. Like the two faces of the Roman god Janus, globalization has both rosy and dark sides.[67] One way to put globalization into perspective is to note that most measures of market integration (such as global trade, investment, and capital flows) have recently scaled new heights, but still fall far short of complete globalization. Such **semiglobalization** is more complex than extremes of total isolation and total globalization, because it suggests that barriers to market integration at national borders are high, but not high enough to completely insulate countries from one another.[68] Overall, (semi) globalization should be neither opposed as a menace nor celebrated as a panacea; but rather, it should be *engaged*.[69]

GLOBAL STRATEGY AND GLOBALIZATION AT A CROSSROADS

The challenge confronting strategists around the globe in the twenty-first century is enormous. The world of semiglobalization calls for more than one strategic experimentation. While total isolation on a nation-state basis suggests a localization strategy and total globalization dictates a standardization strategy, no single right strategy exists in the world of semiglobalization. This results in a wide variety of strategic choices, which this book presents in order to help you make these informed choices.[70] As a backdrop for the remainder of this book, this section makes three key points. First, an understanding of the world economy is necessary. Second, a basic overview of three fundamental events at the dawn of the twenty-first century that define the global landscape is in order. Third, as Sun Tzu taught us a long time ago, knowing yourself and your opponents is imperative.

A Glance at the World Economy

At the beginning of the twenty-first century, the *Economist* estimated the total world output to be approximately $30 trillion. The 2003 gross domestic product (GDP)

FIGURE 1.4   **Estimates of Gross Domestic Products (GDP), 2003—2020**

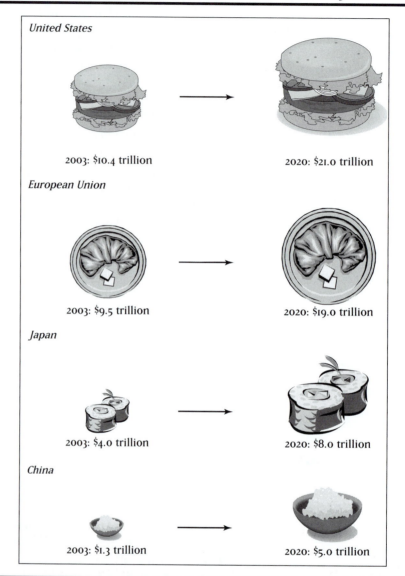

Based on estimates from Economist, 2003, Bergernomics, in The World in 2003 *(p. 30), London: The Economist. 2020 GDP estimates are based on 4 percent annual growth for the US, EU, and Japan, and 9 percent for China. The size of food items is approximately proportional to the size of the economies.*

for the United States was approximately $10.4 trillion, the European Union $9.5 trillion, Japan $4 trillion, and China $1.3 trillion. Assuming US, EU, and Japanese growth rates of 4 percent and Chinese growth rates of 9 percent per year: By 2020, the United States will be producing approximately $21 trillion worth of goods and services a year, the EU $19 trillion, Japan $8 trillion, and China $5 trillion (Figure 1.4).[71]

A frequent observation in the globalization debate is the enormous size of MNEs. Table 1.2 ranks sales of the world's largest MNEs alongside the GDP of the world's

TABLE 1.2   **The Top 100 Economies (GDP) and Firms (Sales), 2003**

RANK	COMPANY	COUNTRY	US$ MILLIONS	RANK	COMPANY	COUNTRY	US$ MILLIONS
1		United States	10,881,609	40		Ireland	148,553
2		Japan	4,326,444	41		Thailand	143,163
3		Germany	2,400,655	42		Iran	136,833
4		United Kingdom	1,794,858	43	General Electric	(US)	134,187
5		France	1,747,973	44		Argentina	129,735
6		Italy	1,465,895	45	Total	(France)	118,441
7		China	1,409,852	46	Allianz	(Germany)	114,950
8		Spain	836,100	47	ChevronTexaco	(US)	112,937
9		Canada	834,390	48	AXA	(France)	111,912
10		Mexico	626,080	49		Israel	103,689
11		South Korea	605,331	50		Malaysia	103,161
12		India	598,966	51	ConocoPhillips	(US)	99,468
13		Australia	518,382	52	Volkswagen	(Germany)	98,637
14		Netherlands	511,556	53	NTT	(Japan)	98,229
15		Brazil	492,338	54	ING Group	(Netherlands)	95,893
16		Russia	433,491	55	Citigroup	(US)	94,713
17		Switzerland	309,465	56		Singapore	91,342
18		Belgium	302,217	57	Intern'l Business		
19		Sweden	300,795		Machines	(US)	89,131
20	Wal-Mart Stores	(US)	263,009	58		Czech Republic	85,438
21		Austria	251,456	59		Venezuela	84,793
22		Turkey	237,972	60		Hungary	82,805
23	BP	(UK)	232,571	61		Egypt	82,427
24	ExxonMobil	(US)	222,883	62	American Internatl		
25		Norway	221,579		Group	(US)	81,303
26		Denmark	212,404	63		Philippines	80,574
27		Poland	209,563	64	Siemens	(Germany)	80,501
28		Indonesia	208,311	65	Carrefour	(France)	79,774
29	Royal Dutch/Shell	(UK/Netherlands)	201,728	66		Colombia	77,559
30	General Motors	(US)	195,324	67	Hitachi	(Japan)	76,423
31		Saudi Arabia	188,479	68		New Zealand	76,256
32		Greece	173,045	69	Hewlett-Packard	(US)	73,061
33	Ford Motor	(US)	164,505	70		Chile	72,416
34		Finland	161,549	71	Honda Motor	(Japan)	72,264
35		South Africa	159,886	72		United Arab	
36		Hong Kong, China	158,596			Emirates	70,960
37	DaimlerChrysler	(Germany)	156,602	73	McKessen	(US)	69,506
38	Toyota Motor	(Japan)	153,111	74		Pakistan	68,815
39		Portugal	149,454	75	US Postal Service	(US)	68,529

(Continued)

TABLE 1.2   **(Continued)**

Rank	Company	Country	US$ Millions	Rank	Company	Country	US$ Millions
76		Puerto Rico	67,897	88	Deutsche Telekom	(Germany)	63,196
77	Verizon			89	Peugeot	(France)	61,385
	Communications	(US)	67,752	90		Peru	61,011
78	Assicurazioni			91	Altria Group	(US)	60,704
	Generali	(Italy)	66,755	92	Metro	(Germany)	60,657
79	Sony	(Japan)	66,366	93		Romania	60,358
80	Matsushita Electric	(Japan)	66,218	94	Aviva	(Britain)	59,719
81		Algeria	65,993	95	ENI	(Italy)	59,304
82	Nissan Motor	(Japan)	65,771	96	Munich Re Group	(Germany)	59,083
83	Nestlé	(Switzerland)	65,415	97	Credit Suisse	(Switzerland)	58,957
84	Home Depot	(US)	64,816	98	State Grid	(China)	58,348
85	Berkshire Hathaway	(US)	63,859	99	HSBC Holdings	(Britain)	57,608
86	Nippon Life Insurance	(Japan)	63,841	100	BNP Paribas	(France)	57,272
87	Royal Ahold	(Netherlands)	63,456				

Sources: Adapted from (1) World Bank, 2004, World Development Indicators database (http://www.worldbank.org, accessed July 25, 2004), and (2) Fortune, 2004, The Fortune Global 500, July 26: F1–F2.

largest countries in 2003. The size of these leading MNEs is indeed striking: forty-eight of the world's top one hundred economic entities are companies. If the largest MNE, US-based Wal-Mart, were an independent country, it would be the twentieth largest economy (its sales are smaller than Sweden's GDP, but larger than Austria's). The sales of the largest EU-based MNE, BP, were larger than the GDP of Norway, Denmark, and Poland. The sales of the largest Asia-Pacific-based MNE, Toyota, were greater than the GDP of Thailand, Malaysia, Singapore, Philippines, and New Zealand. Three of the largest oil companies, BP, ExxonMobil, and Shell, had sales larger than the GDP of the world's largest oil-producing country, Saudi Arabia.

Although the United Nations has identified more than 64,000 MNEs that control 870,000 foreign affiliates, the largest 500 MNEs account for 80 percent of the world's FDI. Total annual sales of these 500 firms are in excess of $11 trillion, about one-third of global output. Table 1.3 documents the changes in the makeup of the 500 largest MNEs since 1990. In general, more than 80 percent of the 500 largest MNEs come from the Triad, with the United States contributing about one-third of these firms, the European Union maintaining a reasonably steady increase, and Japan experiencing the most dramatic variation (roughly corresponding to the boom and bust of its economy with several years of delay). Among MNEs from emerging economies, those from South Korea and Brazil have largely maintained their presence, and those from China have made an increasingly strong showing since the mid-1990s. Critics of globalization do have one valid point: These MNEs, especially those from the Triad, indeed have an enormous impact on the world economy.

TABLE 1.3   **Changes in the Fortune Global 500, 1990–2003**

COUNTRY/BLOC	1990	1991	1992	1993	1994	1995	1996	1997	1998	1999	2000	2001	2002	2003
United States	164	157	161	159	151	153	162	175	185	179	185	178	192	189
European Union	129	134	126	126	149	148	155	155	156	148	136	139	150	147
Japan	111	119	128	135	149	141	126	112	100	107	95	88	88	100
Canada	12	9	8	7	5	6	6	8	12	12	13	5	14	12
South Korea	11	13	12	12	8	12	13	12	9	12	8	12	13	9
Switzerland	11	10	9	9	14	16	14	12	11	11	10	9	11	12
China	0	0	0	0	3	2	3	4	6	10	10	10	11	14
Australia	9	9	9	10	3	4	5	7	7	7	7	6	6	7
Brazil	3	1	1	1	2	4	5	5	4	3	3	4	4	3
Others	50	48	46	41	16	14	11	10	10	11	33	49	11	7
Total	500	500	500	500	500	500	500	500	500	500	500	500	500	500

Sources: Based on data from various issues of Fortune Global 500. *Finland and Sweden are included as "others" prior to 1996 and as European Union after 1996.*

On the other hand, most of the world's MNEs do not make the "Top 100 Economies (GDP) and Firms (Sales)" list shown in Table 1.2, and a large percentage of the world's firms are not even MNEs. They tend to fade into the background in traditional global strategy books. However, firms not making the list in Table 1.2 are often respected competitors in their respective industries and countries. Table 1.4 documents the top twenty largest firms headquartered in emerging economies. Brazil, China, India, Malaysia, Mexico, Russia, South Korea, and Venezuela are represented, and seven of these firms already make the *Fortune* Global 100 list. Current and would-be global strategists ignore these firms at their own peril. This book helps ensure that you won't ignore them.

Three Defining Events

At the dawn of the twenty-first century, at least three sets of sudden, dramatic, and high-profile events occurred that have had significant ramifications for companies and strategists around the world: (1) antiglobalization protests, (2) terrorist attacks, and (3) corporate governance crises. First, **antiglobalization protests** began in December 1999, when more than 50,000 protesters blocked the streets of downtown Seattle in an attempt to derail a World Trade Organization (WTO) meeting. The demonstrators protested against a wide range of issues, including job losses resulting from foreign competition, downward pressure on unskilled wages, and environmental destruction. While protestors battled police in the streets, the delegates failed to reach an agreement inside the meeting halls. Although the protests had little to do with that failure, many believed that the demonstrators had succeeded in derailing the WTO's agenda. Emboldened by the Seattle experience, antiglobalization protestors have made their presence known at just about every major globalization meeting, and have sometimes, beginning in Seattle, resorted to violence (Table 1.5).

TABLE 1.4   **The 20 Largest Firms (by Sales) Headquartered in Emerging Economies, 2003**

Rank (Global 500)	Company	Country	Industry	Sales (US$ million)
1 (46)	State Grid	China	Utilities	58,348
2 (53)	Sinopec	China	Petroleum refining	55,062
3 (54)	Samsung Electronics	S. Korea	Electronics	54,400
4 (65)	Pemex	Mexico	Petroleum refining	49,240
5 (73)	China National Petroleum	China	Petroleum refining	47,046
6 (76)	PDVSA	Venezuela	Petroleum refining	46,000
7 (98)	Hyundai Motor	S. Korea	Motor Vehicles	39,100
8 (119)	SK	S. Korea	Petroleum refining	33,768
9 (144)	Petrobras	Brazil	Petroleum refining	30,797
10 (147)	LG Electronics	S. Korea	Electronics	29,873
11 (167)	Gazprom	Russia	Petroleum refining	27,526
12 (186)	Petronas	Malaysia	Petroleum refining	25,660
13 (189)	Indian Oil	India	Petroleum refining	25,316
14 (241)	China Life Insurance	China	Insurance	20,782
15 (242)	China Mobile Communications	China	Telecommunications	20,764
16 (243)	Industrial & Commercial Bank of China	China	Banking	20,757
17 (263)	Samsung Life Insurance	S. Korea	Insurance	19,159
18 (265)	Korea Electric Power	S. Korea	Utilities	19,114
19 (270)	Sinochem	China	Chemical	18,846
20 (323)	Hanwha	S. Korea	Chemical	16,181

Source: Adapted from Fortune, *2004, "The Fortune Global 500", July 26: F1–F10. Copyright © 2004 Time Inc. All rights reserved. Reprinted by permission.*

TABLE 1.5   **Antiglobalization Protests**

Event	Globalization Organization	Protesters	Arrests
Seattle (December 1999)	World Trade Organization	50,000	600
Washington (April 2000)	World Bank—International Monetary Fund	10,000	1,300
Melbourne (September 2000)	Asia Pacific Economic Cooperation	8,000	12
Prague (September 2000)	World Bank—International Monetary Fund	12,000	900
Davos, Switzerland (January 2001)	World Economic Forum	1,000	121
Quebec City (April 2001)	Summit of the Americas	30,000	400
Genoa, Italy (July 2001)	Summit of the Group of Eight (G-8)	150,000	200 (1 death)
Cancun, Mexico (September 2003)	World Trade Organization	10,000	30

Source: Adapted from (1) Business Week, *2001, When demonstrations turn violent, August 6: 8 and (2)* Economist, *2003, Cancun's charming outcome, September 20: 11.*

Obviously, numerous individuals in many countries believe that globalization has detrimental effects on living standards and the environment. Although both theory and evidence suggest that these fears may be exaggerated,[72] this point has not been communicated clearly enough. Therefore, current and would-be strategists, together with policymakers and scholars, need to do a better job at countering these fears.[73]

A second set of events center on the **terrorist attacks** in New York and Washington on September 11, 2001 and the war on terror since then. Economically, globalization has slowed and become more costly, as evidenced by (1) reduced freedom of international movement as various countries curtail visas and immigration, (2) enhanced security checks at airports, seaports, and land border crossing points that translate into reduced transit speed and efficiency, and (3) cancelled or scaled down FDI projects and trade deals, especially in high-risk regions such as the Middle East.

Finally, the world has been engulfed in a **corporate governance crisis,** which many believe was triggered by Enron's implosion in 2001. Globally, the corporate governance crisis probably erupted in 1997 with the Asian financial crisis, when majority shareholders in many Asian firms, who were often also family owners, abused minority shareholders. Fast forward to America circa 2001, where corporate scandals on such a large scale had been unthinkable. Yet, the scandals of Enron, WorldCom, and Arthur Andersen sent shock waves throughout the world (see Video Cases 3.4, 3.5, and 3.6). Not to be outdone, in 2003, scandals involving the Netherlands' Royal Ahold and Italy's Parmalat hit Europe, earning them the nickname of "Europe's Enron." Investors around the world quickly avoided the few guilty companies and numerous innocent ones, resulting in a chilling effect in financial markets throughout the world. As a result, corporate social responsibility, ethics, and governance, long regarded as "backburners" in strategy discussions, have now increasingly become central topics for many companies throughout the world (see Chapters 4, 11, and 12 in particular).[74]

Future historians will no doubt suggest that these three crucial events changed our world. In a nutshell, current and would-be strategists now have to live with a great deal of uncertainty in the *post-Seattle, post-9/11, post-Enron* world.[75] Without a doubt, other sudden unexpected events will occur too (see Closing Case).

Know Yourself, Know Your Opponents

Many executives, policymakers, and scholars were caught off guard by the antiglobalization protests and the terrorist attacks, because they failed to heed Sun Tzu's most famous teaching: Know *yourself* and *your opponents*. To know yourself calls for a thorough understanding of not only your strengths, but also your limitations. Many individuals fail to understand or simply ignore their limitations. Although, relative to the general public, executives, policymakers, and scholars tend to be better educated and more cosmopolitan, just like everybody else, they are also likely to be biased. In the last two decades, such bias in both developed and emerging economies is toward acknowledging the benefits of globalization.[76]

Although globalization carries both costs and benefits, many executives, policymakers, and scholars fail to take into sufficient account the social, political, and environmental costs associated with globalization. However, the fact that these elites share certain perspectives on globalization does *not* mean that most of the other members of society share the same views. Unfortunately, many elites fail to understand the limits of their beliefs, and mistakenly assume that the rest of the world

TABLE 1.6 Views on Globalization: American General Public versus Business Students

PERCENTAGE ANSWERING "GOOD" FOR THE QUESTION: OVERALL, DO YOU THINK GLOBALIZATION IS GOOD OR BAD FOR	GENERAL PUBLIC[1] (N = 1,024)	BUSINESS STUDENTS (AVERAGE AGE 22)[2] (N = 494)
▪ US consumers like you	68%	96%
▪ US companies	63%	77%
▪ The US economy	64%	88%
▪ Strengthening poor countries' economies	75%	82%

Sources: Based on (1) A. Bernstein, 2000, Backlash against globalization, Business Week, April 24: 43; (2) M. W. Peng & H. Shin, 2003, How do future business leaders view globalization? Working paper, Fisher College of Business, The Ohio State University, http://fisher.osu.edu/mhr/faculty/peng. All differences are statistically significant.

either is or should be more like "us." To the extent that powerful economic and political institutions are largely controlled by these elites, it is not surprising that some powerless and voiceless antiglobalization groups (such as the laid-off steel workers humorously and realistically portrayed in the movie *The Full Monty*) end up resorting to unconventional tactics to make their point.

It is certainly interesting and perhaps alarming to note that, as would-be strategists who will shape the future world economy, current business school students already exhibit values and beliefs in favor of globalization similar to those held by executives, policymakers, and scholars and different from those held by the general public. One study, shown in Table 1.6, finds that, relative to the general public, American business students have significantly more positive—almost one-sided—views toward globalization.[77] This is not surprising, given that both self-selection to study business and socialization within the curriculum, in which free trade is widely regarded as positive, may lead to certain attitudes in favor of globalization. Business majors are often more materialistic and individualistic than the rest of the student population.[78] Consequently, they may focus more on the economic gains of globalization, and be less concerned with its darker sides.

Current and would-be strategists need to be aware of their own bias embodied in such one-sided views toward globalization. Since business schools aspire to train future business leaders by indoctrinating them with the dominant values managers hold, these results suggest that business schools may have largely succeeded in this mission. However, to the extent that there are strategic blind spots in the views of the current managers (and professors), these findings are potentially alarming. They reveal that business students already share these blind spots at a relatively young age (average age of twenty-two years in the study reported in Table 1.6). Aside from possible self-selection in choosing to major in business, there is no denying that student values are shaped, at least in part, by the educational experience business schools provide.[79] Knowing such limitations, business school professors and students need to work especially hard to break out from the straightjacket of these narrow views that almost exclusively favor globalization.[80]

The second part of Sun Tzu's most famous teaching is to know your *opponents*. While competitor analysis (including buyers, suppliers, and substitutes) is always discussed in global strategy books, such analysis appears to be too narrow.[81] Many opponents of globalization, which tend to be **nongovernment organizations** (NGOs), that were active in Seattle—such as environmentalists (Greenpeace), human rights activists (United Students Against Sweatshops), consumer groups (Citizen's Trade Campaign), and farmers (Family Farm Coalition)—are unlikely to be on the traditional radar screen of global strategists.[82] While it is not realistic for individual firms to effectively deal with all these opponents, ignoring them is a grave failure in due diligence when crafting and implementing business strategy around the globe.[83] Instead of viewing NGOs as opponents, many firms view them as partners.[84] NGOs do raise a valid point on the necessity for firms, especially MNEs, to have a broader concern for various stakeholders affected by their actions. At present, this view is increasingly moving from the peripheral to the mainstream.[85] Therefore, it is imperative that strategic analysis of the twenty-first century expand to cover such stakeholders, which may emerge as opponents and/or partners.

In summary, in the *post-Seattle, post-9/11, post-Enron* era, global strategy and globalization are at a crossroads. There is a growing recognition that the traditionally defined, narrow global strategy may not work and that the globalization of the last two decades may have passed its high-water mark. New thinking is called for. This book answers that call.

ORGANIZATION OF THE BOOK

This book is divided into three parts. The first part lays out the *foundations* of global strategy. Following this chapter, Chapters 2, 3, and 4 deal with the three leading perspectives on strategy: industry-, resource-, and institution-based views, respectively. The second part covers *business-level* strategies. In contrast to most global strategy books that focus on large MNEs, we start with the internationalization of small, entrepreneurial firms (Chapter 5), followed by ways to enter foreign markets (Chapter 6), to leverage alliances and networks (Chapter 7), and to manage global competitive dynamics (Chapter 8). Finally, the third part deals with *corporate-level* strategies. Chapter 9 on diversifying, acquiring, and restructuring starts this part; and is followed by strategies to structure, learn, and innovate (Chapter 10), to govern the corporation around the world (Chapter 11), and to strategize with corporate social responsibility (Chapter 12).

A unique organizing principle is the focus on the four fundamental questions of strategy discussed earlier, which are explored in every chapter throughout the text. Following this opening chapter, which contains numerous debates interwoven in the text, every chapter has a substantial "Debates and Extensions" section. Virtually all textbooks uncritically present knowledge "as is" and ignore the fact that the field is alive with a number of debates. Because students are often told "there are no right or wrong answers" and because debates drive practice and research ahead, it is imperative that you be exposed to cutting-edge debates and encouraged to form your own views when engaging in these debates.[86]

Chapter Summary

1. This book focuses on how to effectively strategize and compete around the globe, instead of the traditional, narrowly defined "global strategy," which has often backfired in practice recently.

2. As a *global* global-strategy book, this book provides a more balanced coverage, not only in terms of the traditional "global strategy" and "non-global strategy," but also in terms of both MNEs' perspective and local firms' viewpoint. Moreover, this book substantially goes beyond competition in developed economies by devoting extensive space to competitive battles waged in emerging economies.

3. There is a debate between two schools of thought: "Strategy as plan" and "strategy as action." This book, together with other leading textbooks, follows the "strategy as integration" school.

4. In this book, strategy is defined as a firm's theory about how to compete successfully. Global strategy is defined as the strategy of firms around the globe.

5. Throughout the book, we focus on the four most fundamental questions: (1) Why do firms differ? (2) How do firms behave? (3) What determines the scope of the firm? (4) What determines the international success and failure of firms? The three leading perspectives guiding our exploration are industry-, resource-, and institution-based views.

6. Some view globalization as a recent phenomenon, while others believe that it is a one-directional evolution since the dawn of human history. We suggest that globalization is best viewed as a process similar to the swing of a pendulum, which generally corresponds with the ups and downs associated with market opening around the world.

7. Today's world is perhaps best characterized as semiglobalization—suggesting that barriers to market integration are high, but not high enough to completely insulate countries from each other. Such semiglobalization calls for a wide variety of strategic experimentations around the globe.

8. MNEs, especially large ones from developed economies, are sizeable economic entities in the global economy. However, smaller firms and their strategies also deserve our attention.

9. Three sets of sudden, dramatic, and high-profile events have occurred at the dawn of the twenty-first century. We now live in the uncertainty of the post-Seattle, post-9/11, post-Enron world.

10. Strategists, according to Sun Tzu, need to both "know yourself" and "know your opponents." In light of the fact that globalization has dark sides, current and would-be strategists need to know "yourself," especially the hidden pro-globalization bias. The new strategic radar screen also not only needs to cover traditional competitors, but also nontraditional opponents and/or potential partners (such as NGOs).

Key Terms

emergent strategy	intended strategy	strategy
emerging economies	multinational enterprises (MNEs)	strategy as action
foreign direct investment (FDI)	nongovernment organizations (NGOs)	strategy as integration
formulation	replication	strategy as plan
global strategy	resource-based view	SWOT analysis
implementation	semiglobalization	Triad
industry-based view	strategic management	
institution-based view		

Critical Discussion Questions

1. A skeptical classmate says: "Global strategy is only relevant for top executives such as CEOs in large companies. I am just a student who will struggle to gain an entry-level job, probably in a small company. Why should I care about it?" How do you convince her that she should care about it?

2. Some argue that globalization benefits citizens of rich countries. Others argue that globalization benefits citizens of poor countries. What do you think?

3. In the middle of the debate in Question 2 is the role of MNEs, which through FDI allegedly both exploit the poor in poor countries and take jobs away from rich countries. If you were the CEO of an MNE from a developed economy or from an emerging economy, how would you defend your firm?

4. What are the leading strategic challenges in the post-Seattle, post-9/11, post-Enron world?

5. **ON ETHICS:** What are some of the darker sides (in other words, costs) associated with globalization? How can strategists make sure that the benefits of their various actions (such as outsourcing discussed in Opening Case) outweigh the drawbacks (such as job losses in developed economies)?

6. **ON ETHICS:** Some argue that aggressively investing in emerging economies is not only economically beneficial, but also highly ethical because it may potentially lift many people out of poverty (see Strategy in Action 1.1). However, others caution that in the absence of reasonable hopes of decent profits, rushing to emerging economies is reckless. How would you participate in this debate?

Closing Case: Flextronics and Epidemics

Since its founding in Singapore in 1990, Flextronics (http://www.flextronics.com) *has become a leading original equipment manufacturer (OEM) in electronics. Because Flextronics does not market its own branded products, it is not well known among end-users. Yet, Flextronics is far from being small and obscure. With 2002 revenues of $13 billion, it has operations in twenty-eight countries and employs an army of 70,000 employees. It leads the pack among the more than 3,000 electronics contract manufacturers worldwide with an 11 percent market share.*

Flexitronics' phenomenal growth has resulted from its taking advantage of the trend to outsource manufacturing to OEMs, which as a group may grow from contributing 13 percent of the industry total value at present to 50 percent in the next ten years. With a thin 3 to 5 percent margin, efficiency is key in achieving economies of scale through cost reduction.

Throughout China, Flextronics operates thirty-three factories with a total head count of 34,000. Since 1996, Flextronics has invested $600 million into the heart of its China operations along the southern Pearl River Delta, which neighbors Hong Kong. Inside a 150-acre complex consisting of seven factories, 11,600 workers produce approximately $1 billion worth of products per year. Most of the Microsoft (http://www.microsoft.com) *Xbox game consoles are made there. Other big clients include Dell* (http://www.dell.com), *IBM* (http://www.ibm.com), *Motorola* (http://www.motorola.com), *Palm* (http:// www.palm.com), *and SonyEricsson* (http://www. sonyericsson.com). *The region boasts an excellent combination of low wages, good infrastructure, and efficient logistics. This combination acts as a magnet for foreign investors and the region has become the world's workshop for everything from electronics to toys.*

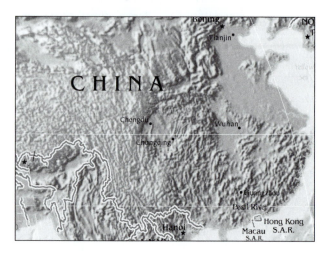

Unfortunately, the Pearl River Delta is also the alleged originator of severe acute respiratory syndrome (SARS), which broke out in early 2003 with global ramifications. The outbreak resulted in the deaths of hundreds of people in several countries and affected several thousand more. Tim Dinwiddie, a forty-year-old Louisville, Kentucky native, who had run the Flextronics complex since 1999 and had dealt with fires, typhoons, and the Y2K bug in his career, claimed that these obstacles all paled in comparison to SARS. Daily on-site visits by current and potential clients and securities analysts dropped to virtually zero. Phone calls, Internet links, and videoconferences kept customers in the loop. As of May 2003, no contract was cancelled, but most major clients indicated that they were considering options elsewhere while closely monitoring whether Flextronics could keep SARS at bay.

In response, Dinwiddie and his management team took the whole complex to a war footing. Like other multinationals in the area, Flextronics enforced a series of rigid procedures to ensure that the epidemic would not penetrate the factories. All staff members who traveled outside the area had to have their temperature taken for ten days, which was believed to be the maximum incubation period. Newly hired workers had to eat in a special section of the canteen for the first ten days and all workers were required to wash their hands before and after eating in the company canteen. All visitors also had their temperature taken. Inside the factories, fear seemed to be abating. In early April, a third of the employees wore masks, but a month later, no one did. Workers showed concern, but did not panic. Overall, Flextronics tried to remain an island of calm amid a sudden storm.

Case Discussion Questions

1. Why has southern China emerged as a global center for manufacturing operations?

2. For Flextronics, what are the benefits and costs of concentrating production in one region?

3. What has fueled Flextronics' strong growth globally and in China?

4. What are the lessons of the SARS epidemic for Flextronics and other MNEs?

Sources: Based on (1) M. Clifford, 2003, Standing guard, Business Week, May 5: 46–48; (2) P. Engardio, 2003, Epidemics and economics, Business Week, April 28: 44–45; (3) B. Einhorn, 2003, Damage in the Delta, Business Week, April 21: 56.

Notes

Abbreviation list

AIM – Advances in International Management

AME – Academy of Management Executive

AMJ – Academy of Management Journal

AMLE – Academy of Management Learning and Education

AMR – Academy of Management Review

APJM – Asia Pacific Journal of Management

ASQ – Administrative Science Quarterly

ASR – American Sociological Review

BW – Business Week

CMR – California Management Review

EMJ – European Management Journal

HBR – Harvard Business Review

JBE – Journal of Business Ethics

JIBS – Journal of International Business Studies

JIM – Journal of International Management

JM – Journal of Management

JMS – Journal of Management Studies

JWB – Journal of World Business

LRP – Long Range Planning

MIR – Management International Review

MS – Management Science

OD – Organizational Dynamics

OSc – Organization Science

OSt – Organization Studies

SMJ – Strategic Management Journal

SMR – MIT Sloan Management Review

1. See, for example, V. Govindarajan & A. Gupta, 2001, *The Quest for Global Dominance*, San Francisco: Jossey-Bass; G. Yip, 2003, *Total Global Strategy II*, Upper Saddle River, NJ: Prentice Hall.

2. C. Baden-Fuller & J. Stopford, 1991, Globalization frustrated, *SMJ*, 12: 493–507.

3. This definition of the MNE can be found in R. Caves, 1996, *Multinational Enterprise and Economic Analysis*, 2nd ed. (p. 1), New York: Cambridge University Press; J. Dunning, 1993, *Multinational Enterprises and the Global Economy* (p. 30), Reading, MA: Addison-Wesley. Other terms are multinational corporation (MNC) and transnational corporation (TNC), which are often used interchangeably with MNE. To avoid confusion, we will use MNE throughout this book.

4. A. Rugman & R. Hodgetts, 2001, The end of global strategy, *EMJ*, 19: 333–343.

5. In the opinion of a German professor, who is the editor of Europe's most respected (and the world's second highest ranked) academic journal in international business,

"even liberal American habits would not allow Coca Cola to show such 'erotic' commercials on US TV screens." See K. Macharzina, 2001, Editorial: The end of pure global strategies? (p. 106), *MIR,* 41: 105–108.

6. United Nations, 2003, *World Investment Report 2003* (p. 6), New York and Geneva: United Nations.

7. K. Ohmae, 1985, *Triad Power,* New York: Free Press.

8. J. Mathews, 2002, *Dragon Multinational,* Oxford: Oxford University Press; L. Wells, 1998, Multinationals and the developing countries, *JIBS,* 29: 101–114; M. Zeng & P. Williamson, 2003, The hidden dragons, *HBR,* 81 (10): 92–104.

9. M. W. Peng, 2000, *Business Strategies in Transition Economies,* Thousand Oaks, CA: Sage Publishing, Inc.

10. "Transnational" and "metanational" have been proposed to extend the traditional notion of "global strategy." See C. Bartlett & S. Ghoshal, 1989, *Managing Across Borders: The Transnational Solution,* Boston: Harvard Business School Press; Y. Doz, J. Santos, & P. Williamson, 2001, *From Global to Metanational,* Boston: Harvard Business School Press. A more radical idea is to abandon "global strategy." See A. Rugman, 2001, *The End of Globalization,* New York: AMACOM.

11. C. Daily, S. T. Certo, & D. Dalton, 2000, International experience in the executive suite, *SMJ,* 21: 515–523; B. Kedia & A. Murkherji, 1999, Global managers, *JWB,* 34: 230–257; A. Yan, G. Zhu, & D. Hall, 2002, International assignments for career building, *AMR,* 27: 373–391.

12. Expatriate managers often command significant premium in compensation. In US firms, their average total compensation package is approximately $250,000–300,000. See C. Hill, 2003, *International Business,* 4th ed. (p. 612), Chicago: McGraw-Hill Irwin; R. Griffin & M. Pustay, 2003, *International Business,* 3rd ed. (p. 583), Upper Saddle River, NJ: Prentice Hall.

13. N. Driffield & M. Munday, 2000, Industrial performance, agglomeration, and foreign manufacturing investment in the UK, *JIBS,* 31: 21–37; Griffin & Pustay, 2003, *International Business* (p. 6); M. Guillen, 2001, *The Limits of Convergence* (p. 125), Princeton, NJ: Princeton University Press; Y. Luo, 2001, *How to Enter China* (p. 14), Ann Arbor: University of Michigan Press.

14. W. Newburry, 2001, MNC interdependence and local embeddedness influences on perceptions of career benefits from global integration, *JIBS,* 32: 497–508.

15. J. Cooper, 2004, The price of efficiency, *BW,* March 22: 38–42.

16. Sun Tzu, 1963, *The Art of War,* translation by S. Griffith, Oxford: Oxford University Press.

17. I. Ansoff, 1865, *Corporate Strategy,* New York: McGraw-Hill; K. Andrews, 1971, *The Concept of Corporate Strategy,* Homewood, IL: Irwin; D. Schendel & C. Hofer, 1979, *Strategic Management,* Boston: Little, Brown.

18. K. Von Clausewitz, 1976, *On War,* London: Kegan Paul.

19. B. Liddell Hart, 1967, *Strategy,* New York: Meridian.

20. H. Mintzberg, 1994, *The Rise and Fall of Strategic Planning,* New York: Free Press. See also C. Grimm & K. Smith, 1997, *Strategy as Action,* Thousand Oaks, CA: Sage Publishing, Inc.

21. S. Cummings & D. Angwin, 2004, The future shape of strategy, *AME,* 18 (2): 21–36; M. Farjourn, 2002, Towards an organic perspective on strategy, *SMJ,* 23: 561–594; R. Grant, 2003, Strategic planning in a turbulent environment, *SMJ,* 24: 491–517; R. Hoskisson, M. Hitt, W. Wan, & D. Yiu, 1999, Theory and research in strategic management, *JM,* 25: 417–456; G. Johnson, L. Melin, & R. Whittington, 2003, Micro strategy and strategizing, *JMS,* 40: 3–22; A. Inkpen & N. Choudhury, 1995, The seeking of strategy where it is not, *SMJ,* 16: 313–323; J. Mahoney, 2004, *Economic Foundations of Strategy,* Thousand Oaks, CA: Sage Publishing, Inc.

22. A. Chandler, 1962, *Strategy and Structure,* Cambridge, MA: MIT Press.

23. L. Greiner, A. Bhambri, & T. Cummings, 2003, Searching for a strategy to teach strategy, *AMLE,* 2: 402–420; C. Hill & G. Jones, 2004, *Strategic Management,* 6th ed., Boston: Houghton Mifflin; M. Hitt, D. Ireland, & R. Hoskisson, 2003, *Strategic Management,* 5th ed., Cincinnati: Thomson South-Western.

24. J. Barney, 2002, *Gaining and Sustaining Competitive Advantage,* 2nd ed. (p. 6), Upper Saddle River, NJ: Prentice Hall; P. Drucker, 1994, The theory of business, *HBR,* 75 (5): 95–105.

25. C. Christensen & M. Raynor, 2003, Why hard-nosed executives should care about management theory, *HBR,* September: 67–74.

26. J. Rivkin, 2001, Reproducing knowledge, *OSc,* 12: 274–293; S. Winter & G. Szulanski, 2001, Replication as strategy, *OSc,* 12: 730–743.

27. W. Boeker, 1997, Strategic change: The influence of managerial characteristics and organizational growth, *AMJ,* 40: 152–170; S. Finkelstein, 2003, *Why Smart Executives Fail,* New York: Portfolio; A. Pettigrew, R. Woodman, & K. Cameron, 2001, Studying organizational change and development, *AMJ,* 44: 697–713; N. Rajagopalan & G. Spreitzer, 1996, Toward a theory of strategic change, *AMR,* 22: 48–79.

28. J. Child, 1972, Organizational structure, environment, and performance: The role of strategic choice, *Sociology,* 6: 1–22; S. Finkelstein & D. Hambrick, 1996, *Strategic Leadership,* St. Paul, MN: West.

29. J. Guntz & R. M. Jalland, 1996, Managerial careers and business strategies, *AMR,* 21: 718–756; D. Hambrick & P. Mason, 1984, Upper echelons: The organization as a reflection of its top managers, *AMR,* 9: 193–206.

30. R. Rumelt, D. Schendel, & D. Teece (eds.), 1994, *Fundamental Issues in Strategy: A Research Agenda* (p. 564), Boston: Harvard Business School Press.

31. M. Koza & J. Thoenig, 1995, Organization theory at the crossroads: Some reflections on European and United States approaches to organizational research, *OSc,* 6: 1–8; R. Whittington & M. Mayer, 2000, *The European Corporation,* Oxford: Oxford University Press.

32. E. Gedajlovic & D. Shapiro, 1998, Management and ownership effects, *SMJ,* 19: 533–553; L. Thomas & G. Waring, 1999, Competing capitalisms, *SMJ,* 20: 729–748.

33. Examples of scholarly articles with the word *keiretsu* in the title include K. Banerji & R. Sambharya, 1996, Vertical *keiretsu* and international market entry, *JIBS,* 27: 89–113; J. Dyer, 1996, Does governance matter? *Keiretsu* alliances and asset specificity as sources of Japanese competitive advantage, *OSc,* 7: 649–666; J. Lincoln, M. Gerlach, & C. Ahmadjian, 1996, *Keiretsu* networks and corporate performance in Japan, *ASR,* 61: 67–88; M. W. Peng, S. Lee, & J. Tan, 2001, The *keiretsu* in Asia: Implications for multilevel theories of competitive advantage, *JIM,* 7 (4): 253–276.

34. M. Boisot & J. Child, 1996, From fiefs to clans and network capitalism, *ASQ,* 41: 600–628; M. W. Peng & P. Heath, 1996, The growth of the firm in planned economies in transition: Institutions, organizations, and strategic choices, *AMR,* 21 (2): 492–528.

35. M. W. Peng, 1997, Firm growth in transition economies: Three longitudinal cases from China, 1989–96, *OSt,* 18

(3): 335–413; M. W. Peng & Y. Luo, 2000, Managerial ties and firm performance in a transition economy: The nature of a micro-macro link, *AMJ,* 43 (3): 486–501.

36. Examples of scholarly articles with the word *guanxi* in the title include S. Park & Y. Luo, 2001, *Guanxi* and organizational dynamics, *SMJ,* 22: 455–477; E. Tsang, 1998, Can *guanxi* be a source of sustained competitive advantage for doing business in China? *AME,* 12 (2): 64–73; K. Xin & J. Pearce, 1996, *Guanxi*: Good connections as substitutes for institutional support, *AMJ,* 39: 1641–1658; I. Yeung & R. Tung, 1996, Achieving business success in Confucian societies: The importance of *guanxi* (connections), *OD,* 25: 54–65.

37. An example of scholarly work with the word *chaebol* in the title is H. Kim, R. Hoskisson, L. Tihanyi, & J. Hong, 2004, The evolution and restructuring of diversified business groups in emerging markets: The lessons from *chaebols* in Korea, *APJM,* 21: 25–48. An example with the word *blat* in the title is S. Michailova & V. Worm, 2003, Personal networking in Russia and China: *Blat* and *guanxi, EMJ,* 21: 509–519.

38. G. Carroll, 1993, A sociological view on why firms differ, *SMJ,* 14: 237–249; J. Child, 2000, Theorizing about organizations cross-nationally, *AIM,* 13: 27–75; S. Hart & C. Banbury, 1994, How strategy-making processes can make a difference, *SMJ,* 15: 251–269.

39. M. Porter, 1980, *Competitive Strategy,* New York: Free Press.

40. J. Barney, 1991, Firm resources and sustainable competitive advantage, *JM,* 17: 99–120.

41. D. North, 1990, *Institutions, Institutional Change, and Economic Performance,* Cambridge, MA: Harvard University Press; M. W. Peng, 2003, Institutional transitions and strategic choices, *AMR,* 28 (2): 275–296.

42. R. Hoskisson, L. Eden, C. Lau, & M. Wright, 2000, Strategy in emerging economies, *AMJ,* 43: 249–267; T. Khanna & J. Rivkin, 2001, The structure of profitability around the world, Working paper, Harvard Business School.

43. S. Chang & J. Hong, 2002, How much does the business group matter in Korea? *SMJ,* 23: 265–274; M. Guillen, 2000, Business groups in emerging economies, *AMJ,* 43: 362–380; T. Khanna & J. Rivkin, 2001, Estimating the performance effects of business groups in emerging markets, *SMJ,* 22: 45–74; M. Li & Y. Wong, 2003, Diversification and economic performance,

APJM, 20: 243–265; M. Makhija, 2004, The value of restructuring in emerging economies, *SMJ,* 25: 243–267; L. Nachum, 2004, Geographic and industrial diversification of developing country firms, *JMS,* 41: 273–294; D. Yiu, G. Bruton, & Y. Lu, 2005, Understanding business group performance in an emerging economy, *JMS* (in press).

44. T. Khanna & K. Palepu, 1997, Why focused strategies may be wrong for emerging markets, *HBR,* July-August: 41–51; K. B. Lee, M. W. Peng, & K. Lee, 2004, From diversification premium to diversification discount during institutional transitions, Working paper, Fisher College of Business, The Ohio State University; M. W. Peng, S. Lee, & D. Wang, 2005, What determines the scope of the firm over time? A focus on institutional relatedness, *AMR* (in press).

45. M. W. Peng, 2004, Identifying the big question in international business research, *JIBS,* 25 (2): 99–108.

46. R. Wiggins & T. Ruefli, 2002, Sustained competitive advantage, *OSc,* 13: 82–105.

47. J. Doh, H. Teegen, & R. Mudambi, 2004, Balancing private and state ownership in emerging markets' telecommunications infrastructure: Country, industry, and firm influences, *JIBS,* 35: 233–250.

48. S. Beldona, A. Inkpen, & A. Phatak, 1998, Are Japanese managers more long-term oriented than US managers? *MIR,* 38: 239–256; K. Laverty, 1996, Economic "short-termism," *AMR,* 21: 825–860.

49. R. Peterson, C. Dibrell, & T. Pett, 2002, Long- versus short-term performance perspectives of Western European, Japanese, and US companies, *JWB,* 37: 245–255.

50. T. Levitt, 1983, The globalization of markets, *HBR,* May-June: 92–102.

51. There is evidence that US companies, on average, are less "global" relative to their Asian and European rivals. See J. Johansson & G. Yip, 1994, Exploiting globalization potential: US and Japanese strategies, *SMJ,* 15: 579–601; M. Makhija, K. Kim, & S. Williamson, 1997, Measuring globalization of industries using a national industry approach, *JIBS,* 28: 679–710; A. Morrison & K. Roth, 1992, A taxonomy of business strategies in global industries, *SMJ,* 13: 399–418.

52. Yip, 2003, *Total Global Strategy II* (p. 7).

53. T. Clark & L. Knowles, 2003, Global myopia, *JIM,* 9: 361–372.

54. A. Giddens, 1999, *Runaway World,* London: Profile; A. Prakash & J. Hart (eds.), 2000, *Coping with Globalization,* London: Routledge; S. Strange, 1996, *The Retreat of the State,* Cambridge: Cambridge University Press.

55. B. Husted, 2003, Globalization and cultural change in international business research, *JIM,* 9: 427–433.

56. K. Moore & D. Lewis, 1999, *Birth of the Multinational,* Copenhagen: Copenhagen Business School Press.

57. D. Yergin & J. Stanislaw, 2002, *The Commanding Heights* (p. 385), New York: Simon & Schuster.

58. P. Doremus, W. Keller, L. Pauly, & S. Reich, 1998, *The Myth of the Global Corporation* (p. 19), Princeton, NJ: Princeton University Press.

59. R. Bettis & M. Hitt, 1995, The new competitive landscape, *SMJ,* 16: 7–19; R. D'Aveni, 1994, *Hypercompetition,* New York: Free Press; G. Hamel & C. K. Prahalad, 1996, Competing in the new economy, *SMJ,* 17: 237–242; G. McNamara, P. Vaaler, & C. Devers, 2003, Same as it ever was: The search for evidence of increasing hypercompetition, *SMJ,* 24: 261–278.

60. J. Stiglitz, 2002, *Globalization and Its Discontents* (p. 9), New York: Norton.

61. The term, "emerging economies," was probably coined in the 1980s by Antonie van Agtmael, a Dutch officer at the World Bank's International Finance Corporation (IFC). See Yergin & Stanislaw, 2002, *The Commanding Heights* (p. 134).

62. United Nations, 2000, *World Investment Report 2000,* New York and Geneva: United Nations.

63. R. Vernon, 1998, *In the Hurricane's Eye,* Cambridge, MA: Harvard University Press.

64. This view is not only shared by ordinary critics of globalization, but also by Joseph Stiglitz, former chair of the Presidential Council of Economic Advisers, former senior vice president and chief economist of the World Bank, and 2001 winner of the Nobel prize in economics. See Stiglitz, 2002, *Globalization and Its Discontents* (especially Chapter 4).

65. J. Oxley & K. Schnietz, 2001, Globalization derailed? *JIBS,* 32: 479–496.

66. United Nations, 2003, *World Investment Report 2003* (overview). New York and Geneva: United Nations.

67. L. Eden & S. Lenway, 2001, Multinationals: The Janus face of globalization, *JIBS,* 32: 383–400.

68. P. Ghemawat, 2003, Semiglobalization and international business strategy, *JIBS,* 34: 138–152.

69. Guillen, 2001, *The Limits of Convergence* (p. 232).

70. J. Ricart, M. Enright, P. Ghemawat, S. Hart, & T. Khanna, 2004, New frontiers in international strategy, *JIBS,* 35: 175–200.

71. *The Economist,* 2003, Bergernomics, in *The World in 2003* (p. 30), London: The Economist.

72. P. Krugman, 1994, Does Third World growth hurt First World prosperity? *HBR,* July-August: 113–121; R. Rajan & L. Zingales, 2003, *Saving Capitalism from the Capitalists,* New York: Crown.

73. J. Bhagwati, 2004, *In Defense of Globalization,* New York: Oxford University Press; A. Rugman & A. Verbeke, 1998, Multinational enterprises and public policy, *JIBS,* 29: 115–136.

74. K. Schnatterly, 2003, Increasing firm value through detection and prevention of white-collar crime, *SMJ,* 24: 587–614; J. Walsh, K. Weber, & J. Margolis, 2003, Social issues and management, *JM,* 29: 859–881.

75. E. Murphy, J. Gordon, & A. Mullen, 2004, A preliminary study exploring the value changes taking place in the United States since the September 11, 2001 terrorist attack on the World Trade Center, *JBE,* 50: 81–96.

76. A. Bird & M. Stevens, 2003, Toward an emergent global culture and the effects of globalization on obsolescing national cultures, *JIM,* 9: 395–407.

77. M. W. Peng & H. Shin, 2003, How do future business leaders view globalization? Working paper, Fisher College of Business, The Ohio State University, *http://fisher.osu.edu/ mhr/faculty/peng.*

78. S. Rynes & C. Trank, 1999, Behavioral sciences in the business school curriculum, *AMR,* 24: 808–824.

79. H. Levitt, 1991, Socializing our MBAs, *CMR,* summer: 127–143.

80. M. Hitt, 1998, Twenty-first-century organizations: Business firms, business schools, and the Academy, *AMR,* 23: 218–224. See also Eden & Lenway, 2001, Multinationals.

81. R. Bettis, 1998, Commentary on "Redefining industry structure for the information age," *SMJ,* 19: 357–361; J. Sampler, 1998, Redefining industry structure for the information age, *SMJ,* 19: 343–355.

82. P. Magnusson, 2000, Meet free traders' worst nightmare, *BW,* March 20: 114.

83. J. Doh & H. Teegen (eds.), *Globalization and NGOs,* New York: Praeger; S. Kobrin, 2001, Sovereignty@Bay, in A. Rugman & T. Brewer (eds.), *The Oxford Handbook of International Business* (pp. 181–205), Oxford: Oxford University Press.

84. D. Rondinelli & T. London, 2003, How corporations and environmental groups cooperate, *AME,* 17 (1): 61–76; S. Hart & M. Milstein, 2003, Creating sustainable value, *AME,* 17 (2): 56–67; H. Teegen, 2003, International NGOs as global institutions, *JIM,* 9: 271–285.

85. J. Garten, 2003, A new year, a new agenda, *Economist,* January 4: 54–56; C. Robertson & W. Crittenden, 2003, Mapping moral philosophies: Strategic implications for multinational firms, *SMJ,* 24: 385–392.

86. D. Ricks, 2003, Globalization and the role of the global corporation, *JIM,* 9: 355–359.

Managing Industry Competition

Outline

- Defining industry competition
- The five forces framework
- Three generic strategies
- Debates and extensions
- Implications for strategists

Opening Case: The Automobile Industry:
From Good Life to Bloodbath at the Top

With a worldwide recession and severe overcapacity, global automobile sales have dropped between 2002 and 2004 and the outlook remains bleak. However, life is not equally stressful for companies in the three broad segments within the industry: Mass-market, luxury, and ultra luxury. The numerous mass-market players, such as Chrysler (http://www.chrysler.com), Ford (http://www.ford.com), General Motors (http://www.gm.com), Honda (http://www.honda.com), Hyundai (http://www.hmc.co.kr), Nissan (http://www.nissandriven.com), Renault (http://www.renault.com), Toyota (http://www.toyota.com), and Volkswagen (http://www.vw.com), are involved in intense competition. For example, it takes an average of $3,300 of incentives per vehicle for the American Big Three (or Big Two and a Half) to move their cars, crushing profit margins, which on average stand at a low 5 percent for all players. The luxury market has fewer players, such as Audi (http://www.audi.com), BMW (http://www.bmw.com), Lexus (http://www.lexus.com), Mercedes (http://www.mercedes-benz.com), and Porsche (http://www.porsche.com). They use fewer gimmicks such as fat rebates or 0 percent financing, and their margins are at a relatively healthy 10 percent. Life in the ultra luxury market seems to be most tranquil. Competition is more "gentlemanly," and changes come at a glacier pace. The handful of players, such as Ferrari (http://www.ferrari. com), Lamborghini (http://www.lamborghini.com), and Rolls-Royce (http://www.rolls-royce.com), produce a small number of cars each year for the world's most discriminating customers: Approximately 7,000 a year (that is, one-hundredth of 1 percent of total global sales) for cars priced above $150,000. Profits per car can exceed $20,000, which is a world apart from the mass-market profits, which can be as low as $150 per car thanks to incentives. Overall, in the ultra luxury group, margins are comfortable, indicating a good life at the top.

However, such a good life may be a thing of the past as it seems that every self-respecting carmaker is rushing to invade the lucrative ultra luxury market, thus unfolding some high-stakes drama not seen before. Mercedes is offering a $320,000 Maybach, which traces its roots to the gull-winged, legendary 1952 SLR model. BMW, which took over Rolls-Royce in 1998, is launching a $360,000 Rolls-Royce Phantom, blending its British heritage with the finest German engineering. Lexus is secretly working on a $150,000 car. Other players such as Acura (http://www.acura.com), Cadillac (http://www.cadillac.com), and Jaguar (http://www.jaguar.com.uk) are all looking forward to entering the fray. Facing such gathering storms, "old timers," such as Aston Martin (http://www.astonmartin.com) *and Maserati* (http://www.maserati.com), *also rush to add new models.*

With 40 to 50 percent growth of supply in the ultra luxury market projected for the next decade, the biggest question is whether so many new entrants will glut the market, repeating what is happening in the mass market now. Carmakers emphasize that their ultra luxury products are unique and are "not about transportation." They are more like jewelry, horses, and other good stuff of the affluent life style. BMW and DaimlerChrysler (http://www.daimlerchrysler.com), *for instance, are confident that they can grow the market by offering wealthy buyers more choices. Carmakers are also eyeing virgin territory. In China (see Integrative Case 1.3 for details), for instance, sales of premium marques have tripled in the past five years. During 2002, Bentley* (http://www.bentleymotors.co.uk), *now owned by BMW, opened a dealership in Beijing and sold twenty-nine cars, all priced at $400,000 or higher. They included three top-of-the-line Pinnacle Bentley Limousines, priced at $1.07 million each (8.88 million yuan, considered a very lucky number in China). However, the United States remains the largest, richest, and most competitive luxury market that can make or break a carmaker. Overall, it seems that a bloodbath is in the making at the top of the global automobile industry.*

Sources: Based on (1) C. Dawson, 2003, Lexus' big test, Business Week, March 24: 68–69; (2) Economist, 2003, Is one Rolls-Royce enough? January 24: 49–50; (3) G. Edmondson, 2003, Classy cars, Business Week, March 24: 62–66; (4) G. Maxton, 2004, A rough road, in The World in 2004 (105–106), London: Economist; (5) D. Roberts, 2003, Bentley Beijing: Chariots on fire, Business Week, March 24: 66; (6) J. Tansky, 2003, Personal communication, July 1; (7) C. Tierney, 2003, Audi, Volvo, Acura ... Chrysler? Business Week, April 14: 68–69.

Why is the ultra luxury car market turning from relative peace and tranquility to more head-on competition? Why are firms that were previously not competing in this market now entering it? What are the responses of existing players (incumbents)? How will components suppliers and car buyers react? Finally, are there any substitutes for these cars? This chapter is designed to help you answer these and other strategic questions. We accomplish this by introducing the industry-based view, which is one of the three leading perspectives on strategy. (The other two, resource- and institution-based views, will be covered in Chapters 3 and 4, respectively).

As noted in Chapter 1, a basic strategy tool is SWOT analysis, which not only deals with internal strengths (S) and weaknesses (W) but also environmental opportunities (O) and threats (T)—SW is internal, while OT is environmental. The focus of this chapter is opportunities (O) and threats (T) from the industry environment (S and W are discussed later in Chapter 3). We start by defining industry competition, and then introduce the five forces framework, followed by a discussion of three generic strategies. Finally, we spell out eight leading debates.

DEFINING INDUSTRY COMPETITION

An **industry** is a group of firms producing products (goods and/or services) that are similar to each other. Industry competition attracted the attention of economists, policymakers, and managers long before the rise of the strategy field. The traditional understanding is based on Adam Smith's (1776) model of **perfect**

competition, in which price is set by the "market," all firms are price takers, and entries and exits are relatively easy. However, such perfect competition is rarely observed in the real world. Consequently, since the late 1930s, a more realistic branch of economics, called **industrial organization (IO) economics** (or **industrial economics**), has emerged.[1] Its primary contribution is a **structure-conduct-performance (SCP) model**. **Structure** refers to the structural attributes of an industry (such as the costs of entry/exit). **Conduct** refers to the firm's actions (such as product differentiation). **Performance** is the result of firm conduct in response to industry structure, which can be classified as (1) average (normal), (2) below-average, and (3) above-average. The model suggests that industry structure determines firm conduct (or strategy), which, in turn, determines firm performance.[2]

However, the original goal of IO economics was *not* to help firms compete; instead, it was to help policymakers better understand how firms compete in order to properly regulate them. In terms of the number of firms in one industry, there is a continuum ranging from thousands of small firms in perfect competition to only one firm in a **monopoly** (in between, there can be an **oligopoly** with only a few players or even a **duopoly** with two competitors). The numerous small firms can only hope to earn average returns at best, whereas the monopolist may earn above-average returns. Economists and regulators are usually alarmed by above-average returns (which they label "excess profits"). Monopoly is usually outlawed, and oligopoly closely scrutinized.

Such an intense focus on above-average firm performance is shared by IO economics and strategy. However, IO economists and policymakers are concerned with the *minimization* rather than the maximization of above-average profits. The name of the game, from the perspective of the profit-maximizing firm, is to try to earn above-average returns, exactly the opposite. Therefore, strategists have turned the SCP model upside down, by drawing on its insights to help firms perform better.[3] This transformation is the heart of this chapter.

THE FIVE FORCES FRAMEWORK

The industry-based view of strategy is underpinned by the **five forces framework,** first advocated by Michael Porter, a Harvard strategy professor, and later extended and strengthened by numerous others. This section traces the framework's roots, introduces its components, and draws important lessons from it.

From Economics to Strategy

In 1980, Porter "translated" and extended the SCP model for strategy audiences.[4] The result is the well-known five forces framework. Shown in Figure 2.1, these five forces are (1) the intensity of rivalry among competitors, (2) the threat of potential entry, (3) the bargaining power of suppliers, (4) the bargaining power of buyers, and (5) the threat of substitutes. A key proposition is that firm performance critically depends on the degree of competitiveness these five forces have within an industry.

FIGURE 2.1   The Five Forces Framework

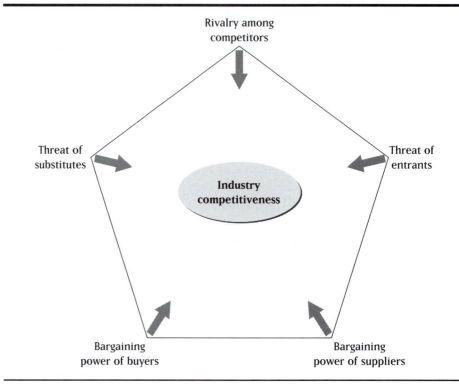

The stronger and more competitive these forces are, the less likely the focal firm is able to earn above-average returns, and vice versa (Table 2.1).

Intensity of Rivalry among Competitors

Actions that indicate a high degree of rivalry include (1) frequent price wars, (2) proliferation of new products, (3) intense advertising campaigns, and (4) high-cost competitive actions and reactions (such as honoring all competitors' coupons). Such intense rivalry threatens firms by reducing profits.[5] The key question is: What conditions lead to intense rivalry?

At least six sets of conditions emerge (Table 2.1). First, the number of competitors is crucial. The more concentrated an industry is, the fewer the competitors are, and the more likely that competitors will recognize their mutual interdependence and restrain their rivalry (see Chapter 8 for details). As shown in the Opening Case, the few luxury car competitors historically do not engage in intense competitive actions (such as deep discounts) typically found among mass-market competitors.

Second, competitors that have a similar size, market influence, and product offerings often vigorously compete with each other. This is especially true for firms that are unable to differentiate their products, such as airlines, which have been hit especially hard recently. Hawaiian, Philippines, Sabena, Swissair, United, and US

TABLE 2.1   **Threats of the Five Forces**

FIVE FORCES	THREATS INDICATIVE OF STRONG COMPETITIVE FORCES THAT CAN DEPRESS INDUSTRY PROFITABILITY
Rivalry among competitors	▪ A large number of competing firms ▪ Rivals are similar in size, influence, and product offerings ▪ High-price, low-frequency purchases ▪ Capacity is added in large increments ▪ Slow industry growth and decline ▪ High exit costs
Threat of potential entry	▪ Little scale-based low-cost advantages (economies of scale) ▪ Little non-scale-based low-cost advantages ▪ Insufficient product differentiation ▪ Little fear of retaliation ▪ No government policy banning or discouraging entry
Bargaining power of suppliers	▪ A small number of suppliers ▪ Suppliers provide unique, differentiated products ▪ Focal firm is not an important customer of suppliers ▪ Suppliers are willing and able to vertically integrate forward
Bargaining power of buyers	▪ A small number of buyers ▪ Products provide little cost savings or quality of life enhancement ▪ Buyers purchase standard, undifferentiated products from focal firm ▪ Buyers are having economic difficulties ▪ Buyers are willing and able to vertically integrate backward
Threat of substitutes	▪ Substitutes superior to existing products in quality and function ▪ Switching costs to use substitutes are low

Airways have all recently flown into bankruptcy (see Video Case 2.4). In contrast, the presence of a dominant player lessens rivalry because it can set industry-wide prices and discipline those firms that deviate too much from the prices set. One example of an industry in which a dominant player sets the standards is the global petroleum industry, which is dominated by the Organization of Petroleum Exporting Countries (OPEC)—eleven countries representing one-third of the global output.

Third, intense rivalry also occurs in industries that produce "big ticket items" that are purchased infrequently (such as mattresses and motorcycles). This is because it can be difficult to establish **dominance** in such industries (that is, the market leader has a very large market share).[6] In contrast, it can be relatively easier for leading firms to dominate in "staple goods" industries with low-price, more-frequently purchased products. Examples include beers, facial tissues, and photographic film, which are dominated by Anheuser Bush (Budweiser), Kimberly-Clark (Kleenex), and Kodak, respectively (see Table 2.2). Consumers for "staple goods" are not likely to spend much time on their purchase decisions, and find it convenient to stick with

TABLE 2.2   **Big Tickets versus Staple Goods**

Product	US Market Leader	Leader's Market Share	Leader's Share Among Top-4 Firms
Big tickets: High-price, less-frequently purchased products			
Athletic footwear	Reebok	25%	40%
Automobile	General Motors	35%	46%
Mattresses	Sealy	25%	46%
Men's jeans	VF Corporation	26%	40%
Motorcycles	Honda	33%	42%
Refrigerators	General Electric	34%	38%
Staple goods: Low-price, more-frequently purchased products			
Beer	Anheuser Busch (Budweiser)	44%	52%
Facial tissues	Kimberly-Clark (Kleenex)	47%	56%
Laundry detergents	Procter & Gamble	53%	59%
Light bulbs	General Electric	59%	62%
Photographic film	Kodak	76%	81%
Processed cheese	Kraft	54%	71%

Source: Adapted from J. Shamsie, 2003, The context of dominance: An industry-driven framework for exploiting reputation (pp. 214–215), Strategic Management Journal, 24: 199–215. All data are average US market share data during 1987–94; numbers are rounded up by the present author.

well-known brands. On the other hand, consumers for "big ticket" items are more interested in searching for a good deal every time they buy, and may not automatically rely on the reputation of leading firms.

Fourth, in some industries, new capacity has to be added in large increments, thus fueling intense rivalry.[7] If three shipping companies, each with one ship of equal size, currently serve the route between two seaports, any existing company's— or new entrant's—addition of merely one ship, adds to the new capacity by one-third. In addition to shipping, hotel, petrochemical, semiconductor, and steel industries periodically experience over-capacity, which leads to price-cutting as a primary coping mechanism.[8]

Fifth, slow industry growth or decline makes competitors more desperate, often unleashing competitive actions not used previously. For instance, when facing declining consumer interest in fast food, McDonald's launched its $1 menu featuring the Big N' Tasty burger, which cost $1.07 to *make* in some restaurants. This action, designed to wear out McDonald's chief competitors, Burger King and Wendy's, squeezed industry-wide margins as a result (see Video Case 1.3).[9]

Finally, industries experiencing high exit costs are likely to see firms continue to operate at a loss. Investments in specialized assets such as specific machines, equipment, and facilities that are of little or no alternative use or cannot be sold off pose as **exit barriers.** In addition, emotional, personal, and career costs, especially on the part of executives admitting failure, can be high. In Japan and Germany, for example, executives may be legally prosecuted if their firms file for bankruptcy.[10] Thus, it is not surprising that these executives try everything before admitting failure and taking their firms out of the industry.

Overall, if only a small number of rivals are led by a few dominant firms, new capacity is added incrementally, industry growth is strong, and exit costs are reasonable, the degree of rivalry is likely to be moderate and industry profits more stable. Conditions opposite from those may unleash intense rivalry. Chapter 8 discusses more about interfirm rivalry.

Threat of Potential Entry

In addition to keeping an eye on existing rivals, established firms in an industry, known as **incumbents,** also have a vested interest in keeping potential new entrants out. New entrants are motivated to enter an industry because of the lucrative, above-average returns some incumbents earn. For example, EMC dominated the global data-storage industry, with gross margins reaching a peak of 59 percent during the booming 1990s. One competitor joked that EMC stood for "Excessive Margin Company." As a result, a powerful pack of heavyweights, led by IBM, HP, and Cisco, have entered this industry to "eat EMC's lunch."[11]

The incumbents' primary weapons are **entry barriers,** defined as the industry structures that increase the costs of entry. For instance, it took Boeing $5 billion to develop the 777, and Airbus spent an estimated $10–$15 billion on its A380. Boeing needs to sell more than 200 aircraft (approximately 15 percent of the *global* market share) just to break even. This means losing money for at least ten to fourteen years. It probably will take much longer for Airbus to recover its investment on the A380.[12] It is not surprising that currently these are the only two competitors in the large commercial aircraft industry, and that all potential entrants, including those backed by the Japanese, Korean, and Chinese governments, have decided to quit (Airbus itself entered the industry in the 1960s with heavy subsidies from the British, French, German, and Spanish governments). The key question is: What conditions have created such high entry barriers?

Shown in Table 2.1, at least five structural attributes are associated with high entry barriers. The first is whether incumbents enjoy **scale-based low cost advantages.** The key concept is **economies of scale,** which refers to reductions in *per unit* costs by increasing the scale of production.[13] This makes sense, because, in general, the more companies perform a certain task, the more efficient they become. Economies of scale can be shown by **experience curves,** namely, the curves on which firms can drive down unit costs based on their experience with expanding scale. New entrants able to ride down the experience curves faster than incumbents are likely to overcome entry barriers based on economies of scale. For example, Galanz, a Chinese microwave producer, produced 200,000 units in 1999. In 2002, it manufactured 15 million microwave ovens for more than 200 brands all over the world. Galanz has become the world's volume leader (although not always using its own brand). Such a high output has enabled Galanz to rapidly ride down the experience curve. Consequently, the Chinese giant launched its own brands in Europe, where it held a 40 percent share of the market in 2002.[14]

Another set of low-cost advantages that incumbents may enjoy is independent of scale. There are four potential sources for **non-scale-based low cost advantages.** First, proprietary technology (such as patents) is helpful. When entrants have to "invent around," the outcome is costly and uncertain. Entrants can also directly copy proprietary technology, which can trigger lawsuits by incumbents for patent violations. This happened to Nexgen, a computer chip maker, when Intel filed such lawsuits. Nexgen paid a heavy price by being forced out of the industry.[15] A second source of such low-cost advantages is **know-how,** the intricate knowledge of how to make products and serve customers that takes years, sometimes decades, to accumulate. New entrants often struggle to duplicate such know-how. A third source is favorable access to raw materials and distribution channels. Because of a long history of dealing with each other, suppliers may be willing to offer incumbents volume discounts and (corporate) buyers happy to provide incumbents with the best distribution channels. Suppliers and buyers are less likely to offer new entrants with little or no track record such good deals, thereby effectively jacking up the cost structure for new entrants. Finally, given that real estate prices tend to rise (in most cases), if incumbents occupy favorable locations for their operations, new entrants are forced to buy or rent at higher prices in similar locations or look for lower-cost, but less-than-desirable locations.

In addition to scale- and non-scale-based low-cost advantages, another entry barrier is **product differentiation,** which refers to the uniqueness of the incumbents' products that customers value. Two underlying sources of differentiation include brand identification and customer loyalty. Incumbents, often through intense advertising, want customers to identify their brands with some unique attributes.[16] For example, BMW brags about its cars being the "ultimate driving machines." Champagne makers in the French region of Champagne argue that competing products made elsewhere are not really worthy of the name, Champagne.

Another source of product differentiation is customer loyalty, especially when switching costs for new products are substantial. Many high-tech industries are characterized by **network externalities,** in which the value a user derives from a product increases with the number (or the network) of other users of the same product.[17] These industries have a "winner take all" property, in which winners (incumbents) whose technology standard is embraced by the market (such as the Microsoft Office package of Word, Excel, and PowerPoint, which has approximately 93 percent global market share as of this writing) are essentially locking out potential entrants. In other words, these industries have an interesting "*increasing* returns" characteristic, as opposed to "*diminishing* returns" taught in basic economics. In the earlier days of the personal computer (PC) standards war, Microsoft's DOS was not technically superior to Apple's Macintosh (Mac). However, through a deal with IBM, Microsoft dramatically increased its installed base and encouraged more software developers to write DOS-based software. After DOS locked in the market, Microsoft was able to spread its costs over a larger base of users, thus reaping increasing returns.[18] Apple, on the hand, chose a "go alone" strategy and suffered from a low installed base, which eventually led even many Mac lovers to switch to DOS.

Another entry barrier is possible retaliation by incumbents. Incumbents often maintain some **excess capacity**, which is designed to punish new entrants (see also Chapter 8). To think slightly outside the box, perhaps the best example is the armed forces maintained by practically every country. They cost taxpayers huge sums of money and do not create much value in peace time. But the armed forces exist for one reason: To deter entry by invading foreign armies. For this reason, no country has ever decided to unilaterally disband its armed forces, and the worst punishment for defeated countries (such as Germany and Japan in 1945 and Iraq in 2003) is to have their military dismantled. In general, new entrants are more likely to be deterred if the threat of retaliation is credible and predictable. For example, Coca-Cola is known to retaliate by slashing prices if any competitor (other than Pepsi) crosses the threshold of 10 percent share in any local market. Facing such a determined incumbent, potential entrants often think twice before making a move.

Finally, government policy banning or discouraging entries can serve as another entry barrier. For example, the US government does not allow foreign entrants to invest in the defense industry and only allows up to 25 percent equity injection from foreign carriers in the airline industry. In many countries, governments practice protectionist policies to ban or discourage foreign entrants, enabling large, established incumbents to carve up domestic markets (see Integrative Case 1.2).[19] In almost every case, lowering government-imposed entry barriers leads to a proliferation of new entrants, threatening the profit margins of incumbents—as illustrated by the Chinese telecommunications service industry (see Strategy in Action 2.1).

Overall, if incumbents can leverage the scale- and/or non-scale-based advantages, provide sufficient differentiation, maintain a credible threat of retaliation, or enjoy regulatory protection, the threat of potential entry becomes weak and incumbents can enjoy higher profits.

Bargaining Power of Suppliers

Suppliers are organizations that provide materials, services, and manpower to firms in the focal industry. The **bargaining power of suppliers** refers to their ability to raise prices and/or reduce quality of goods and services. Four conditions lead to strong bargaining power for suppliers (Table 2.1). First, if a few firms dominate the supply industry, they may gain an upper hand. For example, in the PC industry, the most profitable players are not Dell, IBM, or Sony, but their two suppliers, Microsoft (operating systems) and Intel (microprocessors), which virtually possess monopolies in these two crucial areas. Conversely, numerous individual coffee growers in Africa and Latin America possess little bargaining power when dealing with multinationals such as Nestle and Starbucks.

Second, the bargaining power of suppliers can become substantial if they provide unique, differentiated products with few or no substitutes.[20] For instance, for a

STRATEGY IN ACTION 2.1. *Telecom Service Competition in China, Post-WTO Style*

As a condition for its accession to the World Trade Organization (WTO) (*http://www.wto.org*) in 2001, China reluctantly allowed foreign firms to enter its telecommunications service industry. However, so far, with the exception of a small AT&T (*http://www.att.com*) broadband investment in a tiny portion of Shanghai, no foreign entrant has come. At first glance, this seems odd, given the impression of China being the world's fastest growing telecom service market. More careful examination reveals that avoiding China does not look like a bad idea, because China's telecom gold rush seems to have come to an end. Simply put, there are already too many domestic new entrants.

The industry has experienced dramatic transformation in the past two decades, going from only one incumbent to thousands of players. The incumbent, the state-owned China Telecom (*http://www.chinatelecom. com.cn*), used to be a single, nationwide monopoly that often provided poor services at high prices—a recipe for criticism but a great way to make money. As the mobile market emerged, the government allowed China Unicom (*http://www.chinaunicom.net*) to enter in the mid-1990s. China Mobile (*http://www.chinamobilehk.com*) was then spun off from China Telecom. In 2002, China Telecom itself was split into two halves: The new China Telecom and China Netcom (*http://www.cnc.net.cn*). In addition, the government allowed numerous small players to enter the paging market. At present, more than 2,000 firms are hustling for a slice of the paging market.

While the Chinese telecom service industry has experienced enormous growth, from a 0.4 percent phone penetration (number of subscribers divided by population) in 1980 to 14 percent in 2002, the growth is rapidly slowing down. Most big urban markets have

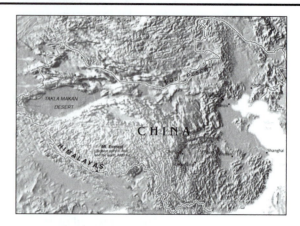

almost reached saturation. Mobile-phone penetration is now more than 50 percent in Shanghai, Beijing, and Guangzhou, a level that ranks with the most developed markets in the world. Over capacity has led to severe price competition. Deep discounting has even affected the high-end market. In January 2002, China Unicom, with great fanfare, rolled out the country's first high-end CDMA mobile network and announced a target of seven million subscribers in one year. It took until June to reach the first million customers. China Unicom had to aggressively slash prices, and in some cities nearly gave away the expensive $350-per-piece phone sets. The upshot is that talk is cheap for consumers, but companies' profit margins are plummeting.

Sources: Based on (1) B. Dolven, 2002, The end of China's telecom gold rush, Far Eastern Economic Review, December 12: 36–42; (2) A. Weintraub, 2002, Go east, young chipmaker, Business Week, December 30: 46; (3) B. Zhang & M. W. Peng, 2000, Telecom competition, post-WTO style, China Business Review, May-June: 12–21.

Coca-Cola bottler, there is only one supplier for Coke syrup. If Coca-Cola hikes up the syrup price, bottlers, which actually bottle, market, and distribute the soda, have to swallow these increases, even if they are unable to pass the price increases to consumers. It is hardly surprising that Coca-Cola's return on equity is substantially higher than that of bottlers (for example, 38 percent versus 6 percent in 2002).[21]

Third, suppliers can exercise strong bargaining power if the focal firm is *not* an important customer. Boeing and Airbus, for example, are not too concerned with losing the business of small airlines, which can only purchase one or two aircraft at a time. Consequently, they often refuse to lower prices. In contrast, they are intensely concerned about losing large airlines, such as American, British, Japan, and Singapore Airlines, which typically buy dozens of aircraft at a time. As a result, lower prices and increased services are often offered to those larger airlines.

Finally, suppliers can enhance their bargaining power if they are willing and able to enter the focal industry by **forward integration.** In other words, suppliers can threaten to become both suppliers *and* rivals. For example, in addition to supplying shoes to traditional department and footwear stores, Nike has established a number of Nike Towns in major cities to directly hawk shoes and sportswear.

In summary, powerful suppliers can squeeze profit out of firms in the focal industry. Firms in the focal industry, thus, have an incentive to strengthen their own bargaining power by reducing their dependence on certain suppliers. For example, Wal-Mart has implemented a policy of not allowing any supplier to account for more than 3 percent of its total purchases.[22]

Bargaining Power of Buyers

From the perspective of buyers (individual or corporate), firms in the focal industry are essentially suppliers. Therefore, the previous discussion on suppliers is relevant here (Table 2.1). Four conditions lead to strong bargaining power of buyers. First, a small number of buyers leads to strong bargaining power. For example, around the world, thousands of automobile component suppliers try to sell to a small number of automakers, such as BMW, GM, and Honda. These buyers frequently extract price concessions and quality improvements by playing off suppliers against each other. When these automakers invest abroad, they often suggest, encourage, or coerce suppliers to invest with them and demand that supplier factories be sited next to the assembly plants—at the suppliers' expense. Not surprisingly, many suppliers comply.[23]

Second, buyers can enhance their bargaining power if products of an industry do not clearly produce cost savings or add value for buyers. For example, repeated and frequent upgrades in software packages are causing a buyer fatigue. Heads of information technology (IT) departments at many buyer companies are increasingly suspicious about whether the costly new systems are really able to help them save money. In consumer electronics (especially wireless communications), the industry has recently unleashed a bewildering array of new products such as cellular phones, personal digital assistants (PDA), and e-mail pagers. For some consumers who already invested in these gadgets only a few years ago, the rationale to replace them with an expensive new device such as Handspring's Treo is not compelling (see Video Cases 1.1 and 1.2). The upshot is that reluctant buyers can either refuse to buy or extract significant discounts.

Third, buyers can have strong bargaining power if they purchase standard, undifferentiated commodity products from suppliers. Although automobile components suppliers as a group possess less bargaining power relative to automakers, suppliers are *not* equally powerless. There are usually several tiers of suppliers.[24]

The top tier suppliers are the most crucial, often supplying nonstandard, differentiated key components such as electrical systems, steering wheels, and car seats. The bottom tier consists of suppliers making standard, undifferentiated commodity products such as seat belt buckles, cup holders, or simply nuts and bolts. Not surprisingly, top-tier suppliers possess more bargaining power than bottom-tier suppliers.

Fourth, buyers can increase their bargaining power when they have economic difficulties. During the early 2000s, individual and corporate consumers in much of the world were reluctant to spend when confronted with the global economic recession and uncertainty. Repeated interest rate cuts by American, European, Japanese, and other authorities did not seem to boost consumption. The upshot is that many goods and services were on sale.

Finally, like suppliers, buyers may enhance their bargaining power by entering the focal industry through **backward integration.** For instance, Qualcomm had a 90 percent market share of code division multiple access (CDMA) chips, which power most of the world's cellular phones. Unfortunately, its two largest buyers, Samsung and Nokia, began making their own CDMA chips, which cut Qualcomm's share to 80 percent by 2004.[25] Many department stores and grocery chains, in addition to buying merchandise from national-brand producers, also procure store-brand products (such as Kroger, Meijer, Kenmore [Sears], and Safeway brands), which compete side-by-side with national brands for shelf space. Store-brand products currently command approximately 39 percent of grocery sales in Britain, 21 percent in France, and 16 percent in the United States.[26]

In summary, powerful or desperate buyers can enhance their bargaining power. Buyers' bargaining power may be minimized if firms can sell to numerous buyers, clearly add value, provide differentiated products, help buyers with difficulties, and enhance entry barriers.

Threat of Substitutes

Substitutes are products of different industries that satisfy customer needs currently met by the focal industry. For instance, while Pepsi is *not* a substitute for Coke (Pepsi is a rival in the same industry), tea, coffee, juice, and water are—that is, they are still beverages, but are in a different product category. Two areas of substitutes are particularly threatening (Table 2.1). First, if substitutes have superior quality and function when compared to existing products, they may rapidly emerge to attract a large number of customers. For example, the emergence of online brokerage houses—such as E*Trade, Ameritrade, and Scottrade, which allow investors more convenient, 24/7 online access at much lower transaction costs—has threatened traditional brokerage houses such as Merrill Lynch. Similarly, digital payment start-ups such as Viewpointe and NetDeposit have significantly jeopardized the business of paper check printing companies such as Deluxe Corporation.[27] Conversely, inferior substitutes have little chance of succeeding. For instance, Eurotunnel threatened to replace ferry services between England and France. Yet, it has not only failed to outcompete ferries, but also been substituted by cut-rate airlines such as Ryanair (see Opening Case in Chapter 3) and easyJet.[28]

Second, substitutes pose significant threats if switching costs are low. For example, consumers incur virtually no costs when switching from sugar to a sugar substitute, Nutrasweet. Both are readily available in restaurants and grocery stores. On the other hand, no substitutes exist for large passenger jets, especially for transoceanic transportation. Given the disappearance of ship-based transoceanic passenger service since the days of the movie *Titanic*, the only other way to go to Hawaii or New Zealand seems to be by swimming (!). As a result, Boeing and Airbus can charge higher prices than if there were substitutes for their products.

Overall, the possible threat of substitutes requires firms to vigilantly scan the larger environment, as opposed to the narrowly defined focal industry. Enhancing customer value (such as price, quality, utility, and location) may reduce the attractiveness of substitutes.

Lessons from the Five Forces Framework

Taken together, the five forces framework provides three significant lessons. First, it reinforces the important point that not all industries are equal in terms of their potential profitability. It sheds light on why, for example, the pharmaceutical industry is always more profitable than the grocery store industry around the world. The upshot is that when firms have the luxury to choose (such as diversified companies contemplating entry into new industries or entrepreneurial start-ups scanning new opportunities), they are better off choosing an industry whose five forces are weak. Michael Dell, the founder of Dell Computer, confessed that he probably would have avoided the PC industry had he known how competitive it could become. Second, the task for strategists is to assess the opportunities (O) and threats (T) underlying each competitive force affecting an industry, and then estimate the likely profit potential of the industry. Finally, according to Porter, the key is "to stake out a position that is less vulnerable to attack from head-to-head opponents, whether established or new, and less vulnerable to erosion from the direction of buyers, suppliers, and substitutes."[29] Consequently, the five forces framework is also known as the **industry positioning** school.

Although Porter put forward the thrust of this framework more than twenty years ago, it has continued to assert strong influence in strategy practice and research today. While it has been debated and modified (as introduced later), its core features remain remarkably insightful when analyzing new phenomena such as e-commerce. Table 2.3 (p. 52) suggests that despite the myth that the Internet may completely rewrite the rules of competition, the contrary may be true. The so-called "New Economy" "appears less like a new economy than like an old economy that has access to a new technology."[30] Unfortunately, from the perspective of the five forces, the benefits of the Internet, such as making information widely available and linking buyers and sellers together, tend to threaten profit margins of the focal firms that try to capture these benefits.[31]

TABLE 2.3   The Five Forces and the Internet

Five Forces	Threats Represented by The Internet
Rivalry among competitors	▪ Reduces differentiation among competitors. ▪ Drives the basis of competition to price. ▪ Increases the number of competitors, which despite having some online presence may be outside the region/country.
Threat of potential entry	▪ Reduces entry barriers such as the need for sales forces and brick-and-mortar channels. ▪ Internet applications are difficult to keep proprietary from new entrants. ▪ Incumbents do not have sufficient advantage to deter entry.
Bargaining power of suppliers	▪ More convenient for suppliers to reach end users, reducing the leverage of the focal firm. ▪ Internet procurement and digital marketplaces may give all companies equal access to suppliers, reducing the value of "special relationships."
Bargaining power of buyers	▪ Buyers possess greater information on the products of the focal firm and of competitors, facilitating comparison shopping. ▪ Buyers can reach producers (suppliers) more easily, reducing the focal firm's bargaining power in distribution industries.
Threat of substitutes	▪ The proliferation of Internet applications may create new substitutes, making the focal firm's products (goods and services) obsolete.

Sources: Based on (1) B. Canzer, 2003, E-Business: Strategic Thinking and Practice, Boston: Houghton Mifflin; (2) M. Porter, 2001, Strategy and the Internet, Harvard Business Review, March: 63–78; (3) S. Rangan & R. Adner, 2001, Profits and the Internet: Seven misconceptions, MIT Sloan Management Review, summer: 44–53.

TABLE 2.4   Three Generic Competitive Strategies

	Product Differentiation	Market Segmentation	Key Functional Areas
Cost leadership	Low (mainly by price)	Low (mass-market)	Manufacturing and materials management
Differentiation	High (mainly by uniqueness)	High (many market segments)	Research and development, marketing and sales
Focus	Low (mainly by price) or high (mainly by uniqueness)	Low (one or a few segments)	Any kind of functional area

THREE GENERIC STRATEGIES

Having identified the five forces underlying industry competition, the next challenge is how to make strategic choices. In 1985, Porter suggested three **generic strategies**, (1) cost leadership, (2) differentiation, and (3) focus, all of which are intended to strengthen the focal firm's position relative to the five competitive forces (see Table 2.4).[32]

Cost Leadership

Recall that our definition of strategy (see Chapter 1) is a firm's theory of how to compete successfully. A **cost leadership** strategy basically indicates that a firm's theory of how to compete successfully centers on low costs and prices. Offering the same product value at a lower price—in other words, better value—tends to attract many more customers. A cost leader often positions its products to target the "average" customers for the mass-market with little differentiation. The key functional areas of cost leaders are manufacturing and materials management, which need to continually ride down the experience curve to keep lowering costs. The hallmark of this strategy is a *high-volume, low-margin* approach.

A great advantage for a cost leader, such as Wal-Mart, is to minimize the threats from the five forces. First, the cost leader is able to charge lower prices and make better profits than higher cost rivals. Second, its low cost advantage is a significant entry barrier that keeps other rivals out. Third, because the cost leader typically buys a large volume from suppliers, it reduces the bargaining power of suppliers.[33] Fourth, the cost leader would be less negatively affected if strong suppliers increase prices or powerful buyers force prices down. Finally, the cost leader challenges substitutes to not only outcompete the utility of its products, but also its prices, a very difficult proposition. Therefore, a true cost leader is relatively safe from these threats. This enviable position is the main reason so many companies try to become cost leaders. However, only a few succeed. For example, Nissan, for decades, has tried, but failed, to outcompete Toyota on a model-by-model basis. This is because Toyota, the cost leader, has a bigger market share, its factories have greater economies of scale for each model, and therefore, its unit costs are usually lower.

However, at least two drawbacks come with being the cost leader. First, the danger of being outcompeted on costs always exists. This forces the leader to *continuously* search for lower costs. For example, a majority of Wal-Mart's nongrocery products are currently produced in low-cost countries such as China, Indonesia, Mexico, and Vietnam. However, twenty years ago, most of them were made in Hong Kong, Singapore, South Korea, and Taiwan, collectively known as the Four Tigers. As the Four Tigers gradually lost their low-cost edge, Wal-Mart switched to even lower-cost countries. The managerial task of replacing hundreds of suppliers in the Four Tigers with an equal or larger number of suppliers in a different set of less economically developed countries is simply mind-boggling. Second, in the relentless drive to cut costs, a cost leader may make trade-offs that compromise the value that customers perceive. A case in point is Toyota's attempt to market a car in Japan with unpainted bumpers. Consumers quickly noticed and rebelled, forcing this model to be withdrawn. The lesson from this experience is not to cut too many corners.

Overall, most companies pursue a cost leadership strategy because they find little alternative basis for distinction. However, a number of other firms have decided to be different by embracing the second generic strategy discussed next.

Differentiation

A **differentiation** strategy focuses on how to deliver products that customers perceive as valuable and different (Table 2.4). While cost leaders serve "typical" customers, differentiators target customers in smaller, well-defined segments who are willing to pay premium prices. The key is a *low-volume, high-margin* approach. The ability to charge higher prices enables differentiators to outperform competitors that are unable to do the same. A Lexus car or a Sony TV is not significantly more expensive to produce than a Chrysler car or a Samsung TV. Yet, customers always pay more to get a Lexus or a Sony, enabling these companies to earn healthy profits. To attract customers willing to pay premiums, differentiated products must have some truly or perceived unique attributes, such as quality, sophistication, prestige, and luxury. The challenge is to identify these attributes and deliver value centered on them for *each* market segment.[34] Therefore, in addition to maintaining a strong lineup for its 3-, 5-, and 7-series, BMW is now filling in the "gaps" by adding new 1- and 6-series as well as the revamped Mini and Rolls-Royce brands.[35] For differentiators, research and development (R&D) is an important functional area through which new features can be experimented with and introduced. Another key function is marketing and sales, focusing on both capturing customers' psychological desires, which lure them to buy, and satisfying their needs after sales through excellent service.

According to the five forces framework, the less a differentiator resembles its rivals, the more protected its products are. For instance, Disney theme parks advertise the unique experience associated with Disney movie characters, whereas Kings Island and Six Flags theme parks brag about how fast and tall their roller coasters are. In cosmetics, while L'Oreal stresses how many patents it has filed, Shiseido makes more concrete claims: Its new Body Creator skin gel can melt 1.1 kilograms (2.4 pounds) of body fat a month without any need to diet or exercise (see Closing Case). The bargaining power of suppliers is relatively less of a problem because differentiators may be better able (as compared to cost leaders) to pass on some (but not unlimited) price increases to customers. Similarly, the bargaining power of buyers is less problematic because differentiators tend to enjoy relatively strong brand loyalty.

On the other hand, a differentiation strategy has two drawbacks. First, the differentiator may have difficulty sustaining the basis of differentiation in the long run. There is always the danger that customers may decide that the price differential between the differentiator's and cost leader's products is not worth paying for. For example, because Mercedes and Chrysler cars increasingly share common parts, Mercedes customers may increasingly wonder why they pay Mercedes prices to get Chrysler material. Second, the differentiator has to confront relentless efforts of competitive imitation. As the overall quality of the industry goes up, brand loyalty in favor of the leading differentiators may decline. For example, IBM's PCs used to command a premium in the 1980s, but not anymore. The upshot is that differentiators must watch out for imitators and avoid pricing their products out of the market.

Overall, a differentiation strategy requires more creativity and capability than a single-minded drive to lower costs. Successful differentiators are able to earn healthy returns.

Focus

A **focus** strategy serves the needs of a particular segment or niche of an industry (Table 2.4). The segment can be defined by geographical market, by type of customer, or by product line. While the breadth of the focus is a matter of degree, focused firms usually serve the needs of a segment so unique that broad-based competitors choose not to serve that same segment. As shown in the Opening Case, a small number of focused competitors dominate the ultra luxury segment of the car industry. During negotiations for such cars, price is usually not much of an issue. The key is to provide "meticulous, 'Wow!' service," according to one Bentley dealer.[36]

In essence, a focused firm is a specialized differentiator or a specialized cost leader. Although it sounds like a tongue twister, a specialized differentiator (such as Bentley) is basically more differentiated than the large differentiator (such as BMW). This approach can be successful when a focused firm possesses intimate knowledge about a particular segment. The logic of how a traditional differentiator can dominate the five forces, discussed before, applies here, the only exception being a much smaller, narrower, but sharper focus. The two drawbacks of differentiation, namely, the difficulty to sustain such expensive differentiation and the challenge of defending against ambitious imitation, also apply here.

A focused firm can also be a specialized cost leader. For example, India's focused IT firms, such as Infosys, Wipro, and TCS, have successfully competed with US giants many times their size, such as Accenture, EDS, and IBM. Indian firms have developed an excellent reputation for providing high-quality services at low costs (see Opening Case in Chapter 1). Their programmers earn approximately $5,000 to $10,000 a year, doing the same (or sometimes better) work performed by their US and European colleagues who are paid five to ten times more. Again, the same rationale for a traditional cost leader to dominate the five forces, described earlier, applies here. The key difference is that a focused cost leader deals with a narrower segment. The two drawbacks, the danger of being outcompeted on costs and of cutting too many corners, are also relevant in the focus strategy.[37]

Lessons from the Three Generic Strategies

The essence of the three strategic choices is whether to *perform activities differently* or to *perform different activities* relative to competitors.[38] Two lessons emerge. First, cost and differentiation are two fundamental strategic dimensions. The key is to choose one dimension and focus on it consistently. Second, companies that are stuck in the middle, that is, neither have the lowest costs nor sufficient differentiation (or focus), can indicate either the lack of a clear strategy or a drifting strategy. Their performance can suffer as a consequence.

DEBATES AND EXTENSIONS

Although the industry-based view is a powerful strategic tool, it is not without controversies. Therefore, as a new generation of strategists, you need to understand some of these debates and extensions, and avoid uncritical acceptance of the traditional view. This section introduces eight leading debates: (1) clear versus blurred boundaries of industry, (2) threats versus opportunities, (3) five forces versus a sixth force, (4) industry rivalry versus strategic groups, (5) integrating versus outsourcing, (6) being "stuck in the middle" versus being "all-rounder," (7) positioning versus hypercompetition, and (8) industry- versus firm- and institution-specific determinants of firm performance.

Clear versus Blurred Boundaries of Industry

The heart of the industry-based view is the identification of a clearly demarcated industry. However, this concept of an industry may be increasingly elusive. For example, consider the television broadcasting industry. The emergence of cable, satellite, and telecommunications technologies has blurred the industry's boundaries. A television in the future may control household security systems, play interactive games, and place online orders—essentially blending with the functions of a computer. To jockey for advantageous positions in preparation for such a future, a large number of mergers and alliances have involved television, telecommunications, cable, software, and movie companies in recent years. In other words, ABC's competitors not only include CBS, NBC, CNN, and Fox, but also AT&T, SkyTV, Microsoft, Apple, Sony, and others.[39] So what exactly is this "industry"?

Threats versus Opportunities

Even assuming that industry boundaries can be clearly identified, the assumption that all five forces are (at least potential) threats seems simplistic and has been challenged on two accounts. First, strategic alliances are on the rise, and even competitors are increasingly collaborating with each other.[40] GM and Toyota manufacture cars together. Samsung provides computer chips to Sony. MiG and Sukhoi, two of Russia's leading aircraft and arms rivals, collaborate on marketing and avionics (see Strategy in Action 7.1 in Chapter 7). In other words, even if these rivals don't love each other, they don't hate each other either. Although distrust will continue, some trust in one's competitors seems imperative for collaboration to work.[41] For example, on any given day, Motorola may find AT&T to be a competitor and a partner (as well as a supplier and a buyer). Compared with the traditional, black-and-white view, this more complicated, but more realistic, view requires a more sophisticated understanding of the nature of competition *and* collaboration today (see Chapter 7 for more details).

Second, even if firms do not directly collaborate with competitors, intense rivalry within an industry, long considered a "no-no," may become an opportunity instead of a threat. Such rivalry drives firms to constantly improve and innovate, which not only creates a higher level of competitiveness within a domestic industry, but also results in stronger international competitiveness—a key finding reported by Porter's more recent work.[42] While this may bode well for firms located in a competitive domestic industry, what about firms located in a country where the domestic rivalry is not strong? Interestingly, instead of staying there and enjoying the relative tranquility as suggested by the five forces framework, a number of ambitious IT companies from India, Israel, Singapore, South Korea, and elsewhere have come to Silicon Valley to seek out the most competitive environment. Their rationale is that only by being closer to "where the action is" can they hope to become globally competitive.[43] In other words, the new strategic motto seems to be: "Love thy competitors! They make you stronger." Overall, it seems that the five forces model may have overemphasized the threat (T) part of the SWOT analysis. A more balanced view needs to highlight both O and T.

Five Forces versus a Sixth Force

The five forces Porter identified in the 1980s are not necessarily exhaustive. In 1990, Porter added related and supporting industries as an important force that affects an industry's competitiveness (see also Chapter 4).[44] This is endorsed by Andrew Grove, the former CEO of Intel, who suggested the term, **complementors.**[45] Basically, complementors are firms selling products that add value to the products of a focal industry.[46] The complementors to the PC industry are firms that produce software applications. When complementors produce exciting products (such as new games), the demand for PCs grows, and vice versa. Therefore, it may be helpful to add complementors as a possible sixth force. This is especially important for high-tech industries with "increasing returns" (in other words, "winner-take-all" markets) as discussed earlier.

Industry Rivalry versus Strategic Groups

While the five forces framework focuses on the industry level, how meaningful it is depends on how an "industry" is defined. In a broadly defined industry such as the automobile industry, not every firm is competing against each other. However, groups of firms within a broad industry *do* compete against each other, such as the mass-market, luxury, and ultra luxury groups in the Opening Case (see also Figure 2.2 on next page). These different groups of firms are known as **strategic groups.** Some argue that strategy within one group tends to be similar: Within the automobile industry, firms in the mass-market group pursue cost leadership, firms in the luxury group pursue differentiation, and firms in the ultra luxury group pursue focus. It is also believed that members within a strategic group also tend to perform similarly.[47]

While this intuitive idea seems uncontroversial, a debate has erupted on three issues. First, how stable are strategic groups? This question boils down to how to identify these groups and how to assess their stability once they are identified. Researchers have explored a number of objective measures (such as R&D intensity), and the results are inconclusive. One side of the debate argues that strategic groups are relatively stable.[48] Another side disagrees, by suggesting that "real" stable strategic groups may not exist, and that documented strategic groups may be simply a

FIGURE 2.2   **Three Strategic Groups in the Global Automobile Industry**

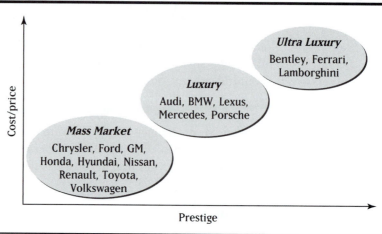

convenient way to summarize firm-level data at one point in time.[49] This problem can be shown in Figure 2.3, which draws on the top five auto firms based on US sales volume to identify *subgroups* within the mass-market strategic group.[50] Panel A uses 1985 data to show that based on quality and aggressiveness, the American Big Three essentially competed with each other in Cell 2 (the low quality–less aggressive subgroup), whereas the two Japanese firms are in the high-quality subgroup (Cells 1 and 3). However, the difficulty of such an analysis becomes evident when we examine Panel B using 1995 data, which shows improvement among *all* competitors. While the Japanese maintained their quality edge, three US firms significantly closed the quality gap. In terms of aggressiveness, again, all three US firms made impressive improvement, with Chrysler possibly joining Toyota and Honda in Cell 3 (the high quality–very aggressive subgroup). In other words, group memberships may change.

Second, assuming strategic groups exist and firms can change group membership, such a change is likely to be a slow and uncertain process. The debate centers on the role of **mobility barriers**, which are within-industry differences that inhibit the movement between strategic groups.[51] A key question is: How important are mobility barriers? The Opening Case shows several luxury carmakers interested in muscling their way into the ultra luxury group.[52] Because of mobility barriers, not all new entrants will succeed.

Finally, because strategic group analysis usually requires large quantities of objective data, how useful is this analysis when data are scarce, especially when entering new markets such as emerging economies? Research in developed economies suggests that while objective measures may change as competition evolves (see Figure 2.3), subjective measures which tap into executives' cognitive inclusion and exclusion of certain firms as competitors may provide more reliable data.[53] This is because executives, when confronting the complexity of industry competition, are likely to use some *simplifying* schemes to better organize their strategic understanding around some identifiable reference points.[54] One recent

FIGURE 2.3   **Subgroups Within the Mass-Market Strategic Group in the US Automobile Industry**

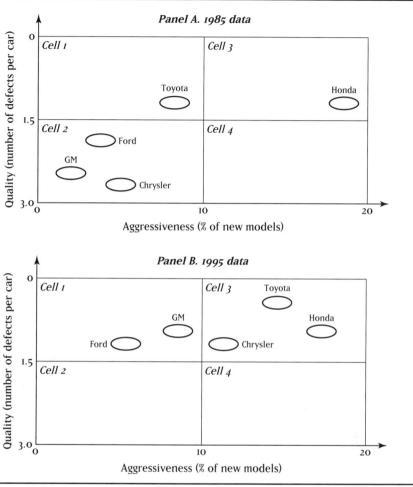

Source: Adapted from R. Hamilton, E. Eskin, & M. Michaels, 1998 "Assessing competitors: The gap between strategic intent and core capability" (p. 413 and 415), Long Range Planning, 31: 406–417. Copyright ©1998. Reprinted with permission from Elsevier.

study in the Chinese electronics industry found that executives may use ownership type, a simple and easily identifiable reference point, to cognitively organize strategic groups.[55] In other words, state-owned enterprises tend to compete with each other, private-owned firms watch each other closely, and foreign entrants benchmark against each other. Their strategic postures (such as defenders, prospectors, and analyzers) also differ accordingly (see Table 2.5 on next page).

Overall, the strategic group analysis has become a useful, but somewhat controversial, middle ground between industry- and firm-level analyses. Regardless of whether "real" strategic groups exist, if the *idea* of strategic groups helps managers simplify the complexity they confront when analyzing an industry, then the strategic group concept seems to have some value.

TABLE 2.5   **Strategic Groups and Ownership Types in the Chinese Electronics Industry**

STRATEGIC GROUP	DEFENDER	ANALYZER	PROSPECTOR
Ownership type	State ownership	Foreign ownership	Private ownership
Customer base	Stable	Mixed	Unstable
Product mix	Stable	Mixed	Changing
Growth strategy	Cautious	Mixed	Aggressive
Managers	Older, more conservative	Mixed	Younger, more aggressive

Source: Adapted from M. W. Peng, J. Tan, & T. Tong, 2004, Ownership types and strategic groups in an emerging economy (p. 1110), Journal of Management Studies, 41 (7): 1105–1129.

Integrating versus Outsourcing

One of the top four most fundamental questions in strategy is how to determine the scope of a firm.[56] As noted earlier, the industry-based view advises the focal firm to consider integrating *backward* (to compete with suppliers) or *forward* (to compete with buyers)—or at least threaten to do so. This strategy is especially recommended when market uncertainty is high, coordination with suppliers/buyers requires tight control because of the highly specialized assets (those with no or little alternative use) involved, and the number of suppliers and/or buyers is small.[57] However, this strategy of integration by acquiring suppliers and/or buyers is very expensive because it takes huge sums of capital to acquire independent suppliers and buyers.

In the last two decades, a great debate has erupted challenging the wisdom of integration. Critics make two arguments. First, they argue that under uncertain conditions, *less* integration (not more) is advisable.[58] When demand is uncertain, a focal firm with no internal component units can simply reduce output by discontinuing or not renewing supply contracts, whereas a firm stuck with its own internal supplier units may keep producing simply to keep these supplier units employed. In other words, integration may reduce *strategic flexibility*, which may have severe performance consequences.[59] Second, critics argue that internal suppliers, which had to work hard for contracts if they were independent suppliers, may lose high-powered market incentives simply because their business is now taken care of by the "family."[60] Over time, these internal suppliers may become less competitive relative to outside suppliers. The focal firm thus faces a dilemma: To go with outside suppliers keeps internal suppliers idle, but to choose internal suppliers sacrifices cost and quality. In the last two decades, clearly these two arguments have won the day. Integration is out, and outsourcing is in. **Outsourcing** is defined as turning over all or part of an activity to an outside supplier to improve the performance of the focal firm (as shown in Opening Case in Chapter 1). Outsourcing not only involves components, but also numerous other functions (such as manufacturing, human resources, logistics, and IT) and numerous countries (such as China, India, Mexico, and Russia). As a part of widespread outsourcing (often in combination with downsizing), the end result is usually a more focused firm doing what it does the best.[61]

The Japanese challenge in the 1980s and 1990s influenced the outsourcing movement. Given that the five forces framework is a product of prevailing Western strategic practices of the 1970s, the Japanese way of managing suppliers, through what is called a *keiretsu* (interfirm network), seems radically different. For example, in the early 1990s, GM, which had 700,000 employees, downsized 90,000 employees, whereas Toyota's *total* headcount was only about 65,000, less than the number of people GM reduced.[62] Many activities that GM performs, such as those in internal supplier units, are undertaken by Toyota's *keiretsu* member firms using non-Toyota employees. Yet, at the same time, Toyota has far fewer suppliers than GM. They tend to be "cherry picked," trusted members of the *keiretsu*. Instead of treating suppliers as adversaries who should be kept at an arm's length, Toyota treats its suppliers (mostly first-tier ones) as collaboration partners by codeveloping proprietary technology with them, relying on them to deliver directly to the assembly line just in time, and helping them when they are in financial difficulty. However, Toyota relies on more than just trust and goodwill. To minimize the potential loss of high-powered market incentive on the part of *keiretsu* members, Toyota often practices a dual sourcing strategy, namely, splitting the contract between a *keiretsu* member and a nonmember (often a local company when Toyota moves abroad).[63] This makes sure that both the internal (*keiretsu*) and external suppliers are motivated to do their best.

Healthy relationships with suppliers may have direct benefits.[64] In 1986, Toyota employed 340 buyers to purchase parts for 3.6 million automobiles (10,560 units per buyer), whereas GM had 3,000 buyers to do the same job for 6 million vehicles (2,000 units per buyer). Such a difference resulted in a $700 cost advantage per car for Toyota, which was nearly 10 percent of the total cost of a small car.[65] Overall, the Japanese approach, exemplified by Toyota, has been widely admired and imitated by firms throughout the world.[66] Such global diffusion has been spearheaded by (1) Japanese firms' replication of the *keiretsu* networks in numerous foreign locations and (2) non-Japanese firms' indigenous learning.[67] Such learning played a major role behind the improvement of US car companies during the 1990s (see Figure 2.3). GM, for example, took a page from the Toyota playbook by spinning off Delphi—now GM is largely out of the components business. Overall, similar to the idea discussed earlier that rivalry may represent opportunities instead of threats, solid value-adding relationships with suppliers (and buyers and other partners) are now widely regarded as a source of competitive advantages.[68]

However, the debate does not end here. In a curious turn of events, while many US firms have become more "Japanese-like," Japanese companies are increasingly under pressure to become more "American-like" (!) when coping with more than a decade of recession in Japan in the 1990s and beyond. This is because some outsourced activities, crucial to the core business, should not have been outsourced; otherwise, the firm risks becoming a "hollow corporation."[69] Supplier relations that are too close may introduce rigidities, resulting in a loss of much-needed flexibility.[70] In Japan, previously rock-solid buyer-supplier links have started to fray. Lead firms are now less willing to help troubled suppliers improve. Even *keiretsu* members, previously discouraged (if not outright forbidden) to seek contracts outside the network, are now encouraged to look for work elsewhere, because lead firms believe that the benefits suppliers learn from dealing with other customers may eventually accrue to lead firms (such as Toyota).[71] Overall, the rise and fall of these two per-spectives in the last two decades suggest the importance of careful analysis when determining the optimal scope of a firm.[72]

Being "Stuck in the Middle" versus Being "All-Rounder"

A key proposition in the industry-based view is that most firms must choose either cost leadership or differentiation. Pursuing both may cause firms to be "stuck in the middle" with poor performance prospects. However, examples abound of highly successful firms, such as Toyota, that stand out as both cost leaders *and* differentiators. As a result, a debate has emerged. First, critics argue that when holding technology constant, the experience curve does not decline continually; instead, at some point the curve bottoms out. Therefore, for firms that are already operating at the maximum efficiency scale, expanding output does not create further cost and efficiency gains.[73] In many industries, several firms, not just one, can attain this minimum-cost position. At that point, the only way for these low-cost firms to distinguish themselves is through some form of differentiation[74] (see Strategy in Action 2.2).

Second, critics suggest that technology may not be constant. Manufacturing technology in the 1970s influenced the idea that differentiators cannot be cost competitive, whereas more recent, **flexible manufacturing technology** has enabled firms to produce differentiated products at a low cost (usually on a smaller batch basis than the large batch typically produced by cost leaders). Thus, the name of the game may become **mass customization,** pursuing cost leadership and differentiation *simultaneously.*[75]

A recent review of seventeen studies confirms that instead of being underdogs, some firms "stuck in the middle" have the potential to be "all-rounders," being both cost competitive and differentiated.[76] Another study finds that for exporters in Brazil, Chile, and Mexico, a cost leadership strategy bodes well for developed economies, whereas a differentiation strategy succeeds in other emerging economies.[77] Thus, in-ternationally ambitious firms from these countries may need to deploy both strategies simultaneously when entering different markets. Although not conclusive, these findings do raise interesting questions and enrich the substance of the debate.

Positioning versus Hypercompetition

Another group of critics argue that the focus on industry positioning and generic strategy selection may be too static, not allowing enough room for dynamic changes associated with industry evolution.[78] The reality in most of the world's industries in the last two decades is that the only constant seems to be change. Thus, critics argue that firms can no longer count on succeeding by choosing a generic strategy once. Over long periods of time, firms are often forced to shift generic strategies (such as cost leaders becoming differentiators). Therefore, any advantage firms may acquire by a single round of positioning is likely to be temporary. Critics argue that competition in many industries has now become **hypercompetition,** whose hallmark is dynamic maneuvering intended to unleash a series of small, unpredictable, but powerful, actions to erode the rival's competitive advantage.[79] In military terms, if

STRATEGY IN ACTION 2.2. *Our Instant Noodles Are Different!*

An instant-noodle war is erupting in Asia. Instant noodles, as a processed, convenient food item, are not cheap compared to traditional noodles. Consumers in low-income countries such as Indonesia and Vietnam are price sensitive, forcing firms to compete on price. The technology is mature, enabling a number of firms to become low-cost producers. The next phase of competition seems to be differentiation, as firms launch a proliferation of new flavors. In 2002, Indofood (*http://www.indofood.co.id*) of Indonesia, the world's largest manufacturer of instant noodles, launched twelve regional flavors to appeal to resurgent local pride sparked by the country's recent political decentralization. Indofood is forced to differentiate, because it is under attack by new players such as Alhami, which undercuts Indofood on price. In addition, Alhami embraces an Islamic image and boasts that its noodles are *halal,* or permissible for Muslims, a message likely to resonate very well in Indonesia, which is the world's most populous Muslim country. Similar drama is unfolding in Vietnam, where three big state-owned companies, forty private firms, and two foreign multinationals, the Anglo-Dutch giant Unilever (*http://www.unilever.com*) and Taiwan's Uni-President Enterprises (*http://www.pec.com.tw*), are all scrambling for a piece of the action. One private firm launched twenty new flavors in 2002, including several Korean-flavored noodles, one of which is a *kimchi* (fermented cabbage) flavor, a quintessential Korean delicacy (anything Korean, ranging from TV shows to

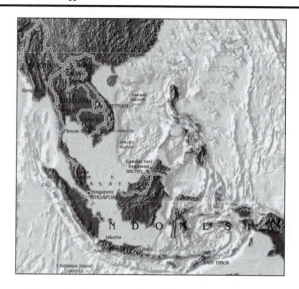

make-up, has been considered hip among Vietnamese lately). Not to be outdone, a usually sleepy state-owned firm launched ten new flavors at the same time, including its own *kimchi* noodles. Interestingly, foreign managers at Unilever and Uni-President, who are not Koreans, are scratching their heads trying to decide whether they want their products to be "Korean" or not.

Sources: Based on (1) A. Granitsas, 2003, The instant-noodle war, Far Eastern Economic Review, January 9: 42–43; (2) M. W. Peng, 2003, Four CEOs in one year: The case of Indofood, unpublished working paper.

the traditional industry-based view can be conceptualized as *static warfare* aimed at occupying certain desirable positions as defendable strongholds, the hypercompetition school argues for *mobile warfare* designed to disrupt, dislodge, and outmaneuver rivals. The name of the game is *not* to seek a sustainable competitive advantage, which is a very difficult proposition in any case; instead, the goal is to disrupt the status quo by seizing the initiative through a series of *temporary* advantages.

While it is easy to appreciate how hypercompetition is played out in fast-moving, high-tech industries such as IT, it is important to note that competition is heating up across the board around the world, including many seemingly low-tech industries such as toys (see Strategy in Action 2.3 on next page).[80] Such a relentless drive to outmaneuver rivals may potentially drive many industries to the Adam Smith world of perfect competition, in which the competitive advantages of all competitors are eliminated and no firm makes above-average returns. While Porter dismissed such hypercompetition as "a self-inflicted wound, not the inevitable

Strategy in Action 2.3. *Managing Hypercompetition in the Toy Industry*

Although toys are fun, surviving in the $50 billion global toy industry requires a steel stomach for uncertainty. Nearly half of the output is consumed by 2 percent of the world's children who live in the United States, and their demand has extreme seasonality. November and December represent approximately 50 percent of annual sales, nearly half of which occur during the last week before Christmas. Because most manufacturing is in Asia, the long transit time rules out the possibility of restocking during the Christmas season. Upfront planning must be flawless. Any breakdown in the supply chain, such as the US West Coast dock workers' strike in 2002, can devastate an entire season. In addition, the hottest new toys may be largely unknown until the buying season is well underway. Hot toys can emerge suddenly, leaving corporate buyers scrambling for whatever stock they can scrounge up around the factories in Asia.

Both based in the United States, Mattel (*http://www.mattell.com*) and Hasbro (*http://www.hasbro.com*) lead this mature industry and control approximately one-third of the market (20 percent versus 13 percent). None of the next top ten players, such as Denmark's LEGO (*http://www.lego.com*) and Hong Kong's VTech (*http://www.vtech.com*), controls more than 3 percent of the market. While thousands of new toys are introduced every year, only a small fraction lasts longer than one or two years—classics such as Mattel's Barbie and Hasbro's Mr. Potato Head are exceptions rather than the rule. Given the fickle demand and changing fads, advantages gained in one year may well be temporary. Even Mattel, which sells 70 percent of new products every year, may be "just one good idea away from going out of business," according to its vice president for product design.

Firms' coping mechanisms focus on (1) reducing seasonality, (2) increasing the number of channels, and (3) building variety. First, through year-round advertising, firms hope to reduce seasonality. Second, toy companies often team with movie studios and fast food chains. While the main distribution channels are discounters such as Wal-Mart (*http://www.walmart.com*) and Target (*http://www.target.com*) and national toy chains such as Toys R Us (*http://www.toysrus.com*), toy companies also hawk toys in gas stations, convenience stores, and entertainment venues.

Third, all toy companies endeavor to add variety (or the appearance of it), such as numerous outfits for the Barbie doll and different products such as cars, ships, and Star Wars action sets all built on the same LEGO building blocks. The most interesting scheme is the rolling mix, which continually introduces slightly different versions of the *same* product. Mattel first experimented with the rolling mix in the mid-1990s when pushing the Hot Wheels die-cast cars. When customers see new products in the store, they are more likely to buy. However, predicting the demand for individual styles and coordinating with manufacturers is difficult. The rolling mix solves this problem by automatically changing 7 to 8 percent of the seventy-two-car assortment every two weeks. The entire product line changes over twice over a year. Retailers love the rolling mix, not only because it increases sales without requiring more shelf space, but also because it eliminates the need to keep different inventories for individual styles—the mix comes from the factory prepackaged. Manufacturers like it too, because they do not have to constantly scramble in response to irregular replenishment requests. This idea has been quickly imitated by competitors. The industry as a whole, thus, has moved to a high-speed, continuously rolling game, with each move aiming to capture some *temporary* advantage, which, by design, will be cannibalized when the next mix arrives.

Sources: Based on (1) D. Ahlstrom, 2003, Personal communication, September 10; (2) C. Bullington, H. Lee, & C. Tang, 1998, Successful strategies for product rollovers, Sloan Management Review, 39 (3): 23–30; (3) M. E. Johnson, 2001, Learning from toys: Lessons in managing supply chain risk from the toy industry, California Management Review, 43 (3): 106–124.

outcome of a changing paradigm of competition,"[81] how rivals strike and counter-strike has become an important part of the strategy repertoire (see Chapter 8).

Industry- versus Firm- and Institution-Specific Determinants of Performance

The industry-based view argues that firm performance is most fundamentally determined by industry-specific attributes.[82] While influential, this view has recently been challenged from two directions. The first is the **resource-based view.** Although the five forces framework suggests that certain industries (such as airlines) are highly unattractive, certain firms, such as Southwest Airlines in the United States and Ryanair in Europe, not only enter, but also succeed. Why did these firms succeed? A short answer is that the performance of these winning firms must be determined by firm-specific resources and capabilities independent from unattractive industry conditions.

A second challenge comes from the critique that the industry-based view "ignores industry history and institutions."[83] In particular, Porter's work may have carried some hidden, taken-for-granted assumptions underpinning the way competition was structured in the United States in the 1970s. As "rules of the game" in a society, institutions obviously affect firm strategies. Therefore, strategists need to understand how institutions affect the way firms compete. This view has become known as the **institution-based view.** Overall, these two views complement the industry-based view, and are introduced in Chapters 3 and 4.

Making Sense of the Debates

The eight debates suggest that the industry-based view—and in fact the strategy field as a whole—is dynamic, exciting, and yet unsettling. All eight debates direct their attention to Porter's work, which has become an *incumbent* in the strategy field. When describing his work, Porter deliberately chose the word "framework" rather than the more formal "model." In his own words, "frameworks identify the relevant variables and the questions that the user must answer in order to develop conclusions tailored to a particular industry and company."[84] In this sense, Porter's frameworks have succeeded in identifying variables and raising questions, while not necessarily providing definitive answers. While some of these debates are more contentious than others, clearly the last word has not been written on any of them.

IMPLICATIONS FOR STRATEGISTS

What are the implications for current and would-be strategists? There are two answers to this question. First, for strategic practice, the industry-based view provides a systematic *foundation* for industry analysis and competitor analysis, upon which more detailed examination, introduced in later chapters, can be added. Second, the industry-based view provides a set of answers to the four fundamental questions in strategy discussed in Chapter 1. The first question is "Why do firms differ?" The industry-based view answers that the five forces in different industries lead to diversity in firm behavior. The answer to the second question, "How do firms behave?," boils down to how they maximize opportunities and minimize threats presented by the five forces. A traditional answer to the third question, "What determines the scope of the firm?," is to examine the bargaining power of the focal firm relative to that of the suppliers and buyers. Integration, which results in an expanded scope of the firm, is often recommended. However, more recent work suggests caution. Companies are advised to leverage outsourcing opportunities, remain focused on their core activities, and be willing to collaborate not only with suppliers and buyers, but also possibly with their competitors. The fourth question is "What determines the international success and failure of firms?" The answer, again, is that industry-specific conditions must have played a very important role in determining firm performance around the world.

Chapter Summary

1. The industry-based view of strategy grows out of industrial organization (IO) economics, which helps policymakers better understand how firms compete in order to properly regulate them.

2. Pioneered by Michael Porter, the five forces framework forms the backbone of the industry-based view of strategy.

3. The stronger and more competitive the five forces are, the less likely that firms in an industry are able to earn above-average returns, and vice versa.

4. The five forces are (1) interfirm rivalry among competitors within an industry, (2) threat of potential entry, (3) bargaining power of suppliers, (4) bargaining power of buyers, and (5) threat of substitutes.

5. The three generic strategies that are intended to strengthen the focal firm's position relative to the five competitive forces are (1) cost leadership, (2) differentiation, and (3) focus.

6. Leading debates in this area include (1) clear versus blurred boundaries of industry, (2) threats versus opportunities, (3) five forces versus a sixth force, (4) industry rivalry versus strategic groups, (5) integrating versus outsourcing, (6) being "stuck in the middle" versus being "all-rounder," (7) positioning versus hypercompetition, and (8) industry- versus firm- and institution-specific determinants of firm performance.

Key Terms

backward integration	differentiation	entry barriers
bargaining power of suppliers	dominance	excess capacity
	duopoly	experience curves
complementors	economies of scale	exit barriers
cost leadership		

five forces framework	industry	oligopoly
flexible manufacturing technology	industry positioning	outsourcing
focus	know-how	perfect competition
forward integration	mass customization	product differentiation
generic strategies	mobility barriers	scale-based low cost advantages
hypercompetition	monopoly	strategic groups
incumbents	network externalities	structure-conduct-performance (SCP) model
industrial organization (IO) economics	non-scale-based low cost advantages	substitutes

Critical Discussion Questions

1. Why do price wars often erupt in certain industries, but less frequently in other industries? What can a firm do to discourage price wars or to better prepare for price wars?

2. Compare and contrast the five forces affecting the airline industry, the fast food industry, the beauty products industry, and the pharmaceutical industry on a *worldwide* or *regional* basis. Which industry holds more promise for earning higher returns? Why?

3. Conduct a five forces analysis of the "business school" industry or the "higher education" industry. Identify the "strategic group" in which your home institution belongs. Use this analysis to explain why your home institution is doing well (or poorly) in the competition for better students, professors, donors, and ultimately rankings.

4. Among the eight debates outlined, choose the debate you feel most strongly about. Assemble the best evidence in support of your position and then be your own "devil's advocate" by assembling the best evidence to support the *opposing* position.

5. **ON ETHICS:** "Excessive profits" coming out of monopoly, duopoly, or any kind of strong market power are targets for government investigation and prosecution (for example, Microsoft was charged by both US and EU competition authorities). Yet, strategists openly pursue above-average profits, which are argued to be "fair profits." Do you see an ethical dilemma here? Make your case either as a government competition official or as a firm strategist (such as Bill Gates).

Closing Case: Competing in the Beauty Products Industry

As a $160 billion-a-year global industry, the beauty products industry encompasses make-up, skin and hair care, perfumes, cosmetic surgery, health clubs, and diet pills. Incumbents have remarkably long staying power in this industry. L'Oreal (http://www.loreal.com) of France, today's industry leader, was founded in 1909. In 1911, both Nivea (http://www.nivea.com) of Germany and Shiseido (http://www.shiseido.co.jp) of Japan were established. In America, Elizabeth Arden (http://www.elizabetharden.com) and Max Factor (http://www.maxfactor.com) were founded at about that same time. All these brands are still around, although not necessarily as independent companies.

Recently, the industry has been growing at 7 percent per year, more than twice the rate of the developed world's GDP. Two groups around the world underpin such strong growth: Richer, aging baby-boomers in developed economies and an increasingly more affluent middle class in emerging economies, such as Brazil, China, India, Russia, and South Korea. Brazil, for example, has a larger army of Avon Ladies (http://www.avon.com), 900,000 strong, than its men and women in the army and navy combined (!).

Three major changes affect this industry. First, a number of new entrants have emerged. Most luxury goods firms, such as Chanel (http://www.chanel.com), Dior (http://www.dior.com), Ralph Lauren (http://www.polo.com), and Yves St Laurent (http://www.ysl.com), now have beauty products. Two consumer goods giants, Proctor & Gamble (P&G, http://www.pg.com) and Unilever (http://www.unilever.com), pose probably the most significant threats. As their traditional products such as diapers and soaps mature, they are pouring more resources into their beauty divisions. Second, changes

in consumer behavior help no-frills retail chains such as Wal-Mart (http://www.walmart.com) gain bargaining power at the expense of fashionable department stores, whose selling costs are high and sales are declining. Wal-Mart, for example, only wants to deal with a handful of big suppliers, which plays into the strength of L'Oreal and P&G. Smaller players, such as Estee Lauder (http://www.esteelauder.com) and Revlon (http://www.revlon.com), which depend more on department stores, are hurting as a result. Finally, incumbents increasingly are fighting back, by emphasizing how unique their products are. L'Oreal, for example, advertised how many patents it has filed. Shiseido made more concrete claims: Its new Body Creator skin gel can melt 1.1 kilograms (2.4 pounds) of body fat a month without any need to diet or exercise. It apparently works, or at least customers believed so: During its first year, 2002, a bottle was bought in Japan every 3.75 seconds (!).

While the market for traditional beauty products becomes more competitive, the industry's real growth may come from areas outside the "radar screen" of the main players: cosmetic surgery and well-being products. First, cosmetic surgery is no longer the exclusive territory of actresses and celebrities. In the United States, it cost $12,000 to reconstruct a woman's breasts ten years ago—now it can be done for $600. More than 70 percent of such customers now earn less than $50,000 a year. The US market for cosmetic surgery, a $20 billion business, has grown 220 percent since 1997. The second area for growth is well-being products, made popular by spas, salons, and clubs linking beauty with natural solutions such as exercise and diet as opposed to chemicals. Numerous entrepreneurs operate a few spas, salons, and clubs here and there and the market is fragmented. Sooner or later, some traditional beauty products companies likely will turn their attention to these new areas as well.

Case Discussion Questions

1. *Why do incumbents have long staying power in this industry?*

2. *How do new entrants overcome entry barriers? How do incumbents react to new entries?*

3. *Why do retail chains gain bargaining power as buyers at the expense of department stores?*

4. *Should traditional competitors focus on expanding new country markets in emerging economies, or on entering hot, new growth product markets in developed economies?*

Sources: Based on (1) Economist, 2003, Pots of promise, May 24: 69–71; (2) Economist, 2003, The color of money, March 8: 59; (3) Economist, 2003, The right to be beautiful, May 24: 9; (4) N. Shute, 2004, Makeover nation, US News & World Report, May 31: 53–63.

Notes

Abbreviation list

AER – *American Economic Review*

AJS – *American Journal of Sociology*

AME – *Academy of Management Executive*

AMJ – *Academy of Management Journal*

AMR – *Academy of Management Review*

APJM – *Asia Pacific Journal of Management*

ASQ – *Administrative Science Quarterly*

BW – *Business Week*

CMR – *California Management Review*

HBR – *Harvard Business Review*

JIBS – *Journal of International Business Studies*

JIM – *Journal of International Management*

JM – *Journal of Management*

JMS – *Journal of Management Studies*

JWB – *Journal of World Business*

LRP – *Long Range Planning*

MDE – *Managerial and Decision Economics*

MIR – *Management International Review*

MS – *Management Science*

OSc – *Organization Science*

OSt – *Organization Studies*

QJE – *Quarterly Journal of Economics*

RES – *Review of Economics and Statistics*

SMJ – *Strategic Management Journal*

SMR – *MIT Sloan Management Review*

1. E. Mason, 1939, Price and production policies of large-scale enterprises, *AER,* 29: 61–74.

2. J. Bain, 1956, *Barriers to New Competition*, Cambridge, MA: Harvard University Press; F. Scherer, 1980, *Industrial Market Structure and Economic Performance*, Boston: Houghton Mifflin.

3. M. Porter, 1981, The contribution of industrial organization to strategic management, *AMR,* 6: 609–620.

4. M. Porter, 1980, *Competitive Strategy*, New York: Free Press.

5. K. Cool & I. Dierickx, 1993, Rivalry, strategic groups, and firm profitability, *SMJ,* 14: 47–59; K. Cool, L. Roller, & B. Leleux, 1999, The relative impact of actual and potential rivalry on firm profitability in the pharmaceutical industry, *SMJ,* 20: 1–14.

6. J. Shamsie, 2003, The context of dominance: An industry-driven framework for exploiting reputation, *SMJ,* 24: 199–215.

7. B. Kim & Y. Lee, 2001, Global capacity expansion strategies, *LRP,* 34: 309–333.

8. J. Campa, 1994, Multinational investment under uncertainty in the chemical processing industries, *JIBS,* 25: 557–578; J. Henderson & K. Cool, 2003, Learning to time capacity expansions, *SMJ,* 24: 393–413.

9. *BW,* 2003, Hamburger hell, March 3: 104–108.

10. S. Lee, M. W. Peng, & J. Barney, 2005, Bankruptcy law and entrepreneurship development: A real options perspective, *AMR* (in press).

11. *BW,* 2002, Everybody wants to eat EMC's lunch, September 2: 76–77.

12. C. Hill, 2003, Boeing versus Airbus, in C. Hill, *International Business,* 4th ed. (p. 295), Boston: McGraw-Hill.

13. F. Katrishen & N. Scordis, 1998, Economies of scale in services: A study of multinational insurers, *JIBS,* 29: 305–324; R. Makadok, 1999, Interfirm differences in scale economics and the evolution of market shares, *SMJ,* 20: 935–952.

14. M. Zeng & P. Williamson, 2003, The hidden dragons, *HBR,* October: 92–99.

15. M. Schilling, 1998, Technological lockout, *AMR,* 23: 267–284.

16. L. Thomas, 1996, Advertising sunk costs and credible spatial preemption, *SMJ,* 17: 481–498.

17. R. Garud & A. Kumaraswamy, 1993, Changing competitive dynamics in network industries, *SMJ,* 14: 351–369; C. Hill, 1997, Establishing a standard: Competitive strategy and technological standards in winner-take-all industries. *AME,* 11 (2): 7–26; M. Schilling, 2002, Technology success and failure in winner-take-all markets, *AMJ,* 45: 387–398; V. Shankar & B. Bayus, 2003, Network effects and competition, *SMJ,* 24: 375–384; C. Shapiro & H. Varian, 1999, *Information Rules,* Boston: Harvard Business School Press.

18. W. B. Arthur, 1996, Increasing returns and the new world of business, *HBR,* July-August: 100–109.

19. H. Chang & F. Tang, 2001, An empirical study on strategic entry barriers in Singapore, *APJM,* 18: 503–517; M. Guillen, 2001, *The Limits of Convergence,* Princeton, NJ: Princeton University Press.

20. M. Bensaou & E. Anderson, 1999, Buyer-supplier relations in industrial markets, *OSc,* 10: 460–481; S. Michael, 2000, Investments to create bargaining power, *SMJ,* 21: 497–514.

21. *BW,* 2002, Coke: The cost of babying bottlers, December 9: 93–94.

22. B. Curtis, B. Dougherty, C. Hackett, R. Patel, & B. Wysong, 2003, *Wal-Mart's Retailing Prospects in Europe,* case study under the supervision of Professor M. W.

Peng, Fisher College of Business, The Ohio State University.

23. M. W. Peng, S. Lee, & J. Tan, 2001, The *keiretsu* in Asia: Implications for multilevel theories of competitive advantage, *JIM,* 7: 253–276.

24. A. Kaufman, C. Wood, & G. Theyel, 2000, Collaboration and technology linkages, *SMJ,* 21: 649–663.

25. A. Weintraub, 2003, Chipping away at Qualcomm's chips, *BW,* June 16: 66–67.

26. *Economist,* 2003, A survey of food (p. 7), December 13: 1–16.

27. T. Mullaney, 2004, E-biz strikes again! (p. 84), *BW,* May 10: 80–90.

28. *Economist,* 2004, The Channel Tunnel: Under water, February 14: 59.

29. M. Porter, 1998, *On Competition* (p. 38), Boston: Harvard Business School Press.

30. M. Porter, 2001, Strategy and the Internet (p. 78), *HBR,* March: 63–78; S. Rangan & R. Adner, 2001, Profits and the Internet: Seven misconceptions, *SMR,* summer: 44–53.

31. Porter, 2001, Strategy and the Internet (p. 66); S. Zaheer & A. Zaheer, 2001, Market microstructure in a global B2B network, *SMJ,* 22: 859–873.

32. M. Porter, 1985, *Competitive Advantage,* New York: Free Press; E. Segev, 1989, A systematic comparative analysis and synthesis of two business-level strategic typologies, *SMJ,* 10: 487–505.

33. W. Lasser & J. Kerr, 1996, Strategy and control in supplier-distributor relationships, *SMJ,* 17: 613–632.

34. W. Desarbo, K. Jedidi, & I. Sinha, 2001, Customer value analysis in a heterogeneous market, *SMJ,* 22: 845–857; M. Kroll, P. Wright, & R. Heiens, 1999, The contribution of product quality to competitive advantage, *SMJ,* 20: 375–384; O. Sorenson, 2000, Letting the market work for you, *SMJ,* 21: 577–592.

35. *BW,* 2003, BMW: Will Panke's high-speed approach hurt the brand? June 9: 57–60.

36. D. Roberts, 2003, Bentley Beijing: Chariots on fire, *BW,* March 24: 66.

37. G. Carroll, 1985, Concentration and specialization, *AJS,* 90: 1262–1283; B. Mascarenhas, 1996, The

founding of specialist firms in a global fragmenting industry, *JIBS,* 27: 27–42.

38. M. Porter, 1996, What is strategy? *HBR,* 74 (6): 61–78.

39. R. Bettis & M. Hitt, 1995, The new competitive landscape, *SMJ,* 16: 7–19.

40. G. Hamel, Y. Doz, & C. K. Prahalad, 1989, Collaborate with your competitors—and win, *HBR,* 67 (1): 133–139.

41. R. Lewicki, D. McAlister, & R. Bies, 1998, Trust and distrust, *AMR,* 23: 438–458.

42. M. Porter, 1990, *The Competitive Advantage of Nations,* New York: Free Press; M. Sakakibara & M. Porter, 2001, Competing at home to win abroad: Evidence from Japanese industry, *RES,* 83: 310–322. See also K. Ito & V. Pucik, 1993, R&D spending, domestic competition, and export performance of Japanese manufacturing firms, *SMJ,* 14: 61–75; G. Miles, C. Snow, & M. Sharfman, 1993, Industry variety and performance, *SMJ,* 14: 163–177.

43. A. Inkpen, A. Sundaram, & K. Rockwood, 2000, Cross-border acquisitions of US technology assets, *CMR,* 42 (3): 50–71; L. Nachum, 2000, Economic geography and the location of TNCs, *JIBS,* 31: 367–385; M. W. Peng & D. Wang. 2000. Innovation capability and foreign direct investment: Toward a learning option perspective, *MIR,* 40 (1): 79–93; R. Pouder & C. St. John, 1996, Hot spots and blind spots: Geographical clusters of firms and innovation, *AMR,* 21: 1192–1225.

44. Porter, 1990, *The Competitive Advantage of Nations.*

45. A. Grove, 1996, *Only the Paranoid Survive,* New York: Doubleday.

46. J. Bonardi & R. Durand, 2003, Managing network effects in high-tech markets, *AME,* 17 (4): 40–52.

47. K. Cool & D. Schendel, 1987, Strategic group formation and performance, *MS,* 33: 1102–1124; A. Nair & S. Kotha, 2001, Does group membership matter? *SMJ,* 22: 221–235; H. Thomas & N. Venkatraman, 1988, Research on strategic groups, *JMS,* 25: 537–555.

48. J. D. Osborne, C. Stubbart, & A. Ramaprasad, 2001, Strategic groups and competitive enactment, *SMJ,* 22: 435–454; S. Tallman, 1991, Strategic management models and resource-based strategies among MNEs in a host country, *SMJ,* 12: 69–82.

49. J. Barney & R. Hoskisson, 1990, Strategic groups: Untested assertions and research proposals, *MDE,* 11: 187–198; D. Dranove, M. Peteraf, & M. Shanley, 1998, Do strategic groups exist? *SMJ,* 19: 1029–1044; R. Wiggins & T. Ruefli, 1995, Necessary conditions for the predictive validity of strategic groups, *AMJ,* 38: 1635–56.

50. R. Hamilton, E. Eskin, & M. Michaels, 1998, Assessing competitors: The gap between strategic intent and core capability, *LRP,* 31: 406–417.

51. R. Caves & P. Ghemawat, 1992, Identifying mobility barriers, *SMJ,* 13: 1–12; R. Caves & M. Porter, 1977, From entry barriers to mobility barriers, *QJE,* 91: 241–261; J. Lee, K. Lee, & S. Rho, 2002, An evolutionary perspective on strategic group emergence, *SMJ,* 23: 727–746.

52. W. Bogner, H. Thomas, & J. McGee, 1996, A longitudinal study of the competitive positions and entry paths of European firms in the US pharmaceutical market, *SMJ,* 17: 85–107.

53. D. Johnson & D. Hoopes, 2003, Managerial cognition, sunk costs, and the evolution of industry structure, *SMJ,* 24: 1057–1068; J. Porac, H. Thomas, F. Wilson, D. Paton, & A. Kanfer, 1995, Rivalry and the industry model of Scottish knitwear producers, *ASQ,* 40: 203–227; M. Peteraf & M. Shanley, 1997, Getting to know you: A theory of strategic group identity, *SMJ,* 18: 165–186; R. Reger & A. Huff, 1993, Strategic groups: A cognitive perspective, *SMJ,* 14: 103–124.

54. A. Fiegenbaum, S. Hart, & D. Schendel, 1996, Strategic reference point theory, *SMJ,* 17: 219–235; G. McNamara, R. Luce, & G. Tompson, 2002, Examining the effect of complexity in strategic group knowledge structures on firm performance, *SMJ,* 23: 151–170.

55. M. W. Peng, J. Tan, & T. Tong, 2004, Ownership types and strategic groups in an emerging economy, *JMS,* 41 (7): 1105–1129.

56. R. Rumelt, D. Schendel, & D. Teece (eds.), 1994, *Fundamental Issues in Strategy,* Boston: Harvard Business School Press. See also A. Afuah, 2003, Redefining firm boundaries in the face of the Internet, *AMR,* 28: 34–53; R. Coase, 1937, The nature of the firm, *Economica,* 4: 386–405.

57. K. Sutcliffe & A. Zaheer, 1998, Uncertainty in the transaction environment, *SMJ*, 19: 1–23; O. Williamson, 1985, *The Economic Institutions of Capitalism*, New York: Free Press.

58. A. Afuah, 2001, Dynamic boundaries of the firm, *SMJ*, 44: 1211–1228; N. Argyres & J. Liebeskind, 1999, Contractual commitments, bargaining power, and governance inseparability, *AMR*, 24: 49–63; K. Harrigan, 1985, *Strategic Flexibility*, New York: Lexington Books.

59. R. D'Aveni & A. Ilinitch, 1992, Complex patterns of vertical integration in the forest products industry: Systematic and bankruptcy risks, *AMJ*, 35: 596–625.

60. J. Mahoney, 1992, The choice of organizational form, *SMJ*, 13: 559–584; A. Vining, 2003, Internal market failure, *JMS*, 40: 431–457; G. Walker, 1994, Asset choice and supplier performance in two organizations—US and Japanese, *OSc*, 5: 583–593.

61. M. Kotabe & S. Swan, 1994, Offshore sourcing, *JIBS*, 25: 115–140; M. Kotabe & H. Zhao, 2002, A taxonomy of sourcing strategic types for MNCs operating in China, *APJM*, 19: 11–27; D. Levy, 1995, International sourcing and supply chain stability, *JIBS*, 26: 343–360.

62. D. E. Westney, 2001, Japanese enterprise faces the twenty-first century, in P. DiMaggio (ed.), *The Twenty-First Century Firm*, (105–143), Princeton, NJ: Princeton University Press.

63. J. Richardson, 1993, Parallel sourcing and supplier performance in the Japanese automobile industry, *SMJ*, 14: 339–350.

64. J. Dyer, 1997, Specialized supplier networks as a source of competitive advantage, *SMJ*, 17: 271–292; C. Hill, 1995, National institutional structures, transaction cost economics, and competitive advantage: The case of Japan, *OSc*, 6: 119–131.

65. J. Dyer & W. Ouchi, 1993, Japanese-style business partnerships, *SMR*, 35: 51–63.

66. J. Womack, D. Jones, & D. Roos, 1990, *The Machine That Changed the World*, New York: Harper & Row.

67. K. Banerji & R. Sambharya, 1996, Vertical *keiretsu* and international market entry, *JIBS*, 27: 89–113; X. Martin, W. Mitchell, & A. Swaminathan, 1995, Recreating and extending Japanese automobile buyer-supplier links in North America, *SMJ*, 16: 589–619; N. Oliver & B. Wilkinson, 1992, *The Japanization of British industry*, Oxford: Blackwell; Peng et al., 2001, The *keiretsu* in Asia.

68. J. Dyer & H. Singh, 1998, The relational view: Cooperative strategy and sources of interorganizational competitive advantage, *AMR*, 23: 660–679.

69. J. Barthelemy, 2003, The seven deadly sins of outsourcing, *AME*, 17 (2): 87–98; A. Takeishi, 2001, Bridging inter- and intra-firm boundaries, *SMJ*, 22: 403–433.

70. M. Kotabe, X. Martin, & H. Domoto, 2003, Gaining from vertical partnerships, *SMJ*, 24: 293–316.

71. C. Ahmadjian & J. Lincoln, 2001, *Keiretsu*, governance, and learning, *OSc*, 12: 683–701; R. Lamming, 2000, Japanese supply chain relationships in recession, *LRP*, 33: 757–778. For evidence showing the persistence of the *keiretsu*, see J. McGuire & S. Dow, 2003, The persistence and implications of Japanese *keiretsu* organization, *JIBS*, 34: 374–388; Peng, et al., 2001, The *keiretsu* in Asia.

72. M. Leiblein, J. Reuer, & F. Dalsace, 2002, Do make or buy decisions matter? The influence of organizational governance on technological performance, *SMJ*, 23: 817–833; C. Nicholls-Nixon & C. Woo, 2003, Technology sourcing and output of established firms, *SMJ*, 24: 651–666.

73. S. Kobrin, 1991, An empirical analysis of the determinants of global integration, *SMJ*, 12: 17–31.

74. C. Hill, 1988, Differentiation versus low cost or differentiation and low cost, *AMR*, 13: 401–412.

75. S. Kotha, 1995, Mass customization, *SMJ*, 16: 21–42; S. Kotha & B. Vadlamani, 1995, Assessing generic strategies, *SMJ*, 16: 75–83; W. Reitsperger, S. Daniel, S. Tallman, & W. Chismar, 1993, Product quality and cost leadership: Compatible strategies? *MIR*, 33: 7–21; R. Sanchez, 1995, Strategic flexibility in product competition, *SMJ*, 16: 135–169; N. Warren, K. Moore, & P. Cardona, 2002, Modularity, strategic flexibility, and firm performance, *SMJ*, 23: 1123–40.

76. C. Campbell-Hunt, 2000, What have we learned about generic competitive strategy? *SMJ*, 21: 127–154.

77. P. Aulakh, M. Kotabe, & H. Teegen, 2000, Export strategies and performance of firms from emerging economies, *AMJ*, 43: 342–361.

78. J. Sampler, 1998, Redefining industry structure for the information age, *SMJ*, 19: 343–355.

79. R. D'Aveni, 1994, *Hypercompetition*, New York: Free Press. See also S. Brown & K. Eisenhardt, 1998, *Competing on the Edge,* Boston: Harvard Business School Press.

80. T. Craig, 1996, The Japanese beer wars, *OSc,* 7: 302–321; A. Ilinitch, R. D'Aveni, & A. Lewin, 1996, New organizational forms and strategies for managing in hypercompetitive environments, *OSc,* 7: 211–220; J. Richardson, 1996, Vertical integration and rapid response in fashion apparel, *OSc,* 7: 400–413.

81. Porter, 1998, *On Competition* (p. 39).

82. A. McGahan & M. Porter, 1997, How much does industry matter, really? *SMJ,* 18: 15–30; R. Schmalense, 1985, Do markets differ much? *AER,* 75: 341–351.

83. S. Oster, 1994, *Modern Competitive Analysis,* 2nd ed. (p. 46), New York: Oxford University Press.

84. M. Porter, 1994, Toward a dynamic theory of strategy, in R. Rumelt, D. Schendel, & D. Teece (eds.), *Fundamental Issues in Strategy* (p. 427), Boston: Harvard Business School Press.

Chapter 3

Leveraging Resources and Capabilities

Outline

- Understanding resources and capabilities
- Resources, capabilities, and the value chain
- The VRIO framework
- Debates and extensions
- Implications for strategists

Opening Case: Ryanair: A Rising Star in the Airline Industry

Devastated by the post-9/11 shocks, global economic recession, war in Iraq, and the SARS outbreak in Asia, the airline industry around the world has had a terrible time, perhaps the worst in the one-hundred-year history of aviation. Yet, the Dublin, Ireland–based Ryanair (http://www.ryanair.com), a low-cost carrier founded in 1985 and modeled after America's much-heralded Southwest Airlines (http://www.iflyswa.com), has defied gravity and scaled new heights. During 2002–03, Ryanair's 30 percent operating profit margin dwarfed British Airways' (http://www.british-airways.com) 3.8 percent, easyJet's (another low-cost competitor in Europe, http://www.easyjet.com) 8.7 percent, and Southwest's 8.6 percent. Ryanair built up $1 billion in cash to order 250 new Boeing 737s during 2001–02, launch 60 new routes in 2002, and negotiate with 40 new airports throughout Western and Eastern Europe in 2003. During 2003, its $5 billion market capitalization exceeded that of major European carriers such as British Airways ($3 billion) and Air France ($2.7 billion, http://www.airfrance. com). In comparison, the big US carriers (excluding Southwest) had a combined market value of approximately $4 billion—American (http://www.aa.com) and Delta (http:// www.delta.com) valued at approximately

$1.4 billion each and Northwest (http://www.nwa.com) and United (http://www.ual.com) between $0.6 billion and $0.75 billion each. Only Southwest, with its $13 billion market value, was worth more than Ryanair in the airline industry.

What are Ryanair's secrets? Plenty. Like Southwest, Ryanair specializes in short-haul flights between European cities using a single type of aircraft, the Boeing 737. Keeping operating costs to a bare minimum and slashing fares aggressively is a hallmark of its strategy. For example, Ryanair's round trip fare between Glasgow and London is $71, whereas easyJet's is $123 and British Airways' is $136. However, there is a catch: The Glasgow and London airports Ryanair uses are smaller airports farther away from these cities, whereas most competitors use major airports closer to the cities. Smaller airports, many of them former military bases, are eager to attract passengers, and they offer Ryanair sweetheart deals on everything from landing and handling fees to marketing support. Flying point-to-point allows Ryanair to quickly turn around flights, whereas hub-and-spoke operators have to let their expensive aircraft sit on the tarmac at a hub to wait for connecting flights to arrive. As a result, Ryanair gets 50 percent more flying hours per day out of its aircraft than conventional carriers. Ryanair has also rented out the overhead storage and seat backs to advertisers. In-flight food and drink? Forget about it—passengers have to buy peanuts. To save ticketing costs, Ryanair sells 90 percent of its tickets online, thus becoming one of Europe's largest e-tailers.

The rise of Ryanair speaks volumes about the dramatic changes in the European commercial aviation industry since deregulation started in 1997. A swarm of discount airlines provide passengers with rock-bottom fares, while stripping away the profits of major carriers and forcing Sabena (http://www.sabena.com) and Swissair (http://www.swissair.com), the flag carriers of Belgium and Switzerland, respectively, into bankruptcy. Having assaulted the majors, the strongest of the discounters are now squaring off against each other. Ryanair, in particular, is turning its guns on easyJet. easyJet may be bigger, with 19 million passengers in 2002 compared to Ryanair's 16 million, but Ryanair is raking in profits, whereas easyJet has been losing money recently. With its $1 billion "war chest," Ryanair believes that it can launch a new price war—lowering fares 5 percent each year for the foreseeable future—and still remain highly profitable. Ryanair may win this war, because its average fares are already 30 percent cheaper than easyJet, and its unit costs are 80 percent less.

While the Ryanair story is remarkable, it is not alone around the world. In the United States, United and US Airways (http://www.usairways.com) have recently flown into bankruptcy and other major carriers are struggling, but the low cost airlines such as Southwest, JetBlue (http://www.jetblue.com), and AirTran (http://www.airtran.com) are expanding and making money. In Asia,

a similar drama is unfolding. Jet Airways (http://www.jetairways.com) is challenging the mighty Air India (http://www.airindia.com) and Indian Airlines (http://www.indian-airlines.nic.in) in the subcontinent. Air Asia (http://www.airasia.com) has grabbed 10 percent of the domestic market in Malaysia, giving the flag carrier, Malaysia Airlines (http://www.malaysiaair.com), more than a headache. In Cambodia, there is Air Mekong (http://www.marveltour.com/mekong); in Indonesia, Air Paradise (http://www.airparadise.co.id); and in United Arab Emirates, Air Arabia (http://www.airarabia.com).

Sources: Based on (1) K. Capell, 2003, Ryanair rising, Business Week, June 2: 40–41; (2) Economist, 2003, Airlines: A way out of the wilderness, May 3: 61–62; (3) Economist, 2003, Low-cost airlines: Cheap and cheerful, May 24: 66–67; (4) C. Prystay, 2002, The sky's the limit, Far Eastern Economic Review, December 5: 34–36; (5) J. Slater, 2002, High-flyer seeks airspace, Far Eastern Economic Review, December 5: 37–40.

Why are Ryanair and other low-cost carriers able to outcompete rivals in a *structurally* unattractive industry? A simple five forces analysis suggests that the airline industry, which provides an undifferentiated commodity service, features tremendous price pressures among rivals and strong bargaining power of suppliers (only two in the world for large jets) and buyers (who cut back on travels). While there are no substitutes for long-haul flights, cars, trains, and ferries can substitute for short-haul flights, such as those in Europe. With deregulation, entry barriers are also lowering. If firms have the luxury of choosing the industry to enter, it is certainly not advisable to compete in this industry. Therefore, the industry-based view suggests that all firms stuck in the airline industry are likely to suffer. In most cases, the performance data support this view. However, certain airlines such as Ryanair have done well. How can they succeed in such an unattractive industry, even during a recession? The answer is that Ryanair and similar firms must have certain resources and capabilities that are not shared by competitors in the same industry. This insight has been developed into a **resource-based view,** which has emerged as one of the three leading perspectives on strategy (the third one will be introduced in Chapter 4).[1] While the industry-based view focuses on how "average" firms within one industry compete (which is an important and insightful perspective), the resource-based view sheds considerable light on how individual firms differ from each other within one industry. Popularized since the 1990s, the resource-based view has emerged in response to the limitations of the industry-based view.[2]

In SWOT analysis, the industry-based view deals with the *external* opportunities (O) and threats (T), and the resource-based view concentrates on the *internal* strengths (S) and weaknesses (W), focusing on what is inside the firm that can generate sustainable competitive advantage. In this chapter, we first define resources and capabilities, and then discuss the value chain analysis. We focus on value (V), rarity (R), imitability (I), and organization (O) through a VRIO framework. Debates and extensions complete the chapter.

UNDERSTANDING RESOURCES AND CAPABILITIES

The concepts of "resources" and "capabilities" are the building blocks of the resource-based view. This section first defines what they are and then provides a series of examples.

Definitions

A basic proposition of the resource-based view is that a firm consists of a bundle of productive resources and capabilities.[3] **Resources** are defined as "the tangible and intangible assets a firm uses to choose and implement its strategies."[4] There is some debate regarding the definition of capabilities. Some authors argue that capabilities are a firm's capacity to dynamically deploy resources. They suggest a critical distinction between resources and capabilities, and advocate a **dynamic capabilities** view.[5] Others prefer the term **core competencies** when referring to a firm's internal attributes that provide a basis for competitive advantage.[6]

TABLE 3.1   **Examples of Resources and Capabilities**

TANGIBLE RESOURCES AND CAPABILITIES	EXAMPLES
Financial	▪ Ability to generate internal funds
	▪ Ability to raise external capital
Physical	▪ Location of plants, offices, and equipment
	▪ Access to raw materials and distribution channels
Technological	▪ Possession of patents, trademarks, and copyrights
Organizational	▪ Formal planning, command, and control systems
	▪ Integrated management information systems

INTANGIBLE RESOURCES AND CAPABILITIES	EXAMPLES
Human	▪ Knowledge
	▪ Trust
	▪ Managerial talents
	▪ Organizational culture
Innovation	▪ A supportive atmosphere for new ideas
	▪ Research and development capabilities
	▪ Capacities for organizational innovation and change
Reputational	▪ Perceptions of product quality, durability, and reliability among customers
	▪ Reputation as a good employer
	▪ Reputation as a socially responsible corporate citizen

Sources: Adapted from (1) J. Barney, 1991, Firm resources and sustained competitive advantage (p. 101), Journal of Management, 17: 101; (2) R. Grant, 1991, Contemporary Strategy Analysis (pp. 100–104), Cambridge, UK: Blackwell; (3) R. Hall, 1992, The strategic analysis of intangible resources (pp. 136–139), Strategic Management Journal, 13: 135–144.

While scholars may engage in academic debates on the distinctions among resources, capabilities, and competencies in theory, these distinctions are likely to "become badly blurred" in practice.[7] For example, is Ryanair's low cost structure a resource, capability, or competence? How about its deals with smaller airports? What about its capability to turn around aircraft quickly? For current and would-be strategists, the key is to understand how these attributes help improve firm performance, as opposed to figuring out whether they are resources, capabilities, or competencies. Therefore, in this book, we will follow leading resource-based theorists, Jay Barney, David Collis, and Cynthia Montgomery, to use the terms "resources" and "capabilities" *interchangeably* and often in *parallel*.[8] In other words, **capabilities** are defined here the same way as resources. To avoid confusion, the term "core competencies" will only be used when discussing diversification strategies (see Chapter 9).

Tangible and Intangible Resources and Capabilities

All firms, including the smallest ones, possess a variety of resources and capabilities. The challenge is how to meaningfully classify such diversity. A useful way is to separate the resources and capabilities into two categories: tangible and intangible (Table 3.1).

Tangible resources and capabilities are assets that are observable and more easily quantified. They can be broadly organized in four categories: (1) financial, (2) physical, (3) technological, and (4) organizational. First, **financial resources and capabilities** refer to the depth of a firm's financial pockets. Examples include the ability to generate internal funds and raise external capital, such as Southwest Airlines' possession of $1.8 billion in cash and an additional $575 million in untapped credit lines during the post-9/11 period when most competitors either lost money or went bankrupt.[9]

Physical resources and capabilities include a firm's plants, offices, equipment, geographic locations, and access to raw materials and distribution channels. For example, while many people attribute the success of Amazon.com to its online savvy (which makes sense), a crucial reason Amazon.com has emerged as the largest bookseller is because it has built some of the largest physical, *brick-and-mortar* book warehouses in key locations around the country.

Technological resources and capabilities refer to skills and assets that generate leading-edge products and services supported by patents, trademarks, copyrights, and trade secrets. For instance, Roomba, a vacuum cleaner that can clean all kinds of floors (carpet, wood, tile) by itself *without* an operator, has recently been released by iRobot Corporation. This entrepreneurial firm's technological capabilities are likely to revolutionize the way people clean floors.

Organizational resources and capabilities refer to a firm's formal planning, command, and control systems and structures. In general, younger firms tend to rely more on the visions of managers (often founders), whereas more established firms usually have more formalized systems and structures. In the early days of Excite.com (founded in 1994), executives often followed hunches with new initiatives that were unsubstantiated by formal analysis. However, those days are long gone, and Excite.com has developed a more elaborate set of formal evaluation criteria.[10]

Intangible resources and capabilities, by definition, are harder to observe and more difficult (or sometimes impossible) to quantify. Yet, we know intangibles exist, because no firm is likely to generate competitive advantage by only relying on tangible resources and capabilities.[11] Shown in Table 3.1, examples of intangible assets include (1) human, (2) innovation, and (3) reputational resources and capabilities.

Human resources and capabilities refer to the knowledge, trust, and talents embedded within a firm that are not captured by its formal, tangible systems and structures.[12] For instance, the knowledge used to serve the most discriminating car customers in the world at ultra luxury carmakers such as Bentley and Ferrari is very difficult for new entrants to replicate (see Opening Case in Chapter 2). In another example, the trust between managers and employees at Southwest Airlines, already strong historically, is likely to grow stronger during the current recession. This is because since 2001, Southwest's six biggest US rivals have laid off more than 70,000 workers and extracted significant pay and pension concessions among surviving employees. On the other hand, Southwest, which has never laid off a soul in its history of three decades, has kept all of its 35,000 people flying.[13]

Innovation resources and capabilities refer to a firm's assets and skills to (1) nurture and generate new ideas, (2) research and develop new products and services, and (3) innovate and change ways of organizing.[14] Some firms are renowned for innovations. For example, more than 60 percent of Canon's products on the market today, including popular digital cameras and digital copiers, have been introduced in the past two years.[15] Similarly, Sony introduces numerous products every year, and often pioneers new *classes* of products, such as the Walkman, the Discman, and the Aibo (e-pet). While competitors attempt to introduce similar products, they often have a hard time keeping up with Canon and Sony's relentless pace of new product development.

Finally, **reputational resources and capabilities** refer to a firm's capabilities to develop and leverage its reputation as a solid provider of goods/services, an attractive employer, and/or a socially responsible corporate citizen. Reputation can be regarded as an outcome of a competitive process in which firms signal their key characteristics to constituents.[16] While firms do not become reputable overnight, it makes sense to leverage reputation after acquiring it.[17] Intel's addition of the new brand sticker, Intel Inside, on the casing of many computers is a classic case in point. The launch of three luxury brands, Lexus, Acura, and Infiniti, by Toyota, Honda, and Nissan, respectively, is indicative of similar strategic thinking. In another example, the Tata Group of India, having made its fame in chemicals, hotels, steel, and tea, is now active in a wider variety of industries, ranging from software and telecom to power generation and airport management. Further, even though not all units used the powerful Tata brand before (for example, ACC, Telco, and Indian Hotels are all member companies), a new wave of restructuring has required that all member companies adopt the Tata brand in an effort to leverage the Tata reputation.[18]

All resources and capabilities discussed previously are merely *examples*; they do not represent an exhaustive list. As firms forge ahead, they will likely discover and leverage new resources and capabilities. Sometimes, the distinction between tangible and intangible resources and capabilities is not clear. For example, Canon and Sony's abilities to generate new products are based on both the tangible capabilities of organizing R&D work and the intangible skills and drives of individual employees. Usually, it is the combination of both tangible and intangible capabilities that leads to a competitive advantage, as noted next in the value chain analysis.

RESOURCES, CAPABILITIES, AND THE VALUE CHAIN

A value chain analysis focuses on how a firm's bundle of resources and capabilities come together to add value. Shown in Figure 3.1 Panel A, most goods and services are produced through a chain of vertical activities (from upstream to downstream) that add value—in short, a **value chain.** The value chain typically consists of two areas: primary activities and support activities.[19] Primary activities are directly associated with developing, producing, and distributing goods and services. Support activities assist primary activities.

FIGURE 3.1   The Value Chain

Panel A. An Example of value chain with firm boundaries

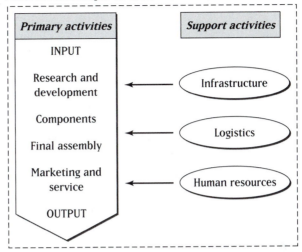

Panel B. An Example of value chain with some outsourcing

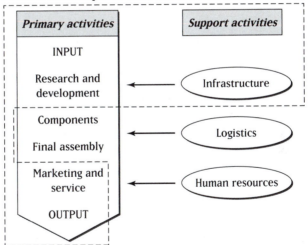

Each primary activity and each support activity requires a number of resources and capabilities. Value chain analysis forces strategists to think about firm resources and capabilities at a very micro, activity-based level.[20] The term "firm resources and capabilities" naturally leads people to think that resources and capabilities reside within the firm; however, because companies typically have numerous units (which may be scattered around the world in the case of multinationals), determining exactly where in the firm resources and capabilities add value is an important

FIGURE 3.2   **A Two-Stage Decision Model in Value Chain Analysis**

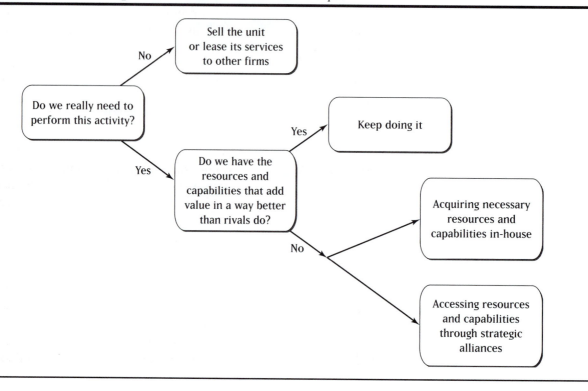

question.[21] Given that no firm is likely to have enough resources and capabilities to be good at all primary and support activities, the key is to examine whether the firm has resources and capabilities to perform a *particular* activity in a manner that is superior to competitors. If the answer is negative, the firm can employ a two-stage decision model to remedy the situation (Figure 3.2). In the first stage, strategists need to ask: "Do we really need to perform this activity?" The answer could be "No," and the firm may decide to sell the unit involved or lease the unit's services to other firms—in other words, exiting (or downsizing). This decision to exit (or downsize) is made because operating multiple stages of activities in the value chain can be cumbersome and result in a loss of strategic flexibility. Imagine if carmakers owned steel mills, the carmakers would have a hard time during a recession to cut back production when customers buy fewer cars because their steel mills might still want to maintain full production. For this reason, although many carmakers such as Ford and GM historically were involved in steel making, none of them does it now.

If the answer to the question, "Do we really need to perform this activity?" is "Yes," but the firm's current resources and capabilities are not up to the task, then there are two second-stage choices (Figure 3.2). First, the firm may want to acquire and develop resources and capabilities in-house so that it can perform this particular activity better. Microsoft's 1980 acquisition of the QDOS operating system (the precursor of the now ubiquitous MS-DOS system) from Seattle Computer Products for only $50,000 is a famous example of how to acquire a useful resource upon which to add more value.[22] Second, if the firm does not have enough skills to develop these resources and capabilities in-house, it may want to access them through **strategic alliances** (see Chapter 7 for more details).

Outsourcing is defined as turning over all or part of an organization's activity to an outside supplier that performs on behalf of the focal firm.[23] For example, many consumer and apparel products companies (such as Nike, The Limited Brands, and United Colors of Benetton), which possess strong resources and capabilities in upstream activities (such as product design and development) and downstream activities (such as marketing), do *not* invest in manufacturing, which is outsourced to suppliers in low-cost countries. Recently, not only are manufacturing activities often outsourced, support activities such as information systems, logistics, and human resources are also increasingly outsourced, leading to a new term, "**business process outsourcing**" (**BPO**) (see Opening Case in Chapter 1). Such outsourcing results in "leaner and meaner" firms that have really strong resources and capabilities in their chosen activities (see Figure 3.1 Panel B).

Value-adding activities may also be geographically dispersed around the world, taking advantage of the best locations to perform certain activities (see Chapter 6 for details).[24] This is illustrated in Figure 3.3 (p. 84), which shows how General Electric units around the world put together a high-technology medical device. In another example, PCs from companies such as Apple, Compaq, Dell, IBM, Samsung, and Sony may be designed in the United States, have advanced components produced in Japan and South Korea, have standard components manufactured in Singapore and Taiwan, be assembled in China and Mexico, and sold as a complete product around the world. Customers in North America are usually given a toll-free telephone number for service needs. Because the computer companies have often outsourced customer service activities, when customers dial this number, the service worker answering the phone may work for an outside service provider and may be in Ireland, India, Jamaica, or the Philippines.

Overall, a value chain analysis engages strategists to ascertain a firm's strengths and weaknesses on an activity-by-activity basis—relative to rivals—in a SWOT analysis.[25] The next section introduces a framework for how to do just that.

THE VRIO FRAMEWORK[26]

The resource-based view focuses on the value (V), rarity (R), imitability (I), and organizational (O) aspects of resources and capabilities, which lead to a **VRIO framework.** Before introducing these crucial aspects, we first outline two crucial assumptions.

Two Key Assumptions

Recall that the industry-based view assumes that firms in the same industry are generally alike except for size (large firms have better economies of scale). The resource-based view challenges this relatively unrealistic assumption, by first assuming that all

FIGURE 3.3   **A Geographically Dispersed Global Value Chain: How General Electric Medical Systems Produces the Proteus Radiographic System**

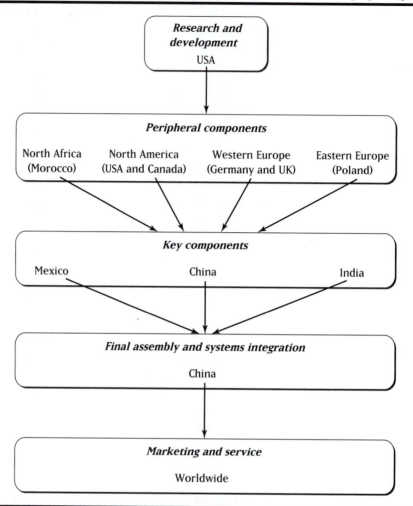

Source: Adapted from T. Khanna & J. Weber, 2002, General Electric Medical Systems, 2002, Harvard Business School case 702–428.

firms, even those within the same industry, have different resources and capabilities—more formally, this is the assumption of **resource heterogeneity.** In other words, while some firms may overlap (using the same software, deploying the same aircraft, having MBAs from the same schools), fundamentally, every firm has a unique *combination* of resources and capabilities and no two firms are "twins."[27] In an interesting "experiment," the seven "Baby Bells," which by law were created as seven (almost) "identical sisters" (in terms of organizational makeup and market size) after the breakup of AT&T in 1984, evolved to become significantly different competitors after a decade.[28] The difference between the resource-based assumption of resource heterogeneity and the industry-based assumption of firm homogeneity is significant. At its core, the industry-based view advises strategists to search for the most structurally attractive industry (segment). However, if all strategists follow this advice, writes leading resource-based theorist Berger Wernerfelt, "why will competition not destroy the attractiveness" of this industry (segment)?[29] On the other hand, the resource-based view urges firms to be entrepreneurial in going after different industries (segments) by taking advantage of their different resources and capabilities.

The second assumption—**resource immobility**—is that resources and capabilities that are unique to one firm cannot easily migrate to competing firms. Competitors often try to imitate the winning firms.[30] However, exactly replicating the "right stuff" that successful firms possess is notoriously difficult, if not impossible. For instance, none of the traditional major airlines' efforts to imitate low-cost carriers such as Southwest and Ryanair has been successful (see Opening Case). Also, the markets for strategic resources are highly imperfect.[31] While buying Microsoft software is easy, purchasing Microsoft's software development capabilities is virtually impossible for competitors. Further, assume that a competitor has amassed an enormous sum of capital to successfully mount a hostile takeover of Microsoft. Conceivably, the acquired Microsoft may no longer be the proverbial goose that laid golden eggs, because of the difficulties in integrating Microsoft with the acquiring firm. Talented managers and software developers may leave Microsoft after the hostile takeover, further degrading its capabilities. While this is a hypothetical case, numerous failures of real acquisitions indicate the reality of these difficulties (see Chapter 9). Overall, the resource immobility assumption highlights the "sticky" nature of resources and capabilities that are associated with one firm and the difficulty of replicating them elsewhere.[32]

Having spelled out the two critical assumptions, next we move on to address the four questions that are at the heart of the VRIO framework. Summarized in Table 3.2, addressing these four important questions has a number of ramifications for competitive advantage.

The Question of Value

Do firm resources and capabilities add value? The value chain analysis suggests that this is the most fundamental question to start.[33] Only value-adding resources can possibly lead to competitive advantage, whereas non-value-adding capabilities may

TABLE 3.2   **The VRIO Framework: Features of a Resource or Capability**

Valuable?	Rare?	Costly to Imitate?	Exploited by Organization?	Competitive Implications	Firm Performance
No	—	—	No	Competitive disadvantage	Below average
Yes	No	—	Yes	Competitive parity	Average
Yes	Yes	No	Yes	Temporary competitive advantage	Above average
Yes	Yes	Yes	Yes	Sustained competitive advantage	Persistently above average

Sources: Adapted from (1) J. Barney, 2002, Gaining and Sustaining Competitive Advantage, 2nd ed. (p. 173), Upper Saddle River, NJ: Prentice Hall; (2) R. Hoskisson, M. Hitt, & R. D. Ireland, 2004, Competing for Advantage (p. 118), Cincinnati: Thomson South-Western.

lead to competitive *disadvantage*. With changes in the competitive landscape, resources and capabilities that previously added value may become obsolete.[34] The evolution of IBM is a case in point. IBM historically has excelled in making hardware, including tabulating machines in the 1930s, mainframes in the 1960s, and PCs in the 1980s. However, as competition for hardware heats up, IBM's core hardware capabilities not only add little value, but also increasingly become core rigidities that stand in the way of the firm moving into new areas.[35] Since the 1990s, under two new CEOs, IBM has been transformed to focus on more lucrative software and services, where it has developed new value-adding resources and capabilities, aiming to become an on-demand computing *service* provider for corporations.[36]

The relationship between valuable resources and capabilities and firm performance is straightforward. Instead of becoming strengths, non-value-adding resources and capabilities, such as IBM's historical expertise in making hardware, may become organizational weaknesses. If firms are unable to get rid of non-value-adding resources and capabilities, they are likely to suffer below-average performance.[37] In the worst case, they may become extinct, a fate IBM narrowly skirted during the early 1990s.

The Question of Rarity

Important as they are, simply possessing valuable resources and capabilities may not be enough. The next question asks: How rare are these valuable resources and capabilities? At best, valuable, but common, resources and capabilities lead to competitive parity, but no advantage. Consider, for example, the identical aircraft used by most airlines that are made by Boeing and Airbus. The aircraft are certainly valuable; yet, it is difficult to derive competitive advantage from these aircraft alone. Airlines have to compete on how to use these same aircraft differently. Similarly, in the oil and gas industry, in which every major firm engages strategic planning (see Closing Case in Chapter 10), such planning in itself is not likely to bring significant performance benefits. However, in the fashion apparel industry, where strategic planning is not widely diffused due to a long-standing entrepreneurial tradition, firms that approach strategic planning in a rigorous and systematic way perform better.[38]

Only valuable and rare resources and capabilities have the potential to provide some temporary competitive advantage.[39] For instance, Ford has gained a temporary advantage through its capabilities to match incentive with changing demand on a region-by-region basis. Ford collects sales data *daily* from dealerships and uses proprietary computer models to calculate which cars need an incentive boost in which regions—and which cars and regions don't. The rationale is simple: Why waste precious incentive cash on vehicles that sell well without it? As a result, in 2003 Ford spent $300 less per car on incentives than GM, whose incentives average $3,800. Although these pricing capabilities seem like common sense, they are surprisingly rare.[40] GM prefers the simplicity of promoting a single deal, say 0 percent financing, across the board in one period. Chrysler is trying to move away from incentives by emphasizing long-term warranties. Japanese and European rivals rely less on incentives.[41] Ford's pricing prowess thus provides some temporary advantage until its rivals figure out how to compete with this capability.

Overall, the question of rarity is a reminder of the cliché: If everyone has it, you can't make money from it. This is especially relevant as firms are often confronted with the latest management fads, such as the rush to quality management, e-commerce, and low-cost countries such as China and Mexico. Adding value in these new areas is certainly commendable; however, if competitors are able to match, then the focal firm lacks a unique and distinctive capability necessary to build competitive advantage. Unless the focal firm is very lucky (and competitors are very unlucky), at best, it can only hope to achieve average performance.

The Question of Imitability

For firms possessing valuable and rare resources and capabilities, the next question is: How challenging is it for competitors to imitate them? Valuable and rare resources and capabilities can be a source of competitive advantage only if competitors have a difficult time imitating them. While imitating a firm's *tangible* resources (such as plants, software, and trucking fleet) is relatively easy, imitating *intangible* resources (such as tacit knowledge, managerial talents, and customer relationships) is much more challenging and often impossible.[42]

Firms can imitate in two ways: direct duplication and substitution. **Direct duplication** is the most difficult form of imitation because it requires competing firms to match the focal firm's organizational components exactly—person-by-person, machine-by-machine, and brand-by-brand. Short of acquiring the focal firm, gaining complete access to its resources and capabilities is virtually impossible. Yet as noted earlier, even after an acquisition, integration may fail and key people may leave (see Chapter 9). **Substitution** involves similar or related capabilities. Compared with direct duplication, it is relatively less challenging, because it does not require a firm to completely match the focal firm's resources and capabilities. However, this is still not easy and in some cases, there are simply no substitutes for certain resources, such as Arnold Schwarzenegger's role in *Terminator 3* (see Strategy in Action 3.1 on next page).

Why is imitation so difficult? The resource-based view suggests three underlying factors: (1) time compression diseconomies, (2) path dependencies, and (3) causal ambiguity. First, **time compression diseconomies** refer to a competitor's inability to successfully acquire in a short period of time the resources and capabilities that the focal firm has developed over a long period of time.[43] Crash programs are usually ineffective when compared with learning that has been accumulated over the years (or decades).[44] For any company interested in competing against Kikkoman, the world's leading producer of soy sauce, it is important to bear in mind that the 350-year-old Japanese company commands one of the world's oldest and best-known brands.[45] To outcompete Kikkoman in the game it has played so long and so well is a tall order. In another example, Mercedes' inability to quickly learn how to "design to cost" has cost it dearly (see Strategy in Action 3.2 on next page). That such a prestigious and otherwise capable company has failed to learn critical new skills in a short period of time indicates how difficult it is for late movers to catch up.

A second barrier to imitation is **path dependencies.** A process is path dependent when events earlier in its evolution have significant effects on subsequent events.[46] Virtually all firms in the world have "a mixed bag of resources—some good, some

STRATEGY IN ACTION 3.1. *The Impossible-to-Imitate Terminator*

Some assets are simply impossible to imitate. For example, who can be a second Arnold Schwarzenegger, the star of *Terminator 1* (1984) and *Terminator 2* (1991)? In *Terminator 3* (*http://www.terminator3.com*), released in July 2003, Schwarzenegger grabbed $30 million upfront and the rights to 20 percent of the merchandise sales. Costing $175 million to produce, *Terminator 3* was produced by Mario Kassar and Andy Vajna. They lined up enough financing to guarantee themselves at least $5 million in return—even *before* the movie sold a single ticket.

Here is how the deal worked: First, Intermedia (*http://www.intermedia.com*), a German film-financing company, invested $20 million to get a piece of the action. Second, Sony (*http://www.sony.com*) and other foreign distributors paid $95 million for most non-US rights, *after* the producers had already collected $20

million by selling the Japanese and German rights. Third, Warner Brothers (*http://www.warnerbros.com*), eager to make sure no other film would disrupt its own 2003 summer blockbuster, *The Matrix Reloaded* (*http://www.whatisthematrix.warnerbros.com*), bid a steep $50 million for US rights. Fourth, additional funding came from sponsors. Toyota (*http://www.toyota.com*), for example, showcased its Tundra truck in the movie, whereas Pepsi (*http://www.pepsi.com*) coughed up $1 million for promotional rights in Russia. Finally, by the luck of timing, Schwarzenegger's entry (and victory) in the California governor's race in summer 2003 added more notoriety.

Sources: Based on (1) Economist, 2003, California's recall race, August 16: 23–24; (2) R. Grover, 2003, Lights! Camera! Investors! Business Week, May 26: 89.

STRATEGY IN ACTION 3.2. *Perennial Kings of the Road?*

Car sales will always ebb and flow, but some cars just seem to sell themselves year in and year out, even if the industry suffers a downturn. For example, at present American consumers just can't get enough of Honda (*http://www.hondacars.com*) Odyssey minivans and Pilot sport-utility vehicles, and are willing to pay dealers a $3,000 premium *over* the $25,000 sticker price. Other seemingly recession-proof cars in the United States include the Toyota Camry (*http://www.toyota.com*), Nissan Altima (*http://www.nissan.com*), and Volkswagen Passat (*http://www.vw.com*).

However, there is no guarantee that today's kings of the road will always be perennial winners. For example, Mercedes (*http://www.mercedes-benz.com*) was embarrassed as its car quality dropped from No. 16 in 2002 to No. 26 in 2003 (the average being No. 18), according to the influential J. D. Power survey (*http://www.jdpower.com*). Such a below-average ranking—trailing Chrysler (*http://www.chrysler.com*)—is a far cry from its

1990 ranking of No. 1 and 1995 ranking of No. 3 by the same survey. One key reason is that Mercedes overhauled the way cars were designed and built. Instead of designing the car first and figuring out the costs later—as practiced before—Mercedes tried to imitate the Japanese capabilities of "design to cost," that is, design a car to meet a predetermined target price. Unfortunately, while Toyota, Honda, and Nissan have perfected these capabilities for decades, Mercedes only started to develop such capabilities in the 1990s and was not very good at them. The embarrassing recent ranking was disproportionately caused by the new M-class sport-utility vehicle and the E-class sedan based on the new design principle.

Sources: Based on (1) L. Armstrong, 2002, Those perennial kings of the road, Business Week, October 14: 50; (2) C. Tierney, 2003, Mercedes' head-on collision with a quality survey, Business Week, July 21: 27.

STRATEGY IN ACTION 3.3. *Resources and Capabilities of the Szczecin Shipyard in Poland*

The Szczecin Shipyard used to be a large state-owned enterprise in Poland. Before 1990, it sold primarily to Eastern bloc countries. When the collapsing former Soviet Union cancelled eight ships already under construction, the shipyard's debt level was pushed from zero in 1990 to $190 million in 1991. Facing a new, noncommunist government unwilling to bail out the firm, the shipyard quickly embarked on its turnaround in three ways. First, it sold non-value-adding assets such as apartments, schools, and resorts. Second, the firm chose a new product strategy to capitalize on its resources and capabilities. A SWOT analysis found that container ships had both substantial demand and price premiums around the world. Moreover, an evaluation of internal strengths and weaknesses determined that the shipyard's strengths lay in 12,500-ton medium-sized container ships. As a result, all capacity was moved to container ships by 1993. Between 1991 and 1993, turnaround for a single ship was reduced from three years to eleven months, a world-class performance. Third, the firm aggressively courted Western buyers, with a high degree of success.

By any measure, the Szczecin Shipyard's turnaround was remarkable. Its share of the worldwide 12,500-ton container ship market rose from an insignificant presence in 1990 to 40 percent by 1993, and the shipyard became the world's dominant producer of ships in this category. All these changes took place when the firm was still a state-owned enterprise. It was privatized in 1993.

Unfortunately, the privatized shipyard went bankrupt in 2002. The reason? The firm did not develop

sufficient capabilities to respond to newer challenges presented by (1) rising Polish wage levels (per capita income doubled from 1992 to 2002 and shipyard workers earned $800 a month in 2002), (2) low-cost rivals from Asia (Chinese shipyard workers, for example, made $20 to $30 a month), and (3) collapsing demand due to the global recession. In late 2002, the Polish government purchased the shipyard for one (1) zloty (US$0.26), and renamed it the Szczecin New Shipyard (*http://www.ssn.pl*), which interestingly has become a state-owned enterprise again.

Source: Based on (1) M. W. Peng, 2000, Business Strategies in Transition Economies (pp. 89–90), Thousand Oaks, CA: Sage; (2) J. Renzema, 2004, Szczecin Shipyard: Full circle, MBA case study, Fisher College of Business, The Ohio State University.

mediocre, and some outright liabilities."[47] For example, numerous firms in emerging economies find imitating Western multinational firms difficult, because their history of operating in a nonmarket system is pulling their legs as they try to learn new tricks in a new market environment.[48] These firms not only typically lack tangible resources, such as technologies and finances, but also fall behind in intangible capabilities such as managerial mindset and marketing know-how.[49] While some firms in emerging economies shed their past and quickly learn the new game (see Strategy in Action 3.3), many other firms struggle because of their troubled past.[50]

A third barrier to imitation is **causal ambiguity,** which refers to the difficulty of identifying the causal determinants of successful firm performance.[51] When firms such as Ryanair, Kikkoman, and Microsoft become very successful, a natural question is: How do they do it? Usually a number of resources and capabilities are nominated, ranging from Ryanair's *short* history (less than 20 years) to Kikkoman's *long* history (350 years), from Microsoft's foresight in discovering a low-cost gem from another firm to the (near) monopoly power of its MS-DOS operating system. While all of these resources and capabilities are plausible, what *exactly* is the determining factor? Finding the answer to this question not only intrigues scholars and students, but can also be hugely profitable for competitors. Unfortunately, outsiders usually have a hard time understanding what a firm does inside its boundaries. We can try, as many competitors have, to identify their recipe for success by drawing up a long list of possible reasons labeled "resources and capabilities" in the classroom. But in the final analysis, as outsiders, we cannot be sure.

Even more interesting for scholars and students and more frustrating for competitors is that often the focal firm's own managers do not know exactly what contributes to their success. When interviewed, they can usually generate a long list of what they do well, such as having a strong organizational culture, pursuing a relentless cost-cutting imperative, and so on. To make matters worse, different managers of the same firm may have different lists. When probed as to which resource or capability is "it," they usually suggest that it is all of the above in *combination*.[52] This is probably one of the most interesting and paradoxical aspects of the resource-based view: If insiders have a hard time figuring out what unambiguously contributes to their firm's performance, it is not surprising that outsiders' efforts to first understand and then imitate these resources and capabilities are usually flawed and often fail.

Overall, valuable, rare, but imitable resources and capabilities may give firms some temporary competitive advantage that leads to above-average performance during some time. However, such advantage is not likely to be sustainable. Only valuable, rare, and hard-to-imitate resources and capabilities potentially lead to a sustained competitive advantage.

The Question of Organization

Even valuable, rare, and hard-to-imitate resources and capabilities may not provide sustained competitive advantage, if a firm is not properly organized. Although movie stars represent some of the most valuable, rare, and hard-to-imitate (as well as highest-paid) resources, *most* movies flop. More generally, the question of organization asks: How should a firm (such as a movie studio) be organized to develop and leverage the full potential of its resources and capabilities?

To answer this question, we must ask a very fundamental question: Why do firms exist? In other words, why do people organize firms? The resource-based view suggests that firms exist to develop and leverage resources and capabilities better than individuals could.[53] For example, when a nineteenth-century entrepreneur discovered some gold deposits, usually he would organize a mining company. Similarly, when a twentieth-century entrepreneur identified some Internet opportunities, she would naturally organize an e-commerce venture. In both cases, firms are created be-cause they can take advantage of opportunities better than individuals can.

Numerous components within a firm are relevant to the question of organiza-tion. In a movie studio, these components include talents in "smelling" good ideas, photography crews, musicians, singers, makeup specialists, animation artists, and managers on the business side who deal with sponsors, distributors, and local sites. These components are often called **complementary assets**[54] because by themselves they would have difficulty generating box office hits. For the movie you saw most re-cently, do you still remember the names of the makeup artists? However, stars alone cannot generate hit movies either; instead, it is the combination of star resources and complementary assets that create hit movies.[55] "It may be that not just a few re-sources and capabilities enable a firm to gain a competitive advantage, but that lit-erally thousands of these organizational attributes, bundled together, generate such advantage."[56]

Another organizational idea is **social complexity,** which refers to the socially complex ways of organizing that are typical of many firms. While the social complexity of the entertainment industry, in which fickle changes in studio formation/dissolution and star affiliation seem to be the norm, is legendary, most firms in most industries are also organized in socially complex ways. In the most ex-treme case, many multinational firms consist of thousands of people scattered in many different countries. How they are organized into one corporate entity and achieve organizational goals is profoundly complex (see Figure 3.3 for an example and Chapters 6, 9, and 10 for details).[57] Often, it is the invisible relationships in such an organization, not formal structures, that add value.[58] Such organizationally embedded resources and capabilities are thus very difficult for rivals to imitate.

Overall, only valuable, rare, and hard-to-imitate resources and capabilities that are organizationally embedded and exploited can possibly lead to sustained compet-itive advantage and persistently above-average performance.[59] The Closing Case draws on the VRIO framework to illustrate how Ispat rose from being an obscure Asian steelmaker to become the second largest player in the global steel industry in a short time.

Lessons from the VRIO Framework

Because resources and capabilities cannot be evaluated in isolation, the VRIO framework presents four interconnected and increasingly difficult hurdles for them to become a source of sustainable competitive advantage (Table 3.2). Building on the two assumptions of resource heterogeneity and immobility, the VRIO frame-work suggests three significant lessons. First, fundamentally, some firms outperform others, even within the same industry, because the winners have some valuable, rare, hard-to-imitate, and organizationally embedded resources and capabilities that are unmatched by competitors. Therefore, the task for strategists is to build firm strengths by identifying, developing, and leveraging such resources and capabilities. In other words, the main strategic task is not necessarily to search for the most attractive industry (or segment). Although positioning in the right industry (or segment) does not hurt if a firm has that luxury, most firms are unable to easily select (or exit) industries due to path dependencies.

Second, imitation is not likely to be a successful strategy. At best, a follower firm that meticulously replicates every resource and capability possessed by a winning firm can hope to attain competitive *parity* with the winning firm. A firm so well endowed with resources to imitate others may be better off developing its own unique capabilities. The best performing firms are often entrepreneurial by creating new ways of adding value.[60]

Finally, a sustained competitive advantage does not imply that it will last forever. In today's global competition, all a firm can hope for is a competitive advantage that can be sustained for as long as possible. However, over time, all advantages may erode. As noted earlier, each of IBM's product-related advantages associated with tabulating machines, mainframes, and PCs sustained for a period of time. But eventually, both competitors' imitation and the industry's evolution nullified these advantages. Therefore, the lesson for all firms, including current market leaders, is to develop strategic *foresight*—"over-the-horizon radar" is a good metaphor—that enables them to anticipate future needs and move early to build up resources and capabilities for future competition.[61]

DEBATES AND EXTENSIONS

Like other theories, the resource-based view has its fair share of controversies and debates. As before, we introduce four leading debates so that a new generation of strategists can put the resource-based view in perspective. These debates are (1) firm- versus industry-specific determinants of performance, (2) static resources versus dynamic capabilities, (3) rent generation versus appropriation, and (4) domestic resources versus international capabilities.

Firm- versus Industry-Specific Determinants of Performance

At the heart of the resource-based view is the proposition that firm-specific resources and capabilities most fundamentally determine firm performance, whereas the industry-based view argues that firm performance is ultimately a function of industry-specific attributes. The industry-based view points out persistently different average profit rates of different industries, such as the pharmaceutical industry versus the grocery industry.[62] The resource-based view, on the other hand, has documented persistently different performance levels among firms within the same industry, such as Ryanair versus other airlines (see Opening Case).[63] While both streams of work are persuasive in their own right, results from studies are split. A number of studies have found industry-specific effects to be more significant.[64] However, a *larger* number of studies are supportive of the resource-based view, that is, firm-specific resources and capabilities are stronger determinants of firm performance than industry-specific effects.[65]

While the debate goes on, beware of declaring one side of the debate to be "winning."[66] There are two reasons for such caution—one methodological and one practical. First, while industry-based studies have used more observable proxies such as entry barriers and concentration ratios, resource-based studies have to confront the challenge of how to measure *unobservable* firm-specific resources and capabilities, such as organizational learning, knowledge management, and managerial talents. While resource-based scholars have created many innovative measures to "get at" these resources, these measures, at best, are "observable consequences of unobservable resources" and can be subject to methodological criticisms.[67] Critics contend that the resource-based view seems to follow the logic that "show me a success story and I will show you a core competence [resource] (or show me a failure and I will show you a missing competence)."[68] Resource-based theorists readily admit that "the source of sustainable competitive advantage is likely to be found in different places at different points in time in different industries."[69] While such reasoning can insightfully *explain* what happened in the past, it is difficult to *predict* what will happen in the future—for example, will the firm do better than its rivals if it matches, say, their equipment and locations?[70]

Second and perhaps more important, a good practical reason exists to believe that the *combination* of industry- and firm-specific attributes collectively drive firm performance. They have in fact been argued to be the two sides of the same "coin" of strategic analysis from the very beginning of the resource-based view's development.[71] Viewing both perspectives as *complementary* to each other seems to make better sense. Several recent studies have indeed underscored this point.[72] For example, one study reports (1) that for industry leaders and losers, firm-specific factors matter significantly more than industry-specific factors, and (2) that for most other firms, the industry effect turns out to be more important for performance than firm-specific factors.[73] Overall, it seems evident that strategic due diligence calls for the blending of these two insightful frameworks, which complement each other.

Static Resources versus Dynamic Capabilities

Another debate stems from the relatively static nature of the resource-based logic, which essentially suggests "Let's identify S and W in a SWOT analysis and go from there." Such a snapshot of the competitive situation may be adequate for slower moving industries (such as meat packing), but it may be less satisfactory for dynamically faster moving industries (such as information technology). Critics, therefore, posit that the resource-based view needs to be strengthened by a heavier emphasis on dynamic capabilities.[74]

More recently, as we advance into a "knowledge economy," a number of scholars argue for a "knowledge-based" view of the firm.[75] Tacit knowledge, probably the most valuable, unique, hard-to-imitate, and organizationally complex resource, may represent the ultimate, dynamic capability a firm has in its quest for competitive advantage.[76] Such invisible assets range from knowledge about customers through years (and sometimes decades) of interaction to knowledge about product development processes and political connections.

Focusing on knowledge-based dynamic capabilities, recent research suggests some interesting, counter-intuitive findings. Summarized in Table 3.3 (p. 94), while

TABLE 3.3   **Dynamic Capabilities in Slow- and Fast-Moving Industries**

	SLOW-MOVING INDUSTRIES	FAST-MOVING (HIGH-VELOCITY) INDUSTRIES
Market environment	Stable industry structure, defined boundaries, clear business models, identifiable players, linear and predictable change	Ambiguous industry structure, blurred boundaries, fluid business models, ambiguous and shifting players, nonlinear and unpredictable change
Attributes of dynamic capabilities	Complex, detailed, analytic routines that rely extensively on existing knowledge ("learning before doing")	Simple, experiential routines that rely on newly created knowledge specific to the situation ("learning by doing")
Focus	Leverage existing resources and capabilities	Develop new resources and capabilities
Execution	Linear	Iterative
Organization	A tightly bundled collection of resources with relative stability	A loosely bundled collection of resources that are frequently added, recombined, and dropped
Outcome	Predictable	Unpredictable
Strategic goal	Sustainable competitive advantage (hopefully for the long term)	A series of short-term (temporal) competitive advantages

Sources: Adapted from (1) K. Eisenhardt & J. Martin, 2000, Dynamic capabilities: What are they? Strategic Management Journal, 21: 1105–1121; (2) G. Pisano, 1994, Knowledge, integration, and the locus of learning, Strategic Management Journal, 15: 85–100.

the hallmark for resources in relatively slow-moving industries, such as hotels and railways, is complexity (which is difficult to observe and results in causal ambiguity), capabilities in very dynamic, high-velocity industries, such as IT, are "simple (not complicated), experiential (not analytic), and iterative (not linear processes)."[77] In other words, while traditional resource-based analysis urges firms to rigorously analyze their strengths and weaknesses and then plot some linear application of their resources ("learning *before* doing"), firms in high-velocity industries have to engage in "learning *by* doing." The imperative for strategic flexibility calls for simple (as opposed to complicated) routines, which helps managers stay focused on broadly important issues without locking them into specific details or requiring them to use inappropriate past experience. For example, Yahoo!'s very successful strategic alliance process is largely unstructured with just two simple rules: (1) no exclusive deals and (2) the basic service provided by the alliance (such as party planning and online greeting cards) must be free. These simple rules afford Yahoo! managers wide latitude for experimenting with a variety of alliance deals and formats.[78]

Overall, recent research on dynamic capabilities suggests that the existing resource-based view may have overemphasized the role of leveraging existing resources and capabilities and underemphasized the role of developing new ones. The assumption that a firm is a tightly bundled collection of resources may break down in high-velocity environments, in which resources are added, recombined, and dropped with regularity.[79] For example, in the chaotic and fickle world of e-commerce, being tightly bundled may be a liability rather than an asset. In a world of hypercompetition in which sustainable competitive advantage may be unrealistic, a series of short-term, unpredictable advantages seems to be the best a firm can hope for.[80]

Rent Generation versus Appropriation

Rents are economic values generated by firm resources and capabilities. If we may regard the resource-based view as a relatively well-developed theory of rent genera-tion,[81] then how about rent appropriation; that is, who gets what?[82] The resource-based view has been criticized for not paying enough attention to this important issue. The debate has focused on two levels: the firm and the individual. First, con-cerning the *firm* level, traditional resource-based logic argues that firms are better off hiding their core assets inside the firm and away from competitors. A "corporate fortress" with hardened firm boundaries is preferred. However, this logic may break down when fixed firm boundaries are no longer possible. As shown earlier in the value chain analysis, long gone are the days when Ford and GM would receive input such as iron ore, coal, sand, and rubber and produce output such as cars (and every-thing in between, including steel and glass). Such a "corporate fortress"—otherwise known as a "black box"—is no longer tenable in today's world, where strategic alliances and outsourcing often penetrate a firm's boundaries.

For example, one important objective for Firm A to establish a strategic alliance with Firm B is to gain access to B's resources and capabilities. An interesting ques-tion is: Why would B grant such access and share rents generated from its resources and capabilities with A? B must believe that a strategic alliance with A will produce net gains after taking into account the cost of rents shared with A (see Chapter 7 for details). However, by opening its boundaries (although only selectively), B runs the risk of having its capabilities imitated by A, which can now observe as a (quasi) in-sider. B, therefore, has to confront the challenge of how to preserve, protect, and strengthen its resources and capabilities while allowing A to access some of them.[83] This is especially challenging when A and B are competitors, such as GM and Toyota in their NUMMI joint venture and Yahoo!'s alliance with Google on search engines. Overall, firm boundaries are not only a buffer, but also a *bridge* connecting two firms. Operating with relatively open boundaries and still appropriating most rents has itself become a particularly useful resource or capability for some firms.[84] In a nutshell, firms need to capture rents both within and across firm boundaries.[85]

The second part of this debate is at the *individual* level. Who reaps the fruits of a firm's resources and capabilities? You might intuitively assume that owners (such as shareholders) reap gains through profits (and stock returns for publicly listed firms), however, this assumption has been hotly debated. The professionalization of man-agement in most modern firms suggests that managers, who are **agents** of owners, have better information about firm-specific resources and capabilities.[86] Managers thus may be able to disproportionately appropriate rents in a fashion that is at odds with the owners' interests—this is known as an **agency problem** (see Chapter 11 for details). For example, at the time of privatization in the early 1990s, the resources and capabilities of state-owned firms in Russia and other former Soviet countries were unknown to outside investors. Only managers had a relatively clear picture of the worth of these assets and they also had connections with politicians who over-saw the privatization process. Not surprisingly, managers as a group reaped the lion's share of these assets.[87]

Corporate governance, namely, how to properly govern the modern corporation whose owners have delegated day-to-day responsibilities to managers, has become a *worldwide* problem (see Chapter 11). Beyond the role of managers, how other stakeholders, such as employees and suppliers, bargain to appropriate rents from a firm's resources and capabilities also remains to be explored (see Chapter 12). Taken together, the "bottom line" may be that much of the rents are "appropriated before the bottom line [traditional performance measures] is calculated."[88] Overall, it seems that the resource-based view needs to develop the rent appropriation side of the story.

Domestic Resources versus International Capabilities

Do firms that succeed domestically have what it takes to succeed internationally? Some firms continue to succeed overseas, whereas many others get burned badly. This question boils down to whether domestic resources and capabilities can be leveraged and developed outside a firm's home country. The answer can be either "Yes" or "No."[89] This debate is an extension of the larger debate on whether international business is different from domestic business. Answering "Yes" to this question is an excellent argument for having stand-alone international business courses (and for having a global strategy textbook like this one). Answering "No" to this question argues that "international business" fundamentally is about "business," which is well covered by marketing, finance, and operations courses (and "mainstream" strategy courses that may also find this "globalized" strategy textbook useful). Due to space constraints, we are unable to discuss this crucial debate at length. However, this debate is confronted head-on in *every* remaining chapter of this book (in particular Chapters 4 and 6).

IMPLICATIONS FOR STRATEGISTS

This chapter suggests three key implications for strategists. First, there is nothing very novel in the proposition that firms "compete on resources and capabilities." The subtlety comes when strategists attempt, via the VRIO framework, to distinguish resources and capabilities that are valuable, rare, hard-to-imitate, and organizationally embedded from those that do not share these attributes. Even if strategists produced a list of all the potentially important resources and capabilities, it would be too long to be of any strategic use. Therefore, strategists must have some sense of what *really* matters.

Second, at the end of the day, strategists should not lose sight that managerial talents represent probably the most valuable, rare, hard-to-imitate, and organizationally embedded resources and capabilities any firm can have. Both forerunners and modern versions of the resource-based view underscore this insight that managers can make or break a firm.[90]

Finally, the resource-based view offers a set of answers to the four fundamental questions in strategy. The assumption of resource heterogeneity, that is, every firm is unique in its bundle of resources and capabilities, directly addresses the first question: Why do firms differ? The answer to the second question—How do firms behave?—boils down to how they take advantage of their strengths that are embodied in resources and capabilities and overcome their weaknesses. To answer the third question—What determines the scope of the firm?—the value chain analysis suggests that how a firm performs different value-adding activities relative to its rivals determines the scope of the firm. A common mistake managers often make when evaluating their resources and capabilities is failing to assess them relative to their competitors' resources and capabilities, thus resulting in an unnecessarily broad scope with some mediocre units. Lastly, what determines the international success and failure of firms? Are winning firms lucky or are they smart? The answer from the resource-based view, again, boils down to firm-specific resources and capabilities, although a stroke of luck certainly helps.[91]

Chapter Summary

1. The resource-based view of strategy grows out of a search for an explanation for some firms' persistent superior performance even in industries that are structurally unattractive.

2. Resources and capabilities are the tangible and intangible assets a firm uses to choose and implement its strategies.

3. A value chain analysis engages strategists to ascertain a firm's strengths and weaknesses on an activity-by-activity basis relative to rivals.

4. A VRIO framework suggests that only resources and capabilities that are valuable, rare, inimitable, and organizationally embedded generate a sustainable competitive advantage.

5. Leading debates in this area include (1) firm- versus industry-specific determinants of performance, (2) static resources versus dynamic capabilities, (3) rent generation versus appropriation, and (4) domestic resources versus international capabilities.

Key Terms

business process outsourcing (BPO)	direct duplication	innovation resources and capabilities
capabilities	dynamic capabilities	intangible resources and capabilities
causal ambiguity	financial resources and capabilities	organizational resources and capabilities
complementary assets	human resources and capabilities	
core competencies		

outsourcing	resource immobility	technological resources and capabilities
path dependencies	resource-based view	time compression diseconomies
physical resources and capabilities	resources	
	social complexity	value chain
rents	substitution	VRIO framework
reputational resources and capabilities	tangible resources and capabilities	
resource heterogeneity		

Critical Discussion Questions

1. Pick any pair of rivals in the same industry (such as Sony/Samsung, GE/Siemens, Coca-Cola/PepsiCo, Ryanair/easyJet, Ispat/USX), and explain why one outperforms another. What resources and capabilities must the non-leading firm acquire to outcompete the leading firm?

2. Conduct a VRIO analysis of your business school in terms of (1) faculty strengths, (2) student quality, (3) administrative efficiency, (4) information systems, and (5) building maintenance, relative to the top three rival schools. If you were the dean with a limited budget, where would you invest precious financial resources to make your school number one among its rivals?

3. Ten years out of college, your former college roommate, who came from China and owned a couple of decent (but not great) Chinese restaurants in the United States since graduation, calls and asks to borrow $20,000 to open a "Western cuisine" restaurant in his hometown in China. He admits that rivalry is intense there and that entry barriers are low. However, he argues that there are plenty of customers (his hometown has 10 million people), that his American experience will enable him to add a "Western" flavor to this new novelty restaurant in the sea of Chinese restaurants (in China), and that his abilities in running restaurants in America can be transferable back home. Assuming you have the money, will you lend him the money? Why or why not?[92]

4. **ON ETHICS:** Ethical dilemmas associated with outsourcing are plenty, ranging from closing plants in the home country to allegedly exploiting lowly paid workers abroad. Pick one of these dilemmas, make a case to either defend your firm's outsourcing activities or recommend that your employer withdraw from such activities (you are allowed to "cheat" by reading Chapter 4).

5. **ON ETHICS:** Because firms read information posted on competitors' Web sites, is it ethical to provide false information on resources and capabilities on corporate Web sites?[93]

Closing Case: Ispat Means Steel Around the World

The global steel industry is chronically plagued with over-capacity., Restructuring, downsizing, and plant closings occurred frequently throughout the 1990s. Yet, in such a structurally "unattractive" industry, Ispat (http://www.ispat.com)—a firm founded in India, incorporated in the Netherlands, headquartered in Great Britain, and listed on the New York and Amsterdam Stock Exchanges—has proven to be an exception rather than the rule. Ispat, which was an obscure Asian steelmaker a decade ago (1.5 million tons in 1992), is currently the world's second largest steel producer with 38 million tons of capacity and $12 billion in revenues (2003). Ispat has acquired facilities in 12 countries (Algeria, Canada, Czech Republic, Germany, France, Indonesia, Kazakhstan, Mexico, Romania, South Africa, Trinidad and Tobago, and the United States), served 5,000 customers in 120 countries, and employed 120,000 people. Overall, it is the first truly global steel company. Ispat is widely regarded in the steel industry as the "Nucor of the twenty-first century." Just as innovative as Nucor (http://www.nucor.com), a leading US mini-mill firm, was seen to be in the 1980s, Ispat adds a crucial international dimension that Nucor has lacked so far.

Mohan Mittal founded Ispat, which means "steel" in Hindi, in Calcutta in 1950 to trade scrap metals. At present, Ispat is 80 percent owned by the LNM Group, which is 100 percent owned by Mohan's son, Lakshmi Niwas Mittal (hereafter referred to as Mittal)—hence the LNM name. In 1976, Mittal, working for his father, went to Indonesia to set up a mini-mill (a small-scale steel factory that melts scrap metal in an electric furnace rather than producing virgin steel from iron ore, coke, and limestone, as an integrated mill would). In 1988, Mittal made his first acquisition by taking over Iscott, a state-owned steel mill in Trinidad and Tobago. Since then, Ispat embarked on a series of acquisitions around the world, taking over plants from the provincial government of Quebec, the municipal government of Hamburg, and the national governments of Mexico, Ireland, and Kazakhstan, as well as the sixth largest steelmaker in the United States, Inland Steel. Ispat often quickly turned around these new units. Given that most acquisitions fail, how can Ispat's acquisitions repeatedly succeed in this seemingly unattractive industry?

A VRIO analysis helps address this question. First, Ispat brings tangible and intangible value to the table. Tangibly, Ispat is a leader in direct reduced iron (DRI), a scrap substitute produced directly from iron ore as opposed to being produced from scrap whose quality is unreliable. The Indonesian factory had a globally pioneering combination of DRI and electric-furnace technology, which Mittal dubbed "an integrated mini-mill." This combination produced steel at consistently lower cost and higher quality than pure integrated mills and mini-mills. However, Ispat is no longer the only DRI practitioner. More importantly, the value it adds stems from intangible sources, notably its unusual capability to identify hidden treasures in underperforming steel mills, acquire them at a fraction of the cost, and turn them around profitably.

The combination of Ispat's tangible and intangible capabilities is rare in the world. When in 1991 the Mexican government privatized its money-losing, state-owned Sicartsa (which cost $2 billion to build in the 1980s), Ispat submitted a bid of $220 million, which was 60 percent higher than the second bid—the third bidder proposed $1 (!). Internally, although Sicartsa had some of the best-trained Mexican engineers, the firm had a culture of relying on external consultants. Ispat managers dismissed all consultants, and encouraged engineers to seek solutions of their own, while allowing for honest mistakes to occur. These engineers have now become the steel experts in Mexico and are often sought after by other firms as consultants.

Ispat's capabilities are not only valuable and unique, but also hard to imitate. Most of the plants Ispat acquired were considered beyond redemption and the owners only resorted to selling them after outside consultants failed. For example, a team of experts from USX (http://www.ussteel.com), the largest US steelmaker, failed to stem the losses of Karmet in Kazakhstan. Yet, after the Ispat takeover, performance has significantly improved. Evidently, USX and many other competitors had the same proprietary information about Ispat's acquisition targets, but they were unable to imitate Ispat's turnaround capabilities.

Ispat also excels in post-acquisition integration and turnaround, a complex organizational challenge that is behind the failure of most acquisitions. Examples of integration and turnaround tactics include (1) daily managers' meetings, (2) better accounting information, (3) internal contracts, and (4) global learning. Heads of various departments meet every day to make decisions on the spot instead of referring to "committees." The cost accounting system in Mexico, for instance, had reported data on a monthly basis three weeks after the month ended—that is, data about cost in March would be available in the fourth week of April. Ispat beefed up the accounting system to capture cost data on a real-time, daily basis. Ispat also initiated a series of precise internal service contracts (such as internal traffic services that provide cranes and trucks

on time for transportation needs within the plant). Finally, "at the core of its management philosophy," according to Ispat's Web site, "is the sharing of knowledge and expertise through the global knowledge integration programs encompassing all functions." Twice each year, the CEOs of all subsidiaries meet as a group for seven days to present and critique their business plans. In addition, these CEOs also sit on the board of directors of their sister subsidiaries. In addition to these formal arrangements, a great deal of informal rapport exists among Ispat managers. "When I have a problem," one CEO shared, "I don't wait until the next [big] meeting. Canada or Trinidad is just one phone call or e-mail away."

Case Discussion Questions

1. Have you heard about this firm before? Why or why not?

2. Why has Ispat been able to grow so strongly in a structurally "unattractive" industry during a time when the industry has gone through a lot of difficulties and turmoil?

3. What is the most important source of Ispat's competitive advantage?

4. Based on this case, why is the question of organization in the VRIO framework so important? (Hint: Social complexity and complementary assets.)

Sources: Based on (1) Ispat International profile, http://www.ispat.com (accessed May 31, 2004); (2) J. Mathews, 2002, Dragon International (pp. 32–33), New York: Oxford University Press; (3) D. Sull, M. Hayward, & G. Piramal, 1998, Spinning steel into gold: The case of Ispat International N.V., European Management Journal, 17: 368–381.

Notes

Abbreviation list

AER – American Economic Review

AME – Academy of Management Executive

AMJ – Academy of Management Journal

AMR – Academy of Management Review

ASQ – Administrative Science Quarterly

BJE – Bell Journal of Economics

BW – Business Week

CMR – California Management Review

HBR – Harvard Business Review

HR – *Human Relations*

JIBS – *Journal of International Business Studies*

JIE – *Journal of Industrial Economics*

JIM – *Journal of International Management*

JM – *Journal of Management*

JMS – *Journal of Management Studies*

JWB – *Journal of World Business*

LRP – *Long Range Planning*

MIR – *Management International Review*

MS – *Management Science*

OSc – *Organization Science*

RES – *Review of Economics and Statistics*

RP – *Research Policy*

SMJ – *Strategic Management Journal*

SMR – *MIT Sloan Management Review*

1. M. W. Peng, 2001, The resource-based view and international business, *JM,* 27 (6): 803–829.

2. J. Barney, 1991, Firm resources and sustained competitive advantage, *JM,* 17: 99–120; K. Conner, 1991, A historical comparison of resource-based theory and five schools of thought within industrial organization economics, *JM,* 17: 121–154; J. Mahoney & J. R. Pandian, 1992, The resource-based view within the conversation of strategic management, *SMJ,* 13: 363–380; M. Peteraf, 1993, The cornerstones of competitive advantage, *SMJ,* 14: 179–191.

3. M. W. Peng & P. Heath, 1996, The growth of the firm in planned economies in transition: Institutions, organizations, and strategic choices, *AMR,* 21 (2): 492–528; E. Penrose, 1959, *The Theory of the Growth of the Firm,* London: Blackwell; M. Pettus, 2001, The resource-based view as a developmental growth process, *AMJ,* 44: 878–896.

4. J. Barney, 2001, Is the resource-based "view" a useful perspective for strategic management research? Yes (p. 54), *AMR,* 26: 41–56.

5. D. Teece, G. Pisano, & A. Shuen, 1997, Dynamic capabilities and strategic management, *SMJ,* 18: 509–533.

6. C. K. Prahalad & G. Hamel, 1990, The core competence of the organization, *HBR,* 68 (2): 57–69.

7. J. Barney, 2002, *Gaining and Sustaining Competitive Advantage,* 2nd ed. (p. 157), Upper Saddle River, NJ: Prentice Hall.

8. Barney, 2002, *Gaining and Sustaining Competitive Advantage* (p. 157); D. Collis & C. Montgomery, 1997, *Corporate Strategy* (p. 9), Chicago: Irwin.

9. W. Zellner, 2003, Holding steady, *BW,* February 3: 66–68.

10. V. Rindova & S. Kotha, 2001, Continuous "morphing," *AMJ,* 44: 1263–1280.

11. H. Itami & T. Roehl, 1987, *Mobilizing Invisible Assets,* Cambridge, MA: Harvard University Press.

12. J. Barney, 1986, Organizational culture: Can it be a source of sustained competitive advantage? *AMR,* 11: 656–665; J. Barney & M. Hansen, 1994, Trustworthiness as a source of competitive advantage, *SMJ,* 15: 175–190; B. Becker & B. Gerhart, 1996, The impact of human resource management on organizational performance, *AMJ,* 39: 779–801; K. Law, D. Tse, & N. Zhou, 2003, Does human resource management matter in a transition economy? *JIBS,* 34: 255–265.

13. Zellner, 2003, Holding steady; W. Zellner, 2003, Coffee, tea, or bile? *BW,* June 2: 56–58.

14. A. Afuah, 2002, Mapping technological capabilities into product markets and competitive advantage, *SMJ,* 23: 171–179; P. Roberts, 1999, Product innovation, product-market competition, and persistent profitability in the US pharmaceutical industry, *SMJ,* 20: 655–670.

15. *Fortune,* 2003, Canon: The power of hybrid management, special advertising section, July 21: S5.

16. C. Fombrun, 1996, *Reputation,* Boston: Harvard University Press; O. Shenkar & E. Yuchtman-Yaar, 1997, Reputation, image, prestige, and goodwill, *HR,* 50: 1361–1381.

17. P. Lee, 2001, What's in a name.com? *SMJ,* 22: 793–804; P. Roberts & G. Dowling, 2002, Corporate reputation and sustained superior financial performance, *SMJ,* 23: 1077–1093.

18. T. Khanna, K. Palepu, & D. Wu, 1998, *House of Tata,* case study, Boston: Harvard Business School.

19. M. Porter, 1985, *Competitive Advantage,* New York: Free Press.

20. G. Johnson, L. Melin, & R. Whttington, 2003, Micro strategy and strategizing, *JMS,* 40: 3–22.

21. J. Birkinshaw & N. Hood, 1998, Multinational subsidiary evolution, *AMR,* 23: 773–795; A. Rugman & A. Verbeke, 2001, Subsidiary-specific advantages in multinational enterprises, *SMJ,* 22: 237–250.

22. R. Makadok, 2001, Toward a synthesis of the resource-based and dynamic capability views of rent creation (p. 388), *SMJ,* 22: 387–401.

23. J. Barthelemy, 2003, The seven deadly sins of outsourcing, *AME,* 17 (2): 87–98.

24. J. Anand & A. Delios, 2002, Absolute and relative resources as determinants of international acquisitions, *SMJ,* 23: 119–134; M. K. Erramilli, S. Agarwal, & S. Kim, 1997, Are firm-specific advantages location-specific too? *JIBS,* 28: 735–757; A. Madhok & T. Osegowitsch, 2000, The international biotechnology industry: A dynamic capabilities approach, *JIBS,* 31: 325–335; S. Tallman & K. Fladmoe-Lindquist, 2002, Internationalization, globalization, and capability-based strategy, *CMR,* 45: 116–135.

25. M. Leiblein & D. Miller, 2003, An empirical examination of transaction- and firm-level influences on the vertical boundaries of the firm, *SMJ,* 24: 839–859.

26. This section draws heavily from Barney, 2002, *Gaining and Sustaining* (pp. 159–174).

27. D. Hoopes, T. Madsen, & G. Walker, 2003, Why is there a resource-based view? Toward a theory of competitive heterogeneity, *SMJ,* 24: 889–902; A. Knott, 2003, Persistent heterogeneity and sustainable innovation, *SMJ,* 24: 687–706; G. Walker, T. Madsen, & G. Carini, 2000, How does institutional change affect heterogeneity among firms? *SMJ,* 23: 89–104.

28. R. Kashlak & M. Joshi, 1994, Core business regulation and dual diversification patterns, *SMJ,* 15: 603–611; T. Noda & D. Collis, 2001, The evolution of intraindustry firm heterogeneity, *AMJ,* 44: 897–925.

29. B. Wernerfelt, 1995, The resource-based view of the firm: Ten years after (p. 172), *SMJ,* 16: 171–174.

30. S. Schnaars, 1994, *Managing Imitation Strategies,* New York: Free Press.

31. J. Barney, 1986, Strategic factor markets: Expectations, luck, and business strategy, *MS,* 32: 1231–1241; T. Chi, 1994, Trading in strategic resources, *SMJ,* 15: 271–290; J. Denrell, C. Fang, & S. Winter, 2003, The economics of strategic opportunity, *SMJ,* 24: 977–990.

32. C. Maritan & T. Brush, 2003, Heterogeneity and transferring practices, *SMJ,* 24: 945–960; G. Szulanski, 1996, Exploring internal stickiness, *SMJ,* 17: 27–43; S. Winter & G. Szulanski, 2000, Replication as strategy, *OSc,* 12: 730–743.

33. S. Lippman & R. Rumelt, 2003, A bargaining perspective on resource advantage, *SMJ,* 24: 1069–1086.

34. C. Helfat & M. Peteraf, 2003, The dynamic resource-based view, *SMJ,* 24: 997–1010.

35. C. Christensen, 1997, *The Innovator's Dilemma,* Boston: Harvard Business School Press; D. Leonard-Barton, 1992, Core capabilities and core rigidities, *SMJ,* 13: 111–125; V. Rindova & C. Fombrun, 1999, Constructing competitive advantage, *SMJ,* 20: 691–710.

36. S. Ante, 2003, The new blue, *BW,* March 17: 80–88.

37. N. Siggelkow, 2001, Change in the presence of fit, *AMJ,* 44: 838–857; G. P. West & J. DeCastro, 2001, The Achilles heel of firm strategy, *JMS,* 38: 417–442.

38. T. Powell, 1992, Strategic planning as competitive advantage, *SMJ,* 13: 551–558.

39. N. Carr, 2003, *Does IT Matter?* Boston: Harvard Business School Press; M. Peteraf & M. Bergen, 2003, Scanning dynamic competitive landscapes, *SMJ,* 24: 1027–1042.

40. S. Dutta, M. Zbaracki, & M. Bergen, 2003, Pricing process as a capability, *SMJ,* 24: 615–630.

41. D. Welch, 2003, Ford tames the rebate monster, *BW,* May 5: 38.

42. D. Collis, 1991, A resource-based analysis of global competition, *SMJ,* 12: 49–68; A. Knott, D. Bryce, & H. Posen, 2003, On the strategic accumulation of intangible assets, *OSc,* 14: 192–208; D. Miller, 2003, An asymmetry-based view of advantage, *SMJ,* 24: 961–976; G. Ray, J. Barney, & W. Muhanna, 2004, Capabilities, business processes, and competitive advantage, *SMJ,* 25: 23–37; R. Schroeder, K. Bates, & M. Junttila, 2002, A resource-based view of manufacturing strategy, *SMJ,* 23: 105–118; B. Skaggs & T. Huffman, 2003, A customer interaction approach to strategy and production complexity alignment in service firms, *AMJ,* 46: 775–786; B. Skaggs & M. Youndt, 2004, Strategic positioning, human capital, and performance in service organizations, *SMJ,* 25: 85–99.

43. I. Dierickx & K. Cool, 1989, Asset stock accumulation and sustainability of competitive advantage, *MS,* 35: 1504–1511.

44. A. Delios & P. Beamish, 2001, Survival and profitability: The roles of experience and intangible assets in foreign subsidiary performance, *AMJ,* 44: 1028–1038; Y. Luo & M. W. Peng, 1999, Learning to compete in a transition economy: Experience, environment, and performance, *JIBS,* 30: 269–296; T. Isobe, S. Makino, & D. Montgomery, 2000, Resource commitments, entry timing, and market performance of foreign direct investments in emerging economies, *AMJ,* 43: 468–484.

45. *Fortune,* 2003, Kikkoman: A recipe for success, special advertising section, July 21: S9.

46. W. Barnett, H. Greve, & D. Park, 1994, An evolutionary model of organizational performance, *SMJ,* 15: 11–28; C. Helfat & R. Raubitschek, 2000, Product sequencing, *SMJ,* 21: 961–980; D. Holbrook, W. Cohen, D. Hounshell, & S. Klepper, 2000, The nature, sources, and consequences of firm differences in the early history of the semiconductor industry, *SMJ,* 21: 1017–1042; S. Karim & W. Mitchell, 2000, Path-dependent and path-breaking change, *SMJ,* 21: 1061–1082; S. Klepper & K. Simons, 2000, Dominance by birthright, *SMJ,* 21: 997–1016; R. Nelson & S. Winter, 1982, *An Evolutionary Theory of Economic Change,* Cambridge, MA: Belknap.

47. D. Collis & C. Montgomery, 1995, Competing on resources (p. 124), *HBR,* 73 (4): 118–128.

48. R. Hoskisson, L. Eden, C. Lau, & M. Wright, 2000, Strategy in emerging economies, *AMJ,* 43: 249–267; M. W. Peng, 2000, *Business Strategies in Transition Economies,* Thousand Oaks, CA: Sage Publishing, Inc.

49. O. Shenkar & J. T. Li, 1999, Knowledge search in international cooperative ventures, *OSc,* 10: 134–143.

50. K. Newman, 2000, Organizational transformation during institutional upheaval, *AMR,* 25: 602–619.

51. S. Lipman & R. Rumelt, 1982, Uncertain imitability: An analysis of interfirm differences in efficiency under competition, *BJE,* 13: 418–438; A. King & C. Zeithaml, 2001, Competencies and firm performance: Examining the causal ambiguity paradox, *SMJ,* 22: 75–99; R. Reed & R. DeFillippi, 1990, Causal ambiguity, barriers to imitation, and sustainable competitive advantage, *AMR,* 15: 88–102.

52. M. W. Peng, 1998, *Behind the Success and Failure of US Export Intermediaries: Transactions, Agents, and Resources,* Westport, CT: Quorum Books.

53. K. Conner & C. K. Prahalad, 1996, A resource-based theory of the firm: Knowledge versus opportunism, *OSc,* 7: 477–501; B. Kogut & U. Zander, 1992, Knowledge of the firm, combinative capabilities, and the replication of technology, *OSc,* 3: 383–397; A. Madhok, 1997, Cost, value, and foreign market entry mode, *SMJ,* 18: 39–62.

54. C. Helfat, 1997, Know-how and asset complementarity and dynamic capability accumulation, *SMJ,* 18: 339–360; D. Teece, 1986, Profiting from technological innovation, *RP,* 15: 285–305.

55. D. Miller & J. Shamsie, 1996, The resource-based view of the firm in two environments, *AMJ,* 39: 519–543.

56. J. Barney, 1997, *Gaining and Sustaining Competitive Advantage* (p. 155), Reading, MA: Addison-Wesley; J. Black & K. Boal, 1994, Strategic resources, *SMJ,* 15: 131–148; S. Thomke & W. Kuemmerle, 2002, Asset accumulation, interdependence, and technological change, *SMJ,* 23: 619–635; P. Yeoh & K. Roth, 1999, An empirical analysis of sustained advantage, *SMJ,* 20: 637–653.

57. D. Collis, 1991, A resource-based analysis of global competition: The case of the bearings industry, *SMJ,* 12: 49–68; S. Tallman, 1991, Strategic management models and resource-based strategies among MNEs in a host market, *SMJ,* 12: 69–82.

58. T. Kostova & K. Roth, 2003, Social capital in multinational corporations and a micro-macro model of its formation, *AMR,* 28: 297–317.

59. S. McEvily & B. Chakravarthy, 2002, The persistence of knowledge-based advantage, *SMJ,* 23: 285–305; T. Powell, 1992, Organizational alignment as competitive advantage, *SMJ,* 13: 119–134; S. Zahra & A. Nielsen, 2002, Sources of capabilities, integration, and technology commercialization, *SMJ,* 23: 377–398.

60. E. Mosakowski, 1998, Entrepreneurial resources and organizational choices, *OSc,* 9: 625–643.

61. I. Cockburn, R. Henderson, & S. Stern, 2000, Untangling the origins of competitive advantage, *SMJ,* 21: 1123–1145; G. Hamel & C. K. Prahalad, 1994, *Competing for the Future,* Boston: Harvard Business School Press; R. Makadok & G. Walker, 2000, Identifying a distinctive competence: Forecasting ability in the money fund industry, *SMJ,* 21: 853–864.

62. R. Schmalensee, 1985, Do markets differ much? *AER*, 75: 341–351.

63. J. Cubbin & P. Geroski, 1987, The convergence of profits in the long run, *JIE*, 35: 427–442; R. Jocobson, 1988, The persistence of abnormal returns, *SMJ*, 9: 415–430; C. Zott, 2003, Dynamic capabilities and the emergence of intraindustry differential firm performance, *SMJ*, 24: 97–125.

64. A. McGahan & M. Porter, 1997, How much does industry matter, really? *SMJ*, 18: 15–30; A. McGahan & M. Porter, 1999, The persistence of shocks to profitability, *RES*, 81: 143–153; G. Waring, 1996, Industry differences in the persistence of firm-specific returns, *AER*, 86: 1253–1265.

65. T. Brush, P. Bromiley, & M. Hendrickx, 1999, The relative influence of industry and corporation on business segment performance, *SMJ*, 20: 519–547; G. Hansen & B. Wernerfelt, 1989, Determinants of firm performance, *SMJ*, 10: 399–411; A. Mauri & M. Michaels, 1998, Firm and industry effects within strategic management, *SMJ*, 19: 211–219; A. McGahan & M. Porter, 2002, What do we know about variance in accounting profitability? *MS*, 48: 834–851; T. Powell, 1996, How much does industry matter? An alternative empirical test, *SMJ*, 17: 323–334; J. Roquebert, R. Phillips, & P. Westfall, 1996, Markets vs. management: What "drives" profitability? *SMJ*, 17: 653–664; T. Ruefli & R. Wiggins, 2003, Industry, corporate, and segment effects and business performance, *SMJ*, 24: 861–879; R. Rumelt, 1991, How much does industry matter? *SMJ*, 12: 167–185; Y. Spanos, G. Zaralis, & S. Lioukas, 2004, Strategy and industry effects on profitability, *SMJ*, 25: 139–165.

66. R. Henderson & W. Mitchell, 1997, The interactions of organizational and competitive influences on strategy and performance, *SMJ*, 18: 5–14.

67. P. Godfrey & C. Hill, 1995, The problem of unobservables in strategic management research (p. 530), *SMJ*, 16: 519–533; R. Henderson & I. Cockburn, 1994, Measuring competence? Exploring firm effects from pharmaceutical research, *SMJ*, 15: 63–84.

68. O. Williamson, 1999, Strategy research: Governance and competence perspectives (p. 1093), *SMJ*, 20: 1087–1108. See also R. Arend, 2003, Revisiting the logical and research considerations of competitive advantage, *SMJ*, 24: 279–284; R. Priem & J. Butler, 2001, Is the resource-based "view" a useful perspective for strategic management research? *AMR*, 26: 22–40; T. Powell, 2003, Strategy without ontology, *SMJ*, 24: 285–291.

69. D. Collis, 1994, How valuable are organizational capabilities (p. 151), *SMJ*, 15: 143–152.

70. M. Javidan, 1998, Core competence: What does it mean in practice? *LRP*, 31: 60–71.

71. B. Wernerfelt, 1984, A resource-based view of the firm (p. 171), *SMJ*, 5: 171–180; C. Lengnick & J. Wolff, 1999, Similarities and contradictions in the core logics of three strategy research streams, *SMJ*, 20: 1109–32.

72. S. Chang & H. Singh, 2000, Corporate and industry effects on business unit competitive position, *SMJ*, 21: 739–752; J. Child, L. Chung, & H. Davis, 2003, The performance of cross-border units in China, *JIBS*, 34: 242–254; D. Griffith & M. Harvey, 2001, A resource perspective of global dynamic capabilities, *JIBS*, 32: 597–606; D. Levinthal & J. Myatt, 1994, Co-evolution of capabilities and industry, *SMJ*, 15: 45–62; Y. Spanos & S. Lioukas, 2001, An examination into the causal logic of rent generation, *SMJ*, 22: 907–934; J. Stimpert & I. Duhaime, 1997, Seeing the big picture, *AMJ*, 40: 560–583; G. Young, K. Smith, & C. Grimm, 1996, "Austrian" and industrial organization perspectives on firm-level competitive activity and performance, *OSc*, 7: 243–255.

73. G. Hawawini, V. Subramanian, & P. Verdin, 2003, Is performance driven by industry- or firm-specific factors? A new look at the evidence, *SMJ*, 24: 1–16.

74. R. Adner & C. Helfat, 2003, Corporate effects and dynamic managerial capabilities, *SMJ*, 24: 1011–1026; Priem & Butler, 2001, Is the resource-based "view" a useful perspective?; Teece, Pisano, & Shuen, 1997, Dynamic capabilities; S. Winter, 2003, Understanding dynamic capabilities, *SMJ*, 24: 991–998; M. Zollo & S. Winter, 2002, Deliberate learning and the evolution of dynamic capabilities, *OSc*, 13: 339–351.

75. J. Birkinshaw, R. Nobel, & J. Ridderstrale, 2002, Knowledge as a contingency variable, *OSc*, 13: 274–289; D. Carr, J. Markusen, & K. Maskus, 2001, Estimating the knowledge-capital model of the multi-national enterprise, *AER*, 91: 693–708; D. DeCarolis & D. Deeds, 1999, The impact of stocks and flows of organizational knowledge on firm performance, *SMJ*, 20: 953–968; A. Grandori & B. Kogut, 2002, Dialogue on organization and knowledge, *OSc*, 13: 224–231; Kogut & Zander, 1992, Knowledge of the firm;

J. Spender & R. Grant, 1996, Knowledge and the firm: Overview, *SMJ,* 17: 5–10.

76. J. Barney, M. Wright, & D. Ketchen, 2001, The resource-based view of the firm: Ten years after 1991, *JM,* 27: 625–641; S. Berman, J. Down, & C. Hill, 2002, Tacit knowledge as a source of competitive advantage in the National Basketball Association, *AMJ,* 45: 13–32; B. Kogut & U. Zander, 1996, What do firms do?, *OSc,* 7: 502–18.

77. K. Eisenhardt & J. Martin, 2000, Dynamic capabilities: What are they? (p. 1113), *SMJ,* 21: 1105–1121.

78. Eisenhardt & Martin, 2000, Dynamic capabilities (p. 1112); Rindova & Kotha, 2001, Continuous "morphing" (p. 1274). This finding, however, is still being contested. See G. Lumpkin & G. Dess, 1995, Simplicity as a strategy-making process, *AMJ,* 38: 1386–1407.

79. S. Brown & K. Eisenhardt, 1998, *Competing on the Edge,* Boston: Harvard Business School Press.

80. R. D'Aveni, 1994, *Hypercompetition,* New York: Free Press; A. Ilinitch, R. D'Aveni, & A. Lewin, 1996, New organizational forms and strategies for managing in hypercompetitive environments, *OSc,* 7: 211–220.

81. R. Amit & P. Shoemaker, 1993, Strategic assets and organizational rent, *SMJ,* 14: 33–46.

82. S. Lippman & R. Rumelt, 2003, The payments perspective, *SMJ,* 24: 903–927.

83. N. Argyres, 1996, Evidence on the role of firm capabilities in vertical integration decisions, *SMJ,* 17: 129–150.

84. J. Dyer & H. Singh, 1998, The relational view, *AMR,* 23: 660–679; A. Lado, N. Boyd, & S. Hanlon, 1997, Competition, cooperation, and the search for economic rents, *AMR,* 22: 110–141; G. Lorenzoni & A. Lipparini, 1999, The leveraging of interfirm relationships as a distinctive organizational capability, *SMJ,* 20: 317–338; A. Madhok & S. Tallman, 1998, Resources, transactions, and rents, *OSc,* 9: 326–339; J. Masters & G. Miles, 2002, Predicting the use of external labor arrangements, *AMJ,* 45: 431–442; S. Matusik & C. Hill, 1998, The utilization of contingent work, knowledge creation, and competitive advantage, *AMR,* 23: 680–698; S. McEvily, S. Das, & K. McCabe, 2000, Avoiding competence substitution through knowledge sharing, *AMR,* 25: 294–311; S. McGaughey, 2002, Strategic interventions in intellectual asset flows, *AMR,* 27: 248–274.

85. L. Araujo, A. Dubois, & L. Gadde, 1993, The multiple boundaries of the firm, *JMS,* 40: 1255–1277; A. Madhok, 2002, Reassessing the fundamentals and beyond, *SMJ,* 23: 535–550.

86. R. Coff, 2003. Bidding wars over R&D-intensive firms, *AMJ,* 46: 74–85; R. Makadok, 2003, Doing the right thing and knowing the right thing to do, *SMJ,* 24: 1043–1056; A. Sharma, 1997, Professional as agent, *AMR,* 22: 758–798.

87. M. W. Peng, T. Buck, & I. Filatotchev, 2003, Do outside directors and new managers help improve firm performance? An exploratory study in Russian privatization, *JWB,* 38 (4): 348–360.

88. M. Blyler & R. Coff, 2003, Dynamic capabilities, social capital, and rent appropriation: Ties that split pies (p. 684), *SMJ,* 24: 677–686.

89. J. Boddewyn, 1997, Is international business a distinct field of inquiry? No and yes, but life goes on, in B. Toyne & D. Nigh (eds.), *International Business: An Emerging Vision* (pp. 639–644), Columbia: University of South Carolina Press; M. W. Peng, 2004, Identifying the big question in international business research, *JIBS,* 35 (2): 99–108.

90. Penrose, 1959, *The Theory of the Growth of the Firm*; C. Bartlett & S. Ghoshal, 1993, Beyond the M-form: Toward a managerial theory of the firm, *SMJ,* 14: 23–46.

91. S. Alvarez & L. Busenitz, 2001, The entrepreneurship of resource-based theory, *JM,* 27: 755–776; A. Lockett & S. Thompson, 2001, The resource-based view and economics, *JM,* 27: 723–754; T. Powell & A. Dent-Micallef, 1997, Information technology as competitive advantage, *SMJ,* 18: 375–406; M. Russo & P. Fouts, 1997, A resource-based perspective on corporate environmental performance and profitability, *AMJ,* 40: 534–559; R. Srivastava, L. Fahey, & H. K. Christensen, 2001, The resource-based view and marketing, *JM,* 27: 777–802; P. Wright, B. Dunford, & S. Snell, 2001, Human resources and the resource-based view of the firm, *JM,* 27: 701–722.

92. Adapted from Barney, 2002, *Gaining and Sustaining Competitive Advantage* (p. 185).

93. Adapted from R. Hoskisson, M. Hitt, & R. D. Ireland, 2004, *Competing for Advantage* (p. 126), Cincinnati: Thomson South-Western.

Emphasizing Institutions, Cultures, and Ethics

Outline

- Understanding institutions
- An institution-based view of strategy
- The strategic role of cultures
- The strategic role of ethics
- A strategic response framework
- Debates and extensions
- Implications for strategists

Opening Case: Behind the Profitability of Big Pharma

The pharmaceutical industry is dominated by large multinational enterprises (MNEs) collectively known as the Big Pharma. They include Merck (http://www.merck.com), Eli Lilly (http://www.lilly.com), Bristol-Myers (http://www.bms.com), and Pfizer (http://www.pfizer.com) of the United States; GlaxoSmithKline (http://www.gsk.com) and Wellcome (http://www.wellcome.ac.uk) of Great Britain; and Hoffman La Roche (http://www.roche.com), Ciba Geigy (http://www.ciba.com), Novartis (http://www.novartis.com), and Sandoz (http://www.sandoz.com) of Switzerland. Characterized by a relentless drive for research and development (R&D), the industry typically ranks among the most profitable in the world.

While industry structure and firm resources can certainly shed light on what is behind Big Pharma's enviable performance, the role of institutional frameworks seems equally important. For example, the US government helps make sure that Big Pharma reaps huge profits. The world's most stringent new drug approval requirements imposed by the Food and Drug Administration (FDA) significantly heighten the barriers to entry and imitation because only the "big boys" can afford to play such a game. Also, the US government does not allow cheaper drugs to be imported. Americans often pay more than twice what Canadians and Europeans pay for the same drugs developed and produced in the United States (Table 4.1 on next page). As a result, Americans spend approximately $240 billion a year on drugs, more than Canada, France, Germany, Great Britain, Italy, Japan, and Spain combined. Elderly and poor people not covered by insurance—approximately 15 percent of the US population—end up paying disproportionately more for the high prices. These international price differentials suggest that there is no global market for drugs. Instead, there are a number of nationally fragmented markets each with different pricing.

Elsewhere in the world, the visible hand of governments is also evident. In Great Britain, the Ministry of Health directly negotiates with drugmakers, each with a different profit margin. British and foreign firms with intensive R&D in the country are able to negotiate higher margins relative to foreign firms that simply export to the country. In Japan, the Ministry of Health and Welfare negotiates the prices with firms. However, once fixed, the price is not allowed to change over the life of the drug. As a result, although manufacturing costs tend to decrease because of economies of scale, prices remain the same. Thus, the oldest—not newest—drugs tend to command the highest margins in Japan.

According to Business Week, "today, most drug prices are determined not by markets, but by clout." This business model is currently under siege. Virtually every American retirement community is reportedly importing cheaper drugs from Canada—mostly through the Internet.

TABLE 4.1   Prices of the Same US Developed Drugs Around the World (2003)

US Developed Drugs	Lipitor	Zoloft	Vioxx	Nexium
2002 global sales	$7.97 billion	$2.74 billion	$2.53 billion	$1.98 billion
Per prescription	20 mg, 30 tablets	50 mg, 30 tablets	25 mg, 30 tablets	20 mg, 28 capsules
US prices	$93.99	$69.99	$78.99	$112.00
Canadian prices	$70.74	$55.30	$47.49	$74.87
Mexican prices	$88.74	Not sold	$56.33	$63.46
French prices	$54.45	$28.96	$49.01	$44.35
Indian prices (generics)	$7.50	$2.24	$2.60	$2.09

The House of Representatives passed a bill in July 2003 allowing for drug imports. Even if Americans are allowed to import drugs only from Canada, the savings reportedly may be up to $38 billion a year—at the expense of Big Pharma.

At the same time, Big Pharma is also challenged by poor countries infested by diseases such as AIDS, malaria, and tuberculosis. These countries demand that their drugmakers be licensed to manufacture cheaper, generic versions of currently patented drugs regardless of the patent holders' wishes—the so-called "compulsory licensing" scheme. The largely symbolic royalty Big Pharma will receive from such licensing hardly compensates for the lucrative profits theses firms stand to lose. Since generic AIDS drugs were introduced in Brazil in 1997, Big Pharma had to drop prices by as much as 65 percent. India not only manufactures a variety of generic drugs for domestic consumption, but also exports them. Recently, Mexico has threatened to do the same.

Big Pharma is fighting these threats at every turn. Firms argue that their wellspring of innovation will run dry if their patents are not protected. In addition, they suggest that the legalization of drug imports in the United States will add to the growing threat of counterfeit drugs that may put patients at risk. Drug companies also worry that the cheap drugs they sell in poor countries may make their way back to rich countries. In addition, such globally differential pricing may give their home governments some added ammunition to cut drug prices at home. Fundamentally, consumers in rich countries, especially the United States, subsidize consumers elsewhere. While American consumers are increasingly sick of doing this, poor countries are essentially demanding that their consumers be subsidized more. From an ethical standpoint, Big Pharma is often challenged for failing to deploy their R&D prowess to combat tropical diseases, the solution of which will have little (or no) profit potential in rich countries. In response, GlaxoSmithKline and Novartis have recently established new units to develop drugs for tropical diseases, and announced that other than earning kudos for corporate social responsibility (see Chapter 12), they do not expect to profit from these new ventures.

Sources: Based on (1) Business Week, 2003, Rethinking the drug business, August 11: 108; (2) J. Carey, 2003, Why do we pay more? Business Week, August 11: 26–28; (3) Economist, 2003, Exotic pursuits, February 1: 52; (4) Economist, 2003, Where the money is, April 26: 53–54; (5) R. Gilmartin, 2003, Drug coverage: Good and bad prescriptions, Business Week, September 8: 12; (6) R. Henderson, L. Orsenigo, & G. Pisano, 1999, The pharmaceutical industry (pp. 267–311), in Sources of Industrial Leadership, eds. D. Mowery & R. Nelson, Cambridge: Cambridge University Press; (7) F. Rothaermel, 2003, personal communication, August 29; (7) G. Smith, 2003, Drugmakers feel the heat in Mexico, Business Week, August 11: 28.

What determines the strategies and performance of firms in the pharmaceutical industry? What is behind the industry's historically high profitability? What about its future? It is evident that the industry- and resource-based perspectives introduced in the previous two chapters, while insightful, are not enough to answer these intriguing questions. It is difficult to imagine how Big Pharma could become so profitable without government-imposed entry barriers. It is equally plausible to hypothesize that Big Pharma's historically fat profit margins may become thinner in the face of heightened competition allowed by domestic and foreign governments. Overall, firm strategies and performance are, to a large degree, determined by institutions, popularly known as "the rules of the game" in a society. In other words, how firms play the game and win (or lose), at least in part, depends on how the rules are made and enforced. Popularized since the 1990s, this **institution-based view,** covering institutions, cultures, and ethics, has emerged as one of the three leading perspectives on strategy, enabling strategists to better appreciate the "big picture" in which competition takes place.

This chapter first introduces the institution-based view, and then discusses the strategic role of cultures and ethics, followed by an examination of a strategic response framework. Debates and implications follow as well.

UNDERSTANDING INSTITUTIONS

This section introduces the concept of institutions, discusses their function, and highlights their abilities to reduce uncertainty.

Definitions

Building on the "rules of the game" metaphor, Nobel laureate Douglas North more formally defines **institutions** as "the humanly devised constraints that structure human interaction."[1] Leading sociologist Richard Scott defines institutions as "regulatory, normative, and cognitive structures and activities that provide stability and meaning to social behavior."[2]

An **institutional framework** is made up of formal and informal institutions governing individual and firm behavior and these institutions, in turn, are supported by three "pillars."[3] Table 4.2 introduces the three pillars: regulatory, normative, and

TABLE 4.2   **Dimensions of Institutions**

DEGREE OF FORMALITY	EXAMPLES	SUPPORTIVE PILLARS
Formal institutions	▪ Laws ▪ Regulations ▪ Rules	▪ Regulatory (coercive)
Informal institutions	▪ Norms ▪ Cultures ▪ Ethics	▪ Normative ▪ Cognitive

cognitive—the former supports formal institutions and the latter two support informal institutions. **Formal institutions** include laws, regulations, and rules (such as competition and regulation policy, intellectual property rights regime, contract law, and their enforcement). Their primary supportive pillar—the **regulatory pillar**—is the coercive power of governments. For example, governments enact and enforce copyright laws. Anyone violating these laws, regardless of how unusual or novel the technologies involved, runs the risk of being caught, as evidenced by the crackdown on individuals who illegally download and share music online in the United States. The penalty for that violation can be as stiff as $150,000 *per song* downloaded.[4]

On the other hand, **informal institutions** include norms, cultures, and ethics. The two main supportive pillars for informal institutions are normative and cognitive. Because norms define how things should be done, the **normative pillar** refers to how the values, beliefs, and norms of other relevant players influence the behavior of individuals and firms. For instance, given some new norms such as to appoint independent directors to the board or to invest in emerging economies such as China and Mexico, many Western firms often imitate each other without a clear understanding of how to make such moves work.[5] In another example, whereas individualism permeates the competitive norms in the United States, collective actions, often in the form of business groups (such as the Japanese *keiretsu* and Korean *chaebol*), underpin the economic norms in Asia. Asians view some trust-based relationships among individuals or firms as normal and beneficial, wheras Americans may view these same relationships as collusion. Despite the recent interest in trust throughout the business world,[6] the existence of *antitrust* (literally, against trust) laws in the West is indicative of the differences in norms of business behavior (see Chapter 8).

The **cognitive pillar** refers to the internalized, taken-for-granted values and beliefs that guide individual and firm behavior. For example, "whistle blowers" reported Enron's and a US Army Iraqi prison unit's wrongdoing because of their beliefs in what was right and wrong.[7] While most other employees and soldiers may not feel comfortable with organizational wrongdoing, the norms are not to "rock the boat." Essentially, whistle blowers choose to follow their internalized beliefs about what is the right thing to do by overcoming the norm that suggests they should keep quiet.[8]

What Do Institutions Do?[9]

While institutions do many things, their key function is to *reduce uncertainty*. Specifically, institutions influence individuals' decision-making by signaling which conduct is acceptable and which is not. Institutions also affect firm strategies by constraining the range of acceptable actions. Basically, institutions define what is legitimate and what is not.[10] It is extremely important to reduce uncertainty because uncertainty can be potentially devastating. Political uncertainty may render long-range planning obsolete. Economic uncertainty, such as failure to carry out transactions as spelled out in contracts, may result in economic losses. Argentina in 2002 is an extreme case of political and economic uncertainty and its devastating impact on firms (Strategy in Action 4.1).

STRATEGY IN ACTION 4.1. *Coping with Institutional Uncertainty in Argentina*

Argentina, despite its rich endowments in natural and human resources, has experienced some dramatic ups and downs characterized by a lack of institutional certainty. Argentina's most recent crisis took place in 2002, during which its GDP shrunk 15 percent, unemployment rose to 23 percent, and riots broke out. The 2002 crisis was triggered by the government's default on its $155 billion public debt, a world record. The government, desperate to maximize revenue, clumsily changed the rules of the economy. It took back control of the central bank and again started to regulate prices for privatized public utilities. All dollar-denominated assets, despite previous legal assurances for their safety, were simply turned into pesos by a new government decree, causing the peso to slip four-fold against the dollar within a few months. A freeze on bank accounts—essentially a straight confiscation for an undetermined period of all deposits—was aimed at curbing a total collapse of the banking system. However, it caused cash to disappear from circulation. With the chain of payments between consumers, firms, and suppliers broken down, the economy entered "coma." Not surprisingly, one of the leading attributes for firms to survive is to be flexible, that is, to know how to adapt quickly to changes. However, even firms capable of being flexible appreciate having a more stable environment. Virtually all interviewed policymakers and executives complain about the lack of clear and credible economic rules and stress the importance of becoming "predictable" if

Argentina is to regain the trust of domestic and international investors.

Sources: Based on (1) A. Carrera, L. Mesquita, G. Perkins, & R. Vassolo, 2003, Business groups and their corporate strategies on the Argentine roller coaster of competitive and anti-competitive shocks, Academy of Management Executive, 17: 32–44; (2) A. Carrera & J. Quiroga, 2003, Marcelo Arguelles, chairman of Grupo de Empresas Farmaceuticas Sidus, on Argentine competitiveness, Academy of Management Executive, 17: 51–55; (3) L. Traverso & J. Quiroga, 2003, Luis Pagani, chairman of Grupo Arcor, on the globalization of Argentine firms, Academy of Management Executive, 17: 56–59.

Uncertainty surrounding economic transactions can lead to **transaction costs,** which are defined as costs associated with economic transactions—or more broadly, costs of doing business. Leading theorist Oliver Williamson refers to frictions in mechanical systems: "Do the gears mesh, are the parts lubricated, is there needless slippage or other loss of energy?" He goes on to suggest that transaction costs can be regarded as "the economic counterpart of frictions: Do the parties to exchange operate harmoniously, or are there frequent misunderstandings and conflicts?"[11]

An important source of transaction costs is **opportunism,** defined as "self-interest seeking with guile."[12] Examples include misleading, cheating, and confusing other parties in transactions. In an effort to reduce these nontrivial transaction costs, institutional frameworks facilitate certainty-enhancing strategies by spelling out the rules of the game so that deviations (such as contract disputes) can be mitigated with relative ease (such as through formal arbitration and courts). In other words, institutional frameworks can provide important strategic planning assumptions.[13]

Without stable institutional frameworks, transaction costs may become prohibitively high, to the extent that certain transactions simply would not take place. For example, in the absence of credible institutional frameworks that protect investors, domestic investors may choose to invest their money abroad, and foreign investors may simply invest in "greener pastures" elsewhere.[14] Consider the oil industry in Argentina. The government in 1955 canceled international contracts signed by a previous president, Peron, in 1952. The next president signed new contracts in 1958, which were nullified in 1963 by a different president. Foreign oil companies were invited to return in 1966, expelled in 1973, and again encouraged to enter after 1976.[15] It is hardly surprising that foreign oil companies are no longer enthusiastic about their prospects in Argentina. Taking such lessons, most governments around the world now compete with each other to provide more investor-friendly institutional frameworks.[16] The global norms are now becoming more friendly to foreign investors (see also Chapters 1 and 6).

How Do Institutions Reduce Uncertainty?

Throughout the world, two primary kinds of institutions—informal and formal—reduce uncertainty in economic transactions. Often called **relational contracting,** the first kind of economic transaction is known as **informal, relationship-based, personalized exchange.** In many parts of the world, there is no need to write an IOU note when you borrow money from your friends. Insisting on such a note, either by you or, worse, by your friends, may be regarded as an insulting lack of trust. While you are committed to paying your friends back, they also believe you will—your transaction is governed by informal norms and cognitive beliefs governing friendship. In case you opportunistically take the money and run, your reputation will be ruined and you will not only lose these friends but also, through word of mouth, lose other friends who may loan you money in the future.

However, in addition to the benefits of friendship, there are costs—remember how much time you have spent with friends and how many gifts you have given them? Graphically (Figure 4.1), initially, at time T1, the costs to engage in relational contracting are high (at point A) and benefits low (at point B), because parties need to build strong social networks through a time- and resource-consuming process to check each other out (such as going to school together). If relationships stand the test of time, then benefits may outweigh costs. Over time, when the scale and scope of informal transactions expand, the costs per transaction move down (from A to C and then E) and benefits move up (from B to C and then D), because the threat of opportunism is limited by the extent to which informal sanctions may be imposed against opportunists, if necessary.[17] There is little demand for costly, formal third-party enforcement (such as an IOU note, which becomes a formal contract, scrutinized by lawyers and notarized by governments). Thus, between T2 and T3, you and your friends—and the economy collectively—are likely to benefit from such relational contracting.[18]

Past time T3, however, the costs of such a mode may gradually outweigh its benefits because "the greater the variety and numbers of exchange, the more complex

FIGURE 4.1   **The Costs and Benefits of Informal, Relationship-Based, Personalized Exchange**

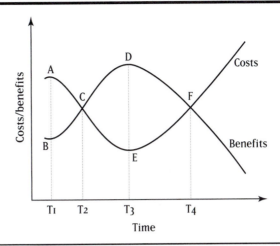

Source: M. W. Peng, 2003, Institutional transitions and strategic choices (p. 279), Academy of Management Review, 28 (2): 275–296. Copyright © 2003. Reprinted by permission of Academy of Management Review via Copyright Clearance Center.

the kinds of agreements that have to be made, and so the more difficult it is to do so" informally.[19] Specifically, the number and strength of network ties an individual or firm can possess is limited. In other words, how many good friends can each person (or firm) have? No one can claim to have one hundred *good* friends (regardless of how "good friends" is defined). When the informal enforcement regime is weak, trust can be easily exploited and abused. What are you going to do if your (so-called) friends borrow money from you and then refuse to pay you back or simply disappear? As a result, the limit of relational contracting is likely to be reached at time T3. Past T4, the costs are likely to gradually outweigh the benefits.

Often termed **arm's-length transactions,** the second institutional mode to govern relationships is **formal, rule-based, impersonal exchange with third-party enforcement.** As the economy expands, the scale and scope of transactions rise (many entrepreneurs want to borrow more money to start up firms), calling for the emergence of third-party enforcement through formal market-supporting institutions. Shown in Figure 4.2 (p. 114), the initial costs per transaction are high, because of the high costs of formal institutions. Services provided by the court system, police forces, and law firms are expensive. Small villages usually cannot afford and do not need them. Over time, however, third-party enforcement is likely to facilitate the widening of markets, because unfamiliar parties, people who are not your friends and who would have been deterred to transact with you before, are now confident enough to trade with you (and others). In other words, with an adequate formal institutional framework, you (or your firm) can now borrow from local banks, out-of-state banks, or even foreign banks. Thus, formal market-supporting institutions facilitate more new entries (such as all the new start-ups you and your fellow entrepreneurs can found and all these banks that provide financing) by lowering transaction costs. Consequently, firms grow and economies expand.

FIGURE 4.2   The Costs and Benefits of Formal, Rule-Based, Impersonal Exchange

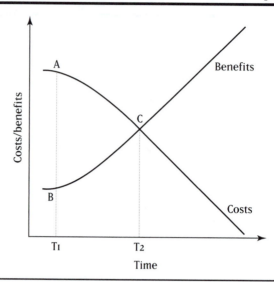

Source: M. W. Peng, 2003, Institutional transitions and strategic choices (p. 280), Academy of Management Review, 28 (2): 275–296. Copyright © 2003. Reprinted by permission of Academy of Management Review via Copyright Clearance Center.

There is no presumption that formal institutions are inherently better than informal ones, because in many situations the demand for formal institutions is not evident. Both forms complement each other. Relational contracting has an advantage when the size of the economy is limited—imagine a small village economy where everyone knows each other. Relational contracting's disadvantage is that it may cause firms to stick with established relationships rather than working with new, untried players, thus creating barriers to entry. As transaction complexity rises, informal dealings within the group may become difficult—imagine a city or national economy in which it would be too difficult to impose informal sanctions against opportunists. Arm's-length transactions, on the other hand, help overcome these barriers, by bringing together formerly distant groups (firms, communities, and even countries) to enjoy the gains from complicated long-distance trade. These rule-based transactions thus become increasingly attractive as more new players enter the game. A global economy simply cannot operate on informal institutions alone. This explains the rise of formal international institutions such as the World Bank (*http://www.worldbank.org*), International Monetary Fund (*http://www. imf.org*), Organization for Economic Cooperation and Development (*http:// www.oecd.org*), and World Trade Organization (*http://www.wto.org*), as well as regional institutions such as the European Union (*http://www.europa.eu.int*) in the past five decades.

Overall, interactions between institutions and firms that reduce transaction costs shape economic activity. In addition, institutions are not static. **Institutional transitions,** defined as "fundamental and comprehensive changes introduced to the formal and informal rules of the game that affect organizations as players,"[20] are widespread in the world, especially in emerging economies. Institutional transitions in some emerging economies, especially those moving from central planning to market competition (such as China, Poland, and Russia), are so pervasive that they are simply called **transition economies** (a subset of "emerging economies"). Managers making strategic choices during such transitions must take into account the nature of institutional frameworks and their transitions (see Integrative Case 2.4), a perspective introduced next.

AN INSTITUTION-BASED VIEW OF STRATEGY

This section first provides an overview of the institution-based view of strategy, which has recently joined the more established industry- and resource-based views to form a "tripod" of three leading perspectives. Then we discuss the two core propositions of the institution-based view.

Overview

Historically, much of the strategy literature, as exemplified by the industry- and resource-based views, does not discuss the specific relationship between strategic choices and institutional frameworks. To be sure, the influence of the "environment" has been noted. However, a "task environment" view, which focuses on economic variables such as market demand and technological change, has dominated much of the existing work on strategy.[21]

For example, consider Porter's influential "diamond" model, which argues that the competitive advantage of different industries in different nations depends on four factors which form a "diamond"[22] (Figure 4.3 on next page). According to this model, first, **firm strategy, structure, and rivalry** within one country are essentially the same as the industry-based view covered in Chapter 2. For example, one reason the Japanese electronics industry is so competitive *globally* is because the rivalry is probably the most intense in the world *domestically*. Second, **factor endowments** refer to the natural and human resource repertoires. Some countries (such as Saudi Arabia) are rich in natural resources but short on population, and others (such as Singapore and South Korea) have large well-educated populations but little natural resources. Third, **related and supporting industries** provide the foundation upon which key industries can excel. Switzerland's global excellence in pharmaceuticals goes hand-in-hand with its dye industry. Finally, tough **domestic demand** propels firms to scale new heights to satisfy such demand. Why is the American movie industry so competitive worldwide? One reason is that American moviegoers demand the very best "sex and violence" (two themes that sell universally if artfully packaged). Endeavoring to satisfy such domestic demand, movie studios unleash *The Mummy Returns* after *The Mummy* and *Terminator 3* after *Terminator 1* and *Terminator 2*—each time packing more excitement than the previous production. Overall, Porter argues that the combination of these four factors explains what is behind the competitive advantage of globally leading industries in different countries.

FIGURE 4.3   The Porter Diamond: Determinants of National Competitive Advantage

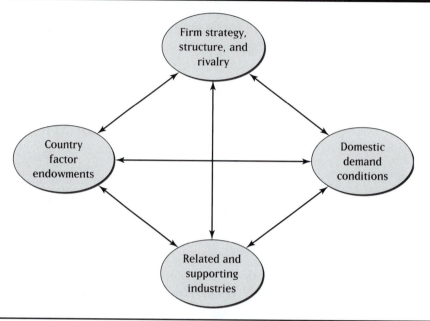

Interesting as the "diamond" model is, critics argue that it ignores histories and institutions.[23] Among strategists, Porter is not alone. Until recently, scholars have rarely looked beyond the task environment (such as what is *behind* firm rivalry).[24] Given that most research focuses on market economies, a market-based institutional framework has been taken for granted and fades into the background—in fact, no other strategy textbook has devoted a full chapter to institutions as this one does.

This omission is unfortunate, because, as practitioners have known for a long time, strategic choices—such as those made by Big Pharma—are made within and constrained by institutional frameworks in developed economies (see Opening Case). Today, this insight becomes more important as more firms do business abroad in general, and Western firms increasingly enter non-Western, emerging economies in particular. The striking institutional differences between developed and emerging economies have propelled the institution-based view to the forefront of strategy discussions.[25] Shown in Figure 4.4, the institution-based view focuses on the dynamic interaction between institutions and firms, and considers strategic choices as the outcome of such an interaction. Specifically, strategic choices are not only driven by industry structure and firm capabilities emphasized by traditional strategic thinking, but also reflect the formal and informal constraints of a particular institutional framework.[26]

Overall, institutions are increasingly recognized as more than background conditions, and many believe that "institutions *directly* determine what arrows a firm has in its quiver as it struggles to formulate and implement strategy and to create

FIGURE 4.4   Institutions, Firms, and Strategic Choices

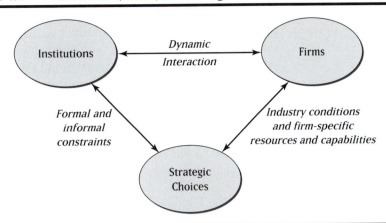

Sources: Adapted from (1) M. W. Peng, 2000, Business Strategies in Transition Economies (p. 45), Thousand Oaks, CA: Sage Publishing; (2) M. W. Peng, 2002, Towards an institution-based view of business strategy (p. 253), Asia Pacific Journal of Management, 19 (2): 251–267.

competitive advantage."[27] At present, the idea that "institutions matter" is no longer novel or controversial. Next, we need to be better understood *how* they matter.

Two Core Propositions

The institution-based view suggests two core propositions. First, managers and firms *rationally* pursue their interests and make strategic choices within institutional constraints. In the pharmaceutical industry (see Opening Case), while the institutional framework in the United States fosters a strategy centered on innovations that command premiums, the institutional framework in Japan *discourages* innovations that make old drugs obsolete—old drugs often are the most profitable ones there. Both strategies are perfectly rational within their own institutional frameworks.

In another example, thousands of firms around the world have pursued a strategy of counterfeiting (see Closing Case). While this is an alarming phenomenon concerning many firms in emerging economies, the key to understanding this strategy is realizing that managers and entrepreneurs who make such a strategic choice are not amoral monsters, but just ordinary people. They have made a *rational* decision (from their standpoint at least), given an institutional environment of weak intellectual protection and availability of certain manufacturing and distribution capabilities.[28] Although firms and governments in developed economies often condemn this strategy, counterfeiting is not restricted to poor countries. Historically, according to the *Economist*, "look back a century or two, many of today's staunch defenders of intellectual property rights in Europe and America were busy doing exactly the same."[29] Of course, to suggest that a strategy of counterfeiting is rational does not deny the fact that it is unethical and illegal. However, without an understanding of its institutional basis, it is difficult to devise effective countermeasures.

The second proposition is that while formal and informal institutions combine to govern firm behavior, in situations where formal constraints fail, informal constraints play a *larger* role in reducing uncertainty and providing constancy to managers and firms. For example, when the formal institutional regime collapsed with the disappearance of the former Soviet Union, it is largely the informal constraints, based on personal relationships and connections (called *blat* in Russian) among managers and officials, that facilitated the growth of many entrepreneurial firms.[30]

Many observers have the impression that relying on informal connections is a strategy only relevant to firms in emerging economies and that firms in developed economies only pursue "market-based" strategies. This is far from the truth. Even in developed economies, formal rules only make up a small (although important) part of institutional constraints, and informal constraints are pervasive. Just as firms compete in product markets, firms also fiercely compete in the political marketplace that is characterized by informal relationships.[31] The best-connected firms are able to reap significant benefits. For instance, in 2003, Halliburton Company, where the sitting Vice President Dick Cheney served as chairman and CEO from 1995 to 2000, was awarded a lucrative contract to rebuild Iraq's infrastructure in the absence of required open bidding. As a result, its revenues rose dramatically from $500 million in 2002 to $3.9 billion in 2003.[32] One study found that when executives are appointed to the US government, on average their firms' share values experience a significant jump of nearly 2 percent, with some firms experiencing an increase of 14 percent.[33] The capital market evidently places a premium on these relationships.

Basically, if a firm cannot be a cost, differentiation, or focus leader, it may still beat the competition on another ground, namely, the nonmarket, political environment that features informal relationships.[34] In many countries, when all else fails, politically sophisticated (or desperate) firms can charge foreign competitors for **dumping** (defined as selling below costs) and can usually count on winning some protection from their governments (see Chapter 8). One study reported that mobilizing political resources to file an antidumping petition is a most lucrative strategy, resulting in a 200 percent return on investment (legal fees for filing) for US firms; another study reports that simply *filing* such a petition resulted in a $46 million increase in market value for listed US firms.[35] To use the resource-based language, political assets can be very valuable, rare, and hard-to-imitate.

THE STRATEGIC ROLE OF CULTURES

While there are hundreds of books and thousands of articles on cultures around the world, in this section we will focus on the strategic aspects of cultures. We first define culture, then we highlight its five dimensions, and finally we link cultures with strategic choices of companies.

Definition of Culture

Although hundreds of definitions of culture have appeared, we will use the one proposed by the world's foremost cross-cultural expert, Geert Hofstede, a Dutch professor. He defines **culture** as "the collective programming of the mind which distinguishes the members of one group or category of people from another."[36] Although most international business textbooks and trade books talk about culture (often presenting numerous details such as how to present business cards in Japan and how to drink vodka in Russia), virtually all strategy books ignore culture. Strategy is usually associated with "hard numbers," and culture is regarded as "too soft." Unfortunately, this belief is narrow-minded in today's global economy.[37] While not touching on the numerous "how-to" aspects (which are certainly important, but can be found elsewhere), here we will focus on the *strategic* role of culture.

Before proceeding, it is important to make two points to minimize confusion. First, although it is customary to talk about American culture or Brazilian culture, no strict one-to-one correspondence exists between cultures and nation-states. Within the United States, numerous subcultures exist, such as the Asian American culture. The same is true for multiethnic countries such as Belgium, China, India, Indonesia, Russia, South Africa, and Switzerland.[38] Second, there are many layers of culture, such as regional, ethnic, and religious cultures. Within a firm, one may find a specific organizational culture (such as the Toyota culture). Having acknowledged the validity of these two points, we will follow Hofstede by using the term "culture" when discussing *national* culture—unless otherwise noted. Although imperfect, this approach is both a matter of expediency and a reflection of the institutional realities of the world, which consists of more than 200 nation-states imposing different institutional frameworks.

Five Dimensions of Culture

While there are a number of ways to identify dimensions of culture,[39] the work of Hofstede has become by far the most influential. He and his colleagues have proposed five dimensions (Table 4.3 on next page). First, **power distance** is the degree of social inequality. For instance, in the United States, subordinates often address their bosses on a first name basis, a reflection of a relatively low power distance. While this boss, Mary or Joe, still has the power to fire you, the distance appears to be shorter than if you have to address this person as Mrs. Y or Dr. Z. In Denmark, a country with one of the lowest power distances, no gates or fences separate the royal palace (guarded by a single soldier) and the regular vehicle and foot traffic passing through a royal square in Copenhagen. In perhaps a most striking example of low power distance, when the king of Sweden went to do some Christmas shopping for his family (an act which would be highly unusual elsewhere), the salesperson demanded to see his "government issued picture identification (ID)" in order to allow him to use his credit card. The king could not produce any ID, and the (lowly) salesperson was not persuaded by other shoppers' argument that "this is our king, I can recognize him on TV"—until the king searched the bottom of his pockets and discovered a coin with his face on it, truly a most authentic piece of government-issued picture ID (!).

Second, **individualism** refers to the perspective that the identity of an individual is fundamentally his or her own, whereas **collectivism** refers to the idea that the identity of an individual is based on the identity of his or her collective group (such as family, village, or company). In individualistic societies (led by the United States), ties between individuals are relatively loose and individual achievement and freedom

TABLE 4.3   **Hofstede Dimensions of Culture**[a]

	1. Power Distance	2. Individualism	3. Masculinity	4. Uncertainty Avoidance	5. Long-Term Orientation
1	Malaysia (104)	USA (91)	Japan (95)	Greece (112)	China (118)
2	Guatemala (95)	Australia (90)	Austria (79)	Portugal (104)	Hong Kong (96)
3	Panama (95)	UK (89)	Venezuela (73)	Guatemala (101)	Taiwan (87)
4	Philippines (94)	Canada (80)	Italy (70)	Uruguay (100)	Japan (80)
5	Mexico (81)	Netherlands (80)	Switzerland (70)	Belgium (94)	South Korea (75)
6	Venezuela (81)	New Zealand (79)	Mexico (69)	El Salvador (94)	Brazil (65)
7	Arab countries (80)	Italy (76)	Ireland (68)	Japan (92)	India (61)
8	Ecuador (78)	Belgium (75)	Jamaica (68)	Yugoslavia (88)	Thailand (56)
9	Indonesia (78)	Denmark (74)	UK (66)	Peru (87)	Singapore (48)
10	India (77)	Sweden (71)	Germany (66)	France (86)	Netherlands (44)
11	West Africa (77)	France (71)	Philippines (64)	Chile (86)	Bangladesh (40)
12	Yugoslavia (76)	Ireland (70)	Colombia (64)	Spain (86)	Sweden (33)
13	Singapore (74)	Norway (69)	South Africa (63)	Costa Rica (86)	Poland (32)
14	Brazil (69)	Switzerland (68)	Ecuador (63)	Panama (86)	Germany (31)
15	France (68)	Germany (67)	USA (62)	Argentina (86)	Australia (31)
16	Hong Kong (68)	South Africa (65)	Australia (61)	Turkey (85)	New Zealand (30)
17	Colombia (67)	Finland (63)	New Zealand (58)	South Korea (85)	USA (29)
18	Salvador (66)	Austria (55)	Greece (57)	Mexico (82)	Great Britain (25)
19	Turkey (66)	Israel (54)	Hong Kong (57)	Israel (81)	Zimbabwe (25)
20	Belgium (65)	Spain (51)	Argentina (56)	Colombia (80)	Canada (23)
21	East Africa (64)	India (48)	India (56)	Venezuela (76)	Philippines (19)
22	Peru (64)	Japan (46)	Belgium (54)	Brazil (76)	Nigeria (16)
23	Thailand (64)	Argentina (46)	Arab countries (53)	Italy (75)	Pakistan (0)
24	Chile (63)	Iran (41)	Canada (52)	Pakistan (70)	
25	Portugal (63)	Jamaica (39)	Malaysia (50)	Austria (70)	
26	Uruguay (61)	Brazil (38)	Pakistan (50)	Taiwan (69)	
27	Greece (60)	Arab countries (38)	Brazil (49)	Arab countries (68)	
28	South Korea (60)	Turkey (37)	Singapore (48)	Ecuador (67)	
29	Iran (58)	Uruguay (36)	Israel (47)	Germany (65)	
30	Taiwan (58)	Greece (35)	Indonesia (46)	Thailand (64)	
31	Spain (57)	Philippines (32)	West Africa (46)	Iran (59)	
32	Pakistan (55)	Mexico (30)	Turkey (45)	Finland (59)	
33	Japan (54)	East Africa (27)	Taiwan (45)	Switzerland (58)	
34	Italy (50)	Yugoslavia (27)	Panama (44)	West Africa (54)	
35	Argentina (49)	Puerto Rico (27)	Iran (43)	Netherlands (53)	
36	South Africa (49)	Malaysia (26)	France (43)	East Africa (52)	
37	Jamaica (45)	Hong Kong (25)	Spain (42)	Australia (51)	
38	USA (40)	Chile (23)	Peru (42)	Norway (50)	

(Continued)

TABLE 4.3   (Continued)

	1. Power distance	2. Individualism	3. Masculinity	4. Uncertainty avoidance	5. Long-term orientation
39	Canada (39)	West Africa (20)	East Africa (41)	South Africa (49)	
40	Netherlands (38)	Singapore (20)	El Salvador (40)	New Zealand (49)	
41	Australia (36)	Thailand (20)	South Korea (39)	Indonesia (48)	
42	Cost Rica (35)	El Salvador (19)	Uruguay (38)	Canada (48)	
43	Germany (35)	South Korea (18)	Guatemala (37)	USA (46)	
44	UK (35)	Taiwan (17)	Thailand (34)	Philippines (44)	
45	Switzerland (34)	Peru (16)	Portugal (31)	India (40)	
46	Finland (33)	Costa Rica (15)	Chile (28)	Malaysia (36)	
47	Norway (31)	Pakistan (14)	Finland (26)	UK (35)	
48	Sweden (31)	Indonesia (14)	Yugoslavia (21)	Ireland (35)	
49	Ireland (28)	Colombia (13)	Costa Rica (21)	Hong Kong (29)	
50	New Zealand (22)	Venezuela (12)	Denmark (16)	Sweden (29)	
51	Denmark (18)	Panama (11)	Netherlands (14)	Denmark (23)	
52	Israel (13)	Ecuador (8)	Norway (8)	Jamaica (13)	
53	Austria (11)	Guatemala (6)	Sweden (8)	Singapore (8)	

a. When the scores are the same, countries are listed according to their alphabetical order. Arab countries, East Africa, and West Africa are clusters of multiple countries. Germany and Yugoslavia refer to the former West Germany and the former Yugoslavia, respectively.

Sources: Adapted from G. Hosftede, 1997, Cultures and Organizations: Software of the Mind (pp. 26, 53, 84, 113, 166), New York: McGraw-Hill. Data on the first four dimensions are based on surveys of IBM employees during 1968–72, first published in G. Hosftede, 1980, Culture's Consequences, Beverly Hills, CA: Sage Publishing. Data on the fifth dimension are based on surveys of students during the 1980s, first published in The Chinese Culture Connections, 1987, Chinese values and the search for culture-free dimensions of culture, Journal of Cross-Cultural Psychology, 18: 143–164.

are highly valued. In contrast, in collectivist societies (such as many countries in Africa, Asia, and Latin America), ties between individuals are close.

Third, the **masculinity** versus **femininity** dimension refers to sex role *differentiation*. In every traditional society, men tend to have occupations that reward assertiveness, such as politicians, soldiers, and executives. Women, on the other hand, usually work in caring professions such as teachers and nurses in addition to being homemakers. High masculinity societies (led by Japan) continue to maintain a sharp differentiation in which men do "men's jobs," and women do "women's work." Low masculinity societies (led by Sweden) feature substantial penetration of both sexes in each other's traditional occupations. Women increasingly become politicians, scientists, and soldiers (consider the movie *GI Jane*), whereas men frequently assume the role of nurses, teachers, and *househusbands*.

Fourth, **uncertainty avoidance** refers to the extent to which members in different cultures accept ambiguous situations and tolerate uncertainty. Members of high uncertainty avoidance cultures (led by Greece) place a premium on job security, career patterns, and retirement benefits. They also tend to resist change, which, by definition, is uncertain. Low uncertainty avoidance cultures (led by Singapore) are characterized by a greater willingness to take risk and less resistance to change.[40]

Finally, **long-term orientation** emphasizes perseverance and savings for future betterment. China, which has the world's longest continuous recorded history of approximately 4,000 years, leads the pack, followed by its East Asian neighbors. On the other hand, members of short-term orientation societies (led by Pakistan in a twenty-three-country sample) prefer relatively quick results and instant gratification.

Overall, Hofstede's dimensions are interesting and informative. While they are not perfect,[41] they represent a *starting point* for strategists trying to figure out the strategic role of culture.

Cultures and Strategic Choices

Many strategic choices have been found to be consistent with Hofstede's cultural dimensions. For example, managers in high power distance countries such as France and Italy tend to have a greater penchant for centralized authority. Therefore, when French and Italian firms set up subsidiaries abroad, they have a greater propensity for majority ownership control (as opposed to minority ownership).[42] In another example, managers' solicitation of subordinate feedback and participation in decision making, widely practiced in low power distance Western countries, is regarded as a sign of weak leadership and low integrity in high power distance countries such as Egypt, India, Mexico, and Russia.[43]

Individualism and collectivism also affect strategic choices. Individualist US firms often try to differentiate themselves, whereas collectivist Japanese firms tend to converge on some defensible positions.[44] Because entrepreneurs are usually willing to take more risk, individualistic societies tend to foster relatively more entrepreneurship, whereas collectivism may result in relatively lower levels of entrepreneurship.[45] When working with alliance partners, individualists rely more on formal contractual safeguards, whereas collectivists emphasize more informal understanding.[46]

Likewise, masculinity and femininity may have strategic implications. At the individual level, the stereotypical manager in masculine societies is "assertive, decisive, and 'aggressive' (only in masculine societies does this word carry a positive connotation)," whereas the stylized manager in feminine societies is "less visible, intuitive rather than decisive, and accustomed to seeking consensus."[47] At the economy level, masculine countries (such as Japan) may have a relative advantage in mass manufacturing, that is, making products efficiently, well, and fast. Feminine countries (such as Denmark) may have a relative advantage in small-scale, customized manufacturing.[48]

Uncertainty avoidance also has a bearing on strategic behavior. Managers in low uncertainty avoidance countries (such as Great Britain) rely more on experience and training, whereas managers in high uncertainty avoidance countries (such as China) rely more on rules and procedures.[49] For example, the 1998 crash of a Swissair flight is indicative of high uncertainty avoidance. The Swissair pilots took their smoke-filled aircraft to the sea to dump fuel before attempting emergency landing. Unfortunately, the aircraft crashed in the sea and everyone on board was killed. A controversy thus broke out as to whether the pilots should have first attempted to land with more fuel (which could explode during landing). With 20/20 hindsight, some US pilots commented that Swissair pilots should have landed the plane as soon as smoke was detected. Swissair officials argued that the pilots did exactly what was required by the written rules. US commentators suggested that under these circumstances, pilots should have exercised independent judgment regardless of the rules—in other words, "rules are there to be broken during an emergency like this," an attitude typical of Americans' uncertainty-accepting norms. Swissair officials, on the other hand, argued that "rules exist exactly for such emergencies."[50]

In addition, cultures with a long-term orientation are likely to nurture firms with long horizons in strategic planning. For instance, Strategy in Action 1.1 in Chapter 1 discusses Matsushita's 250-year plan. While this is certainly an extreme case, Japanese and Korean firms in general are known to be relatively more willing to forego short-term profits and focus more on market share, which, in the long term, may translate into financial gains.[51] In comparison, Western firms tend to focus on relatively short-term profits (often on a quarterly basis).[52] Recently, some Western firms have *shortened* the planning horizon (from a range of ten to fifteen years to five years or less at major oil companies; see Closing Case in Chapter 10).

Overall, strong evidence points out the strategic importance of culture.[53] Sensitivity to cultural differences can not only help strategists better understand what is going on in other parts of the world, but can also avoid strategic blunders. For example, it is hardly surprising that few customers in Latin America bothered to buy the Chevrolet Nova car, which means "no go" in Spanish. It is equally astonishing that a Chinese manufacturer attempted to export to the West a premium brand of battery called White Elephant. More seriously, Mitsubishi Motors, coming from Japan—the world leader in masculinity—encountered major problems when operating in the United States, where more women participate in the labor force (indicative of a relatively higher level of femininity). In 1998, Mitsubishi's North American division paid $34 million to settle sexual harassment charges.

In addition, while cross-cultural differences can be interesting, they can also be unethical and illegal—all depending on the institutional frameworks in which firms are embedded. Thus, it is imperative that current and would-be strategists be aware of the importance of business ethics, as introduced next.

THE STRATEGIC ROLE OF ETHICS

This section first defines ethics from a strategic standpoint, and discusses its impact. This is followed by a particular emphasis on how to manage ethics overseas. This section closes with a discussion of the relationship between ethics and corruption.

Definition and Impact of Ethics

Ethics refers to the norms, principles, and standards of conduct governing individual and firm behavior.[54] Ethics is not only an important part of *informal* institutions, but is also deeply reflected in *formal* laws and regulations. To the extent that laws reflect a society's minimum standards of conduct, there is a substantial overlap between what is ethical and what is legal. However, what is legal may be unethical. For example, laying off thousands of employees in the name of downsizing (as done by Al Dunlap, nicknamed Chainsaw Al, and many other managers) is legal, but widely viewed as unethical.[55]

While in the past few years, corporate scandals around the world, such as Enron (see Video Case 3.4), WorldCom, Royal Ahold, and Parmalat (see Strategy in Action 11.1 in Chapter 11), seem to have pushed business ethics to the forefront of strategy discussions, the global movement to strive for higher levels of business ethics has actually been steadily growing for two decades. By the late 1980s, approximately 75 percent and 41 percent of the large US and European firms, respectively, already had adopted formal codes of conduct.[56] More than a decade later, a majority of large firms in developed economies had such codes in place. The Ethics Officer Association (*http://www.eoa.org*), which was begun in 1992 with twelve firms as members, had nearly a thousand member firms in 2004.

There is a debate concerning what motivates firms to become ethical. A *negative* view suggests that some firms may simply jump onto the ethics "bandwagon" under social pressures to appear more legitimate without necessarily becoming more ethical. A *positive* view maintains that some (although not all) firms may be self-motivated to "do it right" regardless of social pressures.[57] A third, *instrumental* view believes that good ethics simply represent a useful instrument to help make good profits.[58] All sides of the debate, however, agree that it is increasingly clear that ethics can make or break a firm. Firms with an ethical, trustworthy reputation not only earn kudos, but may also gain significant competitive advantage by attracting more investors, customers, and employees.[59]

Perhaps the best way to appreciate the strategic value of ethics is to examine what happens after some crisis. As a "reservoir of goodwill," the value of an ethical reputation is *magnified* during a time of crisis. One study found that all US firms engulfed in crises (such as the Johnson & Johnson Tylenol tampering case and the *Exxon Valdez* oil spill) took an average hit of 8 percent of their market value in the first week. However, after ten weeks, the stock of firms with ethical reputations actually *rose* 5 percent, whereas the stock of firms without such reputations dropped 15 percent.[60] Paradoxically, catastrophes may allow more ethical firms to shine. For example, after the 1998 economic crash in Russia, its fledgling capital market began to differentiate the better-governed, more ethical firms from the less ethical ones. In 1999, there was a 700-fold difference in firm value between the best-governed listed firm (Vimpelcom, a telecom firm) and the worst governed listed ones (several oil firms).[61] The upshot seems to be that ethics pays.

Managing Ethics Overseas

Managing ethics overseas is especially challenging, because what is ethical in one country may be regarded as unethical or even illegal elsewhere.[62] For example, when dealing with under-performing employees who are the primary breadwinners of their families, Korean managers are likely to view keeping them as *ethical* and American managers are likely to view keeping them as *unethical*.[63] Whistle blowers in collectivist societies such as Japan are regarded more as lowly traitors than high-flying heroes. In Nigeria, illegal cross-border trade is so widespread that it becomes the norm.[64] Microsoft's competitive practices, having survived a multiyear trial and been cleared by US antitrust authorities, have been labeled illegal in the European

Union. Facing these and numerous other differences, how can current and would-be strategists prepare themselves instead of getting lost and burned overseas?

According to Thomas Donaldson, a leading business ethicist, two schools of thought deal with ethical dilemmas overseas.[65] First, **ethical relativism** refers to an extension of the cliché, "When in Rome, do as the Romans do." If female employees in Japan and Saudi Arabia are discriminated against, so what? Likewise, if Belgians fail to punish insider trading, who cares? Isn't that the way "Romans" do in "Rome?" Second, **ethical imperialism** refers to the absolute belief that "There is only one set of Ethics (with the big E), and we have it." Around the world, Americans are especially renowned for believing that their ethical values should be applied universally.[66] In other words, if sexual discrimination and insider trading are wrong in the United States, they must be wrong everywhere else. Between the late 1970s and the late 1990s, the United States was the only country that banned its firms from making bribery and other "questionable payments" to foreign government officials. In contrast, until the late 1990s, many EU countries such as Austria, France, Germany, and Netherlands legally allowed bribes that were paid to foreign officials to be tax deductible (!)—a clear sign of ethical relativism.

In practice, however, neither of these schools of thought is realistic. At the extreme, ethical relativism would have to accept any practice that is undertaken within a different culture, whereas ethical imperialism may cause resentment and backlash among locals. Donaldson suggests three "middle-of-the-road" guiding principles. First, *respect for human dignity and basic rights* (such as those concerning health, safety, and the need for education instead of working at a young age) should determine the absolute, minimal ethical thresholds for *all* operations around the world.

Second, *respect for local traditions* suggests cultural sensitivity. If all gift giving is banned, then foreign firms can forget about doing business in China and Japan. While hiring employees' children and relatives instead of more qualified applicants is illegal according to US equal opportunity laws, Indian companies routinely practice such nepotism as a part of the employee benefits that help strengthen employee loyalty. What should US companies setting up subsidiaries in India do? Donaldson advises that such nepotism is not necessarily wrong—at least in India.

Finally, *respect for institutional context* calls for a careful understanding of local institutions. Codes of conduct banning bribery are not very useful unless accompanied by guidelines for the scale and scope of locally appropriate gift giving. For instance, Rhone-Poulenc Rorer, a French pharmaceutical firm, has invited foreign subsidiaries to add locally appropriate supplements to its corporate-wide code of conduct. Overall, these three principles, although far from perfect, have helped managers make decisions about which they and their firms feel relatively comfortable.

Ethics and Corruption

Ethics is important because it helps combat **corruption**, often defined as the abuse of public power for private benefit usually in the form of bribery (in cash or in kind).[67] Corruption distorts the basis for competition, which should be based on products and services, thus causing misallocation of resources and slowing economic

STRATEGY IN ACTION 4.2. *Guinness in Africa: Greasing the Wheels of Commerce with Beer*

Guinness (*http://www.guinness.ie*), a leading Ireland-based beer multinational, operates a brewery in the main port city of Douala, Cameroon in West Africa. Because roads, which disappear in the rainy season, are horrible in general, "just-in-time" delivery is impossible. The factory has to keep forty days of inventory. Wholesalers out in the bush have to carry five months of stock at the beginning of the rainy season. However, the biggest headache is not the roads, but the greedy police officers who man roadblocks throughout the country. One truck delivery to a town 500 kilometers away (313 miles)—about the distance between New York and Pittsburgh—took four days, during which the truck was stopped at roadblocks forty-seven times (!). Corrupt police officers examined papers in the hope of finding errors and checked fire extinguishers, tail lights, and mirrors—all in the name of road safety. Some simply did nothing and merely asked for something. The most frequently requested item was cash, whereas the most plentiful item the driver had was, naturally, beer. By the time the truck finally arrived at its destination, it only carried *two-thirds* of its original load. Despite such unusual management challenges, Guinness is highly profitable in Cameroon, which is its fifth largest market after Britain, Ireland, Nigeria, and America. Its return

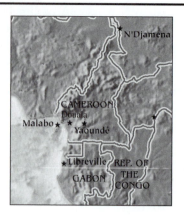

on capital in Cameroon is a healthy 16 percent, and sales have grown 14 percent annually over the past five years. The biggest losers are local customers, especially those who live in the hinterland. A bottle of Guinness that costs $0.53 in Douala is sold at $0.68 in an eastern village, a 28 percent increase because of the high transportation and bribery costs.

Sources: Based on (1) Economist, 2002, The road to hell is unpaved, December 21: 37–39 and (2) http://www.guinness.ie (accessed September 1, 2003).

development[68] (see Strategy in Action 4.2). According to the Germany-based Transparency International (*http://www.transparency.org*), which is probably the most influential anticorruption nongovernment organization (NGO), richer, developed economies tend to be less corrupt than poorer, developing countries (see Table 4.4). The correlation between a high level of corruption and a low level of economic development is strong. Some evidence supports the idea that corruption discourages foreign direct investment (FDI).[69] For example, if the level of corruption in Singapore (which is very low) increases to the level in Mexico (which is in the middle range), it reportedly would have the same negative effect on FDI inflows as raising the tax rate by 50 percent (!)[70]

However, there are paradoxes, such as China and Indonesia, for example. Despite a reportedly high level of corruption, China became the largest host of FDI in the world in 2002. Another case is Indonesia, whose former president Suharto was known as "Mr. Ten Percent," which refers to the well-known (and transparent!) amount of bribes foreign firms were expected to pay him or members

TABLE 4.4 **Transparency International Corruption Rankings**

	CORRUPTION PERCEPTIONS INDEX: 22 LEAST CORRUPT COUNTRIES OUT OF 133 (10: HIGHLY CLEAN — 0: HIGHLY CORRUPT)		CORRUPTION PERCEPTIONS INDEX: 22 MOST CORRUPT COUNTRIES OUT OF 133 (10: HIGHLY CLEAN — 0: HIGHLY CORRUPT)		BRIBE PAYERS INDEX: PROPENSITY OF FOREIGN FIRMS FROM THE FOLLOWING 21 COUNTRIES TO PAY BRIBES (10: NOT LIKELY — 0: EXTREMELY LIKELY)
1	Finland (9.7)	1	Bangladesh (1.3) – #133	1	Australia (8.5)
2	Iceland (9.6)	2	Nigeria (1.4) – #132	2	Sweden (8.4) – #2 (tied)
3	Denmark (9.5) – #3 (tied)	3	Haiti (1.5) – #131		Switzerland (8.4) – #2 (tied)
	New Zealand (9.5) – #3 (tied)	4	Myanmar (1.6) – #129 (tied)	4	Austria (8.2)
5	Singapore (9.4)		Paraguay (1.6) – #129 (tied)	5	Canada (8.1)
6	Sweden (9.3)	6	Angola (1.8) – #124 (tied)	6	Netherlands (7.8) – #6 (tied)
7	Netherlands (8.9)		Azerbaijan (1.8) – #124 (tied)		Belgium (7.8) – #6 (tied)
8	Australia (8.8) – #8 (tied)		Cameroon (1.8) – #124 (tied)	8	UK (6.9)
	Norway (8.8) – #8 (tied)		Georgia (1.8) – #124 (tied)	9	Singapore (6.3) – #9 (tied)
	Switzerland (8.8) – #8 (tied)		Tajikistan (1.8) – #124 (tied)		Germany (6.3) – #9 (tied)
11	Canada (8.7) – #11 (tied)	11	Indonesia (1.9) – #123	11	Spain (5.8)
	Luxembourg (8.7) – #11 (tied)	12	Kenya (1.3) – #122	12	France (5.5)
	United Kingdom (8.7) – #11 (tied)	13	Cote d'Ivoire (2.1) – #118 (tied)	13	Japan (5.3) – #13 (tied)
14	Austria (8.0) – #14 (tied)		Kyrgyzstan (2.1) – #118 (tied)		USA (5.3) – #13 (tied)
	Hong Kong (8.0) – #14 (tied)		Libya (2.1) – #118 (tied)	15	Malaysia (4.3) – #15 (tied)
16	Germany (7.7)		Papua New Guinea (2.1) – #118 (tied)		Hong Kong (4.3) – #15 (tied)
17	Belgium (7.6)	17	Republic of Congo (2.2) – #113 (tied)	17	Italy (4.1)
18	Ireland (7.5) – #18 (tied)		Ecuador (2.2) – #113 (tied)	18	South Korea (3.9)
	United States (7.5) – #18 (tied)		Iraq (2.2) – #113 (tied)	19	Taiwan (3.8)
20	Chile (7.4)		Sierra Leone (2.2) – #113 (tied)	20	China (3.5)
21	Israel (7.0) – #21 tied		Uganda (2.2) – #113 (tied)	21	Russia (3.2)
	Japan (7.0) – #21 tied		Bolivia (2.2) – #113 (tied)	22	Domestic firms (1.9)

Source: Adapted from Transparency International Corruption Perceptions Index 2003 (first two columns) and Bribe Payers Index 2002 (third column), http://www.transparency.org (accessed October 19, 2003).

of his family. Yet, Indonesia is also a popular destination of FDI. There are two possible explanations for the popularity of China and Indonesia as FDI destinations. First, the vast potential of these two economies during the recent reforms may outweigh the drawbacks of dealing with corruption.[71] Second, overseas Chinese (mainly from Hong Kong and Taiwan) and Japanese firms are the leading investors in mainland China and Indonesia, respectively. While Hong Kong, Taiwan, and Japan are relatively "cleaner," they are not in the top league of "cleanest" countries (Table 4.4). Thus, it is possible that "exposure to corruption at home provides a learning experience preparing the individual companies to handle corruption abroad," according to one study, "hence, acquiring skills in managing corruption helps develop a certain competitive advantage."[72]

If that is true, it is not surprising that many US firms complained that they were unfairly restricted by the Foreign Corrupt Practices Act (FCPA), which is a US law enacted in 1977 that bans bribing corrupt foreign officials. They also pointed out that bribery was often tax deductible in many EU countries—at least until the late 1990s. On the other hand, the FCPA has been argued to provide US firms with an ethical *weapon* in the fight against corruption. The law essentially allows US managers to tell corrupt foreign officials, "We would like to pay you, but if we do, we will go to jail. So we can't pay you." Until recently, this weapon was not available to firms from other countries. Preliminary evidence suggests that US firms are not necessarily disadvantaged abroad because of the FCPA.[73]

However, even with the FCPA, no evidence shows that US firms are inherently more ethical than others. The FCPA itself was triggered by the investigation in the 1970s of many corrupt US firms—most notoriously Lockheed, a major aerospace firm, which bribed Japanese officials. Even the FCPA makes exceptions for small "grease" payments to get goods through customs abroad. Further, in 1995, Lockheed was found guilty, again, of bribing an Egyptian official. Most alarmingly, a recent World Bank study reports that despite more than two decades of FCPA enforcement, US firms actually "exhibit systematically *higher* levels of corruption" than other OECD firms (original italics).[74]

Overall, it seems reasonable to regard the FCPA as an institutional weapon in the global fight against corruption. However, despite its formal *regulatory* "teeth," for a long time, there was neither a *normative* pillar nor a *cognitive* pillar—essentially missing two legs in the tripod underpinning any institution. For a long time, the norms among other OECD firms seemed to be pay bribes first and get tax deduction later (!). Only in 1997 did the OECD Convention on Bribery of Foreign Public Officials commit all member countries (essentially all developed economies) to not only remove the tax deductibility of bribes, but also criminalize such behavior. If every country criminalizes bribery and every investor resists corruption, their combined power will eradicate it. However, this will not happen unless FCPA-type legislation is institutionalized *and* enforced in every country.

A STRATEGIC RESPONSE FRAMEWORK

At its core, the institution-based view focuses on how certain strategic choices, under institutional influences, are diffused from a few firms to many. In other words, the attention is on how certain practices (such as switching from relationship- to market-based competition, from being culturally insensitive to sensitive, from agreeing to pay bribes to refusing) become *institutionalized*. How individual firms respond leads to a strategic response framework that features four strategic choices: (1) reactive, (2) defensive, (3) accommodative, and (4) proactive (see Table 4.5).

Reactive Strategy

A reactive strategy is passive. Firms do not feel compelled to act in the absence of disasters and outcries. Even when some problems arise, denial is usually the first line of defense. Put another way, the need to take necessary action is neither

TABLE 4.5 **A Strategic Response Framework**

Institutional Constraints	Primary Underlying Pressures	Strategic Responses	Strategic Behaviors	Examples in the Text
Formal	Regulatory	Reactive	Deny responsibility, do less than required	Ford Pinto fire (the 1970s)
Formal	Regulatory	Defensive	Admit responsibility, but fight it, do the least that is required	Nike (the early 1990s)
Informal	Normative	Accommodative	Accept responsibility, do all that is required	Ford Explorer/Firestone roll-overs (the 2000s)
Informal	Cognitive	Proactive	Anticipate responsibility, do more than is required	Credit Suisse First Boston (the 2000s)

Sources: Based on (1) A. Carroll, 1979, A three-dimensional conceptual model of corporate social performance, Academy of Management Review, 4: 497–505; (2) M. Clarkson, 1995, A stakeholder framework for analyzing and evaluating corporate social performance, Academy of Management Review, 20: 92–117; (3) S. Wartick & P. Cochran, 1985, The evolution of the corporate social performance model, Academy of Management Review, 10: 758–769.

internalized through cognitive beliefs, nor becoming a norm in practice. That only leaves intense formal regulatory pressures to compel firms to act. For example, Ford Motor Company started to market the Pinto in the early 1970s, knowing that its gas tank had a fatal design flaw that could make the car susceptible to exploding in rear-end collisions. Ford decided not to add an $11 per car gas tank improvement because, in its assessment, the total monetary costs outweighed by three times the benefits of the projected 180 lives that could be saved. Sure enough, accidents happened and people were killed and burned in Pintos. Still, for several years Ford refused to recall the Pinto, and more lives were lost. Only in 1978, under intense formal pressures from the government and court cases and informal pressures from the media and consumer groups, did Ford belatedly recall all 1.5 million Pintos built between 1970 and 1976.[75]

Defensive Strategy

A defensive strategy focuses on regulatory compliance. In the absence of regulatory pressures, firms often fight pressures that demand change in their strategies. For example, in the early 1990s, Nike was charged with allegedly running "sweatshops," while in fact these incidents took place in their contractors' factories in Bangladesh, Indonesia, and Vietnam. Although Nike did not own these factories, its initial statement, "We don't make shoes," failed to convey any ethical responsibility or understanding. On the issue of low wages (sometimes called "slave wages" or "below subsistence wages"), Nike argued that these seemingly low wages (such as less than $1 a day) were already reasonable by local standards. Initially, it was clear that Nike would not cooperate. However, when several senators began to suggest legislative solutions and when President Clinton convened a Presidential task force to study the issue—in other words, when regulatory pressures loomed large on the horizon—Nike began to become more serious.[76]

Accommodative Strategy

An accommodative strategy features an emerging organizational norm to accept responsibility and a set of increasingly internalized cognitive beliefs and values toward making certain changes. Further, some new managers who are passionate about or sympathetic toward certain causes may join the organization, whereas some traditional managers may change their outlook to become more sympathetic to certain causes. Further, these normative and cognitive values may be shared by a number of firms, thus leading to some new industry norms. In other words, it becomes legitimate to accept responsibility and do all that is required. Nike, for instance, became more accommodative toward the late 1990s, and the industry as a whole established several coalitions and partnerships with activist groups to try to collectively address the labor issue (see Strategy in Action 12.3 in Chapter 12).

In another example, in 2000, when Ford Explorer vehicles equipped with Firestone tires were reported to have a high likelihood of fatal roll-over accidents, Ford evidently learned the painful lesson from its Pinto fire experience in the 1970s. Ford took aggressive actions, including mobilizing a speedy massive recall, creating a media campaign featuring its CEO, and discontinuing the long-standing relationship with Firestone. In contrast, Firestone's communications were very guarded, reminiscent of Ford's reactive and defensive actions during the Pinto fiasco. The dust is still not settled on the case, but it appears that Ford has largely weathered the storm while Firestone's reputation is at an all time low.

While critics argue that Ford's accommodative strategy was largely intended to place blame squarely on Firestone, the institution-based view suggests that such highly rational actions are to be expected given how institutional pressures work to instill value. Regardless of Ford's actual motive, the fact that it has tangibly embarked on some ethical journey is encouraging, especially when compared with its stonewalling during the 1970s. Even if Ford's public relations campaign was only "window dressing," publicizing a set of ethical criteria against which it can be judged opens doors for more scrutiny by concerned stakeholders. The institutional pressures are likely to encourage its internal transformation to become a more self-motivated, better corporate citizen. It probably is fair to say that Ford was a better corporate citizen in 2000 than it was in 1975.

Proactive Strategy

Proactive firms constantly anticipate institutional changes and endeavor to do more than is required. Top management not only supports and champions these activities, but also views them as a source of differentiation. The recent transformation of Credit Suisse First Boston (CSFB), formerly known as Wall Street's "most free-wheeling" investment bank, is a good example. Brought in 2001, new CEO John Mack argued that "risks to our reputation and our integrity could put us out of business." Mack led CSFB to launch an assault on dubious Wall Street practices. He worked with investigators and legislators, forced star performers to adhere to codes of conduct, and overhauled how the firm does everything to ensure that clients' interests come first. CSFB determined that it would rather lose a deal than lose a client's trust. Accordingly, since 2001, CSFB not only voluntarily withdrew from forty-seven mergers, but also hired a cadre of ethics officers. CSFB already attracted more clients and forced rivals to follow suit to clean up their act, thus helping set newer, more ethical norms for Wall Street. Mack also anticipated that regulators might force all Wall Street firms to separate research from investment banking, and prepared CSFB for such possible requirements in the future.[77]

While a certain element of "window dressing" probably exists, the fact that proactive firms are going beyond the current *regulatory* requirements indicates many managers' *normative* and *cognitive* beliefs about the importance of doing the "right thing."[78]

DEBATES AND EXTENSIONS

Relative to the industry- and resource-based views, the institution-based view is the newest leading perspective on strategy. Not surprisingly, some significant debates emerge, including (1) cultures versus institutions, (2) opportunism versus individualism/collectivism, (3) cultural distance versus institutional distance, and (4) "bad apples" versus "bad barrels."

Cultures versus Institutions

Being the "collective programming of the mind," culture can be considered an essential part of the normative and cognitive pillars underpinning informal institutions in every society. Culture also often asserts its influence on formal institutions.[79] On the other hand, institutions also influence the way culture evolves. Therefore, "institutions are the crystallizations of culture, and culture is the substratum of institutional arrangements."[80] If so, is culture or institution "bigger" or more fundamental? While different scholars argue for each case,[81] Hofstede and his colleagues suggest that from a practical standpoint, such a debate may be "useless hair-splitting,"[82] a position with which we agree. Instead of engaging in such a debate, in this book, we are interested in how cultures, institutions, and/or ethics affect strategic choices and performance outcomes.[83]

Opportunism versus Individualism/Collectivism[84]

The opportunism versus individualism/collectivism debate is practically more important. As noted earlier, opportunism is a major source of uncertainty, and transaction cost theorists maintain that institutions emerge to combat opportunism. However, critics argue that emphasizing opportunism as "human nature" may backfire in practice.[85] For example, if a firm assumes employees will steal and places surveillance cameras everywhere, then employees who otherwise would not steal may be so alienated that they decide to do exactly that. In another example, if firm A insists on specifying minute details in an alliance contract to prevent firm B from behaving opportunistically *in the future*, A is likely to be regarded by B as being opportunistic *now* (see Chapter 7 for details). This is especially the case if B is from a collectivist society whose norm is for the contract to serve as an expression of general principles of cooperation and for parties to hammer out differences later.[86] In a nutshell, attempts to combat opportunism may beget opportunism.

Transaction cost theorists acknowledge that opportunists are a minority in any population. However, theorists contend that because it is difficult to identify such a minority of opportunists *before* they cause any damage, it is imperative to place safe-guards that, unfortunately, treat everybody as a potential opportunist. For example, thanks to the work of only nineteen terrorists, millions of air travelers around the world since September 11, 2001 now have to go through heightened security. Everybody hates it, but nobody argues that it is unnecessary. This debate, therefore, seems deadlocked.

One cultural dimension, individualism versus collectivism, may hold the key to improving our understanding of opportunism. A stereotype is that players from col-lectivist societies (such as China and Japan) are more collaborative and trustworthy, and that those from individualist societies (such as America and Australia) are more competitive and opportunistic. However, recent research suggests that this is *not* necessarily the case. Collectivists are more collaborative *only* when dealing with **in-group** members, that is, individuals and firms regarded as a part of a collective. The flip side is that collectivists discriminate against **out-group** members more harshly. On the other hand, individualists, who believe that every person (firm) is on his or her (its) own, make less distinction between in-group members and out-group members. Therefore, while individualists may indeed be more opportunistic than collectivists when dealing with in-group members (this fits the stereotype), col-lectivists may be *more* opportunistic when dealing with out-group members. In other words, on average Chinese are not inherently more trustworthy than Ameri-cans. For instance, the Chinese motto regarding out-group members is: "Watch out for strangers. They will screw you!" This helps explain why the United States, the leading individualist country, is among the societies with a higher level of sponta-neous trust, whereas greater interpersonal and interfirm *distrust* exists in the large society in China than in the United States.[87] This also explains why it is so impor-tant to establish *guanxi* (relationship) networks for individuals and firms in a collectivist society such as China; otherwise, life can be very challenging in a sea of strangers.

This insight is not likely to help improve airport security screening, but it can help firms better deal with each other. Whereas individualists from the West prefer "business first, relationship afterwards" (have a drink after the negotiations), collec-tivists from China, Japan, Mexico, and Russia often prefer things the other way around (lavish entertainment and social interactions first, talk about business later). Individualists may view social activities as *unrelated* to the business at hand, whereas collectivists believe that such interactions are an *essential* part of doing business.[88] Only through repeated social interactions can collectivists assess whether to accept newcomers as in-group members. If foreigners who, by defini-tion, are from an out-group refuse to show any interest in joining the in-group, then it is a fair game to take advantage of them. This, in part, explains why many cross-culturally naïve Western firms often cry out loud for being taken advantage of in collectivist societies—they are simply being treated as "deserving" out-group members. Conversely, as shown in Strategy in Action 4.3, unsuspecting collectivists may also be astonished by some opportunistic moves made by their individualist partners.

STRATEGY IN ACTION 4.3. *Honda: Got Burned by Individualism?*

For more than a decade (from 1979 to 1994), Honda (*http://www.honda.com*) invested heavily in an alliance with the British automaker Rover (*http://www.mgrover.com*). Honda considered this a long-term relationship, much like a marriage in which trust is first and foremost. Honda shared a great deal of proprietary technology, well beyond what was called for in the alliance agreement, believing that such investments would be reciprocated. As a result, in 1994 Honda executives were dumbfounded when informed by Rover's parent company, British Aerospace (BAe, *http://www.baesystems.com*), that Rover would be sold to BMW (*http://www.bmw.com*), an arch rival of Honda, for £800 million. Coming from a collectivist culture, Honda not only regarded Rover as an "in-group"

member deserving all its trust, but also *assumed* that Rover would do the same. Unfortunately, this assumption was deeply flawed. While Rover executives and employees enjoyed working with Honda, the parent firm, BAe, had virtually no contact with Honda. From BAe's standpoint, since Rover continued to lose money, selling it made great financial sense and was perfectly legal. More importantly, Honda's disproportionate investments made it possible for BAe to ask for *more* from BMW—at Honda's expense.

Sources: Based on (1) J. Sebenius, 2002, The hidden challenge of cross-border negotiations, Harvard Business Review, 80 (3): 76–85; (2) The Times, 2004, Honda signals the severing of partnership with Rover, February 22:1; (3) BBC News, 1994, MPs condemn sale of Rover, February 1.

Cultural Distance versus Institutional Distance

As the previous debate illustrates, doing business with foreigners may entail significantly higher transaction costs than doing business domestically—known as the **liability of foreignness** (see Chapter 6 for details).[89] For instance, Japanese-US joint ventures are not surprisingly shorter lived than Japanese-Japanese joint ventures.[90] Basically, when disputes and misunderstanding arise, it is difficult to ascertain whether the other side is deliberately being opportunistic, or is simply being (culturally) different.[91] As a result, firms in general prefer to first enter culturally close countries. Only after firms gradually exhaust culturally similar countries would they gain enough confidence to enter culturally distant countries. In other words, an identifiable sequence of foreign market entries may be based on the **cultural distance** between the home country and the host country.[92] This view becomes known as the cultural distance hypothesis.

However, critics of the cultural distance hypothesis make five arguments. First, they point out a number of findings inconsistent with this hypothesis.[93] In China, one study reports that joint ventures between local and Western firms outperform those between local and Asian firms.[94] In Italy, one study finds a *positive* association between cultural distance and cross-border acquisition performance.[95] Second, critics contend that given the complexity of foreign-entry decisions, cultural distance, while important, is just one of the many factors to consider.[96] For instance, relative to national culture, *organizational* (firm-specific) culture may be equally important in affecting joint venture and merger performance.[97]

Third, other researchers note that while cultural distance is important *initially*, its importance declines as players get to know each other—as part of the in-group formation process discussed earlier.[98] More generally, cultural distance is gradually shortened because of globalization.[99] Fourth, other critics point out that much of the research is based on Hofstede's data drawing on his surveys of IBM employees between 1968 and 1972. While there is always the question of whether IBM employees are truly representative of their respective cultures (probably not), another problem is that these old data simply fail to capture the cultural *changes* throughout the world in the past three decades.

Finally, some researchers argue that perhaps the cultural distance concept can be complemented (but not replaced) by the **institutional distance** concept. This emerging idea is gathering some momentum, as researchers start to look beyond the Hofstede dimensions and investigate the intricacies of other institutional differences around the world.[100] For instance, if favorite sports can be regarded as "national institutions," the world can be roughly divided into three regions: baseball, cricket, and soccer. This logic suggests that in countries where baseball is the national sport such as Japan and Mexico (except Cuba), US firms are likely to lead in the MNE sector. In countries where cricket captures people's hearts such as Australia and India, British MNEs may take the lead. Finally, in countries where people are crazy about soccer such as Brazil, continental European MNEs are likely to beat their global competitors.[101]

We can take two key lessons from this debate. First, ignoring the potentially important concept of cultural distance is imprudent. Second, we should *not* read too much into culture, which is just one of many variables affecting strategic behavior.[102]

Bad Apples versus Bad Barrels

This bad apples versus bad barrels debate focuses on the root cause of unethical business behavior. One argument suggests that people have ethical or unethical predispositions *before* joining firms. Another side of the debate argues that while there are indeed some opportunistic "bad apples," many times people commit unethical behavior not because they are "bad apples," but because they are spoiled by "bad barrels."[103] Some firms not only condone, but even expect unethical behavior. For example, at the now-defunct Arthur Andersen, the norms were to "make the numbers" no matter what. These expectations became the *normative* and *cognitive* pillars that sustained an unethical organizational culture.

The debate on bad apples versus bad barrels is an extension of the broader debate on "nature versus nurture." Are we who we are because of our genes (nature) or our environments (nurture)? Most studies report that human behavior is the result of both nature *and* nurture. Although individuals and firms (staffed by people) do have some ethical or unethical predispositions that influence their behavior, the institutional environment (such as organizational cultures and national institutions) can also have a significant impact. In a nutshell, even "good apples" may turn bad in "bad barrels."[104]

IMPLICATIONS FOR STRATEGISTS

Strategies are about choices. When trying to understand how these choices are made, practitioners and scholars usually "round up the usual suspects," namely, industry structures and firm capabilities. These views are very insightful, however, they usually do not pay adequate attention to the underlying *context* of structures and capabilities.[105] A contribution of the institution-based view is to emphasize the importance of institutions, cultures, and ethics as the bedrock propelling or constraining strategic choices. Overall, if strategy is about the "big picture," then the institution-based view reminds current and would-be strategists not to forget the "bigger picture."

We conclude this chapter by revisiting the four fundamental questions. First, why do firms differ? The institution-based view points out the institutional frameworks that shape firm differences. Second, how do firms behave? The answer also boils down to institutional differences. Third, what determines the scope of the firm? While we will devote more time to delineate this question in Chapter 9, in short, better developed formal institutional frameworks in the West may call for a reduced corporate scope, whereas more informal institutional frameworks in many emerging economies may provide more benefits for a wider corporate scope.[106] Finally, what determines the international success and failure of firms? The institution-based view argues that firm performance is, at least in part, determined by the institutional frameworks governing strategic choices.

Chapter Summary

1. Commonly known as "the rules of the game," institutions have formal and informal components, each with different supportive pillars (regulatory pillar for formal institutions and normative and cognitive pillars for informal institutions). The key functions of institutions are to reduce uncertainty, curtail transaction costs, and combat opportunism.

2. Institutions reduce uncertainty in two primary ways: (1) through informal, relationship-based, personalized exchange (known as relational contracting) and (2) through formal, rule-based, impersonal exchange with third-party enforcement (known as arm's-length transactions).

3. The institution-based view of strategy suggests two propositions: (1) Managers and firms rationally pursue their interests and make strategic choices within formal and informal institutional constraints; (2) In situations where formal constraints fail, informal constraints play a *larger* role.

4. According to Hofstede's research, national culture has five primary dimensions: (1) power distance, (2) individualism/collectivism, (3) masculinity/femininity, (4) uncertainty avoidance, and (5) long-term orientation. Each dimension has some significant bearing on strategic choices.

5. When managing ethics overseas, two schools of thought are (1) ethical relativism and (2) ethical imperialism. Three "middle-of-the-road" principles focus on respect for (1) human dignity and basic rights, (2) local traditions, and (3) institutional context.

6. The fight against corruption around the world is a long-term, global battle, requiring both formal legislation (such as the Foreign Corrupt Practices Act) and informal norms and cognitions.

7. When confronting institutional pressures, individual firms have four strategic choices: (1) reactive, (2) defensive, (3) accommodative, and (4) proactive.

8. The key debates focus on (1) cultures versus institutions, (2) opportunism versus individualism/collectivism, (3) cultural distance versus institutional distance, and (4) "bad apples" versus "bad barrels."

Key Terms

arm's-length transactions	formal, rule-based, impersonal exchange	long-term orientation
cognitive pillar	individualism	masculinity
collectivism	informal institutions	normative pillar
corruption	informal, relationship-based, personalized exchange	opportunism
culture		out-group
domestic demand	in-group	power distance
dumping	institutional distance	regulatory pillar
ethical imperialism	institutional framework	related and supporting industries
ethical relativism	institutional transitions	relational contracting
ethics	institution-based view	transaction costs
factor endowments	institutions	transition economies
femininity	liability of foreignness	uncertainty avoidance
formal institutions		

Critical Discussion Questions

1. If you were the CEO of an Argentine company in 2002, how would you respond to the economic collapse (see Strategy in Action 4.1)? If you were the CEO of a foreign company operating in Argentina, what courses of action would you take during 2002 (other than exiting the country)? After the crisis is over, what would you do to better prepare your firm (regardless of its nationality) to deal with a similar crisis in the future?

2. Some argue that *guanxi* (relationships and connections) is a unique, Chinese-only phenomenon embedded in the Chinese culture. As evidence, they point out that this word, *guanxi*, has now entered the English language when

describing relationship-based strategies in China and is often used in mainstream media (such as the *Economist*) without explanations provided in brackets. Others disagree, arguing that every culture has a word or two describing what the Chinese call *guanxi*, such as *blat* in Russia, *guan he* in Vietnam, and "old boys' network" in the English-speaking world. They suggest that the intensive use of *guanxi* in China (and elsewhere) is a reflection of the lack of formal institutional frameworks. Which side of the debate would you like to join? Why?

3. ***ON ETHICS:*** Assume you work for a New Zealand company exporting a container of kiwis to Mauritania in West Africa. The customs official informs you that there is a delay in clearing your container through customs and it may last a month. However, if you are willing to pay an "expediting fee" of US$200, he will try to make it happen in one week. What would you do?

Closing Case: Dealing with Counterfeiting

Counterfeiting, despite being unethical and illegal, is a thriving global business. Close to 10 percent of all world trade is reportedly in counterfeits. Different countries have developed "distinctive competences." For example, Russia is emerging as a powerhouse for counterfeit software. Ukraine is famous for bootleg optical discs. Paraguay is well known for imitation cigarettes. Counterfeiting is also not restricted to poor countries. Italy is a leading producer of counterfeit luxury goods. Florida has developed a global reputation for fake aircraft parts. Counterfeiters openly hawk handbags in front of the White House in Washington, DC. At present, the global leader seems to be China, whose own State Council estimated that counterfeiting is a $16 billion a year industry. Chinese counterfeiters target a wide range of products, such as apparel, auto parts, drugs, DVDs, skin-care products, software, and toys, and export many of them around the world.

Counterfeiting is generally regarded as a by-product of an entrepreneurial boom. A fundamental issue is why many entrepreneurs choose a counterfeiting strategy. Industry structures certainly play a role, as counterfeiters tend to converge on industries with low entry barriers. Firm-specific resources are important too—all these products have to be designed (reverse engineered), produced, transported, and sold with reasonable capabilities. However, experts generally agree that the single largest determinant lies in institutional frameworks. A lack of an effective formal intellectual property rights (IPR) regime seems to be a prerequisite for counterfeiting. As a new WTO member since 2001, China has significantly strengthened its IPR laws in line with the WTO Trade-Related Intellectual Property Rights (TRIPS) Agreement. However, enforcement is lacking in China. In America, convicted counterfeiters face fines of up to $2 million and ten years in prison for a first offense. In China, counterfeiters—if they are caught—can get away with a $1,000 fine, which is usually regarded as a (small) cost of doing business. In many cases, local governments and police have little incentive to enforce IPR laws, in fear of losing tax revenues and increasing unemployment. China is not alone in this regard. For example, in Thailand, a 2000 raid to shut down counterfeiters was blocked by a thousand angry people organized by local officials. In most poor countries, currency counterfeiters are severely punished, but other counterfeiters can often count on doing business "as usual."

In the absence of legal protection, the world of counterfeiting is largely regulated by informal norms and beliefs. Operating outside (or underneath) the legal radar screen, players involved in this business, such as financiers, producers, shippers, wholesalers, and retailers, have to rely on relationship-based informal networks. This is especially challenging and dangerous as this business becomes globalized. Despite the drawbacks of having to rely on informal ties, counterfeiting seems to be on the rise globally.

To stem the tide of counterfeits, four "Es" are necessary. The first E, enforcement, even if successful, is likely to be short-lived as long as demand remains high. The other three "Es"—education, external pressures, and economic growth—require much more patient work. Education not only refers to educating IPR law enforcement officials, but also the general public about the perils of counterfeits (fake drugs can kill, so can fake auto parts). Educational efforts hopefully will foster new norms among a new generation of entrepreneurs who will have internalized the values that favor more ethical and legitimate businesses. External pressures have to be applied skillfully. Confronting host governments is not likely to be effective. For example, Microsoft, when encountering extensive software piracy in China, chose to collaborate with the Ministry of Electronics to develop new software instead of challenging it head on (see Video Case 1.7). Microsoft figured that after the

government has a stake in the sales of legitimate Microsoft products, it may have a stronger interest in cracking down on pirated software. Finally, economic growth and home-grown brands are the most effective remedies in the long run. In the 1500s, the Netherlands (an emerging economy at that time) was busy making counterfeit Chinese porcelain. In the 1960s, Japan was the global leader for counterfeits. In the 1970s, Hong Kong grabbed this dubious distinction. In the 1980s, South Korea and Taiwan led the world. Now it is China's turn. As these countries developed their own industries, they also strengthened IPR laws. If past experience around the world is any guide, someday China and other leading counterfeiting nations may hopefully follow the same path.

Case Discussion Questions

1. Why do some entrepreneurs choose a strategy of counterfeiting?

2. What are the pros and cons of operating in the underworld of informal norms and relationships in counterfeiting? For the purposes of this discussion, what would be your key concerns if you were involved in this business?

3. What are the likely attributes of the most "successful" (profitable) counterfeiting firms?

4. What is the recommended course of action if your company's products have been counterfeited?

Sources: Based on (1) D. Chow, 2002, A Primer on Foreign Investment Enterprises and Protection of Intellectual Property in China, Boston: Kluwer; (2) Economist, 2003, Imitating property is theft, May 17: 52–54; (3) Economist, 2003, In praise of the real thing, May 17: 12; (4) T. Moga, 2002, The TRIPS agreement and China, China Business Review, November–December: 12–18; (5) M. W. Peng, 2001, How entrepreneurs create wealth in transition economies, Academy of Management Executive, 15 (1): 95–108; (6) S. Schnaars, 1994, Managing Imitation Strategies, New York: Free Press; (7) T. Trainer, 2002, The fight against trademark counterfeiting, China Business Review, November–December: 20–24.

Notes

Abbreviation list

AME – *Academy of Management Executive*

AMJ – *Academy of Management Journal*

AMLE – *Academy of Management Learning and Education*

AMR – *Academy of Management Review*

APJM – *Asia Pacific Journal of Management*

ASQ – *Administrative Science Quarterly*

BW – *Business Week*

CMR – *California Management Review*

HBR – *Harvard Business Review*

IBR – *International Business Review*

IJCCM – *International Journal of Cross-Cultural Management*

JBE – *Journal of Business Ethics*

JBV – *Journal of Business Venturing*

JIBS – *Journal of International Business Studies*

JIM – *Journal of International Management*

JM – *Journal of Management*

JMS – *Journal of Management Studies*

JR – *Journal of Retailing*

JWB – *Journal of World Business*

LRP – *Long Range Planning*

MIR – *Management International Review*

MS – *Management Science*

OD – *Organizational Dynamics*

OSc – *Organization Science*

RES – *Review of Economics and Statistics*

SMJ – *Strategic Management Journal*

SMR – *MIT Sloan Management Review*

SO – *Strategic Organization*

1. D. North, 1990, *Institutions, Institutional Change, and Economic Performance* (p. 3), New York: Norton.

2. W. R. Scott, 1995, *Institutions and Organizations* (p. 33), Thousand Oaks, CA: Sage Publishing.

3. Scott, 1995, *Institutions and Organizations*.

4. M. France, 2003, Music pirates, you're sunk, *BW,* September 8: 40–41.

5. M. Guillen, 2003, Experience, imitation, and the sequence of foreign entry, *JIBS,* 34: 185–198; J. Lu, 2002, Intra- and inter-organizational imitative behavior, *JIBS,* 33: 19–37; M. W. Peng, 2004, Outside directors and firm performance during institutional transitions, *SMJ,* 25: 453–471.

6. T. Das & B. Teng, 1998, Between trust and control, *AMR,* 23: 491–512; F. Fukuyama, 1995, *Trust,* New York: Free Press; D. Rousseau, S. Sitkin, R. Burt, & C. Camerer, 1998, Not so different after all: A cross-discipline view of trust, *AMR,* 23: 393–404.

7. S. Watkins, 2003, Former Enron Vice President Sherron Watkins on the Enron collapse, *AME,* 17: 119–125.

8. V. Anand, B. Ashforth, & M. Joshi, 2004, Business as usual, *AME,* 18: 39–54.

9. M. W. Peng, 2000, *Business Strategies in Transition Economies* (pp. 42–44), Thousand Oaks, CA: Sage Publishing.

10. M. T. Dacin, J. Goodstein, & W. R. Scott, 2002, Institutional theory and institutional change, *AMJ,* 45: 45–57; W. Powell & P. DiMaggio, 1991, *The New Institutionalism in Organizational Analysis*, Chicago: University of Chicago Press.

11. O. Williamson, 1985, *The Economic Institutions of Capitalism* (pp. 1–2), New York: Free Press.

12. Williamson, 1985, *The Economic Institutions of Capitalism* (pp. 47–48).

13. D. Elenkov, 1997, Strategic uncertainty and environmental scanning, *SMJ,* 18: 287–302; T. Murtha & S. Lenway, 1994, Country capabilities and the strategic state, *SMJ,* 15: 113–129; O. Sawyerr 1993, Environmental uncertainty and environmental scanning activities of Nigerian manufacturing executives, *SMJ,* 14: 287–299.

14. R. Mamamurti, 2003, Can governments make credible promises? *JIM,* 9: 253–269.

15. M. Guillen, 2001, *The Limits of Convergence* (p. 135), Princeton, NJ: Princeton University Press.

16. W. Henisz, 2002, *Politics and International Investment,* Cheltenham, UK: Elgar; B. Koka, J. Prescott, & R. Madhavan, 1999, Contagion influence on trade and

investment policy: A network perspective, *JIBS,* 30: 127–148; E. O'Higgins, 2002, Government and the creation of the Celtic Tiger, *AME,* 16 (3): 104–120; R. Ostergard, 2000, The measurement of intellectual property rights protection, *JIBS,* 31: 349–360.

17. A. Bhappu, 2000, The Japanese family: An institutional logic for Japanese corporate networks and Japanese management, *AMR,* 25: 409–415; J. Hagen & S. Choe, 1998, Trust in Japanese interfirm relations, *AMR,* 23: 589–600.

18. M. W. Peng, 2003, Institutional transitions and strategic choices, *AMR,* 28: 275–296. See also S. Li, 1999, The benefits and costs of relation-based governance: An explanation of the East Asian miracle and crisis, Unpublished working paper, Hong Kong: City University of Hong Kong.

19. North, 1990, *Institutions* (p. 34).

20. Peng, 2003, Institutional transitions and strategic choices (p. 275).

21. L. Brouthers, S. Werner, & E. Matulich, 2000, The influence of Triad nations' environments on price-quality product strategies and MNC performance, *JIBS,* 31: 39–62; B. Kogut, 1991, Country capability and the permeability of borders, *SMJ,* 12: 33–47; S. Kotha & A. Nair, 1995, Strategy and environment as determinants of performance, *SMJ,* 16: 497–518; V. Rindova & C. Fombrun, 1999, Constructing competitive advantage, *SMJ,* 20: 691–710.

22. M. Porter, 1990, *Competitive Advantage of Nations,* New York: Free Press.

23. H. Davies & P. Ellis, 2001, Porter's *Competitive Advantage of Nations*: Time for the final judgment? *JMS,* 37: 1189–1215; H. Moon, A. Rugman, & A. Verbeke, 1998, A generalized double diamond approach to the global competitiveness of Korea and Singapore, *IBR,* 7: 135–151.

24. There are a small number of studies that investigate regulated industries in the West. See K. Ramaswamy, A. Thomas, & R. Litschert, 1994, Organizational performance in a regulated environment, *SMJ,* 15: 63–74; M. Russo, 1992, Power plays, *SMJ,* 13: 13–27.

25. S. T. Cavusgil, P. Ghauri, & M. Agarwal, 2002, *Doing Business in Emerging Markets,* Thousand Oaks, CA: Sage Publishing; R. Hoskisson, L. Eden, C. Lau, & M. Wright, 2000, Strategy in emerging economies, *AMJ,* 43: 249–267; Peng, 2000, *Business Strategies in Transition Economies*; K. Meyer & M. W. Peng, 2004, Identifying leading theories for research on Central and Eastern Europe, Working paper, Copenhagen Business School; M. Wright, I. Filatotchev, R. Hoskisson, & M. W. Peng, 2005, Strategy research in emerging economies: Challenging the conventional wisdom, *JMS* (in press).

26. N. Biggart & R. Delbridge, 2004, Systems of exchange, *AMR,* 29: 28–49; P. Moran & S. Ghoshal, 1999, Markets, firms, and the process of economic development, *AMR,* 24: 390–412; C. Oliver, 1997, Sustainable competitive advantage: Combining institutional and resource-based views, *SMJ,* 18: 679–713; M. W. Peng, 2002, Towards an institution-based view of business strategy, *APJM,* 19: 251–267; M. Ruef, 2003, A sociological perspective on strategic management, *SO,* 1: 241–251.

27. P. Ingram & B. Silverman, 2002, Introduction (p. 20, added italics), in P. Ingram & B. Silverman (eds.), *The New Institutionalism in Strategic Management*: 1–30. Amsterdam: Elsevier. See also U. Haley, 2003, Assessing and controlling business risks in China, *JIM,* 9: 237–253; M. Kotabe & R. Mudambi, 2003, Institutions and international business, *JIM,* 9: 215–217; R. Mudambi & C. Paul, 2003, Domestic drug prohibition as a source of foreign institutional instability, *JIM,* 9: 335–349; T. Ozawa, 2003, Japan in an institutional quagmire, *JIM,* 9: 219–235; A. Parkhe, 2003, Institutional environments, institutional change, and international alliances, *JIM,* 9: 305–216; H. Teegen, 2003, International NGOs as global institutions, *JIM,* 9: 271–285.

28. K. Gillespie, 2003, Smuggling and the global firm, *JIM,* 9: 317–333; K. Gillespie & J. McBride, 1996, Smuggling in emerging markets, *JWB,* 31: 39–54.

29. *Economist,* 2003, In praise of the real thing (p. 12), May 17: 12.

30. M. W. Peng, 2001, How entrepreneurs create wealth in transition economies, *AME,* 15 (1): 95–108.

31. G. Keim, 2001, Business and public policy, in M. Hitt, R. E. Freeman, & J. Harrison (eds.), *The Blackwell Handbook of Strategic Management* (pp. 583–601), Boston: Blackwell; M. Lord, 2003, Constituency building as the foundation for corporate political strategy, *AME,* 17: 112–124; A. McWilliams, D. van Fleet, &

K. Cory, 2002, Raising rivals' costs through political strategy, *JMS,* 39: 707–723; R. Schuler, K. Rehbein, & R. Cramer, 2002, Pursuing strategic advantage through political means, *AMJ,* 45: 659–672; M. Watkins, 2003, Government games, *SMR,* Winter: 91–95.

32. *Economist,* 2003, Halliburton: What we know, February 21: 60–61.

33. A. Hillman, A. Zardkoohi, & L. Bierman, 1999, Corporate political strategies and firm performance: Indications of firm-specific benefits from personal service in the US government, *SMJ,* 20: 67–81.

34. D. Baron, 1995, Integrated strategy: Market and non-market components, *CMR,* 37: 47–65; J. Boddewyn & T. Brewer, 1994, International-business political behavior, *AMR,* 19: 119–143; R. Schuler, 1996, Corporate political strategy and foreign competition, *AMJ,* 39: 720–737.

35. S. Marsh, 1998, Creating barriers for foreign competition, *SMJ,* 19: 25–37; T. Moran, 1985, *MNCs: The Political Economy of FDI,* Lexington, MA: Lexington Books.

36. G. Hofstede, 1997, *Cultures and Organizations: Software of the Mind* (p. 5), New York: McGraw-Hill.

37. P. C. Earley & R. Peterson, 2004, The elusive cultural chameleon, *AMLE,* 3: 100–115.

38. K. Au, 1999, Intra-cultural variation: Evidence and implications for international business, *JIBS,* 30: 799–813; G. Cheung & I. Chow, 1999, Subcultures in Greater China, *APJM,* 16: 369–387; P. Huo & D. Randall, 1991, Exploring subcultural differences in Hofstede's value survey, *APJM,* 8: 159–173; D. Ralston, K. Yu, R. Terpstra, & D. Gustafson, 1996. The cosmopolitan Chinese manager, *JIM,* 2: 79–109.

39. E. Hall & M. Hall, 1987, *Hidden Differences,* Garden City, NY: Doubleday; S. Ronen & O. Shenkar, 1985, Clustering countries on attitudinal dimensions, *AMR,* 10: 435–454.

40. P. Barr & M. Glynn, 2004, Cultural variation in strategic issue interpretation, *SMJ,* 28: 59–67.

41. T. Fang, 2003, A critique of Hofstede's fifth national cultural dimension, *IJCCM,* 3: 351–372; R. Yeh & J. Lawrence, 1995, Individualism and Confucian dynamism, *JIBS,* 26: 655–669.

42. M. K. Erramilli, 1996, Nationality and subsidiary ownership patterns in multinational corporations, *JIBS,* 27: 225–248.

43. C. Fey & I. Bjorkman, 2001, The effect of HRM practices on MNC subsidiary performance in Russia, *JIBS,* 32: 59–75; J. Parnell & T. Hatem, 1999, Behavioral differences between American and Egyptian managers, *JMS,* 36: 399–418; S. Michailova, 2002, When common sense becomes uncommon, *JWB,* 37: 180–187.

44. S. Kotha, R. Dunbar, & A. Bird, 1995, Strategic action generation, *SMJ,* 16: 195–220.

45. T. Begley & W. Tian, 2001, The socio-cultural environment for entrepreneurship, *JIBS,* 32: 537–553; M. Morris, D. Davis, & J. Allen, 1994, Fostering corporate entrepreneurship, *JIBS,* 25: 65–89; A. Thomas & S. Mueller, 2000, A case for comparative entrepreneurship, *JIBS,* 31: 287–301.

46. R. Bhagat, B. Kedia, P. Herveston, & H. Triandis, 2002, Cultural variations in the cross-border transfer of organizational knowledge, *AMR,* 27: 204–221; H. K. Steensma, L. Marino, & K. M. Weaver, 2000, Attitudes toward cooperative strategies: A cross-cultural analysis of entrepreneurs, *JIBS,* 31: 591–609.

47. Hofstede, 1997, *Cultures and Organizations* (p. 94). See also S. Appold, S. Siengthai, & J. Kasarda, 1998, The employment of women managers and professionals in an emerging economy, *ASQ,* 43: 538–565.

48. Hofstede, 1997, *Cultures and Organizations* (p. 95).

49. P. Smith, M. Peterson, & Z. M. Wang, 1996, The manager as mediator of alternative meanings, *JIBS,* 27: 115–137.

50. R. Griffin & M. Pustay, 2003, *International Business,* 3rd ed. (p. 109), Upper Saddle River, NJ: Prentice Hall.

51. G. Hundley, C. Jacobson, & S. Park, 1996, Effects of profitability and liquidity on R&D intensity, *AMJ,* 39: 1659–1674; R. Peterson, C. Dibrell, & T. Pett, 2002, Long- vs. short-term performance perspectives of Western European, Japanese, and U.S. companies, *JWB,* 37: 245–255; L. Thomas & G. Waring, 1999, Competing capitalism, *SMJ,* 20: 729–748.

52. J. Child, D. Faulkner, & R. Pitkethly, 2000, Foreign direct investment in the UK 1985–1994, *JMS,* 37: 141–166; K. Laverty, 1996, Economic "short-termism," *AMR,* 21: 825–860; M. Porter, 1992, Capital disadvantage: America's failing capital investment system, *HBR,* 62 (3): 65–82.

53. H. Barkema, J. Bell, & J. Pennings, 1996, Foreign entry, cultural barriers, and learning, *SMJ,* 17:

151–166; M. de Mooij & G. Hofstede, 2002, Convergence and divergence in consumer behavior, *JR,* 78: 61–69; J. Hennart & J. Larimo, 1998, The impact of culture on the strategy of MNEs, *JIBS,* 29: 515–538; S. Makino & K. Neupert, 2000, National culture, transaction costs, and the choice between joint venture and wholly owned subsidiary, *JIBS,* 31: 705–713; L. Palich & L. Gomez-Mejia, 1999, A theory of global strategy and firm efficiencies, *JM,* 25: 587–606.

54. L. Trevino & K. Nelson, 2004, *Managing Business Ethics,* 3rd ed. (p. 13), New York: Wiley.

55. S. Puffer & D. McCarthy, 1995, Finding the common ground in Russian and American business ethics, *CMR,* 37: 29–46; B. Victor & C. Stephens, 1994, The dark side of the new organizational forms, *OSc,* 5: 479–482.

56. C. Langlois & B. Schlegelmilch, 1990, Do corporate codes of ethics reflect national character? Evidence from Europe and the United States, *JIBS,* 21: 519–539.

57. L. Hosmer, 1994, Strategic planning as if ethics mattered, *SMJ,* 15: 17–34; D. Quinn & T. Jones, 1995, An agent morality view of business policy, *AMR,* 20: 22–42.

58. R. E. Freeman, 1984, *Strategic Management: A Stakeholder Approach,* Boston: Putnam; T. Jones, 1995, Instrumental stakeholder theory, *AMR,* 20: 404–437; D. Swanson, 1995, Addressing a theoretical problem by reorienting the corporate social performance model, *AMR,* 20: 43–64.

59. J. Barney & M. Hansen, 1994, Trustworthiness as a source of competitive advantage, *SMJ,* 15: 175–190; M. Baucus & D. Baucus, 1997, Paying the piper: An empirical examination of longer-term financial consequences of illegal corporate behavior, *AMJ,* 40: 129–151.

60. C. Fombrun, 2001, Corporate reputations as economic assets, in M. Hitt, R. E. Freeman, & J. Harrison (eds.), *The Blackwell Handbook of Strategic Management* (pp. 289–312), Cambridge, UK: Blackwell.

61. M. W. Peng & Y. Ruban, 2005, Institutional transitions and strategic choices: Implications for corporate social responsibility in Russia, in The World Bank (ed.), *Corporate Social Responsibility and Sustainable Competitiveness in Russia,* Washington: The World Bank (in press).

62. V. Brand & A. Slater, 2003, Using a qualitative approach to gain insights into the business ethics experiences of Australian managers in China, *JBE,* 45: 167–182; B. Bucar, M. Glas, & R. Hisrich, 2003, Ethics and entrepreneurs, *JBV,* 18: 261–281; G. Weaver, 2001, Ethics program in global business: Culture's role, *JBE,* 30: 3–15.

63. T. Jackson, 2000, Making ethical judgments, *APJM,* 17: 443–472.

64. A. Fadahunsi & P. Rosa, 2002, Entrepreneurship and illegality, *JBV,* 17: 397–429.

65. The remainder of this section draws heavily from T. Donaldson, 1996, Values in tension: Ethics away from home, *HBR,* September-October: 4–11.

66. D. Vogel, 1992, The globalization of business ethics, *CMR,* Fall: 30–49.

67. P. Rodriguez, K. Uhlenbruck, & L. Eden, 2004, Government corruption and the entry strategies of multinationals, *AMR* (in press).

68. J. Doh, P. Rodriguez, K. Uhlenbruck, J. Collins, & L. Eden, 2003, Coping with corruption in foreign markets, *AME,* 17: 114–127.

69. J. Doh & R. Ramamurti, 2003, Reassessing risk in developing country infrastructure, *LRP,* 36: 337–354; S. Globerman & D. Shapiro, 2003, Governance infrastructure and US foreign direct investment, *JIBS,* 34: 19–39; D. Loree & S. Guisinger, 1995, Policy and non-policy determinants of US equity foreign direct investment, *JIBS,* 26: 281–299.

70. S. Wei, 2000, How taxing is corruption on international investors? *RES,* 82: 1–11.

71. C. Robertson & A. Watson, 2004, Corruption and change: The impact of foreign direct investment, *SMJ,* 25: 385–396.

72. M. Habib & L. Zurawicki, 2002, Corruption and foreign direct investment (p. 295), *JIBS,* 33: 291–307.

73. Wei, 2000, How taxing (p. 2).

74. J. Hellman, G. Jones, & D. Kaufmann, 2002, Far from home: Do foreign investors import higher standards of governance in transition economies (p. 20), Working paper, Washington: The World Bank (*http://www.worldbank.org*).

75. D. Gioia, 2004, Pinto fires, in Trevino & Nelson, 2004, *Managing Business Ethics* (pp. 105–108).

76. J. Burns & D. Spar, 2000, *Hitting the wall: Nike and international labor practices,* HBS case 700–047.

77. E. Thornton, 2002, Can this man be a Wall Street reformer? *BW,* September 23: 90–96.

78. D. Deephouse, 1999, To be different, or to be the same? *SMJ,* 20: 147–166.

79. N. Adler, R. Brahm, & J. Graham, 1992, Strategy implementation, *SMJ,* 13: 449–466; K. Newman & S. Nollen, 1996, Culture and congruence: The fit between management practices and national culture, *JIBS,* 27: 753–779; D. Ralston, D. Holt, R. Terpstra, & K. Yu, 1997, The impact of national culture and economic ideology on managerial work values, *JIBS,* 28: 177–207.

80. G. Hofstede, C. Van Deusen, C. Mueller, T. Charles, & The Business Goals Network, 2002, What goals do business leaders pursue? (p. 800), *JIBS,* 33: 785–803.

81. P. Gooderham, O. Nordhaug, & K. Ringdal, 1999, Institutional and rational determinants of organizational practices, *ASQ,* 44: 507–531; R. Whittington & M. Mayer, 2000, *The European Corporation,* Oxford, UK: Oxford University Press.

82. Hofstede et al., 2002, What goals (p. 800).

83. M. W. Peng, 2002, Cultures, institutions, and strategic choices, in M. Gannon & K. Newman (eds.), *The Blackwell Handbook of Cross-Cultural Management* (pp. 52–66), Cambridge, UK: Blackwell.

84. This section draws heavily from C. Chen, M. W. Peng, & P. Saparito, 2002, Individualism, collectivism, and opportunism: A cultural perspective on transaction cost economics, *JM,* 28: 567–583.

85. S. Ghoshal & P. Moran, 1996, Bad for practice: A critique of the transaction cost theory, *AMR,* 21: 13–47; P. Hirsch, R. Friedman, & M. Koza, 1990, Collaboration or paradigm shift? *OSc,* 1: 87–98.

86. P. Doney, J. Cannon, & M. Mullen, 1998, Understanding the influence of national culture on the development of trust, *AMR,* 23: 601–620; B. Husted, J. Dozier, J. T. McMahon, & M. Kattan, 1996, The impact of cross-national carriers of business ethics on attitudes about questionable practices and form of moral reasoning, *JIBS,* 27: 391–411; J. Sebenius, 2002, The hidden challenge of cross-border negotiations, *HBR,* 80 (3): 76–85.

87. F. Fukuyama, 1995, *Trust;* G. Redding, 1993, *The Spirit of Chinese Capitalism,* New York: Gruyter.

88. J. Graham & N. Lam, 2003, The Chinese negotiation, *HBR,* 81 (10): 82–91.

89. J. Hennart, 1982, *A Theory of Multinational Enterprise,* Ann Arbor: University of Michigan Press; D. Griffith, M. Hu, & J. Ryans, 2000, Process standardization across intra- and inter-cultural relationships, *JIBS,* 31: 303–324; S. Shane, 1994, The effect of national culture on the choice between licensing and direct foreign investment, *SMJ,* 15: 627–642; S. Zaheer, 1995, Overcoming the liability of foreignness, *AMJ,* 38: 341–363.

90. J. Hennart & M. Zeng, 2002, Cross-cultural differences and joint venture longevity, *JIBS,* 33: 699–716.

91. A. Thompson, 1996, Compliance with agreements in cross-cultural transactions, *JIBS,* 27: 375–390.

92. B. Kogut & H. Singh, 1988, The effect of national culture on the choice of entry mode, *JIBS,* 19: 411–432; J. Johanson & J. Vahlne, 1977, The internationalization process of the firm, *JIBS,* 8: 23–32.

93. S. O'Grady & H. Lane, 1996, The psychic distance paradox, *JIBS,* 27: 309–333.

94. J. Li, K. Lam, & G. Qian, 2001, Does culture affect behavior and performance of firms? *JIBS,* 32: 115–31.

95. P. Morosini, S. Shane, & H. Singh, 1998, National cultural distance and cross-border acquisition performance, *JIBS,* 29: 137–158.

96. J. Evans & F. Mavondo, 2002, Psychic distance and organizational performance, *JIBS,* 33: 515–532; C. Hill, P. Hwang, & W. Kim, 1990, An eclectic theory of the choice of international entry modes, *SMJ,* 11: 117–128.

97. V. Pothukuchi, F. Damanpour, J. Choi, C. Chen, & S. Park, 2002, National and organizational culture differences and international joint venture performance, *JIBS,* 33: 243–265; Y. Weber, O. Shenkar, & A. Raveh, 1996, National and corporate culture fit in mergers/acquisitions, *MS,* 42: 1215–1227.

98. R. S. Marshall & D. Boush, 2001, Dynamic decision-making: A cross-cultural comparison of US and Peruvian export managers, *JIBS,* 32: 873–893.

99. M. Heuer, J. Cummings, & W. Hutabarat, 1999, Cultural change among managers in Indonesia? *JIBS,* 30: 599–610; J. Lee, T. Roehl, & S. Choe, 2000, What makes management style similar or distinct across border? *JIBS,* 31: 631–652.

100. K. Brouthers & L. Brouthers, 2001, Explaining the national cultural distance paradox, *JIBS,* 32: 177–189; L. Busenitz, C. Gomez, & J. Spencer, 2000, Country institutional profiles, *AMJ,* 43: 994–1003; R. Calori, M. Lubatkin, P. Very, & J. Veiga, 1997, Modeling the origins of nationally-bound administrative heritages, *OSc,* 8: 681–696; A. Delios & W. Henisz, 2003, Policy uncertainty and the sequence of entry by Japanese firms, 1980–98, *JIBS,* 34: 227–242; C. Lau & H. Ngo, 2001, Organization development and firm performance, *JIBS,* 32: 95–114; T. Kostova, 1999, Transnational transfer of strategic organizational practice, *AMR,* 24: 308–324; O. Shenkar, 2001, Cultural distance revisited, *JIBS,* 32: 519–535; D. Xu & O. Shenkar, 2002, Institutional distance and the multinational enterprise, *AMR,* 27: 608–618.

101. S. Rangan & A. Drummond, 2002, Explaining outcomes in competition among foreign multinationals in a focal host market, *SMJ,* 25: 285–293.

102. J. Salk & M. Brannen, 2000, National culture, networks, and individual influence in a multinational management team, *AMJ,* 43: 191–202.

103. D. Brass, K. Butterfield, & B. Skaggs, 1998, Relationships and unethical behavior: A social network perspective, *AMR,* 23: 14–31; Trevino & Nelson, 2004, *Managing Business Ethics* (p. 10).

104. L. Trevino & M. Brown, 2004, Managing to be ethical, *AME,* 18: 69–81.

105. R. Bettis, 1998, Commentary, *SMJ,* 19: 357–361; J. Cheng, 1994, On the concept of universal knowledge in organizaional science, *MS,* 40: 162–168; A. Madhok, 2002, Reassessing the fundamentals and beyond, *SMJ,* 23: 535–550.

106. M. W. Peng, S. Lee, & D. Wang, 2005, What determines the scope of the firm over time? A focus on institutional relatedness, *AMR* (in press).

Video Case 1.1 (1 minute 57 seconds)
HANDSPRING'S TREO DEBUT

Video Case 1.2 (1 minute 33 seconds)
TREO'S CAPABILITIES

These two related videos showcase how a new technological device—Handspring's Treo communicator—has the potential to substitute for three existing devices—a cell phone, a personal digital assistant (PDA), and an e-mail pager (Blackberry). These video cases relate to the threat of new entrants (Chapter 2), the threat of substitutes (Chapter 2), and the concept of resources and capabilities (Chapter 3). Handspring is a young start-up, which is in alliance with Palm. To a lesser extent, these two videos also relate to entrepreneurial strategies (Chapter 5), "born global" small firms (Handspring, despite being a US firm, introduced its Treo first in tech-savvy Hong Kong—see Chapters 5 and 6), market-seeking foreign entries (Chapter 6), and strategic alliances (Chapter 7).

Video Case 1.3 (2 minutes 40 seconds)

FAST FOOD SQUEEZE

Video Case 1.4 (2 minutes 7 seconds)

MCDONALD'S MARKETING INITIATIVES

Video Case 1.5 (1 minute 38 seconds)

MCDONALD'S IN TROUBLE

These three related videos provide a multidimensional view of the strategic challenges confronting McDonald's. Video Case 1.3, "Fast Food Squeeze," highlights the price war between McDonald's and Burger King, which resulted in McDonald's selling its signature products for under $1, an example mentioned in Chapter 2 when discussing interfirm rivalry. Such rivalry is also discussed in Chapter 8. Video Case 1.4, "McDonald's Marketing Initiatives," indicates how a traditional cost leader is trying to differentiate itself, by providing a self-proclaimed "better experience for customers." The discussion of the two generic strategies, cost leadership and differentiation, in Chapter 2 is directly relevant here. Video Case 1.5, "McDonald's in Trouble," which starts with a clip showing a Broadway chorus line cheering the opening of a new, elegant McDonald's, continues the theme on how to become a more differentiated competitor. The video also documents the fact that Subway now tops McDonald's as the largest fast food chain in the United States. It relates the valuable and unique capabilities of McDonald's, and how easy or difficult it is to compete away such advantages (Chapter 3).

Video Case 1.6 (1 minute 59 seconds)
BLUE LIGHT BLUES

This video provides a snapshot of Kmart filing for bankruptcy in 2001 (*before* the more recent trial and conviction of Martha Stewart, whose products were featured prominently in Kmart). At one time, using a cost leadership strategy, Kmart was the largest US department store chain. Kmart's archrival, Wal-Mart, has been featured extensively in Chapter 2. The key lesson here is that even for a venerable firm such as Kmart, failure to maintain cost leadership relative to the firm's rivals, has grave consequences. The video is also relevant when discussing firm resources and capabilities in Chapter 3. Finally, it is also worth noting that Kmart's CEO announced in the video that "Kmart is not going out of business." Instead, Kmart filed for Chapter 11 bankruptcy reorganization and emerged from Chapter 11 in May 2003, after closing 600 stores (not 500 as indicated in the video). This invites discussions about the sustainability of Kmart's competitive advantages.

Video Case 1.7 (5 minutes 37 seconds)
MICROSOFT IN CHINA

This video shows that Microsoft has willingly agreed to share some of its source code with China, which, according to an analyst in the video, is "like Coca-Cola releasing its formula." While there is some element of interfirm rivalry—Microsoft versus Linux (Chapter 2)—and firm capabilities of maintaining dominance worldwide (Chapters 3 and 6), the most relevant chapter is Chapter 4. The "rules of the game" in China are set up by the Chinese government, and if Microsoft wants to "play" there, it must offer some significant concessions to the Chinese government, which otherwise would support Linux. Microsoft, of course, can choose not to play such a game there. In light of the growing importance of the Chinese economy, however, this does not seem to be an option. An ethical dimension also exists, because one of the purposes for the Chinese government to obtain parts of Microsoft's source code is to better track and control its citizens' Internet usage—in other words, denying Chinese people the right to use the Internet as users in other parts of the world would. While we can debate whether it is ethical for Microsoft to cooperate with the government in these activities, we should also acknowledge that the host country government is one of the stakeholders with some legitimate interest in controlling the activities of foreign entrants (see Chapters 6 and 12).

Video Case 1.8 (2 minutes 46 seconds)
LIK-SANG AND SOFTWARE PIRACY

This video shows the controversy surrounding Lik-Sang, a Hong Kong-based online retailer that sold modification chips (mod chips) used to crack the protection codes of video games. In September 2002, Lik-Sang was jointly sued in Hong Kong by Microsoft, Nintendo, and Sony, which otherwise remain fierce rivals with each other. At the heart of this case is the "rules of the game"—in other words, institutional frameworks (Chapter 4). One side of the debate suggests that mod chips encourage more game play. Another side contends that mod chips should be banned as counterfeiting devices that engage in software piracy. When discussing Chapter 4's Closing Case on counterfeiting, this case can show the human face of alleged counterfeiters, who deny any wrongdoing. In addition to Chapter 4, Chapter 5 on entrepreneurship is also relevant here (see especially Discussion Question 4).

Integrative Case 1.1

GN NETCOM[1]

Klaus E. Meyer

Copenhagen Business School

A Denmark-based, leading global player in telecommunications headsets tries to move part of its global operations to China.

In 2000, GN Netcom (*http://www.gnnetcom.com*), headquartered in Copenhagen, Denmark, was a leading global specialist in the development, production, and marketing of headsets for professional and consumer markets. It was one of the three major divisions of its parent corporation, GN Great Nordic A/S. The other two major divisions were GN ReSound, which focused on hearing aids, and NetTest, which produced testing equipment for communication networks.

GN Netcom presented itself as "among the leading and fastest growing suppliers of hands-free communications solutions, focusing specifically on three market segments: Call centers, offices, and mobile and PC audio."[2] The main products were headsets with microphones and the corresponding amplifiers that were used in offices where staff have a lot of telephone conversations, for example, in call centers or in service and sales departments (see IC-1.1 on next page). Using such a headset, office staff had their hands free, thus increasing the efficiency of their work. Other headsets were produced for consumer

markets, for example, for use with mobile phones in cars. This case focuses on GN Netcom's challenges as its management team, led by a new CEO appointed in 2000, contemplated on how to proceed strategically and globally—in particular, how to move part of its global operations to China.

History

GN Great Nordic A/S had a long and prestigious history that dates back to the nineteenth century. Its predecessor, Great Northern Telegraph Company A/S, was established in 1867. Its primary business was the construction and operation of international telegraph networks, including cross-continent and under-ocean connections. A major part of the telegraph network was the line through Russia to the Far East. The relatively small Danish company entered China for the first time in 1872. Great Northern Telegraph had maintained the connection with and through Russia throughout most of the twentieth century, even during the Stalin years when most foreign investment in Russia was expropriated. The connection with China was, however, disrupted during the years of the Cultural Revolution.

After World War II, the telegraph networks were increasingly taken over by state-owned companies around the world, and GN transformed itself into an industrial conglomerate broadly related to communications technology with most of its activities in

[1] This case was written by Klaus E. Meyer (Copenhagen Business School). It has been prepared solely as a basis for classroom discussion; it is not intended to show the effective or ineffective handling of a management situation. Copyright © Klaus E. Meyer, 2002, 2004. No copying without written permission by the author (*km.cees@cbs.dk*). Reprinted by permission of the author.

[2] *Annual Report 2000*, p. 30.

IC-1.1.   **Selection of Products offered by GN Netcom**

Headsets with microphone and earpiece to be used by office staff.

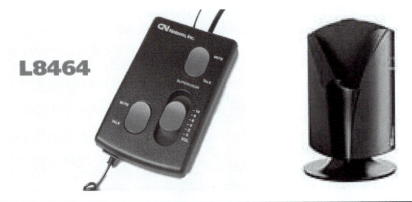

Amplifiers sit on the person's desk, connecting the telephone and the headset and guaranteeing quality of reception. Note that the latest models, based on Bluetooth® technology, are wireless, i.e. there is no fixed connection between headset and amplifier.

A satisfied customer greeting visitors on GN Netcom's website.

Denmark.[3] Throughout the 1990s, GN Great Nordic, as it was now known, changed its strategy to move from a Danish conglomerate to a telecommunications equipment manufacturer operating in related global niche markets. Throughout this long period, GN continuously maintained business relationships with both Russia and China. In May 2000, the then Danish Prime Minister Poul Nyrup Rasmussen attended a special event to mark 130 years of GN in China, organized by NetTest.

Sister Companies

A major business grew in the 1980s and 1990s with GN Danavox producing hearing aids and related products. Following the acquisition of ReSound Corporation and Beltone Electronics in the United States in 1999, this business had been renamed to GN ReSound and headquartered in California. GN Danavox established a joint venture (JV) in China in 1987 as one of the first Danish companies to produce in China. However, when the Chinese partner withdrew, the state-run Danish Fund for Developing Countries (IFU) acquired part of the equity in 1989. In 1999, GN ReSound bought out these shares and became the sole owner of GN ReSound (China).

GN ReSound gradually increased the number of employees in China to about 100 in 1998, when they started a major shift of the production of older models of hearing aids from Præstø, Denmark to Xiamen, China—initially without intentions of reducing employment in Denmark. However, in 2000 approximately 50 Danish employees were laid off due to relocation of production to China. GN ReSound also gradually shifted production from Austria to China, while so far maintaining production facilities in Denmark and the United States. In the first half of 2000, employment in China increased by about 100 to approximately 300 and 70 percent of production had been relocated there. GN ReSound has also been

active in the Chinese market, with an all-Chinese Web site (http://www.gnresound.com.cn).

Another sister company, NetTest (formerly GN Nettest), provided instruments, systems, and other services for testing and optimizing communications networks and was a leader for optical network testing. Providing hardware for the rapidly growing Internet industry, NetTest capitalized on the vast growth potential of the IT industry. It has been a global niche business with strong market positions worldwide. In China it was more active than its sister company in selling to local markets (see IC-1.2). However, due to diminishing synergies with other GN companies, NetTest had been prepared for a spin-off from the parent firm. An IPO had been scheduled for 2001.

GN Netcom's Global Strategy

Headquartered in Copenhagen, GN Netcom had production facilities in the United Kingdom and the United States and R&D centers in New Hampshire, California, and Denmark. Worldwide, GN Netcom had 754 employees in 2000, and achieved a global turnover of DKK 1,479 million and earnings before interest and tax (EBIT) of DKK 272 million (see IC-1.2 on next page and IC-1.3 on page 153 for financial data).

The company had expanded in both Europe and North America through acquisitions, including UNEX in New Hampshire in 1996 and ACS in San José, California in 1998. These companies were largely integrated operationally, although separate brands were still maintained because some key technological interfaces were not compatible. The products varied between Europe and North America, as well as between the different North American brands, which reduced scale economies and efficiencies of the global supply chain.

In 2000, GN Netcom acquired two US companies, Hello Direct and JABRA. These two new acquisitions were primarily aimed at improving the market position of GN Netcom in North America. Hello Direct was a catalogue-based distributor, serving mainly corporate customers, such as large offices where employees frequently use the phone. JABRA manufactured and sold headsets for consumer

---

[3] Martin Iversen (2004): *The governance of GN Great Nordic—in an age of strategic and structural transitions 1939–1988,* PhD dissertation, Copenhagen Business School, ISBN: 87-593-8226-0.

IC-1.2.   GN Great Nordic: Activities by Region, 2000

	EUROPE			AMERICA	ASIA	OTHER
	DENMARK	OTHER NORDIC	OTHER EUROPE			
Revenues, in %						
GN Netcom	43.0			53.0	4.0	—
GN ReSound	42.2			49.4	8.1	0.3
NetTest	42.7			45.5	11.8	—
Other[a]	Sonofon	—	GN Comtext, Telegraph Co.	—	—	—
Total, in %	15.1	5.7	30.7	39.2	8.1	1.2
Total, in DKK million	1,056	399	2,152	2,743	5,68	85
Assets[b]						
Total, in %	7.5	0.6	52.7	38.8	1.0	—
Total, in DKK million	1,794	140	12,398	9,241	236	—

Source: GN Great Nordic Annual Report 2000, p. 24, 32, 40, 46 (for division revenues), p. 64 (for group revenues), p. 75 (for group assets).

Notes: a. GN Comtext is mainly active in the UK and the Telegraph Company mainly in Eastern Europe. Together they contributed DKK 476 million to revenues. Sonofon was sold in 2000 but is still included in the revenue figures for 2000 with DKK 972 million, which were mainly earned in Denmark.
b. The location of assets reflects where the company had undertaken acquisitions in recent years. The assets contain a high proportion of goodwill created through such acquisitions, especially in the case of GN ReSound.

markets (especially for use with mobile phones) and served as an original equipment manufacturer (OEM) for mobile phone companies. These acquisitions, and similar smaller acquisitions in Europe, provided GN Netcom with more control over distribution channels. Following the acquisitions, the operations of these previously independent firms had to be integrated. At the end of 2000, the GN Netcom group comprised three subsidiaries: GN Netcom, Hello Direct, and JABRA.

Although GN Netcom is part of GN Great Northern, a corporation of considerable size with about 6,000 employees and traded on the Copenhagen Stock Exchange, it maintained many features of a medium-sized Danish company. Employees mentioned low levels of hierarchy and a high degree of flexibility as advantages of working at GN Netcom.

Market Position in 2000

Globally, GN Netcom is second behind the market leader, Plantronics. GN Netcom had a stronger position in Europe, while Plantronics is stronger in the United States and Asia. There have been a number of secondary players in the industry, some of which (such

as Hello Direct) had been acquired by GN Netcom recently. Remaining competitors included Andrea, Telex, Hosiden, and Labtec, all of which had single digit market shares and were rather small compared to the two market leaders. After the acquisition of Hello Direct in 2000, GN Netcom was estimated to hold about a quarter of the global market, and Plantronics almost 50 percent. In 2001, Plantronics and GN Netcom collectively controlled 80 to 90 percent of the worldwide market for headsets. As a result, the global competition in the market had developed towards a duopoly.

GN Netcom had not yet established a strong position in Asia. A regional headquarters had been established in Hong Kong in 1998 to coordinate Asia Pacific activities. Vice President Asia-Pacific, Steen Bøge, was based in Hong Kong. Sales offices for the region were in China, Japan, Australia, and Hong Kong. In 2000, GN Netcom earned 4 percent of its revenues in Asia Pacific, where the largest markets were Australia and Japan. China accounted for less than 1 percent of global sales. Yet sales had been growing at a rate of 45 percent over the previous year, far higher than in other regions.

IC-1.3.   GN Financial Data 2000 by Subsidiary (DKK million)

STATEMENT OF INCOME	NETTEST	GN RESOUND	GN NETCOM	OTHER[a]	GROUP
Total revenue	1,817	2,255	1,479	1,452	7,003
Production costs	(903)	(1,194)	(723)	(718)	(3,538)
Gross profit	**914**	**1,061**	**756**	**734**	**3,465**
R&D costs	(128)	(117)	(62)	(8)	(315)
Sales and distribution costs	(408)	(456)	(281)	(347)	(1,492)
Management and administration costs	(141)	(360)	(94)	(287)	(882)
Other operating income	1	17	—	1	19
Share of income from associated companies	2	1	—	(9)	(6)
Earnings before interest, tax, and amortization (EBITA)	**240**	**146**	**319**	**84**	**789**
Amortization of acquired intangible assets	(44)	(22)	(9)	—	(75)
Amortization of goodwill	(99)	(178)	(21)	(18)	(316)
Restructuring of acquired companies	—	(32)	(8)	(49)	(89)
Impairment losses	(58)	(60)	(9)	(57)	(184)
Earnings before interest and tax	**39**	**(146)**	**272**	**40**	**125**
Gains on sale of property	—	—	—	45	45
Gains on sale of companies	7	—	—	12,829	12,836
Gains on sale of other securities	—	—	—	16	16
Financial income	7	34	11	140	192
Financial expenses	(134)	(193)	(20)	147	210
Income before tax and extraordinary items	**(81)**	**(305)**	**263**	**13,127**	**13,004**
ASSETS					
Intangible assets	10,431	5,346	1,407	42	17,226
– of which good will	8,792	4,817	1,051	(62)	14,598
Tangible assets	264	192	101	73	630
Financial assets	575	42	83	100	790
Total noncurrent assets	**11,270**	**5,570**	**1,591**	**215**	**18,646**
Inventories	634	452	283	(1)	1,368
Receivables	793	656	510	585	2,544
– of which trade accounts	689	527	403	221	1,840
Listed bonds and stocks	—	—	—	31	31
Cash and cash equivalent	185	395	193	447	1,220
Total current assets	**1,612**	**1,503**	**986**	**1,062**	**5,163**
Total assets	**12,882**	**7,073**	**2,577**	**1,277**	**23,809**
LIABILITIES					
Equity	**431**	**4,092**	**587**	**14,578**	**19,698**
Provisions	**623**	**347**	**128**	**69**	**1,167**
Long-term debt	572	32	6	438	1,048
Short-term debt	11,256	2,602	1,846	(13,828)	1,896
– of which payables to associated companies	10,560	2,022	1,474	(14,256)	—
Total Debt	**11,828**	**2,634**	**1,852**	**13,383**	**2,944**
Total Liabilities	**12,882**	**7,073**	**2,577**	**1,277**	**23,809**

[a] Includes GN Comtext, the Telegraph Company, Sonofon as well as others and eliminations.

Source: GN Great Nordic Annual Report 2000, p. 76.

GN Netcom's products had been sold to the Chinese market since 1993, initially with an agency agreement and then a JV with a Danish conglomerate with business operations across Southeast Asia. GN later took over the sales network. Marketing and sales in China were coordinated in the country office in Beijing, with additional sales offices in Shanghai and Guangzhou.

The main customers in this region were call centers and, in Hong Kong, Singapore, and Australia, also the office segment. They include especially large firms, for example, mobile phone operators, financial firms, and major foreign multinationals investing in China. The products were designed to increase the efficiency of highly qualified, and thus expensive, office staff. As a result, the potential demand is highest where service industries were well developed and where salaries for office staff were high. This explained some of the regional sales pattern. Within China, the most interesting locations were areas with high growth and foreign investment, such as Shanghai. Typically, companies establishing new offices work with a "solutions provider" or "systems integration" firm that establishes new offices including all the relevant hardware and software. For GN Netcom, these firms are an important channel through which to sell its products.

Marketing in China is different from that in Europe or North America since decision-making processes over procurement are different in Chinese firms. Moreover, many older Chinese firms have excess staff or low staff costs such that increasing the efficiency of their office staff is not a major concern—and they thus were not (yet) interested in GN Netcom's products.

The Chinese market was fragmented, with considerable regional variations and informal trade barriers within the country. Market information was less available than in mature market economies. Roughly one third of the market was supplied by imports including GN Netcom, Plantronics, as well as their Korean competitors. The two largest domestic manufacturers provided one third, and a wide range of small local firms served the remaining third. The domestic firms manufactured mainly products for the lower end of the market, which is below what GN Netcom considered the lower end of its product portfolio. China's anticipated accession to the World Trade Organization (WTO), which eventually did take place in late 2001, may change the competitive dynamics in the industry.

GN Netcom Global Operations in 2000

GN Netcom's headsets for the European markets were based on a modular "click-fit" design, where boom arms with microphones and cord assemblies were manufactured separately. They could be combined in alternative ways, allowing for over one hundred product specifications. Production and final assembly was mainly based in Newcastle, UK. The GN Netcom (UK) subsidiary had established relations with a number of subcontractors mainly in Beijing and with GN ReSound in Xiamen. There had been frequent discussions on how to use outsourcing and relocation of production in China to reduce production costs. Since 1993, the establishment of a JV to manufacture components in China had been discussed, but no suitable partner was found.

The products for the North American market were not necessarily compatible with the European ones. Moreover, GN Netcom maintained both UNEX and ACS product lines in North America in addition to products under GN Netcom's own brand name. This was to continue serving customers who had these products installed. However, firms which had, for example, ACS amplifiers installed in their offices were offered new products that matched these amplifiers.

GN Netcom's main production facility in North American was based in Nashua, New Hampshire. However, this operation had over the years outsourced to over a dozen subcontractors in Guangdong province (north of Hong Kong) and four OEM suppliers. The most important of them was DG Ltd[4] based in Dongguan, which had been manufacturing high volume products, while the facilities in Nashua focused increasingly on smaller volume products. For

---

[4] A pseudonym used to retain anonymity.

IC-1.4.   Key Data on Plantronics

Summary of Plantronics' Income Statement For Financial Years Ending March 31, in Million US$		
	1999	2000
Net sales	**286.3**	**315.0**
Cost of sales	−125.7	−129.5
Gross Profit	**160.6**	**185.5**
R&D and engineering	−19.5	−21.9
Selling, general, and administrative expenses	−57.5	−70.3
Operating Income	**83.5**	**93.3**
Interest expense, including amortization of debt issuance costs	−5.8	−0.1
Interest and other income, net	3.5	1.7
Income before income taxes	**81.3**	**94.9**

Source: Plantronics Annual Report.

some products, DG Ltd would produce the entire product inclusive of packaging and ship it to Nashua. The volume with this partner reached US$18 million in 2000 out of about US$60 million spent on procurement in China. GN Netcom accounts for about 10 percent of sales for DG Ltd and possibly more in terms of profits. Other DG Ltd customers were manufacturers of electronics products unrelated to telecommunications.

These arrangements were in part built by the predecessor firms acquired by GN Netcom. The structures needed to be reassessed in view of the growing volumes of production and the competitive pressures, as well as the more loose relationship among the different GN companies following the changes of corporate strategy implemented from 2000 onwards.

The Competitor[5]

Worldwide, GN Netcom faced one major competitor, Plantronics, which had been manufacturing lightweight communication headsets since 1962 (see

[5] This section is based on archival sources, including Plantronics' website (*www.plantronics.com*, accessed July 2, 2002), an interview with CEO Ken Kannappan in the *Wall Street Corporate Reporter* (*www.wscr.com*, on April 30–May 13, 2001 on pages 17 & 43–44), and Form 10-K report filed by Plantronics with the United States Securities and Exchange Commission for the fiscal year ended March 31, 2001.

IC-1.4). Highlights in its corporate history were the supply of technology to the first Apollo missions and the transmission of Neil Armstrong's historic words from the moon in 1969. Plantronics employed 2,200 associates worldwide. Turnover had been growing from US$286 million in 1999 to US$315 million in the next year. It was ranked 43rd in the list of 200 best small companies by *Forbes* magazine in October 2000, with one of the highest returns on equity. An internal GN Netcom report in 1998 concluded that Plantronics' gross margins were 10 to 14 percent higher than GN Netcom's, although products were selling at similar prices.

Plantronics was headquartered in Santa Cruz, California. The majority of products were manufactured in a single facility in Tijuana, Mexico. It also had smaller manufacturing operations in California, Tennessee, and the United Kingdom. Moreover, Plantronics outsourced a limited number of its consumer products to third parties in China and Taiwan. Components for headset products were purchased in Asia, the United States, Mexico, and Europe.

Plantronics had for many years been the dominant market leader in the United States. Growth had been largely organic without major acquisitions. The main sales segments were call centers (40 percent) and offices (42 percent) with the remainder in accessories to mobile phones (13 percent) and PCs (5 percent). Although Plantronics mainly focused on the US market, its non-US sales reached about 34 percent of total sales in 2000. Plantronics did not have an affiliate in China, but its products were available there through imports. How Plantronics viewed the global competition was documented in its 10-K report:

> *"We believe the principal competitive forces in each market are product features, comfort and fit, product reliability, customer service and support, reputation, distribution, ability to meet delivery schedules, warranty terms, product life, and price. We believe that our brand name recognition, distribution network, extensive and responsive customer service and support programs, large user base and extensive number of product variations, together with our comprehensive experience in designing safe, comfortable, and reliable products and dealing with regulatory agencies, are the key factors necessary in maintaining our position as a leading supplier of lightweight communications headsets."[6]*

However, the business environment and technology were continuously changing. Ken Kannappan, CEO, summarized the main challenges facing Plantronics as follows:[7]

> *"We're undergoing a massive level of change from a business that has been focused in the call center market, purely business to business, with a level of broad consumer awareness that was very low, to a company that is now going into mainstream markets, and needs to build its retail expertise. We need to build up emerging market segments that we haven't been involved with before, namely, mobile and personal computer and grow relationships with the key players in those markets. We're moving up the technology curve very rapidly in terms of wireless and in terms of digital signal processing. All of these changes, in terms of product development and the understanding of markets and needs, in terms of consumer brand awareness and marketing, are major changes for the company"*

New Challenges in 2000

At the corporate level, GN Great Nordic continued its de-diversification and the reorganization of its businesses in 2000.

---

[6] 10-K form, p. 15

[7] *The Wall Street Transcript – JP Morgan H&Q Technology Special,* April 2001, pp. 210–212.

- NetTest had been prepared for an IPO scheduled tentatively for 2001, which necessitated GN Netcom to establish its own independent sales network in China.

- GN ReSound relocated more production to Xiamen, China—and in the process closed facilities in Denmark and Austria. This created further needs to expand capacity in China.

At the subsidiary level, GN Netcom was also rethinking its global strategy. Niels Christiansen had been appointed as CEO of GN Netcom as of January 1, 2000, succeeding Christian Tillisch. Aged thirty-three at the time, Christansen had an undergraduate education in engineering and an MBA from INSEAD. He had four years of consultancy experience with McKinsey and spent two years with Hilti Corp in Liechtenstein with responsibilities for global marketing. He had been with GN Netcom for two years before taking over as CEO.

Christiansen also brought a new management team to GN Netcom. The new team advocated a strategy of continuous improvement across the organization, focusing R&D on new developments at the high end of the market, and better global integration across Europe, North America, and Asia. As part of this strategic change, a Vice President Global Operations, based in New Hampshire, was appointed for the first time. The new management team had to address a number of competitive challenges:

- GN Netcom had acquired two companies in North America in 2000, Hello Direct and JABRA. This strengthened its position in the key US market and the growing worldwide market for headset for mobile phones. Yet, following the acquisitions, the operations of these previously independent firms had yet to be integrated.

- GN Netcom had to address the costs of its operations with production in relative high wage countries (United States and United Kingdom) and the geographic dispersion of the production process involving many suppliers based in Asia.

■ GN Netcom was serving its clients from two main distribution centers in New Hampshire, US and Newcastle, UK as well as three distribution centers operated by firms recently acquired in the United States. Neither of these distribution centers was geographically well located. In particular, distribution in Asia was freight intensive as products were shipped from New Hampshire, even if they were originally manufactured in Asia.

Moving part of the global operations to China appeared to be an avenue to enhance GN Netcom's global position and to address its pertinent challenges. However, this suggestion raised a number of practical questions: Which function should be located in China? Where to locate within China? Which partner to choose? Should it go alone? How quickly to move, and if speed was essential, how to ensure fast and smooth implementation? And, last but not least, how should the new operations be integrated with the existing operations in Asia and around the world?

Case Discussion Questions

1. What are the strengths and weaknesses of GN Netcom relative to its leading competitor Plantronics on a worldwide basis?

2. How should GN Netcom develop its business in Asia to match and support its worldwide strategy?

3. Assuming a decision to manufacture in China is made, what are the consequences for the rest of GN Netcom? For example, what should the company do with the existing resources and capabilities at the production sites in Nashua, US and Newcastle, UK? How to manage the process of downsizing the production facilities in a nondisruptive manner?

4. To implement a strategic decision to manufacture in China, what are your recommended mode(s) of entry (such as a JV, a licensing agreement, an acquisition, or a green-field wholly-owned subsidiary)? Where would be an ideal location? What about timing?

5. What institutional changes might affect the competitive dynamics of this industry in China as it prepares to enter the WTO? How should GN Netcom better position itself in preparation for these changes?

Integrative Case 1.2

BOOKOFF, AMAZON JAPAN, AND THE JAPANESE RETAIL BOOKSELLING INDUSTRY[1]

Charles E. Stevens

Fisher College of Business, The Ohio State University

In the Japanese retail bookselling industry, where discounting is banned by a cartel formed by incumbents, two new entrants, Bookoff and Amazon Japan, have successfully established themselves recently.

The Japanese are voracious readers. As a result, the Japanese retail bookselling industry, at nearly $8 billion in annual sales, is the largest in the world. It is approximately $1 billion larger than its American counterpart, despite the fact that the population of Japan is one-half that of the United States. In Japan, bookstores, magazine stands, and newspaper kiosks can be found everywhere. As of 2001, there were 28,000 bookstores in Japan compared to only 13,465 in the United States.[2] Most of the largest bookstores in Japan have been in existence since the World War II era if not earlier. Maruzen (*http://www.maruzen. co.jp*), the largest and oldest of the Japanese book retailers, has been in business since 1869. However, Japan has no true industry dominators (see IC-1.1 on next page). In the American retail market, Barnes & Noble (*http://www.bn.com*), Borders (*http://www. borders.com*), and Amazon (*http://www.amazon.com*) split the market fairly evenly among themselves.

Barnes & Noble, the largest of the three, has annual sales of nearly $5 billion and over 900 stores throughout the United States. In contrast, Maruzen has annual sales of slightly more than $1 billion but only 31 stores. Kinokuniya (*http://www.kinokuniya.co.jp*) has similar sales with 58 stores throughout Japan. This case introduces the competitive forces shaping the Japanese retail bookselling industry, with an emphasis on interfirm rivalry and two new entrants,

---

[1] This case was written by Charles E. Stevens (Fisher College of Business, The Ohio State University), under the supervision of Professor Mike W. Peng. Yen has been converted at a rate of US$1 = 120 Yen (based on the five-year exchange rate average).

[2] WIDE University: http://www.soi.wide.ad.jp/class/20010003/ slides/10/index_37.html. Reprinted by permission of the author.

IC-1.1.   Net Sales

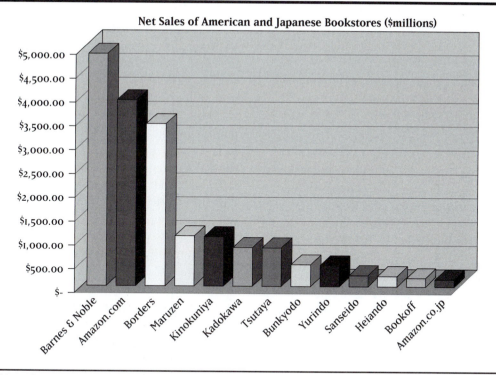

Net Sales of American and Japanese Bookstores ($millions)

Sources: Yahoo! Japan Finance, Hoover's, company Web pages and annual reports. Sales figures are for 2001–2002.

Bookoff (*http://www.bookoff.co.jp*) and Amazon Japan (*http://www.amazon.co.jp*), which recently have made significant inroads.

Suppliers

Book retailers usually buy books from wholesalers and sometimes directly from publishers. Competition in the area of book distribution is very low. Nippon Shuppan Hanbai (*http://www.nippan.co.jp*) and Tohan (*http://www.tohan.jp*), both founded immediately after World War II, traditionally control 70 to 90 percent of the book wholesale market. Also, there is a system in place where retailers and wholesalers can return unsold books to the publisher free of charge, reducing risk and inventory levels. However, the wholesalers are facing a threat that has arisen with the rise of the Internet: publishers and retailers are beginning to link their computers so they can forecast demand in a type of just-in-time system, reducing the need for wholesale services. This is a definite threat that the wholesalers must meet.

Buyers

Two trends among Japanese book buyers are worth noting. First, although the Japanese are intensive readers, they are less active users of the Internet than Americans. As of 2002, approximately 40 percent of Japanese residents regularly used the Internet, compared to 60 to 70 percent of US residents. All phone calls in Japan are relatively expensive, a significant barrier to Internet usage. This means traditional brick-and-mortar bookstores are not significantly threatened by online bookstores. In Japan, there is a long tradition of *tachiyomi* (standing-and-reading), where customers will enter a store, pick up a book or magazine, and stand to read it for as much as an hour or two by the shelf.

Second, Japanese book buyers are increasingly interested in translations of English language books and in imports of foreign-language (mostly English) books from overseas. In 2001, five of the ten best-selling books in Japan were translations of works by American writers. In 2002, Japan imported approximately $515 million worth of foreign books, 35.5 percent of which were from the United States.[3]

Substitutes

Books are used for many different purposes including education and entertainment. While there are alternative sources for education (such as the Internet) and entertainment (such as music, television, audio books, and radio), there is no true substitute for a book. This is not to say that the industry is not evolving, as audio books, e-books, and Internet retailing are beginning to reshape the market. The Internet, perhaps the strongest threat to the book, seems to have had little impact on buying habits in Japan. Sales of books and magazines in Japan have actually increased since the Internet became popular in the 1990s.

Interfirm Rivalry

As noted earlier, interfirm rivalry in this industry is characterized by numerous bookstores but relatively little industry consolidation in the hands of large booksellers. One of the key reasons that there is not a great deal of industry consolidation is the unique price-fixing system that makes it illegal for larger and potentially more efficient booksellers to use price as a weapon to drive out small competitors. Since 1980, laws have allowed publishers to fix the price of new books, music, and newspapers in the bookselling industry. These laws are known as the *Saihanbai Kakaku-iji Seido* ("Resale Price Maintenance System"—commonly known as the *Saihan* system). Despite strong anti-monopolistic legislature in Japan, cartels are illegal only if they "substantially restrained competition contrary to the public

interest."[4] Supporters of the *Saihan* system argue that cartels in the book publishing and retail industry do not run contrary to the public interest nor do they "substantially" restrain competition. They argue that the *Saihan* system increases the number of publishers and booksellers, giving consumers a greater choice of reading materials and booksellers.

While it is true that the number of booksellers, publishers, and book titles are comparatively higher in Japan since the introduction of the *Saihan* system, this has not translated into higher sales. Because of the lack of financial disclosure by Japanese booksellers it is difficult to tell whether profitability has suffered as well, but it seems logical that stagnation in sales along with the steady increase of costs over time has reduced the profitability of both large chains and small stores—see IC-1.2 on next page for an illustration, which compares the lackluster financial performance of three leading Japanese booksellers and that of much more profitable Barnes & Noble.

A book available in multiple bookstores is an undifferentiated commodity. Consequently, competing on price would be a normal competitive strategy for new entrants. However, because of the *Saihan* system, which makes discounting illegal, it would appear that the already oversaturated Japanese retail bookselling industry would be an inhospitable host for new entrants. Nevertheless, there have been two recent new entrants, Bookoff (founded in 1991) and Amazon (entered Japan in 2000), which threaten to revolutionize the bookselling industry in Japan in a surprisingly short time. Despite their similar results, they took dramatically different entry approaches and their successes and setbacks have different implications for the industry. As such, it is advisable to consider each case of the two new entrants separately.

Bookoff

Over the years, Bookoff has been accused of unfair competition, cheating authors out of royalties,

---

[3] JETRO: http://www.jetro.go.jp/ec/e/market/mgb/data_e/3/20.pdf.

[4] M. Kotabe & K. W. Wheiler, 1996, *Anticompetitive Practices in Japan* (p. 86), New York: Praeger.

IC-1.2.   Financial Performance of Three Japanese Industry Leaders and Barnes & Noble

6/3/2003				
	MARUZEN	**KADOKAWA**	**BUNKYODO**	**BARNES & NOBLE**
Stock Price	$2.33	$18.83	$3.38	$22.89
EPS	$0.04	$0.44	$0.12	$1.92
Price/Earnings	65.34	42.98	27.45	17.17
ROE	12.97%	2.00%	3.52%	11.10%
ROA	0.42%	1.33%	0.31%	3.80%

7/28/2004				
Stock Price	$2.05	$33.52	$6.77	$34.23
EPS	−$0.11	$0.76	−$0.01	$2.17
Price/Earnings	−18.71	43.21	−700.93	15.79
ROE	−35.13%	3.06%	−0.25%	14.58%
ROA	−1.39%	2.06%	−0.02%	5.85%

representing a threat to Japanese culture, single-handedly destroying the nation's book industry, and corrupting Japanese youth. However, Bookoff is not a "foreign invader." It is entirely Japanese-owned. The reason why competitors spit venom when they hear founder Takashi Sakamoto's name, and the reason why Bookoff has grown from one store to over 500 (as of June 2004) to become Japan's ninth-largest retailer (see IC-1.1) in only a decade is simple: Bookoff is the only major bookseller that can bypass the *Saihan* system and freely change the prices on their merchandise. The same *Saihan* system that supported the bookselling cartel for over two decades is now handcuffing the industry leaders. Bookoff has taken advantage of the situation, seeing its sales soar to $312 million in 2003 after posting sales of $224 million and $238 million in 2001 and 2002, respectively.

The reason Bookoff can lower prices is due entirely to the fact that it is a used-book store. Used books are a major exemption to the *Saihan* system along with foreign books (i.e., books published outside of Japan). It should be noted that Sakamoto prefers to call Bookoff a "new-used" bookstore. Due to several new technologies that Sakamoto has pioneered, Bookoff is able to rehabilitate used books, using techniques that clean book covers and grind down dog-eared pages to make a used book look practically new. In other

words, Bookoff is able to sell books at new book quality and used book prices—and there is nothing competitors can do about it! Additionally, Bookoff stores are clean and bright, practically identical to the large chain bookstores in appearance.

One difference between Bookoff and its competitors is the organization of the company. Unlike most bureaucracy-laden Japanese companies, Bookoff stores are all franchised and owners and employees are encouraged to act like entrepreneurs. Additionally, unlike traditional used-book stores, Bookoff has a simple buy-back policy: it buys books from customers at 10 percent of their list price and (re)sells them at 50 percent of list price (the list price is the price "fixed" by the publisher, at which other mainstream booksellers must sell new books). In other words, Bookoff might buy a $10 book for $1 and then sell that book, once it has been cleaned, for $5.

At first glance, it may seem miraculous that a used-book store has had such great success in Japan, a country that is traditionally image conscious. However, Japan has been in a recession since the early 1990s, and consumer buying trends reflect financial hardships. Economic realities are reshaping values, and attitudes toward used goods are becoming favorable. Consumers are becoming more focused on the efficient use of a good instead of simply the possession of it. A "new-used" bookstore such as Bookoff is an acceptable compromise for the still image conscious, but increasingly thrifty, Japanese consumer.

Young people in particular are getting on the Bookoff bandwagon. Forty percent of students in Japan now prefer these new-used stores to new stores. The entire used-goods industry in Japan is increasingly being referred to as the "recycle industry" by its members, emphasizing the environmental benefits of "recycling" older goods such as books and CDs instead of simply throwing them away. As Japan moves away from its bubble economy and *kaisute* (buy-and-throw-away) mindset of the 1980s and 1990s and as Japanese youth grow increasingly vocal in voicing their discontent toward the low priority the environment is given by the government and industry, this has become a smooth marketing move that has paid off for self-styled "recycle stores" such as Bookoff. People can make a few yen selling back their old books, save a few by buying new-used ones, and come out feeling frugal and environmentally conscious without suffering a drop-off in the quality of their books. It appears to be a win-win situation for consumers and for stores like Bookoff.

Amazon Japan

Although Amazon Japan has sales revenues similar to Bookoff, given the size of its parent company (see IC-1.1), it has to be considered to be a bit of a disappointment to this point. In seven years (1996 to 2003), Amazon's total sales have grown to nearly $4 billion, but in three years (2000 to 2003), Amazon Japan's sales are still around $150 million, constituting less than 4 percent of Amazon's total global sales. Given the immense size of the Japanese market, Amazon Japan's slow growth seems puzzling. Amazon Japan uses the same formula that brought it great success in North America (Amazon's North American sales are greater than Japan's two largest booksellers *combined!*), but so far, this formula has not resulted in the same success in Japan. Upon close examination, several reasons why Amazon Japan is struggling become clear: (1) Amazon does not have first-mover advantages in Japan that it enjoyed in the United States,

(2) Internet usage is lower in Japan, and (3) the *Saihan* system destroys Amazon's price competitiveness (except for foreign books).

When Amazon entered the American market in 1995, competitors were slow to respond. Barnes & Noble still cannot compete with Amazon's prices, and Borders has given up and is instead involved in a joint venture with Amazon online. In Japan, however, booksellers quickly followed Amazon's lead and went online soon after Amazon revolutionized the American industry. Due to the *Saihan* system, the booksellers could not compete by changing prices, so gaining a foothold in the new e-commerce market was of extra importance for retailers. In 1996, just one year after Amazon opened its English language site, Maruzen, Kinokuniya, and Sanseido (*http://www.books-sanseido.co.jp*) started online sites. The other stores were quick to follow. By the time Amazon entered Japan in 2000, it was a *late* entrant because the Internet bookselling market was already saturated with domestic competitors.

Amazon faced another problem: relatively low Internet usage by the Japanese, as mentioned earlier. Another obstacle lies in the high saturation of bookstores: Japan has twice as many bookstores as the United States for half the population. In other words, for every bookstore per capita in the United States, there are four in Japan, partially negating the convenience of Internet shopping. For example, leading Japanese booksellers often place their stores in locations with a tremendous amount of foot traffic, such as near train stations (some train stations serve as many as three million people a day). Additionally, the time-honored experience of *tachiyomi* (standing-and-reading) in Japan, alluded to earlier, cannot be easily duplicated online. Additionally, Amazon's system of allowing customers to review books online, immensely popular in North America and Europe, is not as popular in a nation where publicly stating one's opinion is generally frowned upon.

Finally, with the exception of non-Japanese books and music, Amazon Japan cannot be price competitive due to the *Saihan* system. Because Amazon does not release detailed figures for its international sales, it

IC-1.3.   Price Competition: Kinokuniya (Online) versus Amazon Japan

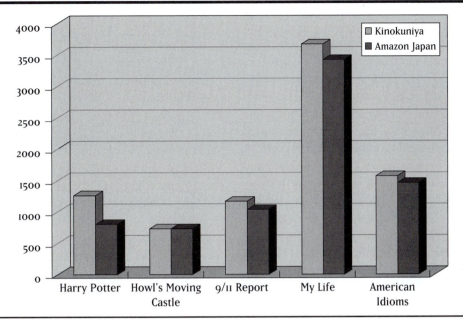

Note: The Saihan law does not apply to foreign (non-Japanese) books, and here Amazon Japan has a clear price advantage. (Prices in yen, from July 31, 2004.)
The books are, respectively, (Kinokuniya Online Price/Amazon Japan Price):
Harry Potter and the Order of the Phoenix (paperback), by J. K. Rowling (1260/803)
Howl's Moving Castle, by Diana Jones (733/731)
9/11 Commission Report, by National Commission on Terrorist Attacks (1166/1034)
My Life, by Bill Clinton (3671/3419)
A Dictionary of American Idioms, by Adam Makkai (1568/1461)
Sources: Web sites for Kinokuniya and Amazon Japan

is impossible to know what percentage of sales is contributed by non-Japanese books and merchandise. However, given the considerable discounts on foreign books by Amazon Japan, along with the increased readership of non-Japanese language books and the popularity of non-Japanese music in Japan, it is presumably significant. However, as expected, the Japanese competitors are quickly closing the gap in terms of discounts on foreign books: the price offered in 2004 on a small sample of best-selling foreign books by Amazon Japan was only 7 percent lower than those sold by a major competitor Kinokuniya (see IC-1.3), in comparison to an almost 30 percent advantage offered in a similar sample just a year earlier in 2003. Overall, with the Saihan system in place, it seems nearly impossible for Amazon to dominate the Japanese market like it has in the American retailing industry.

Still, in spite of these obstacles to success, due to incentives such as offering free shipping on orders over 1500 yen ($13.60) and offering an increasingly wider product selection (most notably opening its Electronics Store in 2003 and Computer Store in 2004), Amazon Japan is starting to make headway. Overall, Amazon's international sales grew at over a 50 percent rate in 2003, and Amazon Japan was called the fastest grower of its international group. However, analysts gave mixed reviews about long-term prospects, citing the Saihan system as a formidable obstacle while crediting the weak dollar for artificially inflating sales data.

Changing the "Rules of the Game"?

The main defining characteristic of the Japanese retail bookselling industry is the Saihan system. This piece of legislature has been in place since 1980. Although there have been several attempts at reform, the government has not been able to garner enough support or motivation to pass anything yet. However, Japanese antitrust laws are currently in a state of flux. With the "unfair" success of Bookoff in getting around aspects of the *Saihan* law, the clamor for reform (if not outright repeal) of the law has dramatically increased both within and outside of the industry.[5] Although the Japanese government has historically been slow to act, given the general malaise of the Japanese economy and the government's desperation to jump start it, many see free competition as inevitable.[6] Booksellers worldwide must continue to focus on this situation. Any change to the "rules of the game" in Japan will radically alter how domestic and foreign booksellers approach this large, influential, and potentially lucrative market.

Case Discussion Questions

1. Why is the profitability of large Japanese retail booksellers relatively poor and their scale relatively small?

2. The *Saihan* system serves as a price-fixing cartel to deter entry. This practice, often labeled as "collusive" and "anticompetitive," would be illegal in many other countries such as the United States. What are the benefits for individual companies and the industry to participate in this system? What are the costs? (You may want to consult Chapter 8.)

3. Draw on the industry-, resource-, and institution-based views to explain the success of Bookoff and the more mediocre performance of Amazon Japan. What is going to happen to them if the *Saihan* system dissolves?

4. If you were a board member of Barnes & Noble or Borders, would you approve a proposal to open a series of bookstores in Japan now? Would you change your mind if the *Saihan* system dissolves?

---

[5] K. Suzumura, 1995, *Competition, Commitment, and Welfare* (p. 222), Oxford, UK: Oxford University Press; *Publishers Weekly* (Reed Business Info): http://publishersweekly.reviewsnews.com/; *Japan Entrepreneur Report:* http://www.japanentrepreneur. com/200302.html.

[6] *Japan Entrepreneur Report:* http://www.japanentrepreneur. com/200302.html, *Asian/Pacific Book Development:* http://www2. accu.or.jp/report/abd/abd3012.html.

Integrative Case 1.3

RACE TO THE GREAT WALL: COMPETING IN THE CHINESE AUTOMOBILE INDUSTRY[1]

Qingjiu (Tom) Tao

Lehigh University

Multinational automakers of all stripes are rushing in to capitalize on China's growth.

The Red-hot Market

For automakers seeking relief from a global price war caused by overcapacity and recession, China is the only game in town. With just 8 vehicles per 1,000 residents in China—as opposed to 940 in the United States and 584 in Western Europe—there seems to be plenty of growth opportunities. Not surprisingly, nearly every major auto company has jumped into China, quickly turning the country into a new battleground for dominance in this global industry.

China's automobile production volume reached 3.25 million units in 2002, a 38.5 percent increase over 2001. This increase represents the first growth peak in the past ten years (see IC-1.1 on next page). Of these 3.25 million vehicles, passenger car production numbers surpassed the 1 million mark for the first time and reached 1.09 million units, a 55 percent increase over 2001. The year 2003 was another excellent year in the development of this industry, with sales up 75 percent compared with 2002. Reports of record sales, new production, and new venture formations were plenty. After China's accession to the World Trade Organization (WTO) in 2001, the industry has been advancing by leaps and bounds. At the global level, China has moved to the fifth position in production behind the United States, Japan, Germany, and

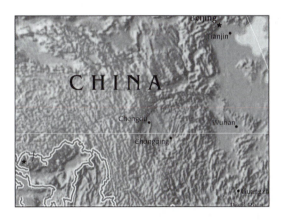

France, and is slated to produce 3.8 to 4 million vehicles in 2004. Already the third largest car market, China may surpass Japan as the second largest market (only behind the United States) by as early as 2007.

Because the Chinese government does not approve wholly owned subsidiaries for foreign carmakers to operate in the country (even after the WTO accession), foreign firms have to set up joint ventures (JVs) or licensing deals with domestic players. By the mid-1990s, most major global auto firms had managed to enter the country through these means (IC-1.2 on next page). Among the European companies, Volkswagen (VW), one of the first entrants (see below), has dominated the passenger car market. In addition, Fiat-Iveco has an important presence in the bus market, and Citroen is expanding its activities.

---

[1] This case was written by Qingjiu (Tom) Tao (Lehigh University). Reprinted with permission of the author.

IC-1.1.   Automobile Production Volume and Growth Rate in China (1992–2002)

YEAR	1992	1993	1994	1995	1996	1997	1998	1999	2000	2001	2002
Volume (Million)	1.062	1.297	1.353	1.453	1.475	1.585	1.629	1.832	2.068	2.347	3.251
Growth rate	49.8%	22.1%	4.3%	7.4%	1.5%	7.5%	2.8%	12.5%	12.9%	13.2%	38.5%

Source: Yearbook of China's Automobile Industry (1992–2002).

IC-1.2.   Timing and Initial Investment of Major Car Producers

JOINT VENTURE	FORMATION	INITIAL INVESTMENT (1990 FIXED MILLION DOLLAR)	FOREIGN EQUITY	CHINESE PARTNER	FOREIGN PARTNER
Beijing Jeep	1983	223.93	42%	Beijing Auto Works	Chrysler
Shanghai Volkswagen	1984	263.41	50%	SAIC	Volkswagen
Guangzhou Peugeot	1985	131.40	22%	Guangzhou Auto Group	Peugeot
FAW Volkswagen	1988	901.84	40%	First Auto Works	Volkswagen
Wuhan Shenlong	1992	505.22	30%	Second Auto Works	Citroen
Shanghai GM	1997	604.94	50%	SAIC	GM
Guangzhou Honda	1998	149.37	50%	Guangzhou Auto Group	Honda

Source: Directory of FDI in China's Automobile Industry (1996, 2000–2001).

Japanese and Korean automakers are relatively late entrants. In 2003, Toyota finally committed $1.3 billion to a 50-50 JV. Guangzhou Honda, Honda's JV, would almost quadruple its capacity in China by 2004. Formed in 2003, Nissan's new JV with Dongfeng, which is the same partner for the Citroen JV, is positioned to allow Nissan to make a full-fledged entry. Meanwhile, Korean auto players are also keen to participate in the China race with Hyundai and Kia having commenced JV production recently.

American auto companies have also made significant inroads into China. General Motors (GM) has an important JV in Shanghai, whose cumulative investment by 2006 would be $5 billion. Although Ford does not have a high-profile JV as GM, Ford nevertheless established crucial strategic linkages with several of China's second-tier automakers. Daimler Chrysler's Beijing Jeep venture, established since the early 1980s, has continued to maintain its presence.

The Evolution of Foreign Direct Investment (FDI) in the Automobile Industry

In the late 1970s, when Chinese leaders started to transform the planned economy to a market economy, they realized that China's urban streets and country roads were largely populated by inefficient, unattractive, and often unreliable vehicles that needed to be replaced. However, importing large quantities of vehicles would be a major drain on the limited hard currency reserves. China thus saw the need to modernize its automobile industry. Attracting FDI through JVs with foreign companies seemed to be ideal. However, unlike the new China at the dawn of the twenty-first century that attracted automakers of every stripe, China in the late 1970s and early 1980s was not regarded as attractive by many global automakers. In the early 1980s, Toyota, for example, refused to establish JVs with Chinese firms even when invited by the Chinese authorities (Toyota chose to invest in a more promising market, the United States, in the 1980s). In the first wave, three JVs were established during 1983 to 1985 by VW, American Motors (later acquired by Chrysler and more recently DaimlerChrysler), and Peugeot, in Shanghai, Beijing, and Guangzhou, respectively. These three JVs thus started the two decades of FDI in China's automobile industry.

There are two distinctive phases of FDI activities in China's automobile industry. The first phase is from the early 1980s to the early 1990s, as exemplified by the three early JVs mentioned above. The

IC-1.3.   Profitability Per Employee of Major Car Producers in China (10,000 Yuan—1999 constant)

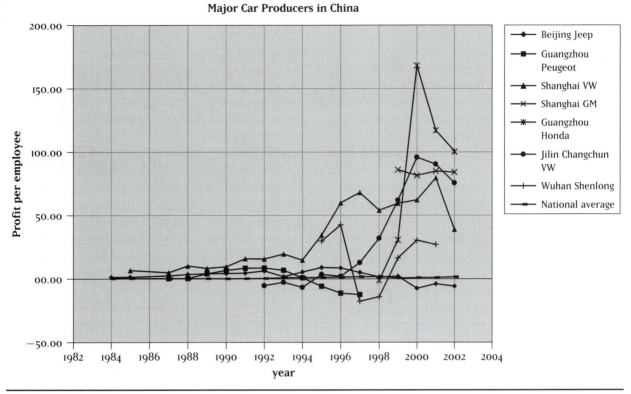

Source: Yearbook of China's Automobile Industry (1992–2004).

second phase is from the mid-1990s to present. Because of the reluctance of foreign car companies, only approximately twenty JVs were established by the end of 1989. FDI flows into this industry started to accelerate sharply from 1992. The accumulated number of foreign invested enterprises was 120 in 1993 and skyrocketed to 604 in 1998 with the cumulated investment reaching $20.9 billion.

The boom of the auto market, especially during the early 1990s, brought significant profits to early entrants such as Shanghai VW and Beijing Jeep. The bright prospect attracted more multinationals to invest. This new wave of investment had resulted in an overcapacity. Combined with the changing customer base from primarily selling to fleets (government agencies, state-owned enterprises, and taxi companies) to private buyers, the auto market has turned into a truly competitive arena. The WTO entry in 2001 has further intensified the competition in the marketplace as government regulations weaken. Given the government mandate for JV entries and the limited number of worthy local firms as partners, multinationals have to fight their way in to secure the last few available local partners. By the end of 2002, almost all major Chinese motor vehicle assemblers had set up JVs with foreign firms. For numerous foreign automakers that entered China, the road to the Great Wall has been a bumpy and crowded one. Some firms (such as Shanghai VW and Shanghai GM) lead, some struggle (Beijing Jeep), and some (Guangzhou Peugeot) had to drop out. IC-1.3 presents the profitability trend of major car producers from 1984 to 2002. The leading players are profiled below.

Volkswagen

After long and difficult negotiations that began in 1978, VW in 1984 entered a JV with the Shanghai Automotive Industrial Corporation (SAIC) to produce the Santana model using completely knocked down (CKD) kits. The 50/50 JV, named Shanghai VW, began trial production in 1985. The Santana went on to distinguish itself as China's first mass-produced modern passenger car. As a result, VW managed to establish a solid market position. Four years later VW built on its first-mover advantage and secured a second opening in the China market when the central authorities decided to establish two additional passenger car JVs. After competing successfully against GM, Ford, Nissan, Renault, Peugeot, and Citroen, VW was selected to set up a second JV with the First Auto Works (FAW) in Changchun in northeast China in 1988 for CKD-assembly of the Audi 100 and the construction of a state-of-the-art auto plant to produce the VW Jetta in 1990.

Entering the China market in the early 1980s, VW took a proactive approach in spite of great potential risks. The German multinational not only committed enormous financial resources but also practiced a rather bold approach in its dealings in China. This involved a great deal of high-level political interaction with China's central and local government authorities for which the German government frequently lent its official support. Moreover, VW was willing to avail the Chinese partners a broad array of technical and financial resources from its worldwide operations. For example, in 1990 VW allowed FAW a 60 percent in its JV while furnishing most of the manufacturing technology and equipment for its new FAW-Volkswagen Jetta plant in Changchun. Moreover, VW has endeavored to raise the quality of locally produced automotive components and parts. Undoubtedly, for the remainder of the 1980s and most of the 1990s VW had a significant first-mover advantage. With a market share of more than 50 percent for passenger cars, VW, together with its Chinese partners, benefited considerably from the scarcity of high-quality passenger cars and the persistence of a sellers' market.

However, by the late 1990s, the market became a more competitive buyers' market. As the leading incumbent, VW has been facing vigorous challenges brought by its global rivals that by the late 1990s made serious commitments to compete in China. Consequently, VW's passenger car market share in China dropped from over 50 percent in 1999 to 26 percent in 2003. In the first four months of 2004, GM's sales doubled, while VW's fell 4.2 percent. How to defend its market position thus is of paramount importance.

General Motors

In 1995, GM and SAIC, which was also Volkswagen's partner, signed a 50/50, $1.57 billion JV agreement—GM's first JV in China—to construct a green-field plant in Shanghai. The new plant was designed to produce 100,000 sedans per year, and it was decided to produce two Buick models modified for China. The plant was equipped with the latest automotive machinery and robotics and was furnished with process technology transferred from GM's worldwide operations. Initially, Shanghai GM attracted a barrage of criticisms about the huge size of its investment and the significant commitments to transfer technology and design capabilities to China. These criticisms notwithstanding, GM management reiterated at numerous occasions that China was expected to become the biggest automotive market in the world within two decades and that China represented the single most important emerging market for GM.

Since launching Buick in China in 1998, GM literally started from scratch. Unlike its burdens at home, GM is not saddled with billions in pensions and health-care costs. Its costs are competitive with rivals, its reputation does not suffer, and it does not need to shell out $4,000 per vehicle in incentives to lure new buyers (see Opening Case in Chapter 2)—even a moribund brand such as Buick is held in high esteem in China. Consequently, profits are attractive: The $437 million profits GM made in 2003 in China, selling just 386,000 cars, compares favorably with $811 million profits it made in North America on sales of 5.6 million autos. In 2004, GM has about 10,000 employees in China and operates six JVs and two wholly owned foreign enterprises (which were allowed to be set up more recently in non-final assembly operations). Boasting a combined manufacturing capacity of 530,000 vehicles sold under the Buick, Chevrolet, and Wuling nameplates, GM offers the widest portfolio of products among JV manufacturers in China.

Peugeot

Together with VW and American Motors (the original partner for the Beijing Jeep JV), Peugeot was one of the first three entrants in the Chinese automobile industry. In 1980 it started to search for JV partners and in 1985 set up a JV, Guangzhou Peugeot, in south China. The JV mainly produced the Peugeot 504 and 505, both out-of-date models of the 1970s. While many domestic users complained about the high fuel consumption, difficult maintenance, and expensive parts, the French car manufacturer netted huge short-term profits of approximately $480 million by selling a large number of CKD kits and parts. Among its numerous problems, the JV also reportedly repatriated most of its profits and made relatively few changes to its 1970s era products, whereas VW in Shanghai reinvested profits and refined its production, introducing a new "Santana 2000" model in the mid-1990s. Around 1991, Guangzhou Peugeot accounted for nearly 16 percent share of the domestic passenger car market. But it began to go into the red in 1994 with its losses amounting to $349 million by 1997, forcing Peugeot to retreat from China. It sold its interest in the JV to Honda in 1998 (see below).

While the sour memories of the disappointing performance of its previous JV were still there, Peugeot—now part of PSA Peugeot Citroen—decided to return to the battlefield in 2003. This time, the Paris-based carmaker seemed loaded with ambitious expectations to grab a slice of the country's increasingly appealing auto market sparked by the post-WTO boom in the auto industry. One of its latest moves in China is an agreement in 2003 under which PSA Peugeot Citroen would further its partnership with Hubei-based Dongfeng Motor, one of China's top three automakers which originally signed up as a JV partner with Citroen, to produce Peugeot vehicles in China. According to the new deal, a Peugeot production platform will be installed at the Wuhan plant of the JV, Dongfeng Citroen. Starting from 2004, the new facility is expected to turn out car models tailored for domestic consumers, including the Peugeot 307, one of the most popular models in Europe since 2003.

Honda

Peugeot's pullout created a vacuum for foreign manufacturers that missed the first wave of FDI into this industry. These late entrants included Daimler-Benz, GM, Opel (a German subsidiary of GM), and Hyundai. Against these rivals, Honda entered and won the fierce bidding war for the takeover of an existing auto plant in Guangzhou of the now defunct Guangzhou Peugeot JV. The partner selection process had followed a familiar pattern: Beijing was pitting several bidders against each other to extract a maximum of capital, technology, and manufacturing capabilities, as well as the motor vehicle types deemed appropriate for China. Honda pledged to invest approximately $200 million and committed the American version of the Honda Accord, whose production started in 1999. Two years later, Guangzhou Honda added the popular Odyssey minivan to its product mix. In less than two years, Honda had turned around the loss-making Peugeot facility into one of China's most profitable passenger car JVs (see IC-1.3).

It is important to note that well before its JV with the Guangzhou Auto Group, Honda had captured a significant market share with exports of the popular Honda Accord and a most effective network of dealerships and service and repair facilities all over China. These measures helped Honda not only to attain an excellent reputation and brand recognition, but also strengthened Honda's bargaining power with the Chinese negotiators.

The Road Ahead

Looking ahead, the trade and non-trade barriers will gradually be removed in post-WTO China. Increasing vehicle imports after trade liberalization will put pressure on the existing JVs that assemble cars in China, and will force them to improve their global competitiveness. Otherwise, locally produced vehicles, even by JVs with multinational automakers, with no advantage as regards models, prices, sales networks, components supply, and client services, will have a hard time surviving.

Despite China's low per capita income overall, there is a large, wealthy entrepreneurial class with significant purchasing power thanks to two decades of economic development. The average price of passenger cars sold in China in 2004 is about $20,000, whereas the average car price in countries such as Brazil, India, and Indonesia is $6,000 to $8,000. China, for example, is BMW's biggest market for the most expensive, imported 7-Series sedan, outstripping even the United States—even though Chinese buyers pay double what Americans pay (thanks to remaining tariffs) and often in cash.

However, vehicle imports will not exceed 8 percent of the market in the foreseeable future. China's automobile industry, which has almost exclusively focused on the domestic market, still has much room for future development and will maintain an annual growth rate of 20 percent for the next few years. The growth rate for major automobile firms could be even higher—GM's sales, for example, grew 75 percent in 2003 and Ford tripled its sales in 2004 (albeit to just 65,000 vehicles).

In the long run, as domestic growth inevitably slows down, there will be fiercer market competition and industry consolidation. The entry barrier will be higher and resource development will be more crucial to the sustainability of competitive advantage. In order to survive and maintain healthy and stable growth, China's JV and indigenous automobile companies, having established a solid presence domestically, must be able to offer its own products that are competitive in the global market.

No doubt, the road to success in China's automobile industry is fraught with plenty of potholes. As latecomers, Toyota, Honda, and Nissan had fewer options in the hunt for appropriate JV partners and market positioning than did the first mover VW during the 1980s. All the way through the early 1990s, foreign auto companies were solicited to enter China and encountered very little domestic competition or challenge. This situation has changed significantly. Today the industry is crowded with the world's top players vying for a share of this dynamic market. Success in China may also significantly help contribute to the corporate bottom line for multinationals that often struggle elsewhere. For example, China, having surpassed the United States, is now Volkswagen's largest market outside of Germany. In 2003, one-quarter of Volkswagen's corporate profits came from China.

There are two competing scenarios confronting strategists contemplating a move into China or expansion in China: (1) At the current rate of rapid FDI and domestic investment, the Chinese industry will rapidly develop significant overcapacity. Given the inevitable cooling down of the overall growth of the economy, a bloodbath propelled by self-inflicted wounds such as massive incentives looms on the horizon (see Opening Case in Chapter 2). (2) Given the low penetration of cars among the vast Chinese population whose income is steadily on the rise, such a rising tide will be able to lift all boats—or wheels—for a long while at least.

Case Discussion Questions

1. Drawing on the industry-based view, explain why the intensity of interfirm rivalry within the Chinese automobile industry has increased in the last two decades.

2. Some early entrants (such as Volkswagen) succeeded and some early entrants (such as Peugeot) failed. Similarly, some late entrants (such as Honda) did well and some late entrants (such as Ford) are struggling. From a resource-based standpoint, how does entry timing play or not play a role in determining performance?

3. Using the institution-based view, how do you explain the initial reluctance of most multinational automakers to enter China in the 1980s? What happened that made them change their minds more recently?

4. If you were a board member at one of the major multinational automakers and you just heard two presentations at a board meeting outlining the two contrasting scenarios for the outlook of the Chinese automobile industry in the last paragraph of the case, would you vote Yes or No for a $2 billion proposal to fund a major FDI project in China?

Sources: Based on (1) W. Arnold, 2003, The Japanese automobile industry in China, Japan Policy Research Institute Working Paper No. 95; (2) Economist, 2003, Cars in China: The great leap forward, February 1: 53–54; (3) G. Edmondson, 2004, Volkswagen slips into reverse, Business Week, August 9: 40; (4) H. Huang, 1999, Policy reforms and foreign direct investment: The case of the Chinese automotive industry, Fourin China Auto Weekly, 9 (1): 3–66; (5) M. W. Peng, 2000, Controlling the foreign agent: How governments deal with multinationals in a transition economy, Management International Review, 40 (2): 141–166; (6) Q. Tao, 2004, The Road to Success: A Resource-Based View of Joint Venture Evolution in China's Auto Industry, Ph.D. dissertation, University of Pittsburgh; (7) D. Welch, 2004: GM: Gunning it in China, Business Week, June 21: 112–115; (8) G. Zeng & W. Peng, 2003, China's automobile industry boom, Business Briefing: Global Automobile Manufacturing & Technology 2003, 20–22.

Integrative Case 1.4

SUNFLOWER COMPANY: ADAPTING TO CHANGING MARKET CONDITIONS[1]

Aldas Pranas Kriauciunas

Purdue University

An entrepreneurial Lithuanian company endeavors to survive and prosper by adapting to changing market conditions in a transition economy.

Business survival in a transition economy encompasses many challenges. Based in the newly independent country of Lithuania, Sunflower has not only survived, but has grown for over ten years under difficult conditions. Through planning and luck, it has met challenges head-on, but the greatest challenges—associated with Lithuania's EU membership—lay ahead. To understand the firm, its history is presented in four periods: start of the firm (1992 to 1994), expansion of the firm (1995 to 1998), crisis period (1999 to 2000), and recovery (2001 to present).

Start (1992 to 1994)

Sunflower was founded in 1992 in Vilnius, the capital of Lithuania. Lithuania is located on the eastern coast of the Baltic Sea and is comparable in size to West Virginia. The country has a population of 3.5 million and had one of the fastest growing economies in Europe from 2001 to 2004. Lithuania's economy is based on a broad industrial base (chemicals, metal processing, construction materials, food processing, and light industry), as well as solid transportation and

service sectors. See IC-1.1 on next page for additional economic information on Lithuania.

The Sunflower company was started with $30,000 initial capital, which the founder earned through metals trading. As indicated in IC-1.2 on next page, the firm started with three employees: the director (founder), the accountant, and a sales agent. In the early 1990s, there were many opportunities in the

---

[1] This case was written by Aldas Pranas Kriauciunas (Purdue University). It is based on interviews with the founder of Sunflower Company. The name of the company has been changed to ensure confidentiality. Reprinted with the permission of the author.

IC-1.1.   Lithuania Macro-Economic Data

Year	GDP Change	Inflation	Cumulative FDI	Average Monthly Wage	Unemployment Rate	Interest Rates
1992	−15.0%	1,150%	***	$18	3.0%	88%
1993	−10.0%	180%	***	$50	4.0%	30%
1994	−5.0%	40%	0.42 billion euros	$100	5.0%	24%
1995	+3.8%	12%	0.55 billion euros	$150	5.5%	24%
1996	+4.5%	7%	0.8 billion euros	$175	6.8%	16%
1997	+7.0%	3%	1.2 billion euros	$225	7.5%	12%
1998	+5.0%	0%	1.9 billion euros	$300	8.5%	13%
1999	−4.0%	0%	2.4 billion euros	$285	10.1%	13%
2000	+3.0%	1%	2.7 billion euros	$270	11.5%	11%
2001	+7.9%	0.6%	3.1 billion euros	$273	12.5%	8%
2002	+6.8%	−1.0%	3.8 billion euros	$348 ($288ª)	11.3%	6%
2003	+9.0%	−1.3%	4.0 billion euros	$441 ($304ª)	10.3%	5%

a. On February 2, 2002, Lithuania changed its exchange rate system to peg its currency to the euro, rather than the US dollar. Average monthly wages for 2002 and 2003 are reported based on the floating exchange rate. Figures in parentheses are dollar amounts based on the previous fixed exchange rate.

IC-1.2.   Annual Company Data

Year	# of Employees	Revenue	Pre-Tax Profits
1992	3	$15,000	N/A
1993	10	$150,000	−$7,000
1994	11	$185,000	$10,000
1995	17	$366,000	$20,000
1996	12	$455,000	$14,000
1997	23	$1,375,000	$149,000
1998	28	$1,576,250	$30,000
1999	36	$1,375,000	$18,000
2000	48	$1,650,000	$12,000
2001	45	$2,100,000	$23,000
2002	54	$2,700,000	$24,000
2003	52	$3,500,000	$22,000

All information based on December 31 of the calendar year.

new economy. It was easy to register a new company, demand for new products was high, and competition was still low. However, annual inflation exceeded 500 percent, the country did not have its own currency, and organized crime robbed firms or required protection money to leave firms alone.

In the early 1990s, it was very difficult to get a loan from a bank. Domestic banks were primarily interested in large companies and had little interest in new or start-up companies. There were no foreign banks in the country and the laws forbade companies from borrowing money from private individuals. To get around these restrictions, many companies had two sets of books. One set was presented to tax authorities and another set reflected the actual financial situation of the company including loans from individuals. However, by 1994 banks started giving short-term loans to new firms.

The newly reestablished Republic of Lithuania had to create its own legal foundation, along with financial and fiscal systems. Therefore, many new laws were passed—about 3,200 by 1996. The fast pace of legal development made it hard to operate a business, since the laws were not well prepared and were amended frequently. For example, the value-added tax (VAT) law was amended eighteen times over four years. There was little consideration regarding the impact of the laws on businesses.

Internally, one problem for the firm was deciding what work to focus on. As IC-1.3 shows, the firm sold metal and many other products in its first years. It

IC-1.3.   Product Lines by Year

PRODUCT	1992	1993	1994	1995	1996	1997	1998	1999	2000	2001	2002	2003
Washing Machines	+	+										
Tea	+	+	+									
Ferrous Metals	+	+	+									
Soup		+	+									
Spices		+	+									
Matches		+	+									
Chocolate Cream		+	+									
Shoes		+	+									
Coffee		+	+									
Detergent		+	+									
Candy		+	+									
Cookies		+	+									
Bras		+	+									
Calculators			+									
Light Bulbs			+	+								
Store Display Systems			+	+	+	+	+	+	+	+	+	+
Service Station Equipment			+	+	+	+	+	+	+	+	+	+
Tire Repair Materials			+	+	+	+	+	+	+	+	+	+
Tires				+	+	+	+	+	+			
Car Windshields				+	+							
Service Station Tools									+	+	+	+
Auto Diagnostic Equipment								+	+	+	+	+
Kitchen Cabinets									+	+	+	+
Office Furniture											+	+
Hotel Furniture											+	+

even tried selling sandwiches and snacks during the visit of Pope John Paul II to Lithuania in 1993. Each product was introduced with the intent of meeting some niche demand. Since there were almost no management books or journals written in Lithuanian, small companies relied on a hit-or-miss approach in deciding what to sell.

Expansion (1995 to 1998)

As the firm grew, the set of problems and opportunities changed. Finding qualified employees continued to be a problem. This problem became even more acute during 1997 to 1998 when the prime minister significantly raised the salaries for government workers. Since these workers made up one-third of all employed people in the country, this put upward pressure on all wages. The increasing number of foreign companies in Lithuania also paid premium wages. Therefore, it became harder for small companies to hire good employees. To keep turnover low, the company ensured salaries were paid on time, lent money to employees for personal needs, and let employees use company vehicles over the weekend. This increased employee loyalty to the firm. During this period, working with banks became easier. In late 1994, the company received its first loan—for six months at an annual rate of 40 percent. Western suppliers noticed the success of the company and began to sell equipment through a credit line, allowing payment after the sale was made. In this stage of growth, the product lines of the company changed significantly. The firm shifted its attention to two new areas: tire repair and store display systems.

Development of the Tire Repair Division. In 1994, the competition in the current product lines increased while at the same time, the demand for new products was also increasing. At that time, there were only two companies in Lithuania selling tire repair equipment. Both demand and competition were growing, which provided an opportunity for Sunflower to enter into this new market. The director's education background was in transportation, so he was interested in expanding in this area. He saw that the volume of cars was growing in Lithuania, indicating increased demand for tire and car repair services. Additionally, he looked to the experience of Poland, which was three years ahead of Lithuania in regards to the tire repair market. In Poland, car repair shops were already updating their equipment.

To receive training, the firm's technicians traveled to Poland to visit tire repair equipment vendors. These vendors became Sunflower's initial partners and were very helpful as the company entered this market in Lithuania. The Polish partners provided training on the product, on market analysis, and on strategies for success. In late 1995, the company began to bypass the Polish middlemen and buy directly from Western suppliers. Buying direct helped reduce the purchase costs of the equipment.

The competition in this market increased annually. The company decided to deal with competition by specializing in a key segment. Sunflower chose tire-repair as the area of specialty and was able to provide everything associated with that line of work: equipment, materials, and consultations. Entry was achieved through three stages: (1) Establishing a network of sales agents throughout the country, (2) starting an advertising campaign, and (3) helping companies prepare business plans so that they could get financing to buy the firm's equipment. At one time, the company had 50 percent of its target market, largely by attracting clients that no one had targeted before.

Development of the Store Display Division. In the mid-1990s, there was an increase in the number of small stores in Lithuania as well as remodeling of existing stores. These stores needed new shelves, display cases, layout design, and related products. Since one of Sunflower's employees was an architect, this seemed like an area of high potential for the company. To learn about designing in-store displays, the company's staff took trips to Poland to learn about the market and materials used and began to import store display case and shelving materials.

The market for store displays, cases, and shelves can be split into two parts: food stores and non-food stores. Sunflower targeted both parts of the market, but as a result, did not do well in either market segment. Food stores needed refrigeration systems, but the company did not have sufficient technical experience for that line of work. Attention to the food stores took time and energy away from focusing on the non-food stores where the company could have done well. Additionally, two changes occurred in the market in a short period of time. The first change was that the competition moved from using Polish suppliers to using Italian suppliers for higher quality materials. The second change was that the competition began to produce display cases and shelves from raw materials rather than purchasing completed units. These two changes allowed the competition to increase quality and cut prices. The sales in this area for Sunflower fell in 1998 and 1999.

Crisis (1999 to 2000)

In August 1998, Russia devalued its currency, the ruble. At first, the impact on Lithuania was small, but as time went on, the effect became worse, especially during the winter of 1999/2000. The demand for product lines in both divisions fell as the economy contracted. For example, although the sales of gasoline and retail sales fell 15 percent, the money spent on investments fell 50 percent. This significantly affected Sunflower, since both its product lines were investment-type goods and fewer retail stores and tire-repair shops were opening up.

Tire-Repair Equipment. It became more difficult for companies to finance purchases and investments. Banks tightened up on lending, making it difficult for smaller companies to get loans. One solution initiated by Sunflower's director was to broker agreements between Lithuanian service stations and foreign companies like Shell, Mobil, and British Petroleum (BP). The agreement provided for the Lithuanian service station distributing only one kind of motor oil and the foreign company financing tire repair materials and equipment, which Sunflower would supply. The second solution was for Sunflower to become involved in the leasing process. Since Lithuanian collateral laws were not fully developed, many leasing companies sprung up whereby they would hold title to equipment and allow companies to use that equipment until such a time that the equipment was paid off. Sunflower learned how to prepare documents for leasing companies, so that leasing companies only had to process the paperwork. In this way, the leasing company financed the equipment, Sunflower kept sales going, and the service stations received the equipment they needed.

Store Display. Sunflower was being pushed out of the store display market. The management decided to enter store furniture production and predicted that

the Russian crisis would end in the fall of 1999. The strategy was to start up production when the market would be in the recovery stage and market entry would be easier. Unfortunately, the opposite happened. The economic crisis grew worse and production began during the worst phase of the recession. The company director was ready to initiate lay-offs. However, a large unexpected contract with a new store in Uzbekistan (Central Asia) to install all its shelving and display cases allowed the division to keep working even when local demand was low.

Kitchen Cabinet Production. Production of store displays began in November 1999 and kitchen furniture production began in December 1999. This was, to some extent, an extension of the store display work. The kitchen cabinet market had a lot of competition. To compete, Sunflower purchased multi-task equipment with short set-up times. This allowed them to undertake special orders at half the price as the competition. Additionally, the competition was laying off production workers and managers due to the impact of the Russian economic crisis. Sunflower hired these employees and quickly built a strong production division. Through these steps, in March 2000, Sunflower won one of the top awards in Lithuania's largest annual furniture exhibition for its kitchen furniture, even though the competition was much larger with annual revenues of $15 to $20 million and employed from 500 to 800 workers.

Recovery (2001 Onward)

As Lithuania's economy began to recover, the company prepared itself to take advantage of predicted demand increase. The firm standardized production processes to improve quality and delivery times; it established ties with strategic partners and suppliers; it increased the length of loans to three years, and invested $150,000 to purchase and renovate much larger production facilities.

The tire-repair market faced a different set of challenges. The number of small, independent service stations was falling and the importance of large, domestic service station chains was increasing. The surviving independent chains were forming their own networks to give themselves better bargaining power, but they only made up 15 percent of the market. Foreign companies were trying to lock-in local companies in long-term contracts and also establishing contracts with service stations in smaller cities. Competition in this area was at an all-time high.

On May 1, 2004, Lithuania became a member of the European Union. Overnight, the country became part of a market with over 350 million inhabitants. Sunflower's revenues had increased 20 percent over the past year due to increased foreign interest. Exports westward were rising but the quality, price, and delivery requirements were stricter than what the company had faced previously. The company had already paid fines due to late delivery. Foreign companies expanding in Lithuania were placing orders for Sunflower's furniture and store display systems. However, the orders were based on low labor costs which were likely to increase in the future. Being part of the EU meant the firm could focus even more than before, but it was not clear what to focus on. The director was considering how to adjust the firm's strategy, handle the continued growth of the company, and take advantage of increased demand.

Case Discussion Questions

1. Why has Sunflower been successful even though it has frequently changed its product line and strategy? Would this approach work in established markets?

2. What are the drawbacks and advantages for Sunflower to continue having divergent business lines?

3. How should Sunflower take advantage of Lithuania's EU membership?

BUSINESS-LEVEL STRATEGIES

chapter 5

GROWING AND INTERNATIONALIZING THE ENTREPRENEURIAL FIRM

Outline

- Entrepreneurship, entrepreneurs, and entrepreneurial firms
- A comprehensive model of entrepreneurship
- Five entrepreneurial strategies
- Internationalizing the entrepreneurial firm
- Debates and extensions
- Implications for strategists

Opening Case: All A Cart Eyes International Markets

All A Cart (http://www.allacart.com) *is a Columbus, Ohio–based small firm specializing in designing and manufacturing customized mobile vending systems. All A Cart began in 1972, with just president Jeff Morris and his wife, Bonnie. Starting with push carts, All A Cart's products now include trailers, trucks, step vans, modular and drive-up buildings for serving food and other merchandise. All A Cart's customers range from mom-and-pop operators to multinationals such as McDonald's and Merrill Lynch. All A Cart works extensively with every customer to customize mobile vending systems. The company now has a staff of more than thirty and operates seven days a week.*

Over the past three decades, not only has All A Cart's product selection expanded, but its customers now also come from developed countries such as Canada, Germany, and Japan, as well as developing countries such as Sierra Leone and United Arab Emirates. "Every day we are contacted by people from all over the world who are interested in starting their own business," stated Morris. "I take great pride in assisting these entrepreneurs, many of whom come from foreign lands. They are eager to work in the streets, selling their wares, just as their forefathers did."

In 1995, All A Cart began to use the Internet—"more of an afterthought," according to Morris. Thomas Register (http://www.thomasregister.com), an industrial ency- *clopedia publisher with whom All A Cart had placed an advertisement each year, invited Morris to consider the Internet. Thomas Register was beginning to convert its publications online. Morris submitted a brochure that became All A Cart's first web site. The site at that time cost $175* per month, *a striking price tag compared with today's average of $9.99 per month.*

Although international sales currently only make up approximately 6 percent of total sales (based on eighty inquiries in 2002), they are all a result of the Internet. In 1990, All A Cart had only two overseas inquiries and no export sales. In 1995, the first year the firm went online, the number of overseas inquiries jumped ten-fold (to twenty) and export sales reached 2 percent of total sales. On a large wall in Morris' office, a world map full of pushpins represents the countries in which All A Cart has had inquiries and sales. Every continent is represented. This seemed unimaginable back in 1972 when this company began. It even seemed unimaginable in 1995, as Morris said, "I never dreamed that this thing called the Internet would be so big."

"The Internet is responsible for the growth of this company," according to Morris. Not only has All A Cart enjoyed increased sales, it has also benefited from more efficient communication. "I no longer have to talk to every customer," said Morris, "We can communicate through e-mail and I can show or send them pictures of the items." Communication is key for All A Cart to cater to customer needs, especially concerning international sales. A customer's personalized food cart is designed, manufactured,

and then photographed. The photo is then sent (via e-mail) to the customer for approval. If changes are needed, All A Cart makes the necessary changes before shipping the product overseas.

"For All A Cart's future, the only way is up," stated Morris confidently. "I would like to work with other cultures and possibly in the future we will have a more aggressive strategy for international sales. Right now I have potential customers in Moldova asking for modular buildings for an amusement park. But it is hard work to develop relationships internationally." To compensate for the company's shortage in international resources, Morris utilizes state and city government resources such as the State of Ohio International Trade Division to aid in building his international relations.

Source: This case was written by Tara Wedwaldt (Fisher College of Business, The Ohio State University), under the supervision of Professor Mike W. Peng as a basis for class discussions. It is based on interviews with Jeff Morris, who granted permission to use the case for educational purposes. Reprinted by permission of the author.

How do **small- and medium-sized enterprises** (**SMEs**)—usually defined as firms with less than 500 employees—such as All A Cart grow? How do they enter international markets? What are the challenges and constraints they face? This chapter deals with these and other strategic questions. This is different from many strategy textbooks, which only focus on large firms. To the extent that *every* large firm today started small and that some (although not all) of today's SMEs may become tomorrow's multinational enterprises (MNEs), current and would-be strategists cannot gain a complete picture of the strategic landscape by focusing only on large firms. More importantly, because SMEs (in contrast to most large firms, which often have to downsize) generate most jobs now (60 to 90 percent of employment, depending on the country), most students will join SMEs when entering the job market. Some readers of this book may also start up SMEs, which makes it even more imperative to focus our attention on these numerous "Davids" instead of on the smaller number of "Goliaths."

More broadly, this chapter on entrepreneurship starts Part II (Chapters 5, 6, 7, and 8), which focuses on **business-level strategy**, defined as the way to build competitive advantage in a discrete and identifiable market. This can be accomplished through an entrepreneurial venture (this chapter), an entry into a foreign country (Chapter 6), a strategic alliance (Chapter 7), and/or a set of competitive maneuvers

(Chapter 8). After this part, Part III (Chapters 9, 10, 11, and 12) will focus on **corporate-level strategy,** defined as how a firm creates value through the configuration and coordination of its multimarket activities.

This chapter first defines entrepreneurship, and then follows with a discussion on the nature of entrepreneurship. Next, we outline a comprehensive model of entrepreneurship informed by the three leading perspectives on strategy, and then we introduce five major strategies and multiple ways for entrepreneurial firms to internationalize. As before, debates and extensions follow.

ENTREPRENEURSHIP, ENTREPRENEURS, AND ENTREPRENEURIAL FIRMS

Although entrepreneurship is often associated with smaller and younger firms, no rule bans larger and older firms from being "entrepreneurial." In fact, many large firms, which tend to be more established and bureaucratic, are often urged to become more entrepreneurial. Therefore, what exactly is entrepreneurship? Recent research suggests that firm size and age are *not* defining characteristics of entrepreneurship. Instead, **entrepreneurship** is defined as "the identification and exploitation of previously unexplored opportunities."[1] Specifically, entrepreneurship is concerned with "the sources of opportunities; the processes of discovery, evaluation, and exploitation of opportunities; and the set of individuals who discover, evaluate, and exploit them."[2] These individuals are **entrepreneurs**, who may be founders and owners of new businesses or managers of existing firms. Consequently, **international entrepreneurship** is defined as "a combination of innovative, proactive, and risk-seeking behavior that crosses national borders and is intended to create wealth in organizations."[3]

Although these definitions suggest that SMEs are not the exclusive domain of entrepreneurship, many people associate entrepreneurship with SMEs, which, on average, may indeed be more entrepreneurial than large firms. To minimize confusion, in the remainder of this chapter, we will follow such a convention, although it is not totally accurate. That is, while we acknowledge that some managers at large firms can be very entrepreneurial, we will limit the use of the term "entrepreneurs" to owners, founders, and managers of SMEs. Further, we will use the term "entrepreneurial firms" when referring to SMEs (less than 500 employees). We will refer to firms with more than 500 employees as "large firms," and will use the term "corporate entrepreneurship" when discussing entrepreneurship in large firms.[4]

SMEs are important around the world. Although frequently ignored by the business press, SMEs account for more than 95 percent of the number of firms, create approximately 50 percent of total value added, and generate 60 to 90 percent of employment (depending on the country) worldwide.[5] Each year, approximately 4 to 6 percent of the adult working population in North America, Western Europe, and Central and Eastern Europe attempt (but do not necessarily succeed) to start a new venture.[6] Obviously, entrepreneurship has both rewarding and punishing aspects. Many will try, many will fail (approximately 60 percent of start-ups in the United States fail within six years),[7] and only a small number will succeed.

A COMPREHENSIVE MODEL OF ENTREPRENEURSHIP

The three leading perspectives on strategy, namely, the industry-, resource-, and institution-based views, help us understand the entrepreneurship phenomenon, and result in a comprehensive model illustrated in Figure 5.1.

Industry-Based Considerations

The industry-based view, exemplified by the Porter five forces first introduced in Chapter 2, suggests that (1) interfirm rivalry, (2) entry barriers, (3) bargaining power of suppliers, (4) bargaining power of buyers, and (5) threats of substitute products have a bearing on entrepreneurship. First, the intensity of the *interfirm rivalry* has a direct impact on whether a new start-up will make it.[8] The fewer the number of incumbent firms, the more likely they will form some sort of collusion to prevent newcomers from gaining market shares (see Chapter 8 for details). In the worst case, a monopoly incumbent, such as Microsoft, may become so dominant that it can potentially stifle innovation brought about by SMEs—this was the key reason Microsoft was prosecuted by the US and EU antitrust authorities.

FIGURE 5.1   A Comprehensive Model of Entrepreneurship

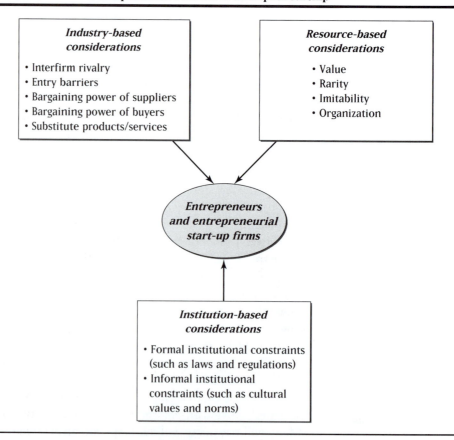

Entry barriers also impact entrepreneurship. Not surprisingly, new firm entries cluster around low entry barrier industries, such as restaurants. Conversely, capital-intensive industries hinder the entrepreneur's chance to succeed. For example, at present no entrepreneurs in their right mind would bet their money on competing against Boeing or Airbus, which are in a capital-intensive industry with very high entry barriers.

When the *bargaining power of suppliers* becomes too large, entrepreneurs may seek solutions to reduce such bargaining power. For instance, Microsoft, which of course has been very entrepreneurial, is the monopoly supplier of operating systems to virtually all personal computer (PC) makers in the world; these PC makers feel uncomfortable, but compelled, to get Microsoft products. As a result, LINUX is becoming more popular as an emerging alternative (see Video Case 1.7).

Similarly, entrepreneurs who can reduce the *bargaining power of sellers* may also find a niche for themselves. For example, a small number of national chain ("brick and mortar") bookstores used to represent the only major outlets through which hundreds of publishers could sell their books. Entrepreneurial Internet bookstores, led by Amazon, have provided more outlets for publishers, thereby reducing the bargaining power of traditional bookstores.

Substitute products/services may allow great opportunities for entrepreneurs. Given that it is difficult to compete against larger, more established incumbents in industries with high entry barriers (noted previously), entrepreneurs who bring in substitute products that redefine the game can effectively chip away some of the competitive advantages held by incumbents. For instance, e-mail, attachments, and online payments, pioneered by entrepreneurial firms, are now substituting for a large proportion of faxes, express mails, and paper check printing and processing, leaving incumbent firms in those industries powerless to fight back.

Obviously, entrepreneurs need to understand the nature of the industries they intend to join. However, one important paradox is that the basics underlying the five forces may not be known, especially in emerging, turbulent industries. For example, it is often difficult to predict consumer preferences, price innovative products, and build capacity. However, even when the industry is conducive for entries, entrepreneurs are not guaranteed success. Consider e-commerce, for example. Several years ago, incumbents did not have much market power in this field, entry barriers were relatively low (in part due to plentiful venture capital financing), sellers and buyers had limited bargaining power because of their lack of expertise in this domain, and the threat of substitutes was negligible. Yet, the bloodbath of the past several years suggests that in this industry, just like many others, only a few strong firms (such as Amazon and eBay) emerge as winners and many others disappear. This outcome, clearly, speaks to the importance of firm-specific resources and capabilities, as outlined next.

Resource-Based Considerations

The resource-based view, represented by the VRIO framework first introduced in Chapter 3, focuses on entrepreneurship's *v*alue, *r*arity, *i*mitability, and *o*rganizational aspects (refer to Figure 5.1). First, entrepreneurial resources must create *value*.[9]

STRATEGY IN ACTION 5.1. *Ski in Southern Africa, Anyone?*

It is hard to believe, but entrepreneurs in South Africa and neighboring Lesotho have built ski resorts on the slopes of the Drakensberg mountains. These mountains are not tall by Alpine standards (3,000 meters/ 9,900 feet), snow is irregular, and getting in and out is difficult. Yet, Tiffindell Resort (*http://www.tiffindell.co. za*) on the South Africa side has managed to produce a ski season every year. Between May and September (the southern hemisphere winter), more than 5,000 skiers arrive at the resort. When real snow is scarce, skiers enjoy themselves on 1.5 hectares (3.7 acres) of artificial snow. This entrepreneurial venture taps into an un-tapped demand: Rich, young customers are interested in coming to *practice* skiing to prepare for more serious winter holidays in Europe or North America. Some Tiffindell skiers may join South Africa's first-ever team for the winter Olympics. Tiffindell's rising notoriety has brought in some international competition. Afri-Ski (*http://www.afriski.co.za*), a rival ski resort, is opening up across the border on the Lesotho side. If Afri-Ski succeeds, Tiffindell may lose some of its novelty value. To stay ahead of the game, Tiffindell has begun a

150 million rand ($20 million) expansion, although the venture is not reliably profitable yet.

Sources: Based on (1) Economist, 2003, No business like snow busi-ness, August 2: 57; (2) http://www.afriski.co.za (accessed October 15, 2003); (3) http://www.tiffindell.co.za (accessed October 15, 2003).

For instance, networks and contacts are great potential resources for would-be entrepreneurs. However, unless they channel such networks and contacts into meaningful ways of creating economic value, usually through starting up new ven-tures, such resources remain just *potential* resources.

Second, resources must be *rare*. As the cliché goes, "If everybody has it, you can't make money from it." The best-performing entrepreneurs tend to have the rarest knowledge and insights about business opportunities. For example, only some of the most creative and insightful minds would have thought about building ski resorts in Africa (see Strategy in Action 5.1).

Third, resources must be *inimitable*. For instance, Amazon's success has prompted many online bookstores to directly imitate it. Of course, being a first mover does not ensure good performance. The best-performing entrepreneurs excel at *execution*, namely, aggressively leveraging their knowledge and insights by ex-ploiting the opportunities unknown to others. In the absence of a proven business model, Amazon rapidly built the world's largest book warehouses, which ironically are "brick-and-mortar." It is Amazon's "best in the breed" physical inventories—not its online presence—that are more challenging to imitate. In addition, Amazon has also developed great capabilities to deliver directly to consumers. As Amazon branches out to other commodities (for example, toys), incumbents such as Toys R

Us find it difficult to imitate such capabilities. Thus, Toys R Us turned to Amazon to handle its online business.

Fourth, entrepreneurial resources must be *organizationally* embedded. A key strategy is to use observable actions to signal that entrepreneurs are organizationally credible. Therefore, the best-performing entrepreneurs are likely to be those with the best signaling capabilities.[10] For example, one way to signal credibility to consumers is to specialize in one area.[11] Many Internet entrepreneurs deliberately specialize in highly standardized commodities, such as books, CDs, and airline tickets, to alleviate buyers' concerns about product quality. The bankruptcy of WebVan, which specialized in nonstandardized, perishable fresh groceries, has been largely attributed to its specialization in the wrong industry.[12]

Another key signal that entrepreneurs rely on is reputation. For air travelers in North America and Europe looking for great deals, the reputation of entrepreneurial discount airlines such as Southwest, easyJet, and Ryanair (see Opening Case in Chapter 3) and e-commerce sites such as Travelocity and Priceline—for always providing the most price-competitive deals—serves as a tremendous draw. If smaller, entrepreneurial firms do not have a strong reputation, they may want to team up with large firms as strategic alliances to enhance their legitimacy and credibility.[13] For instance, in the early 1980s, Microsoft benefited significantly when IBM endorsed its MS-DOS operating system.

Finally, another key signal is the willingness to take ownership of intermediated goods and services.[14] Instead of working on commissions (as traditional travel agencies do), Expedia and Priceline purchase airline tickets by bulk. Traditionally, airlines were always concerned about how aggressive outside travel agents, who work on commissions, market their tickets relative to those of competing airlines. Taking title to the tickets by Expedia and Priceline solves this problem: If Expedia and Priceline are unable to (re)sell the airline tickets, they are stuck. Consequently, airlines are happy to sell them tickets, even at a deep discount. Similarly, in export trade, entrepreneurial trading companies able and willing to take title to the goods, relative to competitors who are unable or unwilling to do so, tend to perform better for the same reason.[15]

Overall, the resource-based view suggests that on top of industry conditions, firm-specific (and in many cases entrepreneur-specific) resources and capabilities largely determine entrepreneurial success and failure. In addition, institutional conditions also make a huge difference, as outlined next.

Institution-Based Considerations

First introduced in Chapter 4, both formal and informal institutional constraints, as rules of the game, affect entrepreneurship. Although entrepreneurship is thriving around the globe in general, its development is unequal. Whether entrepreneurship is facilitated or retarded significantly depends on formal institutions governing how entrepreneurs start up new firms.[16] A recent World Bank study reports some striking differences in government regulations concerning start-ups such as registration, licensing, incorporation, taxation, and inspection (Table 5.1 on next page).[17] In

TABLE 5.1   The Costs of Starting Up a New Firm in Forty-Two Countries

Country	Number of Procedures	Time (Days)	Direct Costs (% of per Capita GDP)	Time + Direct Costs (% of per Capita GDP)	Per Capita GDP 1999 ($US)
Canada	2	2	1.45	2.25	19,320
Australia	2	2	2.25	3.05	20,050
New Zealand	3	3	0.53	1.73	13,780
Denmark	3	3	1.00	1.12	32,030
Ireland	3	16	1.16	1.80	19,160
United States	4	4	0.50	1.69	30,600
Norway	4	18	4.72	11.92	32,880
United Kingdom	5	4	1.43	3.03	22,640
Hong Kong	5	15	3.33	9.33	23,520
Mongolia	5	22	3.31	12.11	350
Finland	5	24	1.16	10.76	23,780
Israel	5	32	21.32	34.12	15,860
Sweden	6	13	2.56	7.76	25,040
Zambia	6	29	60.49	72.09	320
Switzerland	7	16	17.24	23.64	38,350
Singapore	7	22	11.91	20.71	29,610
Latvia	7	23	42.34	51.54	2,470
Netherlands	8	31	18.41	30.81	24,320
Taiwan	8	37	6.60	21.40	13,248
Hungary	8	39	85.87	101.47	4,650
South Africa	9	26	8.44	18.84	3,160
Thailand	9	35	6.39	20.39	1,960
Nigeria	9	36	257.00	271.40	310
Chile	10	28	13.08	24.28	4,740
Germany	10	42	15.69	32.49	25,350
Czech Republic	10	65	8.22	34.22	5,060
India	10	77	57.76	88.56	450
Japan	11	26	11.61	22.01	32,230
Egypt	11	51	96.59	116.99	1,400
Poland	11	58	25.46	48.66	3,960
Spain	11	82	17.30	50.10	14,000
Indonesia	11	128	53.79	104.99	580
China	12	92	14.17	50.97	780
South Korea	13	27	16.27	27.07	8,490
Brazil	15	63	20.14	45.34	4,420
Mexico	15	67	56.64	83.44	4,400
Italy	16	62	20.02	44.82	19,710
Vietnam	16	112	133.77	178.57	370

(Continued)

TABLE 5.1   (Continued)

Country	Number of Procedures	Time (Days)	Direct Costs (% of per Capita GDP)	Time + Direct Costs (% of per Capita GDP)	Per Capita GDP 1999 ($US)
Madagascar	17	152	42.63	103.43	250
Russia	20	57	19.79	42.59	2,270
Bolivia	20	88	265.58	300.78	1,010
Dominican Republic	21	80	463.09	495.09	191
Global average	10.48	47.49	47.08	65.98	8,226

Source: Adapted from S. Djankov, R. La Porta, F. Lopez-de-Silanes, & A. Shleifer, 2002, The regulation of entry (pp. 18–20), Quarterly Journal of Economics, 67: 1–37. Drawing on a major World Bank study, the table is based on the ascending order of (1) the total number of procedures domestic entrepreneurs must fulfill, (2) the number of days to obtain legal status to start up a firm, and (3) the direct costs, as a percentage of per capita GDP, to do so. The measure, time + direct costs, captures the monetized value of entrepreneurs' time in addition to direct costs. Global average is based on the full sample of eighty-five countries, and this table reports on forty-two of them.

general, governments in developed economies impose fewer procedures (as low as two procedures and two days in Australia and Canada) and a lower total cost (less than 2 percent of per capita GDP in Denmark, Ireland, New Zealand, and the United States). On the other hand, entrepreneurs confront harsher regulatory burdens in poor countries. As a class of its own, the Dominican Republic requires twenty-one procedures and a total cost of 4.63 times the per capita GDP. Bolivia, Egypt, Hungary, Indonesia, Nigeria and Vietnam require a total cost that is more than their per capita GDP. Madagascar leads the world in requiring entrepreneurs to spend 152 days to obtain legal clearance to start a new firm. As expected, the more entrepreneur-friendly these formal institutional requirements are, the more entrepreneurship flourishes, and the more developed the economies will become—and vice versa.

In addition to formal institutions, informal institutions such as cultural values and norms also affect entrepreneurship. For example, because entrepreneurs necessarily take more risk, individualistic and low uncertainty avoidance societies tend to foster relatively more entrepreneurship, whereas collectivistic and high uncertainty avoidance societies may have relatively lower levels of entrepreneurship.[18] Chapter 4 discussed this issue at length, so we will not repeat that material here other than to stress the importance of informal institutions. Overall, the institution-based view suggests that institutions matter.[19] How they matter can be seen in the following discussion.

FIVE ENTREPRENEURIAL STRATEGIES

This section discusses five entrepreneurial strategies, (1) growth, (2) innovation, (3) network, (4) financing/governance, and (5) harvest/exit. A sixth strategy, internationalization, is highlighted in the next section. Before proceeding, it is important to note that these strategies are not mutually exclusive and that they are often pursued in combination by entrepreneurial firms.

Growth

For many individuals, it is the excitement associated with a growing firm that attracts them to become entrepreneurs.[20] Recall from the resource-based view that

STRATEGY IN ACTION 5.2. *Premji's Wipro Takes Off from India*

With a net worth of $5.3 billion, Azim Premji, chairman of software-services provider Wipro (*http://www. wipro.com*), is the richest man in India and probably third or fourth richest in the world. Yet, this entrepreneur has been working as hard as ever. He gets up at 4:30 am throughout the year. By noon, he has already worked seven hours, with another seven to go. Premji's father founded Wipro in 1945 as a small producer of cooking oil, Western India Vegetable Products Ltd.—hence "Wipro." In 1977, India's government booted out IBM (*http://www.ibm.com*), leaving a vacuum for local firms. Wipro and other Indian firms leaped at the opportunity, initially in hardware. Soon, Premji noticed that local rivals were not investing in after-sales services, an IBM tradition that he thought deserved to be carried forward. This insight led to Wipro's new focus on software services starting in the early 1980s. By the 1990s, it emerged as a major player behind India's rise as a global IT powerhouse. Wipro's winning formula? Excellent quality, reliability, and cost savings of 40 percent relative to the costs of much larger Western rivals. From 1998 to 2002, Wipro's sales and earnings increased, respectively, by 25 percent and 52 percent

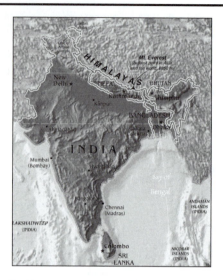

annually. Yet, Premji seems to focus on just one goal: even more success.

Sources: Based on (1) M. Kripalani, 2003, Global designs for India's tech king, Business Week, October 13: 56–58; (2) R. Ramamurti, 2001, Wipro's chairman Azim Premji on building a world-class Indian company, Academy of Management Executive, 15: 13–16. See also Opening Case in Chapter 1.

a firm can be conceptualized as a bundle of resources and capabilities. The growth of an entrepreneurial firm can thus be viewed as an attempt to more fully utilize currently underutilized resources and capabilities.[21] With start-up firms, these resources and capabilities are primarily entrepreneurial vision, drive, and leadership.[22] While young firms are usually short on tangible resources (such as capital), they often have an abundant supply of intangible resources (such as entrepreneurial drive). The attempt to leverage such an entrepreneurial drive has been motivating Azim Premji, chairman of India's Wipro and the country's richest man, to get up at 4:30 am, day in and day out (Strategy in Action 5.2).

A hallmark of entrepreneurial growth is a dynamic, flexible, guerrilla strategy. As underdogs, entrepreneurial SMEs cannot compete head-on with their larger and more established rivals. "Going for the crumbs" (at least initially), SMEs often engage in indirect and subtle attacks that large rivals may not immediately recognize as competitive challenges.[23] Entrepreneurial firms conserve scarce resources for crucial battles. They often use speed and stealth to create disruption by preempting competitors, resulting in substantial first mover advantages. Amazon in the US bookstore industry, Wipro in the Indian software industry, and Li Ning in the Chinese sporting goods industry (see Closing Case) all exemplify such a strategy.

Firms with an entrepreneurial growth strategy place more emphasis on action and less on analysis. While many large firms with strong analytical resources often become incapable of seizing opportunities (known as "paralysis by analysis"), many entrepreneurial firms grow by seizing certain opportunities with relatively little analysis, a classic "emergent" strategy at work.[24] For example, one study of the fastest growing firms in the United States found that 41 percent had no formal business plan at all and that the other 26 percent had only a rudimentary, "back-of-the-envelope" plan—only 28 percent developed full-blown business plans.[25] Of course, all new ventures need and benefit from some analysis and planning.[26] However, research documents that entrepreneurs who spent a long time in planning are no more likely to outperform individuals who seized opportunities with relatively little planning.[27]

On the other hand, over-aggressiveness can cause failure as well. Entrepreneurs, of *all* nationalities, have a tendency to be overconfident.[28] The e-commerce crash since 2000 reminds us of the perils of such overconfidence. The best entrepreneurs embrace uncertainty, yet protect themselves against excessive downside risk. For example, some venture capitalists, who are entrepreneurs themselves, employ well-known financing milestones ("rounds") to stage and sequence their commitment to risky projects based on performance in the previous round. Entrepreneurs failing to do so may end up suffering huge losses.

In essence, an entrepreneurial growth strategy relies on an abundant supply of intangible entrepreneurial and managerial resources to compensate for the lack of tangible resources. However, the finite availability of capable entrepreneurs and managers naturally constrains such growth.[29] Therefore, upon reaching a certain point, the momentum of rapid growth may slow down, and the room for filling in niches unnoticed by large rivals may become limited. For example, Kola Real's challenge to Coca-Cola and Pepsi in Peru and Mexico has been noticed by these two giants, which retaliated (see Strategy in Action 5.3 on next page).

Innovation

Innovation is at the heart of an entrepreneurial mindset.[30] On average, there is a positive relationship between a high degree of innovation and superior profitability.[31] An innovation strategy is a specialized form of differentiation strategy (see Chapter 2).[32] Specifically, it offers three advantages. First, innovation allows for a potentially more sustainable basis for competitive advantage. Firms first to introduce new goods or services are likely to earn (quasi) "monopoly profits" until competitors emerge. If entrepreneurial firms come up with "disruptive technologies" (from the standpoint of incumbent firms), then they may redefine the rules of competition, thus wiping out the advantages of incumbents.[33] For example, consider the impact of Microsoft, Ryanair, and Wipro on their respective industries.

Second, innovation should be regarded broadly. Technological breakthroughs are not the only innovations; less novel but still substantially new ways of doing business are also innovations. Most start-ups reproduce existing organizational routines, but *recombine* them to create some novel product/service offerings, such as Federal

STRATEGY IN ACTION 5.3. *Cola War in Mexico: One David versus Two Goliaths*

Mexico is the world's second largest soft-drinks market, with a per-capita consumption of 101 liters per year, only slightly less than the Americans at 113 liters. Coca-Cola (*http://www.coca-cola.com*) and Pepsi (*http://www.pepsi.com*) have long regarded Mexico as their backyard. Coca-Cola controls 70 percent of the market, which contributes 11 percent of its global sales. Pepsi has 15 percent of the market. Facing such giants, the 2002 entry of Kola Real (*http://www.kolareal.com*) from Peru, which started only fifteen years ago, has turned the cola war into David-and-Goliath proportions. Kola Real has had considerable success in Peru, with a 17 percent market share. It has also expanded into Ecuador and Venezuela, but its real target is Mexico. Before Kola Real entered Mexico, the equivalent bottle of cola cost $1.00 in the United States, but cost $1.40 in Mexico, a much poorer country. Entrepreneurs at Kola Real think that Mexico is ripe for a similar product at a lower price. Consequently, in Mexico, Kola Real has begun to market an equivalent bottle for 90 cents, which may go even lower to 81 cents. In its first year, Kola Real has grabbed a respectable 3.5 percent market share in Mexico. In response, Coca-Cola and Pepsi have slashed prices, intensified marketing, and pushed retailers to

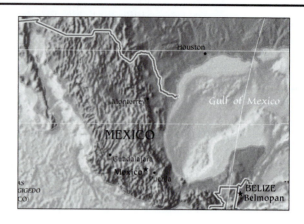

stock their cola exclusively. Undeterred, Kola Real believes that it can gain a 10 percent market share in five years, widely regarded as an unrealistic goal by observers. But then, before David killed Goliath, nobody had much respect for the little boy either.

Source: Based on (1) The Atlantic Journal-Constitution, 2003, Coke pervades Mexico, September 7 (http://www.ajc.com, accessed October 15, 2003); (2) Economist, 2003, Cola down Mexico way, October 11: 69–70.

Express's (re)combination of existing air and ground assets to create a new market.[34] For another example, consider *Hola!*, a high-society weekly in Spain, which exported its winning formula with a new focus on British celebrities and launched *Hello!* in Britain. Edited and printed in Spain, *Hello!* has become the fastest growing British magazine.[35] In short, these firms used organizational innovation instead of technological innovation.

Finally, entrepreneurial firms are uniquely ready for innovation. Owners, managers, and employees at entrepreneurial firms tend to be more innovative and risk-taking than those at large firms.[36] In fact, many SMEs are founded because former employees of large firms are frustrated by their inability to translate innovative ideas into realities. Intel, for instance, was founded by three former employees—one of them was Andy Grove—who quit Fairchild Semiconductor in 1968. Innovators at large firms also have limited ability to personally profit from innovations, whose property rights usually belong to the corporation. In contrast, innovators at entrepreneurial firms are better able to reap the financial gains associated with innovations, thus fueling their motivation to charge ahead.

Network

A network strategy refers to intentionally constructing and tapping into the relationships, connections, and ties that individuals and organizations have. The two kinds of networks—personal and organizational—are both important. Prior to and during the founding phase of the entrepreneurial firm, these two networks overlap significantly —that is, an entrepreneur's personal network is essentially the same as the firm's organizational network.[37] The essence of entrepreneurship is "translating" personal networks into value-adding organizational networks. While practically all firms (including large ones) need to nurture and cultivate networks, a network strategy is more important for smaller firms. Three attributes, urgency, intensity, and impact, distinguish entrepreneurial networking.

First, entrepreneurial firms have a high degree of *urgency* to develop and leverage networks. Essentially, they confront a **liability of newness,** defined as the inherent disadvantage that entrepreneurial firms experience as new entrants.[38] In the absence of a track record and of tangible products—many start-ups only have an idea—start-ups do not inspire confidence and lack legitimacy in the eyes of suppliers, customers, financiers, and other stakeholders. Therefore, start-ups urgently need to draw upon entrepreneurs' existing social networks and construct new ones to overcome the liability of newness. Convincing more legitimate and well-established individuals (as cofounders, management team members, investors, or board directors) and organizations (as alliance partners, sponsors, or customers) to lend a helping hand can boost the legitimacy of SMEs. In other words, legitimacy is an intangible and highly important resource that can be transferred. For instance, the stock price of Net2Phone, a little-known Internet carrier, jumped more than 50 percent right after it announced strategic alliances with Compaq and Sprint.[39] On the other hand, entrepreneurial firms must guard against being taken advantage of by their larger and more powerful partners[40] (a topic to be discussed in Chapter 7).

A second characteristic that distinguishes entrepreneurial networking is its *intensity.* Network relationships can be classified as either strong ties or weak ties. **Strong ties** are more durable, reliable, and trustworthy relationships, whereas **weak ties** are less durable, reliable, and trustworthy.[41] Efforts to cultivate, develop, and maintain strong ties are usually more intense than weak ties. Entrepreneurs often rely on strong ties—typically five to twenty individuals—for advice, assistance, and support. Strong ties can result in trust, which grows from a long history of friendly interaction. Strong ties also lead to predictability, which refers to one party's ability to confidently predict how the other party will behave under some new circumstances. Not surprisingly, entrepreneurs, such as Li Ning (see Closing Case), often initially rely on strong ties, such as family members, old classmates, and long-time friends, to accomplish organizational goals.[42] Over time, this may change, and the benefits of weak ties may become more prevalent (discussed later in the "Financing and Governance" section).

Finally, because the firm is small, the contributions of entrepreneurs' personal networks tend to have a stronger *impact* on the firm's performance.[43] In comparison, the impact of similar networks cultivated by managers at large firms may be less pronounced because of the sheer size of these firms. Moreover, being private owners, entrepreneurs can directly pocket the profits if their firms perform well, thereby motivating them to make these networks work.

Overall, strong evidence supports that both personal and organizational networks represent significant resources and opportunities, and that successful networking may lead to entrepreneurial success.[44] The most advantageous positions are those well connected to a number of players who are otherwise not connected—in other words, more *centrally* located network positions are helpful. Armed with useful ties and contacts, entrepreneurs, in a nutshell, "add value by brokering the connection between others."[45]

Financing and Governance

All start-ups need to raise capital. Other than an entrepreneur's own resources, strong ties—especially family and friends—are the most likely sources of financing. Here is a quiz (also a joke): Other than family and friends, who is the other "F" in the "3F" model of entrepreneurial financing? The answer is . . . fools! Although this is a joke, it strikes a chord in the entrepreneurial world: Given the well-known failure risks of start-ups (a *majority* of them will fail), why would anyone other than fools be willing to invest in start-ups? In reality, most outside, strategic investors, who can be angels (wealthy individual investors), venture capitalists, banks, foreign entrants, and government agencies, are not foolish. They often examine business plans, require a strong management team, and scrutinize financial reviews and analysis.[46] They also demand some assurance (such as collateral) that entrepreneurs will not simply "take the money and run." Entrepreneurs need to develop relationships with these outside investors, some of whom are weak ties. Turning weak-tie contacts into willing investors is always challenging.[47]

While dealing with strong-tie contacts can be informal (based on handshake deals or simple contracts), working with weak-tie contacts is usually more formal. In the absence of a long history of interaction, weak-tie investors, such as angels and venture capitalists, often demand a more formal **governance** strategy to safeguard their investment, such as a significant percentage of equity (for example, 20 to 40 percent), a corresponding number of seats on the board of directors, and a set of formal rules and policies.[48] In extreme cases, when business is not going well, venture capitalists may exercise their formal voting power and dismiss the founding CEO.[49] Entrepreneurs, therefore, must make tradeoffs to balance the need for larger-scale financing and the need to cede a significant portion of their "dream" firms' ownership and control rights (see Chapter 11).

Given the well-known hazards associated with start-up failures, anything that entrepreneurs can do to improve their odds is helpful. Research indicates that the odds for survival during the crucial early years are significantly correlated with firm size—the larger the firm, the better (Table 5.2). The upshot is that the faster start-ups can reach a certain size, the more likely they will survive the first few years in the face of the liability of newness. Because it takes a significant amount of capital

TABLE 5.2   **One- and Four-Year Survival Rates by Firm Size**

Firm Size (Employees)	Chances of Surviving After 1 Year	Firm Size (Employees)	Chances of Surviving After 4 Years
0–9	78%	0–19	50%
10–19	86%	20–49	67%
20–99	95%	50–99	67%
100–249	95%	100–499	70%
250+	100%		

Source: Adapted from J. Timmons, 1999, New Venture Creation *(p. 33), Boston: Irwin McGraw-Hill, based on US data.*

(among other things) to reach a large size, entrepreneurs often choose to accept more outside investment and agree to give up some ownership and control rights.

Internationally, the extent to which entrepreneurs draw on the resources of family and friends vis-à-vis outside investors is different. In the West, only a handful of minority groups (such as Chinese and Korean immigrants) can count on much financial support from family and friends, whereas in Asia, these two "Fs" (of the "three Fs" referred to earlier) typically contribute a great deal more.[50] This can be explained by the informal cultural norms of collectivism and the lack of formal market-supporting institutions such as venture capitalists and credit-reporting agencies in Asia.[51] Interestingly, this pattern persists after Asian immigrants arrive in the West. For example, one study in Great Britain found that 33 percent of Asian immigrant entrepreneurs borrowed capital from family and 49 percent of these entrepreneurs borrowed capital from friends. In contrast, only 10 percent of native-born British entrepreneurs tapped into family resources and 3 percent of them tapped into friends' resources.[52]

Harvest and Exit

Entrepreneurial harvest and exit can take a number of routes: (1) selling an equity stake, (2) selling the business, (3) merging with another firm, (4) considering an **initial public offering** (IPO), which is the first round of public trading of company stock, and/or (5) declaring bankruptcy. First, selling an equity stake to an outside, strategic investor, discussed earlier, can substantially increase the firm's value and therefore offer an excellent harvest option. However, entrepreneurs must be willing to give up some ownership and control rights. Second, selling the firm to other private owners or companies may be done at a painful discount if the business is failing or at a happy premium if the business is booming. An entrepreneurial firm can be sold via auction or negotiations.[53] Regardless of the sale price or method, selling the firm is typically one of the most significant and emotionally charged events entrepreneurs confront. It is important to note that "selling out" does not necessarily mean failure. Many entrepreneurs deliberately build up businesses in anticipation of being acquired by larger corporations and profiting handsomely. For example, the founders of Dangdang.com, the number one online bookstore in China explicitly modeled after Amazon, indicated in interviews that as an exit strategy, they hope to sell the business to Amazon for a profit when Amazon eventually enters that country.[54]

Third, when business is not doing well, merging with another company is another alternative. The drawbacks are that the firm may lose its independence and some entrepreneurs may have to personally exit the firm (after receiving some compensation) to leave room for executives from another company. Obviously, a lackluster entrepreneurial firm is not in a great position to bargain for a good deal. However, if properly structured and negotiated, a merger allows entrepreneurs to reap the rewards for which they have worked so hard (see also Chapter 9).

Fourth, entrepreneurs can take their firms through an IPO, which is the goal of many entrepreneurs. An IPO has several advantages and disadvantages (Table 5.3). First and foremost among the advantages is financial stability, in that the firm no longer has to constantly "beg" for money. For entrepreneurs themselves, an IPO can potentially result in financial windfalls. For the firm, stock options can be issued as incentives to attract, motivate, and retain capable employees. The IPO also signals that the firm has "made it." Such an enhanced reputation enables the firm to raise more capital to facilitate future growth such as acquisitions.

On the other hand, an IPO carries a number of disadvantages. The firm is subject to the rational and irrational exuberance (and also pessimism) of the financial market. For example, the late 1990s saw many companies go through an IPO, whereas fewer have done so in the new millennium (thanks to the collapse of the bubble). In the IPO process, founding entrepreneurs may gradually lose their majority control. The firm, legally speaking, is no longer "theirs." Instead, founding entrepreneurs now have the new fiduciary duty to look after the interests of outside shareholders. As a result, the entrepreneurs' freedom of action is constrained. Securities authorities, shareholders, the media, and other stakeholder groups (such as NGOs) are now scrutinizing the entrepreneurs, often forcing firms to focus on the short term (see Chapter 11). Privacy is also compromised, as information about personal wealth, shareholding, and compensation often must be disclosed. Some entrepreneurs, such as Ingvar Kamprad, founder of the Swedish furniture chain

TABLE 5.3   Advantages and Disadvantages of an Initial Public Offering (IPO)

ADVANTAGES	DISADVANTAGES
▪ Improved financial condition	▪ Subject to the whims of financial market
▪ Access to more capital	▪ Forced to focus on the short term
▪ Diversification of shareholder base	▪ Loss of entrepreneurial control
▪ Ability to cash out	▪ New fiduciary responsibilities for shareholders
▪ Management and employee incentives	▪ Loss of privacy
▪ Enhanced corporate reputation	▪ Limits on management's freedom of action
▪ Greater opportunity for future acquisition	▪ Demands of periodic reporting

Source: Based on text in J. Kaplan, 2003, Patterns of Entrepreneurship (pp. 428–430), New York: Wiley.

IKEA, and Tadao Yoshida, founder of the Japanese zipper maker YKK, have refused to go public to avoid being forced toward a short-term focus by the stock market.[55]

Finally, while taking the firm through an IPO is the most triumphant way to harvest, many failing entrepreneurial firms do not have such a luxury. The only viable exit is often to declare bankruptcy. Approximately 38,000 US businesses, most of which were start-ups, filed for bankruptcy each year from 2000 to 2002.[56] During the 1990s, the annual average number of bankrupt firms was approximately 14,000 to 15,000 in Japan; 52,000 in France; 47,000 in Great Britain; and 21,100 in Germany.[57]

Overall, a number of harvest and exit options are available to entrepreneurs. Entrepreneurs should think about the exit plan early in the business cycle and aim at maximizing the gains from the fruits of their labor.[58] Otherwise, they may end up having to eventually declare bankruptcy and face the consequences, definitely not something they planned for.

INTERNATIONALIZING THE ENTREPRENEURIAL FIRM

There is a myth that only large MNEs do business abroad and that SMEs mostly operate domestically. This myth, which is based on historical stereotypes, is being increasingly challenged as more and more SMEs, such as All A Cart (see Opening Case), Kola Real (see Strategy in Action 5.3), and Li Ning (see Closing Case), become internationalized. Further, some start-ups attempt to do business abroad from their inception. These firms are often called **born global** firms (or "international new ventures").[59] This section examines *how* entrepreneurial firms internationalize.

Transaction Costs and Entrepreneurial Opportunities

Compared to transaction costs domestically, transaction costs internationally are qualitatively higher.[60] On the one hand, numerous innocent differences in formal institutions and informal cultures and norms appear as barriers (see Chapter 4). On the other hand, a high level of deliberate opportunism may exist, which is hard to detect and remedy. For example, if foreign payment is not arriving on time, it is difficult to assess whether punctual payment is simply not the norm for firms in that country or whether that particular buyer is being opportunistic. If the latter is the case, determining how to go after the opportunistic foreign buyer becomes more than a headache. All these factors add to the complexity and uncertainty of doing business abroad to such an extent that many firms, especially SMEs, choose not to pursue international opportunities. Therefore, there are always opportunities to innovatively lower some of these transaction costs by bringing distant groups of people, firms, and countries together.[61]

Shown in Table 5.4 (p. 196), while entrepreneurial firms can internationalize by entering foreign markets, they can also add an international dimension without going abroad. Next, we discuss how entrepreneurial firms actually undertake some of these strategies.

TABLE 5.4   **Internationalization Strategies for Entrepreneurial Firms**

ENTERING FOREIGN MARKETS	STAYING IN DOMESTIC MARKETS
■ Direct exports ■ Licensing/franchising ■ Foreign direct investment (through strategic alliances, green-field wholly owned subsidiaries, and/or foreign acquisitions)	■ Indirect exports (through domestic export intermediaries) ■ Supplier of foreign firms ■ Licensee/franchisee of foreign brands ■ Alliance partner of foreign direct investors ■ Harvest and exit (through sell-off to and acquisition by foreign entrants)

International Strategies for Entering Foreign Markets

There are three broad strategies for entering foreign markets: (1) direct exports, (2) licensing/franchising, and (3) foreign direct investment (see Chapter 6 for more details). First, **direct exports** entail selling products made by entrepreneurial firms (such as All A Cart in Opening Case) in their home country to customers in other countries. This strategy is attractive because entrepreneurial firms can reach foreign customers directly. When domestic markets experience some downturns, sales abroad may compensate for such drops (see Integrative Case 2.2).[62] However, a major drawback is that these firms may not have enough resources to go after international opportunities. They may also be unfamiliar with how to turn these opportunities into sales and profits. The way All A Cart reaches foreign customers is called **sporadic** (or **passive**) **exporting,** prompted by unsolicited foreign inquiries. To actively and systematically pursue export customers is a different ball game, and All A Cart, as well as numerous other SMEs, may not be up to the task.

A second way to enter international markets is via licensing/franchising. Usually used in *manufacturing* industries, **licensing** refers to Firm A's agreement to give Firm B the rights to use A's proprietary technology and trademark for a royalty fee paid to A by B. For example, assuming (hypothetically) that All A Cart cannot keep up with demand in Saudi Arabia, All A Cart may consider granting a Saudi firm the license to use All A Cart's technology and trademark for a fee. **Franchising** represents essentially the same idea, except it is typically used in *service* industries, such as fast food. A great advantage is that licensors and franchisors can expand abroad with relatively little capital of their own—this is very attractive to typically resource-constrained SMEs.[63] Foreign firms interested in becoming licensees/franchisees have to put their own capital up front. For instance, it now costs approximately $1 million and $0.5 million to earn a franchise from McDonalds and Wendy's, respectively. However, the flip side is that licensors and franchisors may suffer a loss of control over how their technology and brand are used. That is, if All A Cart's (hypothetical) Saudi licensee produces substandard products that damage the brand, it will be very difficult for All A Cart to remedy the situation. If the licensee refuses to improve quality, All A Cart is left with two difficult, complicated, and costly choices: (1) suing its licensee in an unfamiliar Saudi court (where no one speaks English) or (2) discontinuing the relationship.

A third entry strategy is **foreign direct investment** (FDI), defined as a firm's direct investment in production and/or service activities abroad. FDI may entail strategic alliances with foreign partners (such as joint ventures), foreign acquisitions, and/or "green-field" wholly owned subsidiaries (that is, building new, foreign-based facilities from scratch). The key word here is "direct," which emphasizes hands-on, managerial involvement in foreign operations. FDI has several distinct advantages. By planting some roots abroad, a firm becomes more committed to serving foreign markets because it is physically and psychologically close to foreign customers. Relative to licensing/franchising, a firm is better able to control how its proprietary technology and brand name are used because it now directly participates in the management of foreign operations.[64] However, FDI's major drawbacks are cost and complexity. FDI requires both a nontrivial sum of capital and a significant managerial commitment. Some evidence supports that in the long run, FDI by SMEs may lead to higher performance, and that some entrepreneurial SMEs can come up with sufficient resources to engage in FDI.[65] However, many SMEs are simply unable to engage in FDI.

In general, the complexity level and required resources increase from direct exports, to licensing/franchising, and finally to FDI. Because of this, traditional thought is that most firms must go through these different "stages" of internationalization, and that SMEs (perhaps with few exceptions) are unable to take on FDI. These ideas—collectively known as **stage models**—posit that even for some SMEs that eventually internationalize, it entails a very slow, stage-by-stage, evolutionary process.[66] For example, it took thirty years for All A Cart's overseas sales to reach 6 percent of total sales (see Opening Case). Starbucks first blanketed the United States in about a decade. Only more recently has Starbucks started to invest more aggressively abroad (see Opening Case in Chapter 6).

However, enough counterexamples of *rapidly* internationalizing entrepreneurial firms exist to challenge stage models. Consider Logitech, now a global leader in computer peripherals.[67] Entrepreneurs from Switzerland and the United States established this firm and set up dual headquarters in these two countries. R&D and manufacturing were initially split between Switzerland and the United States, and then quickly spread to Ireland and Taiwan through FDI. Logitech's first commercial contract was with a Japanese company. Another interesting example is a medical equipment venture, Technomed, which was set up in France. From its inception, the founder did not see it as a French company; instead, it was viewed as a global company with English as its official language—very uncharacteristic of French firms. Only nine months after it began, Technomed established a subsidiary through FDI in a key market, the United States. In another example, most Internet firms, because of their instant worldwide reach, have rapidly concluded that the world is their market—although their degree of success varies.[68]

Given that most SMEs still fit the stereotype of slow (or no) internationalization and that some very entrepreneurial SMEs seem to be "born global," a key question is: What leads to rapid internationalization? The key differentiator between rapidly and slowly (or not at all) internationalizing SMEs appears to be the entrepreneurs' international experience.[69] If founders, owners, and managers have solid previous experience abroad (such as working and studying overseas and immigrating from certain countries), then doing business internationally is not so intimidating. Otherwise, the "fear and loathing" factor associated with the unfamiliar foreign business world may take over, causing entrepreneurs to avoid overseas troubles.

While many entrepreneurial firms have aggressively gone abroad, a majority of SMEs probably will be unable to do so—struggling domestically is already giving them enough headaches. However, interestingly, some SMEs can still internationalize by staying in their home countries, as discussed next.

International Strategies for Staying in Domestic Markets

Shown in Table 5.4, entrepreneurial SMEs can choose from at least five strategies for internationalizing without leaving their home countries: (1) indirect exports, (2) become suppliers of foreign firms, (3) become licensees/franchisees of foreign brands, (4) become alliance partners of foreign direct investors, and (5) harvest and exit through sell-offs. First, whereas direct exports may be lucrative, many SMEs simply do not have the resources to handle such work. However, they can still reach overseas customers through **indirect exports,** namely, exporting through domestic-based export intermediaries. **Export intermediaries** are "specialist firms that function as export departments of several manufacturers in noncompetitive lines."[70] Entrepreneurs themselves, these intermediaries, such as Asia Trade (see Strategy in Action 5.4), perform an important "middleman" function by linking sellers and buyers overseas that otherwise would not have been connected.[71] These intermediaries greatly facilitate the internationalization of many SMEs (such as Brown Lumber in Integrative Case 2.2). Export intermediaries, such as export trading and management companies, handle approximately 50 percent of total exports in Japan and South Korea, 38 percent in Thailand, and 5 to 10 percent in the United States.[72]

A second strategy is to become suppliers of foreign firms that come to do business in one's home country. Most foreign firms look for local suppliers in order to cut costs. For example, one Northern Irish bakery secured supply contracts for chilled part-bake bread with an American firm, Subway, which entered Ireland in the mid 1990s. So successful was this relationship that the firm now supplies Subway franchisees throughout Europe.[73] SME suppliers thus may be able to internationalize by "piggybacking" on the larger foreign entrants.

Third, entrepreneurial firms may consider becoming licensees or franchisees of foreign brands. Foreign licensors and franchisers provide training and technology transfer—for a fee, of course. SMEs consequently can learn much about how to operate at world-class standards. Further, licensees and franchisees do not have to be permanently under the control of the licensors and franchisors. If enough has been learned and enough capital has been accumulated, it is possible to discontinue the relationship and reap greater entrepreneurial profits. For example, in Thailand, Minor Group, which had held the Pizza Hut franchise for twenty years, broke away

Strategy in Action 5.4. *Asia Trade Exports to the Russian Far East*

Asia Trade (*http://www.asiatrade.com*) is a small, Seattle-based export trading company founded by a recent Russian immigrant and his American wife in 1992. The collapse of the Soviet Union created chaos as well as opportunities. The breakdown of the centrally administered trading system hit the distant Russian Far East especially hard. Asia Trade took advantage of the general food shortage there by bringing canned foods, beverages, and flour, mostly sourced from the Pacific Northwest, to that new market. As a virgin market, the Russian Far East had all the attractions for first movers. Yet, it also possessed all the dangers that would scare away many who were less determined. Locals would not do business with strangers unless they had become friends. This cultural norm, reinforced by decades of communist rule, created deep suspicion about foreigners in a region guarded as a military reserve and deterred many interested foreign firms. Asia Trade had an advantage because one of the co-founders was born and raised there and had seven years of trading experience. Asia Trade carved out a niche for itself by knowing who to talk to and being able to reliably source

products in America. Two years after its founding, Asia Trade's per-capita export sales more than doubled the average among the population of small US export intermediaries.

Source: Based on author's interviews, adapted from M. W. Peng, 1998, Behind the Success and Failure of US Export Intermediaries: Transactions, Agents, and Resources (pp. 86–87), Westport, CT: Quorum.

from the relationship. Minor Group's new venture, The Pizza Company, is now the market leader in Thailand.[74]

A fourth strategy is to become alliance partners of foreign direct investors. Facing an onslaught of aggressive MNEs, many entrepreneurial firms stand little chance of successfully defending their market positions. In this case, following the old adage, "If you can't beat them, join them," makes sense. While "dancing with the giants" is tricky, it is much better than being crushed by them (see Chapters 6, 7, and 8 for more discussion).[75]

Finally, as a harvest and exit strategy, entrepreneurs may contemplate selling an equity stake or the entire firm to foreign entrants. For example, an American couple, originally from Seattle, built a Starbucks-like coffee chain called Seattle Coffee with sixty stores in Britain. When Starbucks entered Britain, the couple sold the chain to Starbucks for a hefty $84 million (see Opening Case in Chapter 6). Because acquisitions provide the fastest route to establish market presence, foreign entrants such as Starbucks are often willing to pay a premium (see Chapters 6 and 9). In light of the high failure rates of start-ups, being acquired by foreign entrants may help preserve the business in the long run.

Overall, while some entrepreneurial firms venture abroad, others can be successfully internationalized without getting their feet wet in unfamiliar foreign waters.[76]

DEBATES AND EXTENSIONS

The recent boom in entrepreneurship throughout the world has continued to attract significant controversies and debates.[77] This section introduces three leading debates: (1) traits versus institutions, (2) slow versus rapid internationalization, and (3) antifailure biases versus entrepreneur-friendly bankruptcy laws.

Traits versus Institutions

This debate, which probably is the oldest debate on entrepreneurship, focuses on the question: What motivates entrepreneurs to establish new firms, while most others are simply content to work for bosses? The "traits" school of thought argues that personal traits make the difference. Compared with nonentrepreneurs, entrepreneurs seem more likely to possess a stronger desire for achievement, have a stronger locus of control (the belief that they can largely control their own fate), and are more willing to take risks and tolerate ambiguities. Overall, entrepreneurship "inevitably implies a deviation from customary behavior,"[78] and this deviation seems to be in the "blood" of entrepreneurs. For example, some people are **serial entrepreneurs** who start, grow, and sell several businesses throughout their career. One example is Wayne Huizenga, who has founded a series of successful firms such as Waste Management, Blockbuster, and AutoNation.[79]

Critics, however, argue that some of these traits, such as a strong achievement orientation, are not necessarily limited to entrepreneurs, but instead are characteristic of many successful individuals. Moreover, the diversity among entrepreneurs makes any attempt to develop a standard psychological or personality profile futile.[80] Critics suggest that it is institutions, namely, the environments which set formal and informal rules of the game, that matter.[81] For example, consider the Chinese, who have exhibited a high degree of entrepreneurship throughout Southeast Asia where as an ethnic minority group (usually less than 10 percent of the population in countries such as Indonesia and Thailand), they control 70 to 80 percent of the wealth. Yet, in mainland China, for nearly three decades (the 1950s through the 1970s), there had been virtually no entrepreneurship, thanks to harsh communist policies. In the last two decades, as government policies in China become more entrepreneur-friendly, the institutional transitions have opened the floodgates of entrepreneurship, contributing to a booming economy.[82] In a nutshell, it is not what is in people's "blood" that makes or breaks entrepreneurship; it is what institutions encourage or constrain that explains it.

Beyond the macro societal-level institutions, more micro institutions also matter. Some socially or culturally disadvantaged groups (such as immigrants) may have difficulty finding employment in the mainstream corporate sector and be driven to self-employment. Family background and educational attainment also correlate with entrepreneurship. Children of wealthy parents, especially those who own businesses, are more likely to start their own firms, so are people who are better educated.[83] Taken together, informal norms governing one's socioeconomic group, in terms of whether starting a new firm is legitimate or not, assert some powerful influence on the propensity to create new ventures.

Overall, this debate between "traits" and "institutions" is an extension of the broader debate on "nature versus nurture." Most scholars now agree that human behavior such as entrepreneurship is the result of nature *and* nurture. A relevant issue is whether entrepreneurship can be taught in formal business education. Alex DeNoble, an entrepreneurship professor, suggested that

> *You can't teach someone to acquire the drive, the hunger, the passion, and the tenacity to pursue an entrepreneurial path. However, give us someone who has such "fire in their belly" and we can help them to develop critical entrepreneurial skills which will guide them along their journey.*[84]

Slow Internationalizers versus "Born Global" Start-ups

This debate has two components: (1) *Can* SMEs internationalize faster than traditional stage models suggest? (2) *Should* they rapidly internationalize? The dust has largely settled on the first component—it is possible for some (but not all) SMEs to make very rapid progress in internationalization. What is currently being debated is the second component.

On the one hand, some advocates argue that every industry has become "global" and that entrepreneurial firms need to rapidly go after these opportunities.[85] On the other hand, stage models suggest that firms need to enter culturally and institutionally close markets first, spend enough time there to accumulate overseas experience, and then gradually move from more primitive modes such as exports to more sophisticated strategies such as FDI in distant markets. Consistent with stage models, Sweden's IKEA, for example, waited twenty years (1943–1963) before entering a neighboring country, Norway. Only more recently has it accelerated its internationalization.[86] Stage models caution that inexperienced swimmers may be drowned in unfamiliar and turbulent foreign waters if they attempt to plunge into the ocean too fast.

A key strategic issue, therefore, is whether it is better for entrepreneurs to start the internationalization process soon after founding (as "born global" firms do) or to postpone until the firm has accumulated significant resources (as IKEA did). One study in Finland supported rapid internationalization.[87] Specifically, firms following the prescription of stage models, when eventually internationalizing, must overcome substantial inertia because of their domestic orientation. In contrast, firms that internationalize earlier need to overcome fewer of these barriers. Therefore, SMEs without an established domestic orientation (such as Logitech and Technomed discussed earlier) may outperform their rivals who wait longer to internationalize. In other words, contrary to the inherent disadvantages in internationalization associated with SMEs as suggested by stage models, there may be "inherent advantages" of being small while venturing abroad.[88]

In contrast, one study in the United States found no performance difference between aggressive and passive internationalizers.[89] One study in Hungary reported that foreign sales during the first few years of the new venture may *reduce* its chances for survival.[90] Consequently, indiscriminate advice for new ventures to "go global" is not warranted. Capitalizing on such findings, other writers argue that "the born-global view, although appealing, is a dangerous half-truth." They maintain that "you must first be successful at home, then move outward in a manner that anticipates and genuinely accommodates local differences."[91] They suggest that not all Internet start-ups are able to go global, because potential customers abroad must trust these firms enough to do business on their sites. To win such trust, a great deal of *local* marketing and services—country by country—is necessary, as eBay, Schwab, and Yahoo! have done. The only way to do that well is to follow the teachings of stage models.

Given that findings continue to be split, there are no hard and fast rules on whether entrepreneurial firms should rapidly internationalize. While the entrepreneurial urge to "be bold" should be encouraged, entrepreneurs also need to be reminded of the virtues of "not being too bold."[92]

Antifailure Bias versus Entrepreneur-Friendly Bankruptcy Laws[93]

Given that a majority of entrepreneurial firms will fail, failure looms large on the entrepreneurial horizon. However, entrepreneurs, scholars, journalists, and government officials all share an "antifailure" bias.[94] That is, everyone is interested in entrepreneurial success, and high-flying entrepreneurs, such as Meg Whitman at eBay and Richard Branson at the Virgin Group, are often elevated to rock star status. Relative to the attention given to entrepreneurial success, the attention given to entrepreneurial failure is scant—and this criticism applies to this chapter as well (!).

One of the leading debates is how to treat failed entrepreneurs who file for bankruptcy. Although we are confident that many start-ups will end up in bankruptcy, it is impossible to predict beforehand which ones will go under. Therefore, from an institutional standpoint, if entrepreneurship is to be encouraged, the pain associated with bankruptcy must be eased by means such as allowing entrepreneurs to walk away from debt, a legal right bankrupt American entrepreneurs appreciate. In contrast, bankrupt German entrepreneurs may remain liable for unpaid debt for up to thirty years. Further, German and Japanese managers of bankrupt firms can also be liable for criminal penalties, and some bankrupt Japanese entrepreneurs have committed suicide. Not surprisingly, many failed entrepreneurs in Germany and Japan try to avoid business exit despite escalating losses. Therefore, as rules of the "end game," harsh bankruptcy laws become grave *exit* barriers. They can also create significant *entry* barriers, as fewer would-be entrepreneurs may decide to launch their ventures.

At a societal level, if many would-be entrepreneurs abandon their ideas in fear of failure, there will not be a thriving entrepreneurial sector. Given the risks and uncertainties, many entrepreneurs do not make it the first time. However, if they are given second, third, or more chances, some of them will succeed. For example, approximately 50 percent of American entrepreneurs who had filed bankruptcy between 1989 and 1993 resumed a new venture by 1993, in part due to the more entrepreneur-friendly bankruptcy laws.[95] On the other hand, a society that severely punishes failed entrepreneurs through harsh bankruptcy laws is not likely to foster widespread entrepreneurship. Failed entrepreneurs have nevertheless accumulated a great deal of experience and lessons on how to avoid their mistakes. If they drop out of the entrepreneurial game (or, in the worst case, kill themselves), their wisdom will be permanently lost.[96]

Overall, institutionally, there is an urgent need to remove some of our antifailure biases and design and implement entrepreneur-friendly bankruptcy policies so that failed entrepreneurs are given more chances. At a societal level, entrepreneurial failures may be beneficial because through a large number of entrepreneurial experimentations—although many will fail—winning solutions will emerge, entrepreneurship will flourish, and economies will develop.

IMPLICATIONS FOR STRATEGISTS

Entrepreneurs and their firms are quintessential engines of the "creative destruction" process underpinning global capitalism first described by Joseph Schumpeter, an Austrian American scholar in the early twentieth century.[97] All three leading perspectives on strategy can help explain entrepreneurship. The industry-based view suggests that entrepreneurial firms tend to choose industries with lower entry barriers and often generate more innovative competing or substitute products. The resource-based view posits that largely intangible resources, such as vision, drive, and willingness to take risk, fuel entrepreneurship. Finally, the institution-based view argues that the larger institutional frameworks explain a great deal about what causes the differences in entrepreneurial and economic development around the world.

We conclude this chapter by revisiting the four fundamental questions in strategy. Because start-ups are an embodiment of their founders' personal characteristics, the answers to why firms differ (Question 1) and how they behave (Question 2) can be found in how entrepreneurs differ from nonentrepreneurs. What determines the scope of the firm (Question 3) boils down to how successful entrepreneurs can employ growth, innovation, network, and financing/governance strategies to expand the business. Finally, what determines the international success and failure of firms (Question 4) depends on whether entrepreneurs can select the right industry, leverage their capabilities, and take advantage of formal and informal institutional resources, both at home and abroad.

Chapter Summary

1. Entrepreneurship is the identification and exploration of previously unexplored opportunities Although large firms can be entrepreneurial, the term "entrepreneurship" is most commonly associated with small- and medium-sized enterprises (SMEs) that employ less than 500 people.

2. A comprehensive model of entrepreneurship draws on industry-, resource-, and institution-based perspectives to illuminate the entrepreneurship phenomenon.

3. Five leading entrepreneurial strategies are (1) growth, (2) innovation, (3) network, (4) financing/governance, and (5) harvest/exit, which are often pursued in combination.

4. Entrepreneurial firms can internationalize by entering foreign markets through entry modes such as (1) direct exports, (2) licensing/franchising, and (3) foreign direct investment (FDI).

5. Entrepreneurial firms can also internationalize without venturing abroad by (1) exporting indirectly, (2) supplying foreign firms, (3) becoming licensees/franchisees of foreign firms, (4) joining foreign entrants as alliance partners, and (5) harvesting and exiting through sell-offs to foreign entrants.

6. The leading debates concerning entrepreneurship are (1) traits versus institutions, (2) slow versus rapid internationalization, and (3) antifailure biases versus entrepreneur-friendly bankruptcy laws.

Key Terms

born global	foreign direct investment	serial entrepreneurs
business-level strategy	franchising	small- and medium-sized enterprises (SMEs)
corporate-level strategy	governance	
	indirect exports	sporadic (or passive) exporting
direct exports	initial public offering	stage models
entrepreneurs		
	international entrepreneurship	strong ties
entrepreneurship		weak ties
export intermediaries	liability of newness	
exporting	licensing	

Critical Discussion Questions

1. Why is entrepreneurship most often associated with SMEs, as opposed to larger firms?

2. Given that most entrepreneurial start-ups fail, why do entrepreneurs found so many new firms? Why are (most) governments interested in promoting more start-ups?

3. Some suggest that foreign markets are graveyards for entrepreneurial firms that overextend themselves. Others argue that foreign markets represent the future for SMEs. If you were the owner of a small, reasonably profitable firm, would you consider expanding overseas? Why or why not?

4. **ON ETHICS:** Your former high school buddy invites you to join an entrepreneurial start-up (such as Hong Kong's Lik-Sang—see Video Case 1.8) that specializes in cracking the codes of the protection software that protects CDs, VCDs, and DVDs from being copied. He has developed the pioneering technology and lined up financing. The worldwide demand for this technology appears to be enormous. He offers you the job of CEO and 10 percent equity of the firm. How would you respond to his proposition?

5. **ON ETHICS:** Everything is the same as in Question 4, except the technology involved is the manufacturing technology for more affordable generic drugs to combat HIV/AIDS, which would potentially help millions of patients worldwide who cannot afford the high prices of the patented drugs produced by the Big Pharma (see Opening Case in Chapter 4). How would you respond?

Closing Case: Li Ning: From Olympic Gold Medallist to Star Entrepreneur

Li Ning, founder and president of Li Ning Sports Goods Company (http://www.english.lining.com.cn), *is an Olympic gold medallist in gymnastics. At the age of 21, Li Ning, in the 1984 Los Angeles games, captured three gold medals and became a national hero in China. He retired in the late 1980s and founded his company in 1990. The start-up adopted a differentiation strategy by positioning itself at an intermediate price/value range between the low price/poor quality products generated by the state-owned Chinese sportswear industry and the very expensive international brands such as Nike* (http://www.nike.com) *and Adidas* (http://www.adidas.com). *Li Ning Sports Goods Company focused on leveraging the almost 100 percent recognition of the Li Ning name in China.*

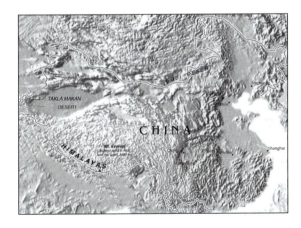

Like all start-ups, Li Ning's early years were full of frustrations. The firm had no research and development (R&D), its products were of low quality, and money was tight. However, Li Ning had one key asset, his relationships and connections among numerous fellow athletes and sports officials, who often retire to enter the sports business. Intense networking by Li Ning and his top management team eventually paid off, as many athletes and sports officials invested in the venture and opened doors.

The biggest transition occurred when the firm moved from family-style management to professional management in 1995. During the early years, Li Ning relied heavily on family, friends, and former teammates (the "three Fs") for managing and financing. However, he found that the loyalty and passion of the "three Fs," which were necessary to get the firm off the ground, were not sufficient for further growth. Most of the "three F" individuals lacked knowledge about business management. In what Li called "a single knife chop," he dismissed without exception all "three F" employees. They were all given a lucrative number of shares, but no longer allowed to be members of the top management team. Not surprisingly, many relatives, friends, and former teammates accused Li of having a "lack of humanism." But Li persisted.

After professionalizing the management team, the company experienced a period of solid growth. It has now become the market leader in China, controlling approximately 50 percent of the market share—Nike, Adidas, and a host of other players fight for the other half. Li Ning has more than 360 company-owned specialty stores, more than 600 shop-within-shops, and approximately 3,000 selling points throughout rural China, a vast market largely ignored by foreign entrants. Li Ning has opened the only sportswear R&D center in the country. Li Ning in recent years has invested 10 percent of its one billion yuan (US$122 million) revenue in marketing, as opposed to the previous 5 percent.

Li Ning has also embarked on internationalization. Li Ning has used Italian designers and designed products with a blend of Chinese and European flavors. In addition to sponsoring a number of Chinese teams, Li Ning also sponsored the French and Czech Republic gymnastics teams at the 2000 Sydney Olympics. Li Ning has opened two retail shops in Spain and Russia, and currently has distributors/partners throughout Asia, Europe, and Latin America. By 2008, when the Olympics come to Beijing, Li Ning plans to maximize its home court advantage by having a large number of sponsorships aiming at further globalizing the brand.

During an interview, Li attributed his entrepreneurial success to his athletic training, summarized as (1) self-expression ("sports encourage you to show your best"), (2) discipline, (3) respect for competitors, and (4) knowing your competition. "In sports, people don't get excited about ordinary plays. They only remember the extraordinary plays." Li concluded, "We are looking for the extraordinary plays in our business."

Case Discussion Questions

1. What are the critical resources fueling the growth of this entrepreneurial start-up?

2. What are the pros and cons of having the "three Fs" for managing and financing?

3. Why was Li Ning able to become the largest sportswear player in China in slightly over a decade, in the face of multinational competition from Nike, Adidas, and other foreign entrants?

4. What strategies of internationalization has Li Ning used? Evaluate their likely effectiveness.

5. What are the personal traits that underpin Li Ning's success? What are the institutional factors?

Sources: Based on (1) Economist, 2003, "Just do it" Chinese-style, August 2: 59; (2) Time Asia, 2002, The mainland's sneaker king, August 5 (http://www.timeasia.com, accessed October 15, 2003); (3) A. Tsui, 2001, The story of Li Ning Sports Goods Company, HKUST Hang Lung Center for Organizational Research Newsletter, 6: 2–5.

Notes

Abbreviation list

AER – American Economic Review

AIM – Advances in International Marketing

AJS – American Journal of Sociology

AJSB – American Journal of Small Business

AME – Academy of Management Executive

AMJ – *Academy of Management Journal*

AMR – *Academy of Management Review*

AP – *American Psychologist*

APJM – *Asia Pacific Journal of Management*

ASQ – *Administrative Science Quarterly*

ASR – *American Sociological Review*

ETP – *Entrepreneurship Theory and Practice*

FEER – *Far Eastern Economic Review*

HBR – *Harvard Business Review*

IBR – *International Business Review*

JBV – *Journal of Business Venturing*

JEL – *Journal of Economic Literature*

JF – *Journal of Finance*

JIBS – *Journal of International Business Studies*

JIM – *Journal of International Management*

JM – *Journal of Management*

JMS – *Journal of Management Studies*

JPE – *Journal of Political Economy*

LRP – *Long Range Planning*

MS – *Management Science*

OSc – *Organization Science*

OSt – *Organization Studies*

QJE – *Quarterly Journal of Economics*

SBE – *Small Business Economics*

SMJ – *Strategic Management Journal*

SMR – *MIT Sloan Management Review*

SP – *Sociological Perspectives*

1. M. Hitt, R. D. Ireland, M. Camp, & D. Sexton, 2001, Strategic entrepreneurship: Entrepreneurial strategies for wealth creation (p. 480), *SMJ,* 22: 479–491. See also T. Brown, P. Davidsson, & J. Wiklund, 2001, An operationalization of Stevenson's conceptualization of entrepreneurship as opportunity-based firm behavior, *SMJ,* 22: 953–968; S. Shane, 2001, Technological opportunities and new firm creation, *MS,* 47: 205–220.

2. S. Shane & S. Venkataraman, 2000, The promise of entrepreneurship as a field of research (p. 218), *AMR,* 25: 217–226.

3. P. McDougall & B. Oviatt, 2000, International entrepreneurship (p. 903), *AMJ,* 43: 902–906.

4. G. Ahuja & C. Lampert, 2001, Entrepreneurship in the large corporation, *SMJ,* 22: 521–543; B. Barringer & A. Bluedorn, 1999, The relationship between corporate entrepreneurship and strategic management, *SMJ,* 20: 421–444; J. Birkinshaw, 2000, *Entrepreneurship in the Global Firm*, London: Sage; C. Covin & M. Miles, 1999, Corporate entrepreneurship and the pursuit of competitive advantage, *ETP,* 23: 47–63; G. Dess, G. Lumpkin, & J. McGee, 1999, Linking corporate entrepreneurship to strategy, *ETP,* 23: 85–102; S. Floyd & B. Wooldridge, 1999, Knowledge creation and social networks in corporate entrepreneurship, *ETP,* 23: 123–143; W. Guth & A. Ginsberg, 1990, Corporate entrepreneurship, *SMJ,* 11: 5–15; S. Zahra & D. Garvis, 2000, International corporate entrepreneurship and firm performance, *JBV,* 15: 469–492.

5. G. Knight, 2001, Entrepreneurship and strategy in the international SME, *JIM,* 7: 155–171; R. Wright & H. Etemad, 2001, SMEs and the global economy, *JIM,* 7: 151–154.

6. H. Aldrich, 1999, *Organizations Evolving* (p. 75), London: Sage Publishing; M. W. Peng, 2001, How entrepreneurs create wealth in transition economies (p. 96), *AME,* 15 (1): 95–108.

7. J. Timmons, 1999, *New Venture Creation* (pp. 32–34), Boston: Irwin McGraw-Hill.

8. N. Huyghebaert & L. Van de Gucht, 2004, Incumbent strategic behavior in financial markets and the exit of entrepreneurial start–ups, *SMJ,* 25: 669–688.

9. E. Mosakowski, 1998, Entrepreneurial resources, organizational choices, and competitive outcomes, *OSc,* 9: 625–643.

10. A. Spence, 1973, *Market Signaling*, Cambridge, MA: Harvard University Press.

11. B. Mascarenhas, 1996, The founding of specialist firms in a global fragmenting industry, *JIBS,* 27: 27–42.

12. J. de Figueiredo, 2000, Finding sustainable profitability in electronic commerce, *SMR,* 41: 41–52.

13. B. Gomes-Casseres, 1997, Alliance strategies of small firms, *SBE,* 9: 33–44; T. Stuart, H. Hoang, & R. Hybels, 1999, Interorganizational endorsements and the performance of entrepreneurial ventures, *ASQ,* 44: 315–349.

14. M. W. Peng & H. Wang, 2002, An intermediation-based view of entrepreneurship, in M. Hitt, R. Amit, C. Lucier, & R. Nixon (eds.), *Creating Value: Winners in the New Business Environment* (pp. 48–60), Oxford, UK: Blackwell.

15. M. W. Peng, 1998, *Behind the Success and Failure of US Export Intermediaries: Transactions, Agents, and Resources*, Westport, CT: Quorum Books.

16. W. Baumol, 1990, Entrepreneurship: Productive, unproductive, and destructive, *JPE*, 98: 893–921; A. Fadahunsi & P. Rosa, 2002, Entrepreneurship and illegality, *JBV*, 17: 397–429.

17. S. Djankov, R. La Porta, F. Lopez-de-Silanes, & A. Shleifer, 2002, The regulation of entry, *QJE*, 67: 1–37.

18. T. Begley & W. Tan, 2001, The socio-cultural environment for entrepreneurship, *JIBS*, 32: 537–553; L. Busenitz & C. Lau, 1996, A cross-cultural cognitive model of new venture creation, *ETP*, summer: 25–39.

19. A. Thomas & S. Mueller, 2000, A case for comparative entrepreneurship, *JIBS*, 31: 287–301; S. Venkataraman, 2004, Regional transformation through technological entrepreneurship, *JBV*, 19: 153–167; A. Zacharakis, D. Shepherd, & J. Coombs, 2003, The development of venture-capital-based Internet companies, *JBV*, 18: 217–231.

20. J. Covin & D. Slevin, 1991, A conceptual model of entrepreneurship as firm behavior, *ETP*, 6: 7–25; W. Gartner, 1985, A conceptual framework for describing the phenomenon of new venture creation, *AMR*, 10: 696–706; S. Lee & P. Wong, 2004, An exploratory study of technopreneurial intentions, *JBV*, 19: 7–28; T. Nelson, 2003, The persistence of founder influence, *SMJ*, 24: 707–724; S. Park & Z. Bae, 2004, New venture strategies in a developing country, *JBV*, 19: 81–105.

21. G. Bruton & Y. Rubanik, 2002, Resources of the firm, Russian high-technology start-ups, and firm growth, *JBV*, 17: 553–576; E. Mosakowski, 1998, Entrepreneurial resources, organizational choices, and competitive outcomes, *OSc*, 9: 625–643; E. Penrose, 1959, *A Theory of the Growth of the Firm*, New York: Wiley.

22. G. D. Meyer & K. Sheppard, 2000, *Entrepreneurship as Strategy*, Thousand Oaks, CA: Sage Publishing; R. McGrath & I. MacMillan, 2000, *The Entrepreneurial Mindset*, Boston: Harvard Business School Press; G. Rowe, 2001, Creating wealth in organizations: The role of strategic leadership, *AME*, 15: 81–94.

23. M. Chen & D. Hambrick, 1995, Speed, stealth, and selective attack, *AMJ*, 38: 453–482; A. Fiegenbaum & A. Karnani, 1994, Output flexibility—a competitive weapon for small firms, *SMJ*, 12: 101–114; M. K. Erramilli & D. D'Souza, 1993, Venturing into foreign markets, *ETP*, 17: 29–41.

24. H. Mintzberg, 1989, *Mintzberg on Management*, New York: Free Press; S. Sarasvathy, 2001, Causation and effectuation, *AMR*, 26: 243–264.

25. A. Bhide, 1994, How entrepreneurs craft strategies that work (p. 152), *HBR*, March-April: 150–161.

26. F. Delmar & S. Shane, 2003, Does business planning facilitate the development of new ventures? *SMJ*, 24: 1165–85.

27. B. Honig & T. Karlsson, 2004, Institutional forces and the written business plan, *JM*, 30: 29–48.

28. L. Busenitz & J. Barney, 1997, Differences between entrepreneurs and managers in large organizations, *JBV*, 12: 9–30; A. Cooper, W. Dunkelberg, & C. Woo, 1988, Entrepreneurs' perceived chances for success, *JBV*, 3: 97–108; M. Kroll, L. Toombs, & P. Wright, 2000, Napoleon's tragic march home from Moscow, *AME*, 14: 117–128; M. Manimala, 1992, Entrepreneurial heuristics, *JBV*, 7: 477–504; R. McGrath & I. MacMillan, 1992, More like each other than anyone else? *JBV*, 7: 419–429; D. Miller, 1990, *The Icarus Paradox*, New York: Harper.

29. M. W. Peng & P. Heath, 1996, The growth of the firm in planned economies in transition: Institutions, organizations, and strategic choice, *AMR*, 21 (2): 492–528.

30. R. Amit & C. Zott, 2001, Value creation in e-business, *SMJ*, 22: 493–520; P. Drucker, 1985, *Innovation and Entrepreneurship*, New York: Harper; R. D. Ireland, M. Hitt, M. Camp, & D. Sexton, 2001, Integrating entrepreneurship actions and strategic management actions to create firm wealth, *AME*, 15: 49–63; G. Lumpkin & G. Dess, 1996, Clarifying the entrepreneurial orientation construct and linking it to performance, *AMR*, 21: 135–172.

31. H. Lee, K. Smith, C. Grimm, & A. Schomburg, 2000, Timing, order, and durability of new product advantages with imitation, *SMJ*, 21: 23–30; H. Li & K. Atuahene-Gima, 2001, Product innovation strategy and the performance of new technology ventures in China, *AMJ*, 44: 1123–1134; T. Man, T. Lau, & K. Chan, 2002, The competitiveness of small and medium enterprises, *JBV*,

17: 123–142; P. Reynolds, 1997, New and small firms in expanding markets, *SBE,* 9: 79–84; P. Roberts, 1999, Product innovation, product-market competition, and persistent profitability, *SMJ,* 20: 655–670.

32. Z. Acs & D. Audretsch, 1988, Innovation in large and small firms, *AER,* 78: 678–690; N. Carter, T. Stearns, P. Reynolds, & B. Miller, 1994, New venture strategies, *SMJ,* 15: 21–41; S. Zahra & W. Bogner, 1999, Technology strategy and software new ventures' performance, *JBV,* 15: 135–173.

33. R. Arend, 1999, Emergence of entrepreneurs following exogenous technological change, *SMJ,* 20: 31–47; C. Christensen, 1997, *The Innovator's Dilemma,* Boston: Harvard Business School Press; G. Hamel, 2000, *Leading the Revolution,* Boston: Harvard Business School Press.

34. C. Brush, P. Greene, & M. Hart, 2001, From initial idea to unique advantage *AME,* 15: 64–78.

35. M. Guillen, 2001, *The Limits of Convergence* (p. 117), Princeton, NJ: Princeton University Press.

36. Z. Acs & D. Audretsch, 1990, *Innovation and Small Firms,* Cambridge, MA: MIT Press; S. Graves & N. Langowitz, 1993, Innovative productivity and returns to scale in the pharmaceutical industry, *SMJ,* 14: 593–605; G. Qian & L. Li, 2003, Profitability of small- and medium-sized enterprises in high-technology industries, *SMJ,* 24: 881–887.

37. S. Birley, 1985, The role of networks in the entrepreneurial process, *JBV,* 1: 107–117; P. Dubini & H. Aldrich, 1991, Personal and extended networks are central to the entrepreneurial process, *JBV,* 6: 305–313; A. Larson, 1992, Network dyads in entrepreneurial settings, *ASQ,* 37: 76–104; D. Lee & E. Tsang, 2001, The effects of entrepreneurial personality, background, and network activities on venture growth, *JMS,* 38: 583–602; H. Hoang & B. Antonic, 2003, Network-based research in entrepreneurship, *JBV,* 18: 165–187.

38. D. Ahlstrom & G. Bruton, 2001, Learning from successful local private firms in China: Establishing legitimacy, *AME,* 15: 72–83; H. Aldrich & C. M. Fiol, 1994, Fools rush in? The institutional context of industry creation, *AMR,* 19: 645–670; A. Henderson, 1999, Firm strategy and age dependence, *ASQ,* 44: 281–314; S. Human & K. Provan, 2000, Legitimacy building in the evolution of small-firm multilateral networks, *ASQ,* 45: 327–365; M. Lounsbury & M. Glynn, 2001, Cultural entrepreneurship, *SMJ,* 22: 545–564; C. Oliver, 1990, Determinants of interorganizational relationships, *AMR,* 15: 241–265; M. Zimmerman & G. Zeitz, 2002, Beyond survival: Achieving new venture growth by building legitimacy, *AMR,* 27: 414–431.

39. S. Alvarez & J. Barney, 2001, How entrepreneurial firms can benefit from alliances with large partners (p. 139), *Academy of Management Executive,* 15: 139–148.

40. D. Deeds & C. Hill, 1998, An examination of opportunistic action within research alliances, *JBV,* 14: 141–163.

41. M. Granovetter, 1973, The strength of weak ties, *AJS,* 78: 1360–1380.

42. N. Nicolaou & S. Birley, 2003, Social networks in organizational emergence, *MS,* 49: 1702–1725.

43. M. W. Peng & Y. Luo, 2000, Managerial ties and firm performance in a transition economy: The nature of a micro-macro link, *AMJ,* 43: 486–501.

44. B. Batjargal, 2003, Social capital and entrepreneurial performance in Russia, *OSt,* 24: 535–556; J. Baum, T. Calabrese, & B. Silverman, 2000, Don't go it alone: Alliance network composition and start-ups' performance in Canadian biotechnology, *SMJ,* 21: 267–294; J. Florin, M. Lubatkin, & W. Schulze, 2003, A social capital model of high-growth ventures, *AMJ,* 46: 374–384; R. Gulati, N. Nohria, & A. Zaheer, 2000, Strategic networks, *SMJ,* 21: 203–215; C. Lee, K. Lee, & H. Pennings, 2001, Internal capabilities, external networks, and performance, *SMJ,* 22: 615–640; Peng & Luo, 2000, Managerial ties and firm performance; M. Sarkar, R. Echsmbadi, & J. Harrison, 2001, Alliance entrepreneurship and firm market performance, *SMJ,* 22: 701–711.

45. R. Burt, 1997, The contingent value of social capital (p. 342), *ASQ,* 42: 339–365.

46. J. Hall & C. Hofer, 1993, Venture capitalists' decision criteria in venture evaluation, *JBV,* 8: 25–42; A. Zacharakis & G. D. Meyer, 1998, A lack of insight: Do venture capitalists really understand their decision process? *JBV,* 13: 57–76.

47. D. Cable & S. Shane, 1997, A prisoners' dilemma approach to entrepreneur-venture capitalist relationship, *AMR,* 22: 142–176; D. Harrison, M. Dibben, & C. Mason, 1997, The role of trust in the informal investors' investment decision, *ETP,* 21: 63–81.

48. W. Bygrave & J. Timmons, 1992, *Venture Capital at the Crossroads,* Boston: Harvard Business School Press; J.

Lerner, 1995, Venture capitalists and the oversight of private firms, *JF,* 50: 301–318.

49. G. Bruton, V. Fried, & R. Hisrich, 1997, Venture capitalists and CEO dismissal, *ETP,* 21: 41–54; A. Ranft & H. O'Neill, 2001, Board composition and high-flying founders, *AME,* 15: 126–138; J. Rosenstein, A. Bruno, W. Bygrave, & N. Taylor, 1993, The CEO, venture capitalists, and the board, *JBV,* 8: 99–113; H. Sapienza & A. Gupta, 1994, Impact of agency risks and task uncertainty on venture capitalist-CEO interaction, *AMJ,* 37: 1618–1632.

50. Aldrich, 1999, *Organizations Evolving* (p. 83); T. Bates, 1997, Financing small business creation: The case of Chinese and Korean immigrant entrepreneurs, *JBV,* 12: 109–124.

51. G. Bruton & D. Ahlstrom, 2003, An institutional view of China's venture capital industry, *JBV,* 18: 233–59.

52. C. Zimmer & H. Aldrich, 1987, Resource mobilization through ethnic networks, *SP,* 30: 422–455.

53. I. Arikan, 2003, How should an entrepreneurial firm be sold? Auctions versus negotiations, Working paper, Fisher College of Business, The Ohio State University.

54. *Economist,* 2003, China's Amazon, August 23: 52–53.

55. R. Larsson, K. Brousseau, M. Driver, M. Holmqvist, & V. Tarnovskaya, 2003, International growth through cooperation (p. 15), *AME,* 17 (1): 7–21.

56. *http://www.aibworld.org* (accessed October 14, 2003).

57. S. Claessens & L. Klapper, 2002, Bankruptcy around the world, Working paper 2865, The World Bank.

58. J. Gimeno, T. Folta, A. Cooper, & C. Woo, 1997, Survival of the fittest? *ASQ,* 42: 750–783.

59. G. Knight & S. T. Cavusgil, 2004, Innovation, organizational capabilities, and the born-global firm, *JIBS,* 35: 124–141; T. Madsen & P. Servais, 1997, The internationalization of born globals, *IBR,* 6: 561–583; B. Oviatt & P. McDougall, 1994, Toward a theory of international new ventures, *JIBS,* 25: 45–64.

60. A. Zacharakis, 1998, Entrepreneurial entry into foreign markets: A transaction cost perspective, *ETP,* spring: 23–39.

61. M. W. Peng, C. Hill, & D. Wang, 2000, Schumpeterian dynamics versus Williamsonian considerations: A test of export intermediary performance, *JMS,* 37 (2): 167–184.

62. R. Chen & M. Martin, 2001, Foreign expansion of small firms, *JBV,* 16: 557–574.

63. J. Combs & D. Ketchen, 1999, Can capital scarcity help agency theory explain franchising? *AMJ,* 42: 196–207; J. Combs & D. Ketchen, 2003, Why do firms use franchising as an entrepreneurial strategy? *JM,* 29: 443–465; S. Michaels, 2000, Investments to create bargaining power, *SMJ,* 21: 497–515; S. Shane, 1996, Hybrid organizational arrangements and their implications for firm growth and survival, *AMJ,* 39: 216–234; O. Sorenson & J. Sorensen, 2001, Finding the right mix, *SMJ,* 22: 713–724.

64. Z. Acs & L. Preston, 1997, Small- and medium-sized enterprises, technology, and globalization, *SBE,* 9: 1–6; H. Boter & C. Holmquist, 1996, Industry characteristics and internationalization processes in small firms, *JBV,* 11: 471–487; S. Preece, G. Miles, & M. Baetz, 1998, Explaining the international intensity and global diversity of early-state technology-based firms, *JBV,* 14: 259–281.

65. M. Jones, 2001, First steps in internationalization, *JIM,* 7: 191–210; T. Kohn, 1997, Small firms as international players, *SBE,* 9: 45–51; J. Lu & P. Beamish, 2001, The internationalization and performance of SMEs, *SMJ,* 22: 565–586; S. Zahra, R. D. Ireland, & M. Hitt, 2000, International expansion by new venture firms, *AMJ,* 43: 925–950.

66. J. Johanson & J. Vahlne, 1977, The internationalization process of the firm, *JIBS,* 4: 20–29; L. Li, D. Li, & T. Dalgic, 2004, Internationalization process of small and medium-sized enterprises, *MIR,* 44: 93–116.

67. P. McDougall, S. Shane, & B. Oviatt, 1994, Explaining the formation of international new ventures, *JBV,* 9: 469–487.

68. S. Kotha, V. Rindova, & F. Rothaermel, 2001, Assets and actions: Firm-specific factors in the internationalization of U.S. Internet firms, *JIBS,* 32: 769–791; J. Tiessen, R. Wright, & I. Turner, 2001, A model of e-commerce use by internationalizing SMEs, *JIM,* 7: 211–233.

69. A. Portes, W. Haller, & L. Guarnizo, 2002, Transnational entrepreneurs: An alternative form of immigrant economic adaptation, *ASR,* 67: 278–298; A. B. Reuber & E. Fischer, 1997, The influence of the management team's international experience on the internationalization behaviors of SMEs, *JIBS,* 28: 807–825; P. Westhead, M. Wright, & D. Ucbasaran, 2001, The internationalization of new and small firms, *JBV,* 16: 333–358.

70. F. Root, 1994, *Entry Strategies for International Markets* (p. 102), Lexington, MA: Lexington Books.

71. M. W. Peng & A. York, 2001, Behind intermediary performance in export trade: Transactions, agents, and resources, *JIBS,* 32: 327–346; H. Trabold, 2002, Export intermediation: An empirical test of Peng and Ilinitch, *JIBS,* 33: 327–344.

72. M. W. Peng & A. Y. Ilinitch, 1998, Export intermediary firms: A note on export development research, *JIBS,* 29: 609–620.

73. J. Bell, R. McNaughton, & S. Young, 2001, "Born-again global" firms (p. 184), *JIM,* 7: 173–189.

74. R. Tasker, 2002, Pepperoni power, *FEER,* November 14: 59–60.

75. N. Dawar & T. Frost, 1999, Competing with giants, *HBR,* March-April: 119–129; D. Lavie & A. Fiegenbaum, 2000, The strategic reaction of domestic firms to MNC dominance, *LRP,* 33: 651–72.

76. Z. Acs, R. Morck, & B. Yeung, 201, Entrepreneurship, globalization, and public policy, *JIM,* 7: 235–251.

77. L. Busenitz, G. P. West, D. Shepherd, T. Nelson, G. Chandler, & A. Zacharakis, 2003, Entrepreneurship research in emergence: Past trends and future directions, *JM,* 29: 285–308; P. Phan & M. Foo, 2004, Technological entrepreneurship in emerging regions, *JBV,* 19: 1–5.

78. R. Brenner, 1987, National policy and entrepreneurship (p. 95), *JBV,* 2: 95–101; C. McClelland, 1967, *The Achieving Society,* New York: Free Press.

79. D. Sexton, 2001, Wayne Huizenga: Entrepreneur and wealth creator, *AME,* 15: 40–48; P. Westhead & M. Wright, 1998, Novice, portfolio, and serial founders, *JBV,* 13: 173–204.

80. M. Low & I. MacMillan, 1988, Entrepreneurship, *JM,* 14: 119–135.

81. L. Busenitz, C. Gomez, & J. Spencer, 2000, Country institutional profiles, *AMJ,* 43: 994–1003; A. Chua, 2004, *World on Fire,* New York: Anchor Books; R. Mitchell, B. Smith, K. Seawright, & E. Morse, 2000, Cross-cultural cognitions and the venture creation decision, *AMJ,* 43: 974–993; J. Oxley & B. Yeung, 2001, E-commerce readiness: Institutional environment and international competitiveness, *JIBS,* 32: 705–724; H. K. Steensma, L. Marino, M. Weaver, & P. Hickson, 2000, The influence of national culture on the formation of technology alliances by entrepreneurial firms, *AMJ,* 43: 951–973; H. Yeung, 2002, Entrepreneurship in international business, *APJM,* 19: 29–61.

82. L. Busenitz & C. Lau, 1997, A cross-cultural cognitive model of new venture creation, *ETP,* summer: 25–39; Peng, 2001, How entrepreneurs create wealth in transition economies; J. Tan, 2002, Culture, nation, and entrepreneurial strategic orientations, *ETP,* summer: 95–111; E. Tsang, 1994, Threats and opportunities faced by private businesses in China, *JBV,* 9: 451–468.

83. A. Cooper & W. Dunkelberg, 1987, Entrepreneurial research: Old questions, new answers, and methodological issues, *AJSB,* 11: 1–20.

84. Quoted in J. Kaplan, 2003, *Patterns of Entrepreneurship* (p. 11), New York: Wiley.

85. V. Govindarajan & A. Gupta, 2001, *The Quest for Global Dominance,* San Francisco: Jossey-Bass.

86. K. Kling & I. Goteman, 2003, IKEA CEO Anders Dahlvig on international growth, *AME,* 17: 31–45.

87. E. Autio, H. Sapienza, & J. Almeida, 2000, Effects of age at entry, knowledge intensity, and imitability in international growth, *AMJ,* 43: 909–924.

88. P. Liesch & G. Knight, 1999, Information internationalization and hurdle rates in small and medium enterprise internationalization, *JIBS,* 30: 383–394.

89. P. McDougall & B. Oviatt, 1996, New venture internationalization, strategic change, and performance, *JBV,* 11: 23–40.

90. M. Lyles, T. Saxton, & K. Watson, 2004, Venture survival in a transition economy, *JM,* 30: 351–373.

91. S. Rangan & R. Adner, 2001, Profits and the Internet (pp. 49–50), *SMR,* summer: 44–53

92. Peng, Hill, & Wang, 2000, Schumpeterian dynamics versus Williamsonian considerations.

93. This section draws heavily from S.-H. Lee, M. W. Peng, & J. Barney, 2005, Bankruptcy law and entrepreneurship development: A real options perspective, *AMR* (in press).

94. R. McGrath, 1999, Falling forward: Real options reasoning and entrepreneurial failure, *AMR,* 24: 13–30.

95. Lee, Peng, & Barney, 2004, Bankruptcy law.

96. D. Shepherd, 2003, Learning from business failure, *AMR,* 28: 318–328.

97. J. Schumpeter, 1942, *Capitalism, Socialism, and Democracy,* New York: Harper.

Entering Foreign Markets

Outline

- Why go abroad?
- A comprehensive model of foreign market entries
- Where to enter?
- When to enter?
- How to enter?
- Debates and extensions
- Implications for strategists

Opening Case: Bringing Starbucks Coffee to the World

Maintaining a 20 percent annual sales growth since going public in 1992, Starbucks (http://www.starbucks.com) now has more than 5,000 stores across the United States. However, even in such a large market, further growth will be difficult, leading to jokes such as "A new Starbucks opens in the restroom of an existing Starbucks." To maintain the momentum, overseas expansion is a must. In 1996, Starbucks entered its first overseas market, Japan. In 2000, founder and chairman Howard Schultz stepped down as CEO and named himself "chief global strategist." At present, Starbucks operates more than 1,500 stores in thirty-one countries outside of North America. Relative to its home market, Starbucks believes that there is plenty of room to grow internationally. However, these overseas stores, which account for 23 percent of its stores and yet only 9 percent of sales, are a net money loser. In 2003, Starbucks closed 6 stores in Israel and downsized its overseas expansion by 50 stores to 400 a year.

A number of factors play a part in the difficulty Starbucks is having overseas. First, while Starbucks is relatively more successful in Asia, it has met stronger resistance in Europe. The Starbucks coffee house concept itself, in fact, was inspired by its European origin, which was brought back by Schultz after a trip to Italy. Many European café-goers view Starbucks as an overpriced imitation of the real thing. In London, for instance, a Starbucks tall latte sells for $2.93, while a rival, Caffe Nero (http://www.caffenero.com), sells the same drink for $2.12. This is not to say that Starbucks' future is hopeless in Europe. In Austria, for example, it has attracted a younger clientele, who consider Starbucks trendy and hip. But overall, Europe has been a tougher nut to crack.

Second, Starbucks' entry timing has been an issue. In the United States, Starbucks is lucky in that as a first mover, it has no nationwide competitor. However, in many countries strong local rivals are already entrenched, thus forcing Starbucks to be a late mover with all its trappings. For example, in Great Britain, an American couple originally from Seattle established a thriving chain called Seattle Coffee with sixty retail stores. Instead of challenging it head-on, Starbucks acquired the chain for $84 million.

Finally, how Starbucks enters foreign markets contributes to its problems overseas. In the United States, all stores are company owned. Although adding more stores in one location cannibalizes each other's sales, the firm is still maximizing total revenue. However, Starbucks makes less money on each overseas store because most of them are operated with local partners (through franchising or joint venture deals). For example, it relies on a 50/50 joint venture (JV) with Taiwan's Uni-President (http://www.starbucks.com.tw) to expand in Taiwan and China. While these shared entry modes make it easier to open *foreign markets, they reduce Starbucks' share to only 20 to 50 percent of total profits. Also, relationships with foreign partners are not always cozy. In South Korea, Starbucks initially franchised its format to ESCO in 1999. Although ESCO soon opened ten stores, Starbucks felt ESCO was not aggressive enough in growing the chain. In 2001, it formed a JV with Shinsegae* (http://www.shinsegae.com), *the parent company of ESCO, to gain greater control over the growth strategy. In Thailand, Starbucks spent $12 million to acquire its franchisee, Coffee Partners, which had failed to open twenty stores as initially agreed upon. Likewise, Starbucks bought out its partner, Bon Appetit* (http://www.bon-appetit.ch), *in its troubled Swiss and Austrian stores. Overall, Starbucks has not yet replicated its winning formula outside the home market. Turning its bitter brew overseas to sweet profits, as they say at Starbucks, has been a double tall order so far.*

Sources: Based on (1) Business Week, 2003, Starbucks, December 8: 11; (2) C. Hill, 2003, International Business, 4th ed. (pp. 203–204), Chicago: Irwin McGraw-Hill; (3) S. Holmes, 2002, Planet Starbucks, Business Week, September 9: 99–110; (4) S. Holmes, 2003, For Starbucks, there's no place like home, Business Week, June 9: 48.

How do numerous companies such as Starbucks enter foreign markets? Why do they enter certain countries, but not others? Why do some of their entry strategies (such as licensing, joint ventures, and acquisitions) change over time? These are some of the key questions we address in this chapter. Entering foreign markets probably represents one of the most important strategy topics in international business; otherwise, there would only be domestic business to speak of. While Chapter 5 discussed how smaller, entrepreneurial firms internationalize, this chapter pays more attention to larger, multinational enterprises (MNEs). This chapter first focuses on the rationale behind going abroad, and then introduces a comprehensive model of the "2W1H" factors concerning (1) *where* to enter, (2) *when* to enter, and (3) *how* to enter. As before, debates and implications follow.

WHY GO ABROAD?

This section focuses on the motivation of venturing abroad. It starts by introducing the concept of the liability of foreignness, which has to be overcome. Then it outlines a simple model of the propensity to internationalize among four types of firms.

Overcoming the Liability of Foreignness

Why go abroad? When answering this question, typical reasons include (1) to reach larger economies of scale by selling to more customers in other countries, (2) to reduce the risk of overdependence on one country by spreading sales in multiple countries, and (3) to replicate the success at home in new settings. However, succeeding in an unfamiliar environment is not easy. Foreign firms must overcome a **liability of foreignness,** which is the *inherent* disadvantage foreign firms experience in host countries because of their nonnative status.[1] This liability is manifested in at least two dimensions. First, numerous differences exist in formal and informal institutions that govern the rules of the game in different countries (such as regulatory, language, and cultural differences). While local firms are already well versed in these rules, foreign firms have to learn them quickly. Failure to learn these rules may cost foreign firms dearly. Mitsubishi Motors, for example, paid a huge cost ($34 million) in 1998 to settle sexual harassment charges in its American plant, which is governed by a different set of formal legal and regulatory standards and informal norms relative to those in Japan.

Second, although customers in this age of globalization *supposedly* no longer discriminate against foreign firms, the reality is that foreign firms are still often discriminated against, sometimes formally and other times informally. For example, in government procurement, most governments prefer to "buy national" (such as "Buy American"). The discrimination against foreign firms is less with consumer products, but it is still far from disappearing. Even *after* formal discriminatory policies imposed by their governments were removed, for years individual consumers in Japan and Europe informally resisted buying American rice and beef, which were suspected (although never proven) to contain long-term health hazards because of genetic modification.

Against such significant odds, foreign firms primarily deploy overwhelming resources and capabilities that, after offsetting the liability of foreignness, still offer some competitive advantage.[2] These resources and capabilities can be in three forms. First, superior technologies help tackle overseas markets. In many countries, photocopying is the same as "Xeroxing," which explains a great deal of Xerox's global success. Australian firm INCAT's world-leading wave-piercing technology has pierced through the protective walls of the US military, which normally does not even *consider* buying weaponry from non-US firms (see Strategy in Action 6.1 on next page). Second, superior organizational and marketing capabilities may overcome some liability of foreignness. For instance, Manchester United, a highly successful English soccer team, is trying to enter the intensely competitive American professional sports market by leveraging both its star power and marketing muscles (see Strategy in Action 6.2 on next page). Finally, superior knowledge about the institutional intricacies in various countries contributes to overseas success.[3] For example, in the early 1980s when most MNEs were clueless about China, Volkswagen entered China by leveraging its knowledge of how centrally planned economies worked based on the firm's experience in Eastern Europe. For two decades, Volkswagen has remained the "king of the road" in China. In 2004, one-third of Volkswagen's total corporate profits came from China (see Integrative Case 1.3).

Understanding the Propensity to Internationalize

Despite recent preaching by some gurus that every firm should go abroad, not every firm is ready for it. Prematurely venturing overseas may be detrimental to the firm's overall performance, especially for smaller firms whose margin for error is very small.[4] Therefore, strategists need to carefully decide whether doing business abroad is warranted for their particular firms. So what motivates some firms to go abroad while others are happily staying at home?

STRATEGY IN ACTION 6.1. *A Warship Named* Joint Venture

With a military budget larger than that of the next five powers combined, the United States is the world's largest defense market. For non-US firms, however, this is also the toughest nut to crack because the US military is famously protective of US firms. Remarkably, one Australian shipbuilder, INCAT (*http://www.incat.com.au*), has overcome substantial liability of foreignness by whetting the appetite of *all* branches of the US military (except the Air Force). Its secret? A world-leading technology in high-speed wave-piercing catamarans that has given INCAT approximately 50 percent global market share of high-speed commercial ferries. With relatively slight modifications, this technology can be adapted for military sealift and amphibious operations. In 2001, INCAT produced a 96-meter ship, appropriately named *Joint Venture* (HSV-X1), as an evaluation platform for the joint forces of the US Navy, Marine Corps,

Army, and Coast Guard. In 2003, *Joint Venture* successfully acted as a command, control, and staging platform for the special operations forces that took the Iraqi port of Umm Qasr. Its sister ship, *Spearhead* (TSV-1X), left Australia and sailed straight to the Persian Gulf in 2002. *Spearhead* also excelled in Iraq in 2003. The overwhelming interest from US forces led INCAT to set up a joint venture with Bollinger (*http://www.bollingershipyards.com*), a builder of US Navy and Coast Guard patrol boats—Bollinger/INCAT USA (*http://www.bollingerincatusa.com*)—to capitalize on such opportunities.

Sources: Based on (1) http://www.bollinger-incatusa.com *and (2)* http://www.incat.com.au *(both accessed July 15, 2004). See also Integrative Case 2.3,* The INCAT-AFAI Joint Venture: Technology Transfer with a Loose Contract.

STRATEGY IN ACTION 6.2. *Manchester United Charges into America*

Manchester United (*http://www.manutd.com*), the most popular sports team in the world with a following of 53 million fans around the globe, is trying to enter America. Man U fosters a global business that spreads far beyond soccer. In 2002, the publicly traded club produced $50 million profits on $230 million revenues. The primary revenues come from ticket sales and lucrative TV deals. In addition, Man U sells everything from coffee mugs to bed sheets. Man U runs its own subscription television service called Manu.TV that airs six hours a day, seven days a week. The club also sells credit cards, home mortgages, consumer loans, and insurance policies. There is even a major motion picture, *Bend It Like Beckham,* about a girl who idolized the team's (former) star, David Beckham (who joined a Spanish team in 2003).

Coming to America, Man U's goals are to penetrate the $15 billion-a-year professional sports market. Currently, four million Man U fans reside in the United States and the team's four-match US promotion tour in the summer of 2003 sold out. However, the club needs

millions more fans. Although 28 million Americans play soccer, the US women's team dominates the world, and the US men's team reached the quarterfinals of the 2002 World Cup, soccer struggles to gain a foothold in the crowded American sports market. Despite steady progress, Major League Soccer continues to lose money. The United States remains one of the world's last untapped soccer markets. Other than a few Canadian teams, no foreign sports team—in soccer or other sports—has successfully penetrated the US market. If any foreign team could make a successful run in America, it seems that Man U could be it. For Man U, which is quickly approaching market saturation in Europe and Asia, the million-dollar question is: Will Man U score in America?

Sources: This case was written by Tara Wedwaldt (Fisher College of Business, The Ohio State University) under the supervision of Professor Mike W. Peng. It is based on (1) Business Week, *2003, Bend it like— somebody else, August 11: 10; (2)* Economist, *2003, Branded as Beckham, July 5: 56–57; (3) S. Holmes, 2003, Can Man U score in America?* Business Week, *June 23: 108–109. Reprinted by permission of the author.*

FIGURE 6.1   Firm Size, Domestic Market Size, and Propensity to Internationalize

Size of the Firm

Size of the Domestic Market	(Cell 1) Enthusiastic internationalizer	(Cell 2) Follower internationalizer	*Small Domestic Market*
	(Cell 3) Slow internationalizer	(Cell 4) Occasional internationalizer	*Large Domestic Market*
	Large Firm	*Small Firm*	

At the risk of oversimplification, we can identify two underlying factors, (1) the size of the firm and (2) the size of the domestic market, which lead to a 2×2 framework (Figure 6.1). In Cell 1, large firms in a small domestic market are likely to be very **enthusiastic internationalizers,** because they can quickly exhaust opportunities in a small country. Consider ABB of Switzerland, which specializes in large power-generation equipment (and many other products). The demand for such equipment in Switzerland is rather limited. As a result, 97 percent of ABB's sales, 95 percent of its assets, and 95 percent of its employees are outside of Switzerland, making ABB the most internationalized firm according to the United Nations' *World Investment Report.*[5]

In Cell 2, many small firms in a small domestic market are labeled **follower internationalizers,** because they often follow their larger counterparts abroad as suppliers.[6] Even small firms that do not directly supply large firms may similarly venture abroad because of the inherently limited size of the domestic market. A considerable number of small firms from small countries such as Austria, Finland, Ireland, Hong Kong, New Zealand, Singapore, and Taiwan are active overseas.

In Cell 3, large firms in a large domestic market are labeled **slow internationalizers,** because their overseas activities are usually (but not always) slower than those of enthusiastic internationalizers in Cell 1. For instance, Wal-Mart started to enter foreign markets (first in Mexico in 1991) only after largely exhausting domestic opportunities. Wal-Mart's internationalization is considered "slow" when compared with its two global competitors, Carrefour of France and Metro of Germany, which are both based in relatively smaller domestic economies. (On the other hand, Wal-Mart's degree of internationalization clearly exceeds that of its three large US competitors, Kmart, J. C. Penny, and Sears.[7])

Finally, as shown in Cell 4, most small firms in a large domestic market confront a "double whammy" on the road to internationalization because of their relatively poor resource base and the limited size of their domestic market. For example, many small firms in the United States do not feel compelled to go abroad in the absence of a strong nationwide market position. To the extent that small firms engage in some overseas sales, the deals are likely to be initiated by unsolicited foreign buyers, such as those at All A Cart (see Opening Case in Chapter 5). Overall, small firms in a large domestic market can be labeled **occasional internationalizers** (that is, if they have any international business at all).

Of course, this framework presents some crude generalizations and cannot capture patterns outside these four cells. For example, as discussed in Chapter 5, some small firms (Cells 2 and 4) are born global. In addition, firms do not have to stay in one cell. For instance, Starbucks (see Opening Case) started in Cell 4 with no internationalization and moved to Cell 3 as it became larger. These exceptions and migrations notwithstanding, the framework in Figure 6.1 does depict the basic propensity to internationalize among various types of firms in most cases.

A COMPREHENSIVE MODEL OF FOREIGN MARKET ENTRIES

Assuming the decision to internationalize is a "go," strategists must make a series of decisions regarding the location, timing, and mode of entry, collectively known as the *where, when,* and *how* (2W1H) aspects, respectively. Underlying each decision is a set of strategic considerations drawn from the three leading perspectives discussed earlier, which form a comprehensive model (Figure 6.2).

Industry-Based Considerations

These considerations are primarily drawn from the five forces framework first introduced in Chapter 2. First, rivalry among established firms may prompt certain moves. Firms, especially those in oligopolistic industries, often match each other in foreign entries.[8] If Komatsu and Federal Express enter a new country—let's say Afghanistan—Caterpillar and DHL, respectively, probably would feel compelled to follow. Sometimes, firms may enter foreign markets to retaliate. For example, Texas Instrument (TI) entered Japan not to make money, but to *lose* money. The reason was that TI faced the low price Japanese challenge in many markets, whereas rivals such as NEC and Toshiba were able to charge high prices in Japan and use domestic profits to cross-subsidize their overseas expansion. By entering Japan and slashing prices there, TI retaliated by incurring a loss. This forced the Japanese firms to defend their profit sanctuary at home, where they had more to lose.

Second, the higher the entry barriers, the more intensely firms will attempt to compete abroad. A firm's strong presence in an overseas market in itself can be seen as a major entry barrier for other firms contemplating entry into the same country. By tapping into wider and bigger markets, international sales can increase scale economies and deter entry. For instance, it would be mind-boggling to imagine how high the costs of Boeing and Airbus aircraft would be in the absence of international sales. Research and development (R&D) acts as another entry barrier. Consider Big Pharma (see Opening Case in Chapter 4). Relative to rivals operating in a single

FIGURE 6.2   **A Comprehensive Model of Foreign Market Entries**

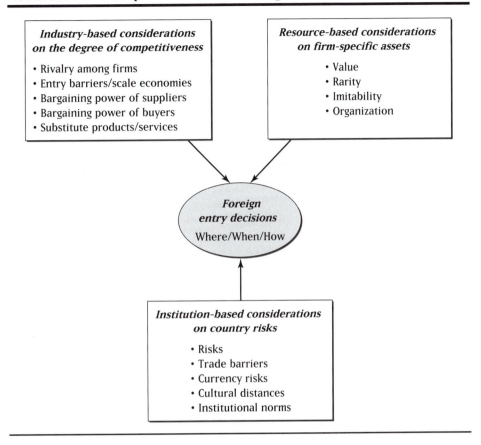

country, Big Pharma can afford to develop more costly, but potentially more lucrative, drugs primarily because they can spread expensive R&D costs on a worldwide—as opposed to a national—basis. Heavy marketing and advertising centered on distinctive product differentiation, ranging from the "just do it" spirit of Nike to the "ultimate driving machine" of BMW, also serves as an entry barrier. Many firms are often motivated to leverage such brand equity around the world.

Third, the bargaining power of suppliers may prompt certain foreign market entries, often called **backward vertical integration** because they involve multiple stages of the value chain (see Chapter 3). Many extractive industries feature extensive backward integration overseas (such as bauxite mining), in order to provide a steady supply of raw materials to late stage production (such as aluminum smelting). Because natural resources are not always found in politically stable countries, many firms have no choice but to enter politically uncertain countries. Remember the 1998 James Bond movie, *The World Is Not Enough*? The storyline features a Caspian Sea oil intrigue involving Western MNEs, former Soviet republics, and Middle Eastern countries, and the plot thickens with an attempted nuclear explosion in Istanbul, Turkey. While the movie is fictitious, the real world of oil exploration is perhaps no less risky (or exciting). At present, Western oil exploration vessels are surveying the South China Sea. Each boat is escorted by naval warships from China, Indonesia, Malaysia, the Philippines, and Vietnam—all armed to the teeth with real guns and missiles aimed at each other (!). Why do these Western MNEs go through such trouble to secure oil supply? Evidently, the costs of such trouble are still less than the costs of having to deal with strong, unfriendly suppliers such as OPEC.

Fourth, the bargaining power of buyers may lead to certain foreign market entries, often called **forward vertical integration.** Sony, for example, entered downstream activities abroad by acquiring Columbia Pictures and Sony Music. Despite the huge financial costs, under certain circumstances the benefits outweigh the costs.

Finally, the market potential of substitute products may encourage firms to bring them abroad. If as promised, the third-generation (3G) wireless technology, in addition to being a cell phone, can substitute for a videoconferencing system, a camera, a camcorder, an e-mail system, and a game machine, people in a variety of countries may demand it. Based on this belief, Hutchison Whampoa has embarked on an ambitious, but risky, campaign to bring 3G to nine countries (see Closing Case).

Overall, how an industry is structured and how its five forces are played out significantly affect foreign entry decisions.[9] Next, we examine the influence of resource-based considerations.

Resource-Based Considerations

The VRIO framework introduced in Chapter 3 sheds considerable light on entry decisions by focusing on their *v*alue, *r*arity, *i*mitability, and *o*rganization aspects (Figure 6.2).[10] First, the value of firm-specific resources and capabilities plays a key role behind decisions to internationalize. Often the superb value of firm-specific assets allows foreign entrants to overcome the liability of foreignness. Therefore, the higher the value of these assets (especially intangible assets such as brands, know-how, and software), the more likely firms will aggressively leverage them overseas.[11] INCAT's highly valuable wave-piercing technology serves as a case in point (see Strategy in Action 6.1).

Second, the rarity of firm-specific assets encourages firms that possess them to leverage such assets overseas. Patents, brands, and trademarks legally protect the rarity of certain product features. Not surprisingly, patented and branded products, such as cars, cigarettes, and CDs, are often aggressively marketed overseas.[12] However, here is a paradox: Given the uneven protection of intellectual property rights, the more countries these products are sold in (becoming less rare), the more likely counterfeits will pop up somewhere around the globe (see Closing Case in Chapter 4). The question of rarity, therefore, directly leads to the next issue of imitability.

Third, if firms are concerned that their imitable assets might be expropriated in certain countries, they may choose *not* to enter. In other words, the **transaction costs** may be too high primarily because of **dissemination risks,** defined as the risks associated with the unauthorized diffusion of firm-specific assets. If a foreign company grants a license to a local firm to manufacture or market a product, "it runs the risk of the licensee, or an employee of the licensee, disseminating the know-how or using it for purposes other than those originally intended."[13] Although both sides *in* *theory* can enter into a comprehensive contract to specify their rights and obligations, *in practice,* given the inherent uncertainties and changes in the real world, it is impossible to draw up a truly comprehensive contract that foresees every possible contingency. There are always some possible, unanticipated contingencies that may lead to opportunistic behavior against which the foreign firm has little recourse.[14] A firm's worst nightmare is to nurture a competitor, as Pizza Hut found out in Thailand. Pizza Hut's long-time franchise operator in Thailand disseminated its know-how and established a direct competitor, simply called The Pizza Company, which recently controlled 70 percent of the market in Thailand.[15]

Finally, organizing firm-specific resources and capabilities as a *bundle* favors firms with strong complementary assets integrated as a system and encourages them to use these assets overseas. Many MNEs are organized in a way that protects them against entry and favors them as entrants into other markets—consider the near total vertical integration at ExxonMobil and BP, which often allows them to win oil and gas exploration contracts in various countries.

In summary, the resource-based view suggests that an important set of considerations underpin entry decisions. In the case of imitability and dissemination risk, these issues are obviously related to property rights protection, which leads to the next topic.

Institution-Based Considerations

Chapter 4 already illustrated a number of *informal* institutional differences such as cultural differences, so here the focus is on the three major *formal* institutional constraints confronting foreign entrants: (1) regulatory risks, (2) trade barriers, and (3) currency risks.

Regulatory Risks

These risks are associated with unfavorable government policies. Some governments may demand that foreign entrants share technology with local firms, in effect, *increasing* the dissemination risk. Even as a WTO member, the Chinese government continues its historical practice of only approving joint ventures for foreign automakers and banning foreign firms from setting up wholly-owned subsidiaries in the automobile industry (see Integrative Case 1.3). The government's openly proclaimed goal has been to "encourage" local automakers to learn from their foreign partners.

Although governments, as regulators, set the formal rules of the game governing competition, they sometimes directly enter such competition. These governments, thus, are both referees and players in the same game in which foreign entrants attempt to play. A well-known phenomenon is the **obsolescing bargain,** referring to the deals struck by MNEs and host governments, which change their requirements *after* the entry of MNEs.[16] The obsolescing bargain typically unfolds in three rounds. In Round One, the MNE and the government negotiate a deal. The MNE usually is not willing to enter without some reasonable government assurance concerning property rights, earnings, and even incentives (such as tax holidays). In Round Two, the MNE enters and, if all goes well, earns profits that may become visible to politicians, journalists, and envious domestic firms. In Round Three, the government, often pressured by domestic political groups, may demand renegotiations of the deal that seems to yield "excessive" profits to the foreign firm (the foreign firm, of course, regards these as "fair" and "normal" profits). The previous deal, therefore, becomes obsolete. The government's tactics include removing incentives, demanding a higher share of profits and taxes, and even confiscating foreign assets—in other words, **expropriation.** The Indian government in the 1970s, for example, demanded that Coca-Cola share its secret formula, something that the MNE did not even share with the US government. At this time, the MNE has already invested substantial sums of resources (called **sunk costs**) and often has to accommodate some new demands; otherwise, it may face expropriation or exit at a huge loss (as Coca-Cola did in India). Coca-Cola's experience in India, unfortunately, is not isolated. Numerous governments in Africa, Asia, and Latin America in the 1950s, 1960s, and 1970s expropriated MNE assets through **nationalization** by turning them over to state-owned enterprises (SOEs).[17] Not surprisingly, foreign firms do not appreciate the risk associated with such obsolescing bargains.[18]

Recently, some decisive changes around the world have been in favor of foreign entries (see Chapter 1) because many governments realize that nationalizing foreign MNE assets does not necessarily maximize their national interests. While expropriation drives MNEs away, SOEs are often unable to run the operations as effectively as MNEs and most SOEs end up losing money and destroying value. Therefore, the global trend since the 1980s and 1990s has been **privatization,** which, as the opposite of nationalization, turns state-owned assets over to private firms (see Chapter 11). Interestingly, many private bidders are MNEs.[19] During this new era, MNEs often push for transparency and predictability in host-government decision-making *before* committing to new deals. Coca-Cola, for example, agreed to return to India in the 1990s with an explicit commitment from the government that its secret formula would be untouchable. Many governments have realized that investor-friendly institutions are likely to attract more foreign entrants. Otherwise, foreign investors may either avoid certain countries or withdraw from them.[20] Indonesia, for example, suffered a net *outflow* of $1.7 billion FDI in 2002 due to its worsening corruption and chaos.[21]

Overall, host governments (especially those in the developing world) are competing to transform their relationships with MNEs from confrontational to cooperative.[22] China's recent success in attracting FDI (from zero inflow thirty years ago to *the* largest FDI recipient in the world) can be directly attributed to a new post-Mao policy of welcoming FDI. In 2002 alone, seventy countries, more than one third of the total number of countries in the world, changed FDI regulations to become more favorable to foreign entrants (Table 6.1). Overall, while regulatory risks, especially those associated with expropriation, have decreased significantly around the world, individual countries still vary considerably, thus calling for very careful analysis of such risks.[23]

Trade Barriers

Trade barriers include (1) tariff and nontariff barriers, (2) local content requirements, and (3) restrictions on certain entry modes. **Tariff barriers,** taxes levied on

TABLE 6.1   **Changes in National Regulations of Foreign Direct Investment (FDI), 1991–2002**

	1991	1992	1993	1994	1995	1996	1997	1998	1999	2000	2001	2002
Number of countries	35	43	57	49	64	65	76	60	63	69	71	70
Number of changes	82	79	102	110	112	114	151	145	140	150	208	248
More favorable to FDI	80	79	101	108	106	98	135	136	131	147	194	236
Less favorable to FDI	2	0	1	2	6	16	16	9	9	3	14	12

Source: Changes in National Regulations of Foreign Direct Investment (FDI) from World Investment Report 2003, p. 13. Reprinted by permission of United Nations.

imports, are government-imposed entry barriers. **Nontariff barriers** are more subtle. For example, the Japanese customs inspectors, in the name of detecting unwanted bacteria from abroad, often insist on cutting *every* tulip bulb exported from the Netherlands vertically down the middle. The Dutch argument that their tulips have been safely exported to just about every other country in the world has not been persuasive. These barriers effectively encourage foreign entrants to produce locally and discourage them from exporting.

However, even after foreign entrants set up factories locally, they can still export completely knocked down (CKD) kits to be assembled in factories in host countries (see Integrative Case 1.3). Such factories are nicknamed "screwdriver plants" because only screwdrivers plus local labor are needed. In response, many governments have imposed **local content requirements,** mandating that a "domestically produced" product can still be subject to tariff and nontariff barriers unless a certain fraction of its value (such as 51 percent in the United States) is truly produced domestically. Although made-in-USA Toyota Camrys and Honda Accords have now met local content requirements, the popular press and most of the public continue to call these cars "imports"—with a good historical reason.

There are also **restrictions on entry modes.** Many countries limit or even ban wholly foreign-owned subsidiaries. For example, while Mexico had practiced these policies (until 1994 when it joined NAFTA), the United States has also selectively protected certain industries. In the United States, foreign airlines are not allowed to operate wholly owned subsidiaries or acquire US airlines. They are allowed to control no more than 25 percent equity of any US airlines (a ceiling reached by KLM Royal Dutch Airlines in Northwest Airlines).

Currency Risks

These risks stem from the unfavorable currency movements to which firms are exposed. For instance, Nestle's sales volume in Brazil grew by 10 percent between 1998 and 2002, but because of currency deterioration, its Brazil revenues in Swiss francs actually went *down* by 30 percent during the same period.[24] Honda is similarly hurt by the strong yen, which appreciated against the dollar since 2000. Because Honda made 80 percent of its profits in the United States, their value, when translated into the Japanese yen, became much lower ($889 million lower in 2003).[25] If the Chinese yuan appreciates from its current (2004) peg of 8.3 yuan to $1, domestic and foreign firms in China may lose a significant chunk of their low cost advantage.

In response, firms can speculate or hedge.[26] **Speculation** involves committing to stable currencies. However, this can be risky if firms bet on the wrong currency movements. For example, Japan Airlines (JAL) needed US dollars to purchase Boeing aircraft, but its revenues were mostly in yen. In 1985, JAL entered a ten-year contract with foreign exchange traders at a rate of $1 to 185 yen. This looked like a great deal given the 1985 exchange rate of $1 to 240 yen. However, by 1994, the yen had surged against the dollar to a rate of $1 to 99 yen. Because JAL was bound by the contract to purchase dollars at the rate of $1 to 185 yen, it was paying 86 percent (!) more than it needed to for every Boeing aircraft it bought.[27] **Hedging** means spreading out activities in a number of countries in different currency zones to offset the currency losses in certain regions through gains in other regions.[28] This was one of the key motivations behind Toyota's 1998 decision to set up a new factory in France, instead of expanding its existing British operations (which would cost less in the short run). Being in France which is in the Euro zone allows Toyota to more effectively hedge than in Britain which is not in the Euro zone.

In addition to *formal* institutional constraints, firms contemplating foreign entries also must develop a sophisticated understanding of numerous *informal* aspects such as cultural distances and institutional norms. Chapter 4 has already discussed these issues at length, so we will not repeat them here other than to stress their importance; we will revisit some of the informal aspects in the next section.

Overall, the institution-based perspective's core proposition that "institutions matter" is *magnified* in foreign entry decisions.[29] Rushing abroad without a solid understanding of institutional differences can be hazardous and even disastrous.

Synthesis

While the comprehensive model illustrates how *each* of the three leading perspectives sheds light on foreign entry decisions, it is important to note that different considerations may pull the foreign entrant in different directions. For example, the industry-based view may suggest that foreign entries would be necessary in the face of rivals' entries into certain countries. However, the resource-based view may question whether the firm's key assets would be valuable enough to compensate for its liability of foreignness, and the institution-based view may caution against such moves given some inherent institutional risks in certain countries. In practice, how to make an optimal decision given these conflicting considerations is challenging. Nevertheless, strategists often have to make a series of entry decisions along the 2W1H dimensions, as detailed in the next three sections.

WHERE TO ENTER?

Like real estate, the motto for international business is "location, location, location." In fact, such a *spatial* perspective (that is, doing business outside of one's home country) is a defining feature of international business.[30] Two sets of considerations drive the location of foreign entries: (1) strategic goals and (2) cultural and institutional distances. Each is discussed next.

Location-Specific Advantages and Strategic Goals

Favorable locations in certain countries may give firms operating there **location-specific advantages.** The continuous expansion of international business can be regarded as an unending saga of searching for location-specific advantages. Certain locations simply possess geographical features that are difficult for others to match. Singapore, for instance, is an ideal stopping point for sea and air traffic connecting Europe/the Indian Ocean basin and East Asia/Australia. Austria is an attractive site as MNE regional headquarters for Central and Eastern Europe. Turkey is a great launch pad for the Middle East, Caucasus, and Central Asia. Miami, which advertises itself as the "Gateway of the Americas," is an attractive location both for North American firms looking south and Latin American companies coming north. Although difficult, firms may be able to imitate some of these geographic advantages. For example, Italy is often associated with high-quality fashion and leather products. The internationally successful, Italian-sounding Giordano brand of fashion clothing, however, does not come from Italy. It actually originates from Hong Kong with no Italian roots.

Beyond geographical advantages, location-specific advantages also arise from clustering economic activities in certain locations, usually referred to as **agglomeration.** The basic idea dates back at least to Alfred Marshall, a British economist who first published it in 1890. Essentially, location-specific advantages stem from (1) knowledge spillovers among closely located firms that attempt to hire individuals from competitors, (2) industry demand that creates a skilled labor force whose members may work for different firms without having to move out of the region, and (3) industry demand that facilitates a pool of specialized suppliers and buyers also located in the region.[31] For instance, the Netherlands grows and exports two-thirds of the world's exports of cut flowers due to significant agglomeration benefits. Slovakia has been producing more cars per capita than any other country in the world, thanks to the quest for agglomeration benefits by Hyundai, Kia, Peugeot-Citroen, and Volkswagen in this relatively small country of 5.4 million people.[32]

Given that different locations offer different benefits, strategic goals, such as seeking (1) natural resources, (2) market, (3) efficiency, or (4) innovation, must be matched with locations (Table 6.2). First, for firms interested in **seeking natural resources,**

TABLE 6.2   Matching Strategic Goals with Locations

STRATEGIC GOALS	LOCATION-SPECIFIC ADVANTAGES	ILLUSTRATIVE LOCATIONS MENTIONED IN THE TEXT
Natural resource seeking	Possession of natural resources and related transport and communication infrastructure	Oil in the Middle East and Russia; bananas in Central America and the Caribbean
Market seeking	Abundance of strong market demand and customers willing to pay	Seafood in Japan; soft drinks in Mexico
Efficiency seeking	Economies of scale and abundance of low-cost factors	Manufacturing in China; IT in India
Innovation seeking	Abundance of innovative individuals, firms, and universities	IT in Silicon Valley and India; financial services in New York and London; cosmetics in France; chemicals in Germany; aerospace in Russia

Source: First two columns adapted from J. Dunning, 1993, Multinational Enterprises and the Global Economy (pp. 82–83), Reading, MA: Addison-Wesley.

certain resources are tied to particular foreign locations, such as oil and gas in the Middle East and Russia. In another example, the nickname "Banana Republics" probably best indicates the location-specific advantages of certain Central American and Caribbean countries in banana production.

Second, **market-seeking** firms go after countries that offer the highest price and strongest demand for their products and services. For example, the Japanese appetite and willingness to pay for seafood has motivated seafood exporters around the world—ranging from the nearby China and Korea to the distant Norway and Peru—to ship their catch to Japan for top dollars (or yens). With *every* man, woman, and child washing down 101 liters of cola every year (that is, about one big 2-liter bottle every week), Mexicans' thirst for soft drinks is second in the world (slightly less than the Americans at 113 liters). Consequently, Mexico has attracted numerous beverages companies from around the world to compete for "a share of the throat" (see Strategy in Action 5.3 in Chapter 5).

Third, **efficiency-seeking** firms often single out the most efficient locations that feature a combination of scale economies and low cost factors.[33] Numerous MNEs have entered China to build products for the rest of the world. The city of Shanghai alone reportedly hosts a cluster of more than 300 of the *Fortune* Global 500 firms. Likewise, India, especially the city of Bangalore, has emerged as a leading location for information technology (IT) (see Opening Case in Chapter 1). Most efficiency-seeking firms do not necessarily go after the locations with the lowest labor costs. China and India do not present the absolutely lowest labor costs in the world, and Shanghai and Bangalore are some of the *highest* cost cities in China and India, respectively. However, these cities are attractive because they are able to lower foreign entrants' *total* costs. Given that the key efficiency concern is lowest total costs, it is also not surprising that some nominally "high cost" countries (such as the United States) continue to attract significant FDI. For instance, Grupo Mexico, the world's third largest copper producer, has considered moving its energy-thirsty refining operations from "high-cost" Mexico to "low-cost" Texas, where electricity costs 4 cents per kilowatt hour as opposed to 8.5 cents in Mexico.[34]

Finally, **innovation-seeking** firms target countries and regions renowned for generating world-class innovations, such as Silicon Valley and India (IT), New York and London (financial services), France (cosmetics), Germany (chemicals), and Russia (aerospace). Such entries can be viewed as "an option to maintain access to innovations resident in the host country, thus generating information spillovers that may lead to opportunities for future organizational learning and growth."[35] Such location-specific advantages may help foreign entrants develop new innovation capabilities (see Chapter 10).[36]

Overall, these four strategic goals, while analytically distinct, are *not* mutually exclusive. For instance, MNEs may enter certain emerging economies to seek production efficiency for high-end products exported to high-income countries (such as 3G cell phones currently costing $1,000 each in the West). Currently, firms assume that customers in low-income countries cannot afford these cell phones. However, over time, MNEs may increasingly find a market in low-income countries when income rises. Further down the road, these countries may develop some world-class R&D capabilities, attracting innovation-seeking MNEs. Thus, in a country such as China or India, some MNEs may be efficiency-, market-, and innovation-seeking *simultaneously.*

Another important consideration is that location-specific advantages may grow, evolve, and/or decline. However, if policymakers fail to maintain the institutional attractiveness and raise taxes and if companies overcrowd and bid up factor costs (such as land, office, and talents), some firms may move out of certain locations that were previously considered advantageous.[37] For instance, Mercedes and BMW, which had proudly projected a 100 percent "Made in Germany" image until the early 1990s, are now replacing that image with "Made by Mercedes" and "Made by BMW" products manufactured in countries such as Brazil, China, Mexico, South Africa, the United States, and Vietnam. Such an emphasis on *firm*-specific (as opposed to *location*-specific) advantages illustrates both the relative decline of Germany's location-specific advantages and the rise of other countries' advantages.

Cultural/Institutional Distances and Foreign Entry Locations

Another set of considerations centers on cultural/institutional distances (see also Chapter 4). **Cultural distance** is the difference between two cultures along some identifiable dimensions (such as those advocated by Hofstede in Chapter 4).[38] Considering culture as an informal part of institutional frameworks governing a particular country, **institutional distance** is "the extent of similarity or dissimilarity between the regulatory, normative, and cognitive institutions of two countries."[39]

Two schools of thought have emerged. The first is associated with **stage models,** arguing that firms will enter culturally similar countries during their first stage of internationalization, and that they may gain more confidence to enter culturally distant countries in later stages.[40] This idea is intuitively appealing because it makes sense for Canadian and Austrian firms to enter, respectively, the United States and Germany first, taking advantage of common cultural and language traditions. On average, business between countries that share a language is three times greater than business between countries without a common language. Firms from common-law countries (English-speaking countries and their former colonies) are more likely to be interested in other common-law countries. Colony-colonizer links (such as Britain's ties with the Commonwealth, France's ties with the franc zone of West Africa, and Spain's ties with Latin America) boost trade by 900 percent.[41] Some evidence documents that certain performance benefits come from competing in countries that are culturally and institutionally adjacent to one another.[42]

Citing numerous counterexamples, a second school of thought argues that strategic goals such as market and efficiency are more important than cultural/institutional considerations.[43] For instance, natural resource-seeking firms have some compelling reasons to enter culturally and institutionally distant countries (such as Papua New Guinea for bauxite, Zambia for copper, and Nigeria for oil). Market-seeking firms tend to go after the largest markets regardless of cultural/institutional distances, which, for example, explains why Norwegian fishery exporters are so eager to enter Japan.[44] Further, some counterintuitive (although inconclusive) evidence exists that firms operating in culturally/institutionally distant countries do not necessarily underperform those from neighboring countries.[45]

Overall, in the complex calculus that underpins entry decisions, locations represent only one of several important sets of considerations.[46] As shown next, entry timing and modes are also important.

WHEN TO ENTER?[47]

Unless a firm is approached by unsolicited foreign customers which may lead to "passive" entries, conscientious entry timing considerations center on whether compelling reasons exist to be early or late entrants when moving into certain countries. Often firms prefer **first mover advantages,** defined as the advantages that first movers enjoy and that later movers do not.[48] However, first movers may also encounter significant disadvantages, which in turn become **late mover advantages.**

Shown in Table 6.3, first mover advantages stem from (1) gaining proprietary, technological leadership, (2) preempting scarce assets, (3) establishing entry barriers, (4) avoiding clashes with dominant firms in domestic markets, and (5) creating good relationships with key stakeholders such as customers and governments. First, first movers may gain advantage through innovations in proprietary technology. They also ride down the learning curve in pursuit of scale and scope economies in new countries, as evidenced by eBay in online auction and INCAT in wave-piercing technology (see Strategy in Action 6.1).

Second, first movers may also make preemptive investments. A number of Japanese MNEs, for instance, have "cherry picked" leading local suppliers and distributors as new members of the expanded *keiretsu* networks in Southeast Asia, and sought to block access to them by late entrants from the West.[49]

Third, first movers may erect significant entry barriers for late entrants, such as customer switching costs. For example, parents who have decided to buy one brand of disposable diapers (such as Huggies or Pampers) for their first child often stick with this brand for their other children. Buyers of expensive equipment are likely to stick with the same producers for components, training, and other services for a long time. That is why American, British, French, German, and Russian aerospace firms competed intensely for Poland's first post–Cold War order for fighter jets—America's F-16 eventually won.

TABLE 6.3   First Mover Advantages and Late Mover Advantages

FIRST MOVER ADVANTAGES	LATE MOVER ADVANTAGES (OR FIRST MOVER DISADVANTAGES)
▪ Proprietary, technological leadership	▪ Opportunity for free ride on first mover investments
▪ Preemption of scarce resources	▪ Resolution of technological and market uncertainty
▪ Establishment of entry barriers for late entrants	▪ First mover's difficulty to adapt to market changes
▪ Avoidance of clash with dominant firms at home	
▪ Relationships and connections with key stakeholders such as customers and governments	

Fourth, intense domestic competition may drive some nondominant firms to seek fortunes abroad to avoid clashing with dominant firms head-on in their home market.[50] For example, among Japanese MNEs active in the United States, Sony, Honda, and Epson all entered ahead of their domestic industry leaders, Matsushita, Toyota, and NEC, respectively.

Finally, first movers may build up precious relationships and connections with key stakeholders such as customers and governments. Motorola, for example, entered China in the early 1980s and now benefits from its long-time presence in the country. In 1996, China adopted Motorola's technology as its national paging standard, locking out other rivals. Similarly, American International Group (AIG) has a sweetheart deal with the Chinese authorities which authorized AIG to be the only foreign insurer to operate wholly owned subsidiaries. Other foreign insurers (as of 2004) must settle for minority joint ventures.

On the other hand, the potential advantages of first movers may be counterbalanced by various disadvantages. Specifically, late movers may benefit from (1) the opportunity to take a free ride on first mover investments, (2) the resolution of technological and market uncertainty, and (3) the difficulty of first movers to adapt to changing market needs. There are numerous examples of first mover firms losing their advantages in their industries, such as EMI in CT scanners, de Haviland in jet airliners, and Netscape in Internet browsers. Late mover firms, such as GE, Boeing, and Microsoft (Explorer), respectively, captured significant advantages in these industries.

Specifically, late mover advantages are manifested in three ways. First, late movers may be able to take a free ride on first movers' investments. For example, a first mover in 3G technology such as Hutchison Whampoa must incur huge advertising expenses to educate customers on *both* what 3G technology is and why its offering is the best (see Closing Case). A late mover can free ride on such customer education by only focusing on why its particular product is the best, thus getting more "bang" for the marketing investment.

Second, as explorers of uncharted territories, first movers assume considerably more operational risks and face numerous technological and market uncertainties. After some of these uncertainties are removed, late movers may join the game with massive firepower. Some MNEs such as IBM and Matsushita are known to have such a tendency.

Finally, as incumbents, first movers may be locked into a given set of fixed assets or be reluctant to cannibalize existing product lines in favor of new ones. Late movers may be able to take advantage of first movers' inflexibility by *leapfrogging* over them.

Overall, while some evidence points out first mover advantages,[51] other evidence supports a late mover strategy.[52] Unfortunately, a mountain of research is still unable to conclusively recommend a particular entry timing strategy. Although first movers may have an *opportunity* to exploit advantages, their pioneering status is not a birthright for success.[53] For example, among all three first movers that entered the Chinese automobile industry in the early 1980s, Volkswagen captured significant advantages, Chrysler had very moderate success, and Peugeot failed and had to exit. Among late movers that entered in the late 1990s, many are struggling, but GM,

Citroen, and Honda have gained significant market shares (see Integrative Case 1.3). Obviously, entry timing per se is not the only factor that determines whether a foreign entry will succeed or fail. It is through *interaction* with other strategic variables that entry timing has an impact on performance.[54]

HOW TO ENTER?

This section first focuses on the larger versus small scale of entry. Then it introduces a hierarchical model guiding market entry decisions. The first step in this model is to determine whether the modes of entry would be equity- or non-equity-based. This crucial decision differentiates an MNE (which employs equity modes) from a non-MNE (which relies on non-equity modes). Finally, we outline the second step in this model, which details the pros and cons of various groups of equity and non-equity modes.

Scale of Entry: Commitment and Experience

Another key dimension in foreign entry decisions is the **scale of entry.** Large-scale entries are costly. For instance, a number of European financial services firms, such as ABN Amro, HSBC, and ING Group, have recently spent several billion dollars to enter the United States by making a series of acquisitions. These large-scale entries benefit from a **strategic commitment** to certain markets, which both assures local customers and suppliers (by saying "We are here for the long haul!") and deters potential entrants. The drawbacks of such large-scale, hard-to-reverse strategic commitment are (1) limited strategic flexibility elsewhere and (2) huge losses if these large-scale "bets" turn out to be wrong. Chapter 9 provides more details on the sad reality that most acquisitions fail.

Small-scale entries are less costly. They focus on accumulating experience by getting a firm's "feet" wet while limiting the downside risk. The emphasis is on **organizational learning** through "learning by doing" in host countries.[55] For example, to enter the market of Islamic finance where no interest can be charged, Citibank set up a subsidiary Citibank Islamic Bank, HSBC established Amanah, and UBS launched Noriba, all of which were designed to experiment with different interpretations of the Koran on how to make money while not committing religious sins.[56] Acquiring such an experience is impossible outside the Islamic world. Overall, some evidence supports the view that the longer foreign firms stay in host countries, the less liability of foreignness they experience.[57] The drawback of small-scale entries is a lack of strong strategic commitment, which may lead to difficulties in building market share and capturing first mover advantages.

Modes of Entry: The First Step

Among numerous modes of entry, strategists are unlikely to consider all of them at the same time. Given the complexity of entry decisions, strategists must *prioritize,* by considering only a few manageable, key variables first, and then considering other variables later. The **hierarchical model** shown in Figure 6.3 and explained in Table 6.4 (p. 232) is helpful in this endeavor.[58]

FIGURE 6.3   The Choice of Entry Modes: A Hierarchical Model

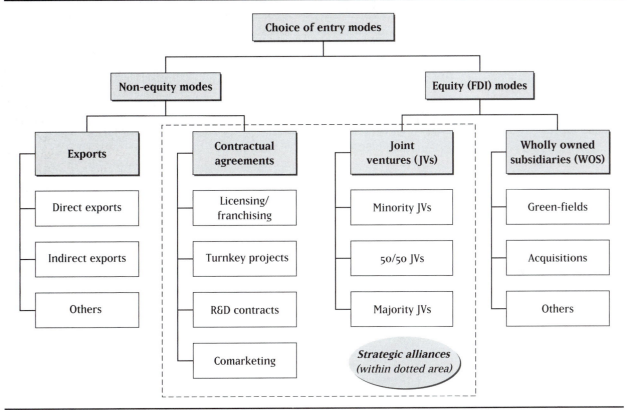

Source: Adapted from Y. Pan & D. Tse, 2000, The hierarchical model of market entry modes (p. 538), Journal of International Business Studies, 31: 535–554.

In the first step, considerations for small- versus large-scale entries usually boil down to the equity (ownership) issue. **Non-equity modes** (exports and contractual agreements) tend to reflect relatively smaller commitments to overseas markets, whereas **equity modes** (joint ventures and wholly owned subsidiaries) indicate relatively larger, harder-to-reverse commitments. Equity modes call for establishing independent organizations overseas (partially or wholly controlled). Non-equity modes do not require such independent organizations. Overall, these modes differ significantly in terms of cost, commitment, risk, return, and control (see numerous examples in the next section).

The distinction between equity and non-equity modes is not trivial. In fact, this crucial distinction is what defines an MNE: An MNE enters foreign markets via equity modes through **foreign direct investment** (FDI), which refers to direct control and management of value-adding activities overseas (see Chapter 1).[59] A firm that merely exports/imports with no FDI is usually not regarded as an MNE. Why would a firm, say, an oil importer, want to become an MNE by directly investing in the oil-producing country, instead of relying on the market mechanism by purchasing oil from an exporter in that country?

TABLE 6.4   Modes of Entry: Advantages and Disadvantages

ENTRY MODES	ADVANTAGES	DISADVANTAGES
1. Non-equity modes: Exports		
Direct exports	▪ Economies of scale in production concentrated in home country ▪ Better control over distribution (relative to indirect export)	▪ High transportation costs for bulky products ▪ Marketing distance from customers ▪ Trade barriers
Indirect exports	▪ Concentration of resources on production ▪ No need to directly handle export processes	▪ Less control over distribution (relative to direct exports) ▪ Inability to learn how to operate overseas
2. Non-equity modes: Contractual agreements		
Licensing/Franchising	▪ Low development costs ▪ Low risk in overseas expansion	▪ Little control over technology and marketing ▪ May create competitors ▪ Inability to engage in global coordination
Turnkey projects	▪ Ability to earn returns from process technology in countries where FDI is restricted	▪ May create efficient competitors ▪ Lack of long-term presence
R&D contracts	▪ Ability to tap into the best locations for certain innovations at low costs	▪ Difficult to negotiate and enforce contracts ▪ May nurture innovative competitors ▪ May lose core innovation capabilities
Comarketing	▪ Ability to reach more customers	▪ Limited coordination
3. Equity modes: Joint ventures	▪ Sharing costs and risks ▪ Access to partners' knowledge and assets ▪ Politically acceptable	▪ Divergent goals and interests of partners ▪ Limited equity and operational control ▪ Difficult to coordinate globally
4. Equity modes: Wholly owned subsidiaries		
Green-field projects	▪ Complete equity and operational control ▪ Protection of technology and know-how ▪ Ability to coordinate globally	▪ Potential political problems and risks ▪ High development costs ▪ Slow entry speed (relative to acquisitions)
Acquisitions	▪ Same as green-field (above) ▪ Fast entry speed	▪ Same as green-field (above), except slow speed ▪ Post-acquisition integration problems

Relative to a non-MNE, an MNE has two principal advantages: ownership and internalization. By owning assets in both oil-importing and oil-producing countries, the MNE is better able to manage and coordinate cross-border activities, such as delivering crude oil to the oil refinery in the importing country right at the moment its processing capacity becomes available (just-in-time delivery), instead of letting crude oil sit in expensive ships or storage tanks for a long time. This advantage is therefore called **ownership advantage.** Another advantage stems from removing the market relationship between an oil importer and an oil exporter, which may suffer from high transaction costs. Using the market, deals have to be negotiated, prices agreed upon, and deliveries verified, all of which entails significant costs. More costly, however, is the possibility of opportunism on both sides. For example, the oil importer may refuse to accept a shipment *after* its arrival citing unsatisfactory quality, but the real reason could be the importer's inability to sell refined oil downstream. The exporter is thus forced to find a new buyer for a shipment of crude oil on a last-minute, "fire sale" basis. On the other hand, the oil exporter may demand higher-than-agreed-upon prices, citing a variety of reasons ranging from inflation to natural disasters. The importer thus has to either (1) pay more than the agreed-upon prices or (2) refuse to pay and suffer from the huge costs of keeping expensive refinery facilities idle. These transaction costs increase international market inefficiencies and imperfections. By replacing such a market relationship with a single organization spanning both countries (a process called **internalization,** basically transforming external markets with in-house links), the MNE thus reduces cross-border transaction costs and increases efficiencies. This advantage is called an **internalization advantage.**[60] According to John Dunning, a leading MNE scholar, relative to a non-MNE, an MNE, which operates in certain desirable locations, enjoys a combination of ownership (O), location (L—discussed earlier), and internalization (I) advantages. These are collectively known as the **OLI advantages.**[61]

Overall, the first step in entry mode considerations is extremely critical. A strategic decision must be made concerning whether to undertake FDI and become an MNE by selecting equity modes.

Modes of Entry: The Second Step

During the second step, strategists consider variables within *each* group of non-equity and equity modes. If the decision is to export, then the next question is direct exports or indirect exports (also discussed in Chapter 5). **Direct exports** represent the most basic mode of entry, which capitalizes on economies of scale in production concentrated in the home country and affords better control over distribution.[62] However, if the products involved are bulky (such as cars, refrigerators, and TVs), transportation costs may be prohibitive, as China's Haier found out (see Strategy in Action 6.3 on next page). This strategy essentially treats foreign demand as an extension of domestic demand, and the firm is geared toward designing and producing for the domestic market first and foremost. While direct exports may work if the export volume is small, it is not optimal when the firm has a large number of foreign buyers. "Marketing 101" suggests that firms need to be closer—both physically and

STRATEGY IN ACTION 6.3. *Haier Spreads Its Wings*

While Made-in-China goods sporting American brands are common everywhere, Chinese brands are a rare commodity outside of China—even more rare are Chinese-branded products made in the USA. Haier (*http://www.haier.com*), China's largest and the world's fifth largest appliance maker, is trying to change that. At home, it battled giants such as Electrolux (*http://www.electrolux.com*), Siemens (*http://www.siemens.com*), and Matsushita (*http://www.panasonic.jp*) to become the leader in China by the early 1990s. Since then, Haier has launched an export push, now commanding approximately 50 percent market share for compact refrigerators and 60 percent for wine coolers in the United States, and 8 percent for air conditioners in the European Union. Although Haier manufactures 250 refrigerator, air conditioner, dishwasher, and oven models, its US entry, starting in 1994, side-stepped market leaders such as GE (*http://www.ge.com*) and Whirlpool (*http://www.whirlpool.com*) by focusing on small (sub-180 liter) refrigerators that serve in hotel rooms and dorms—a segment that the incumbents had dismissed as peripheral and low margin. Haier's second foray was equally cautious: It entered the specialized wine coolers market in 1997. Since the 1990s, Haier has successfully penetrated nine of the ten largest US retail chains, including Wal-Mart (*http://www.walmart.com*) and Target (*http://www.target.com*), which carried the Haier brand.

Haier has also become a foreign direct investor by setting up factories in emerging economies such as India, Indonesia, and Iran. Since 2000, it has invested $30 million to build a green-field factory in Camden, South Carolina. Why would a Chinese multinational already blessed with a low-wage workforce at home want to open a plant in high-wage America? Haier officials suggest that shipping refrigerators across the Pacific is costly and can take forty days, thus offsetting China's wage advantage. Better to build close to the customer and place the "Made in USA" tag on the product, which is a tie-breaker among American consumers. The factory brings other, less tangible benefits as well. It shows a commitment to the US market, which should increase retailers' confidence in carrying the brand. Also, it is "politically correct" when Chinese exports are being criticized for taking away American jobs. By 2002, Haier's US sales, of which 15 percent were locally made, reached $500 million and its US unit was profitable.

Sources: Based on (1) D. Biers, 2001, Taking the fight to the enemy, Far Eastern Economic Review, March 29: 52–54; (2) R. Crawford & L. Paine, 1998, The Haier Group (A), Harvard Business School case 9-398-101; (3) B. Wysocki, 2002, Chinese firms aim for global market, Asian Wall Street Journal, January 29: 1; (5) M. Zeng & P. Williamson, 2003, The hidden dragons, Harvard Business Review, 81 (10): 92–104.

psychologically—to where the customers are, prompting firms to consider more intimate overseas involvement such as FDI.

In addition, direct exports may provoke protectionism. In the late 1970s, the success of direct auto exports from Japan led the US government, which usually calls itself a "free trader," to threaten the enactment of protectionist mechanisms unless the Japanese curtailed their exports. In 1981, both governments signed a **voluntary export restraint** (VER) agreement in which the Japanese "voluntarily" agreed to limit their auto exports. The Japanese, of course, did not really voluntarily agree to do so: They only agreed to it under explicit threats of far more damaging tariffs. While the VER is a euphemism for protectionism, it is indicative of the perils of a (successful) direct export strategy.

Another export strategy is **indirect exports,** namely, exporting through domestically based **export intermediaries.**[63] This is usually undertaken by small firms unable to export on their own or by large firms exploring unfamiliar countries (see Integrative Case 2.2). This strategy not only enjoys the economies of scale in domestic production (similar to direct exports), it is also relatively worry-free. A significant amount of export trade in commodities (such as textiles, woods, and meats), which compete primarily on price, is indirect through intermediaries.[64] Indirect exports have some drawbacks because of the introduction of third parties (such as export trading companies) with their own agendas and objectives that are not necessarily the same as the exporter's objectives.[65] The primary reason exporters chooses intermediaries is because of information asymmetries concerning risks and uncertainties associated with foreign markets (that is, information regarding foreign markets is asymmetrically distributed with intermediaries knowing a lot more than exporters). As first discussed in Chapter 5, intermediaries, which have international contacts and knowledge, essentially make a living by taking advantage of such information asymmetries. They may have a vested interest in making sure that such asymmetries are not reduced. Intermediaries, for example, may repackage the products under their own brand and insist on monopolizing the communication with overseas customers. Overall, indirect exports do not provide exporters much opportunity to know how its products are doing overseas.

The next major group of non-equity entry modes refers to contractual agreements that consist of (1) licensing/franchising, (2) turnkey projects, (3) R&D contracts, (4) comarketing, and others. First, as introduced in Chapter 5, in **licensing/franchising** agreements, the licensor/franchiser sells the rights to intellectual property such as patents and know-how to the licensee/franchisee for a royalty fee. The licensor/franchiser, therefore, does not have to bear the full costs and risks associated with foreign market expansion. On the other hand, the licensor/franchiser does not have tight control over production and marketing.[66] This mode may create potential competitors and can lead to contractual hazards, such as the disputes Pizza Hut has experienced in Thailand (discussed earlier in this chapter).

Turnkey projects refer to projects in which clients pay contractors to design and construct new facilities and train personnel. At their completion, contractors hand clients the proverbial "key" to the facilities ready for operations—hence the term "turnkey." Turnkey projects make it possible to earn returns from process technology in countries where FDI is restricted (such as power generation). The drawbacks are twofold. First, if foreign clients are competitors, selling them state-of-the-art technology through turnkey projects may boost their competitiveness. Second, turnkey projects do not allow for a long-term presence after the "key" is handed to clients. To obtain a longer-term presence, **build-operate-transfer agreements** (BOT) are often used instead of the traditional build-transfer type of turnkey projects. For example, an international consortium of Italian, German, and Iranian firms obtained a large-scale BOT power-generation project in Iran. After its completion, the consortium will operate the project for 20 years, before transferring it to the Iranian government.[67]

R&D contracts refer to outsourcing agreements in R&D between firms (that is, firm A agrees to perform certain R&D work for firm B). These contracts allow firms to tap into the best locations for certain innovations at relatively low costs, such as IT work in India and aerospace research in Russia. However, three principal drawbacks may emerge. First, given R&D's uncertain and multidimensional nature, these contracts are often difficult to negotiate and enforce. While delivery time and costs are relatively easy to negotiate, quality is often difficult to assess. Second, such contracts may nurture competitors. A number of Indian IT firms, nurtured by such work, are now on a global offensive to take on their Western rivals (see Opening Case in Chapter 1). Finally, firms that rely on outsiders to perform a lot of R&D may lose some of their core R&D capabilities in the long run.

Comarketing refers to agreements among a number of firms to jointly market their products and services. Fast food restaurants, for instance, often launch comarketing campaigns with movie studios and toy makers to hawk toys based on certain movie characters (see Video Case 1.4). Through code sharing, airline alliances such as One World and Star Alliance extensively engage in comarketing (see Video Case 2.3). The advantage is the capability to reach more customers. The drawbacks center on limited control and coordination because everything has to be negotiated between the firms that are comarketing.

The next group is called **equity modes,** all of which entail some FDI. They transform firms into MNEs.[68] A **joint venture** (JV) is a "corporate child" that is a new entity given birth and jointly owned by two or more parent companies (see Strategy in Action 6.1). A JV can have three principal forms: Minority JV (less than 50 percent equity), 50/50 JV, and majority JV (more than 50 percent equity). JVs have three advantages. First, an MNE shares costs and risks with a local partner, leading to a certain degree of control while limiting risk exposure. Second, the MNE gains access to the local partner's knowledge about the host country; the local firm, in turn, benefits from the MNE's expertise in technology, capital, and management. Third, JVs may be politically more acceptable than WOS. In terms of disadvantages, first, JVs often involve partners from different backgrounds, divergent goals, and incompatible capabilities. Partners may collaborate for some time, yet in the long run their goals diverge. Second, effective equity and operational control may be difficult to achieve because everything must be shared and negotiated (and, in some cases, fought over). Finally, the nature of the JV may not give an MNE the tight control over a foreign subsidiary that it needs for global coordination (such as simultaneously launching new products around the world). Overall, all sorts of non-equity-based contractual agreements and equity-based JVs can be broadly considered **strategic alliances** (within the *dotted area* in Figure 6.3). Chapter 7 will discuss strategic alliances in detail.

The last group of entry modes refers to **wholly owned subsidiaries** (WOS). There are two primary means to set up a WOS.[69] The first one is to establish new **green-field operations,** which refers to building factories and offices from scratch (on a proverbial piece of "green field" formerly used for agricultural purposes). Toyota and Honda, for example, built green-field factories in the United States in the 1980s. There are three primary advantages associated with green-field operations. First, a green-field WOS gives an MNE complete equity and management control, thus eliminating the headaches associated with JVs. Second, this undivided control leads to better protection of proprietary technology and know-how. Third, a WOS allows for centrally coordinated global actions.[70] Sometimes, a subsidiary (such as

TI's in Japan discussed earlier) is ordered to launch actions that by design will *lose* money. Local licensees/franchisees or JV partners are unlikely to accept such a subservient role. In terms of drawbacks, a green-field WOS tends to be very expensive and risky, not only financially, but also politically. The conspicuous foreignness embodied in such a WOS may become a target for nationalistic sentiments in some countries. Another drawback is the slow entry speed (relative to acquisitions), given that it generally takes at least one to two years (or more) to start up.

The second strategy to establish a WOS is through an **acquisition.** Although this is the last mode discussed here, the acquisition is probably the most important mode given the amount of capital involved (representing approximately 60 percent of global FDI).[71] In addition to sharing all the benefits of green-field WOS, acquisitions also enjoy an additional advantage, namely, faster entry speed. For example, in less than a decade (the 1990s), two leading banks in Spain with little prior international experience, Santander and Bilbao Vizcaya, became the largest foreign banks in Latin America through some 20 acquisitions (see Integrative Case 3.2). In terms of drawbacks, acquisitions share all the disadvantages of green-field WOS, except slow entry speed. In addition, acquisitions have to shoulder a unique and potentially devastating disadvantage—post-acquisition integration problems. While there is no evidence that acquisitions necessarily outperform (or under perform) green-field WOS,[72] these complicated issues are beyond the scope of our discussion here (see Chapter 9 for detailed discussions).

Making Strategic Choices

Trade-offs are inevitable in foreign market entry decisions. Three additional considerations are in order. First, while we have focused on how to make one entry into one country, firms in practice are not limited by any single entry choice. The same MNE may establish JVs in some countries and engage in acquisitions in others. Second, entry strategies may change over time, as shown by Starbucks' in the Opening Case.[73] In general, as suggested by stage models, firms' international involvement has a tendency to migrate from simple strategies (such as non-equity-based modes) in culturally/institutionally adjacent countries to complex strategies (such as equity-based modes) in distant countries. While these models are not always accurate, they make a lot of sense under many circumstances.[74] Finally, everything discussed in this chapter so far has focused on entries. Although important, entry strategies, even when successful, do not guarantee international success.[75] Post-entry strategies, noted in Chapters 8, 9, and 10, are equally or more important.

DEBATES AND EXTENSIONS

The entire body of practice and research on how to enter foreign markets consists of numerous debates, some of which are already covered (such as first mover versus late mover advantages and small-scale versus large-scale entries). This section illustrates three particularly heated debates in *recent* discussions.

High Control versus Low Control

In the hierarchical model (Figure 6.3), moving from non-equity to equity modes, the underlying theme is *increasing* organizational control of activities abroad, which is underpinned by a fundamental deliberation about whether the firm wants to become an MNE by engaging in FDI. A debate has emerged on the importance of such control.[76] The "high control" school argues that given the inherent uncertainties overseas, a higher level of control, preferably in WOS, is likely to hold the winning key. Advocates point out numerous cases of transaction hazards in low-control modes such as licensing and JVs. They recommend that foreign entrants jettison their low-control operations and set up high-control ones, such as converting JVs into WOS.[77]

On the other hand, the "low control" school makes four arguments. First, *no* conclusive evidence suggests that WOS always outperform JVs.[78] Successful JVs with mutually satisfactory partners certainly exist—SonyEricsson, Fuji Xerox, and Shanghai Volkswagen, to name a few. Asserting one party's control rights, even when justified based on a majority equity position in a JV, may irritate the other party.[79] Second, recent research finds that a series of "low control," minority JVs may afford a firm more opportunities for future growth, whereas a bundle of "high control," majority JVs and WOS may have exhausted such opportunities.[80] Third, there are some differences in the preference for "high control" between manufacturing and service industries. When dealing with environmental uncertainty, manufacturers may prefer JVs, whereas service providers may be more interested in WOS presumably because of their higher needs to control their people-intensive operations.[81] Therefore, one-directional advice for "high control" may fail to take into account the differences between manufacturing and service industries. Finally, some evidence suggests that firms coming from cultures (such as Japan) that feature high power distance and high uncertainty avoidance prefer "high control."[82] For instance, Japanese firms investing in the United States have a two-to-one preference for WOS (relative to JV). In contrast, US firms investing in Japan have a two-to-one preference for JV (relative to WOS).[83] Clearly, "high control" is not universally preferred among firms of all nationalities. Recommending a "high control" strategy to firms not comfortable with it may backfire.

Developed Economies versus Emerging Economies[84]

The bulk of international business takes place among **developed economies,** also described as high-income countries, Western (plus Japanese) economies, and the First World, which contribute approximately 80 percent of the global GDP. The UN defines these fifty-four countries (primarily North America, European Union, Australia, Japan, and New Zealand) as having per capita incomes in excess of $9,000. A great debate has erupted as to whether it is appropriate to continue to focus on these economies in the twenty-first century.

Also referred to as developing economies, less developed countries, low-income nations, and the Third World, the term **emerging economies** has caught on since the 1990s. One side of the debate argues that emerging economies are the markets

TABLE 6.5   **Major Emerging Economies**

▪ Argentina ▪ Brazil ▪ China	▪ India ▪ Indonesia ▪ Mexico	▪ Poland ▪ Russia ▪ South Africa	▪ South Korea ▪ Thailand ▪ Turkey

of tomorrow (also known as **emerging markets**). This argument is certainly both true *and* false. Emerging economies consist of 156 countries in various stages of development, which account for 84 percent of the world's population and 76 percent of its landmass, but only 20 percent of its output. Some of these economies are indeed rapidly emerging on the global stage, whereas many others are destined to be submerging (if not sinking!) in the years to come.

Even advocates for emerging economies concede that foreign firms need to focus on the *major* emerging economies, the top twelve collectively representing approximately 73 percent of this group's GDP (Table 6.5). The relative economic firepower of even some of the largest emerging economies is limited. For example, the GDP of Russia (141 million people) is smaller than that of the Netherlands (16 million), and India (1 billion) has less GDP than California (34 million). However, the growth potential of some (although not all) emerging economies, such as Brazil, China, and India, is exciting. Therefore, if Western firms want to grow, they must participate in such growth. This argument seems compelling in light of very slow growth throughout developed economies. For instance, demand for durables such as washers, dryers, and cars is primarily based on replacement needs in the West, whereas in many emerging economies, rising income levels afford numerous first-time purchases of these big-ticket items. At present, FDI inflows to emerging economies trail behind inflows to developed economies by an approximately one-to-three margin. To combat this trend, the argument goes, Western firms need to *disproportionately* invest in emerging economies, that is, invest more than 20 percent of the total corporate resources as justified by these economies' current contributions to the global GDP.[85]

On the other hand, strong arguments have been made against aggressively moving into emerging economies given their numerous risks and uncertainties. Most emerging economies are going through chaotic institutional transitions. Transitions in a *subset* of emerging economies (consisting of former and weakened communist countries, such as China, Hungary, and Russia, transitioning toward market capitalism) are so pervasive that these countries are simply labeled **transition economies.**[86] Emerging economies often experience tremendous booms and busts.[87] The Asian economic "miracle" was suddenly replaced by a major crisis in 1997. Central and Eastern Europe experienced the euphoria of the removal of communism in 1989, which was quickly replaced by a deep recession worsened by the Russian default in 1998 (see Integrative Case 1.4). In the last decade, every major economy in Latin America experienced significant economic crises: Mexico (1995), Brazil (1998), Argentina (2001), and Venezuela (2003).

Overall, emerging economies represent the classic combination of high risk and high (potential) return. A sensible strategy for Western MNEs is to strike a balance between developed and emerging economies. The expertise of Western MNEs, profiting from high-income customers in affluent economies, must be significantly adapted to work in emerging economies. Otherwise, Western MNEs may be "trapped by their devices in gilded cages, serving the affluent few but ignoring the potential of the billions of new customers that attracted them in the first place."[88] For instance, bragging about shampoo-and-conditioner-in-one (otherwise known as 2-in-1) is of little relevance to customers who have never used conditioner—or shampoo. Entering emerging economies with a warehouse-style retail format suitable for markets with a high level of car ownership (such as COSTCO and Sam's Club) is unlikely to reach the masses, which usually do not have cars.

Finally, despite significant regional and country differences, emerging economies have enough common underlying logic to justify developing an alternative business model based on price/value trade-offs different from those in developed economies.[89] Whereas Western MNEs often find it tough going in these unfamiliar territories, some new MNEs from emerging economies—sometimes called Third World multinationals or "dragon multinationals"—that are well versed in such an alternative business model are capturing the hearts, minds, and wallets of customers in emerging economies.[90] In the Philippines, Jollibee beats the mighty McDonald's and is now venturing out to Southeast Asia and the Middle East. In China, until recently, the single largest foreign investor was the C. P. Group from Thailand. In Africa, Asia, and Central America, South African Breweries (now SABMiller) runs neck-and-neck with Heineken, Carlsberg, and Anheuser-Busch. Out of Taiwan, Acer has emerged as a strong contender in the global IT industry. In a nutshell, there is money to be made in emerging economies, despite their high risks. How to make such money, however, remains one of the leading strategic challenges in the twenty-first century (see Strategy in Action 1.1 in Chapter 1).[91]

Cyberspace Entries versus Conventional Entries

The arrival of e-commerce has sparked two new debates. The first is concerned with the *revolutionary* versus *evolutionary* nature of e-commerce. Despite the argument that the Internet may completely revolutionize competition, the contrary seems to have happened (also see Chapters 2 and 5). The Internet does not indiscriminately "globalize" every firm and not all new e-commerce firms are "born global." The comprehensive model (Figure 6.2), originally developed for "brick-and-mortar" entries, is quite capable of understanding cyberspace entries.[92] For example, reputation, a key source of differentiation according to the industry-based view, is found to be behind e-commerce firms' internationalization. Capabilities to coordinate globally dispersed activities, a key firm-specific asset according to the resource-based view, have a direct bearing on the success and failure of international e-commerce. Finally, respect for the rule of law, long considered a key formal institution by the institution-based view, is significantly related to a country's e-commerce competitiveness.

The Internet does facilitate a greater dispersion of economic activities via remote access, which, in turn, may reduce the agglomeration benefits of certain locations. However, only activities whose quality and quantity can be clearly specified and

STRATEGY IN ACTION 6.4. *Did Yahoo! Really Enter France?*

In the late 1990s, Yahoo! (*http://www.yahoo.com*), an American Internet portal, hosted third-party auctions, some of which sold Nazi memorabilia. Although perfectly legal (indeed protected under the First Amendment of the Constitution) in the United States, sales of Nazi items are illegal in France. Yahoo! was thus challenged in a French court. During the process, Yahoo! removed Nazi materials from its French language portal to comply with the French law. However, in November 2000, the French court ruled that Yahoo! must prevent French computer users from accessing any Yahoo! site—*in any language*—on which such items were sold or face a fine of 100,000 French francs (US$17,877) per day. Yahoo! first counterattacked by asking a US court to declare that this decision could not be enforced in the United States because it violates the First Amendment and that American firms were not obliged to follow French rules outside of France. A US court supported this argument. However, by early 2001,

Yahoo! changed its mind and decided to self censor, removing all items that "promote or glorify violence or hatred" from its site.

At the heart of this case is the controversy over whether France has the legal right to assert its law to order Yahoo!, which apparently only had a virtual presence in France, to change behavior that was in full compliance with US law. The fundamental question is whether national territorial jurisdiction applies to cyberspace. Some analysts saw the French decision as a dangerous one, because taken to the extreme, it would imply that every jurisdiction on the planet regulates everything on the Internet. Others contend that cyberspace entries into foreign markets, just like brick-and-mortar entries, have to follow local rules.

Sources: Based on (1) S. Kobrin, 2001, Territoriality and the governance of cyberspace, Journal of International Business Studies, 32: 687–704; (2) P. Lasserre, 2003, Global Strategic Management (p. 390), London: Palgrave.

measured are best suited for remote access (such as call centers in Ireland and basic accounting in the Philippines). Tacit knowledge spillovers will remain highly localized through face-to-face contact. This is "not likely to be affected by the Internet, which allows long distance 'conversations' but not 'handshakes'."[93] To truly succeed abroad, e-commerce firms, just like all other firms, must plant some roots overseas by engaging in a great deal of *local* marketing and services. Overall, the consensus seems to be that the Internet and e-commerce are likely to have an evolutionary rather than revolutionary impact on foreign entries.[94]

Compared with the first debate, the second debate concerning the governance of e-commerce has only begun. Despite numerous repetitions that globalization is compromising the power of national governments, little evidence suggests that the modern nation-state system, in existence since the 1648 Treaty of Westphalia, is retreating. Legally, it may be argued that there is no such a thing as a *multinational* enterprise. Because incorporation is only possible under national law, at its core every MNE represents a bunch of *national* companies (subsidiaries) registered in various countries.[95]

Although some suggest that geographic jurisdiction may be meaningless in cyberspace, others argue that the Internet is "no more a borderless medium than the telephone, telegraph, postal service, facsimile, or smoke signal."[96] In principle, governments have every right to regulate e-commerce. As the Yahoo! in France case (see Strategy in Action 6.4) illustrates, when the *formal* institutional constraints governing e-commerce between France and the United States clash, *informal* institutional constraints will rise—as evidenced by Yahoo!'s self censorship, which affects its business strategy. In the absence of harmonizing formal national regulations concerning cyberspace, such informal constraints will become more important in governing cross-national cyberspace activities, a classic prediction derived from the institution-based view on strategy.

IMPLICATIONS FOR STRATEGISTS

Foreign market entries represent a *foundation* for strategic actions in overseas settings. Without these crucial first steps, firms will remain domestic players. Internationalization features daunting challenges, enormous complexities, and high stakes. Strategists should prioritize the complex tasks suggested by the hierarchical model when making such decisions.

Not surprisingly, this chapter sheds considerable light on the four fundamental questions in strategy. Why firms differ in their propensity to internationalize (Question 1) boils down to the size of the firm and the domestic market (Figure 6.1). How firms behave (Question 2) in foreign entries depends on how considerations for industry competition, firm capabilities, and institutional differences influence their decisions (Figure 6.2). What determines the scope of the firm (Question 3)—in this case, the scope of its international involvement—fundamentally depends on how to acquire and leverage the three-pronged set of ownership, location, and internalization (OLI) advantages. Firms committed to owning some assets overseas through equity modes of entry and thus becoming MNEs are likely to have a broader scope overseas than those unwilling to do so. Finally, what determines the international success and failure of firms (Question 4) certainly has something to do with entry strategies. With inappropriate entry strategies (such as licensing in countries where there is no respect for and protection of intellectual property rights), overseas ventures are doomed to fail. However, appropriate entry strategies, while certainly important, are only a *beginning*. To succeed overseas requires much more, such as making alliances work, managing competitive dynamics, and creating flexible structures, all of which will be covered in later chapters.

Chapter Summary

1. When entering foreign markets, firms confront a liability of foreignness.

2. The propensity to internationalize is often influenced by (1) the size of the firm and (2) the size of the domestic market. An understanding of foreign market entries can be enhanced by drawing on industry-, resource-, and institution-based perspectives in a comprehensive model.

3. Where to enter depends on certain foreign countries' location-specific advantages and the firm's strategic goals, such as seeking (1) natural resources, (2) market, (3) efficiency, and (4) innovation.

4. When to enter boils down to whether firms are interested in (1) first mover advantages or (2) late mover advantages. However, entry timing is not the sole determinant of whether a foreign entry succeeds or fails.

5. How to enter depends on the scale of entry. Large-scale entries demonstrate strategic commitment, whereas small-scale entries focus on organizational learning.

6. A hierarchical model of the choice of foreign entries first focuses on the equity (ownership) issue. The distinction between equity and non-equity modes is important because it defines an MNE, which, by definition, engages in FDI via equity modes. The MNE has three principal advantages: (1) ownership, (2) location, and (3) internalization—collectively known as the OLI advantages.

7. After deciding the equity issue, the second step suggested by the hierarchical model focuses on making the actual selection of entry modes, such as exports (direct and indirect exports), contractual agreements (licensing/franchising, turnkey projects, R&D contracts, and comarketing), joint ventures, and wholly owned subsidiaries (green-field projects and acquisitions). Each has a number of pros and cons.

8. Three leading debates discussed are (1) high control versus low control, (2) developed economies versus emerging economies, and (3) cyberspace entries versus conventional entries.

Key Terms

acquisition	enthusiastic internationalizers	institutional distance
agglomeration	equity modes	internalization advantage
backward vertical integration	export intermediaries	internalization
build-operate-transfer agreements	expropriation	joint venture
comarketing	first mover advantages	late mover advantages
cultural distance	follower internationalizers	liability of foreignness
currency risks	foreign direct investment	licensing/franchising
developed economies	forward vertical integration	local content requirements
direct exports	green-field operations	location-specific advantages
dissemination risks	hedging	market-seeking
efficiency-seeking	hierarchical model	nationalization
emerging economies	indirect exports	non-equity modes
emerging markets	innovation-seeking	nontariff barriers

obsolescing bargain	restrictions on entry modes	sunk costs
occasional internationalizers	scale of entry	tariff barriers
OLI advantages	seeking natural resources	trade barriers
organizational learning	slow internationalizers	transaction costs
ownership advantage	speculation	transition economies
privatization	stage models	turnkey projects
R&D contracts	strategic alliances	voluntary export restraint
regulatory risks	strategic commitment	wholly owned subsidiaries

Critical Discussion Questions

1. Are there exceptions to the examples used in Figure 6.1 (such as large firms located in a large domestic market that are *not* slow internationalizers and instead are enthusiastic internationalizers)? Why?

2. During the 1990s, many North American, European, and Asian MNEs set up manufacturing operations in Mexico, tapping into its location-specific advantages such as (1) its geographic proximity to the world's largest economy (the United States), (2) its market-opening policies associated with NAFTA membership (since 1994), and (3) its abundant, low cost, and high quality labor. None of these has changed much. Yet, by the tenth anniversary of NAFTA, many MNEs are curtailing or shutting down operations in Mexico and moving to China. Use industry-, resource-, and institution-based perspectives to explain why this is the case. (Hint: It is helpful to focus on a particular industry.)

3. Pick any industry (such as oil or furniture), select a pair of firms from the same home country (such as Great Britain) entering the same host country (such as Russia), which use different entry modes (such as direct exports versus local production via a joint venture). How would you explain these differences?

4. ***ON ETHICS:*** Entering foreign markets, by definition, means not investing in a firm's home country. For example, since 2000, GN Netcom shut down some operations in its home country, Denmark, while adding headcounts in China (see Integrative Case 1.1). Lucent laid off thousands of people in the United States and beefed up operations in India. Nissan closed factories in Japan and added a new factory in the United States. What are the ethical dilemmas here? What are your recommendations?

Closing Case: 3G: A Cell Phone Too Far?

The third-generation (3G) wireless technology is promising, yet risky. In addition to being a cell phone, it can take pictures, send e-mails (including the pictures just snapped), play video games, display maps (using the global positioning system), download media (both video and music), and hold videoconferences (see the person you are talking to). The problem is that there seems to be little demand for it. This is a painful conclusion reached by the European telecommunications industry that burned $150 billion bidding for 3G licenses, but wrote off plans for network roll-out. Similarly, the performance of NTT DoCoMo (http://www.nttdocomo.com) *and KTF* (http://www.ktf.com), *which recently launched 3G in Japan and South Korea, respectively, is not encouraging.*

However, Hutchison Whampoa (http://www.hutchisonwhampoa.com), *a conglomerate controlled by Hong Kong's most influential tycoon, Li Ka-shing, begs to differ. It is charging into 3G at a breakneck speed by spending $17.5 billion to set up nine operators (through JVs and WOSs) in Australia, Austria, Denmark, Great Britain, Hong Kong, Ireland, Israel, Italy, and Sweden. As a first mover, Hutchison is betting that it can pioneer and dominate a new business. Its global brand is simply called "3." Except Hong Kong and Australia, where Hutchison has been a telecom player, 3 will be a first-time entrant not only in 3G, but also in the entire telecom industry in the other seven countries. Therefore, 3 will confront the "double whammy" of having to overcome both the liability of foreignness as an unknown player and the liability of new technology.*

The countries Hutchison seeks to enter are developed markets saturated by strong local competitors. The number of cell phone users there has peaked, and 3 will have to take market share away from incumbents, an action sure to invite retaliation. Adding license fees, a 3G network costs at least 50 percent more to build than a traditional mobile network. To subscribe to 3's services, customers will also have to buy a new handset, which would cost US$960 in Britain and close to US$2,000 in Hong Kong. In comparison, the most fancy 2G cell phones hardly sell for more than US$550. In addition, to break even in Britain by 2006, 3 UK (the British subsidiary) would have to squeeze US$350 out of an average subscriber each month. Experts note that there has been no precedent for any firm to command that kind of market power from zero in saturated markets. Hutchison executives argue that 3G is a whole new ball game and that customers will have an unprecedented motive to switch. For example, they stress the excitement of being able to download a video clip of the latest sports games. The question is how much that convenience will cost. Given the sticker shock, none of the gadgets appears to be a "must have."

Even on the technology side, the early 3G experience from Japan and South Korea is that handsets would be big, heavy, and short on battery life—in addition to being expensive. With so many applications provided by hundreds of companies, nobody can guarantee whether they will work smoothly with each other. Early customers may even find conversations cut off when crossing into an area with no 3G coverage.

As a well-run global conglomerate, not a pure telecom player, Hutchison can survive a total disaster in its 3G ventures. In 2002, only 13 percent of its revenues came from telecom. Its "bread and butter" businesses are ports, infrastructure, retail, and property, which generated 46 percent of the group's profits. Nevertheless, Hutchison's shares already took a beating, dropping 41 percent in 2002 primarily because of its exposure to 3G risks. The stakes clearly are high. There are many well-wishers for 3's pioneering efforts. Equipment makers such as Ericsson (http://www.ericsson.com), NEC (http://www.nec.com), and Nokia (http://www.nokia.com) desperately want 3 to succeed. Even rivals all wish 3 well. "They are doing all the explaining about 3G for us," commented a strategist at Orange (http://www.web.orange.co.uk), a British competitor. Coming from a late mover, this comment is indeed not a half-hearted one.

Case Discussion Questions

1. *Why doesn't Hutchison Whampoa launch 3G services in its home market first, and then enter foreign*

countries? In other words, what are the benefits of launching in nine countries simultaneously?

2. *While all European telecom players have taken a "wait-and-see" attitude toward 3G (even after spending billions to acquire licenses), what motivates Hutchison to strategize differently?*

3. *If you were a Hutchison board member, would you vote "go" or "no go" for the 3G ventures?*

4. *If you were a board member at Orange, what would be your strategic advice for Orange?*

Sources: Based on (1) K. Au, M. W. Peng, & D. Wang, 2000, Interlocking directorates, firm strategies, and performance in Hong Kong, Asia Pacific Journal of Management, 17: 29–47; (2) H. A. Bolande, 2002, High wireless act, Far Eastern Economic Review, October 31: 36–40; (3) A. Latour, 2002, Market leader or spoiler? Far Eastern Economic Review, October 31: 40; (4) T. Standage, 2004, Crunch time for 3G, in The World in 2004 (pp. 99–100), London: Economist; (5) Standard (Hong Kong), 2003, Troubled 3 UK, December 19: A6.

Notes

Abbreviation list

AIM – *Advances in International Management*

AMJ – *Academy of Management Journal*

AMR – *Academy of Management Review*

APJM – *Asia Pacific Journal of Management*

ASQ – *Administrative Science Quarterly*

BW – *Business Week*

CMR – *California Management Review*

EMJ – *European Management Journal*

FEER – *Far Eastern Economic Review*

HBR – *Harvard Business Review*

HJE – *Hitotsubashi Journal of Economics*

IMR – *International Marketing Review*

JIBS – *Journal of International Business Studies*

JIM – *Journal of International Management*

JM – *Journal of Management*

JMS – *Journal of Management Studies*

LRP – *Long Range Planning*

MIR – *Management International Review*

MS – *Management Science*

SMJ – *Strategic Management Journal*

SMR – *MIT Sloan Management Review*

TIBR – *Thunderbird Intl Business Review*

1. S. Hymer, 1976, *The International Operations of National Firms*, Cambridge, MA: MIT Press; J. Mezias, 2002, Identifying liabilities of foreignness and strategies to minimize their effects, *SMJ*, 23: 229–244; S. Miller & A. Parkhe, 2002, Is there a liability of foreignness in global banking?, *SMJ*, 23: 55–75; S. Zaheer, 1995, Overcoming the liability of foreignness, *AMJ*, 38: 341–363.

2. S. Chang & P. Rosenzweig, 2001, The choice of entry mode in sequential foreign direct investment, *SMJ*, 22: 747–776; Y. Luo & J. Mezias, 2002, Liabilities of foreignness, *JIM*, 8: 217–221; S. Miller & M. Richards, 2002, Liability of foreignness and membership in a regional economic group, *JIM*, 8: 323–337; L. Nachum, 2003, Liability of foreignness in global competition? *SMJ*, 24: 1187–1208; B. Petersen &

T. Pedersen, 2002, Coping with liability of foreignness, *JIM,* 8: 339–350.

3. M. Calhoun, 2002, Unpacking liability of foreignness, *JIM,* 8: 301–321; D. Sethi & S. Guisinger, 2002, Liability of foreignness to competitive advantage, *JIM,* 8: 223–240.

4. M Lyles, T. Saxton, & K. Watson, 2004, Venture survival in a transition economy, *JM,* 30: 351–373; K. Miller, 1992, A framework for integrated risk management in international business, *JIBS,* 23: 311–331; W. Mitchell, J. M. Shaver, & B. Yeung, 1992, Getting there in a global industry, *SMJ,* 13: 419–432.

5. United Nations, 2003, *World Investment Report* (p. 5), New York and Geneva: United Nations.

6. K. Banerji & R. Sambharya, 1996, Vertical *keiretsu* and international market entry, *JIBS,* 27: 89–113; X. Martin, A. Swaminathan, & W. Mitchell, 1998, Organizational evolution in the interorganizational environment, *ASQ,* 43: 566–602.

7. A. Gupta & V. Govindarajan, 2004, *Global Strategy and Organization* (pp. 50–52), New York: Wiley.

8. F. Knickerbocker, 1973, *Oligopolistic Reaction and Multinational Enterprise,* Boston: Harvard Business School Press; V. Terpstra & C. Yu, 1988, Determinants of foreign investment of US advertising agencies, *JIBS,* 19: 33–45.

9. B. Elango & R. Sambharya, 2004, The influence of industry structure on the entry mode choice of overseas entrants in manufacturing industries, *JIM,* 10: 107–124.

10. M. W. Peng, 2001, The resource-based view and international business, *JM,* 27 (6): 803–829. See also D. Griffith & M. Harvey, 2001, A resource perspective of global dynamic capabilities, *JIBS,* 32: 597–606; D. Tan & J. Mahoney, 2002, Examining the Penrose effect in an international business context, Working paper, University of Illinois at Urbana-Champaign; S. Tallman, 1991, Strategic management models and resource-based strategies among MNEs in a host market, *SMJ,* 12: 69–82; S. Zahra, R. D. Ireland, & M. Hitt, 2000, International expansion by new venture firms, *AMJ,* 43: 925–951.

11. J. Denekamp, 1995, Intangible assets, internalization, and FDI in manufacturing, *JIBS,* 26: 493–504.

12. R. Larsson, K. Brousseau, M. Driver, M. Holmqvist, & V. Tarnovskaya, 2003, International growth through cooperation, *AME,* 17 (1): 7–21.

13. C. Hill, P. Hwang, & C. Kim, 1990, An eclectic theory of the choice of international entry mode (p. 124), *SMJ,* 11: 117–128.

14. A. Thompson, 1996, Compliance with agreements in cross-cultural transactions, *JIBS,* 27: 375–390.

15. R. Tasker, 2002, Pepperoni power, *FEER,* November 14: 59–60.

16. T. Brewer, 1992, An issue-area approach to the analysis of MNE-government relations, *JIBS,* 23: 295–309; N. Fagre & L. Wells, 1982, Bargaining power of multinationals and host governments, *JIBS,* 21: 1–22; T. Murtha & S. Lenway, 1994, Country capabilities and the strategic state, *SMJ,* 15: 113–129.

17. T. Poytner, 1982, Government intervention in less developed countries, *JIBS,* 13: 9–25.

18. A. Delios & W. Henisz, 2000, Japanese firms' investment strategies in emerging economies, *AMJ,* 43: 305–323; J. Doh & R. Ramamurti, 2003, Reassessing risk in developing country infrastructure, *LRP,* 36: 337–353; W. Henisz & A. Delios, 2001, Uncertainty, imitation, and plant location, *ASQ,* 46: 443–475; M. Makhija, 1993, Government intervention in the Venezuelan petroleum industry, *JIBS,* 24: 531–555.

19. J. Doh, 2000, Entrepreneurial privatization strategies, *AMR,* 25: 551–572; K. Meyer & S. Estrin, 2001, Brownfield entry in emerging markets, *JIBS,* 32: 574–584; N. Uhlenbruck & J. DeCastro, 2000, Foreign acquisitions in Central and Eastern Europe, *AMJ,* 43: 381–402.

20. J. Zhao, S. Park, & J. Du, 2003, The impact of corruption and transparency on foreign direct investment, *MIR,* 43: 41–62.

21. *Economist,* 2003, Indonesia: Still living dangerously, October 25: 58.

22. K. Brouthers & G. Bamossy, 1997, The role of key stakeholders in international joint venture negotiations, *JIBS,* 28: 285–308; Y. Luo, 2001, Toward a cooperative view of MNC-host government relations, *JIBS,* 32: 401–419; R. Ramamurti, 2001, The obsolescing bargaining model? *JIBS,* 32: 23–40.

23. T. Agmon, 2003, Who gets what, *JIBS,* 34: 416–427; M. Minor, 1994, The demise of expropriation as an instrument of LDC policy, 1980–1992, *JIBS,* 25: 177–188; J. Oetzel, R. Bettis, & M. Zehner, 2001, Country risk measures, *JWB,* 36: 128–145; R. Vernon, 2001, Big business and national governments, *JIBS,* 32: 509–518.

24. *Economist,* 2003, Selling to the developing world, December 13: 8.

25. D. Welch, 2004, How Honda is stalling in the US, *BW,* May 24: 62–63.

26. L. Jacque & P. Vaaler, 2001, The international control conundrum with exchange risk, *JIBS,* 32: 813–832; D. Miller & J. Reuer, 1998, Firm strategy and economic exposure to foreign exchange rate movements, *JIBS,* 29: 493–514.

27. C. Hill, 2003, *International Business,* 4th ed. (p. 307), Chicago: Irwin McGraw-Hill.

28. B. Kogut & N. Kulatilaka, 1994, Operating flexibility, global manufacturing, and the option value of a multinational network, *MS,* 40: 123–139; S. Lee & M. Makhija, 2003, Environmental uncertainty and the value of Korean firms' international investments, Working paper, University of Texas at Dallas; C. Pantzalis, B. Simkins, & P. Laux, 2001, Operational hedges and the foreign exchange exposure of US multinational corporations, *JIBS,* 32: 793–812.

29. J. Bonardi, 2004, Global and political strategies in deregulated industries, *SMJ,* 25: 101–120; P. Davis, A. Desai, & J. Francis, 2000, Mode of international entry, *JIBS,* 31: 239–258; S. Estrin & K. Meyer, 2004, *Investment Strategies in Emerging Economies,* Cheltenham, UK: Elgar; J. Laurila & M. Ropponen, 2003, Institutional conditioning of foreign expansion, *JMS,* 40: 725–751; K. Meyer, 2001, Institutions, transaction costs, and entry mode choice in Eastern Europe, *JIBS,* 32: 357–367; D Tse, Y Pan, & K. Au, 1997, How MNCs choose entry modes and form alliances, *JIBS,* 28: 779–805.

30. P. Buckley & N. Hashai, 2004, A global system view of firm boundaries, *JIBS,* 35: 33–45; J. Dunning, 1998, Location and the multinational enterprise: A neglected factor?, *JIBS,* 29: 45–66.

31. T. Chen, H. Chen, & Y. Ku, 2004, Foreign direct investment and local linkages, *JIBS,* 35: 320–333; S. Feinberg & S. Majumdar, 2001, Technology spillovers from FDI, *JIBS,* 32: 421–437; A. Kalnins & W. Chung, 2004, Resource–seeking agglomeration, *SMJ,* 25: 689–699; L. Nachum, 2000, Economic geography and the location of TNCs, *JIBS,* 31: 367–385; M. Porter, 1998, *On Competition,* Boston: Harvard Business School Press; R. Pouder & C. St. John, 1996, Hot spots and blind spots, *AMR,* 21: 1192–1225; L. Rosenkopf & P. Almeida, 2003, Overcoming local search through alliances and mobility, *MS,* 49: 757–766; S. Tallman, M. Jenkins, N. Henry, & S. Pinch, 2004, Knowledge, clusters, and competitive advantage, *AMR,* 29: 258–271.

32. *Economist,* 2004, European carmaking: Going east, March 26: 60.

33. D. Sethi, S. Guisinger, S. Phelan, & D. Berg, 2003, Trends in FDI flows, *JIBS,* 34: 315–326.

34. G. Smith, 2003, Mexico: Was NAFTA worth it? (p. 72), *BW,* December 22: 66–72.

35. M. W. Peng & D. Wang, 2000, Innovation capability and foreign direct investment (p. 80), *MIR,* 40: 79–93.

36. A. Madhok, 1997, Cost, value, and foreign market entry mode, *SMJ,* 18: 39–61.

37. W. Chung & A. Kalnins, 2001, Agglomeration effects and performance, *SMJ,* 22: 969–988; J. M. Shaver & F. Flyer, 2000, Agglomeration economies, firm heterogeneity, and foreign direct investment in the United States, *SMJ,* 21: 1175–93.

38. B. Kogut & H. Singh, 1988, The effect of national culture on the choice of entry mode, *JIBS,* 19: 411–432.

39. D. Xu & O. Shenkar, 2002, Institutional distance and the multinational enterprise (p. 608), *AMR,* 27: 608–618. See also L. Busenitz, C. Gomez, & J. Spencer, 2000, Country institutional profiles, *AMJ,* 43: 993–1003.

40. T. Chen, 2003, Network resources for internationalization, *JMS,* 40: 1107–1130; K. Gillespie, L. Riddle, E. Sayre, & D. Sturges, 1999, Diaspora interest in homeland investment, *JIBS,* 30: 623–634; J. Johansson & J. Vahlne, 1977, The internationalization process of the firm, *JIBS,* 8: 23–32.

41. P. Ghemawat, 2001, Distance still matters, *HBR,* September, 79 (8): 137–147.

42. H. Barkema, J. Bell, & J. Pennings, 1996, Foreign entry, cultural barriers, and learning, *SMJ,* 17: 151–166; A. Rugman & A. Verbeke, 2004, A perspective on regional

and global strategies of multinational enterprises, *JIBS,* 35: 3–18.

43. G. Benito & G. Gripsrud, 1992, The expansion of foreign direct investments, *JIBS,* 23: 461–476; A. Harzing, 2004, The role of culture in entry-mode studies, *AIM,* 15: 75–127; J. Hennart & J. Larimo, 1998, The impact of culture on the strategy of multinational enterprises, *JIBS,* 29: 515–538; O. Shenkar, 2001, Cultural distance revisited, *JIBS,* 32: 519–535.

44. G. Gripsrud, 1990, The determinants of export decisions and attitudes to a distant market, *JIBS,* 21: 469–485.

45. J. Evans & F. Mavondo, 2002, Psychic distance and organizational performance, *JIBS,* 33: 515–532; P. Morosini, S. Shane, & H. Singh, 1998, National cultural distance and cross-border acquisition performance, *JIBS,* 29: 137–158; S. O'Grady & H. Lane, 1996, The psychic distance paradox, *JIBS,* 27: 309–333.

46. J. Anand & A. Delios, 1996, Location specificity and the transferability of downstream assets to foreign subsidiaries, *JIBS,* 28: 579–603; M K. Erramilli & S. Agarwal, 1997, Are firm-specific advantages location-specific too? *JIBS,* 28: 735–57.

47. This section draws heavily from Y. Luo & M. W. Peng, 1998, First mover advantages in investing in transition economies, *TIBR,* 40: 141–163.

48. M. Lieberman & D. Montgomery, 1988, First-mover advantages, *SMJ,* 9: 41–58.

49. M. W. Peng, S. Lee, & J. Tan, 2001, The *keiretsu* in Asia, *JIM,* 7 (4): 253–276.

50. B. Mascarenhas, 1986, International strategies of nondominant firms, *JIBS,* 17: 1–25

51. T. Isobe, S. Makino, & D. Montgomery, 2000, Resource commitment, entry timing, and market performance of foreign direct investments in emerging economies, *AMJ,* 43: 468–484; R. Makadok, 1998, Can first-mover and early-mover advantages be sustained in an industry with low barriers to entry/imitation?, *SMJ,* 19: 683–696; B. Mascarenhas, 1992, Order of entry and performance in international markets, *SMJ,* 13: 499–510; W. Mitchell, 1991, Dual clock, *SMJ,* 12: 85–100; R. Sinha & C. Noble, 1997, The performance consequences of subfield entry, *SMJ,* 18: 465–481; X. M. Song, C. Nenedetto, & Y. Zhao, 1999, Pioneering advantages in manufacturing and service industries, *SMJ,* 20: 811–836; B. Tan &

I. Vertinsky, 1996, Foreign direct investment by Japanese electronics firms in the United States and Canada, *JIBS,* 27: 655–681.

52. L. Fuentelsaz, J. Gomez, & Y. Polo, 2002, Followers' entry timing, *SMJ,* 23: 245–264; H. Lee, K. Smith, C. Grimm, & A. Schomburg, 2000, Timing, order, and durability of new product advantages with imitation, *SMJ,* 21: 23–30; J. Shamsie, C. Phelps, & J. Kuperman, 2004, Being late than never, *SMJ,* 25: 69–84; L. Tegarden, D. Hatfield, & A. Echols, 1999, Doomed from the start, *SMJ,* 20: 495–518.

53. V. Gaba, Y. Pan, & G. Ungson, 2002, Timing of entry in international market, *JIBS,* 33: 39–55; M. Lieberman, 2002, Did first-mover advantage survive the dot-com crash? Working paper, UCLA; K. Miller & T. Folta, 2002, Option value and entry timing, *SMJ,* 23: 655–665.

54. M. W. Peng, 2000, Controlling the foreign agent: How governments deal with multinationals in a transition economy, *MIR,* 40 (2): 141–165; T. Q. Tao, 2004, The road to success: A resource-based view of joint ventures evolution in China's auto industry, PhD dissertation, Pittsburgh: Katz School of Business, University of Pittsburgh.

55. A. Delios & P. Beamish, 2001, Survival and profitability: The roles of experience and intangible assets in foreign subsidiary performance, *AMJ,* 44: 1028–1038; Y. Luo & M. W. Peng, 1999, Learning to compete in a transition economy: Experience, environment, and performance, *JIBS,* 30: 269–296; J. M. Shaver, W. Mitchell, & B. Yeung, 1997, The effect of own-firm and other-firm experience on foreign direct investment survival in the United States, 1987–92, *SMJ,* 18: 811–824.

56. *Economist,* 2003, Islamic finance: West meets East, October 25: 69.

57. A. Delios & W. Henisz, 2003, Political hazards, experience, and sequential entry strategies, *SMJ,* 24: 1153–1164; M. K. Erramilli, 1991, The experience factor in foreign market entry behavior of service firms, *JIBS,* 22: 479–502; P. Padmansbhan & K. Cho, 1999, Decision specific experience in foreign ownership and establishment strategies, *JIBS,* 30: 25–44.

58. Y. Pan & D. Tse, 2000, The hierarchical model of market entry modes, *JIBS,* 31: 535–554. See also E. Anderson & H. Gatignon, 1986, Modes of foreign entry, *JIBS,* 16: 1–26.

59. R. Caves, 1996, *Multinational Enterprise and Economic Analysis* (p. 1), New York: Cambridge University Press.

60. P. Buckley & M. Casson, 1976, *The Future of the Multinational Enterprise,* London: Macmillan; J. Campa & M. Guillen, 1999, The internalization of exports, *MS,* 45: 1463–1478; W. Davidson & D. McFetridge, 1985, Key characteristics of the choice of international technology transfer mode, *JIBS,* 17: 5–21.

61. J. Dunning, 1993, *Multinational Enterprises and the Global Economy* (p. 79), Reading, MA: Addison-Wesley. See also S. Agarwal & S. Ramaswami, 1992, Choice of foreign market entry mode, *JIBS,* 23: 1–27.

62. L. Leonidou & C. Katsikeas, 1996, The export development process, *JIBS,* 27: 517–551.

63. G. Balabanis, 2000, Factors affecting export intermediaries' service offerings, *JIBS,* 31: 83–99; R. Castaldi, A. De Noble, & J. Kantor, 1992, The intermediary service requirements of Canadian and American exporters, *IMR,* 9: 21–40; A. Perry, 1992, *The Evolution of US Trade Intermediaries,* Westport, CT: Quorum Books; T. Roehl, 1983, A transaction cost approach to international trading structures, *HJE,* 24: 119–135.

64. M. W. Peng, 1998, *Behind the Success and Failure of US Export Intermediaries,* Westport, CT: Quorum Books; M. W. Peng & A. Ilinitch, 1998, Export intermediary firms: A note on export development research, *JIBS,* 29 (3): 609–620; H. Trabold, 2002, Export intermediation: An empirical test of Peng and Ilinitch, *JIBS,* 33: 327–344.

65. P. Ellis, 2003, Social structure and intermediation, *JMS,* 40: 1683–1708; L. Li, 2003, Determinants of export channel intensity in emerging markets, *APJM,* 20: 501–516; D. Skarmeas, C. Katsikeas, & B. Schlegelmilch, 2002, Drivers of commitment and its impact on performance in cross-cultural buyer-seller relationships, *JIBS,* 33: 757–783; C. Zhang, S. T. Cavusgil, & A. Roath, 2003, Manufacturer governance of foreign distributor relationships, *JIBS,* 34: 550–566.

66. A. Arora & A. Fosfuri, 2000, Wholly owned subsidiary versus technology licensing in the worldwide chemical industry, *JIBS,* 31: 555–572; P. Aulakh, S. T. Cavusgil, & M. Sarkar, 1998, Compensation in international licensing agreements, *JIBS,* 29: 409–420; J. Combs & D. Ketchen, 1999, Can capital scarcity help agency theory explain franchising? *AMJ,* 42: 196–207; K. Fladmoe-Lindquist & L. Jacque, 1995, Control modes in international service operations, *MS,* 41: 1238–1249; S. Shane, 1996, Hybrid organizational arrangements and their implications for firm growth and survival, *AMJ,* 39: 216–234; X. Yin & E. Zajac, 2004, The strategy/governance structure fit relationship, *SMJ,* 25: 365–383.

67. Y. Luo, 2002, *Multinational Enterprises in Emerging Markets* (p. 202), Copenhagen, Denmark: Copenhagen Business School Press.

68. S. Chen & J. Hennart, 2002, Japanese investors' choice of joint ventures versus wholly-owned subsidiaries in the US, *JIBS,* 33: 1–18; J. Hennart & Reddy, 1997, The choice between mergers/acquisitions and joint ventures, *SMJ,* 18: 1–12.

69. H. Barkema & F. Vermeulen, 1998, International expansion through start-up or acquisition, *AMJ,* 41: 7–26; A. Harzing, 2002, Acquisitions versus green-field investments, *SMJ,* 23: 211–227.

70. W. C. Kim & P. Hwang, 1992, Global strategy and multinationals' entry mode choice, *JIBS,* 23: 29–53.

71. United Nations, 2003, *World Investment Report 2003* (p. 2).

72. J. M. Shaver, 1998, Accounting for endogeneity when assessing strategy performance, *MS,* 44: 571–585.

73. J. Hagedoorn & B. Sadowski, 1999, The transition from strategic technology alliances to mergers and acquisitions, *JMS,* 36: 87–107; B. Peterson, D. Welch, & L. Welch, 2000, Creating meaningful switching options, *LRP,* 33: 688–705.

74. R. Grosse & L. Trevino, 1996, Foreign direct investment in the United States, *JIBS,* 27: 139–155; L. Melin, 1992, Internationalization as a strategy process, *SMJ,* 13: 99–118; D. Yiu & S. Makino, 2002, The choice between joint venture and wholly owned subsidiary, *OSc,* 13: 667–683.

75. J. Child, L. Chung, & H. Davies, 2003, The performance of cross-border units in China, *JIBS,* 34:242–254; J. Mata & P. Portugal, 2000, Closure and divestiture by foreign entrants, *SMJ,* 21: 549–562; A. Sharma, 1998, Mode of entry and ex-post performance, *SMJ,* 19: 879–900; F. Vermeulen & H. Barkema, 2002, Pace, rhythm, and scope, *SMJ,* 23: 637–653.

76. J. Brown, C. Dev, & Z. Zhou, 2003, Broadening the foreign market entry mode decision, *JIBS,* 34: 473–488;

J. Li, 1995, Foreign entry and survival, *SMJ,* 16: 333–351; C. P. Woodcock, P. Beamish, & S. Makino, 1994, Ownership-based entry mode strategies and international performance, *JIBS,* 25: 253–273.

77. W. Vanhonacker, 1997, Entering China: An unconventional approach, *HBR,* March-April: 130–140.

78. A. Delios & P. Beamish, 2004, Joint venture performance revisited, *MIR,* 44: 69–91; Y. Pan & P. Chi, 1999, Financial performance and survival of multinational corporations in China, *SMJ,* 20: 359–374.

79. H. K. Steensma & M. Lyles, 2000, Explaining IJV survival in a transition economy through social exchange and knowledge-based perspectives, *SMJ,* 21: 831–851.

80. T. Tong, J. Reuer, & M. W. Peng, 2004, International joint ventures and the value of growth options, Working paper, Fisher College of Business, The Ohio State University.

81. K. Brouthers & L. Brouthers, 2003, Why service and manufacturing entry mode choices differ, *JMS,* 40: 1179–1204; F. Contractor, S. Kundu, & C. Hsu, 2003, A three-stage theory of international expansion, *JIBS,* 5–18; R. Grosse, 1997, International technology transfer in services, *JIBS,* 27: 781–800; J. Murray & M. Kotabe, 1999, Sourcing strategies of US service companies, *SMJ,* 20: 791–809; P. Rivoli & E. Salorio, 1996, FDI under uncertainty, *JIBS,* 27: 335–357.

82. M. K. Erramilli, 1996, Nationality and subsidiary ownership patterns in multinational corporations, *JIBS,* 27: 225–248; Y. Pak & Y. Park, 2004, Global ownership strategy of Japanese multinational enterprises, *MIR,* 44: 3–21; S. Shane, 1994, The effect of national culture on the choice between licensing and direct foreign investment, *SMJ,* 15: 627–642.

83. J. Hennart, 1991, The transaction costs theory of joint ventures, *MS,* 37: 483–497; S. Makino & K. Neupert, 2000, National culture, transaction costs, and the choice between joint venture and wholly owned subsidiary, *JIBS,* 31: 705–713.

84. This section draws from R. Hoskisson, L. Eden, C. Lau, & M. Wright, 2000, Strategy in emerging economies, *AMJ,* 43: 249–267; M. W. Peng, 2000, *Business Strategies in Transition Economies,* Thousand Oaks, CA: Sage Publishing.

85. C. K. Prahalad & K. Lieberthal, 1998, The end of corporate imperialism, *HBR,* July-August: 68–79.

86. M. W. Peng, 2003, Institutional transitions and strategic choices, *AMR,* 28: 275–296.

87. D. McCarthy, S. Puffer, & P. Simmonds, 1993, Riding the Russian roller coaster, *CMR,* 36: 99–115.

88. N. Dawar, 2002, Rethinking marketing programs for emerging markets (p. 457), *LRP,* 35: 457–474.

89. D. Arnold & J. Quelch, 1998, New strategies in emerging markets, *SMR,* 39: 7–20; S. Miller & A. Parkhe, 1998, Patterns in the expansion of US banks' foreign operations, *JIBS,* 29: 359–390.

90. P. Aulakh, M. Kotabe, & H. Teegen, 2000, Export strategies and performance of firms from emerging economies, *AMJ,* 43: 342–361; S. Makino, C. Lau, & R. Yeh, 2002, Asset-exploitation versus asset-seeking, *JIBS,* 33: 403–421; J. Mathews, 2002, *Dragon Multinationals,* New York: Oxford University Press.

91. M. Levesque & D. Shepherd, 2004, Entrepreneurs' choice of entry strategy in emerging and developed markets, *JBV,* 19: 26–54; S. T. Cavusgil, P. Ghauri, & M. Agarwal, 2002, *Doing Business in Emerging Markets,* Thousand Oaks, CA: Sage.

92. S. Kotha, V. Rindova, & F. Rothaermel, 2001, Assets and actions, *JIBS,* 32: 769–792; J. Oxley & B. Yeung, 2001, E-commerce readiness, *JIBS,* 32: 705–723; B. Peterson, L. Welch, & P. Liesch, 2002, The Internet and foreign market expansion by firms, *MIR,* 42: 207–221; S. Rangan & R. Adner, 2001, Profits and the Internet, *SMR,* summer: 44–53; N. Singh & S. Kundu, 2002, Explaining the growth of e-commerce corporations, *JIBS,* 33: 679–697; S. Zaheer & S. Manrakhan, 2001, Concentration and dispersion in global industries, *JIBS,* 32: 667–686.

93. E. Leamer & M. Storper, 2001, The economic geography of the Internet age (p. 641), *JIBS,* 32: 641–665.

94. J. de la Torre & R. Moxon, 2001, E-commerce and global business, *JIBS,* 32: 617–639; S. Globerman, T. Roehl, & S. Standifird, 2001, Globalization and electronic commerce, *JIBS,* 32: 749–768.

95. S. Kobrin, 2001, Sovereignty@bay, in A. Rugman & T. Brewer (eds.), *The Oxford Handbook of International Business* (pp. 181–205), Oxford, UK: Oxford University Press.

96. J. Goldsmith, 2000, cited in P. Lasserre, 2003, *Global Strategic Management* (p. 390). New York: Palgrave.

MAKING STRATEGIC ALLIANCES AND NETWORKS WORK

Outline

- Defining strategic alliances and networks
- A comprehensive model of strategic alliances and networks
- Formation
- Evolution
- Performance
- Debates and extensions
- Implications for strategists

Opening Case: General Motors and Daewoo: Married, Divorced, and Married Again

In 1984, General Motors (GM, http://www.gm.com) and Daewoo (http://www.daewoo.com) *formed a 50/50, South Korea–based joint venture (JV), named the Daewoo Motor Company, with each partner contributing $100 million of equity. The JV would produce the Pontiac Le Mans, based on GM's popular Opel Kadett model (Opel* [http://www.opel.com] *is a wholly owned German subsidiary of GM). Commentators hailed the JV as a brilliant outcome of a corporate "marriage" of German technology and Korean labor (whose cost was low at that time). As a win-win combination, GM would tackle the small car market in North America and eventually expand into Asia, whereas Daewoo would gain access to superior technology and to the world's largest car market, the United States.*

However, by the late 1980s, Korean workers became more assertive in the new democratic era. Demanding higher wages, the JV workers launched a series of bitter strikes. Ultimately, the JV had to more than double their wages. It thus became cheaper to build cars in Germany than in Korea. Even though German wages were high, German productivity was even higher, which led to lower labor costs per vehicle in Germany than in Korea. Equally problematic was the poor quality of the Le Mans. Electrical systems often crashed, and brakes had a tendency to

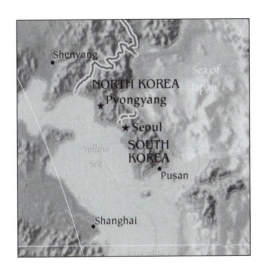

fail. US sales plummeted to 37,000 vehicles in 1991, down 86 percent from the 1988 high.

However, Daewoo argued that the poor sales were not primarily due to quality problems, but due to GM's poor marketing efforts, which had not treated the Le Mans as one of GM's own models. Further, Daewoo was deeply frustrated by GM's determination to block its efforts to export cars to Eastern Europe, which Daewoo saw as its ideal market. GM's reasoning was that Eastern Europe was Opel's territory.

Gradually, Daewoo shifted its efforts toward independently developing car models in anticipation of a breakdown of the JV, while GM initially was unaware of these activities. After Daewoo openly launched competing car models, the troubles associated with this JV, long rumored by the media, became strikingly evident. The picture of an "ideal couple" with a "perfect kid" (the JV) was now replaced by the image of a dysfunctional family where everyone was pointing a finger at each other.

In 1991, GM and Daewoo renegotiated. Daewoo demanded that each partner invest another $100 million. GM refused and delivered a blunt counterproposal: Sell your stake or buy ours. Much to GM's surprise, Daewoo agreed to buy out GM's equity for $170 million. GM exited the problematic JV in 1992, which left GM without a manufacturing base in Korea. Daewoo, on the other hand, embarked upon one of the most ambitious marches into emerging economies, building a dozen auto plants in countries such as Indonesia, Iran, Poland, Ukraine, Vietnam, and Uzbekistan. In the process, Daewoo borrowed an astounding $20 billion, which led to the collapse of the group during the 1997 Asian economic crisis (also see Closing Case in Chapter 9).

In an interesting turn of events, GM and Daewoo joined hands again. Despite Daewoo's grave financial difficulties, it attempted to avoid a takeover by GM and strongly preferred a takeover by Ford (http://www.ford.com). When Ford backed out, GM entered the negotiation, eventually forming a new JV, called GM Daewoo Motor (http://www.daewoous.com), with Daewoo's Korean creditors in 2001. The terms of this marriage were quite different from the previous one. Instead of a 50/50 split, GM was now in the driver's seat, commanding a 67 percent stake (with a $400 million investment). Some observers suggested that this was really a GM takeover in disguise (also see Video Case 2.2).

Sources: Based on (1) C. Hill, 2000, General Motors and Daewoo, International Business, 3rd ed., Boston: Irwin McGraw-Hill; (2) L. Kraar, 2003, Wanted, Fortune, February 3: 102–108; (3) M. W. Peng and O. Shenkar, 2002, Joint venture dissolution as corporate divorce, Academy of Management Executive, 16 (2): 92–105.

Why did GM and Daewoo establish strategic alliances? Among many forms of strategic alliances, why did they choose the JV form both times? Why did the equity distribution in the two JVs change from an equal contribution to an unequal contribution? Why do some strategic alliances succeed, while others fail? These are some of the key questions we discuss in this chapter.

In 1966, GM boldly declared in its annual report that "unified ownership for coordinated policy control of all of our operations throughout the world is essential for our effective performance as a worldwide corporation."[1] GM has evidently changed its mind. As globalization intensifies, strategic alliances and networks have proliferated around the world, resulting in an "explosion in alliances."[2] "The least attractive way to try to win on a global basis," according to GE's former chairman and CEO Jack Welch, "is to think you can take on the world all by yourself."[3] In the United States in 1990, only 7 percent of the revenues of the top 1,000 public firms were generated through alliances and networks. By the end of the 1990s, alliances and networks produced approximately one-quarter of the revenues of these firms.[4]

Similar strategic alliance and network proliferation is now evident in just about every industry and every country. Yet, 30 to 70 percent of all alliances and networks, such as the first GM-Daewoo JV, reportedly fail to meet the parent firm's objectives,[5] thus necessitating our attention to the cause of these failures.

This chapter first defines strategic alliances and networks, followed by an introduction of a comprehensive model that draws upon the three leading perspectives on strategy. We then discuss the formation, evolution, and performance of alliances and networks, followed by debates and extensions.

DEFINING STRATEGIC ALLIANCES AND NETWORKS

Strategic alliances are "voluntary agreements between firms involving exchanging, sharing, or codeveloping of products, technologies, or services."[6] Shown in Figure 7.1, strategic alliances are *compromises* between short-term, pure market transactions (such as spot transactions) and long-term, complete ownership solutions (such as mergers and acquisitions [M&As]—see Chapter 9).[7] First introduced in Chapter 6, alliances fall into two broad categories: contractual (non-equity) and equity-based. **Contractual alliances** include comarketing, research and development (R&D) contracts, turnkey projects, strategic suppliers, strategic distributors, and licensing/franchising (see Chapter 6 for definitions). They entail a relatively low level of commitment and are often limited in scope and duration. **Equity-based alliances** call for a higher level of commitment. Examples include **strategic investment** (one partner invests in another as a strategic investor) and **cross-shareholding** (both partners invest in each other). **Joint venture** is a special case of equity-based alliance that establishes a new legally independent entity (in other words, a new firm which is the JV) whose equity is provided by two (or more) alliance partners.

Although JVs are often used as examples of strategic alliances (see Opening Case), *not* all strategic alliances are JVs. Essentially, a JV is a "corporate child" given birth by two (or more) parent firms—such as SonyEricsson set up by Sony and Ericsson.[8] A non-JV, equity-based alliance can be regarded as two firms "getting married," but not having "children." The Renault-Nissan alliance is such an example

FIGURE 7.1   The Variety of Strategic Alliances

(see Opening Case in Chapter 9): Renault is a strategic investor in Nissan, but both automakers still operate independently and they have *not* given birth to a new car company (which would be a JV if they did).

The term "strategic networks" is derived from the term "social networks" highlighting the social aspects of interfirm relationships.[9] For the purposes of this chapter, we define **strategic networks** as strategic alliances formed by *multiple* firms to compete against other such groups and against traditional single firms.[10] For example, the three multipartner alliances in the airline industry—Star Alliance (consisting of United Airlines, Lufthansa, Air Canada, SAS, and others), Sky Team (Delta, Air France, Korean Air, and others), and One World (American Airlines, British Airways, Cathay Pacific, Qantas, and others)—are strategic networks, which are sometimes also called **constellations** (see Video Case 2.3). Such multilateral strategic networks are inherently more complex than single alliance relationships between two firms (such as the alliance between KLM Royal Dutch Airlines and Northwestern Airlines).[11] Overall, we use the terms "strategic alliances" and "strategic networks" to refer to **cooperative interfirm relationships**.

A COMPREHENSIVE MODEL OF STRATEGIC ALLIANCES AND NETWORKS

Despite the diversity of cooperative interfirm relationships, underlying each decision to engage in alliances and networks is a set of strategic considerations drawn from the three leading perspectives on strategy discussed in earlier chapters.[12] These form a comprehensive model of strategic alliances and networks (see Figure 7.2).

Industry-Based Considerations

According to the traditional industry-based view, firms are independent players interested in maximizing their own performance. In reality, most firms in any industry are embedded in a number of competitive and/or collaborative relationships, thus we must consider firms' alliance and network ties to realistically understand the dynamics of the five forces.[13]

First, because rivalry often reduces profits, firms do not compete against each other on all occasions. Instead, many competitors collaborate by forming strategic alliances (often called **horizontal alliances**).[14] For example, GM and Toyota formed a JV, NUMMI, to jointly manufacture small cars in the United States. This does not suggest that these two firms are no longer competing; they still are, in most cases. What is interesting is that they decided to collaborate on a limited basis, for different purposes. GM was interested in learning how to profitably manufacture small cars, whereas Toyota was interested in learning how to operate in the United States (in anticipation of its forthcoming wholly owned subsidiaries [WOS]). These two firms are not alone. Recently, approximately half of all strategic alliances are between competitors (see Strategy in Action 7.1 on p. 258).[15] Sometimes, the goal of an alliance is simply to tie up a competitor.

FIGURE 7.2   A Comprehensive Model of Strategic Alliances and Networks

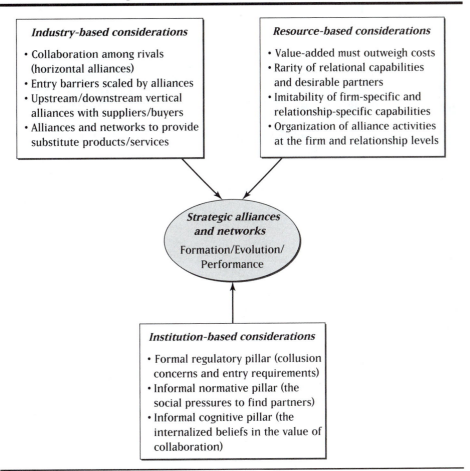

Second, while high entry barriers may deter individual firms, firms may form strategic alliances and networks to scale these walls. For instance, both Coca-Cola (Coke) and Nestle were interested in entering the hot canned drinks market (such as hot coffee and tea) in Japan. However, domestic players led by Suntory built formidable entry barriers and neither Coke nor Nestle, despite their global experience, had any expertise in this particular segment largely unknown outside of Japan. Although Suntory was better than Coke at soluble coffee and tea and had a larger distribution network than Nestle, when Coke and Nestle formed an alliance, Suntory was unable to match the combined strengths of these two giants.[16] Overall, combining forces allows the partner firms to enter new and unknown markets at a lower cost and lower risk.

Third, although suppliers are traditionally regarded as threats, that is not necessarily the case. First introduced in Chapter 2, firms can establish strategic alliances with suppliers (often called **upstream vertical alliances**), as exemplified by the Japanese *keiretsu* networks. In essence, strategic supply alliances transform an adversarial

STRATEGY IN ACTION 7.1. *Russia's MiG and Sukhoi Join Hands*

During the Cold War, thousands of MiG fighter jets made by the Mikoyan Moscow Production Organization (MAPO) were synonymous with "bogeys" widely recognized and respected by military pilots in the free world. In the post-Cold War era, MAPO ran into great difficulties because the Russian government cut back its orders (no orders for new aircraft from 1992 to 1998) and, with the dissolution of the Warsaw Pact, Central and Eastern European air forces started to import fighters from the West. Poland, for example, ordered F-16s from the United States. MAPO thus was forced to look for new export markets. However, in new markets, MAPO found that its previously popular MiG aircraft were not as successful as those made by its traditional rival, Sukhoi Aircraft Military and Industrial Group (*http://www.sukhoi.org*). While Sukhoi jets had not been as famous as MiGs, Sukhoi scored big hits in the 1990s

by securing high-profile contracts from China, India, and Vietnam, including more than 150 Su-27s as direct exports and 300 under licensed production. Even more impressive was that the Indonesian and South Korean air forces, traditionally exclusive markets for US fighters, expressed a strong interest in Sukhoi (although eventually had to cancel because of the 1997 Asian financial crisis). In comparison, MAPO only sold 80 MiG-29s to India and Malaysia in the 1990s. As a result, MAPO had little choice but to cooperate with Sukhoi. To be sure, initial cooperation was limited, involving only a joint marketing strategy and sharing some avionics. Such cooperation, however, was expected to intensify as competition in the global arms market heats up.

Source: Adapted from M. W. Peng, 2000, Business Strategies in Transition Economies *(p. 96), Thousand Oaks, CA: Sage Publishing, Inc.*

relationship centered on hard bargaining to a collaborative relationship featuring knowledge sharing and mutual assistance. Instead of negotiating contracts with a large number of suppliers on a frequent, short term basis (such as 2.3 years, the average length of US auto supply contracts in the 1990s), strategic supply alliances award contracts to a smaller number of key suppliers for longer terms (such as 8 years, the average length of Japanese auto supply contracts in the 1990s).[17] This helps align the focal firm's interests with the supplier's interests, which makes the suppliers more willing to make specialized investments to produce better components.[18] This is not to say that bargaining power becomes irrelevant. Instead, buyer firms increase their dependence on a smaller number of strategic suppliers, whose bargaining power may, in turn, *increase*.[19] However, collaboration softens some rough edges of bargaining power, by transforming a zero-sum game into a win-win proposition.

Fourth, similarly, instead of treating buyers and distributors as possible threats, establishing strategic distribution alliances (also called **downstream vertical alliances**) may bind the focal firm, buyers, and distributors together. For example, numerous hotels, publishers, airlines, and car rental companies find that alliances with leading Internet distributors such as Amazon, Expedia, Priceline, and Travelocity enable them to reach more customers.

Finally, the market potential of substitute products may encourage firms to form strategic alliances and networks to materialize the commercial potential of these new products. For instance, in the drive to bring 3G wireless technology to replace existing wireless technology in nine countries, Hutchison Whampoa has formed a number of alliances with local firms (see Closing Case in Chapter 6).

Resource-Based Considerations

The resource-based view, embodied in the VRIO framework, illustrates a number of crucial issues concerning the *v*alue, *r*arity, *i*mitability, and *o*rganizational aspects of strategic alliances and networks.

Value

Strategic alliances and networks must create value.[20] Table 7.1 identifies four broad categories of advantages that add value. First, relative to relying on pure market transactions and/or M&As, strategic alliances and networks may reduce costs, risks, and uncertainties.[21] The three global airline networks, for example, reduce ticket costs booked on two-stage flights by 18 to 28 percent compared with separate flights on the same route if these airlines were not allied.[22] Second, strategic alliances and networks allow firms to tap into their partner's complementary assets. Only through such pooling of partner capabilities has Airbus become a viable competitor of Boeing. Third, alliances and networks provide innovation and learning opportunities for partners, as evidenced by the GM-Toyota JV.[23]

Finally, an important advantage of alliances and networks lies in their "real options" value. An **option** is an investment instrument that enables its holder, who has paid for a small fraction of an asset's value, the right (but not the obligation) to increase his/her investment to eventually acquire the asset. A **real option** is an option investment in real operations as opposed to financial capital.[24] A real options perspective suggests two steps: (1) An investor first makes a small, initial investment to buy an option, which leads to the right to future investment without being obligated to do so; and (2) the investor holds the option until a decision point arrives in the second phase, and then decides between exercising the option or abandoning it. Firms that are interested in, but not sure about, eventually acquiring other companies, can

TABLE 7.1   **Strategic Alliances and Networks: Advantages and Disadvantages**

ADVANTAGES	DISADVANTAGES
Reduce costs, risks, and uncertainties	Possibilities of choosing the wrong partners
Gain access to complementary assets and capabilities	Costs of negotiation and coordination
Opportunities to learn from partners	Possibilities of partner opportunism
Possibilities to use alliances and networks as real options	Risks of helping nurture competitors (learning race)

STRATEGY IN ACTION 7.2. *Sendo versus Microsoft: Whose Fault?*

Although Sendo (*http://www.sendo.com*), a British start-up, had the dream for a Web-enabled "smartphone" with PC-like functions, it did not have enough resources to bring this idea to fruition. Therefore, it searched for partners. After a year of courtship, in 2000 Sendo and Microsoft (*http://www.microsoft.com*) agreed to collaborate on a smartphone due out in 2001, which would be the first to use the mobile version of Windows, known by the code name Stinger. As a strategic investor, Microsoft invested $12 million in Sendo for a 5 percent stake and a board seat. Naturally, Sendo was thrilled for the Microsoft endorsement of its endeavor.

Because the launch of the Sendo smartphone depended on the timely delivery of Stinger by Microsoft, Sendo had to keep pushing back the delivery of its smartphone because of Microsoft's failure to deliver the code (among other problems). By late 2001, Sendo, short on cash, faced bankruptcy, and Microsoft offered a $14 million loan. In exchange, Microsoft demanded a four-day technical audit of Sendo's progress. In September 2002, Sendo finally got the code from Microsoft and its phone was scheduled to hit the market in November. However, two weeks before the scheduled release, another smartphone equipped by Microsoft software, made by High Tech Computer (HTC, *http://www.htc.com.tw*) of Taiwan, was unexpectedly released.

Sendo was furious. Its CEO quickly ended the contract with Microsoft, essentially writing off two years of hard work and as much as $300 million in lost revenue. Sendo signed up to use the rival Nokia (*http://www.nokia.com*) software instead. Arguing that Microsoft had "double-crossed" Sendo, in December 2002, Sendo filed a lawsuit against Microsoft, which alleged that Microsoft had a "plan" to gain its trust, "plunder" its technology, and drive the company "to the brink of bankruptcy." In particular, Sendo claimed that Microsoft provided HTC with test versions of the Sendo smartphone to help HTC develop a rival version. Microsoft denied these charges. The case is ongoing as of this writing (July 2004).

Sources: Based on (1) B. Brewin, 2003, Phone designer takes Microsoft to court, pcworld.com (December 27); (2) A. Reinhardt, 2003, Death of a dream, Business Week, February 10: 44–45; (3) G. Wearden, 2003, Microsoft suit stays in Texas, CNET News.com (October 1).

use an alliance to get an insider view to evaluate partners. Because acquisitions are not only costly but also risky (see Chapter 9), alliances and networks, in essence, permit firms to *sequentially* increase their investment should they decide to pursue acquisitions. On the other hand, if firms find, through working together with potential target companies, that acquisitions are not a good idea, they are not obligated to make such acquisitions. Overall, strategic alliances and networks, especially JVs, have emerged as great instruments of real options because of the flexibility embodied in the stepwise, sequential investment, which enables firms to scale up or scale down the investment as needed.[25]

Conversely, alliances and networks have a number of important drawbacks. First, there is always the possibility of being stuck with the wrong partner(s). A prospective alliance partner should choose a mate with caution, preferably a firm it already knows (such as through satisfactory market transactions). Yet, the mate should also be sufficiently differentiated to provide some complementary (nonoverlapping) capabilities.[26] Just like many individuals have a hard time figuring out the true colors of their spouses before marriage, many firms find it difficult to evaluate the true intentions and capabilities of their prospective partners until it is too late (see Strategy in Action 7.2).[27]

Second, the costs of negotiation and coordination are nontrivial. During the early 1980s, American Motors (later acquired by Chrysler), Volkswagen, and Peugeot, spent four, six, and five *years*, respectively, to negotiate JV deals with Chinese partners.[28] After the negotiations, the costs to coordinate operations may be mind-boggling. In another example—the airline industry—imagine how hard it must be to coordinate the thousands of flight schedules of multiple partners involved in Star Alliance, One World, and Sky Team spanning the globe.

A third possible disadvantage is partner opportunism. While opportunism is likely in any kind of economic relationship (see Chapter 4), the alliance/network setting may provide especially strong incentives for some (but not all) partners to be opportunistic. This is because cooperative relationships always entail some elements of trust, which can be easily abused.[29] For instance, in a JV with Lotte, the leading Japanese chocolate maker, Nestle transferred its technology to produce Nestle's Crunch bar to Japan. To Nestle's dismay, Lotte introduced an imitation product called Crunky. In the first year of the JV, Lotte sold 300 tons of Nestle's Crunch and 3,000 tons of its own Crunky bar.[30] Unfortunately, such an example is not an isolated incident (see Strategy in Action 4.3 in Chapter 4 for another example).

Finally, alliances and networks, especially those between rivals, can be dangerous because they may help competitors. Because firm-specific competitive advantage, by definition, lies within firm boundaries, firms are traditionally advised to make their capabilities hard to observe and imitate. By opening their "doors" to outsiders, alliances and networks may make it *easier* for competitors to observe and imitate firm-specific capabilities. In horizontal alliances between competitors, there is a potential **learning race** in which partners aim to outrun each other by learning the "tricks" from the other side as fast as possible.[31] Probably the most challenging alliances to manage are those with competitors—also known as "dancing with the wolf" (or the "bear").[32] For example, the alliance between GE and Rolls Royce to jointly develop jet engines collapsed because both firms could not solve issues raised by their long-standing rivalry.[33] Some believe that certain alliances and networks are "Trojan horses" that are designed by one partner to weaken another.[34] Although empirical evidence does not fully support this view,[35] the point of the potentially devastating effect of certain alliances and networks is well made.

Rarity

The second component in the VRIO framework is rarity, which has two dimensions: (1) capability rarity and (2) partner rarity. First, the capabilities to successfully manage interfirm relationships—sometimes called **relational** (or **collaborative**) **capabilities**—may be rare. Managers involved in alliances and networks require relationship skills rarely covered in the traditional business school curriculum, which emphasizes competition as opposed to collaboration. To truly derive benefits from alliances and networks, managers must foster trust with partners, while at the same time guarding against opportunism.[36] Consistently taking advantage of (or being abused by) partners does not enhance a firm's reputation.[37]

As much as alliances and networks represent a strategic and economic arrangement, they also constitute a social, psychological, and emotional phenomenon: words such as "courtship," "marriage," and "divorce" often surface.[38] Given that the interests of partner firms do not fully overlap and are often in conflict, managers involved in alliances and networks live a precarious existence, trying to represent the interests of their respective firms while attempting to make the complex relationship work.[39] Given the general shortage of good relationship management skills among people (remember, for example, that 50 percent of marriages in the United States fail), it is not surprising that managers with sound relational capabilities to successfully manage alliances and networks are in short supply. Firms with these rare relational capabilities, such as Sweden's IKEA and Ericsson, naturally try to leverage them.[40]

A second aspect of rarity is **partner rarity,** defined as the difficulty to locate partners with certain desirable attributes. This stems from two sources: (1) industry structure and (2) network position. From an *industry structure* standpoint, in many oligopolistic industries, the number of available players as potential partners is limited. In some emerging economies where only a few local firms may be worthy partners, latecomers may find that all potential partners have already been "cherry picked" by rivals. In the Chinese automobile industry (where WOSs are not allowed), Ford Motor Company, as a late mover, ended up allying with partners, Jiangling and Changan, which are not first-tier carmakers even in China. Not surprisingly, Ford's presence in China has been insignificant (see Integrative Case 1.3).

In addition, from a *network position* perspective, firms located in the center of interfirm networks may have access to better and more opportunities (such as information, access, capital, goods, and services), and consequently may accumulate more power and influence.[41] In contrast, peripheral firms may not have these attractive properties. The upshot is that firms with a high degree of **network centrality**—defined as the extent to which the firm's position is pivotal with respect to others in the interfirm network—are likely to be more attractive partners. Unfortunately, such firms are rare, and they are often very choosy in the kind of relationships they enter. Citibank, Sony, and Carrefour, for example, routinely turn down alliance proposals coming from all over the globe.

Imitablility

The issue of imitability pertains to two levels: (1) firm level and (2) alliance/network level. First, as noted earlier, one firm's resources and capabilities may be imitated by partners. For instance, in the late 1980s, McDonald's set up a JV with the Moscow Municipality Government, which helped it enter Russia. However, during the 1990s, the Moscow mayor set up a rival fast food chain, The Bistro, which replicated numerous McDonald's products, practices, and processes. McDonald's could do very little, because no one sues the mayor in Moscow and hopes to win.

Another issue pertaining to the imitability of strategic alliances and networks stems from their complexity. Successful alliances and networks are often based on socially complex relations among partners, which makes it very difficult for members of rival alliances and networks to observe and outcompete. Successful relationships are often built on trust, understanding, and friendship—in other words, "chemistry." Firms without such "chemistry" may have a hard time imitating such activities.

Organization

Similarly, the organizational issues also affect both the firm level and the alliance/network level. First, at the firm level, how firms are organized to benefit from alliances and networks is an important issue.[42] When firms have only a few alliances and networks, many firms adopt a trial-and-error approach. Not surprisingly, the number of "misses" is often very high. What is problematic is that even for successful "hits," this ad hoc approach does not allow firms to systematically learn from these experiences. This obviously is a hazardous way of organizing for large multinational enterprises (MNEs) engaging in numerous alliances and networks around the globe. In response, many firms have been developing a dedicated alliance function (parallel with traditional functions such as finance and marketing), often headed by a vice president or director with his/her own staff and resources.[43] Such a dedicated function acts as a focal point for leveraging lessons from prior and ongoing relationships. Hewlett-Packard, for example, developed a 300-page decision-making manual on alliances, including sixty different tools and templates (such as alliance contracts, metrics, and checklists). HP also organized a two-day course that is taught three times a year to diffuse such learning about alliances to its managers worldwide.

At the alliance/network level, some of these relationships are organized in a way that makes it difficult for others to replicate. There is much truth behind Tolstoy's opening statement in *Anna Karenina*: "All happy families are like one another; each unhappy family is unhappy in its own way." Just as individuals in unhappy marriages find it difficult to improve their relationship (despite an army of professional marriage counselors, social workers, friends, and family), firms in unsuccessful alliances and networks (for whatever reason) often find it exceedingly challenging—if not impossible—to organize and manage their interfirm relationships better.

Institution-Based Considerations

Because institutions that govern economic activities include both formal and informal constraints supported by regulatory and normative/cognitive pillars, respectively, this section examines them in turn.

Formal Institutions Supported by Regulatory Pillars

Strategic alliances and networks function within a set of formal legal and regulatory frameworks. These formal institutions impact (1) antitrust (or collusion) concerns and (2) entry mode requirements. First, although the number of alliances between competitors is on the rise, explicit collusion between competitors to fix prices is anticompetitive and banned by antitrust authorities. Cooperation between rivals is usually suspected of at least some tacit collusion (see Chapter 8).[44] However, because the integration and coordination within alliances/networks are usually not as tight as those in full M&As of competitors (which would eliminate one competitor), antitrust authorities are more likely to approve alliances/networks than M&As. For instance, the proposed merger between American Airlines and British Airways was blocked by the antitrust authorities of both countries; however, these two airlines have been allowed to form an alliance, One World.

Another way formal institutions affect strategic alliances and networks is through formal requirements imposed on foreign market entry modes (see also Chapter 6). In many countries, governments have discouraged or simply banned WOSs, which leaves some sort of alliances with local firms as the only equity-based entry choice for foreign firms. For instance, the pre-NAFTA Mexican government not only limited foreign MNEs' entries to JVs, but also dictated the maximum ceiling of their equity position to be 49 percent (these policies have been abolished since the beginning of NAFTA in 1994).[45] In another example, the Fuji Xerox JV was originally proposed in 1962 as a sales company to market Xerox products in Japan. However, the Japanese government refused to approve the JV unless Xerox transferred some technology to Fuji.

Recently, two trends are emerging concerning formal government policies on entry mode requirements. First, there is a general trend toward more liberal policies. Many governments (such as those in Mexico and South Korea) that historically only approved JVs have now allowed WOSs as an entry mode. A second trend is that despite such general movement toward more liberal policies, many governments still impose considerable requirements. For example, while WOSs are in principle welcome in most Chinese and Russian industries, only alliances such as JVs are permitted in the strategically important Chinese automobile assembly industry (see Integrative Case 1.3) and the Russian oil and gas industry. In another case, US regulations only permit up to 25 percent of the equity of any US airline to be held by foreign carriers, and EU regulations limit non-EU ownership to 49 percent of EU-based airlines.

Informal Institutions Supported by Normative and Cognitive Pillars

The first set of informal institutions centers on collective norms, supported by a normative pillar. The institutional perspective suggests that because firms act to enhance or protect their legitimacy, copying other reputable organizations—even without knowing the direct performance benefits of doing so—may be a low-cost way to gain legitimacy. Therefore, when competitors have a variety of alliances, jumping on the alliance "bandwagon" may be perceived as joining the norm as opposed to ignoring industry trends. In other words, informal, but powerful, normative pressures from the business press, investment community, and board deliberations probably drove late-mover firms such as Ford to ally with relatively obscure partners in China (discussed earlier) as opposed to having no partner and hence no presence there. For the same reason that some unmarried adults experience social pressures to get married, firms insisting on "going alone," especially when they experience performance problems, often confront similar pressures and criticisms from peers, analysts, investors, and the media. Although not every alliance/network decision is driven by imitation, this motivation seems to explain a lot of these activities.[46] The flipside of such a behavior is that many firms rush into interfirm relationships without adequate due diligence and then get burned.

A second set of informal institutions stresses the cognitive pillar, which centers on the internalized, taken-for-granted values and beliefs that guide firm behavior. British Aerospace (now BAE Systems) announced in the 1990s that *all* its future aircraft development programs would involve alliances. Managers at such firms as British Aerospace often take a proactive approach, endeavoring to visualize the desired network structure of their interfirm relationships in the future and then work backward to define their current alliance strategy. For example, after their proposed merger was torpedoed because of antitrust concerns, American Airlines and British Airways joined hands in a strategic alliance, which they deliberately positioned as the core relationship in a multipartner network, One World.

Overall, both of the core propositions that underpin the institution-based view (first introduced in Chapter 4) are applicable. The first proposition—individuals and firms rationally pursue their interests and make strategic choices within institutional constraints—is illustrated by the constraining and enabling power of the formal regulatory pillar; the informal, but powerful, normative pillar; and the internalized, but evident, cognitive pillar. The second proposition—when formal constraints fail, informal constraints may play a larger role—is also evident. Similar to the institutions governing human marriages, formal regulations and contracts can only govern a small (although important) portion of alliance/network behavior. The success and failure of such relationships, to a large degree, depends on the day-in and day-out interaction between partners influenced by informal norms and cognitions.[47] This point will be expanded in more detail in the next three sections on the formation, evolution, and performance of strategic alliances and networks.

FORMATION[48]

The process of forming strategic alliances and networks can be illustrated by a three-stage managerial decision model (Figure 7.3 on next page), which is discussed in this section.

Stage One: To Cooperate or Not to Cooperate?

In Stage One, the firm makes a strategic choice concerning whether to form cooperative interfirm relationships or to rely on pure market transactions or M&As to grow the firm. To grow by pursuing pure market transactions, the firm must be able to independently confront competitive challenges. This is a very demanding hurdle even for resource-rich MNEs.[49] To pursue M&As not only costs huge sums of financial capital, but is also fraught with significant transaction costs. Unlike the regular market for goods and services whose price and quality can be reasonably assessed, the market for buying and selling companies is often full of "noises" that make it difficult to ascertain whether the seemingly attractive deals are indeed good ones. As a result, many M&As end up destroying value (see Chapter 9). After ruling out pure market transactions and M&As as possible growth strategies, many managers conclude that alliances and networks are the way to go. Further, these relationships do not necessarily preclude future upgrading into possible M&As or downgrading

FIGURE 7.3   **A Three-Stage Decision Model of Strategic Alliance and Network Formation**

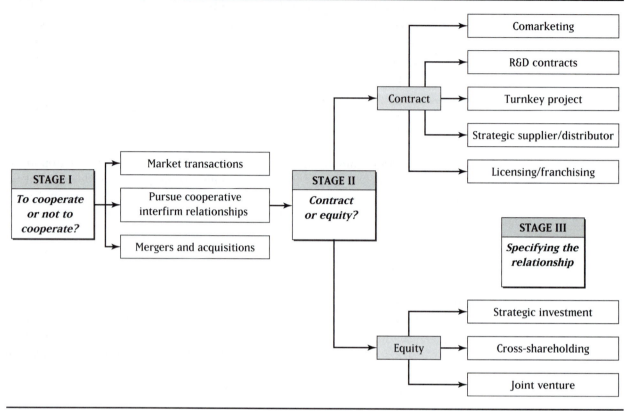

Source: Adapted from S. Tallman & O. Shenkar, 1994, A managerial decision model of international cooperative venture formation (p. 101), Journal of International Business Studies, 25 (1): 91–113.

into arm's-length market transactions by phasing out ties. In a nutshell, alliances and networks may be a flexible *intermediate* solution to solve strategic growth problems.

The next step is: How to find partners? Firms usually find partners in three ways. First, an informal method involves managers who translate their *interpersonal* ties (at the micro, individual level) with executives at other firms into *interfirm* relationships (at the macro, firm level)—in other words, managers create a **micro-macro link**.[50] This is especially crucial for smaller, entrepreneurial firms, whose founders are interested in leveraging their interpersonal ties (such as *guanxi* in China and *blat* in Russia).[51] Interestingly, many large firms also rely on such a largely informal process to find partners. These contacts come about in several ways, such as trade shows, industry associations, professional workshops, charitable events, as well as associated social activities. In general, managers with previously successful alliance/network experiences are likely to look into new relationships more favorably.[52]

While useful, the informal way to find partners is inherently limited by the number of trustworthy personal friends (and friends of friends) managers have. While this strategy may be reasonable for smaller entrepreneurial firms, it obviously will not work for larger MNEs. A second way to find partners is to rely on successful previous business dealings (see Integrative Case 2.3). Because successful previous transactions inevitably lead to some good social relationships among managers from both sides, their alliances/networks may start on a firmer foundation, require less extensive contract negotiation, and have a higher likelihood (although not a guarantee) of success (see Integrative Case 2.3).[53] In some cases, two firms from two different countries have had such a satisfactory business relationship that they form an alliance to enter a *third* country.[54] For example, this was how Coke and Swire Pacific (Hong Kong) entered China.

A third way to find partners is through formal, systematic scanning around the world to identify candidates that present both strategic fit and organizational fit. **Strategic fit** refers to whether the partner firm possesses complementary, "hard" skills and resources that the focal firm cannot acquire easily, such as technology, capital, and distribution channels.[55] **Organizational fit** focuses on whether the partner firm possesses certain "soft" organizational traits, such as goals, experiences, and behaviors, that facilitate cooperation.[56] Firms that have a rich history of successful collaborative experiences are often sought after. This is particularly important in emerging economies such as India, Russia, and Vietnam because local firms with some collaborative experiences with Western MNEs are likely to become more Western-like (although not necessarily Westernized) in their managerial styles, which may facilitate mutual understanding between partners (see Strategy in Action 7.3 on next page).[57]

Managers need to be aware that these three methods are not mutually exclusive. Any one method alone is likely to be inadequate. Relying on interpersonal relationships alone without assessing the strategic and organizational fit between firms may lead to some dissatisfaction because good friends are not necessarily good alliance partners. On the other hand, solely using the impersonal scanning of strategic and organizational traits may not necessarily result in good interfirm relationships either, because of the absence of "chemistry" among key players. A combination of these approaches seems to work better in determining quality interfirm relationships.[58]

Stage Two: Contract or Equity?

As first noted in Chapter 6, the choice between contract and equity is a key distinction. The four driving forces behind this choice are identified in Table 7.2 on next page. First, the key concern is the kind of resources and capabilities that are shared. The more tacit (that is, hard to describe and codify) they are, the more likely firms will prefer equity involvement. Conversely, the easier it is to specify the shared resources and capabilities, the more likely firms will pursue contractual agreements. The core consideration here is **organizational learning,** defined as how an organization learns from its experience to carry out new tasks.[59] Although not the only source of learning, **learning by doing** is perhaps the most effective way to learn *complex* know-how. Just like reading cookbooks, driving manuals, or parenting handbooks alone will not teach individuals how to cook, drive, or become parents,

STRATEGY IN ACTION 7.3. *How to Select Partners? A Local Firm Perspective*

As in marriages where both sides choose mates, international strategic alliances involve prospective partners from two (or more) countries each selecting partners for different purposes. Yet, much of the literature focuses on how foreign MNEs select partners in emerging economies, implicitly assuming that local firms are relatively passive and waiting to be selected. This, of course, is far from the truth. Some firms in emerging economies have very strong capabilities and suitors line up to seek relationships with them. For example, the Shanghai Automobile Industrial Corporation (*http://www.saicgroup.com*) managed to have both Volkswagen (*http://www.vw.com*) and GM (*http://www.gm.com*), two fierce rivals elsewhere, to be its partners in two successful JVs in China. Likewise, Baosteel (*http://www.baosteel.com*), China's biggest steel maker, has managed to attract a number of global rivals, such as Arcelor (*http://www.arcelor.com*), Nippon Steel (*http://www.nsc.co.jp*), and ThyssenKrupp (*http://www.thyssenkrupp.com*), each of which has a JV with it. Evidently, these MNEs have to swallow their pride and put up with such "polygamy" to access the booming Chinese economy. Similarly, the alliance portfolio of India's Tata Group (*http://www.tata.com*) reads like a "Who's Who" in the Global 500, with partners such as American Express (*http://www.americanexpress.com*), Bell Canada (*http://www.bell.ca*), and Hitachi (*http://www.hitachi.com*). Although many local firms do not care about the global rivalry among MNEs, local firms are often interested in using alliances to beat their own domestic rivals. As a result, if *domestic* rivals have MNE partners (let's say Heineken [*http://www.heineken.com*] or DHL [*http://www.dhl.com*]), local firms in retaliation often enlist the MNE competitors of their domestic rivals' MNE partners (such as Carlsberg [*http://www.carlsberg.com*] or Federal Express [*http://www.fedex.com*]). In terms of goals, while foreign MNEs are in search of partners with desirable local knowledge, production facilities, and distribution channels, local firms often use a different set of criteria. For example, Chinese, Mexican, Polish, Romanian, and Russian firms tend to focus on foreign partners' financial strengths and willingness to share expertise as their most important criteria in partner selection. While the benefits of having financially strong foreign partners are self-evident, having willing "teachers" to share knowledge—in combination with the local partners' capacity to learn—also directly contributes to the performance of both the alliances and the parent firms, as found by studies in Hungary and elsewhere.

Sources: Based on (1) M. Hitt, D. Ahlstrom, T. Dacin, E. Levitas, & L. Svobodina, 2004, The institutional effects on strategic alliance partner selection in transition economies, Organization Science, 15: 173–185; (2) M. Kotabe, P. Aulakh, & H. Teegen, 2000, Strategic alliances in emerging Latin America, Journal of World Business, 35: 114–125; (3) P. Lane, J. Salk, & M. Lyles, 2001, Absorptive capacity, learning, and performance in international joint ventures, Strategic Management Journal, 22: 1139–1161; (4) M. W. Peng, 2000, Business Strategies in Transition Economies, Thousand Oaks, CA: Sage Publishing.; (5) O. Shenkar & J. Li, 1999, Knowledge search in international cooperative ventures, Organization Science, 10: 134–143; (6) H. K. Steensma & M. Lyles, 2000, Explaining IJV survival in a transition economy through social exchange and knowledge-based perspectives, Strategic Management Journal, 21: 831–851.

TABLE 7.2   Equity-Based versus Non-Equity-Based Strategic Alliances and Networks

DRIVING FORCES	EQUITY-BASED ALLIANCES/NETWORKS	NON-EQUITY-BASED ALLIANCES/NETWORKS
Nature of shared resources (degree of tacitness and complexity)	High	Low
Importance of direct organizational monitoring and control	High	Low
Potential as real options	High (for possible upgrading to M&As)	High (for possible upgrading to equity-based relationships
Influence of formal institutions	High (when required or encouraged by regulations)	High (when required or encouraged by regulations)

firms attempting to produce new cars or operate in an unfamiliar country will find that no amount of learning from books and reports (disseminating codified knowledge) is enough.[60] Beyond books and reports, a lot of implicit, tacit, uncodifiable knowledge can only be acquired by doing, preferably with individuals and firms that are masters of their domains.

More importantly, a lot of tacit knowledge that deals with complex skills and know-how is embedded in specific organizational settings and is "sticky" (that is, hard to isolate out of the particular firm that possesses it).[61] For example, if Toyota could codify all the tacit knowledge associated with the legendary Toyota production system (TPS)—impossible to do in reality, of course—and sell it, purchasing firms would probably find that no matter how hard they tried, they could not completely replicate it. This is because the TPS, which is by definition firm-specific, is highly "sticky" to Toyota. Short of completely acquiring Toyota (an extremely costly proposition), no other firm can hope to totally master this system. Further, if many Toyota employees leave after the acquisition (a realistic scenario at most acquired firms), again, the acquiring firm would find its mastery of the system incomplete. Therefore, the most realistic way to access the TPS is to establish an equity-based alliance in order to learn how to "do it" side-by-side with Toyota, as GM did through its JV with Toyota. In general, equity-based alliances/networks are more likely to be formed when dealing with more complex technology and know-how (such as the Airbus consortium) than with less complex skills that can be more efficiently transferred between two organizations (such as McDonald's franchising).

Although involving less tacit knowledge, contractual relationships are only simpler in a *relative* sense, that is, in comparison with equity relationships. When viewed on their own, contractual relationships, especially those dealing with relatively more complex technology (such as R&D contracts), can still be very complicated.[62] Firms that fail to realize this crucial point can get burned. For example, Intentia, a Swedish software maker, rushed to India to sign an R&D contract, expecting to cut costs by 40 percent (see Opening Case in Chapter 1), but the savings never materialized. The software code the Indian partner delivered was riddled with errors and Intentia's own engineers had to redo it from scratch. A recent study found that half of such "offshoring," contractual-based projects fail to deliver anticipated savings.[63]

A second driving force is the importance of direct monitoring and control. As first discussed in Chapter 6, equity relationships allow firms to have at least some partial direct control over joint activities on a continuing basis, whereas contractual relationships usually do not allow that.[64] In general, firms prefer equity alliances (and a higher level of equity) if they fear that their intellectual property may be expropriated by partners. Given the possibility of partner opportunism, equity-based mechanisms (such as board seats, key managerial positions, and reporting procedures) provide some hands-on opportunities for direct monitoring and control (see Closing Case for a recent example).[65]

A third driver is real options thinking. Some firms prefer to first establish contractual relationships, which can be viewed as real options (or stepping stones) for possible upgrading into equity alliances should the interactions turn out to be mutually satisfactory. For instance, the Airbus consortium (originally consisting of two partners, France's Aerospatiale and Germany's Deutsche Aerospace, in the 1960s) first initiated contractual relationships with Spain's CASA and the UK's British Aerospace, which proved to be satisfactory. Later in the 1970s, CASA and British Aerospace became full-fledged equity members of the Airbus consortium. On the other hand, as noted earlier, equity relationships can also be used as real options for possible scaling up to WOSs through M&As (also see Chapter 9).

Finally, the choice between contract and equity also boils down to institutional constraints. For instance, many governments of oil-rich countries, in fear of foreign dominance, ban equity alliances between domestic and foreign oil firms (and WOSs) in their oil and refinery sectors. Therefore, the only relationships foreign energy firms can establish with domestic firms are contractual ones, such as turnkey projects (see Chapter 6). On the other hand, some governments in emerging economies that are eager to help domestic firms climb the technology ladder either require or actively encourage equity alliances to be formed between foreign and domestic firms, in particular JVs, which permit domestic firms access to greater organizational learning (see Integrative Case 1.3).

Overall, the choice between contract and equity is a crucial one. In the case of international market entries, having equity relationship through strategic alliances and networks (together with WOSs) is a hallmark of MNEs, whereas firms only having contractual relationships overseas are not usually considered to be MNEs (see Chapter 6 for details).[66] Not surprisingly, large MNEs are more likely to prefer equity alliances and/or a higher equity stake within these relationships.[67] Some firms, such as Starbucks, initially believe that they can rely on their contractual partners to get the job done, but over time when performance is poor they often switch to equity relationships (see Opening Case in Chapter 6).

Stage Three: Positioning the Relationship

In the context of foreign market entries, Chapter 6 has already discussed each specific type of interfirm relationships at length so we will not repeat them here. What we highlight here is how to position a particular alliance or network within a number of relationships. Although forming strategic alliances has historically been assumed to occur between two partners (such as one foreign partner and one local partner), the proliferation of interfirm relationships suggests that such thinking may need to be expanded.[68] Each firm likely has multiple interfirm relationships, which makes it important to manage the relationships as a corporate *portfolio* (or network).[69] Most firms approach the design of interfirm relationships by attempting to optimize each individual alliance/network. However, combining several individually "optimal" relationships may not create an optimal relationship portfolio for the entire firm, in light of some tricky alliances with competitors.[70] In a world of multilateral intrigues, one step down the alliance path, which may open some doors, may foreclose other opportunities. In other words, the age-old strategic motto, "My friend's enemy is my enemy, and my enemy's enemy is my friend," is still valid in modern competition.[71] Therefore, to prevent an "alliance gridlock," carefully assessing the impact of each individual relationship on the firm's other relationships *prior to its formation* is increasingly important. In particular, the scope of a new relationship needs to be properly defined to prevent substantial overlapping with other relationships.[72] Some seemingly optimal relationships may become detrimental to the overall portfolio, such as introducing a major competitor of several current partners. Such relationships—despite their individual merits—may need to be avoided.

EVOLUTION

All relationships evolve—some grow, others fail.[73] This section highlights two aspects of relationship evolution: (1) minimizing the threat of opportunism and (2) evolving from strong ties to weak ties.

Minimizing the Threat of Opportunism

As noted earlier, the threat of opportunism often looms large on the horizon. Except for a small number of firms that deliberately enter alliances and networks to opportunistically exploit the other side, most firms want to make their relationship work, but also want to protect themselves in case the other side is opportunistic.[74] While it is difficult to completely eliminate opportunism, it is possible to minimize the threat by (1) walling off critical skills and technologies through contractual safeguards and (2) swapping critical skills and technologies through credible commitments.

First, both sides can contractually agree to wall off critical skills and technologies not meant to be shared. For example, GE and SNECMA of France cooperated to build aircraft engines, yet GE was not willing to completely share its proprietary technology with SNECMA. GE thus presented several sealed "black box" components, to the inside of which SNECMA had no access, while permitting SNECMA access to the final assembly. In another similar example, Boeing collaborated with several Japanese firms to produce the 767. Boeing walled off critical research, design, and marketing skills and only shared production technologies with Japanese partners.[75] In a nutshell, this type of relationship, in human marriage terms, is like married couples whose premarital assets are protected by prenuptial agreements. Parties are able to wall off certain assets through such agreements. As long as both sides are willing to live with these agreements that are designed to minimize the threat of opportunism, the relationships can prosper.

The second approach, swapping skills and technologies, is the exact *opposite* of the first approach. Both sides agree not to hold critical skills and technologies back, and also make credible commitments to hold each other as a "hostage."[76] Motorola, for instance, licensed its microprocessor technology to Toshiba, which, in turn, licensed its memory chip technology to Motorola. In international alliances, setting up a parallel and reciprocal relationship in the foreign partner's home country may increase the incentives for both partners to cooperate. For example, the agreement between France's Pernod-Ricard and America's Heublein to distribute Heublein's Smirnoff vodka in Europe was balanced by another agreement in which Heublein agreed to distribute Pernod-Ricard's Wild Turkey bourbon in the United States. In a nutshell, such mutual "hostage taking" reduces the threat of opportunism. To think slightly outside the box, the precarious nuclear peace during the Cold War between the

United States and the (former) Soviet Union can be regarded as yet another case of successful mutual "hostage taking." For various reasons, both sides had incentives to launch a first nuclear strike, yet neither decided to do so partly because both sides held each other hostage. As long as the victim of the first strike had only *one* nuclear ballistic missile submarine (such as an American Ohio class boat or a Soviet Typhoon class boat) left, this single submarine had enough retaliatory firepower to wipe the top twenty US or Soviet cities off the surface of the earth, an outcome neither superpower found acceptable (see the movie *The Hunt for Red October* for an illustration). Strangely (and scarily), the Cold War did not heat up in part because of such a mutually assured destruction (MAD!) strategy, which is a real jargon in the military.

In strategic alliances and networks, both walling off critical skills and swapping skills help relationships evolve to minimize the threat of opportunism. While these approaches emphasize contractual safeguards, highlighting the soft, relational aspects of the evolution of interfirm cooperation is also important, as discussed next.

Evolving from Strong Ties to Weak Ties[77]

First introduced in Chapter 5, **strong ties** are more durable, reliable, and trustworthy relationships cultivated over a long period of time.[78] Strong ties have two advantages. First, strong ties are associated with exchanging finer-grained, higher-quality information. Second, although interpersonal and interfirm relationships may be fraught with potential opportunism, strong ties serve as an informal, social control mechanism that is an alternative to formal contracts for combating opportunism.[79] Formal contracts are often ineffective because they cannot fully cover all contingencies; in fact, emphasizing formal contracts may even indicate a lack of trust and thus undermine collaboration. Not surprisingly, many strategic alliances and networks are initially built upon strong ties among individuals and firms.

Defined as relationships that are characterized by infrequent interaction and low intimacy, **weak ties,** paradoxically, are more wide-ranging and likely to provide more opportunities. Weak ties, despite their limited capability to serve as a social control mechanism, enjoy two advantages. First, weak ties are less costly (requiring less time, energy, and money) to maintain. Second and more importantly, weak ties excel at connecting with distant others who possess unique and novel information for strategic actions—often regarded as the *strength* of weak ties.[80] Specifically, the broader a firm's weak ties network, the more likely it is to identify suitable partners. This may be especially critical as firms search for new knowledge for cutting-edge technologies and practices.

In the same way that individuals tend to have a combination of a small number of good friends (strong ties) and a large number of acquaintances (weak ties), firms at any given point in time are likely to have a combination of strong ties and weak ties in their interfirm relationships. Both strong and weak ties "are beneficial to firms, but under different conditions, for different purposes, and at different times."[81] In some ways, firms' strategies are primarily designed to *exploit* current resources (such as existing connections) or *explore* new opportunities (such as future technologies). Of particular interest is the distinction between "exploitation" and "exploration" noted by James March, a leading organization theorist. **Exploitation** refers to "such things as refinement, choice, production, efficiency, selection, and execution," whereas **exploration** includes "things captured by terms such as search, variation, risk taking, experimentation, play, flexibility, discovery, and innovation."[82] Both kinds of strategic activities are important and often occur simultaneously, but there is a trade-off between the two because firms have limited resources.[83] Thus, an *emphasis* on either set of the ties is often necessary during a particular period. In environments conducive for exploitation, strong ties may be more beneficial. Conversely, in environments suitable for exploration, weak ties may be preferred.

Many interfirm relationships evolve from an emphasis on strong ties to a focus on weak ties. Examples from two contexts illustrate these dynamics. First, in an entrepreneurial context, a new start-up often first concentrates on dense, strong ties because it "seeks to exploit the current external networks and resources of the founding entrepreneur(s) to ensure its survival."[84] In the next phase, after having largely exploited (and exhausted) the initial set of opportunities, the firm searches for new opportunities. Therefore, the firm shifts into exploration and actively seeks new opportunities, thus calling for more weak ties with greater diversity. Amazon's changing alliance portfolio is indicative of such evolution. Initially, Amazon established strong ties–based strategic alliances with a few key publishing and distributing firms. As Amazon expanded to cover new products (videos and electronics) and new business models (auctions), it formed numerous weak ties–based alliances with a variety of large retail suppliers, small merchants, auction houses, outsourcing partners, and sales and distribution partners.

A second example is international JVs formed by two partners, which represent strong ties. Because of opportunism, international JVs are often characterized by conflicts. However, for our discussion purposes, even if we assume no such deliberate opportunism exists, JVs may still be riddled with conflicts. This is because over time, as the initial set of opportunities are exploited and exhausted by the JV, partners, as they embark on new searches, may prefer to establish some relationships based on weak ties with a diverse set of players. In other words, the strong ties within the JV may become too limiting.[85] However, original partners will naturally become upset, thus triggering conflicts—in a human marriage it is easy to appreciate the fury of one spouse when the other spouse is exploring other relationships (even though only weak ties!).

While this section has focused on the evolution from strong ties to weak ties, it is important to note that not all alliances and networks follow this path. Certainly, some relationships evolve from weak ties to strong ties, such as moving from market transactions to JVs (as discussed elsewhere).

PERFORMANCE

Performance is a central focus for strategic alliances and networks.[86] This section discusses (1) the performance of strategic alliances and networks and (2) the performance of parent firms.

TABLE 7.3   Alliance- and Network-Related Performance Measures

Alliance/Network Level	Parent Firm Level
Objective	*Objective*
▪ Financial performance (for example, profitability)	▪ Financial performance (for example, profitability)
▪ Product market performance (for example, market share)	▪ Product market performance (for example, market share)
▪ Stability and longevity	▪ Stock market reaction
Subjective	*Subjective*
▪ Level of top management satisfaction	▪ Assessment of goal attainment

The Performance of Strategic Alliances and Networks

Despite high rates of alleged failures, there is no consensus on what constitutes alliance/network performance.[87] A combination of objective and subjective measures can be used to determine performance, as shown in Table 7.3. Traditional measures in financial and product market performance are often difficult to obtain because firms usually do not report such data on each interfirm relationship. Further, maximizing financial and product market performance may not be the goals for entering these relationships (for example, some goals may be to tie up competitors). Instability, such as a change in ownership structure, may not necessarily constitute failure because the change may be in line with the objectives of at least one partner. Many studies use the objectively measurable longevity (or termination) as a performance measure, based on the belief that alliances and networks "perceived by their parents as performing more successfully are more likely to remain in operation than those that are evaluated as being less successful."[88] However, this belief may be questionable in some cases because many successful alliances are predestined to terminate after a certain point as agreed by the partners at the outset.

In addition, subjective measures, such as the level of managers' perceived satisfaction, are also important. However, sometimes the objective and subjective measures *diverge*. For example, some interfirm relationships are not necessarily designed to make money, but to learn from partners. Therefore, managers may rate the performance of certain loss-making alliances as "satisfactory." Further, subjectively measured performance may be *asymmetric,* in that one partner may have achieved its objectives and is happy, whereas the other partner(s) may fail to do so and be unhappy. Clearly, the performance dimensions that are emphasized depend on the particular strategic goals of the firms.

Four factors may influence the performance of alliances and networks: (1) equity, (2) learning and experience, (3) nationality, and (4) relational capabilities. However, none of them is able to assert an unambiguous, direct impact on performance. Instead, these factors may have some *correlations* with performance. First, the level of equity may be crucial. A lower level of equity contribution (or none) may indicate a firm's relative lack of commitment and attention. On the other hand, a higher level of equity stake (such as in majority-equity JVs) indicates that a firm has stronger interest, higher-quality resources committed, stronger bargaining power, and better opportunities for monitoring and control—all of which are likely to result in higher performance.[89] This is not to say that all firms should increase their equity stake in alliances and networks, because there are obvious costs for doing so.[90]

Second, whether firms have successfully learned from their partners features prominently when assessing alliance/network performance.[91] Because organizational learning is abstract and difficult to measure, experience, which is relatively easy to measure, is often used as a proxy.[92] While experience certainly helps, its impact on performance is not linear, because a limit exists beyond which further increase in experience may not necessarily provide additional performance benefits.[93] Further, an increase in the experience of one partner may bring *instability* into the relationship, because it reduces the need to rely on the other partner.

Third, nationality may affect performance. For the same reason that marriages between people of dissimilar backgrounds can be less stable than those with similar backgrounds, dissimilarities in national culture may create strains in interfirm relationships.[94] Not surprisingly, international alliances and networks tend to have more problems than domestic relationships.[95] When disputes and conflicts arise, it is often difficult to ascertain whether the other side is deliberately being opportunistic or is simply being (culturally) different. As a result, firms usually prefer to first ally with culturally close partners; only after acquiring some experience will firms consider culturally distant partners.

As first noted in Chapter 4, nationality is not only a proxy for national culture, but also an embodiment of the institutional environment in which a firm is embedded. For instance, many Western firms ally with Hong Kong firms when entering mainland China. The *cultural* distance between a Western country (such as Canada) and Hong Kong (98 percent ethnic Chinese in the population) and such distance between Canada and mainland China is about the same, yet the *institutional* distance is much shorter with Hong Kong (a common colonial history, language, and rule of law). In another example, when assessing alliances in emerging economies, the satisfaction level of Korean firms is higher than that of firms from developed economies.[96] Evidently, common institutional features confronting emerging economies enable Korean firms to better cope with the difficulties in other emerging economies despite cultural distances.

Lastly, while equity, experience, and nationality are relatively easy to measure, alliance and network performance fundamentally boils down to "soft," hard-to-measure relational capabilities. As discussed earlier, the art of relational capabilities, which is firm-specific and difficult to codify, describe, and transfer, may make or break interfirm relationships.[97] Table 7.4 (p. 276) outlines a number of "do's" and don'ts" for relationship management. Overall, it would be naïve to think that any of these single factors—equity, learning, nationality, and relational capabilities—would guarantee success. It is the *combination* of these factors that jointly increases the odds for successful strategic alliances and networks.

The Performance of Parent Firms

Do parent firms benefit from engaging in strategic alliances and networks? This goes back to the value-added aspect of these relationships (discussed earlier). Compared with the relative lack of consensus on alliance/network performance, there has been some convergence on firm performance benchmarks, such as profitability, product market share, and stock market reaction, in addition to the more subjective measure of goal attainment as perceived by management (see Table 7.3).

A number of studies report that a higher level of collaboration and shared technology is associated with better profitability and more product market share for parent firms.[98] However, because a firm's overall performance is influenced by numerous other activities, these findings document correlations, but not necessarily causalities. Another group of studies focused on stock market reactions, by treating each decision to enter or exit a relationship as an "event." If the event window is short enough (several days prior to and after the event), the "abnormal" stock returns can be viewed as directly caused by that particular event. A number of studies found that the stock market responds favorably to alliance activities, but only under certain circumstances, such as (1) complementary resources, (2) previous alliance experience, (3) ability to manage the host country's political risk, and (4) partner buyouts.[99] Anheuser-Busch, for example, has skillfully used a variety of alliances around the world, thus creating significant value for its shareholders (see Strategy in Action 7.4). Overall, strategic alliances and networks can create value for their parent firms, although how to make that happen remains a challenge.[100]

TABLE 7.4　　Relationship Lessons for Managers in Strategic Alliances and Networks

AREAS	DO'S AND DON'TS
Contract versus "chemistry"	No contract can cover all elements of the relationship. Relying on a detailed contract does not guarantee a successful relationship and it may indicate a lack of trust.
Warning signs	Identify symptoms of frequent criticism, defensiveness (always blaming others for problems), and stonewalling (withdrawal during a fight).
Investment in the relationship	Like married individuals working hard to invigorate their ties, alliances require continuous nurturing. Once a party starts to waver, it is difficult to turn back.
Conflict resolution mechanisms	"Good" married couples also fight. Their secret weapon is to find mechanisms to avoid unwarranted escalation of conflicts. Managers need to handle conflicts—inevitable in any relationship—in a credible, responsible, and controlled fashion.

Source: Based on text in M. W. Peng & O. Shenkar, 2002, Joint venture dissolution as corporate divorce (pp. 101–102), Academy of Management Executive, 16 (2): 92–105.

DEBATES AND EXTENSIONS

The rise of alliances and networks has generated a number of debates. Three of them are introduced here: (1) learning race versus cooperative specialization, (2) majority JVs as control mechanisms versus minority JVs as real options, and (3) alliances versus acquisitions.

STRATEGY IN ACTION 7.4. *How Anheuser-Busch Creates Shareholder Wealth Through Alliances*

Anheuser-Busch (*http://www.anheuser-busch.com*) is a leader in the US beer market. Because the domestic market growth was slow, Anheuser-Busch looked for ways to expand overseas. From 1996 to 1998, while the firm's invested capital grew by only $1.9 billion, its stock market value grew by about $13.4 billion. Such a stellar performance was not due to significant large-scale investments overseas, because as of 1996, Anheuser-Busch still made 95 percent of its beer domestically. Then, how could the firm create $11.5 billion in market value added over a three-year period? An examination of its alliance strategy reveals some suggestive answers. An important element of this strategy was to establish minority JVs with local breweries (with equity ranging from 5 percent to 50 percent) in emerging economies with uncertain, albeit fast-growing demand for beer. These involved such prominent players as Grupo Modelo (*http://www.gmodelo.com*) in Mexico, AmBev (*http://www.ambev.com.br*) in Brazil, Asia

Brewery (*http://www.asiabrewery.com*) in the Philippines, and Tsingtao (*http://www.tsingtaobeer.com*) in China. These small equity stakes represent tremendous opportunities to expand should demand in these countries grow favorably in the future, yet help limit Anheuser-Busch's downside risk if positive developments do not actually materialize. These international JVs therefore provide Anheuser-Busch managers great opportunities to better understand the foreign markets and the flexibility to condition their further investments on how these markets evolve. Evidently, this logic has been appreciated and rewarded by investors.

Sources: This case was written by Tony W. Tong (State University of New York at Buffalo). It is based on (1) T. Arnold & R. Shockley, 2001, Value creation at Anheuser-Busch, Journal of Applied Corporate Finance, 14 (2): 41–50; (2) T. W. Tong, J. J. Reuer, & M. W. Peng, 2004, International joint ventures and the value of growth options, Working paper, Fisher College of Business, The Ohio State University. Reprinted by permission of the author.

Learning Race versus Cooperative Specialization[101]

An influential school of thought is the "learning race" view, contending that firms enter alliances, especially JVs, to learn and acquire partners' capabilities as quickly as possible.[102] Consequently, managers are advised to sharpen their firms' "learning edge" to win in such a race. However, critics argue that suggesting partners should enter a JV with a racing mindset is not always justified. They question two assumptions of the learning race view that may be unrealistic. First, the learning race view assumes that acquiring know-how from partners is always cost effective. However, a major reason for entering alliances in the first place is that in-house development may be inefficient. Second, the learning race view assumes that other than the focal firm being eager to learn and win, other partners are passively being exploited. In reality, other partners may be able to block access to key resources.

The second group, collectively known as the "cooperative specialization" school, posits that different firms in a relationship may want to specialize in different tasks in exchange for access to partners' contributions. This is not to suggest that learning races do not occur. To the extent that these races occur, they represent more of the relationship *pathologies* rather than the norms. Firms can reduce these pathologies in two ways. First, mutually taking hostages, such as cross-licensing (discussed earlier), can reduce pathologies. Second, making an effort to prevent spillovers should also reduce pathologies. Choosing noncompeting partners is most ideal, of course. When dealing with rivals, one lesson is that if the first GM-Daewoo JV

(Opening Case) had been given a global mandate to be in charge of the development and production for all of GM's subcompact cars, it would have reduced Daewoo's incentives to independently expand to Eastern Europe. For this reason, Shin Caterpillar Mitsubishi, a JV between Caterpillar and Mitsubishi, became successful after both partners completely merged their hydraulic excavator business, thus eliminating the incentives to transfer the JV know-how to each firm's own business.

From a negative and a positive standpoint, the learning race and cooperative specialization views seem to be two sides of the same coin. It is difficult to dismiss either one's validity. However, overemphasizing one side, such as the learning race view, is probably not warranted.

Majority JVs as Control Mechanisms versus Minority JVs as Real Options

Similar to the "high control versus low control" debate in Chapter 6, a long-standing debate focuses on the appropriate level of equity in JVs. While the logic of having a higher level of equity control in majority JVs is straightforward, its actual implementation is often problematic. Asserting one party's control rights, even when justified based on a majority equity position and stronger bargaining power, may irritate the other party. This is especially likely in international JVs in emerging economies, where local partners often resent the dominance of Western MNEs. For example, despite the obvious needs for foreign capital, technology, and management, Russian managers often refuse to acknowledge that their country, which in their view is still a superpower, is an emerging, let alone developing, country.[103] Consequently, some authors advocate a 50/50 share of management control even when the MNE has majority equity.[104]

While a "low control" strategy has a number of benefits as noted in Chapter 6, a key additional benefit alluded to earlier is associated with real options thinking. In general, the more uncertain the conditions, the higher the value of real options. In highly uncertain, but potentially promising industries and countries, M&As or majority JVs may be inadvisable because the cost of failure may be tremendous. Therefore, minority JVs are recommended *toehold* investments as possible stepping stones for future scaling up—if necessary—while not exposing the firm too heavily to the risks.[105] For example, when entering emerging economies (where majority JVs are often recommended by proponents of the "high control" school), minority JVs may provide significant growth opportunities. This seems to be a key factor behind Anheuser-Busch's stellar performance in emerging economies (see Strategy in Action 7.4). On the other hand, real options thinking is often difficult to implement, in part because firms often find it difficult to abandon their options by killing unsuccessful relationships ("What if they get better if we try harder?").[106]

Because the real options thinking is relatively new, its applicability is still being debated.[107] What has emerged out of the "majority JV versus minority JV" debate is the realization that a minority equity position can be a potential source of competitive advantage.[108]

TABLE 7.5   Alliances versus Acquisitions

	ALLIANCES	ACQUISITIONS
Resource interdependence	Low	High
Ratio of soft to hard assets	High	Low
Source of value creation	Combining complementary resources	Eliminating redundant resources
Level of uncertainty	High	Low

Source: Based on text in J. Dyer, P. Kale, & H. Singh, 2003, Do you know when to ally or acquire? Choosing between acquisitions and alliances, Working paper, Brigham Young University.

Alliances versus Acquisitions[109]

Despite the proliferation of strategic alliances, some writers are debating whether they represent the best forms of firm growth. There is an alternative to alliances, namely, M&As (see Chapter 9). Many firms seem to pursue M&As and alliances in isolation.[110] While many large MNEs have an M&A function and some have set up an alliance function (discussed earlier), virtually no firm has established a combined "mergers, acquisitions, *and* alliances" function. In practice, it may be advisable to explicitly consider alliances vis-à-vis acquisitions within a single decision framework.[111]

Shown in Table 7.5, alliances, which tend to be loosely coordinated among partners, cannot work in a setting that requires a high degree of interdependence; such a setting would call for acquisitions. Alliances work well when the ratio of soft to hard assets is relatively high (such as a heavy concentration of tacit knowledge), whereas acquisitions may be preferred when such a ratio is low. Alliances create value primarily by combining complementary resources, whereas acquisitions derive most value by eliminating redundant resources. Finally, consistent with real options thinking, alliances are more suitable when conditions are uncertain, and acquisitions are preferred when conditions are more certain.

Failure to compare some of these factors may cost firms dearly. Consider the 50/50 JV between Coke and Procter and Gamble (P&G), which combined the fruit drinks businesses of Coke (such as Minute Maid) and P&G (such as Sunny Delight) in 2001. The goal was to combine Coke's global distribution system with P&G's R&D capabilities in consumer products, which seemed reasonable. However, the stock market sent a mixed signal, by pushing P&G's stock 2 percent *higher* and Coke's 6 percent *lower* on the day of the announcement. For three reasons, Coke probably could have done better by acquiring P&G's fruit drinks business. First, a higher degree of integration would be necessary to derive the proposed synergies. Second, because Coke's distribution assets were relatively easy-to-value hard assets whereas P&G's R&D capabilities were hard-to-value soft assets, the risk was higher for Coke. Finally, there was little uncertainty regarding the popularity of fruit drinks and investors found it difficult to understand why Coke would share 50 percent of this fast-growing business with P&G, a laggard in this industry. Not surprisingly, the JV was terminated within six months.

On the other hand, many M&As (such as DaimlerChrysler) probably would have been better off by pursuing alliances, at least initially (see Chapter 9). In general, alliances seem to outperform acquisitions in terms of creating stock market value. For US listed firms, the difference in "abnormal returns" (namely, additional returns caused by the event) is 0.76 percent for alliances and merely break even for acquirers.[112] On average, the alliance returns translate into a nontrivial increase in market value of approximately $40 million. Overall, acquisitions may be overused as a first step to access resources in another firm, whereas alliances, because of their real options properties, have some unique advantages.

Finally, while the real options logic is straightforward, its practice, when applied to acquiring JVs, is messy because most JV and other alliance contracts do not specify a previously agreed upon price for one party to acquire and the other to divest the assets. Most contracts only give the rights of first refusal to the parties, which agree to negotiate in "good faith." It is understandable that "neither party will be willing to buy the JV for more than or sell the JV for less than its own expectation of the venture's wealth generating potential."[113] Because alliances are based on private negotiations involving no external market valuation of affected assets, reaching an agreement on a "fair" price is tricky. In international JVs, especially those with a lot of political involvement from host governments, such negotiations are very challenging—as evidenced by Alcatel's attempt to acquire its JV in China (see Closing Case).

IMPLICATIONS FOR STRATEGISTS

While, traditionally, firm strategy is about how a single firm strategizes, the recent rise of alliances and networks has significantly expanded the strategic horizon by highlighting *interfirm* strategy. This process is driven by both the institution-level transitions of globalization and liberalization and the firm-level evolution in search of core competencies and competitive advantages around the world. Globalization of markets and production has necessitated the search for partners throughout the globe. Liberalization of many formerly regulated industries and countries has permitted firms to explore many new relationships, including those among competitors, which would have been banned in a previous era (see Chapter 8). The quest for core competencies means focusing on what firms can do best and—for something that they are not particularly good at—what they can access via interfirm relationships. Increasingly, strategists realize that competitive advantages do not have to reside within the boundaries of their own firms. This "alliance revolution" has introduced a new perspective to the strategy field. Instead of concentrating on competition only, a new generation of strategists must be savvy at *both* competition and cooperation—in other words, "co-opetition."[114]

Not surprisingly, this chapter sheds more light on the four fundamental questions in strategy. The answers to Questions 1 (Why firms differ?) and 2 (How firms behave?) boil down to how different industry-, resource-, and institution-based considerations drive alliance and network actions. What determines the scope of the firm (Question 3)—or more specifically, the scope of the alliance in this context—can be found in the strategic goals behind these relationships. Some relationships may have a wide scope in anticipation of an eventual merger (such as the Renault-Nissan alliance), whereas others may have a limited scope while the partners may be fiercely competitive in other aspects (such as the GM-Toyota JV). Finally, the international success and failure of strategic alliances and networks (Question 4) is fundamentally determined by how firms develop, possess, and leverage "soft," relational capabilities when managing their interfirm relationships in addition to "hard" assets such as technology and capital. In conclusion, strategic alliances and networks are difficult to manage, but managing is hardly ever simple, whether managing external relationships or internal units.

Chapter Summary

1. Strategic alliances are voluntary agreements between firms involving exchanging, sharing, or codeveloping products, technologies, or services. There are two broad alliance categories: contractual (non-equity) and equity-based. Joint ventures are a type of equity-based alliance that involves establishing a new legal entity.

2. Strategic networks are strategic alliances formed by multiple firms to compete against other such groups and against traditional single firms.

3. Industry-, resource-, and institution-based considerations form the backbone of a comprehensive model of strategic alliances and networks.

4. Principal phases of alliance and network formation include (1) deciding whether to cooperate or not, (2) determining whether to pursue contractual or equity modes, and (3) positioning the particular relationship.

5. Two aspects of relationship evolution highlighted (there are many other aspects not mentioned) are (1) minimizing the threat of opportunism and (2) evolving from strong ties to weak ties.

6. Performance issues associated with strategic alliances and networks can be found at two levels: (1) the performance of strategic alliances and networks themselves and (2) the performance of parent companies.

7. Three leading debates are (1) learning race versus cooperative specialization, (2) majority JVs as control mechanisms versus minority JVs as real options, and (3) alliances versus acquisitions.

Key Terms

constellations	cross-shareholding	exploitation
contractual alliances	downstream vertical alliances	exploration
cooperative interfirm relationships	equity-based alliances	horizontal alliances

joint venture	organizational learning	strategic investment
learning by doing	partner rarity	strategic networks
learning race	real option	strong ties
micro-macro link	relational capabilities	upstream vertical alliances
network centrality	strategic alliances	
option	strategic fit	weak ties
organizational fit		

Critical Discussion Questions

1. Some argue that at a 30 to 70 percent failure rate (depending on different studies), strategic alliances and networks have a strikingly high failure rate and that firms need to scale down their alliance and network activities. Others suggest that this failure rate is not particularly higher than the failure rate of new entrepreneurial start-ups, internal corporate ventures, and new products launched by single companies. Therefore, such a failure rate is not of grave concern. How would you join this debate?

2. Some firms prefer strategic networks (multifirm alliances), and other firms prefer bilateral (two-firm) relationships. What are their pros and cons? Which approach would you prefer? Why?

3. Although strategic alliances are commonly referred to as "corporate marriages" and, when terminated, as "corporate divorces," few strategists in their writings have drawn on the massive literature on human marriages and divorces. Some argue that given that the success or failure of strategic alliances and networks depends on relationship management, the strategy field has a lot to learn from the human marriage and divorce experience (and its literature). Others contend that strategic alliances and networks are fundamentally different and that strategists do not need to waste time to draw on that literature. What do you think?

4. ***ON ETHICS:*** Firms often do not reveal (and try to hide) their true intentions during the courtship and negotiation stages prior to forming strategic alliances and networks. What are the ethical dilemmas here?

5. ***ON ETHICS:*** Some argue that engaging in a "learning race" is unethical. Others believe that a "learning race" is part and parcel of alliance relationships, especially those with competitors. What do you think?

Closing Case: Alcatel Acquires Its Joint Venture, Shanghai Bell

Alcatel (http://www.alcatel.com) is a Paris-based, leading global telecommunications solutions supplier with sales of 31 billion Euro in 2000, 25 billion in 2001, and 17 billion in 2002 (thanks to a global recession in the telecom sector). In 1985, Alcatel formed a JV in China, named Shanghai Bell, in which it had 32 percent of equity. Its state-owned Chinese partner PTIC (http://www.ptic.com.cn) had 60 percent, and Fund for Development Corporation of the Belgian government (http://www.belgium.be) had 8 percent. The JV became a leading player in the booming telecom equipment sector in China, reaching a $1.3 billion annual turnover in 2000. Shanghai Bell supplied one-third of the installed base of fixed line switches in China and was the number one producer worldwide. However, Shanghai Bell was almost a single product company, too heavily dependant on fixed line switches. The competition from low-cost Chinese rivals pulled the price per line down from $100 to $9 in five years, and made the JV unable to afford R&D expenses to develop new products other than fixed lines. Clearly, despite its past success, the JV was in need of some major strategic changes.

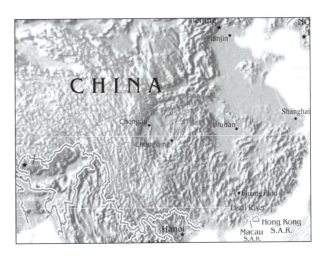

Under these circumstances, Alcatel sought to convert this JV into one of its fully consolidated units. The primary rationales were to put this JV under tighter leash as competition intensified as well as to better capitalize on the continued growth of the Chinese economy. Alcatel initiated the negotiations in early 2000, with the goal of acquiring an additional 18 percent of equity plus one share. Yet by August 2001, one and a half years later, Alcatel

had made no concrete progress. A lot had changed during that period. Just a year before, the telecom sector was the darling of investors worldwide, whereas by August 2001, it was in the middle of a profound crisis. The share value of Alcatel had lost 75 percent during 2001 (from $63.92 in January to $16.39 in December). The mandate from corporate headquarters—to use this acquisition in one of the few remaining bright spots in the global economy, to add value to the entire corporation—became more important as the global recession worsened.

Although Alcatel had been a seasoned player in China and generally had good working relationships with its partner, negotiations showed that Alcatel did not know enough about its partner. One of the first problems Alcatel encountered was identifying who would really make the decision to sell the shares. It took Alcatel a while to realize that PTIC was not necessarily the decision maker to dispose of the shares. While the theoretical owner of the Chinese partner is the State Assets Bureau, the actual decision would come from the Ministry of Information Industry (MII) in charge of the telecom industry—and they are two completely different government bodies. As Shanghai Bell was perceived as a crown jewel of the Chinese telecom industry, even the MII would not want to make a decision to sell, which might turn out to be politically incorrect. In the end, the problem reached the highest political level, where during a meeting, Chinese Premier Zhu Rongji told Serge Tchuruk, chairman and CEO of Alcatel, "Sell? Yes, it is for sale, but subject to a reasonable price."

Finding this "reasonable price" took Alcatel and Chinese negotiators one and a half years to negotiate, but they remained at a standstill by August 2001. On the Chinese side, the "reasonable price" was not just an economic term, it was predominantly political. What was a "reasonable price" for Shanghai Bell? A JV which had been nurtured by the Shanghai municipality government since the beginning—most importantly, nurtured personally during the period when President Jiang Zeming and Premier Zhu Rongji had been the mayor and communist party boss of Shanghai, respectively. Any price could be challenged by others for "cheaply selling state-owned assets to foreigners," and the career consequence for an official making the decision could be disastrous.

On the Alcatel side, the headquarters instructed the negotiation team to drop the deal if it could not close by the second quarter of 2002. The longer the negotiations took, the stronger the oppositions within Alcatel emerged. "Why spend so much money to acquire a weak majority in a company that has no future?" according to one argument, which pointed out that Alcatel had eighteen other units in China all in need of investment.

Another argument suggested that Alcatel might be perceived as a hostile predator by the Chinese government rather than a friendly foreign investor. Finally, there were some reservations about post-acquisition integration problems.

Eventually, an agreement was reached and announced on October 23, 2001. The financial market reacted positively with a 5 percent same-day jump of Alcatel stock. Alcatel agreed to spend $312 million to acquire Shanghai Bell, but the deal was more comprehensive than simply increasing Alcatel's shares in Shanghai Bell. The deal entailed completely restructuring and consolidating twelve of Alcatel's JVs in China under a new organizational structure with a much larger scope called Alcatel Shanghai Bell (ASB, http://www.alcatel-sbell.com.cn). Alcatel holds 50 percent plus one share and Chinese shareholders hold the remainder—the Belgian shares were bought out. Alcatel did not ask for 60 percent because it wanted to be a partner, rather than a controlling shareholder. Nevertheless, the "50/50+1" method has given Alcatel, which does not want to have the last word on every minute decision, the ultimate say with respect to key decisions. In exchange, Alcatel agreed to let ASB gain full access to the global repertoire of its technology, something the firm was reluctant to do when dealing with the old Shanghai Bell and other JVs in China.

With 6,500 employees, ASB covers the fixed, mobile, and broadband networking solutions and applications. ASB also has a key R&D center with 15 percent of Alcatel's global R&D budget, developing original technology for Alcatel's customers in China and the world. In addition, Alcatel has also moved its Asia Pacific headquarters to Shanghai. Overall, ASB endeavors to stay ahead of multinational rivals in China and in the Asia Pacific region.

Case Discussion Questions

1. What possible reasons motivated Alcatel to consider acquiring Shanghai Bell?

2. Why did the negotiations take so long?

3. Alcatel only acquired 50 percent plus one share in this "acquisition," which in essence is still a JV. Yet, this deal was able to add value to the Alcatel stock. Why?

4. Why was the scope of the new Alcatel Shanghai Bell dramatically widened? Identify the pros and cons.

Sources: Based on the author's interviews and non-proprietary materials provided by Alcatel executives.

Notes

Abbreviation list

AME – Academy of Management Executive

AMJ – Academy of Management Journal

AMR – Academy of Management Review

ASQ – Administrative Science Quarterly

ASR – American Sociological Review

BH – Business Horizons

BW – Business Week

CMR – California Management Review

EMJ – European Management Journal

HBR – Harvard Business Review

IBR – International Business Review

JEBO – Journal of Economic Behavior and Organization

JIBS – Journal of International Business Studies

JIM – Journal of International Management

JLEO – Journal of Law, Economics, and Organization

JM – Journal of Management

JMS – Journal of Management Studies

LRP – Long Range Planning

MIR – Management International Review

MS – Management Science

OSc – Organization Science

SMJ – Strategic Management Journal

SMR – MIT Sloan Management Review

SO – Strategic Organization

1. Cited in A. Parkhe, 1996, International joint ventures (p. 429), in B. J. Punnett & O. Shenkar (eds.), *Handbook for International Management Research* (429–459), Oxford, UK: Blackwell.

2. P. Beamish & P. Killing (eds.), 1997, *Cooperative Strategies* (3 volumes), San Francisco: New Lexington; F. Contractor & P. Lorang (eds.), 2002, *Cooperative Strategies and Alliances,* Amsterdam: Elsevier; J. Dunning, 1995, Reappraising the eclectic paradigm in an age of alliance capitalism, *JIBS,* 26: 461–491; R. Osborn & J. Hagedoorn, 1997, The institutionalization and evolutionary dynamics of interorganizational alliances and networks, *AMJ,* 40: 261–278; K. Smith, S. Carroll, & S. Ashford, 1995, Intra– and interorganizational cooperation, *AMJ,* 38: 7–23.

3. Cited in J. Reuer, 2004, Introduction (p. 2), in J. Reuer (ed.), *Strategic Alliances,* New York: Oxford University Press.

4. J. Dyer, P. Kale, & H. Singh, 2003, Do you know when to ally or acquire? Working paper, Brigham Young University.

5. J. Bamford, B. Gomes-Casseres, & M. Robinson, 2003, *Mastering Alliance Strategy,* San Francisco: Jossey-Bass.

6. R. Gulati, 1998, Alliances and networks (p. 293), *SMJ,* 19: 293–317.

7. J. Hennart, 1988, A transaction costs theory of equity joint ventures, *SMJ,* 9: 361–374; R. Osborn & C. Baughm, 1990, Forms of interorganizational governance for multinational alliances, *AMJ,* 33: 503–519; O. Williamson, 1991, Comparative economic organization, *ASQ,* 36: 269–296.

8. W. Danis & A. Parkhe, 2002, Hungarian-Western partnerships, *JIBS,* 33: 423–455.

9. Gulati, 1998, Alliances and networks; J. Jarillo, 1988, On strategic networks, *SMJ,* 9: 31–41.

10. T. Das & B. Teng, 2002, Alliance constellations, *AMR,* 27: 445–456; B. Gomes-Casseres, 1996, *The Alliance Revolution,* Cambridge: Harvard University Press; S. Human & K. Provan, 1997, An emergent theory of structure and outcomes in small-firm strategic manufacturing networks, *AMJ,* 40: 368–404; C. Jones, W. Hesterly, K. Fladmoe-Lindquist, & S. Borgatti, 1998, Professional service constellations, *OSc,* 9: 396–410.

11. C. Dhanaraj & A. Parkhe, 2003, Orchestrating innovation networks, Working paper, Indiana University; M. Zeng & X. Chen, 2003, Achieving cooperation in multiparty alliances, *AMR,* 28: 587–605.

12. F. Contractor & S. Kundu, 1998, Modal choice in a world of alliances, *JIBS,* 29: 325–358.

13. R. Gulati, N. Nohria, & A. Zaheer, 2000, Strategic networks, *SMJ,* 21: 203–215; K. Harrigan, 1985, *Strategies for Joint Ventures,* Lexington, MA: Lexington Books; M. Sakakibara, 2002, Formation of R&D consortia, *SMJ,* 23: 1033–1050.

14. W. Burgers, C. Hill, & W. C. Kim, 1993, A theory of global strategic alliances, *SMJ,* 14: 419–432; D. Deeds & C. Hill, 1996, Strategic alliances and the rate of new product development, *JBV,* 11: 41–55.

15. D. Gnyawali & R. Madhavan, 2001, Cooperative networks and competitive dynamics (p. 431), *AMR,* 26: 431–445.

16. J. Dyer & H. Singh, 1998, The relational view (p. 667), *AMR,* 23: 660–679.

17. J. Dyer, 1997, Effective interfirm collaboration, *SMJ,* 18: 543–556.

18. M. Subramani & N. Venkatraman, 2003, Safeguarding investments in asymmetric relationships, *AMJ,* 46: 46–62.

19. D. Harrison, 2004, Is a long-term business relationship an implied contract? *JMS,* 41: 107–125.

20. A. Boateng & K. Glaister, 2003, Strategic motives for international joint venture formation in Ghana, *MIR,* 43: 107–128; P. Brews & C. Tucci, 2003, Internetworking, *AME,* 17 (4): 8–24; R. D. Ireland, M. Hitt, & D. Vaidyanath, 2002, Alliance management as a source of competitive advantage, *JM,* 28: 413–446; H. Li & K. Atuahene-Gima, 2001, Product innovation strategy and the performance of new technology ventures in China, *AMJ,* 44: 1123–1135; A. Madhok & S. Tallman, 1998, Resources, transactions, and rents, *OSc,* 9: 326–339; N. Park, J. Mezias, & J. Song, 2004, A resource–based view of strategic alliances and firm value in the electronic marketplace, *JM,* 30: 7–27; M. Schilling & H. K. Steensma, 2001, The use of modular organizational forms, *AMJ,* 44: 1149–1169.

21. P. Dussauge & B. Garrette, 1995, Determinants of success in international strategic alliances, *JIBS,* 26: 505–530.

22. *Economist,* 2003, Open skies and flights of fancy (p. 67), October 4: 65–67.

23. J. Goes & S. Park, 1997, Interorganizational links and innovation, *AMJ,* 40: 673–696; M. Kotabe & S. Swan, 1995, The role of strategic alliances in high-technology new product development, *SMJ,* 16: 621–636.

24. D. Hurry, A. Miller, & E. Bowman, 1993, Calls on high-technology, *SMJ,* 13: 85–101; B. Kogut, 1991, Joint ventures and the option to expand and acquire, *MS,* 37: 19–33; R. McGrath, 1997, A real options logic for initiating technology positioning investments, *AMR,* 22: 974–996.

25. T. Chi & D. McGuire, 1996, Collaborative ventures and value of learning, *JIBS,* 27: 285–307; T. Folta & K. Miller, 2002, Real options in equity partnerships, *SMJ,* 23: 77–88; T. Folta & J. O'Brien, 2004, Entry in the presence of dueling options, *SMJ,* 25: 121–138; R. McGrath & A. Nerkar, 2004, Real options reasoning and a new look at the R&D investment strategies of pharmaceutical firms, *SMJ,* 25: 1–21; K. Miller, 1998, Economic exposure and integrated risk management, *SMJ,* 19: 497–514; K. Miller & Z. Shapira, 2004, An empirical test of heuristics and biases affecting real option valuation, *SMJ,* 25: 269–284; S. Rangan, 1998, Do multinationals operate flexibly? *JIBS,* 29: 217–37; P. Rivoli & E. Salorio, 1996, Foreign direct investment under uncertainty, *JIBS,* 27: 335–357; C. Young-Ybarra & M. Wiersema, 1999, Strategic flexibility in information technology alliances, *OSc,* 10: 439–459.

26. R. Hill & D. Hellriegel, 1994, Critical contingencies in joint venture management, *OSc,* 5: 594–607.

27. S. Balakrishnan & M. Koza, 1993, Information asymmetry, adverse selection, and joint ventures, *JEBO,* 20: 99–117.

28. M. W. Peng, 2000, Controlling the foreign agents: How governments deal with multinationals in a transition economy, *MIR,* 40 (2): 141–165.

29. P. Aulakh, M. Kotabe, & A. Sahay, 1996, Trust and performance in cross–border marketing partnerships, *JIBS,* 27: 1005–1032; S. Currall & A. Inkpen, 2002, A multilevel approach to trust in joint ventures, *JIBS,* 33: 479–495; T. Das & B. Teng, 1998, Between trust and control, *AMR,* 23: 491–512; J. Johnson, J. Cullen, T. Sakano, & H. Takenouchi, 1996, Setting the stage for trust and strategic integration in Japanese-US cooperative alliances, *JIBS,* 27: 981–1004; B. Nooteboom, H. Berger, & N. Nooderhaven, 1997, Effects of trust and governance on relational risk, *AMJ,* 40: 308–338.

30. M. Porter, H. Takeuchi, & M. Sakakibara, 2000, *Can Japan Compete?* (p. 89), Cambridge, MA: Perseus.

31. G. Hamel, 1991, Competition for competence and inter-partner learning within strategic alliances, *SMJ,* 12: 83–103.

32. S. Alvarez & J. Barney, 2001, How entrepreneurial firms can benefit from alliances with large partners, *AME,* 15: 139–148; P. Kale, H. Singh, & H. Perlmutter, 2000, Learning and protection of proprietary assets in alliances, *SMJ,* 21: 217–237.

33. J. Lampel & J. Shamsie, 2000, Probing the unobtrusive link (p. 590), *SMJ,* 21: 593–602.

34. R. Reich & E. Mankin, 1986, Joint ventures with Japan give away our future, *HBR,* March-April: 78–90.

35. M. Bear, 1998, How Japanese partners help US manufacturers to raise productivity, *LRP,* 31: 919–926; J. Hennart, T. Roehl, & D. Zietlow, 1999, "Trojan horse" or "workhorse"? *SMJ,* 20: 15–29.

36. D. Ahlstrom, M. Young, & A. Nair, 2002, Deceptive managerial practices in China, *BH,* November–December: 49–59; L. Huff & L. Kelley, 2003, Levels of organizational trust in individualistic versus collectivist societies, *OSc,* 14: 81–90; R. Kashlak, R. Chandran, & A. Benedetto, 1998, Reciprocity in international business, *JIBS,* 29: 281–304; B. McEvily, V. Perrone, &

A. Zaheer, 2003, Trust as an organizing principle, *OSc,* 14: 91–103.

37. M. Dollinger, P. Golden, & T. Saxton, 1997, The effect of reputation on the decision to joint venture, *SMJ,* 18: 127–140; T. Saxton, 1997, The effects of partner and relationship characteristics on alliance outcome, *AMJ,* 40: 443–461.

38. M. W. Peng & O. Shenkar, 2002, Joint venture dissolution as corporate divorce, *AME,* 16 (2): 95–105.

39. O. Shenkar & Y. Zeira, 1992, Role conflict and role ambiguity of chief executive officers in IJVs, *JIBS,* 23: 55–75.

40. G. Lorenzoni & A. Lipparini, 1999, The leveraging of interfirm relationships, *SMJ,* 20: 317–338.

41. B. McEvilly & A. Zaheer, 1999, Bridging ties, *SMJ,* 20: 1133–1156; J. Pennings, K. Lee, & A. Witteloostujin, 1998, Human capital, social capital, and firm dissolution, *AMJ,* 41: 425–440; T. Pollock, J. Porac, & J. Wade, 2004, Constructing deal networks, *AMR,* 29: 50–72; G. Walker, B. Kogut, & W. Shan, 1997, Social capital, structural holes, and the formation of an industry network, *OSc,* 8: 109–125.

42. D. Gerwin, 2004, Coordinating new product development in strategic alliances, *AMR,* 29: 241–257.

43. J. Dyer, P. Kale, & H. Singh, 2001, How to make strategic alliances work, *SMR,* summer: 37–43.

44. A. Millington & B. Bayliss, 1995, Transnational joint ventures between UK and EU manufacturing companies and the structure of competition, *JIBS,* 26: 239–254.

45. S. Weiss, 1990, The long path to the IBM-Mexico agreement, *JIBS,* 21: 565–97.

46. C. Garcia-Pont & N. Nohria, 2002, Local versus global mimetism, *SMJ,* 23: 307–321; M. Guillen, 2002, Structural inertia, imitation, and foreign expansion, *AMJ,* 45: 509–525; M. Kraatz, 1998, Learning by association? *AMJ,* 41: 621–643; J. Lu, 2002, Intra- and inter-organizational imitative behavior, *JIBS,* 33: 19–38; S. Majumdar & S. Venkatraman, 1998, Network effects and the adoption of new technology, *SMJ,* 19: 1045–1062.

47. F. Jeffries & R. Reed, 2000, Trust and adaptation in relational contracting, *AMR,* 25: 873–882; S. Lui & H. Ngo, 2004, The role of trust and contractual safeguards

on cooperation in non-equity alliances, *JM*, 30: 471–485; Y. Luo, 2002, Contract, cooperation, and performance in international joint ventures, *SMJ*, 23: 903–919; A. Nordberg, A. Campbell, & A. Verbeke, 1996, Can market-based contracts substitute for alliances in high technology markets? *JIBS*, 27: 963–980; A. Parkhe, 2003, Institutional environments, institutional change, and international alliances, *JIM*, 9: 305–316; L. Poppo & T. Zenger, 2002, Do formal contracts and relational governance function as substitutes or complements? *SMJ*, 23: 707–725; P. Ring & A. Van de Ven, 1994, Developmental processes in cooperative interorganizational relationships, *AMR*, 19: 90–118; P. Saparito, C. Chen, & H. Sapienza, 2004, The role of relational trust in bank-small firm relationships, *AMJ*, 47: 400–410; A. Zaheer & N. Venkatraman, 1995, Relational governance as an interorganizational strategy, *SMJ*, 16: 373–392.

48. This section draws heavily from S. Tallman & O. Shenkar, 1994, A managerial decision model of international cooperative venture formation, *JIBS*, 25: 91–113. See also Y. Doz, P. Olk, & P. Ring, 2000, Formation of research and development consortia, *SMJ*, 20: 239–266; P. Kenis & D. Knoke, 2002, How organizational field networks shape interorganizational tie-formation rates, *AMR*, 27: 275–294.

49. S. Park, R. Chen, & S. Gallagher, 2002, Firm resources as moderators of the relationship between market growth and strategic alliances in semiconductor start-ups, *AMJ*, 45: 527–545.

50. M. W. Peng & Y. Luo, 2000, Managerial ties and firm performance in a transition economy: The nature of a micro-macro link, *AMJ*, 43: 486–501. See also L. Abrams, R. Cross, E. Lesser, & D. Levin, 2003, Nurturing interpersonal trust in knowledge-sharing networks, *AME*, 17: 64–77; D. Hambrick, J. Li, K. Xin, & A. Tsui, 2001, Composition and processes of IJV management groups, *SMJ*, 22: 1033–1053; J. Johnson, A. Korsgaard, & H. Sapienza, 2002, Perceived fairness, decision control, and commitment in international joint venture management teams, *SMJ*, 23: 1141–1160; Y. Luo, 2001, Antecedents and consequences of personal attachment in cross-cultural cooperative ventures, *ASQ*, 46: 177–201; M. Seabright, D. Levinthal, & M. Fichman, 1992, Role of individual attachments in the dissolution of interorganizational relationships, *AMJ*, 35: 122–160; I. Williamson & D. Cable, 2003, Organizational hiring

patterns, interfirm network ties, and interorganizational imitation, *AMJ*, 46: 349–358.

51. S. Borgatti & R. Cross, 2003, A relational view of information seeking and learning in social networks, *MS*, 49: 432–445; K. Eisenhardt & C. Schoonhoven, 1996, Resource–based view of strategic alliance formation, *OSc*, 7: 136–150; P. Wong & P. Ellis, 2002, Social ties and partner identification in Sino-Hong Kong IJVs, *JIBS*, 33: 267–289; B. Uzzi & R. Lancaster, 2003, Relational embeddedness and learning, *MS*, 49: 383–399.

52. P. Dickson & K. M. Weaver, 1997, Environmental determinants and individual-level moderators of alliance use, *AMJ*, 40: 404–425; B. Tyler & H. K. Steensma, 1998, The effects of executives' experiences and perceptions on their assessment of potential technological alliances, *SMJ*, 19: 939–965.

53. S. Chung, H. Singh, & K. Lee, 2000, Complementarity, status similarity, and social capital as drivers of alliance formation, *SMJ*, 21: 1–22; U. Elg, 2000, Firms' home-market relationships, *JIBS*, 31: 169–177; R. Gulati, 1995, Does familiarity breed trust? *AMJ*, 38: 85–112; S. Li & T. Rowley, 2002, Inertia and evaluation mechanisms in partner selection, *AMJ*, 45: 1104–1119.

54. Y. Pan & D. Tse, 1996, Cooperative strategies between foreign firms in an overseas country, *JIBS*, 27: 929–946.

55. M. Geringer, 1991, Strategic determinants of partner selection criteria in international joint ventures, *JIBS*, 22: 41–62.

56. B. Borys & D. Jemison, 1989, Hybrid arrangements as strategic alliances, *AMR*, 14: 234–249.

57. I. Bjorkman & Y. Lu, 1999, A corporate perspective on the management of human resources in China, *JWB*, 34: 16–25; E. Weldon & J. Li, 1999, International joint ventures in China, *JWB*, 34: 1–2.

58. G. Ahuja, 2000, The duality of collaboration, *SMJ*, 21: 317–343.

59. L. Argote, B. McEvily, & R. Reagans, 2003, Managing knowledge in organizations, *MS*, 49: 571–582; M. Fiol & M. Lyles, 1985, Organization learning, *AMR*, 10: 803–813.

60. M. Colombo, 2003, Alliance form, *SMJ*, 24: 1209–1229; A. Inkpen & A. Dinur, 1998, Knowledge management processes and international joint ventures,

OSc, 9: 454–468; B. Kogut, 1988, Joint ventures, *SMJ,* 9: 319–322; B. Kogut & U. Zander, 1993, Knowledge of the firm and the evolutionary theory of the multinational corporation, *JIBS,* 24: 625–645; R. Kumar & K. Nti, 1998, Differential learning and interaction in alliance dynamics, *OSc,* 9: 356–367; P. Lane & M. Lubatkin, 1998, Relative absorptive capacity and interorganizational learning, *SMJ,* 19: 461–477; B. Uzzi & J. Gillespie, 2002, Knowledge spillovers in corporate financing networks, *SMJ,* 23: 595–619.

61. G. Szulanski, 1996, Exploring internal stickiness, *SMJ,* 17: 27–43.

62. A. Gopal, K. Sivaramakrishnan, M. Krishnan, & J. Mukhopadhyay, 2003, Contracts in offshore software development, *MS,* 49: 1671–1683.

63. S. Ante, 2004, Shifting work offshore? Outsourcer beware, *BW,* January 12: 36–37.

64. M. Makhija & U. Ganesh, 1997, The relationship between control and partner learning in learning-related joint ventures, *OSc,* 8: 508–527; H. Mjoen & S. Tallman, 1997, Control and performance in international joint ventures, *OSc,* 8: 257–274.

65. J. Oxley, 1997, Appropriability hazards and governance in strategic alliances, *JLEO,* 13: 387–409.

66. P. Beamish & J. Banks, 1987, Equity joint ventures and the theory of the multinational enterprise, *JIBS,* 19: 1–16.

67. Y. Pan & X. Li, 2000, Joint venture formation of very large multinational firms, *JIBS,* 31: 179–189.

68. S. Makino & P. Beamish 1998, Performance and survival of JVs with non-conventional ownership structures, *JIBS,* 29: 797–818.

69. B. Gomes-Casseres, 2003, Competitive advantage in alliance constellations, *SO,* 1: 327–335; E. Tsang, 1998, Can *guanxi* be a sustainable competitive advantage for doing business in China? *AME,* 12: 64–73.

70. B. Silverman & J. Baum, 2002, Alliance-based competitive dynamics, *AMJ,* 45: 791–806.

71. S. Parise & A. Casher, 2003, Alliance portfolios, *AME,* 17 (4): 25–39.

72. T. Khanna, 1998, The scope of alliances, *OSc,* 9: 340–355.

73. Y. Doz, 1996, The evolution of cooperation in strategic alliances, *SMJ,* 17: 55–83; M. Koza & A. Lewin, 1998, The co-evolution of strategic alliances, *OSc,* 9: 255–264; J. Reuer, M. Zollo, & H. Singh, 2002, Post-formation dynamics in strategic alliances, *SMJ,* 23: 135–152; J. Robins, S. Tallman, & K. Fladmoe-Lindquist, 2002, Autonomy and dependence of international cooperative ventures, *SMJ,* 23: 881–901.

74. S. Jap & E. Anderson, 2003, Safeguarding interorganizational performance and continuity under ex post opportunism, *MS,* 49: 1684–1701.

75. C. Hill, 2005, *International Business,* 5th ed. (p. 503), Chicago: McGraw-Hill Irwin.

76. Y. Zhang & N. Rajagopalan, 2002, Inter-partner credible threat in international joint ventures, *JIBS,* 33: 457–478.

77. This section draws heavily from M. W. Peng, 2003, From strong ties to weak ties in emerging economies, Working paper, Fisher College of Business, The Ohio State University.

78. M. Granovetter, 1973, The strength of weak ties, *AJS,* 78: 1360–1380.

79. P. Adler & S. Kwan, 2002, Social capital, *AMR,* 27: 17–40; J. Hagen & S. Choe, 1998, Trust in Japanese interfirm relations, *AMR,* 23: 589–600; B. Koka & J. Prescott, 2002, Strategic alliances as social capital, *SMJ,* 23: 795–816; A. Larson, 1992, Network dyads in entrepreneurial settings, *ASQ,* 37: 76–104; S. Park & Y. Luo, 2001, *Guanxi* and organizational dynamics, *SMJ,* 22: 455–477; B. Uzzi, 1996, Social structure and competition in interfirm networks, *ASQ,* 42: 35–67; G. Walker, B. Kogut, & W. Shan, 1997, Social capital, structure holes, and the formation of industry networks, *OSc,* 8: 109–125.

80. R. Burt, 1992, *Structural Holes,* Cambridge: Harvard University Press; M. Granovetter, 1973, The strength of weak ties, *AJS,* 78: 1360–1380.

81. T. Rowley, Behrens, & Krackhardt, 2000, Redundant governance structures (p. 383), *SMJ,* 21: 369–386. See also G. Ahuja, 2000, Collaboration networks, structural holes, and innovation, *ASQ,* 45: 425–455.

82. J. March, 1991, Exploration and exploitation in organizational learning (p. 71), *OSc,* 2: 71–87.

83. F. Rothaermel & D. Deeds, 2004, Exploration and exploitation alliances in biotechnology, *SMJ,* 25: 201–221.

84. J. Hite & W. Hesterly, 2001, The evolution of firm networks (p. 282), *SMJ*, 22: 275–286; R. Madhavan, B. Koka, & J. Prescott, 1998, Networks in transition, *SMJ*, 19: 439–459.

85. C. Jones, W. Hesterly, & S. Borgatti, 1997, A general theory of network governance, *AMR*, 22: 911–945.

86. J. Child & Y. Yan, 2003, Predicting the performance of international joint ventures, *JMS*, 40: 284–320; R. Pearce, 1997, Toward understanding joint venture performance and survival, *AMR*, 22: 203–225.

87. A. Arino, 2003, Measures of strategic alliance performance, *JIBS*, 34: 66–79; X. Lin & R. Germain, 1998, Sustaining satisfactory joint venture relationships, *JIBS*, 29: 179–196; A. Yan & M. Zeng, 1999, International joint venture instability, *JIBS*, 30: 397–414.

88. M. Geringer & L. Hebert, 1991, Measuring performance of international joint ventures (p. 258), *JIBS*, 22: 249–263; J. Reuer & M. Koza, 2000, Asymmetric information and joint venture performance, *SMJ*, 21: 81–88.

89. M. Geringer & L. Hebert, 1989, Control and performance in international joint ventures, *JIBS*, 20: 235–254; J. Killing, 1983, *Strategies for Joint Venture Success*, New York: Praeger; A. Parkhe, 1993, Strategic alliance structuring, *AMJ*, 36: 794–829; A. Yan & B. Gray, 1994, Bargaining power, management control, and performance, *AMJ*, 37: 1478–1517.

90. C. Dhanaraj & P. Beamish, 2004, Effect of equity ownership on the survival of international joint ventures, *SMJ*, 25: 295–305.

91. J. Child & L. Markoczy, 1993, Host country managerial behavior and learning in Chinese and Hungarian joint ventures, *JMS*, 30: 611–631; P. Lane, J. Salk, & M. Lyles, 2001, Absorptive capacity, learning, and performance in international joint ventures, *SMJ*, 22: 1139–1161; M. Lyles & J. Salk, 1996, Knowledge acquisition from foreign parents in international joint ventures, *JIBS*, 27: 877–903; G. Osland, 1994, Successful operating strategies in the performance of US-China joint ventures, *JIM*, 2: 53–78; B. Simonin, 1997, The importance of collaborative know-how, *AMJ*, 40: 1150–1174; E. Tsang, 2002, Acquiring knowledge by foreign partners from international joint ventures in a transition economy, *SMJ*, 23: 835–854.

92. H. Barkema, O. Shenkar, F. Vermeulen, & J. Bell, 1997, Working abroad, working with others, *AMJ*, 40: 426–442; M. K. Erramilli, 1991, The experience factor in foreign market entry behavior of service firms, *JIBS*, 22: 479–501; M. Lyles, 1988, Learning among joint venture sophisticated firms, *MIR*, 28: 85–98; B. Simonin, 1999, Ambiguity and the process of knowledge transfer in strategic alliances, *SMJ*, 20: 595–623.

93. Y. Luo & M. W. Peng, 1999, Learning to compete in a transition economy: Experience, environment, and performance, *JIBS*, 30: 269–296; S. Makino & A. Delios, 1996, Local knowledge transfer and performance, *JIBS*, 27: 905–927.

94. H. K. Steensma, L. Marino, K. M. Weaver, & P. Dickson, 2000, The influence of national culture on the formation of technology alliances by entrepreneurial firms, *AMJ*, 43: 951–974; A. Parkhe, 1991, Interfirm diversity, organizational learning, and longevity in global alliances, *JIBS*, 22: 579–602; D. Sirmon & P. Lane, 2004, A model of cultural differences and international alliance performance, *JIBS*, 35: 306–319.

95. H. Barkema & F. Vermeulen, 1997, What differences in the cultural backgrounds of partners are detrimental for international joint ventures? *JIBS*, 28: 845–864; J. Hennart & M. Zeng, 2002, Cross-cultural differences and joint venture longevity, *JIBS*, 33: 699–716; A. Inkpen & P. Beamish, 1997, Knowledge, bargaining power, and the instability of international joint ventures, *AMR*, 22: 177–202; S. Park & G. Ungson, 1997, The effect of national culture, organizational complementarity, and economic motivation on joint venture dissolution, *AMJ*, 40: 279–307.

96. C. Lee & P. Beamish, 1995, The characteristics and performance of Korean joint ventures in LDCs, *JIBS*, 26: 637–654.

97. A. Arino & J. de la Torre, 1998, Learning from failure, *OSc*, 9: 306–325; C. Fey & P. Beamish, 2000, Joint venture conflict, *IBR*, 9: 139–162; J. Mohr & R. Spekman, 1994, Characteristics of partnership success, *SMJ*, 15: 135–152; S. Park & M. Russo, 1996, When competition eclipses cooperation, *MS*, 42: 875–890; M. Serapio & W. Cascio, 1996, End-games in international alliances, *AME*, 10: 62–73; A. Zaheer, B. McEvily, & V. Perrone, 1998, Does trust matter? *OSc*, 9: 141–161.

98. A. Afuah, 2000, How much do your co-opetitors' capabilities matter in the face of technological change? *SMJ,* 21: 387–404; J. Baum, T. Calabrese, & B. Silverman, 2000, Don't go it alone, *SMJ,* 21: 267–294; J. Combs & D. Ketchen, 1999, Explaining interfirm cooperation and performance, *SMJ,* 20: 867–888; A. Kaufman, C. Wood, & G. Theyal, 2000, Collaboration and technology linkages, *SMJ,* 21: 649–664; W. Mitchell & H. Singh, 1996, Survival of business using collaborative relationships, *SMJ,* 17: 169–195; P. Olk & C. Young, 1997, Why members stay or leave an R&D consortium, *SMJ,* 18: 855–877; K. Singh, 1997, The impact of technological complexity and cooperation on business survival, *AMJ,* 40: 339–367.

99. B. Anand & T. Khanna, 2000, Do firms learn to create value? *SMJ,* 21: 295–316; S. Das & P. Sen, 1998, Impact of strategic alliances on firm valuation, *AMJ,* 41: 27–42; J. Koh & N. Venkatraman, 1991, Joint venture formations and stock market reactions, *AMJ,* 34: 869–892; H. Merchant, 2003, Joint venture characteristics and shareholder value creation, *MIR,* 43: 21–40; H. Merchant & D. Schendel, 2000, How do international joint ventures create shareholder value? *SMJ,* 21: 723–737; J. Reuer, 2001, From hybrids to hierarchies, *SMJ,* 22: 27–44.

100. J. Hagedoorn & J. Schakenraad, 1994, The effect of strategic alliances on company performance, *SMJ,* 15: 291–309.

101. This section draws heavily from M. Zeng & J. Hennart, 2002, From learning races to cooperative specialization, in F. Contractor & P. Lorange (eds.), *Cooperative Strategies and Alliances* (pp. 189–210), Amsterdam: Elsevier.

102. Hamel, 1991, Competition for competence. See also P. Dussauge, B. Garrette, & W. Mitchell, 2000, Learning from competing partners, *SMJ,* 21: 99–126; P. Dussauge, B. Garrette, & W. Mitchell, 2004, Asymmetric performance, *SMJ,* 25: 701–711.

103. J. Barnes, M. Cook, T. Koybaeva, & E. Stafford, 1997, Why do our Russian alliances fail? *LRP,* 30: 540–550; N. Napier & D. Thomas, 2004, *Managing Relationships in Transition Economies,* New York: Prager; S. Puffer, D. McCarthy, & N. Alexander, 2000, *The Russian Capitalist Experiment,* Cheltenham, UK: Edward Elgar.

104. L. Blodgett, 1992, Factors in the instability of international joint ventures, *SMJ,* 13: 475–481; C. Choi & P. Beamish, 2004, Split management control and international joint venture performance, *JIBS,* 35: 201–215; H. K. Steensma & M. Lyles, 2000, Explaining IJV survival in a transition economy, *SMJ,* 21: 831–851.

105. T. Tong, J. Reuer, & M. W. Peng, 2004, International joint ventures and the value of growth options, Working paper, Fisher College of Business, The Ohio State University.

106. R. Adner & D. Levinthal, 2004, What is *not* a real option? *AMR,* 29: 74–85; B. Peterson, D. Welch, & L. Welch, 2000, Creating meaningful switching options in international operations, *LRP,* 33: 688–705.

107. R. McGrath, W. Ferrier, & A. Mendelow, 2004, Real options as engines of choice and heterogeneity, *AMR,* 29: 86–101; J. Reuer & M. Leiblein, 2000, Downside risk implications of multinationality and international joint ventures, *AMJ,* 43: 203–214; A. Zardkoohi, 2004, Do real options lead to escalation of commitment? *AMR,* 29: 111–119.

108. B. Kogut & N. Kulatilaka, 2001, Capabilities as real options, *OSc,* 12: 744–758.

109. This section draws heavily from Dyer, Kale, & Singh, 2003, Do you know when to ally or acquire?

110. J. Hagedoorn & B. Sadowski, 1999, The transition from strategic alliances to mergers and acquisitions, *JMS,* 36: 87–107.

111. J. Hennart & S. Reddy, 1997, The choice between mergers/acquisitions and joint ventures, *SMJ,* 18: 1–12; P. Kale, J. Dyer, & H. Singh, 2002, Alliance capability, stock market response, and long-term alliance success, *SMJ,* 23: 747–767.

112. Calculated by Dyer, Kale, & Singh, 2003, Do you know when to ally or acquire? See also N. Park, 2004, A guide to using event study methods in multi-country settings, *SMJ,* 25: 655–668.

113. T. Chi, 2000, Option to acquire or divest a joint venture (p. 671), *SMJ,* 21: 665–687.

114. A. Brandenburger & B. Nalebuff, 1996, *Co-opetition,* New York: Doubleday.

chapter

8

MANAGING GLOBAL COMPETITIVE DYNAMICS

Outline

- Strategy as action
- A comprehensive model of global competitive dynamics
- Attack and counterattack
- Cooperation, accommodation, and collusion
- Local firms versus multinational enterprises
- Debates and extensions
- Implications for strategists

Opening Case: The Pacific War: Kodak versus Fuji

When a major trade dispute erupted between Kodak (http://www.kodak.com) and Fuji (http://www.fujifilm.com) in 1996, both had approximately the same worldwide revenue of $15 billion. Both controlled a 70 percent market share of their home countries, Kodak maintained a 12 percent market share in Japan, and Fuji a 14 percent market share in the United States. In markets outside the United States and Japan, Kodak had a 36 percent share and Fuji 33 percent.

During their long rivalry, Kodak and Fuji employed a variety of moves and countermoves, including (1) pricing, (2) innovation, (3) marketing, (4) distribution, and (5) political components. Given that there was no real differentiation between the products of both companies, which products were superior fundamentally depended on consumers' perceptions. In the 1950s, both American and Japanese consumers regarded Kodak as a superior product

deserving higher prices. Through price-cutting, Kodak tripled its market share in Japan from 6 percent in 1971 to 18 percent in 1981. However, in status-conscious Japan, lowering prices might have inadvertently hurt Kodak's image, allowing Fuji to take the lead with higher prices. By the early 1990s, Kodak's market share went down to 10 percent in Japan.

In terms of innovations, while Kodak had an early lead, Fuji's first break-through was the 1973 introduction of mini-labs for one-hour photo processing, which used Fuji supplies. Kodak did not respond with its own mini-labs until 1987. By 1994, Fuji controlled 45 percent of Japan's mini-labs, whereas Kodak had just 20 percent. In 1987, Fuji also unleashed the one-time use camera ahead of Kodak. Kodak fought back in 1989, by introducing the new RA-4 papers. However, Fuji quickly responded with higher quality RA-4 papers.

Both firms competed intensely with advertising. In 1984, Fuji won the official sponsorship of the Los Angeles Olympics, which not only solidified its quality image in the United States, but also strengthened it in Japan. In Japan, Fuji capitalized on American consumers' increasing acceptance of its products, advertising that Kodak was "dethroned" in its own home country. In 1998, Kodak belatedly got its revenge by winning the sponsorship of the Nagano Winter Olympics in Japan.

Distribution was another contested arena. While large retail outlets such as department stores had long carried Kodak products (often side by side with Fuji) in Japan, these outlets only represented 15 percent of the total number of outlets and 30 percent of sales. The majority of sales were handled by small shops, which typically only carried Fuji. Fuji, through exclusive arrangements with the four principal wholesalers, essentially controlled these small retail outlets. Kodak approached the four wholesalers to distribute its products in Japan, but was refused.

Finally, the rivalry also had a significant political dimension. In 1993, as Fuji's RA-4 papers flooded the United States, Kodak charged Fuji of dumping (selling below cost). Fuji subsequently agreed to raise prices. In addition, in 1995, Kodak requested that the US Trade Representative (USTR) impose "Super 301" trade sanctions on Japan, because Fuji allegedly conspired to prevent Kodak from reaching 85 percent of the Japanese retail outlets. According to Kodak, these small outlets were Fuji's captive profit sanctuary, which unfairly funded its global expansion. Fuji denied all charges, pointing out that both Fuji and Kodak had equal market shares in their home countries because of their natural home court advantage. In 1996, although the USTR ruled in favor of Kodak, it did not initiate Super 301 sanctions. Instead, the World Trade Organization (WTO) was asked to adjudicate this dispute. In 1997, a WTO panel consisting of Brazil, New Zealand, and Switzerland unanimously ruled in favor of Fuji and Japan, and the United States did not appeal the WTO ruling.

In the new digital era, although both firms' traditional chemical-based business is threatened, Fuji started relatively earlier with digital cameras, with approximately 11 percent of the worldwide market share as of 2004. Kodak followed with an 8 percent market share. In late 2003, Kodak announced that it would stop selling 35 mm photo film in North America and Western Europe and focus on digital products. Nevertheless, the rivalry is hardly over, as both firms will compete intensely on digital cameras, online kiosks, and mini-labs.

Sources: Based on (1) D. Baron, 1997, Integrated strategy and international trade disputes: The Kodak-Fujifilm case, Journal of Economics and Management Strategy, 6: 291–346; (2) H. D. Hopkins, 2003, The response strategies of dominant US firms to Japanese challengers, Journal of Management, 29: 5–25; (3) W. Symonds, 2003, The Kodak revolt is short-sighted, Business Week, November 3: 38; (4) Y. Tsurumi & H. Tsurumi, 1999, Fujifilm-Kodak duopolistic competition in Japan and the United States, Journal of International Business Studies, 30: 813–830; (5) http://www.fujifilm.com.

During the long rivalry between Kodak and Fuji, why did they take certain actions, but not others? After one side initiates an action, how does the other respond? What are the performance consequences of these actions and responses? These are some of the key questions we will discuss in this chapter, which focuses on such competitive dynamics around the world. **Competitive dynamics** refers to actions and responses undertaken by competing firms. In any competitive setting, one firm's actions to enhance its advantage are rarely unnoticed by rivals. Therefore, the initiating firm not only needs to know its own strengths and weaknesses associated with its planned actions *before* it makes a move, but the firm also needs to predict the kind of response competitors might make. By anticipating rivals' actions, the initiating firm may want to both revise its planned initial actions and prepare to deal with its rivals' responses in the next round. This process is called **competitor analysis,** advocated a long time ago by Sun Tzu's teaching to not only know "yourself," but also "your opponents."

Recall that Chapter 1 introduced the "strategy as plan" and "strategy as action" schools. Firms certainly need to carefully plan their actions. However, as military officers have long known, a good plan never lasts longer than contact with the enemy. Firms must constantly adapt to rivals' attacks and counterattacks. This chapter first outlines the basic tenets of the "strategy as action" school, followed by a comprehensive model drawing on the three leading perspectives on strategy. Next, we discuss the two main actions: attack/counterattack and cooperation. As before, debates and extensions follow.

STRATEGY AS ACTION

In essence, the "strategy as action" perspective, first discussed in Chapter 1 and summarized in Figure 8.1, suggests that the heart of strategy is interaction, which is actions and responses that lead to competitive advantage.[1] Firms, like militaries, often compete aggressively—note the expressly military tone of terms such as "attacks," "counterattacks," and "price wars." In other words, it often seems that "business is war."

So, business is war—or is it? Obviously, military principles cannot be completely applied in business, because the marketplace, after all, is not a battlefield whose motto is "Kill or be killed." For example, it is well known that continuous price wars may ruin profits for an entire industry. If fighting to the death destroys the "pie," there will be nothing left. In business, it is possible to compete and win without having to kill the opposition. If firms try to destroy rivals, governments may sometimes intervene alleging firms of predatory pricing or dumping (discussed later in this chapter). Therefore, the motto is "Live and let live." In a nutshell, business is simultaneously war *and* peace.[2]

FIGURE 8.1   Strategy as Action

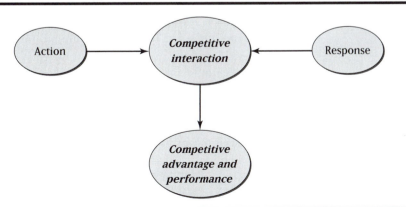

Source: From Strategy in Action, Industry Rivalry and Coordination, *1ˢᵗ edition by C.M. Grimm and K.G. Smith, p. 62. Copyright © 1997. Reprinted with permission of South-Western, a division of Thomson Learning: www.thomsonrights. com <http://www.thomsonrights.com>. Fax (800) 730-2215.*

While militaries fight over territories, waters, and air spaces, firms compete in markets. Markets can be defined along **product** dimensions (such as a product niche, a broad industry, or multiple industries) and **geographic** lines (such as one city, country, or continent). **Multimarket competition** occurs when firms engage the same rivals in multiple markets.[3] Because a multimarket competitor can respond to an attack not only in the attacked market, but also in other markets in which both firms meet, its challenger has to think twice before launching an attack. In other words, while multimarket firms "act local," they have to "think global." For instance, when Kodak aggressively cut prices in Japan in the 1980s, Fuji responded not by matching the price reductions in Japan, but by slashing prices in the United States, where Kodak, being the dominant player, had more to lose. Consequently, Kodak stopped its low-price campaigns in Japan and Fuji reciprocated in the United States. Because firms recognize their rivals' capability to retaliate in multiple markets, such multimarket competition may result in the *reduction* of competitive intensity among rivals, an outcome known as **mutual forbearance,**[4] which is discussed in more detail next.

A COMPREHENSIVE MODEL OF GLOBAL COMPETITIVE DYNAMICS

The three leading perspectives on strategy, which help explain how competitive dynamics unfold around the world, suggest a comprehensive model outlined in Figure 8.2.

Industry-Based Considerations

Industry-based considerations first focus on the nature of collusion, followed by a discussion of the relationship between industry structures and firms' propensity to collude (as opposed to compete).

Collusion and Prisoners' Dilemma

Shown in Figure 8.2, industry-based considerations are fundamentally concerned with the very first of the Porter five forces, interfirm rivalry. Issues associated with entry barriers for entrants with similar products and with substitute products, the other two of the five forces, also figure prominently. Because Chapter 2 has already discussed interfirm rivalry at length, we will not repeat it here. What we highlight here is that most firms in an industry, if given a choice, would probably prefer a reduced level of competition. "People of the same trade seldom meet together, even for merriment and diversion," wrote Adam Smith in *The Wealth of Nations* (1776), "but their conversation often ends in a conspiracy against the public." In modern jargon, this means that competing firms in an industry may have an incentive to engage in **collusion,** defined as collective attempts to reduce competition.

Collusion can be tacit or explicit. **Tacit collusion** occurs when firms *indirectly* coordinate actions by signaling to others their intention to reduce output and maintain pricing above competitive levels. Mutual forbearance can be regarded as a form of tacit collusion in multiple markets.[5] **Explicit collusion** exists when firms *directly*

FIGURE 8.2   **A Comprehensive Model of Global Competitive Dynamics**

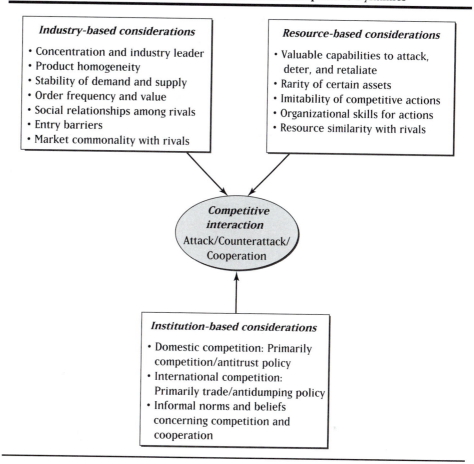

Industry-based considerations

- Concentration and industry leader
- Product homogeneity
- Stability of demand and supply
- Order frequency and value
- Social relationships among rivals
- Entry barriers
- Market commonality with rivals

Resource-based considerations

- Valuable capabilities to attack, deter, and retaliate
- Rarity of certain assets
- Imitability of competitive actions
- Organizational skills for actions
- Resource similarity with rivals

Competitive interaction
Attack/Counterattack/Cooperation

Institution-based considerations

- Domestic competition: Primarily competition/antitrust policy
- International competition: Primarily trade/antidumping policy
- Informal norms and beliefs concerning competition and cooperation

negotiate output and pricing and divide markets to reduce competition. Explicit collusion leads to the formation of a **cartel,** which is an output- and price-fixing entity involving multiple competitors. A cartel is also known as a **trust,** because members have to trust each other for honoring their agreements. Historically, cartels, such as the Seven Sisters in the oil industry a hundred years ago when cartels were legal, regulated many industries. Today, cartels are often labeled "anticompetitive" and outlawed by antitrust laws. Even though cartels are illegal in most countries today, they have not become relics of the past. It is possible that globalization, by increasing competition in many formerly protected markets, has *increased* firms' incentive to participate in cartels. At present, OPEC (with eleven member countries) is probably the most visible cartel in the world. While it is impossible to "convict" member countries of OPEC, companies are likely to be convicted if found to be involved in cartels. Since 1990, US and EU competition authorities have convicted over forty cartels with several hundred member firms from more than thirty countries.[6]

In addition to antitrust laws, collusion is often crushed by the weight of its own incentive problems. Chief among these problems is the **prisoners' dilemma,** which underpins **game theory.** The term "prisoners' dilemma" derives from a simple game in which two prisoners suspected of a major joint crime (such as burglary) are separately interrogated and told that if either one confesses, the confessor will get a one-year sentence while the other will go to jail for ten years. If neither confesses, both will be convicted of a lesser charge (such as trespassing) each for two years. If both confess, both will go to jail for ten years. At first glance, the solution to this problem seems clear enough. The maximum *joint* payoff would be for neither of them to confess. However, even if both parties agree not to confess before they are arrested, there are still tremendous incentives to confess.

Translated to an airline setting, Figure 8.3 illustrates the payoff structures for both airlines A and B in a given market, let's say, between Sydney, Australia and Auckland, New Zealand. Assuming a total of 200 passengers, Cell 1 represents the most ideal outcome for both airlines to maintain the price at $500—each gets 100 passengers and makes $50,000 and the "industry" (hypothetically consisting of two airlines) revenue reaches $100,000. However, in Cell 2, if B maintains its price at $500 while A drops it to $300, B is likely to lose all customers. Assuming perfectly transparent pricing information on the Internet, who would want to pay $500 when you can get a ticket for $300? Thus, A may make $60,000 on 200 passengers and B gets nothing. In Cell 3, the situation is reversed. In both Cells 2 and 3, although the industry *decreases* revenue by 40 percent, the price dropper *increases* its revenue by 20 percent. Thus, both A and B have strong incentives to reduce the price and hope the other side to become a "sucker." However, neither likes to be a "sucker." Thus,

FIGURE 8.3   A Prisoners' Dilemma for Airlines and Payoff Structure (assuming a total of 200 passengers)

		Airline A	
		Action 1 A keeps price at $500	Action 2 A drops price to $300
	Action 1 B keeps price at $500	(Cell 1) A: $50,000 B: $50,000	(Cell 2) A: $60,000 B: 0
Airline B	Action 2 B drops price at $300	(Cell 3) A: 0 B: $60,000	(Cell 4) A: $30,000 B: $30,000

both A and B may want to chop price, as in Cell 4, so that each still gets 100 passengers. But both firms as well as the industry end up with a 40 percent decrease of revenue. A key insight of game theory is that even if A and B have a prior agreement to fix the price at $500, both still have strong incentives to cheat, thus pulling the industry to Cell 4, where both are clearly worse off.

Industry Characteristics and Collusion vis-à-vis Competition

Given the benefits of collusion and incentives to cheat, what industries are conducive for collusion vis-à-vis competition? Eight factors emerge (Table 8.1). The first relevant fact is the number of firms or, more technically, the **concentration ratio,** defined as the percentage of total industry sales accounted for by the top four, eight, or twenty firms. In general, the higher the concentration, the easier it is to organize collusion. In a high-concentration, two-firm interaction (Figure 8.3), when the situation deteriorates to Cell 2, B may choose *not* to respond with "tit-for-tat" because it would land in the undesirable Cell 4. Instead, B may choose to retaliate by dropping prices in other markets. This sends a relatively clear signal urging A to go back to Cell 1 in the Sydney-Auckland market. Now imagine that ten airlines compete in the Sydney-Auckland market (a low-concentration situation) and six launch some price-cutting. The situation becomes much more complicated. Because the remaining four airlines prefer not to join such a campaign in this particular market, they may use low-price retaliation elsewhere that is intended to signal to the six price droppers to "come to their senses." However, this low-price retaliation may send an ambiguous signal, because the six price droppers may (mis)interpret the retaliatory actions in their other markets not as a response to their price reductions in the Sydney-Auckland market, but rather, as an "invasion" of their other markets. Therefore, instead of increasing prices in the Sydney-Auckland market (as the four retaliating firms hoped), the six airlines that initiated price reductions in the Sydney-Auckland market may also drop prices in other markets. Given the high likelihood that the six airlines that drop prices in the first place may not "get it," the

TABLE 8.1   **Industry Characteristics and Possibility of Collusion vis-à-vis Competition**

COLLUSION POSSIBLE	COLLUSION DIFFICULT (COMPETITION LIKELY)
▪ Few firms (high concentration)	▪ Many firms (low concentration)
▪ Existence of an industry price leader	▪ No industry price leader
▪ Homogeneous products	▪ Heterogeneous products
▪ Stability of demand, supply, and technology	▪ Rapidly growing demand, supply, and technology
▪ High-frequency, low-value orders	▪ Low-frequency, high-value orders
▪ Friendly social relationships among rival managers	▪ Distant social relationships among rival managers
▪ High entry barriers	▪ Low entry barriers
▪ High market commonality (mutual forbearance)	▪ Lack of market commonality (no mutual forbearance)

four remaining airlines may well decide to simply slash their prices in the Sydney-Auckland market, thus pushing the entire industry to a downward spiral. This seems to be what is going on in many industries, each with numerous rivals, where price competition is the norm.

Second, the existence of a **price leader**—defined as a firm that has a dominant market share and sets "acceptable" prices and margins in the industry—helps maintain the order and stability needed for tacit collusion. The price leader can signal to the entire industry with its own pricing behavior when it is appropriate to raise or reduce prices, without jeopardizing the overall industry structure. The price leader also possesses the **capacity to punish,** defined as having sufficient resources to deter and combat defection. To combat cheating, the most frequently used punishment entails undercutting the defector by flooding the market, thus making the defection fruitless. Such punishment is very costly because it brings significant financial losses to the price leader (as well as the entire industry) in the short run. However, if small-scale cheating is not dealt with, defection may become endemic, and the price leader will have the most to lose if collusion collapses. Thus, the price leader (such as De Beers in the diamond industry) has both the willingness and capabilities to carry out punishments and bear the costs (see Closing Case and Integrative Case 2.4). On the other hand, an industry without an acknowledged price leader is likely to be more chaotic. For example, prior to the 1980s, GM played the price leader role, announcing in advance the percentage of price increases and expecting Ford and Chrysler to follow (which they often did). Should the latter two step "out of bounds," GM would punish them. However, more recently, when Asian and European challengers in the US automobile market refuse to follow GM's lead, GM is no longer willing and able to play this role. As a result, the industry has become much more competitive (see Opening Case in Chapter 2).

Third, an industry with homogeneous products, in which rivals are forced to compete on price (rather than differentiation), is likely to lead to collusion. Because price competition is often "cut-throat," firms may have stronger incentives to collude. Since 1990, many firms in commodity industries around the globe, such as shipping, steel beams, and sugar, have been convicted for price fixing.

Fourth, the stability of demand, supply, and technology makes it difficult to expand the total size of the "pie," which provides strong incentives for incumbent firms to carve it up via collusion. Conversely, rapidly growing demand, supply, and technology, typical of younger, high-technology industries, may offer a growing "pie," making collusion unnecessary.

Fifth, an industry characterized by low-frequency, high-value orders is not conducive for collusion. Collusion requires both restraint (resisting the urge to defect) and trust (believing that one firm's "sacrifice" will be reciprocated by others in the future), which impose significant costs—popularly known as the "sucker's costs" if others defect. In "big ticket" industries such as aircraft, shipbuilding, and subway systems, securing a single contract may provide earnings and profits for years or even decades. Lockheed, for example, has been producing the C-130 Hercules military transport aircraft since the 1950s (!). On the other hand, being a "sucker" only once may force a firm to downsize or even go out of business. Thus, firms are likely to abandon collusion and compete intensely for these long-term contracts, even in industries with a small number of competitors (such as aircraft).

Sixth, friendly social relationships among managers of rival firms may facilitate collusion.[7] These managers may have gone to school together, worked for the same firm before, served together on the board of certain firms, or interacted in charity functions, social clubs, and parent-teacher meetings at their children's schools . For example, when rival firms cluster around a small area (such as Hong Kong), chances for their managers to develop some friendly social relationships are greater.[8]

Seventh, an industry with high entry barriers for new entrants with established technologies (such as shipbuilding) is more likely to facilitate collusion than an industry with low entry barriers (such as restaurants). New entrants are likely to ignore the existing industry "order," to introduce less homogeneous products with newer technologies (in other words, "disruptive technologies"),[9] and to violate industry norms cultivated through social relationships. As "mavericks," new entrants "can be thought of as loose cannons in otherwise placid and calm industries."[10]

Finally, **market commonality,** defined as the degree that two competitors' markets overlap, also has a significant bearing on the intensity of rivalry.[11] Multimarket firms may respect their rivals' spheres of influence in certain markets and their rivals may reciprocate, leading to tacit collusion.[12] To make that happen, firms need to establish multimarket contact, by following each other to enter new countries. In other words, when Kodak enters a new country, Fuji will not be far behind; and the reverse is also true. Such mutual forbearance primarily stems from two factors: (1) deterrence and (2) familiarity. **Deterrence** is important because a high degree of market commonality suggests that if a firm attacks in one market, its rivals have the capability to engage in **cross-market retaliation,** leading to a costly all-out war nobody can afford. During the Cold War, mutually assured destruction (MAD), the capability of US and Soviet nuclear forces to retaliate and wipe each country off the face of the earth *after* absorbing a first nuclear strike, successfully served as a deterrent to prevent each side from launching a nuclear attack. **Familiarity** is the extent to which tacit collusion is enhanced by a firm's awareness of the actions, intentions, and capabilities of rivals. Repeated interactions in a number of markets lead to such familiarity, resulting in more mutual understanding and respect. On the other hand, a low degree of market commonality may intensify competition. For example, Rupert Murdoch's News Corporation aggressively launched the Fox TV network to enter the United States. In violation of the norms to which the American Big Three (ABC, NBC, and CBS) adhered, Fox raided their affiliate stations. Unfortunately, there was little mutual forbearance: Because the Big Three had few overseas operations that overlapped with News Corporation's, they were not able to retaliate.[13]

Overall, the industry-based perspective has generated a voluminous body of insights on competitive dynamics. Recall from Chapter 2 that this perspective's predecessor is industrial organization (IO) economics, whose goal is to facilitate competition through regulation. IO economics has been influential in competition/antitrust policy. For example, concentration ratios used to be mechanically applied by US antitrust authorities. For many years (until 1982), if an industry's top-four firm concentration ratio exceeded 20 percent, it would *automatically* trigger an antitrust investigation. However, since the 1980s, such a mechanical approach has been abandoned, in part because "cartels have formed in markets that bear few of the suggested structural criteria and have floundered in some of the supposedly ideal markets."[14] Evidently, industry-based considerations, while certainly insightful, are unable to tell the complete story, thus calling for contributions from resource- and institution-based perspectives to shed light on competitive dynamics, as outlined in the next two sections.

Resource-Based Considerations

A number of resource-based imperatives, informed by the VRIO framework, drive decisions and actions associated with competitive dynamics (see Figure 8.2).

Value

Firm resources must create value when engaging in strategic actions. For example, the capability to attack in multiple markets—as Gillette did when it launched its Sensor razors in twenty-three countries *simultaneously*—throws rivals off balance, thus adding value. Likewise, the capability to rapidly respond to challenges also adds value.[15] Failing to respond to rivals' actions (such as international expansion) in a timely manner may lead to lost opportunities.[16] Owning the dominant position in key markets (such as flights in and out of hub cities for airlines) is also value enhancing. Such a strong sphere of influence poses credible threats to rivals, which understand that the firm will defend its core markets vigorously.

Rarity

Either by nature or nurture (or both), certain assets are very rare, thus generating significant advantage. Saudi Arabia's vast oil reserves enable it to become the enforcer of OPEC cartel agreements. Singapore Airlines, in addition to claiming one of the best locations connecting Europe/Indian Ocean Basin and East Asia/Australia as its home base, has often been rated as the world's best airline. This combination of such geographic advantage and man-made reputational advantage is rare, allowing significant room for Singapore Airlines' competitive actions.

Imitability

Most rivals watch each other and probably have a fairly comprehensive (although not necessarily accurate) picture of how their rivals compete. However, the next hurdle lies in how to imitate some of the more successful rivals. For example, rivals that are competitively aggressive, carry out complex actions (that is, a variety of difficult-to-execute maneuvers), and move quickly often have better financial and market performance.[17] Even when armed with this knowledge, competitively passive, single-action-based (such as cost-cutting), and slow-moving firms will find it exceedingly difficult to imitate rivals' actions. For decades, numerous major airlines have sought to imitate successful discount carriers such as Southwest Airlines and Ryanair (see Opening Case in Chapter 3), but have failed repeatedly.

Organization

Whether opting for competition or cooperation, firms need to be organizationally prepared to engage in desirable actions. Some firms are better organized for competitive actions, such as stealth attacks, rapid responses, and willingness to answer challenges "tit-for-tat."[18] This intensely competitive, "warrior-like" culture not only requires top management commitment, but also employee involvement down to the "soldiers in the trenches." Historically slow-moving, conservative firms find it very difficult to suddenly wake up and become more aggressive.[19]

On the other hand, some firms are better organized to engage in collusion such as mutual forbearance. More centrally coordinated firms may be better mutual forbearers than firms whose units are loosely controlled. For an MNE competing with rivals across many countries, a mutual forbearance strategy requires some units, out of respect for the rivals' sphere of influence, to sacrifice their maximum market gains by withholding some efforts.[20] Of course, such coordination aims at helping other units with dominant market positions to maximize performance, thus helping the MNE as a whole. Successfully carrying out such mutual forbearance calls for organizational reward systems and structures (such as those concerning managerial bonuses and promotions) that encourage cooperation between units, instead of promoting interunit competition (see Chapter 10). Conversely, if a firm has competitive reward systems and structures, unit managers may be unwilling to give up market gains for the greater benefits of other units and the whole firm, thus undermining mutual forbearance.[21]

Resource Similarity

Resource similarity is defined as "the extent to which a given competitor possesses strategic endowment comparable, in terms of both type and amount, to those of the focal firm."[22] Firms that have a high degree of resource similarity are likely to have similar strengths and weaknesses, which results in similar competitive actions. For example, Coca-Cola and PepsiCo may have a higher degree of resource similarity than the degree of resource similarity between Coca-Cola and Nestle.

Combining resource similarity and market commonality (discussed earlier) yields a competitor analysis framework for any pair of rivals (Figure 8.4 on next page). In Cell 4, because two firms have a high degree of resource similarity, but a low degree of market commonality (little mutual forbearance), their rivalry is likely to be the most intense. Conversely, in Cell 1, because both firms have little resource similarity, but a high degree of market commonality, their rivalry may be the least intense. Cells 2 and 3 present an intermediate level of competition. Although some multimarket rivalry may result from chance encounters (for example, conglomerates expanding to multiple industries),[23] such conscientious mapping can help managers sharpen their analytical focus and allocate resources in proportion to the threat each rival presents. Such mapping can also help managers select ideal attack targets, such as least direct rivals (in Cell 1) or more direct ones (in Cells 2 or 3).

FIGURE 8.4   A Framework for Competitor Analysis Between a Pair of Rivals

Resource Similarity

		Low	High
Market Commonality	High	**(Cell 1)** Intensity of rivalry *Lowest*	**(Cell 2)** Intensity of rivalry *Second lowest*
	Low	**(Cell 3)** Intensity of rivalry *Second highest*	**(Cell 4)** Intensity of rivalry *Highest*

Sources: Adapted from (1) M. Chen, 1996, Competitor analysis and interfirm rivalry: Toward a theoretical integration (p. 108), Academy of Management Review, 21: 100–134 and (2) J. Gimeno & C. Y. Woo, 1996, Hypercompetition in a multimarket environment: The role of strategic similarity and multimarket contact in competitive de-escalation (p. 338), Organization Science, 7: 322–341.

Institution-Based Considerations

Despite the importance of institutions (Chapter 4), strikingly, the existing global (or mainstream) strategy textbooks have relatively little (or sometimes no) coverage of the institutions governing competitive dynamics. This is unfortunate because not understanding these institutions may land otherwise successful firms (such as Microsoft) in deep trouble. In a nutshell, the institution-based view argues that free markets are not necessarily free. This section focuses on formal institutions governing domestic and international competition as well as informal norms and beliefs.

Formal Institutions Governing Domestic Competition

These institutions are broadly labeled as **competition policy**, which "determines the institutional mix of competition and cooperation that gives rise to the market system."[24] Of particular relevance to us is one branch called **antitrust policy** that is designed to combat monopolies, cartels, and trusts. Competition/antitrust policy seeks to balance efficiency and fairness. While efficiency is relatively easy to understand, it is often hard to agree on what fairness is. In the United States, fairness means equal opportunities for incumbents and new entrants. In Japan, fairness refers to rewarding loyalty. As a result, Japanese firms such as Fuji often characterize loyalty toward and from their wholesalers and suppliers as "only fair," whereas US firms such as Kodak allege this to be an "unfair" collusion (see Opening Case).

Table 8.2 illustrates the three major US antitrust laws and five landmark cases. Although the United States has the world's longest-running and most influential antitrust laws, other countries have increasingly strengthened their antitrust regulations as well. Competition/antitrust policy focuses on (1) collusive price setting,

TABLE 8.2   Major Antitrust Laws and Landmark Cases in the United States

Major Antitrust Laws	Landmark Cases
Sherman Act of 1890	*Standard Oil (1911)*
■ It is illegal to monopolize or attempt to monopolize in an industry.	■ Had a US market share exceeding 85 percent.
■ "Every person who shall monopolize, or attempt to monopolize, or combine or conspire with any person or persons, to monopolize any part of the trade or commerce among the several states, or with foreign nations, shall be deemed guilty of a misdemeanor."	■ Found guilty of monopolization. ■ Dissolved into several smaller firms. *Aluminum Company of America (ALCOA) (1945)* ■ Had 90 percent of the US aluminum ingot market.
■ Explicit collusion is clearly illegal.	■ Found guilty of monopolization.
■ Tacit collusion is in a gray area, although the spirit of the law is against it.	■ Ordered to subsidize rivals' entry and to sell plants.
Clayton Act of 1914	*IBM (1969–82)*
■ Created the Federal Trade Commission (FTC) to regulate the behavior of firms.	■ Had 70 percent of the US computer market.
■ Empowered the FTC to prevent firms from engaging in harmful business practices.	■ Sued by DOJ for monopolization, unfair product bundling, and predatory pricing. ■ Case dropped by the Reagan Administration.
Hart-Scott-Rodino (HSR) Act of 1976	*AT&T (1974–82)*
■ Empowered the Department of Justice (DOJ) to require firms to submit internal documents.	■ A legal "natural monopoly" since the 1900s.
■ Empowered state attorneys general (AGs) to initiate triple-damage suits.	■ Still sued by DOJ for monopolization, in particular its efforts to block new entrants. ■ Reached a settlement with the Reagan Administration resulting in a breakup.
	Microsoft (1990–2001)
	■ MS-DOS and Windows had an 85 percent US market share.
	■ Sued by DOJ, FTC, and twenty-two state AGs for monopolization and illegal product bundling.
	■ Settled in 1994, ordered to split into two in 2000, judgment to split the firm reversed on appeal in 2001, settled again in 2001.
	■ Found guilty by the EU in 2004.

(2) predatory pricing, and (3) extraterritoriality. First, **collusive price setting** refers to monopolists or collusion parties setting prices at a level higher than the competitive level. Even without an actual monopoly with a 100 percent market share, dominant firms such as Standard Oil and ALCOA have been convicted of monopolization. In general, the rule of thumb suggests that a 75 to 80 percent market share is a

threshold that may trigger US government actions against monopolization.[25] For an example of price fixing among a cartel, we can look to Germany during the first Oil Shock (1973–74). The six leading oil producers in Germany—BP, Exxon, Gevelsberg, Shell, Texaco, and VEBA—drastically raised prices citing a 30 percent increase in crude oil prices. However, their profits skyrocketed by 300 percent. The German government consequently sued them for collusive price setting.[26]

A second area of concern is **predatory pricing,** which is defined by US laws as (1) setting prices below costs in the short run to destroy rivals *and* (2) intending to raise prices to cover losses in the long run after eliminating rivals (legally referred to as "an attempt to monopolize"). This is an area of significant contention. First, what qualifies as "costs" is not exactly clear. Second, even if certain firms are found to be selling below average variable costs (a frequently used measure), US courts have ruled that such firms' pricing behavior cannot be labeled "predatory" if the industry has too many rivals for them to eliminate—in other words, inability to eliminate rivals makes it impossible to recoup losses by jacking up prices later.

Most industries seem to have a large number of rivals. Therefore, while predatory pricing may exist in theory, the two legal tests—selling below average variable costs *and* an industry conducive for recoupment—have made it extremely difficult to win a predation case in the United States. In contrast, EU antitrust laws only require evidence that firms sell below average variable costs. The ability to recoup losses by raising prices after eliminating a rival is *not* necessary.[27] The upshot is that US firms have a relatively higher degree of freedom in pricing, whereas EU firms have to be more careful.

A third area of concern is **extraterritoriality,** which is defined as the reach of one country's laws to other countries. US courts have taken it upon themselves to *unilaterally* punish non-US cartels (some of which may be legal elsewhere) that have a substantial adverse impact on US markets. Not surprisingly, such US actions often irritate foreign governments and firms. For example, during the 1970s, the US and Canada were in a severe antitrust "war" with each other over the uranium cartel case (see Strategy in Action 8.1). More recently, the EU evidently has taken a page from the US antitrust playbook by threatening to veto the merger between Boeing and McDonnell Douglas and successfully torpedoing the proposed merger between GE and Honeywell. In 2004, Microsoft, which cleared antitrust hurdles with the US government, was subject to antitrust penalties imposed by the EU.

Without a doubt, in the age of globalization, applying domestic competition/antitrust laws extraterritorially creates tension among governments and firms. The United States historically took an ideological approach, labeling almost all cartels to be illegal (with a small number of exceptions). However, in Japan and the EU, crisis cartels, which involve firms in an industry facing a severe crisis, are legally allowed.[28] Foreign critics make two points. First, US policy, despite its pro competition ideology, may be actually mercantilist (seeking to advance US interests at the expense of foreign rivals). They point out that US laws permit *export* cartels (see the next section on "Formal Institutions Governing International Competition"). Second, US policy itself is in flux and seems more permissive recently, thus weakening US arguments.

STRATEGY IN ACTION 8.1. *The Uranium Cartel and Extraterritoriality of US Antitrust Laws*

Uranium is a vital, nonsubstitutable raw material for nuclear weapons and power generation. In the 1960s, the US Congress banned foreign uranium imports, at the urging of American uranium firms interested in monopolizing the US markets. Foreclosed from two-thirds of their worldwide customers in the United States, uranium firms in Australia, Canada, France, and South Africa, supported by their governments, formed a cartel in 1972 to fix prices. In 1971, the uranium spot price was $3.55 a pound. However, from 1973 to 1975, the price *quadrupled*, from $6.50 to $26 per pound. In 1976, the US government, Westinghouse (a major US producer of nuclear power generators), and more than a dozen US utilities brought antitrust charges against the cartel responsible for such an increase of worldwide (and US) uranium prices.

At issue was whether US antitrust laws had jurisdiction over activities that were legal outside the United States. The US side argued that its antitrust laws had extraterritorial power to prosecute this non-US cartel (nicknamed a "uranium OPEC"), which had a sub-

stantial adverse impact on US markets. Foreign governments and firms argued otherwise and criticized the US protectionism of its own markets. The Canadian government, which took the lead in organizing the cartel, was especially irritated. In protest of US intrusion into their sovereignty, the Canadians passed legislation banning any Canadian citizen or firm to release any information to foreign authorities concerning the cartel. Other countries also passed similar legislature. Eventually, all lawsuits were settled out of court, with payments reportedly in excess of $400 million. Devastated by such notoriety as well as a host of internal problems (notably cheating), the cartel collapsed and the industry went back to cut-throat price competition.

Sources: Based on (1) D. Rosenthal & P. Nicolaides, 1997, Harmonizing antitrust: The less effective way to promote international competition, in E. Graham & J. D. Richardson (eds.), Global Competition Policy (pp. 355–383), Washington: Institute for International Economics; (2) D. Spa, 1994, The Cooperative Edge: The Internal Politics of International Cartels, Ithaca, NY: Cornell University Press.

Since the Reagan era, US antitrust enforcement has indeed become more permissive. It is not an accident that strategic alliances among competitors have proliferated since the 1980s (see Chapter 7). The National Cooperative Research Act of 1984, which legally permitted rivals to join hands in research and development (R&D), was a crucial step. The blessing of the Boeing-McDonnell Douglas merger in 1996, which eliminated the last remaining US rival of Boeing, is indicative of this increased permissiveness. However, despite improved clarity and permissiveness, the legal standards for interfirm cooperation are still ambiguous in the United States and elsewhere. In the absence of international harmonization of antitrust policy, it is crucial that firms be aware of these ambiguities when planning their actions, especially when under the jurisdiction of multiple governments.

Formal Institutions Governing International Competition

These are primarily concerned with international trade/antidumping and secondarily with export cartels. In the same spirit of predatory pricing, **dumping** is defined as (1) an exporter selling below cost abroad and (2) planning to raise prices after eliminating local rivals. Interestingly, while domestic predation is usually labeled "anticompetitive," cross-border dumping is often emotionally accused to be "unfair."[29]

Consider the following two scenarios. First, a steel producer in Indiana enters a new market, Texas. In Texas, it offers prices lower than those in Indiana, resulting in a 10 percent market share in Texas. Texas firms have two choices. The first one is to initiate a lawsuit against the Indiana firm for "predatory pricing." However, it is difficult to prove (1) that the Indiana firm is selling below cost *and* (2) that its pricing is an "attempt to monopolize." Under US antitrust laws, a case like this will have no chance of succeeding. In other words, domestic competition/antitrust laws offer no hope for protection. Thus, Texas firms are most likely to opt for their second option—to retaliate in kind by offering lower prices to customers in Indiana, leading to lower prices in both Texas and Indiana.

Now in the second scenario, the "invading" firm is not from Indiana, but India. Holding everything else constant, Texas steel firms can argue that the Indian firm is dumping, causing "material injury" in the form of lost sales, profits, and jobs. Under US antidumping laws, Texas steel producers "would almost certainly obtain legal relief on the very same facts that would not support an antitrust *claim*, let alone antitrust relief."[30] Note that imposing antidumping duties on Indian steel imports reduces the incentive for Texas firms to counterattack by entering India, resulting in *higher* prices in both Texas and India, where consumers are hurt. These two scenarios are highly realistic. An OECD study in Australia, Canada, the EU, and the US reported that 90 percent of the practices found to be unfairly dumping in these countries would never have been questioned under their own antitrust laws if used by a domestic firm in making a domestic sale.[31] In a nutshell, foreign firms are often discriminated against by the formal rules of the game in many countries.

Discrimination is also evident in the actual investigation of antidumping. A domestic firm usually files a case with the relevant government authorities—in the United States, they are the International Trade Administration (a unit of the Department of Commerce) and International Trade Commission (an independent government agency). These government agencies then send lengthy questionnaires to accused foreign firms, requesting comprehensive, proprietary data on their cost and pricing in English using US generally accepted accounting principles (GAAP) within 45 days. Many foreign defendants fail to provide such data on time because they are not familiar with US GAAP.

The investigation can have four outcomes. First, if no data are forthcoming from abroad, the data provided by the accusing firm become the evidence upon which the accusing firm can easily win. Second, if foreign firms do provide cost data, the accusing firm can still argue that these "unfair" foreigners have lied—"There is no way their costs can be so low!" For example, in the case of Louisiana versus Chinese crawfish growers, the authenticity of the average $9 per *week* salary made by Chinese workers was a major point of contention. Third, even if the low cost data are verified (as the Chinese crawfish growers were able to do), US (and EU) antidumping laws allow the complainant to argue that these data are not "fair." In the case of China, the argument goes, its cost data reflect huge distortions due to government intervention because China is still a "nonmarket" economy. Therefore, it is only "fair" to calculate how much it costs to raise hypothetical crawfish in a market economy (in this particular case, Spain was chosen). Because Spanish costs were about the same as Louisiana costs, the Chinese, despite their vehement objections, were found guilty of dumping (that is, selling below *Spanish* costs). Consequently, 110 to 123 percent import duties were levied on Chinese crawfish.[32] The fourth possible outcome is that the defendant wins the case, but this seems highly unlikely.[33]

Overall, the direct implication for domestic firms under competitive pressures from imports is clear: file an antidumping petition. One study found that simply filing such a petition (regardless of the outcome) resulted in a statistically significant 1 percent increase of the stock price of US listed firms (an average of $46 million increase in market value).[34] As a result, it is not surprising that antidumping cases now proliferate throughout the world. Although the US and the EU have initiated the largest number of cases, actually a number of emerging economies on *per dollar of imports* are the most eager practitioners of antidumping. On per dollar of imports, Argentina and South Africa have twenty times more cases than the US, India seven times, and Brazil five times.[35] China, whose firms lead the world by attracting 15 percent of antidumping cases worldwide, has recently returned the "favor" by enforcing its own antidumping laws since 1999.

In addition to antidumping, another weapon available to US firms to combat "unfair" foreign trade practices is to urge the US government to invoke Section 301 sanctions (such as tariffs and import quotas) of the 1974 Trade Act against offending foreign countries. Popularly known as the **Super 301,** this is the action Kodak sought when alleging that Fuji unfairly blocked its market access in Japan (see Opening Case). Super 301, which no other country has, gives the United States a big club in its negotiations with trading partners. Consequently, many targets of Super 301 actions are resentful.

Another formal institution governing international competition is regulations permitting domestic firms to organize **export cartels,** defined as alliances of firms that cooperate in exporting (including quota- and price-fixing). To the extent that export cartels do not spill over to domestic competition, competition laws in virtually all countries legalize such collusion. In other words, collusion punishable in a domestic setting may be allowed and even encouraged if such activities promote exports. For example, the US Congress passed the Webb-Pomerene Act of 1918 and the Export Trading Company Act of 1982, both of which grant export cartels an antitrust exemption. Given the general competitiveness of most international markets, export cartels have played a relatively minor role (affecting approximately 2 percent of US exports).[36] Nevertheless, this is another example of how formal institutions give domestic firms added advantages at the expense of foreign rivals.

While some argue that the differences between domestic and international business are only a matter of degree, in the case of antidumping and export cartels (and "Super 301"), we see some fundamental differences in how domestic and international firms are treated. Ironically, the rising tide of globalization in the last two decades has been accompanied by the rising proliferation of antidumping cases, which are allowed under the WTO. The message to firms interested in doing business abroad is clear: Their degree of freedom in overseas pricing is significantly less than that in domestic pricing.

Informal Norms and Beliefs

Informal norms and beliefs also play a significant role in governing competitive dynamics. Since Chapters 4–7 have already dealt with these issues at length, we will not expand on this point here other than stressing their importance.

In summary, the institution-based view suggests that institutional conditions such as the availability of antidumping protection are not just the "background." They directly determine which weapons a firm has in its arsenal to wage competitive battles. Next, we outline the two main action items of attack and counterattack.

ATTACK AND COUNTERATTACK

In the form of price cuts, advertising campaigns, market entries, and new product introductions, **attack** can be defined as an initial set of actions to gain competitive advantage, and **counterattack** is consequently defined as a set of actions in response to attacks.[37] This section focuses on answering the following two questions: (1) What are the main kinds of attacks? and (2) What kinds of attacks are more likely to be successful?

Three Main Types of Attack[38]

As in the military, business strategists face the choice of initiating frontal attacks that will provoke retaliation or making discrete moves that may fail to elicit retaliation. The three main types of attacks are (1) thrust, (2) feint, and (3) gambit. **Thrust** is the classic frontal attack with brute force. Figure 8.5 displays a thrust, in which firm A launches a direct attack on target market X against firm B. A case in point is the

FIGURE 8.5   **Thrust**

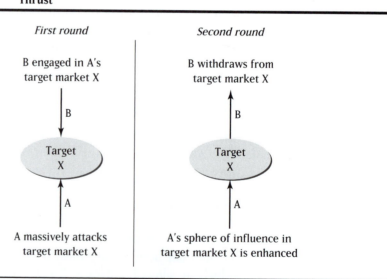

Source: Adapted from R. G. McGrath, M. Chen, & I. C. MacMillan, 1998, Multimarket maneuvering in uncertain spheres of influence: Resource diversion strategies (p. 729), from Academy of Management Review, 23: 724–740. Copyright © 1998. Reprinted by permission of Academy of Management Review via Copyright Clearance Center.

"browser war" between Microsoft and Netscape. In 1996, Netscape's Navigator had 90 percent of the market, whereas Microsoft's Explorer had less than 5 percent. When Microsoft realized the importance of the browser market, it mobilized its formidable resources, including cold cash (such as paying $150 million to Apple and $10 million to KPMG), to launch a frontal attack. Bill Gates was personally involved in wooing some of the biggest clients, by bluntly asking them, "How much do we need to pay you to screw Nestcape?" By 1998, Netscape's market share fell to 14 percent and Microsoft's rose to 86 percent. In late 1998, Netscape withdrew, agreeing to be acquired by AOL.[39]

The success or failure of a thrust is determined largely by (1) the relative strengths of the two rivals and (2) the relative importance of the focal market recognized by each of them. Obviously, the attacker needs to have some overwhelming strengths. In traditional military attacks, the attacker needs to have at least a three-to-one advantage. If the defender feels that the attacked market is crucial, it will be more willing to commit more resources to defend it.[40]

Feint is a firm's attack on a focal arena important to a competitor, but not the attacker's true target area. The feint is followed by the attacker's commitment of resources to its actual target area. The attacker initiating a feint seeks to compel its opponent to divert resources to defend the focal area. Figure 8.6 illustrates a feint executed by the attacker, firm A, on market Y, which is firm B's focal market. In response, B diverts resources to defend Y. A then attacks its real target, market X, where B's defense is weakened because of resource transfers to market Y.

The "Marlboro war" between Philip Morris and R. J. Reynolds (RJR) is indicative of a feint that worked. In the early 1990s, their traditional focal market, the

FIGURE 8.6   Feint

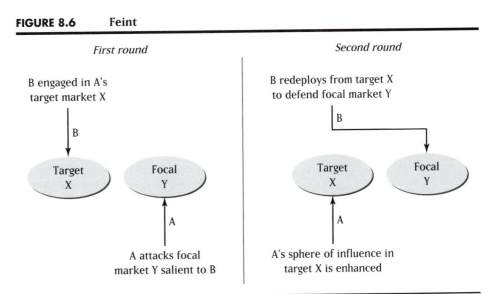

Source: Adapted from R. G. McGrath, M. Chen, & I. C. MacMillan, 1998, Multimarket maneuvering in uncertain spheres of influence: Resource diversion strategies (p. 731), from Academy of Management Review, *23: 724–740. Copyright © 1998. Reprinted by permission of Academy of Management Review via Copyright Clearance Center.*

United States (Y), annually sold 500 billion cigarettes and experienced a 15 percent decline over the previous decade. Both were interested in the emerging Central and Eastern Europe (CEE) market (X), whose total demand was 700 billion cigarettes and growing rapidly. Philip Morris executed a feint in the United States by dropping the price of its flagship brand, Marlboro, by 20 percent on one *day* (April 2, 1993, which became known as the "Marlboro Friday"). To RJR, this move, full of ferocity and suddenness, appeared to be a frontal thrust. RJR consequently diverted substantial resources, which were originally earmarked for use in the CEE market, to defend its US market. RJR thus left the CEE market wide open and Philip Morris was able to rapidly establish its dominant sphere of influence in CEE.[41]

For a feint to work, three conditions have to be met: (1) A's attack on Y must capture B's attention, (2) Y must be of considerable importance to B, and (3) B must perceive A's move to be serious and credible. Conversely, if B has a dominant market position in Y, a less-than-all-out attack by A on Y may appear to be less threatening. In such a case, the feint would fail.

Gambit, in chess, is a move that sacrifices a low-value piece in order to capture a high-value piece. The competitive equivalent is for a firm to withdraw from a low-value market to attract rival firms to divert resources into the low-value market so that the original withdrawing firm can capture a high-value market. Withdrawal can be unilaterally removing products, increasing prices, and reducing marketing and sales. As a daring strategic move, gambit is not for the faint of heart. In Figure 8.7, a gambit is illustrated by firm A's withdrawal from market Y. In essence, A is enticing B to move into Y. Then A is in a position to attack its real target market, X.

How Gillette battled Bic is indicative of a gambit. Both competed in razors (X) and lighters (Y). Gillette was strong in razors and mediocre in lighters. Bic had a

FIGURE 8.7   Gambit

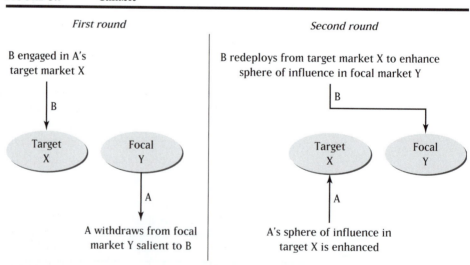

Source: Adapted from R. G. McGrath, M. Chen, & I. C. MacMillan, 1998, Multimarket maneuvering in uncertain spheres of influence: Resource diversion strategies (p. 733), from Academy of Management Review, *23: 724–740. Copyright © 1998. Reprinted by permission of Academy of Management Review via Copyright Clearance Center.*

stronger position in lighters, which made much better profits than razors. Gillette in 1984 withdrew *entirely* from lighters and devoted its attention to razors. Bic accepted the gambit and diverted razor resources to lighters. At the same time, Gillette capitalized on its more abundant and now focused resources in razors, which led to a dominant position. The gambit, in essence, can be regarded as an exchange of the spheres of influence between Gillette and Bic, each with a stronger position in one market. To make the gambit work, three conditions are necessary: (1) A's withdrawal from Y must capture B's attention, (2) B has a significant stake in Y, and (3) B must perceive A's withdrawal from Y to be serious and credible.

While these three sets of actions are analytically distinct, in reality they are often used in combination (a gambit in Y coupled with a thrust in X). More complicated than our simple examples, the real-world combinations of thrusts, feints, and gambits on multiple fronts and at different times can create virtually endless strategic choices for actions (see Strategy in Action 8.2 on next page for an example).

Attacks, Counterattacks, and Firm Performance

Obviously, attacks that are unopposed are more likely to be successful. Consequently, the attacking firm's performance is more likely to be improved. Therefore, attackers need to be aware of what drives counterattacks and consequently attempt to minimize the chances of counterattacks. In general, there are three drivers of counterattacks: (1) awareness, (2) motivation, and (3) capability.[42] First, awareness is generally considered a prerequisite for any counterattack. If an attack is so subtle that rivals are not aware of it, then the attacker's objectives are likely to be attained. Awareness usually increases with a high degree of market commonality and resource similarity (see Figure 8.4). Second, having identified an attack, a firm needs to be motivated to counterattack. If the attacked market is only marginally valuable or if other more important markets are being attacked simultaneously, managers may decide not to counterattack. Finally, even if an attack is identified and a firm is motivated to respond, counterattacks require strong capabilities, which are not necessarily possessed by all firms. Overall, attacks that can minimize the awareness, motivation, and capabilities of the opponents are more likely to succeed.

To the extent that firms often fight like "cats and dogs," an interesting typology of competitive actions (puppy dog, top dog, lean and hungry, fat cat) is outlined in Table 8.3 on next page. These different actions differ in their (1) subtlety, (2) frequency, (3) complexity, and (4) predictability, each with different odds of provoking counterattacks. First, a subtle, "puppy dog" attack, on average, is expected to be more effective than a brute force attack.[43] This echoes generations of military wisdom. Chinese strategist Sun Tzu wrote that "the expert general approaches his object indirectly." British guru Liddell Hart similarly instructed that strategy "has for its purposes the reduction of fighting to the slenderest possible proportions." For example, in the 1960s, the standard product in the US motorcycle market, dominated by US and UK firms, was a large 300-400cc machine with a $1,000 to $1,500 price tag. Honda entered with a 50cc, $250 machine that looked more like a bicycle than a motorcycle. Its larger US and UK rivals did not bother to pay much attention to

STRATEGY IN ACTION 8.2. *Unilever Fights Procter & Gamble*

With twin headquarters in the United Kingdom and the Netherlands, Unilever (*http://www.unilever.com*) competes in three major geographical areas in Europe, the Americas, and Asia-Pacific-Africa (APA). Unilever contests in three product markets: foods (such as Knorr soups), personal care (such as Calvin Klein cosmetics), and fabric care (such as Omo detergent). Combining the geographic and product markets, Unilever thus has presence in nine (3 x 3) specific markets. Its main global rival in these nine markets is the US-based Procter & Gamble (P&G, *http://www.pg.com*), whose leading brands include Folgers coffee (foods), Pampers diapers (personal care), and Tide detergent (fabric care).

For Unilever, a fundamental strategic question is: How to channel resources that can provide the best opportunities to outcompete P&G in this global "war"? A table outlining the attractiveness of various markets and the clout of P&G helps answer this question. Because both Unilever and P&G dominate their home markets, room for further growth in Europe is limited and chances in the Americas are not great. Thus, developing the fast-growing APA markets becomes imperative. Unilever may want to plot feints (such as cutting prices) and/or gambits (such as raising prices) in the Americas

to distract P&G. Because P&G has more at stake there, it probably will defend its turf and/or invest further. Consequently, Unilever can thrust into APA foods where P&G is still weak. For example, Hindustan Lever (*http://www.hll.com*), its Indian subsidiary, quickly acquired a number of local firms, boosting its market share in ice cream from 0 percent in 1992 to 74 percent in 1997. In APA fabric care, because P&G's strengths are also strong, Unilever had to assemble massive forces to launch price wars. For instance, Unilever China (*http://www.unilever.com.cn*) dropped the price of its Omo detergents by 40 percent in 1999. Because P&G was distracted elsewhere, it took two years to match Unilever's prices, thus ceding its position as a leading foreign branded detergent in China to Unilever. While winning these "campaigns" does not guarantee that Unilever will win the global "war," such systematic thinking definitely is helpful.

Sources: Based on (1) Author's own interviews and case research in Asia, 2003–04; (2) C. Hill, 2003, International Business, 4th ed. (pp. 242, 433–434), Chicago: Irwin McGraw-Hill; (3) I. MacMillan, A. van Putten, & R. McGrath, 2003, Global gamesmanship, Harvard Business Review, May: 62–71.

	UNILEVER ATTRACTIVENESS	PROCTER & GAMBLE CLOUT
Europe foods	High	Low
Europe personal care	High	Moderate
Europe fabric care	High	Low
Americas foods	Low	High
Americas personal care	Low	High
Americas fabric care	Low	High
Asia-Pacific-Africa foods	High	Low
Asia-Pacific-Africa personal care	High	High
Asia-Pacific-Africa fabric care	High	High

TABLE 8.3   A "Cats and Dogs" Typology of Competitive Actions

LABEL	ACTION	EXAMPLE DISCUSSED IN TEXT
Puppy dog	Maintaining a subtle, nonthreatening posture	Honda's and Haier's entry into the US market
Top dog	Aggressively confronting each other	Netscape versus Microsoft
Lean-and-hungry look	Seeking all sorts of advantages to outrun rivals	Microsoft attacks CA; Nike dethrones Reebok
Fat cat	Actively investing in nonthreatening ways	IKEA focuses on self-assembly furniture

this "crazy little bike"—until it was too late.[44] A less well-known but more recent case is Haier's entry into the US white goods market in the 1990s. Although Haier dominates its home country, China, with a broad range of refrigerators, air conditioners, and microwaves, it chose to enter the US market in a nonthreatening segment, mini-bars for hotels and dorms. Incumbents such as GE and Whirlpool had dismissed this segment as peripheral and low margin, failing to recognize the threat of this "puppy dog." Haier now commands a 50 percent US market share in compact refrigerators (see Strategy in Action 6.3 in Chapter 6).

Compare Honda's and Haier's stealth, "puppy dog" actions with Netscape's name-calling, "top dog" attack on Microsoft. In the mid-1990s, Netscape drew tremendous publicity by labeling Microsoft the "Death Star" (of the movie *Star Wars* fame) and predicting that the Internet would make Windows obsolete. Although Microsoft previously had *not* viewed Netscape as a main rival, such a challenge helped make Netscape Microsoft's enemy number one, leading to the demise of Netscape.[45] An underdog openly challenging a top dog, not surprisingly, is likely to be crushed by the top dog.

Another hallmark of successful attacks is their frequency. "Lean-and-hungry" firms frequently initiate new actions, confusing rivals and delaying their actions. For example, in the prepackaged software industry—spreadsheets, word processors, and database management—Microsoft aggressively moved from number four behind Lotus, WordPerfect, and leader Computer Associates (CA) to number one in 1991. On average, Microsoft carried out 43 *more* new actions (such as pricing, upgrades, and advertising) than CA per year. Between 1991 and 1993, Microsoft carried out 131 *more* new actions every year.[46]

In addition, the complexity of attacks forces rivals to busily defend multiple fronts, delay their responses, and stretch their resources. Nike, playing "lean and hungry," dethroned Reebok in the 1990s via a variety of complex actions, including pricing, new products, promotions, licensing, and market segmenting (such as children's shoes, Air Jordan basketball shoes, and walking shoes). In contrast, Reebok focused single-mindedly on new advertising campaigns. The Closing Case has another example of how a nondominant firm, Lev Leviev of Israel, challenges the mighty De Beers through a series of complex actions. In short, competitive complexity is helpful. Competitive simplicity may hurt long-run performance, especially during periods of intense and uncertain "wars."[47]

Finally, unpredictability increases the odds for successful attacks, whereas predictability destroys the element of surprise. When Kmart predictably advertised its weekly specials through expensive direct mailing, Wal-Mart, which was reluctant to follow because of its "*every* day low price" policy, creatively posted Kmart's weekly circulars at the front of Wal-Mart stores and promised to match or beat Kmart's specials. The word of mouth quickly spread, creating a dilemma for Kmart: The more it advertised, the more it drove customers to Wal-Mart. In other words, Wal-Mart used Kmart's advertising budget to underwrite its own promotion. Kmart eventually had to file for bankruptcy (see Video Case 1.6). In the bloodbath between CA and Microsoft (discussed earlier), while CA predictably emphasized new products,

Microsoft unleashed a number of unconventional actions, including a controversial attack called "vaporware." Vaporware refers to the announcement of future software development several years down the road, some of which Microsoft did not intend to actually carry out. It is important to note that vaporware is regarded by many as unethical and even illegal, and it was a focus of the US government's investigation of Microsoft's competitive conduct during the 1990s.

Overall, rivals will be prepared for methodical frontal, infrequent, simple, and predictable attacks.[48] Inspired by the wisdom of Sun Tzu and Liddell Hart, modern militaries have converged on a doctrine called "maneuver warfare."[49] Similarly, modern business competition has evolved into its own maneuver warfare in which winning firms excel at making subtle, frequent, complex, but unpredictable, attacks to reduce rivals' awareness of attacks, minimize their motivation to act, and undermine their capabilities to counterattack.

COOPERATION, ACCOMMODATION, AND COLLUSION

What motivates some firms to cooperate whereas others opt to fight? Chapter 7 alluded to this question when dealing with formal strategic alliances legally cleared by competition authorities. This section deals with informal cooperation with competitors for the purposes of *reducing* competitive intensity, some of which may not be cleared by competition authorities.

Signaling

Short of illegally talking directly to competitors about reduced rivalry, firms have to resort to signaling—that is, "While you can't talk to your competitors on pricing, you can always *blink* at them." We outline five means of such blinking: (1) nonaggression ("fat cat"), (2) market entry, (3) truce seeking, (4) communication via governments, and (5) strategic alliances. First, a nonaggression strategy refers to active investment in nonthreatening ways so as not to provoke attacks on a firm's core markets (see Table 8.3). For example, Sweden's IKEA actively invests in the wooden, self-assembly segment of the furniture market. At the same time, being a soft "fat cat," it does *not* enter the factory-assembled, upholstered segment, signaling its intention not to raise competition there in order not to attract these firms to enter its core market.[50]

Interestingly, while a "fat cat" strategy reduces competition by not entering new markets, a second strategy, market entry, may also have the same effect. Firms may enter new markets, not to challenge the incumbents there, but to seek mutual forbearance. For example, MNEs often chase each other, entering one country after another.[51] Airlines that meet in many routes are often less aggressive than airlines that meet in one or a few routes.[52] Recently, while UPS, traditionally strong on ground delivery, expanded its air express service, Federal Express built up a ground network in response. Because a high degree of mutual forbearance may significantly constrain freedom of action and a low degree of mutual forbearance may result in excessive competition, firms often prefer to enter markets with a *moderate* level of mutual forbearance (Cells 1 and 2 in Figure 8.4).[53]

Third, firms can send a signal for a truce, such as announcing a price increase in the middle of a price war. Because a protracted price war hurts the profits of all rivals, others often follow. However, this is not always the case, because a truce may be interpreted as a sign of weakness. Some rivals thus may keep up the pressure. For instance, after more than two years of an "incentive war" that began after the September 11, 2001 terrorist attacks (see Opening Case in Chapter 2), GM announced in December 2003 that it would stop 0 percent financing. However, rivals actually *increased* their incentives. Consequently, GM within one month slapped 0 percent financing on its lineup again.

Fourth, sometimes firms can send a signal to rivals by enlisting the help of government restrictions. Because direct negotiations with rivals on what constitutes "fair" pricing is illegal, holding such discussions, including some exchanges of highly proprietary cost and pricing data, is legal under the auspices of government investigations. Therefore, filing an antidumping petition or suing a rival does not necessarily indicate a totally hostile intent; sometimes, it signals to the other side: "We don't like what you are doing; it's time to talk." Cisco, for instance, sued a Chinese rival, Huawei, in 2003 for its alleged intellectual infringement. Cisco dropped the case after both firms negotiated a solution in 2004.

Finally, firms can openly organize strategic alliances with rivals for cost reduction. Although price fixing is illegal, reducing cost by 10 percent through an alliance, which is legal, has the same impact on the financial bottom line as collusively raising price by 10 percent. One of the most striking examples is the oil country tabular goods cartel, consisting of four European and four Japanese firms. The EU convicted all of them in 1999 for price fixing. After the breakup of the cartel, *all* former members joined one of the three international alliances.[54] Granted, these alliances may have a number of legitimate benefits such as cost reduction, technology sharing, and market access as noted in Chapter 7. However, these legitimate motives are not mutually exclusive with a continued interest in possible collusion.

Behind the Success and Failure of Cooperation and Accommodation[55]

Reduced to its core, cooperation among competitors fundamentally boils down to a repeated game in which players accommodate each other to avoid conflict. Thomas Schelling, a leading theorist on conflict resolution, argues that conflict is essentially a way of bargaining and that maintaining cooperation is a protracted series of successful bargains.[56] Sometimes such bargaining is explicit. However, explicit bargaining can easily become explicit collusion and is no longer allowed legally. As a result, "bargaining" often takes place through signals and actions, which in theory speak louder than words. However, conflicting objectives, imperfect information processing, and deliberate actions to mislead (such as feints noted earlier) often result in misunderstandings, which tend to lead to an escalation of competition and consequently a collapse of cooperation. Because of significant incentive problems (noted earlier), collusion is often difficult to sustain. For example, the average duration of cartels convicted by US and EU authorities since 1990 was only six years.[57]

This reasoning, therefore, begs an answer to the question: Why do certain collaborations such as the global diamond cartel centered on De Beers (see Integrative Case 2.4) succeed while many others fail? Three issues emerge: (1) secrecy, (2) exclusivity, and (3) informality. First, secrecy facilitates more straightforward bargaining, including issuing threats. If such bargaining is in the public domain where all players have a reputation to protect, cooperation may collapse. Second, cooperation as a game is best played by a small, exclusive group of like-minded players. Repeated interactions among them foster mutual understanding, resulting in fewer surprises. For instance, firms led by CEOs who have a long tenure in an industry are often more restrained in their competitive action, honoring mutual forbearance. On the other hand, firms led by newer CEOs often pay less attention to mutual forbearance.[58] Third, counterintuitively, a *lack* of formal rules helps facilitate cooperation. Most happily married couples do not have a formal contract governing their behavior and they constantly engage in give-and-take kinds of negotiations. For interfirm relationships, while formal rules have a number of benefits (such as transparency), their lack of flexibility may hinder cooperation.

Overall, because of the sensitive nature of interfirm cooperation designed to reduce competition, we do not know a lot about these schemes. However, to the extent that business is both war and peace, strategists need to pay as much attention to making peace with rivals as fighting wars against them.

LOCAL FIRMS VERSUS MULTINATIONAL ENTERPRISES

While strategists, students, and journalists are often fascinated by MNE rivals such as Sony/Samsung, Unilever/Nestle, and Caterpillar/Komatsu, much less is written and known about how local firms cope. This is especially crucial for local firms in emerging economies, which typically cannot match the expertise, experience, and endowments of MNEs. However, local firms are not necessarily sitting ducks. Given the broad choices of competing and/or cooperating, local firms can adopt four strategic postures, depending on (1) the industry conditions and (2) the nature of competitive assets. Shown in Figure 8.8, these factors suggest four strategic actions.[59]

In Cell 3, in some industries, the pressures to globalize are relatively low and local firms' primary strengths lie in a deep understanding of local markets. Therefore, a **defender** strategy that leverages local assets that MNEs are either weak in or unaware of is often called for. For example, Bimbo is the largest bread producer in Mexico, and blankets the country with 420,000 deliveries daily to 35,000 corner stores. Managers considered cutting out a number of these daily runs, some of which might only generate sales of $10 per delivery. However, when confronted with PepsiCo's aggressive entry in the 1990s, Bimbo changed its plan. While PepsiCo focused on sales to large supermarkets, Bimbo believed that its corner store distribution network was the key to defending its home turf. Such a network taps into Mexican consumers' preference for freshness and shopping daily at a nearby

FIGURE 8.8   How Local Firms in Emerging Economies Respond to MNE Actions

Competitive Assets

		Customized to home markets	Transferable abroad
Industry Pressures to Globalize	High	(Cell 1) *Dodger*	(Cell 2) *Contender*
	Low	(Cell 3) *Defender*	(Cell 4) *Extender*

Source: Reprinted with permission of Harvard Business Review from "Competing with giants: Survival strategies for local companies in emerging markets" (p. 122) by N. Dawar & T. Frost, March-April 1999. Copyright © 1999 by the Harvard Business School Publishing Corporation; all rights reserved.

corner store. Therefore, instead of reducing deliveries, Bimbo increased them, thus creating a huge barrier for PepsiCo. In another example, facing an onslaught from MNE cosmetics firms in Israel, a number of Israeli firms turned to focus on products suited to the Middle Eastern climate and managed to defend their turf. Ahava has been particularly successful, in part because of its highly unique components extracted from the Dead Sea, which MNEs cannot find elsewhere.[60] In essence, we can view such a defender strategy as a *gambit*, through which local firms cede some markets (such as supermarkets in Mexico and mainstream cosmetics in Israel) to MNEs while building strongholds in other markets.

In Cell 4, in some industries where pressures for globalization are relatively low, local firms may possess some skills and assets that are transferable overseas, thus leading to an **extender** strategy. This strategy centers on leveraging home-grown competencies abroad by expanding into similar markets. For instance, Jollibee, a fast food chain in the Philippines, not only survived an invasion from McDonald's in its home country, but also successfully expanded to Hong Kong, the Middle East, and California, where large Filipino populations reside. In another example, Asian Paints controls 40 percent of the house paint market in India despite aggressive entries by MNEs. Asian Paints developed strong capabilities tailored to the unique environment in India, characterized by thousands of small retailers serving numerous illiterate consumers who only want small quantities of paint that can be diluted to save money. Such capabilities are not only a winning formula in India, but also in much of Asia, Africa, and the Pacific. In contrast, MNEs, whose business model typically centers on affluent customers in developed economies, have had a hard time coming up with profitable low-end products (see Strategy in Action 1.1 in Chapter 1). Overall, Jollibee and Asian Paints' strategy can be viewed as a *thrust* charging into new markets.

Cell 1 depicts a most difficult situation for local firms that compete in industries with high globalization pressures. In this case, competitive assets based on a superior understanding of local markets are not enough. Consequently, a **dodger** strategy is necessary. This is largely centered on cooperating through joint ventures (JVs) with MNEs, sell offs to MNEs, and/or becoming MNE suppliers and service providers. In the Chinese automobile industry, *all* major local automakers have entered JVs with MNEs (see Integrative Case 1.3). In the Czech Republic, Skoda, the leading state-owned automaker, was sold by the government to Volkswagen. In Mexico, numerous manufacturers have reoriented themselves to become suppliers and service providers to the newly arrived MNEs. The essence of this strategy is that to the extent that local firms are unable to successfully compete head-on against MNEs, cooperation becomes necessary. In other words, if you can't beat them, join them!

Finally, in Cell 2, some local firms find some hope even in industries with high globalization pressures. Through a **contender** strategy, these local firms engage in rapid learning to approach the capabilities of the MNEs and then expand overseas. For example, a number of Chinese cellular phone makers, such as TCL and Bird, have rapidly caught up with global heavyweights, such as Motorola and Nokia. By 2003, local firms, from a 5 percent market share five years ago, commanded more than 50 percent market share in China. Engaging in a "learning race," TCL and Bird first directly purchased handset modules from leading-edge foreign suppliers such as France's Wavecome and South Korea's Pantech and Telson, and then engaged in design innovations such as diamond-studded phone casings and fish skin surfaces to appeal to local tastes. TCL and Bird have now developed proprietary technology and embarked on overseas expansion, first through exports to Southeast Asia and more recently through acquisitions of Western firms such as Schneider in Germany and some units of Thomson in France. These local firms have taken advantage of the readily available world-class core technology and then developed combinative capabilities by integrating core technology with locally adapted design and marketing to allow them to *thrust* overseas.[61]

Overall, as MNEs march into more countries, how local firms respond is increasingly important for managers worldwide. In countries such as China, evidence is now emerging that after the initial dominance, MNEs are not necessarily always "kings of the hill." In numerous industries (such as cellular phone, personal computer, home appliance, and telecom network), many MNEs have been "dethroned" in China.[62] While weak local players are washed out, winning firms are often skilled at making subtle, frequent, complex, yet unpredictable, moves. According to Porter's "diamond" model, which suggests that strong domestic competition drives global competitiveness (see Chapter 4),[63] it is not surprising that some of these leading local players, having won the game in the highly competitive domestic environment, are now able to challenge MNEs overseas. In the process, they become a new breed of MNEs themselves (see Strategy in Action 6.3 in Chapter 6). As a group, foreign MNEs in China are not as profitable as local firms (except state-owned ones).[64] The upshot is that when facing the onslaught of MNEs, local firms may not be as weak as many people believe. Carefully making strategic choices concerning competition and/or cooperation may allow some local firms to not only survive, but also prosper.

DEBATES AND EXTENSIONS

This sensitive area sparks numerous debates. We outline two of the most significant ones: (1) strategy versus IO economics and antitrust policy and (2) competition versus antidumping.

Strategy versus IO Economics and Antitrust Policy[65]

This debate is between strategy and IO economics and its public policy brainchild, competition/antitrust policy. Modern ideas of strategy, pioneered by Michael Porter, have turned IO economics "on its head." While IO economics attempts to prevent any firm from gaining sustained competitive advantage, the very purpose of strategy is to gain such advantage. Intended to encourage competition and "fair play," antitrust laws are based on the assumption that large firms are especially capable of building sustainable advantage through monopoly or oligopoly. Therefore, they need to be "tamed."

While this debate goes on in many parts of the world, it is most heavily contested in the United States. Because the United States has the world's oldest and most developed antitrust frameworks (dating back to the 1890 Sherman Act), the US debate is also the most watched in the world. Therefore, our discussion here primarily draws on US materials. This does not mean that we are adopting a US-centric perspective here (which is a tendency this book endeavors to *combat*); we just use the crucial US debate as a *case study* that may have global implications elsewhere.

In this debate, strategists make five arguments. First, strategists argue that dominated by IO economics, antitrust laws were created in response to the old realities of mostly domestic competition. However, the new realities of largely international competition indicate that the elusive quest for long-term sustainable advantage is exceedingly difficult (and probably impossible) to accomplish. The "strategy as action" perspective suggests that *all* advantages are temporary and that they may disappear when rivals launch new attacks. Richard D'Aveni, who coined the term "hypercompetition," argues that "applying traditional US antitrust enforcement in an environment of hypercompetition is like driving a Model T on an expressway. The law moves too slowly to keep up with the traffic."[66]

Second, to the extent that competition is increasingly global and that foreign antitrust laws are more permissive, US antitrust laws may become "a self-imposed impediment to US economic performance."[67] Numerous successful American firms have found themselves in court (Table 8.2). In 1945, the Aluminum Company of America (ALCOA) was forced to spin off its Canadian operations as a standalone, Canadian firm ALCAN. Now ALCAN has been challenging ALCOA on a

STRATEGY IN ACTION 8.3. *Intel Dodges Trustbusters*

A number of leading US firms ranging from Standard Oil (1911) to Oracle (2004) have been charged for antitrust violations. How can a dominant firm such as Intel (*http://www.intel.com*), whose chips power 83 percent of the world's PCs, avoid a dreaded encounter with "trustbusters?" Taking a lesson from the Microsoft ordeal, Intel has instituted a conservative safety margin. Intel began by training all the executives and sales forces and emphasizing no price fixing with rivals, no exclusive contracts, and no aggressive memos (such as "Let's kill the competition"). Its legal department carried out random searches of managers' files. These files would then be used in mock depositions, in which Intel lawyers acted as government prosecutors to cross-examine managers in front of the executive staff. Such role-playing served as a dramatic wake-up call. "I could have written that memo," noted the then CEO Andy Grove, who went on to emphasize the necessity for proactive *anti*-antitrust efforts. Nevertheless, in 2004, Intel was investigated by the European Union for possible antitrust violations.

Sources: Based on (1) Business Week, 2004, The EU's hard look inside Intel, June 21: 13; (2) Economist, 2004, Of God, Larry Ellison, and antitrust, March 6: 17; (3) D. Yoffie & M. Kwak, 2001, Judo Strategy (pp. 196–200), Boston: Harvard Business School Press.

worldwide basis. The US government thus directly created a strong *foreign* rival for a US firm. The costs, even for firms that are not guilty, are considerable. A grueling thirteen-year (1969 to 1982) pursuit—eventually dropped by the government—dampened IBM's aggressiveness, including passing up an opportunity to acquire Microsoft. The end result? IBM almost went out of business in the early 1990s. Thus, proactive firms such as Intel have to do all they can, at great costs, to avoid an encounter with "trustbusters" (see Strategy in Action 8.3).

Third, the very actions accused of being "anticompetitive" may actually be highly "competitive" or "hypercompetitive." For instance, in 1945, ALCOA was found guilty, in the words of the judge, for "embracing each new opportunity" to aggressively defend itself against rivals. In 1972, the US government accused Kellogg, General Mills, General Foods, and Quaker Oats of product proliferation. In the 1990s, Microsoft was charged for *not* voluntarily helping its competitors (!).

Fourth, US antitrust laws create strategic confusion. Because the intent to destroy rivals is a smoking gun of antitrust cases, America thus has become a "fantasyland" in which many firms go bankrupt, but none is destroyed by a competitor (at least theoretically). Strategists are forced to use milder language; otherwise, they may end up in court. For example, in a successful antitrust case against the National Football League (NFL) in 1984, the "smoking gun" was a presentation made by Michael Porter to NFL managers that encouraged them to "conquer" a rival league. "When one of the leading US strategic thinkers comes under attack for merely talking about aggressive competitive actions," according to D'Aveni, "it is clear that the American defense of free speech does not extend to statements of good business strategy."[68] In contrast, foreign firms often use war-like language: Komatsu is famous for "Encircling Caterpillar!" and Honda for "Annihilate, crush, and destroy Yamaha!" The inability to talk straight creates confusion among lower level managers and employees, who have a hard time figuring out what top managers are really talking about. A confused firm is not likely to be aggressive.

Finally, US antitrust laws, designed to combat "unfair" practice, may be unfair. First, the laws are ambiguous. If a firm's prices are viewed as too low, it can be charged for predatory pricing. Conversely, if prices are seen as too high, a firm can be sued for tacit collusion with rivals. When firms are not being sued, no one really knows what is acceptable. Antitrust laws thus create a chilling effect on firms' aggressiveness, causing them to be averse to risk. A second issue is that these laws discriminate *against* US firms. Joint manufacturing among US rivals is banned. This forces US firms to jointly manufacture with foreign rivals, which ironically is often allowed. For example, IBM can team with Siemens and Toshiba to jointly develop and manufacture new chips, whereas its JV with Apple and Motorola can only develop, not manufacture, new chips. This does not seem very fair.

Overall, strategists argue that monopolization, feared in nineteenth century America, is not likely in most industries in the global economy of the twenty-first century. This view, however, has not yet been fully accepted by antitrust policymakers. Thus, strategists in both practice and academia need to make their case more vocally.[69] Unfortunately, *none* of the other strategy textbooks discusses such a crucial debate. They may be doing the field a disservice by not confronting this debate head-on. Outside the United States, strategists elsewhere engage in similar debates with economists and policymakers in their countries. Their outcome may to a large degree shape future competition in the world.

Competition versus Antidumping

In international business, there are two arguments against antidumping. First, because dumping centers on selling "below cost," it is often difficult (if not impossible) to prove the case given the ambiguity concerning "cost." The second argument is that if foreign firms are indeed selling below cost, so what? This is simply a (hyper)competitive action. When entering a new market, virtually all firms lose money on day one (and often year one). Until some point in the future when the firm breaks even, it will lose money because it sells below cost. Domestically, there are numerous cases of such dumping, which are perfectly legal. For example, we all receive numerous coupons in the mail offering free or cheap goods. Coupon items are frequently sold (or given away) below cost. Do consumers complain about such good deals? Probably not. Likewise, "if the foreigners are kind enough (or dumb enough) to sell their goods to our country below cost," one argument goes, "why should we complain?"[70]

Of course, a classic argument is: What if, through "unfair" dumping, foreign rivals drive out local firms and then jack up prices? The answer is similar to the answer to the predatory pricing charge in a domestic setting. Given the competitive nature of most industries, it is often difficult (if not impossible) to eliminate all rivals and then recoup dumping losses by charging higher monopoly prices. Therefore, special interest groups often exaggerate the fear of foreign monopoly. In reality, antidumping duties protect certain firms, industries, and regions while consumers in the entire country pay higher prices. Antidumping laws, therefore, are fundamentally at odds with the spirit of promoting competition, which underpins competition/antitrust laws in the first place. Antidumping laws are also at odds with the recent trends toward more globalization. In the words of Joseph Stiglitz, a Nobel laureate in economics and then chief economist of the World Bank, antidumping duties "are simply naked protectionism" and one country's "fair trade laws" are often known elsewhere as "unfair trade laws."[71]

The significant differences between domestic competition/antitrust laws and international trade/antidumping laws (legal actions domestically can be illegal dumping internationally) call for some streamlining. One solution is to phase out antidumping laws and use the same standards against domestic predatory pricing when dealing with foreign firms. Such a waiver of antidumping charges against each other has been in place between Australia and New Zealand, between Canada and the United States, and within the European Union. That is, a Canadian firm, essentially treated as a US firm, can be accused of predatory pricing, but cannot be accused of dumping within the United States. However, domestically, as noted earlier, a predation case is very difficult to make. In such a way, competition can be fostered, aggressiveness rewarded, and "dumping" legalized.

IMPLICATIONS FOR STRATEGISTS

If capitalism, according to Joseph Schumpeter, is about "creative destruction," then the "strategy as action" perspective highlights how the power of creative destruction is unleashed in the marketplace. However, unlike the ideal of Adam Smith, this marketplace is not necessarily governed by the "invisible hand." Instead, the "visible hand" of governments is evident. Therefore, strategists not only need to become masters of strategic actions (both confrontation and cooperation), but also experts in government regulations if they aspire to successfully navigate the global competitive landscape.

In terms of the four fundamental questions, why firms differ (Question 1) and how firms behave (Question 2) boil down to how industry-, resource-, and institution-based considerations influence their competitive/cooperative actions. What determines the scope of the firm (Question 3) is driven, in part, by an interest to establish mutual forbearance with multimarket rivals. When under attack from multimarket rivals, single market firms may find it beneficial to broaden their scope by entering markets in which these rivals operate—in other words, as in military and sports, "the best defense is offense." Finally, what determines the international success and failure of firms (Question 4), to a large extent, depends on how firms carry out their actions around the world. In competitive attacks and counterattacks, subtlety, frequency, complexity, and unpredictability are helpful. When cooperating, secrecy, exclusivity, and informality may be better. Overall, given that business is simultaneously war *and* peace, a winning formula, as in war and chess, is "Look ahead, reason back."

Chapter Summary

1. Underpinning the "strategy as action" perspective, competitive dynamics refers to actions and responses undertaken by competing firms.

2. Multimarket competition occurs when firms engage the same rivals in multiple markets. Through mutual forbearance, multimarket competition, as a form of tacit collusion, may reduce competition.

3. Industry-, resource-, and institution-based perspectives combine to suggest a comprehensive model of competitive dynamics. In particular, institutional issues concerning antitrust and antidumping, which are hardly discussed in other strategy books, are very important for domestic and international competition.

4. The three main types of attacks are (1) thrust, (2) feint, and (3) gambit. Counterattacks are driven by (1) awareness, (2) motivation, and (3) capability.

5. Competitive actions differ in their (1) subtlety, (2) frequency, (3) complexity, and (4) predictability.

6. Without talking directly to competitors, firms can signal to rivals. To a large degree, the success and failure of cooperation and accommodation depend on (1) secrecy, (2) exclusivity, and (3) informality.

7. When confronting MNEs, local firms can choose from a variety of strategies: (1) defender, (2) extender, (3) dodger, and (4) contender. Local firms may not be as weak as many people believe.

8. The two key debates are (1) strategy versus IO economics and (2) competition versus antidumping.

Key Terms

antitrust policy	concentration ratio	explicit collusion
attack	contender	export cartels
capacity to punish	counterattack	extender
cartel	cross-market retaliation	extraterritoriality
collusion	defender	familiarity
collusive price setting	deterrence	feint
competition policy	dodger	gambit
competitive dynamics	dumping	game theory
competitor analysis		market commonality

multimarket competition	price leader	Super 301
mutual forbearance	prisoners' dilemma	tacit collusion
predatory pricing	resource similarity	thrust

Critical Discussion Questions

1. You are the CEO of the second largest firm in your industry. In the middle of a price war, the industry leader has announced a price increase. How are you going to react?

2. You are the CEO of an MNE (firm A) whose market coverage overlaps with your main rival (firm B) in twenty countries. You are planning to launch an attack on B in country 1. However, before you attack, B has launched its own attack on your firm (A) in countries 2, 3, and 4. How would you react?

3. As the CEO of a Chinese firm, you are concerned about the prospects of MNEs rushing to your previously protected domestic industry (such as banking and insurance) because of China's commitment as a new WTO member (since 2001). What strategic options do you have to better prepare your firm?

4. **ON ETHICS:** As an executive, you feel that the price war in the industry is killing profits for all firms. However, you have been warned by your corporate counsels not to openly discuss sensitive issues such as pricing with your rivals, whom you know personally (you and rival managers went to school together). How would you signal your intentions without violating antitrust laws?

5. **ON ETHICS:** As a CEO, you are concerned that your firm and your industry in the United States are being devastated by foreign imports. However, you are not sure about the cost structure of foreign rivals. Nevertheless, trade lawyers suggest filing an antidumping case against leading foreign rivals (such as those in China) and assure you a win. Would you file an antidumping case or not? Why?

6. **ON ETHICS:** As part of a feint attack, your firm (firm A) announces that in the next year, it intends to enter country X where the competitor (firm B) is very strong. Your firm's real intention is to march into country Y where B is very weak. There is actually *no* plan to enter X. However, in the process of trying to "fool" B, customers, suppliers, investors, and the media are also being intentionally misled. What are the ethical dilemmas here? Do the pros of this action outweigh its cons?

Closing Case: Lev Leviev Fights De Beers

(see also Integrative Case 2.4)

In the diamond industry, De Beers (http://www. debeersgroup.com) of South Africa has been the undisputed "king of the hill" for more than a hundred years. It has skillfully organized a cartel known as the Diamond Syndicate whose purposes were to keep supply low and price high. Historically dominating the global diamond production (mostly in South Africa), De Beers sold rough diamonds only to a select group of merchants (called "sightholders") from around the world at take-it-or-leave-it prices. De Beers thus was able to control how many stones entered the market and at what price. Today, De Beers still controls approximately 45 percent of worldwide production. For independent producers, De Beers often urged them to sell rough diamonds only to De Beers. De Beers would purchase all of the output at prices it set. In exchange, the producers reaped the benefits of a cartel: stable prices, guaranteed purchases, and little competition. At present, De Beers still controls approximately 50 to 60 percent of worldwide rough diamond sales.

As in all cartels, the incentives to cheat are tremendous: Producers and buyers are all interested in cutting De Beers out. De Beers' reactions are typically swift and ruthless. In 1981, Zaire broke away from De Beers to directly market its diamonds. De Beers drew on its stockpiles to flood the market, forcing the Zairians to change their mind. In 1978, some Israeli sightholders began hoarding rough diamonds, creating their own stockpiles. De Beers ruthlessly purged one-third of sightholders, forcing many Israeli buyers out of business.

It is against such formidable forces that the Lev Leviev Group (http://www.africa-israel.com) of Israel has risen.

Lev Leviev is a Russian-speaking, Uzbeki-born Israeli citizen. As one of Israel's largest diamond polishers, Leviev was invited to become a sightholder by De Beers in 1985. However, Leviev has proven to be De Beers' worst enemy. His actions are characterized by their subtlety, frequency, complexity, and unpredictability. Leviev has subtly cultivated political connections in key countries. Dating back to the Soviet days, Russia had always sold its rough diamonds to De Beers. Leviev befriended Russian leaders such as Yeltsin and Putin, and convinced the state-owned Russian producer, now called Alrosa (http://www.eng. alrosa.ru), to set up a JV with him, which cuts $140 million worth of diamonds a year. "Lean and hungry," Leviev's actions are also frequent, as he is constantly in search of opportunities to beat De Beers around the world.

Leviev has cultivated a complex web of businesses scattered in numerous industries and countries. The Russian venture is only the tip of the iceberg of his deals in the former Soviet Union. In Angola, De Beers was engulfed in a public relations disaster associated with "conflict diamonds." In 1996, Leviev took advantage of the De Beers fiasco by putting together an Angola Selling Corporation, in which he gave the government a 51 percent share in exchange for exclusive rights to purchase Angolan rough diamonds. In Namibia, where locals also preferred to process their own diamonds instead of selling them to De Beers, Leviev first set up a joint diamond-polishing factory with local players and then bought out their shares. In addition, Leviev has also diversified his holdings, owning a gold mine in Kazakhstan, commercial real estate in Europe,

Fina gas stations and 7-Eleven stores in the US Southwest, and a 33 percent stake in Israel's first toll road.

Finally, Leviev's actions are often unpredictable in the tradition-bound diamond business largely dictated by De Beers. Leviev has become the first diamond dealer with his finger on every facet of the value chain, from mining and cutting to polishing and retailing. Leviev is innovatively branding his best stones, dubbed the Vivid Collection. In his "spare time," he has also brokered meetings between Putin and American Jewish leaders as well as Israeli politicians. Every year, he donates at least $30 million to Jewish charities.

Outraged, De Beers kicked Leviev out as a sightholder in 1995. De Beers has also set up a diamond-polishing factory in Namibia and sought to launch its own brand. Today, as the world's largest cutter and polisher and a primary source of rough diamonds, Leviev has become De Beers' enemy number one.

Case Discussion Questions

1. What characteristics made the De Beers cartel long lasting? (See also Integrative Case 2.4.)

2. What competitive and cooperative actions have made Leviev De Beers' enemy number one?

3. Discuss the future of the rivalry between De Beers and Leviev, especially in the new arena of retail competition with branded jewelry. What does the future hold for both firms?

Sources: Based on (1) P. Berman & L. Goldman, 2003, The billionaire who cracked De Beers, Forbes, September 15: 108–115; (2) Economist, 2004, Rumors are forever, February 28: 62; (3) Economist, 2004, The cartel isn't forever, July 17: 60–62; (4) C. Kaira, 2004, Lev Leviev squares up with De Beers, The Namibia Economist, February 6 (http://www.economist.com.na); (5) D. Spa, 1994, The Cooperative Edge: The Internal Politics of International Cartels, Ithaca, NY: Cornell University Press.

Notes

Abbreviation list

AME – *Academy of Management Executive*

AMJ – *Academy of Management Journal*

AMR – *Academy of Management Review*

APJM – *Asia Pacific Journal of Management*

ASQ – *Administrative Science Quarterly*

BW – *Business Week*

CBR – *China Business Review*

CMR – *California Management Review*

HBR – *Harvard Business Review*

ICC – *Industrial and Corporate Change*

IE – *International Economy*

JEBO – *Journal of Economic Behavior and Organization*

JEP – *Journal of Economic Perspectives*

JIBS – *Journal of International Business Studies*

JIM – *Journal of International Management*

JM – *Journal of Management*

JMktg – *Journal of Marketing*

JMS – *Journal of Management Studies*

LRP – *Long Range Planning*

OSc – *Organization Science*

OSt – *Organization Studies*

RES – *Review of Economics and Statistics*

SMJ – *Strategic Management Journal*

SMR – *MIT Sloan Management Review*

SO – *Strategic Organization*

1. M. Chen, 1996, Competitor analysis and interfirm rivalry, *AMR*, 21: 100-134; W. Ferrier, 2001, Navigating the competitive landscape, *AMJ*, 44: 858–878; C. Grimm & K. Smith, 1997, *Strategy as Action*, Cincinnati: Thomson South-Western.

2. A. Brandenburger & B. Nalebuff, 1996, *Co-opetition* (p. 4), New York: Currency Doubleday.

3. W. Barnett, H. Greve, & D. Park, 1994, An evolutionary model of organizational performance, *SMJ*, 15: 11–28; A. Karnani & B. Wernerfelt, 1985, Multiple point competition, *SMJ*, 6: 87–96.

4. C. Edwards, 1955, Conglomerate bigness as a source of power, *Business Concentration and Price Policy* (pp. 331–352), Princeton: Princeton University Press; J. Gimeno & C. Woo, 1999, Multimarket contact, economics of scope, and firm performance, *AMJ,* 43: 239–259.

5. S. Jayachandran, J. Gimeno, & P. R. Varadarajan, 1999, The theory of multimarket competition, *JMktg,* 63: 49–66.

6. S. Evenett, M. Levenstein, & V. Suslow, 2001, International cartel enforcement, *IE,* 24 (9): 1221–1245.

7. P. Ingram & P. Roberts, 2000, Friendships among competitors in the Sydney hotel industry, *AJS,* 106: 387–423; M. W. Peng & Y. Luo, 2000, Managerial ties and firm performance in a transition economy, *AMJ,* 43 (3): 486–501.

8. K. Au, M. W. Peng, & D. Wang, 2000, Interlocking directorates, firm strategies, and performance in Hong Kong: Towards a research agenda, *APJM,* 17 (1): 29–47.

9. C. Christensen, 1997, *The Innovator's Dilemma,* Boston: Harvard Business School Press.

10. J. Barney, 2002, *Gaining and Sustaining Competitive Advantage* (p. 359), Upper Saddle River, NJ: Prentice Hall.

11. M. Chen, 1996, Competitor analysis and interfirm rivalry (p. 106).

12. F. Smith & R. Wilson, 1995, The predictive validity of the Karnani and Wernerfelt model of multipoint competition, *SMJ,* 16: 143–160.

13. H. Ma, 1998, Mutual forbearance in international business (p. 140), *JIM,* 4: 129–147.

14. D. Spar, 1994, *The Cooperative Edge: The Internal Politics of International Cartels* (p. 5), Ithaca, NY: Cornell UP.

15. J. R. Baum & S. Wally, 2003, Strategic decision speed and firm performance, *SMJ,* 24: 1107–1129.

16. X. Martin, A. Swaminathan, & W. Mitchell, 1998, Organizational evolution in the interorganizational environment, *ASQ,* 43: 566–601; V. Terpstra & C. Yu, 1988, Determinants of foreign investment of US advertising agencies, *JIBS,* 19: 33–55.

17. W. Ferrier, K. Smith, & C. Grimm, 1999, The role of competitive action in market share erosion and industry dethronement, *AMJ,* 42: 372–388.

18. K. Smith, C. Grimm, M. Gannon, & M. Chen, 1991, Organizational information processing, competitive responses, and performance in the US domestic airline industry, *AMJ,* 34: 60–85.

19. C. Pegels, Y. Song, & B. Yang, 2000, Management heterogeneity, competitive interaction groups, and firm performance, *SMJ,* 21: 911–923.

20. W. C. Kim & P. Hwang, 1992, Global strategy and multinationals' entry mode choice, *JIBS,* 23: 29–53.

21. B. Golden & H. Ma, 2003, Mutual forbearance: The role of intrafirm integration and rewards, *AMR,* 28: 479–493; A. Kalnins, 2004, Divisional multimarket contact within and between multiunit organizations, *AMJ,* 47: 117–128.

22. Chen, 1996, Competitor analysis and interfirm rivalry (p. 107).

23. H. Korn & J. Baum, 1999, Chance, imitative, and strategic antecedents to multimarket contact, *AMJ,* 42: 171–193.

24. E. Graham & D. Richardson, 1997, Issue overview (p. 5), in E. Graham & D. Richardson (eds.), *Global Competition Policy* (pp. 3–46), Washington: Institute for International Economics.

25. Grimm & Smith, 1997, *Strategy as Action* (p. 151).

26. K. Kuhn, 1997, Germany (p. 128), in E. Graham & D. Richardson (eds.), *Global Competition Policy* (pp. 115–149), Washington: Institute for International Economics.

27. E. Fox, 1997, US and EU competition law (pp. 351–352), in E. Graham & D. Richardson (eds.), *Global Competition Policy* (pp. 339–354), Washington: Institute for International Economics.

28. M. Porter, H. Takeuchi, & M. Sakakibara, 2000, *Can Japan Compete?* (p. 25), Cambridge, MA: Perseus.

29. M. Finger, F. Ng, & S. Wangchuk, 2001, Antidumping as safeguard policy (p. 6), Working paper, World Bank.

30. R. Lipstein, 1997, Using antitrust principles to reform antidumping law (p. 408, original italics), in E. Graham & D. Richardson (eds.), *Global Competition Policy* (pp. 405–438), Washington: Institute for International Economics.

31. OECD, 1996, *Trade and Competition: Frictions After the Uruguay Round* (p. 18), Paris: OECD.

32. C. Hill, 2003, *International Business*, 4th ed. (p. 140), Chicago: McGraw-Hill Irwin.

33. P. Engardio, 2004, Wielding a heavy weapon against China, *BW,* June 21: 56–57; D. Robin & W. C. Sawyer, 1998, The ethics of antidumping petitions, *JWB, 33:* 315–328.

34. S. Marsh, 1998, Creating barriers for foreign competitors, *SMJ,* 19: 25–37.

35. Finger, Ng, & Wangchuk, 2001, Antidumping as safeguard policy (p. 6).

36. M. W. Peng, 1998, *Behind the Success and Failure of US Export Intermediaries,* Westport, CT: Quorum Books.

37. M. Chen & K. Stucker, 1997, Multinational management and multimarket rivalry, *Academy of Management Best Papers Proceedings,* 2–6.

38. This section draws heavily from R. McGrath, M. Chen, & I. MacMillan, 1998, Multimarket maneuvering in uncertain spheres of influence, *AMR,* 23: 724–740.

39. D. Yoffie & M. Kwak, 2001, *Judo Strategy* (p. 193), Boston: Harvard Business School Press.

40. W. Boeker, J. Goodstein, J. Stephen, & J. Murmann, 1997, Competition in a multimarket environment, *OSc,* 8: 126–142; M. Chen & I. MacMillan, 1992, Nonresponse and delayed response to competitive moves, *AMJ,* 35: 359–370.

41. I. MacMillan, A. van Putten, & R. McGrath, 2003, Global gamesmanship, *HBR,* May: 62–71.

42. Chen, 1996, Competitor analysis and interfirm rivalry (p. 110).

43. M. Chen & D. Miller, 1994, Competitive attack, retaliation, and performance, *SMJ,* 15: 85–102.

44. A. Mair, 1999, Learning from Honda, *JMS,* 36: 25–44; R. Pascale, 1996, The Honda effect, *CMR,* 38 (4): 80–94.

45. M. Cusumano & D. Yoffie, 1998, *Competing on Internet Time,* New York: Free Press.

46. K. Smith, W. Ferrier, & C. Grimm, 2001, King of the hill (p. 66), *AME,* 15: 59–70.

47. D. Miller & M. Chen, 1996, The simplicity of competitive repertoires, *SMJ,* 17: 419–439.

48. P. Chattopadhyay, W. Glick, & G. Huber, 2001, Organizational actions in response to threats and opportunities, *AMJ,* 44: 937–955.

49. E. Clemons & J. Santamaria, 2002, Maneuver warfare, *HBR,* 80 (4): 57–65.

50. Barney, 2002, *Gaining and Sustaining Competitive Advantage* (p. 353).

51. J. Anand & B. Kogut, 1997, Technological capabilities of countries, firm rivalry, and foreign direct investment, *JIBS,* 28: 445–465; J. Gimeno, 1999, Reciprocal threats in multimarket rivalry, *SMJ,* 20: 101–128; J. Hennart & Y. Park, 1994, Location, governance, and strategic determinants of Japanese manufacturing investment in the United States, *SMJ,* 15: 419–436; K. Ito & E. Rose, 2002, Foreign direct investment location strategies in the tire industry, *JIBS,* 33: 593–602; F. Knickerbocker, 1973, *Oligopolistic Reaction and Multinational Enterprise,* Boston: Harvard Business School Press; L. Thomas & K. Weigelt, 2000, Product location choice and firm capabilities, *SMJ,* 21: 897–909.

52. J. Baum & H. Korn, 1996, Competitive dynamics of interfirm rivalry, *AMJ,* 39: 255–291.

53. H. Haveman & L. Nonnemaker, 2000, Competition in multiple geographic markets, *ASQ,* 45: 232–267.

54. Evenett et al., 2001, International cartel enforcement (p. 1229).

55. This section draws heavily from Spar, 1994, *The Cooperative Edge* (pp. 15–38).

56. T. Schelling, 1980, *The Strategy of Conflict,* Cambridge, MA: Harvard University Press.

57. Evenett et al., 2001, International cartel enforcement (p. 1226).

58. J. Stephen, J. Murmann, W. Boeker, & J. Goodstein, 2003, Bringing managers into theories of multimarket competition, *OSc,* 14: 403–421.

59. This section draws heavily from N. Dawar & T. Frost, 1999, Competing with giants, *HBR,* March-April: 119–129.

60. D. Lavie & A. Fiegenbaum, 2000, The strategic reaction of domestic firms to foreign MNC dominance: The Israeli experience (p. 663), *LRP,* 33: 651–672.

61. M. Zeng & P. Williamson, 2003, Why foreign and local firms dominate different industries in China, Working paper, INSEAD.

62. White & G. Linden, 2002, Organizational and industrial response to market liberalization, *OSt,* 23: 917–948.

63. M. Porter, 1990, *The Competitive Advantage of Nations*, New York: Free Press; M. Sakakibara & M. Porter, 2001, Competing at home to win abroad: Evidence from Japanese industry, *RES*, 83: 311–326.

64. Y. Pan & D. Xu, 2004, Competitiveness: Local versus foreign firms, *HBR China*, February: 14–17.

65. This section draws heavily from R. D'Aveni, 1994, *Hypercompetition* (appendix), New York: Free Press.

66. D'Aveni, 1994, *Hypercompetition* (p. 358); J. Kerstetter, 2004, Trustbusters are on the wrong trail, *BW*, June 21: 48.

67. T. Jorde & D. Teece, 1990, Innovation and cooperation: Implications for antitrust (p. 76), *JEP*, 4: 75–96.

68. D'Aveni, 1994, *Hypercompetition* (p. 376).

69. J. Barney, 2001, Competence explanations of economic profits in strategic management: Some policy implications, in J. Ellig (ed.), *Dynamic Competition and Public Policy* (pp. 45–64), Cambridge, UK: Cambridge University Press.

70. R. Griffin & M. Pustay, 2003, *International Business*, 3rd ed. (p. 241), Upper Saddle River, NJ: Prentice Hall.

71. J. Stiglitz, 2002, *Globalization and Its Discontent* (pp. 172–173), New York: Norton.

Video Case 2.1 (1 minute 52 seconds)

APPLE ITUNES

This case illustrates Apple's introduction of iTunes, a product that is probably familiar to many students. The most relevant chapter is Chapter 5 on entrepreneurship. Apple is one of the quintessential entrepreneurial firms and Steve Jobs, its two-time CEO, is also a quintessential entrepreneur. Given the high cost of music CDs ($18 a copy) and the possibility of free downloads, it is not surprising that CD sales have dropped significantly. However, because rules banning free downloads and file sharing have been tightened, a market is opening for Apple iTunes, which allows legal downloads of thousands of songs at 99 cents each. In the long run, the issue is whether Apple can sustain such a first mover advantage, especially when considering that it lost the "PC war" in which it had a similar early lead in the 1980s.

Video Case 2.2 (2 minutes 11 seconds)

GM AND DAEWOO

This video captures the most recent episode of the GM-Daewoo relationship portrayed in Chapter 7's Opening Case. GM and Daewoo first had a joint venture in the 1980s, which was then dissolved in the early 1990s due to a number of problems. However, in an interesting turn of events, GM and Daewoo joined hands again in 2001. In addition to Chapter 7, this case is also directly relevant for the liability of foreignness concept (Chapter 6), the difficulty associated with international takeovers (Chapter 9), and the necessity to manage key stakeholder groups such as employees (Chapter 12).

Video Case 2.3 (2 minutes 2 seconds)
STATE OF THE WORLD AIRLINE INDUSTRY

This video shows the difficulties of the world airline industry from the European point of view. Although the discussion on country-based landing rights is relevant for the "rules of the game" concept (Chapter 4), the most relevant chapter is Chapter 7, especially its discussion on multipartner alliances (also known as networks or constellations). Chapter 7 extensively discusses all three such networks: Star Alliance, Sky Team, and One World. One of the most crucial points raised in the chapter is most directly supported by this video, namely, strategic alliances are a compromise, an intermediate step between single, stand-alone companies and full mergers (see Figure 7.1). Should European airlines pursue full mergers, they stand to lose some US landing rights and hence some lucrative trans-Atlantic business. Therefore, cooperating strategically, short of pursuing full mergers, seems to be a better alternative.

Video Case 2.4 (1 minute 57 seconds)
UNITED AIRLINES

Related to Video Case 2.3, this video further underscores the difficulty of the airline industry, this time from a US perspective. United Airlines filed for bankruptcy, specifically a Chapter 11 reorganization that allowed it to skip interest payments on debts and to extract significant concessions from employees. However, like Kmart (Video Case 1.6), United Airlines was not going out of business. Passengers interviewed did not seem to be concerned. Although not directly portrayed in the video, how the bankrupt United Airlines deals with its Star Alliance partners (Chapter 7), how it unleashes aggressive competitive actions, and how rivals respond (Chapter 8) can also be interesting class discussions.

Integrative Case 2.1

PEARL RIVER PIANO GROUP'S INTERNATIONAL STRATEGY[1]

Lu Yuan

Chinese University of Hong Kong

The CEO of China's leading piano maker seeks advice on how to enter international markets.

In March 2000, Tong Zhicheng, CEO of China's Pearl River Piano Group (PRPG) Corporation (*http://www.pearlriverpiano.com*), received a group of professors from business schools in Hong Kong and the United States. He enthusiastically showed them around the company's product presentation hall and workshops. "Do you think American customers would like my products?" he asked an American professor. "Yeah, why not?" the professor replied, "They are good pianos with low prices. However, the American piano market has matured and therefore it is not easy to be there."

"How to enter the American market?" It was the major strategic challenge confronting Tong for a long time. Over the past few years, the company began to export to Asian and European markets. However, Tong believed that it was the right time to think about the US market.

Company Background

PRPG was a state-owned enterprise. The group corporation was developed from a piano factory established in 1956 in the southern city of

Guangzhou. When the factory was founded, it had less than one hundred employees and produced thirteen pianos a year (one was exported to Hong Kong). As most production procedures involved manual skills, the factory's capacity was limited to less than 1,000 units a year. The factory branded its products "Pearl River Piano," since it was located next to the Pearl River. Throughout the 1960s and the 1970s, Pearl River pianos were not well known in China. The better-known brands were the Star Sea made by the Beijing Piano Factory and the Ni Er (named after a famous musician) made by the Shanghai Piano Factory.

A strategic turnaround occurred in the early 1980s after the Chinese government decided to embark on economic reforms. One of China's early

---

[1] This case was written by Dr. Lu Yuan (Chinese University of Hong Kong). It is intended to be used for class discussions rather than to illustrate either effective or ineffective handling of an administrative situation. The author would like to thank Mr. Tong Zhicheng for his kindness in offering opportunities for interviews and visits to the company. Reprinted by permission of the author.

reform programs was to delegate decision autonomy to enterprise levels. In the mid-1980s, the factory was granted autonomy for imports and exports, which encouraged it to search for partners and markets abroad. It became the first piano builder in China to import foreign technologies and expatriate experts. In 1987, the factory was expanded to become Pearl River Piano Industrial Corporation. In 1996, after merging with a few smaller musical instrument companies, it formed Pearl River Piano Group Corporation.

The piano originated in Europe where the first stringed instrument was the harp in ancient times. The modern piano took a long time to develop. For instance, keyed monochords were developed approximately in the twelfth century. In 1709, Bartolomeo Cristofori, an Italian harpsichord maker, made an instrument which was regarded as the first piano. He called it in his time *gravicembalo col piano e forte*, or "harpsichord that plays soft and loud." In the late eighteenth century, piano making flourished in Vienna. The piano at that time had a wood frame, two strings per note, and leather-covered hammers. Mozart, for example, composed his concertos and sonatas on such a piano. The eighteenth and nineteenth centuries were the most exciting time for piano builders since the Industrial Revolution brought innovations, such as high quality steel for making strings, in piano production. In terms of basic technology, today's piano is almost the same as that of the late nineteenth century.

A piano is made up of more than 8,000 components, requiring more than 200 labor hours, through more than 300 production procedures. Normally, piano builders introduce production assembly lines in order to improve efficiency, but it was commonly believed that a high quality piano could only be made by craftsmen using their skills and experience to make and tune each product.

1992 to 1999: Tong's Strategy

Tong joined the piano factory when he was sixteen and started his career as a piano builder by first working as a junior craftsman. He recalled his career development:

> PRPG was a small-scale company at that time [when I joined it], so I was able to try a variety of jobs. I worked as a repairman, and then I became the head of the repair department. Afterwards, I was promoted to be the head of three other departments: overseas sales, domestic sales, and supplies. After that, I was sent to Macau [a former Portuguese colony south of Guangzhou which was returned to Chinese sovereignty in 1999] to set up a new factory. In 1991, I was sent back to the headquarters and in 1992, I was appointed CEO.[2]

After Tong assumed the CEO position, he introduced two strategic pillars: innovation and quality. Innovation included the importation of new technology in production, quality measurement, and product innovation by developing a wide range of pianos to meet the high-, medium-, and low-end markets. PRPG invested approximately $60 million to upgrade production lines. The company established an expert team consisting of more than forty technicians using computerized product design, tuning, and product quality analysis. It further developed more than seventy different styles and eight families of pianos.

The second strategic pillar was to enhance quality. The company introduced Total Quality Management in 1988. In 1996 it introduced ISO 9000 and was certified in 1998. The company also established a joint venture with Yamaha in 1995. The joint venture licensed Yamaha technology to make key components (such as framework) and then became a key supplier to Yamaha in China. Through this partnership, PRPG learned how to make a world-class, high-quality product.

As CEO, Tong did not like to stay in his office, but maintained his tradition of walking around production lines and chatting with workers. He once said to

---

[2] *Hang Lung Center for Organizational Research Newsletter,* Fall 2000. Globalization ambition and management philosophy: An interview with Mr. Tong Zhicheng, CEO of Pearl River Piano Group.

visitors, "Every piano is my son." He told employees:

> *By striving to compete with other manufacturers that have a much longer history of building pianos, Pearl River has put its employees and management on notice that we will accept nothing short of perfection.*[3]

Tong realized that innovation and quality improvement were perhaps not enough to make his products competitive with Western-built pianos. Since the piano was traditionally a European musical instrument, it is imperative that a Chinese piano builder, such as PRPG, identify a distinctive position in the marketplace in order to beat the competition.

Chinese Pianos with Western Cultural Properties

Piano builders can be categorized as those targeting high-, medium-, and low-end markets. A company targeting the high-end market typically developed competitive advantages based on a long history of reputation, sophisticated procedures, luxury materials, beautiful styles and painting, and high quality piano performance. Usually, European pianos targeted the high-end market. Customers in this market segment included professionals for world-class concerts, upper-class households, and collectors. However, although European piano makers enjoyed their long history of developing pianos, the United States became an important piano building base as well as a large market. For example, Steinway pianos were usually regarded as the best in the world. The company, which is now based in the United States, was created in 1853 by German immigrant Henry Engelhard Steinway. For 150 years, Steinway has been dedicated to the ideal of making the finest pianos in the world. Due to sophisticated production procedures, as well as characteristics of the small market niche, companies in this market segment usually had a small production volume. For instance, Steinway only produced about 2,000 pianos a year. To compete by this strategy, handcraft skills,

history, reputation, and preferences of well-known piano players became the key factors to success.

Many piano builders, particularly late entrants from Asia to this industry, targeted the medium- and low-end markets. The strategy adopted by these companies focused on efficiency which was achieved through large-scale production. For example, Yamaha was the largest piano builder in the world. Its production capability could reach over 150,000 units a year. Companies positioning themselves to target the medium- and low-end markets competed primarily on price.

PRPG adopted the second strategy and focused on the mass customer market as its dominant niche. However, Tong's ambition was to produce the best pianos in the world, like Steinway. He clearly knew that it was difficult to replicate Steinway's success. His strategic ambition therefore was to upgrade Pearl River Piano as an upper-class brand while improving both product quality and reputation. Tong believed that he could make the best product next only to Steinway. To achieve this goal, he must make his pianos better than the products of most overseas piano builders, particularly those produced by Asian competitors.

How to do that? Tong believed that the piano is a distinctive piece of work that integrates both technology and culture, and that he must make his piano sound like European products and project an image of "European culture." He said that although PRPG could take a few years to catch up to the world-class piano builders by importing technologies and expert knowledge for quality enhancement, it would take a much longer time to understand and master the piano culture.

To make employees and managers understand not only technology, but also the Western culture associated with pianos, Tong invited seven expatriates from Germany and the United States as consultants and advisors who came every six months to work with PRPG technicians and workers. Moreover, Tong stressed the necessity to maintain manual work in key production procedures, although the company installed two computerized laboratories to test products. "Do you know the difference between products made by machine and made by hand?" Tong once said

---

[3] Pearl River Piano Group homepage: *http://www.pearlriverpiano.com/eprp/aboutus.html#Origins.*

to his employees, "A piano made by machine sounds like a machine. A piano made by hands sounds like a human being. The best piano should be made by heart not by machine." To make handcrafted pianos, Tong trained one hundred highly skilled technicians who tested and adjusted every product manually. He also encouraged managers to learn to play piano, while he himself was an excellent pianist.

Building Sales Networks and Brand

Tong had rich experiences in sales and marketing both domestically and internationally. PRPG was the first piano builder in China to establish a nationwide distribution network. Tong created strategic alliances with distributors, musical schools and colleges, and invited numerous famous pianists to be advisors to promote Pearl River pianos. By 2000, PRPG had more than 130 strategic alliances over the country, in addition to 208 sales units.

Tong's ambition was to build Pearl River Piano as a world-class brand. In fact, when he began to introduce innovation and quality strategies, he noted the importance of brand. Since 1996, he consciously promoted Pearl River Piano as a national brand. His strategy was to make his brand known in domestic and international markets by enlisting famous pianists. Tong sponsored various types of piano concerts and competitions, such as the Chinese Works Piano Competition 2000 in Hong Kong. Tong also established close personal relationships with many world-renowned piano players (such as Lazar Berman) and recommended them to play Pear-River pianos in their concerts.

The Internationalization Challenge

By the end of 2000, PRPG was the largest piano builder in China, and the second largest in the world (next to Yamaha), with an annual production capacity of over 100,000 pianos. The company had more than 4,000 employees with a total asset value of approximately $130 million. While it also diversified into other musical instruments, its center of gravity was definitely the piano, with more than 50 percent of the piano market in China. However, Tong did not seem satisfied with this progress. Although there was room to grow in China, competition became tougher than a few years ago. Hundreds of private companies began entering the market and competing with their low quality and low price products.

Tong thus turned his eyes on international markets, specifically the US market. When asked "What would PRPG's prospects be without globalization?" he answered:

> *The company could still survive [by staying in China] under some constraints. However, it is impossible for an entrepreneur to stay at the same position permanently. In fact, an entrepreneur is an aggressor in the business world. . . . We are still developing. We have made some progress, but not yet a great success . . . PRPG has laid the foundations for globalization, but we cannot claim that our global outreach is well established yet. I guess it will take another three years to build a more solid foundation.*[4]

When compared with other Chinese piano builders, PRPG had gained some experience in exporting. Tong believed that although the piano market in the United States was mature, his products could carve out a market niche. Because of the expensive labor costs in the United States and the necessity to rely on manual skills when building pianos, Pearl River pianos could take advantage of cheap labor costs in China combined with high product quality to eventually win American customers.

The company actually started making efforts to enter the US market a few years ago. While relying upon traditional direct exports, Tong also tried to seek a US piano builder as a partner to penetrate the market, but this attempt did not succeed. He realized that most Americans still viewed Chinese products as cheap and low quality. In addition, it was difficult to get a strategic alliance partner because an American piano builder would perceive him as a competitor instead of a partner. To build a strategic alliance with

---

[4] *Hang Lung Center for Organizational Research Newsletter,* Fall 2000. Globalization ambition and management philosophy: An interview with Mr. Tong Zhicheng, CEO of Pearl River Piano Group.

an American company, PRPG might also have to introduce the American partner to the Chinese market, as an exchange for PRPG's entry to the US market. This would add a new rival in China's increasingly crowded domestic market. Therefore, Tong needed to calculate carefully what he could offer to the partner and what he wanted from the partnership.

Searching various alternatives to enter the US market did not stop Tong's pace. In 1999, he set up a sales subsidiary in the United States as the platform upon which to further expand. However, he believed that although direct exports might be effective in the short run, the company should do something else in the long run. He viewed the mission to enter the US market as a crucial stage to build the Pearl River Piano brand name internationally. "What should I do next?" he frequently asked this question to his managers and consultants. In that morning of March 2000, he asked the same question to Hong Kong and American professors who visited him.

Case Discussion Questions

1. Drawing on industry-, resource-, and institution-based views, explain how PRPG, from its humble roots, managed to become China's largest and the world's second largest piano producer.

2. Why did Tong believe that PRPG must engage in significant internationalization (other than the current direct export strategy) at this point?

3. If you were one of those professors who visited Tong in March 2000, how would you brief him on the pros and cons of various foreign market entry options?

4. Again, if you were one of those professors, how would you specifically point out a direction to tackle the US market for PRPG?

Integrative Case 2.2

BROWN LUMBER: CHOOSING THE OPTIMAL EXPORT STRATEGY[1]

Asda Chintakananda

University of North Carolina at Chapel Hill

Anne York

University of Nebraska at Omaha

The owner and CEO of Brown Lumber weighs his options among export strategies: (1) short-term relationships with multiple export intermediaries, (2) a long-term relationship with an exclusive intermediary, or (3) export directly.

Jimmy Brown, owner of the Atmore, North Carolina–based Brown Lumber Manufacturing, was considering his export options. Overseas Unlimited, an export intermediary firm that Brown had worked with on and off for more than a decade, was not bringing him as much business as in the past and was not offering the margins he had seen in past years. In all fairness, the global softwood lumber supply had increased dramatically throughout the 1990s. At the same time, many new substitute products, especially those from Eastern Europe, Asia, and Russia, entered the market and softwood lumber prices had fallen accordingly. This drop in demand for southern pine lumber was especially troubling, as Brown had learned years ago that competing in the price-based domestic market was a losing proposition for small, rural, low-tech firms like his own. As a result, Brown had increasingly targeted export markets, which absorbed, on average, about two-thirds of his sales during the past three years (see Exhibit IC-2.1 and on page 341 Exhibit IC-2.2).

Recently, Brown Lumber had been approached by Mark Ward, owner of Woodnet, a cooperative that boasted the highest market share of softwood lumber export sales in the world. Impressed with the quality of Brown's products, Ward promised that if Brown could meet specifications with regard to quality and deadlines, Woodnet would, after a trial period, pay

---

[1] Company names have been disguised to ensure confidentiality. "Cooperative or Competitive? Structuring an Export Partnership" by Asda Chintakananda and Anne S. York. Reprinted by permission of the authors.

IC-2.1.   Brown Lumber Manufacturing, Inc. Income Statement, 2001–2003

		2001	2002	2003
				(In Thousands)
Sales:	$		$	$
Export sales..		12,568	8,945	12,039
Domestic sales...		5,432	4,620	7,387
Total sales...		18,000	13,565	19,426
Costs and Expenses:				
Cost of Goods Sold		11,414	11,116	10,395
Selling, General and Administrative		767	758	762
Export intermediary expenses		702	541	777
Total Costs and Expenses		12,883	12,415	11,934
Operating Income		5,117	1,150	7,492
Interest Expense		869	869	865
Interest Income		-	-	-
Gain on Disposition of Assets - Net		-	-	-
Other (Expense) Income - Net		98	91	97
Net Income	$	4,150	$ 190	$ 6,530

Source: Brown Lumber Manufacturing Accounting Statements
Note: - *Cubic meters of lumber sold*

	2001	2002	2003
Export sales..	*37,405*	*35,216*	*31,268*
Domestic sales..	*22,354*	*22,983*	*23,158*
	59,759	*58,199*	*54,426*

- *Export sales are for 1" × 4" boards sold to Japan, Mexico, and Spain through Overseas Unlimited.*

a guaranteed higher price than Brown was currently getting from Overseas Unlimited and also guarantee a relatively steady demand. Brown had heard that Woodnet was a tricky company to get on with due to the required trial period and exclusivity. However, he had also heard that once accepted as a partner by Woodnet and its existing clients, Brown probably would have a solid relationship for life.

However, another possibility that intrigued Brown was to go it alone and handle exports directly. Brown had heard through the grapevine that at least one or two firms had been quite successful taking this route, although these firms were not popular with other manufacturers, which tended to be a close knit group that frequently shared information. While potential margins from going the direct route could be higher, there were also more risks, both financially and market-wise. Brown settled down to run some numbers and also to consider what direction he was most comfortable following (see IC-2.1 and IC-2.2).

The Softwood Lumber Industry

Softwood lumber is manufactured from trees such as pine and spruce that are known for their strength and durability. In the United States, these species are most often found in the Southeast and the Pacific Northwest. Similar species are grown in Scandinavia, South America, Europe, and Russia. Approximately

IC-2.2.   **Brown Lumber Manufacturing, Inc. Balance Sheet, 2001–2003**

	2001	2002	2003
			(In Thousands)
ASSETS			
Current Assets:			
Cash and Cash Equivalents .... $	1,016	$ 914	901
Accounts Receivable	689	682	651
Inventories	1,278	999	997
Other Current Assets	918	910	909
	3,901	3,505	3,458
Timber and Timberlands - Net	4,287	4,012	3,971
Property, Plant and Equipment - Net	2,058	2,032	2,028
Deferred Tax Asset	-	-	-
Other Assets	226	207	265
Total Assets .... $	10,472	$ 9,757	9,722
LIABILITIES			
Current Liabilities:			
Current Portion of Long-Term Debt .... $	235	$ 234	234
Line of Credit	823	823	823
Accounts Payable	985	997	982
Interest Payable	-	-	-
Other Current Liabilities	395	495	481
	2,437	2,549	2,520
Long-Term Debt	893	814	801
Deferred Income	234	192	232
Other Liabilities	66	69	68
Total Liabilities	3,630	3,624	3,620
STOCKHOLDERS' EQUITY			
Additional Paid-In Capital	2,941	2,961	2,938
Retained Earnings	3,852	3,121	3,121
Other Equity	49	51	43
Total Stockholders' Equity..................................	6,842	6,133	6,102
Total Liabilities and Stockholders' Equity ..... $	10,472	$ 9,757	9,722

Source: Brown Lumber Manufacturing Accounting Statements

IC-2.3.   **US Softwood Domestic Production, Consumption, Exports, and Imports (billion board feet)**

YEAR	US Production	US Exports	US Imports	US Consumption
1983	31.2	1.8	11.9	41.3
1984	31.3	1.6	13.3	43.0
1985	35.3	1.4	14.6	48.5
1986	38.3	1.9	14.2	50.6
1987	38.1	2.5	14.7	50.3
1988	37.5	3.2	13.5	47.8
1989	36.1	3.3	14.9	47.7
1990	33.6	3.7	12.9	42.8
1991	35.6	2.9	11.5	44.2
1992	31.9	2.6	13.2	42.5
1993	33.1	2.3	15.1	45.9
1994	31.6	2.1	16.2	45.7
1995	33.6	1.9	17.2	48.9
1996	34.8	1.8	18.0	51.0
1997	34.9	1.7	18.0	51.2
1998	36.7	1.1	18.7	54.3
1999	35.7	1.4	19.2	53.5
2000	34.3	1.4	19.5	52.4
2001	35.9	0.9	20.1	55.1
2002	36.3	0.9	20.9	56.3
2003	36.3	0.7	20.5	56.1

Source: Southern Products Forest Association, Western Woods Products Association, US International Trade Commission

80 percent of the softwood lumber produced in the United States is used in the construction industry for home building and remodeling. The US market consumes 50 to 60 billion board feet of softwood lumber annually (see IC-2.3). In addition, the United States produces an additional 2 million cubic meters of softwood for exports, in which more than half is exported to Canada, Japan, and Mexico. The United States also imports a large volume of wood primarily from Canada as well (see IC-2.4 on page 343). Most softwood lumber manufacturers produce just a few sizes or dimensions, as it is difficult to cut softwood lumber into several different dimensions within the same mill using the same equipment. The quality of softwood lumber (and often the price, at least in export markets)

depends on the thickness of the finished boards, their clarity or lack of staining, the absence or small size of knots, and the durability of the wood.

The US softwood lumber industry grew rapidly between 1980 and 1987, mainly due to the global construction and building boom. It rose from 38 billion board feet in 1980 to 50 billion board feet in 1987, a 34 percent increase over seven years. In response to growing market demand, many mills expanded rapidly. In addition, the level of US exports also grew rapidly from 1.5 billion board feet in 1980 to 3.7 billion board feet in 1990, a 146 percent increase over ten years. However, in the late 1990s, due to the US domestic economic slump, the level of construction activity declined by 20 percent, which had a

IC-2.4.   Value of US Exports and Imports of Softwood Lumber by Country (1993–2002)

Export value										(thousand US$)
	1993	1994	1995	1996	1997	1998	1999	2000	2001	2002
Canada	129,545	131,714	132,537	130,106	162,513	122,879	130,551	136,402	96,225	94,858
Japan	612,240	625,884	618,481	649,749	447,983	189,991	204,956	206,159	123,984	80,143
Mexico	189,344	129,490	55,625	34,437	38,987	42,997	49,565	55,815	48,200	47,690
Dominican Republic	35,540	43,567	45,147	33,218	50,540	40,180	45,429	41,505	38,909	33,833
Spain	43,630	60,096	57,517	48,545	52,086	52,732	62,314	57,701	39,189	28,359
China	398	422	287	627	1,712	1,297	1,213	2,322	12,624	19,634
Italy	67,355	54,719	53,065	41,332	47,686	41,814	42,862	24,439	13,670	13,865
Philippines	1,323	1,714	6,913	17,292	13,069	13,360	24,457	16,958	15,421	11,206
Indonesia	277	110	636	2,355	1,664	3,132	5,484	9,431	7,954	10,443
Others	291,760	261,948	240,187	215,572	234,797	179,507	170,290	159,504	91,898	81,532
Total	**1,371,412**	**1,309,664**	**1,210,395**	**1,173,233**	**1,051,037**	**687,889**	**737,121**	**710,236**	**488,074**	**421,563**

Export volume										(cubic meters)
	1993	1994	1995	1996	1997	1998	1999	2000	2001	2002
Japan	2,472,744	2,263,134	2,056,491	2,032,180	1,483,927	703,095	681,022	648,578	425,367	271,738
Canada	622,056	666,961	737,007	736,455	776,419	545,287	603,896	625,776	439,848	408,865
Mexico	745,521	573,908	232,102	191,919	204,364	253,767	314,056	316,408	272,964	274,889
Dominican Republic	166,530	197,544	214,193	161,491	208,344	175,558	204,053	190,422	175,725	154,144
Spain	141,109	157,514	151,223	139,684	145,232	146,734	180,064	156,704	100,457	78,304
The Bahamas	31,440	45,950	46,576	33,220	75,764	49,715	146,323	47,308	25,015	24,387
Italy	174,783	126,530	125,021	108,597	135,534	128,058	134,533	67,146	30,450	31,950
Philippines	4,780	5,479	18,676	51,589	36,828	40,809	70,791	48,979	44,342	34,059
Germany	108,284	98,971	77,953	57,790	77,758	87,571	52,691	41,633	13,198	12,261
UK	57,868	49,817	40,322	29,041	40,792	39,657	41,675	26,314	16,068	13,598
Australia	266,472	156,751	222,503	137,117	106,531	48,702	38,911	39,332	14,484	11,240
Others	570,765	554,763	495,160	544,142	591,362	449,440	515,952	586,789	329,049	380,619
Total	**5,362,352**	**4,897,322**	**4,417,227**	**4,223,225**	**3,882,855**	**2,668,393**	**2,983,967**	**2,795,389**	**1,886,967**	**1,696,054**

Import value										(thousand US$)
	1993	1994	1995	1996	1997	1998	1999	2000	2001	2002
Canada	4,643,831	5,532,621	4,944,175	6,241,175	6,589,904	5,906,255	6,784,139	5,958,289	5,654,293	5,176,326
New Zealand	39,404	55,185	59,063	46,368	58,628	68,658	96,275	90,997	134,127	164,536
Chile	57,389	75,876	85,662	62,413	87,655	92,381	142,796	135,992	126,766	164,228
Germany	66	31	48	278	852	508	7,762	42,100	70,472	148,390
Brazil	12,679	44,194	63,932	68,188	104,231	112,440	153,551	132,985	119,679	134,635
Sweden	513	1,248	1,778	1,790	5,645	10,455	33,918	41,160	79,816	131,635
Austria	12	0	6	484	11,438	27,763	47,514	45,767	51,220	75,815
Others	43,536	46,549	61,278	98,338	127,429	91,048	87,619	101,457	132,867	145,412
Total	**4,797,430**	**5,755,704**	**5,215,942**	**6,519,034**	**6,985,782**	**6,309,508**	**7,353,574**	**6,548,747**	**6,369,240**	**6,140,977**

Import volume										(cubic meters)
	1993	1994	1995	1996	1997	1998	1999	2000	2001	2002
Canada	35,060,590	37,457,026	39,602,000	41,519,906	40,675,739	42,097,724	42,552,200	42,727,253	43,667,044	44,657,774
Germany	92	39	397	1,202	4,493	2,167	32,112	275,420	471,224	960,899
Brazil	47,679	174,789	234,809	240,819	387,516	495,035	675,695	693,718	591,553	703,229
Chile	155,728	177,605	209,546	170,634	260,147	300,167	487,628	526,046	505,482	616,278
Sweden	2,975	6,867	6,199	5,837	15,273	39,143	119,706	170,325	357,474	564,952
New Zealand	99,879	156,837	167,575	145,420	170,113	220,881	314,378	316,834	479,357	520,605
Austria	30	0	65	2,112	51,251	135,886	221,930	212,780	244,630	381,793
Others	162,801	176,427	299,351	361,440	410,216	281,265	298,634	373,747	508,792	639,722
Total	**35,529,774**	**38,149,590**	**40,519,942**	**42,447,370**	**41,974,748**	**43,572,268**	**44,702,283**	**45,296,123**	**46,825,556**	**49,045,252**

Source: US Department of Agriculture, Foreign Agriculture Service
Note: Data above are for softwood lumbers only, does not include processed softwood such as softwood moulding, flooring, plywood, veneer, and chips.

IC-2.5.   US Softwood Lumber Price Trends (Domestic)

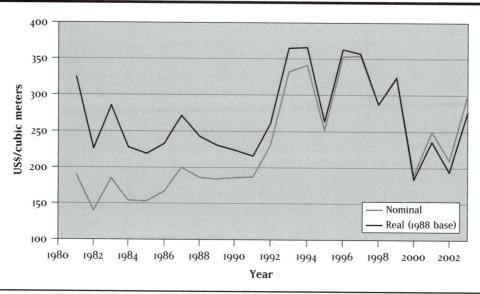

Source: Bank of Montreal Consumer Price Reports

significantly negative impact on the softwood lumber industry. In addition, the influx of pine imports from Canada, Germany, Brazil, Mexico, Chile, and Sweden as well as many new substitute products from Eastern Europe, Asia, and Russia reduced the price of softwood lumber in the United States (see IC-2.5 for price trends).

Accordingly, many US softwood manufacturers began seeking overseas outlets for their excess production which provided them, on average, approximately 25 percent higher sales margins. In some cases, export prices could be as much as 70 percent higher than domestic prices. The exporting of softwood lumber was primarily conducted in two ways. First, larger manufacturers with overseas knowledge and the capacity to export and negotiate with overseas customers mainly exported directly (many of these large firms had sales of $100 million or above and more than 500 employees). Second, most of the smaller manufacturers tended to rely on export intermediaries to reach overseas markets (many of these smaller firms had sales of less than $50 million and less than 100 employees). Using export intermediaries helped

small firms overcome the impediments of time and resource limitations in developing export capabilities within their firm. In such relationships, manufacturers and export intermediaries are highly dependent on each other's resources—inventory from the manufacturer's side and either knowledge or financial resources from the export intermediary's side. Manufacturers typically pay export intermediaries approximately 2.5 to 5 percent of total export sales as a commission for their services.

Brown Lumber's Export History

Brown Lumber was established by Jimmy Brown's grandfather in 1965. Until the late 1980s, Brown Lumber had only produced for the US domestic market. However, in the early 1990s, when Jimmy Brown took over as CEO, he realized that the US domestic market was very cyclical (see IC-2.5) and had intense competition, and that Brown Lumber would either have to scale down production or seek outlets overseas in order to survive. Exporting not only required Brown to search for customers overseas, an activity never undertaken before, but also required Brown to develop capabilities to handle a variety of tasks such as the paperwork, legal issues, payment settlements via wire transfers, hedging of currencies, negotiation of the best freight rates, and risk management. Developing such capabilities would have been costly and risky for a small firm like Brown. In addition, finding overseas customers that had the exact needs that Brown could meet would have been difficult. In many instances, foreign companies require specifications of lumber that are different from products intended for sale within the US market, such as cutting in metric dimensions, thicker sizes, kiln drying, sorting, and so forth. The development of such products could require Brown to make substantial changes in production techniques, which, if done incorrectly, could result in large portions of unused wood and lower profits. Finally, the substantial changes required in the manufacturing process to accommodate foreign buyers' needs might also make it difficult to produce for domestic markets.

Through trade shows, Brown met several export intermediaries and chose United Exporting as its first agent. United Exporting appeared to already have a large existing demand in Israel for $1'' \times 4''$ boards, Brown's specialty. However, the relationship lasted for only four months. After Brown fulfilled its obligations, United Exporting was not able to continue to provide the same high margins and the relationship ended. Despite this, United Exporting continued to maintain regular contact with Brown, hoping to work with it again when United Exporting could identify new demands for $1'' \times 4''$ boards.

After the relationship with United Exporting ended, Brown continued to search for export opportunities, working with three other export intermediaries, including Overseas Unlimited, on a one-time or spot transaction basis. However, despite the multiple export intermediaries that Brown had developed relationships with, all of the relationships were short term and, except for Overseas Unlimited, had ended when the export intermediaries lowered the export prices offered, found alternative arrangements with other manufacturers, or failed to find new customers. Such

terminations required Brown to continually search for new export intermediaries. Once an export intermediary was selected, Brown then had to carefully monitor its performance. After numerous problems, Brown decided to do most of its business through Overseas Unlimited. Overseas Unlimited had a large established network all over Europe and, in the past, had been able to seek markets for Brown's excess supply or capacity. In this relationship, all Brown needed to do was to ensure that the specifications of its wood dimensions matched the detailed spec sheet provided by Overseas Unlimited, which included sawing, wrapping, banding, and packing. Overseas Unlimited handled all the customer negotiations and shipping processes. It also took title to the shipments and dealt with any problems that arose, such as late payments and damages to the goods. However, export prices, terms, and conditions continued to be negotiated prior to each export transaction.

In early 2004, after an almost thirteen-year relationship with Overseas Unlimited, Brown realized that Overseas Unlimited had been providing more business to a rival manufacturer that produced primarily 5-1/4″ wood, a dimension of cut that provided Overseas Unlimited with higher margins. While Brown understood that the overall softwood lumber market, especially the demand for the $1'' \times 4''$ size that his firm specialized in, had not been strong, he also realized that if he wanted to increase sales for his firm, he would need to arrange other export alternatives.

The Woodnet Option

Around the time of his disenchantment with Overseas Unlimited, Jimmy Brown was approached by Mark Ward, owner of Woodnet. Ward contacted Brown because of a recommendation of another softwood lumber firm which had cooperated with Brown in the past and which was one of Woodnet's lumber manufacturing partners. Woodnet, which like Brown was also located in North Carolina, not only claimed to have the highest market share of softwood lumber export sales in the world but also boasted of having the best working relationship with its softwood lumber partners. Woodnet's track record included working

IC-2.6.   Three Strategic Choices

Competitive partnership model

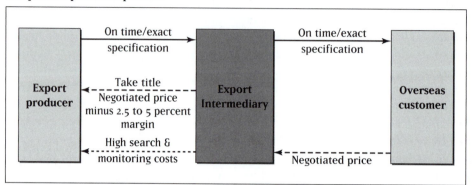

Cooperative partnership model

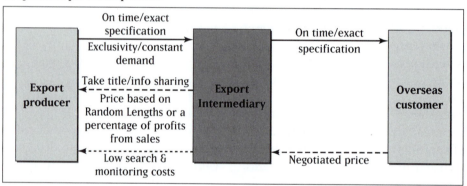

Direct export model

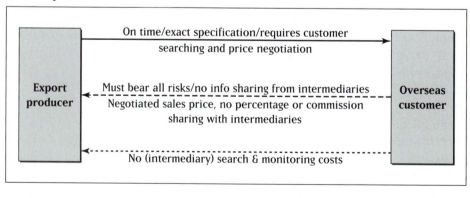

Note: A mixed model comprises a mixture of elements from both the competitive partnership model and the cooperative partnership model

exclusively with eighteen firms that had never left Woodnet to work with other intermediaries, some having worked with Woodnet for as long as fifteen years. Ward stated, "We've never booted a company nor has there been a company that has left us . . . Once we've committed to a manufacturer, we stick with them." Woodnet's strategy was to put together a consortium of small, noncompeting lumber manufacturers which typically did not manufacture the same products in order to offer export customers a full line of products from one source.

Ward offered Brown a one-year trial period in which Brown would provide Woodnet with specific amounts of $1'' \times 4''$ lumber, a dimension that members within Woodnet's consortium did not currently produce. Brown would also be required to meet Woodnet's stringent high quality, on-time production and delivery specifications on an exclusive basis for export markets. In return, Woodnet would export an agreed-upon quantity of Brown's products and guarantee fair industry prices, as published by Random Lengths, a trusted industry source of information. After this trial period, if there was mutual satisfaction on both sides, Woodnet would formally accept Brown into its exclusive consortium and guarantee a steady export demand at a relatively high price. Ward assured Brown, "Our number one job is to provide you a price advantage. It is important not to compete on pricing as it will be harmful in the long run. Our customers may buy only 15 percent of your quantity, but this could make 40 percent of your US dollar earnings. Such pricing and volume consideration makes a tremendous difference!" Also, through working with Woodnet, Jimmy Brown would have the opportunity to observe the entire exporting process first hand, traveling with Ward on overseas marketing trips to meet end customers and better understand their needs. Finally, Ward promised to co-brand Brown's products, which meant that both Woodnet and Brown Lumber stamps would appear on all lumber sold. Through this process, Brown's lumber would benefit from the long-term reputation for quality developed by Woodnet over the years.

Brown's Choice

Brown realized that he was faced with at least three very different and possibly conflicting export strategy options, each with its own risks and rewards (see IC-2.6 on page 346). The first, competitive partnership strategy, was to continue with short-term, spot relationships with multiple intermediaries such as Overseas Unlimited. Maintaining such relationships, especially when it involved trusting agents to operate in Brown's best interests, was difficult and time-consuming, although they allowed Brown to maintain the flexibility of working with multiple intermediaries and sometimes, at least potentially, to make higher one-time profits. A second option, cooperative partnership strategy, was to work with Woodnet, perhaps giving up some short-term profits but trusting that Woodnet would operate in Brown's best interest in the long term. This partnership would save Brown from having to continually search for new agents and monitor them in order to receive the best possible deals. It would also assure a steady stream of revenues and profits. Such a relationship would also allow Brown to gradually develop its own export skills, knowledge, and brand recognition. A third strategy, which was the riskiest and required the most front-end investment but which also carried the highest revenue potential because no commissions would have to be paid, was to export directly. Woodnet had asked for a commitment within a week, as it was considering an alternate $1'' \times 4''$ manufacturer as well as Brown. What should Brown do?

Case Discussion Questions

1. What were Brown's primary motivations to focus on export as opposed to domestic markets?

2. Thus far, what was Brown's strategy to overcome its liability of foreignness in export markets?

3. Brown can export directly or indirectly (through export intermediaries). What are their pros and cons? Why did Brown always use export intermediaries?

4. Of the three strategic choices Brown was contemplating, which one would you recommend?

Integrative Case 2.3

THE INCAT-AFAI JOINT VENTURE: TECHNOLOGY TRANSFER WITH A LOOSE CONTRACT[1]

Sara L. McGaughey

Copenhagen Business School

Peter W. Liesch

University of Queensland

Duncan Poulson

University of Tasmania

Despite the often noted concern for intellectual property violation in joint ventures, Australia's INCAT entered a joint venture with Hong Kong's AFAI with a very loose contract.

One of the leading concerns in joint venture (JV) management is one party's unauthorized appropriation of technology from another party. Typical remedies are extensive legal contracts specifying the rights and responsibilities of each side. But there are still numerous cases of legal disputes. However, there are exceptions. The China-based JV between INCAT (*http://www.incat.com.au*), an Australian company that produces high-speed ferries, and AFAI (*http://www.afaiships.com*), a Hong Kong shipbuilder, is one interesting exception.

INCAT

Established in 1978 as International Catamarans Pty Ltd, INCAT has been a dominant player in the world market for high-speed car- and passenger-carrying ferries. As a "born global," it started with a strong export orientation from the outset. Its innovative design and production have allowed INCAT to grow from 31 employees in 1978 to 1,000 in 2000. It has built approximately 50 percent of high-speed car- and passenger-carrying ferries currently in operation worldwide. INCAT's success was made possible due to a program of cutting-edge research and development (R&D) to improve product design and performance. The program's result has been an improved wave-piercing vessel that could travel easily through oncoming waves and for long distances. INCAT is particularly known for two successful high-speed ferry designs. The first is a large, wave-piercing catamaran and the second is a small "k class" catamaran created

---

[1] This case was based on S. L. McGaughey, P. W. Liesch, & D. Poulson, 2000, An unconventional approach to intellectual property protection: The case of an Australian firm transferring shipbuilding technologies to China, *Journal of World Business*, 35 (1): 1–20. Reprinted by permission of the authors.

for sheltered ferry trips. These two designs have set world standards for ocean-based transport around the world for cars and passengers, and have recently attracted the attention of Australian and US militaries (see Strategy in Action 6.1 in Chapter 6).

The Joint Venture

Unable to fill orders, INCAT licensed shipyards to build vessels in Australia, New Zealand, Hong Kong, Singapore, the United States, and the United Kingdom. For several reasons, INCAT decided in mid-1995 to form a JV with another shipbuilder for offshore production. One reason was the increasing global demand for its high-speed ferries, which far outweighed its capabilities with its single Tasmania-based shipyard. A second reason was that the Australian government was attempting to abolish the subsidies that helped the Australian shipbuilding industry to compete overseas. Third, INCAT had a disadvantage in delivering ships to the very distant northern hemisphere, due to high costs and rivalry.

A number of shipyards from China, Hong Kong, Malta, Sweden, the United States, and the United Kingdom expressed strong interest in a JV with INCAT. In 1996, INCAT chose to enter a JV with one of its former Hong Kong licensees, AFAI High Performance Ships Ltd., for the production of its "k class" catamaran. Under the agreement, INCAT held 49 percent of the equity whereas AFAI controlled 51 percent. Production was to take place at AFAI's shipyard in Panyu, southern China. Prior to entering this JV, AFAI constructed boats for INCAT from 1982 to 1989 with no formal licensing agreement ever being signed. The trust that was built through this prior relationship was a major reason why INCAT chose AFAI. AFAI is also a company that is well versed in Western business and culture, due to its other JVs in addition to that with INCAT. Although these other JVs are in the shipbuilding industry, they were not competitors to INCAT. Yet a third attractive point was that AFAI's shipyard in Panyu began during a time of rapid growth of high-speed transport in the Pearl River Delta in southern China, enabling AFAI

to gain valuable skills in the repair, maintenance, and development of high-speed ferries. AFAI's purpose built, 50,000-square-meter specialist shipyard in Panyu is, according to AFAI's Web site, "the only one of its kind in Asia, reflecting a fastidious attention to finished detail that is almost unnerving to our competitors."[2]

As part of the JV, INCAT was responsible for the design of the vessels as well as supplying the Chinese shipyard with the machinery and prefabricated components for the "k class" catamarans. INCAT had lower component costs than AFAI, due to its significant buying power. Production in China further strengthened buying power. AFAI's responsibilities were to supply the labor and management to build the vessels as well as technical assistance. Through this arrangement, INCAT has been able to achieve economies of scale by specializing in its large wave-piercing catamarans in Tasmania, while the Chinese shipyard concentrated on the smaller, "k class" vessels.

Different from the previous licensing relationship that INCAT had with AFAI, INCAT had much more control in the JV arrangement. All vessels had to be made according to INCAT's instruction. However, while control increased, so did the associated risk levels and commitment of resources from INCAT. As part of the agreement, INCAT agreed to bear all costs related to the supply of equipment and components to AFAI until the vessel was sold. In addition, INCAT was to receive no payment for the knowledge and technology that it supplied to AFAI. Therefore, INCAT had the potential to suffer financially if the construction or sale of its product was delayed, unlike the previous arrangement. Each "k class" vessel was worth US$17 million, whereas the vessels constructed in the previous arrangement were worth US$1.3 to $2 million.

Unlike most international licensing and JV agreements, the joint production arrangement between these two companies was unusual in that the agreement

---

[2] *http://www.afaiships.com/resources.html* (accessed July 9, 2004).

did *not* specify exactly what each partner would contribute in technological expertise to the JV. Neither company intended to restrict the contribution of the other partner. Rather, both parties agreed to do whatever was necessary (within reason) to construct "k class" vessels for the world market. This type of agreement exemplifies a great deal of flexibility. But it will only succeed if a relationship based on trust exists between the parties. Both INCAT and AFAI stated that they trust the other partner to get their half of the bargain accomplished. This statement, coupled with the Chinese business culture known as *guanxi*, which is based on trust, reciprocity, and obligation, has allowed this partnership to succeed. In 1998, the JV delivered an 80-meter catamaran with a carrying capacity of 400 people and 89 cars, with an impressive speed of 47 knots when fully loaded and much lower operation costs than conventional ferries.[3]

Why Such a Loose Contract?

Given the often-voiced concern for intellectual property protection, why did INCAT choose such a loose contract in its JV arrangement with AFAI? This is primarily because INCAT's management is not concerned with legally defined intellectual property to protect its global market share. INCAT had not registered patents or designs. In fact, INCAT had not even registered a trademark to protect its name and logo. One could attribute this to the fact that INCAT is a smaller, privately owned company. One could also consider the costs and ineffectiveness associated with legally protecting intellectual property. In fact, only a small proportion of the total package of technology being transferred by INCAT to its JV partner could be protected by intellectual protection laws. However, neither of these appears to be the major reason why INCAT did not engage in such activities. INCAT continued to demonstrate a lack of concern over the possibility of AFAI taking away its designs and/or

processes. This is especially interesting since the Chinese government–operated company, Guangzhou Maritime Shipping Bureau, was affiliated with the shipyard. The JV agreement did afford a certain degree of protection from outside parties by including confidentiality clauses designed to prevent AFAI from disclosing INCAT's proprietary information to third parties. Although these clauses existed, INCAT recognized the limited extent of protection that they provide.

INCAT's primary sources of competitive advantage lie in (1) a relentless emphasis on innovation, (2) an ongoing commitment to clients, and (3) a strong reputation for safety. The first item, an emphasis on innovation, is one explanation as to why INCAT is not interested in securing intellectual property rights legally. INCAT believes that it will sustain its technological superiority with intense R&D activity. While all vessels sold in the international market by INCAT include paper and electronic plans explaining how the product was built, INCAT's management insists that simple plans are not as valuable as they may seem. In addition to the plans, all the background information and research that went into the process is needed if a competitor wishes to build or adapt one of INCAT's designs. Yet a vast array of essential knowledge is not embodied in the plans. This essential knowledge includes mechanical principles underlying the design that are codified, as well as critical tacit knowledge. This tacit knowledge is built up over years of experience, and cannot be easily taken away ("stolen").

Second, INCAT's commitment to clients is evident through its ability to provide maintenance assistance via its computerized design system. When a client experiences a problem, INCAT can design a solution and electronically send it to minimize downtime for the customer. This system also tracks each vessel that INCAT has produced throughout its lifetime, even through ownership changes. Learning is transferred and customer service is enhanced through this mechanism.

To continue upholding its reputation for safety, INCAT recreates via a computerized simulation every

---

[3] *http://www.incat.com.au/uploaded/18/63234–04k50-marketing-002.doc* (accessed July 23, 2004).

possible incident that occurs with sea ferries, in order to ascertain and improve its vessels' ability to withstand a potential disaster. These results are distributed to interested parties worldwide to demonstrate the company's dedication to keeping passengers safe and minimizing risks. INCAT also participates in international marine advisory boards and works closely with companies that specialize in safety components.

Overall, INCAT's avoidance of formal means of intellectual property protection in China, a country reportedly with rampant intellectual property violations, can be explained by the implicit protection afforded through its abilities to uniquely combine capabilities relating to innovation, client commitment, and safety, in which its proprietary technology and know-how is embedded and renewed. According to INCAT's managing director:

What we do have is mostly in our heads and it is a sort of intellectual property which is far more valuable than being on paper.

Case Discussion Questions

1. Why did INCAT want to establish a JV as opposed to relying on licensing agreements as before?

2. Why is INCAT comfortable with a loose JV agreement which does not delineate the details of technological expertise each party is to contribute?

3. What are the drawbacks and advantages of INCAT's approach? (Hint: See the debate on "learning race versus cooperative specialization" in Chapter 7).

Integrative Case 2.4

ARE DIAMONDS FOREVER? BEHIND THE LONGEVITY OF THE DE BEERS CARTEL[1]

Mike W. Peng

Fisher College of Business, The Ohio State University

South Africa's De Beers not only managed the global diamond cartel throughout the twentieth century, but is also endeavoring to meet new challenges in the twenty-first century.

The Cartel

The longest running and probably the most successful cartel in the modern world is the international diamond cartel headed by De Beers (*http://www. debeersgroup.com*) of South Africa. The cartel system underpinning the $60 billion a year industry is, according to the *Economist*, "curious and anomalous—no other market exists, nor would anything similar be tolerated in a serious industry."

Although historically diamonds were rare, the discovery of South African diamond mines by the end of the nineteenth century brought an avalanche of stones to the global market. A key reason diamond prices were so high was because of the deeply ingrained perception of scarcity. Consequently, if there was an oversupply, prices could plummet. Cecil Rhodes, an English tycoon who founded the De Beers Mines in

South Africa in 1875, sought to solve this problem by focusing on two areas. First, Rhodes realized that supply from South Africa, the only significant producer in the world at that time, should be limited. Second, because producers (diggers) had little control over the quality and quantity of their output, they preferred to deal with an indiscriminate buyer willing to purchase both spectacular and mediocre stones. On the other hand, buyers (merchants) needed to secure a steady supply of stones (both high and low ends) in order to generate sufficient volume. Rhodes's solution was to

[1] This case was written by Mike W. Peng (Fisher College of Business, The Ohio State University) and supported by a National Science Foundation CAREER grant (SES-0238820) for educational purposes. It is entirely based on published sources. The views expressed are those of the author and not those of the NSF. All errors remain the author's. This case is best used as a companion case for the Chapter 8 Closing Case, "Lev Leviev Fights De Beers."

create an ongoing agreement between a single producer and a single buyer in which supply was kept low and prices high.

Putting his idea in action, Rhodes bought out all the major South African mines in the 1890s and formed a diamond merchants' association in the country, called the "Diamond Syndicate," to which he would sell his output. In such "single-channel marketing," all members of the Syndicate pledged to buy diamonds from Rhodes and sell them in specific quantities and prices. With such an explicit scheme of quantity- and price-fixing, the diamond cartel was born. After Rhodes's death in 1902, the De Beers empire was strengthened by Ernest Oppenheimer, a German diamond merchant who had founded his own company, Anglo-American (*http://www.angloamerican.co.uk*), in South Africa. Through cross shareholdings, members of the Oppenheimer family still control both De Beers and Anglo-American to this day.

Industry Attributes

Most cartels collapse due to organizational and incentive problems. The longevity of the De Beers cartel, now running for more than one hundred years, thus is an amazing case study of how to effectively run a cartel. At least three industry attributes contribute to the cartel's longevity. First, the industry has an extraordinarily high concentration. In Rhodes's day, De Beers not only controlled all of South African (and hence virtually worldwide) production, but also controlled all sales through its wholly owned subsidiary, Central Selling Organization (CSO), in London. Second, De Beers is the undisputed price leader. Sales of rough diamonds (called "sights") are managed by the CSO to an exclusive group of "cherry picked" merchants (known as "sightholders") from cities such as Antwerp, Johannesburg, New York, Mumbai, and Tel Aviv. Sightholders would inform the CSO of their preferences for quantity and quality. The CSO then matched them with inventory. During each sight, the CSO offered each sightholder a preselected parcel. The buyer either took it or left it—no bargaining was permitted. Generally, buyers took the parcel. If buyers did not like the system, they would not be invited again. This tactic allowed De Beers to control, down to the carat, exactly what and how many stones entered the market and at what price. To maintain the exclusivity of the sightholders, their number was reduced from approximately 350 in the 1970s to 120 in the 1990s. There were less than 100 sightholders in 2004. Third, the friendly social relationships among participants of the cartel—for the most part—facilitate its long-term viability. "It's a personal business, face to face," said De Beers' current chairman Nicky Oppenheimer (Ernest's grandson). "In uranium, everybody brings their lawyers. In diamonds, there are no lawyers sitting around. It's a handshake business."

Firm Capabilities

At least three firm-specific attributes are also behind the longevity of De Beers' cartel. First, De Beers has a very clear strategy: Expand demand, limit supply, and maximize long-term profit. In the postwar decades, thanks to De Beers advertising (which amounted to $180 million in 2003, in addition to $270 million spent by its clients), diamond engagement rings became almost compulsory in North America, Western Europe, and Japan. Increasingly anniversary rings are made of diamonds as well. The purpose of the recent "diamonds are forever" campaign is simply to prevent the emergence of a market for second-hand diamonds, which would have significantly increased supply. Consequently, De Beers historically has been able to take advantage of very inelastic demand to set prices, largely constrained only by the number of engagements and to a lesser extent major anniversaries in any given year.

Second, De Beers exhibits a high level of flexibility to adapt to new challenges. By the 1950s, South Africa was no longer the leading producer. Today, the top eight producing countries are Botswana, Canada, Russia, South Africa, Angola, Democratic Republic of Congo (formerly Zaire), Namibia, and Australia, of which only 11 percent of the worldwide production is from South Africa. Out of necessity, De Beers had to reach out to other producers. De Beers offered its capital and expertise to African producers in Botswana,

Angola, and Namibia. As a result, De Beers still controls approximately 45 percent of the worldwide production—it is still the biggest diamond miner but no longer that dominant. If producers declined offers for joint production, De Beers would urge them to sell to De Beers. Appreciating the benefits of cooperation and the hazards of oversupply, many producers agreed. Even during the heyday of the former Soviet Union, which for political reasons did not acknowledge any business dealings with the then Apartheid-era South Africa, the Soviet government entered secret agreements with De Beers to participate in such collusion. The producers typically agreed to sell rough diamonds only to De Beers, which set prices. De Beers promised to purchase all of the output, rain or shine (prices might fluctuate due to changing demand), resulting in its huge stockpiles of diamonds. In exchange, the producers reaped the traditional benefits of a cartel: relatively stable prices, guaranteed purchases, and little competition. At present, De Beers still controls approximately 50 to 60 percent of the rough diamond sales worldwide.

Perhaps most strikingly, De Beers possesses both the unique will and capability to enforce cartel arrangements. As in all cartels, the incentives to cheat are tremendous: Both producers and buyers are interested in cutting De Beers out of the process. De Beers' reactions are typically swift and powerful. In 1981, President Mobutu Seko of Zaire announced that his country, the world's leading producer of industrial diamonds, broke away from De Beers by directly marketing its diamonds. Although only 3 percent of De Beers' sales were lost, its "world order" would be at stake if such actions were unpunished. Consequently, De Beers drew on its stockpiles to flood the market, driving the price of Zairian industrial diamonds from $3 per carat to $1.80 and wiping out any financial gains the Zairians hoped to grab. While incurring disproportional losses, De Beers made its point. In 1983, Zaire crawled back on its knees and De Beers agreed, but only at terms much less favorable than those offered before.

In another example, many sightholders in Tel Aviv, a major diamond cutting and trading center, began to hoard diamonds purchased from the CSO in the late 1970s, hoping to combat Israel's rampant inflation. The disappearance of a substantial amount of diamonds from global circulation tightened supply, leading to skyrocketing prices and encouraging merchants elsewhere also to hoard and profit. While De Beers actually benefited from such higher prices in the short run, it realized that in the long run such an uncontrolled speculative bubble would burst. In response, in 1978, De Beers purged one-third of CSO sightholders and kicked out the most aggressive Israeli speculators and some non-Israeli merchants who had done business with the Israelis. Cut off from their CSO supplies, speculative merchants were forced to draw down their stockpiles, thus restoring prices to normal levels and leading to a "soft landing" from the speculative fever.

Institutional Constraints and Maneuvers

De Beers is also a skillful player in understanding and manipulating the rules of the game. In South Africa, half of the stock market is composed of the stocks of De Beers, Anglo-American, and their vast empire of related firms in the conglomerate. They control the pillar of South Africa's economy, namely, strategic minerals. For obvious reasons, the South African government—both during and after the Apartheid—is on friendly terms with De Beers, whose cartel has no fear of being prosecuted. Likewise, De Beers maintains friendly relationships with most governments of diamond-producing countries. Its secret deals with the former Soviet government were indicative of its superb persuasive power, driving home the point that economics was more important than ideology. De Beers does face one major institutional headache: the US government thinks that it is in clear violation of US antitrust laws, and has unsuccessfully tried to prosecute it in 1945, 1974, and 1994. Thus far, De Beers has managed to stay beyond the extraterritorial reach of US laws. It has no legal presence and no (direct) sales in the US. All its diamonds are sold in London, and then sightholders can export them to the US, which is legal. Technically, the imported diamonds are no longer De Beers'—they belong to independent sightholders.

Current Challenges

Overall, the De Beers group, which is now widely diversified despite its center of gravity in diamonds, has been highly successful. In its more than one hundred years of history, it only lost money in 1915 and 1932. In 2003, it employed approximately 24,000 people in nineteen countries, including twenty mines currently in production in Africa and joint ventures and partnerships in Canada, Russia, and Australia. In 2003, it produced healthy profits of $676 million on record sales of $5.5 billion. Although 2003 was a very difficult year given the general weakness of the global economy and the substantial uncertainties associated with the war in Iraq and SARS in Asia, De Beers' profits increased 18 percent when compared with 2002. However, it is not without challenges. Three main challenges lie in (1) adapting to the changing industry structure, (2) dealing with pressures for corporate social responsibility, and (3) overcoming formal institutional barriers preventing it from directly operating in its largest market, the United States.

First, in terms of industry structure, De Beers has been transformed from a monopolist to a leading player in an oligopoly which increasingly has to accommodate new players. The rise of the then Soviet and now Russian mines in Siberia, which now produce 22 percent of the global output, poses sufficient market power to threaten De Beers' standing. The leading Russian producer, Alrosa (*http://www.eng.alrosa.ru*), has collaborated with Lev Leviev Group (*http://www.africa-israel.com*), a leading Israeli diamond merchant headed by a Russian-speaking, Uzbeki-born Israeli citizen (see Closing Case in Chapter 8). The Russians have reduced sales of rough diamonds to De Beers, polished more diamonds in Russia, and marketed them directly. Outraged, De Beers, which invited Lev Leviev to become a sightholder in 1985, removed its privileges of a sightholder in 1995. But the tide is difficult for De Beers to turn back. However, on the bright side, with the increasingly difficult-to-control cartel, De Beers no longer needs to focus exclusively on defending the cartel. Instead, it has more freedom to make decisions

to maximize profits, such as buying fewer stones at uneconomic prices. It is not an accident that its recent profits, noted earlier, soared.

Second, De Beers has been facing mounting pressures for corporate social responsibility, on at least three fronts. The first was the $1.2 billion worth of "conflict diamonds" that floated to the global market as a result of the civil war in Angola in the 1990s. In its traditional role of a buyer of last resort, De Beers felt compelled to purchase the new supply; otherwise, it risked losing its tight grip on global supply. However, with "blood on its hands," De Beers encountered a public relations disaster, especially after the UN imposed sanctions on purchases of "conflict diamonds." Eventually, under tremendous pressure of consumer boycotts and activist campaigns, De Beers in 2000 initiated a "Kimberly Process" which, together with almost seventy governments and all the big industry players, committed the industry to a strict certification process for the legitimate origin of diamonds. The "Kimberly Process" has been in effect since 2003. The second is the HIV/AIDS disaster, reportedly affecting 25 percent of the adult population in southern Africa. In 2003, De Beers became the first mining company to extend health insurance free of charge to HIV positive employees and their spouses in South Africa, Botswana, and Namibia. This insurance coverage would remain in effect to employees after retirement or retrenchment. The third area is environmental protection. Diamond mining, if not properly managed, can easily cause environmental problems. De Beers thus has to pay careful attention to the environmental footprint of its operations. All its major operations have been ISO14001 certified.

Finally, facing competition, De Beers has sought to develop a De Beers brand of diamonds and other luxury goods. In 2000, it formed a joint venture with a leading luxury goods firm, LVMH (*http://www.lvmh.com*), and opened a De Beers LV store in London and three stores within stores in Tokyo. However, its plan to open a flagship store in New York has been frustrated, because of the US government ban on its business due to its alleged antitrust violations. Nicky

Oppenheimer, De Beers' current chairman, openly wrote in his "chairman's statement" in the *2003 Annual Report* that De Beers' core strategy was "to bend all our efforts to increasing worldwide demand for our product and ensure that diamond jewelry would henceforth outperform the rest of the luxury goods market"—in other words, increase demand, limit supply, and jack up price, exactly the "criminal" acts charged by the US government. Openly acknowledging "guilty as charged," Oppenheimer's 1999 speech to alumni of the Harvard Business School contained the following statements:

- *We set out, as a matter of policy, to break the commandments of Mr. Sherman [principal lawmaker for the Sherman Act of 1890]. We make no pretence that we are not seeking to manage the diamond market, to control supply, to manage prices, and to act collusively with our partners in the business.*

- *This form of single-channel marketing has exercised an extraordinary beneficial influence upon the whole of the diamond industry and particularly to many of the economies of Africa.*

- *It is no accident that diamond prices have been more stable when compared with other commodities. The positive trend in rough diamond prices is due to De Beers' marketing efforts. And this is an effort which is in the interest of both the producer and the consumer, a strange and illogical coming together of opposites.*

- *I believe that the attitude of the [US] Justice Department is at odds with American foreign policy which seeks to support the reconstruction and development of Africa . . . It is always hard to argue that you are the exception to the rule but in the case of De Beers and the ultimate luxury—diamonds—I believe a review of US antitrust laws should form part of a new framework for engagement with Africa. Indeed, it would be in line with the spirit of the African Growth and Opportunity Act.*

Postscript

Before this book went to press, in July 2004, in an Ohio court, De Beers finally pleaded guilty to charges of price-fixing of industrial diamonds and agreed to pay a $10 million fine to settle, thus ending a sixty-year impasse—it was first charged by the US government in 1945 and this recently settled case was initiated in 1994. De Beers' top executives may now travel to the United States without fear of arrest and the firm will be able to operate directly in the world's largest diamond market, which consumes approximately 48 percent of the retail diamonds.

Case Discussion Questions

1. Most cartels fail within a short period of time due to organizational and incentive problems. Why is the diamond cartel so long lasting (spanning the entire twentieth century and still going, despite some recent loss of power)?

2. Drawing on industry-, resource-, and institution-based views, explain why De Beers has been phenomenally successful.

3. Given the multidimensional current challenges, what are the opportunities for De Beers? What are the threats? What strengths and weaknesses does De Beers have when dealing with these challenges?

4. Discuss the future of the rivalry between De Beers and Leviev, especially in the new arena of retail competition with branded jewelry. What does the future hold for both firms? (Consult Closing Case in Chapter 8.)

Sources: Based on (1) T. Allison, 2002, Rough stones and the Russian connection, *Asian Times*, November 28 (http://www.atimes.com); (2) P. Berman & L. Goldman, 2003, The billionaire who cracked De Beers, *Forbes*, September 15: 108–115; (3) J. Burns & D. Spa, 2000, Forever: De Beers and U.S. Antitrust Law, Harvard Business School case study 9–700–082; (4) A. Cockburn, 2002, Diamonds: The real story, *National Geographic*, March: 2–35; (4) *Economist*, 2004, Rumors are forever, February 28: 62; (5) *Economist*, 2004, The cartel isn't forever, July 17: 60–62; (6) E. Muller, 2003, De Beers faces second US price-fixing action, *Red Herring*, December 17 (http://www.myneweconomy.com); (7) D. Spa, 1994, The Cooperative Edge: The Internal Politics of International Cartels, Ithaca, NY: Cornell University Press.

part 3

CORPORATE-LEVEL STRATEGIES

chapter 9

DIVERSIFYING, ACQUIRING, AND RESTRUCTURING

Outline

- Product diversification
- Geographic diversification
- Combining product and geographic diversification
- A comprehensive model of diversification
- Acquisitions
- Restructuring
- Debates and extensions
- Implications for strategists

Opening Case: Renault/Nissan and DaimlerChrysler/Mitsubishi: A Tale of Two Acquisitions

As part of the recent restructuring in the global automobile industry, Renault (http://www.renault.com) acquired Nissan (http://www.nissan.co.jp) in 1999 and DaimlerChrysler (http://www.daimlerchrysler.com) acquired Mitsubishi (http://www.mitsubishimotors.com) in 2000. Acquiring these Japanese firms enabled the two European automakers to broaden their geographic scope by expanding to Asia, where they had been weak. The problem was that both Japanese firms, despite their historical glory, had faded brands, awesome debt loads, and uncertain futures.

Although none of these takeovers—called "partnerships" as a euphemism—resulted in 100 percent foreign control (37 percent equity of Nissan and 34 percent of Mitsubishi were sold for $5.4 billion and $2.1 billion to new owners, respectively), foreign managers undoubtedly were in charge now. Specifically, Carlos Ghosn (nicknamed "Le Cost Cutter") and Rolf Eckrodt (nicknamed "Mr. Fix-It") were named CEOs of Nissan and Mitsubishi, respectively, initiating some gut-wrenching restructuring on a scale unheard of in Japan. Since 1999, Ghosn shut down five plants in Japan, reduced the workforce by 23,000 (14 percent of the total—all in Japan),

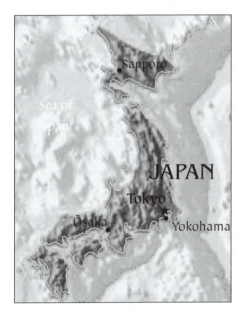

and shifted more production to the United States. Nissan returned to profitability in 2001. Today Nissan boasts one of the best margins in the industry and a number of bold new models.

Since Eckrodt's arrival at Mitsubishi in 2001, he had slashed costs by 15 percent, cut the workforce by 16 percent, and doubled research and development spending from 2000 levels. Yet, critics argued that he and his team could have turned more "stones," such as closing at least one plant in Japan and another in Australia, killing off money-losing models, and cracking down on quality and financing problems. For instance, to help US sales, Mitsubishi resorted to a high-risk financing campaign for consumers—no money down and no payments for a year. The result? Almost half a billion dollars in bad loans.

By 2004, the contrast between the two acquisitions could not have been clearer. In April, Ghosn reported record profits for Nissan, while Eckrodt stepped down at Mitsubishi, which posted a $660 million loss. Even worse, DaimlerChrysler's supervisory board refused to pump in an additional $7 billion to bail out the debt-laden Mitsubishi.

One acquisition succeeded. Another failed. What happened? In the words of Ghosn himself, writing in the Harvard Business Review, *the key was to balance the needs for radical strategic changes and the respect for Nissan's identity and the self-esteem of its employees.*

Those two goals—making changes and safeguarding identity—can easily come into conflict; pursuing them both entails a difficult and sometimes

precarious balancing act. This was particularly true in this case. I was, after all, an outsider—non-Nissan, non-Japanese . . . I knew that if I tried to dictate changes from above, the effort would backfire, undermining morale and productivity. But if I was too passive, the company would simply continue its downward spiral.

On the one hand, Ghosn and his team ditched the time-honored seniority system in Nissan and installed a performance-based promotion system. Not surprisingly, they received a lot of flak for undermining Japanese "culture." On the other hand, they created nine cross-functional teams involving 500 Nissan managers. The teams were not only responsible for coming up with recommendations that became the input for the corporate-wide revival plan, but were also the watchdogs for their implementation. These teams, according to Ghosn, were "my way of making sure that Nissan stays awake."

Sources: Based on (1) B. Bremner, 2004, Japan, Business Week, May 10: 42; (2) Economist, 2004, The wheels come off, May 1: 65–66; (3) C. Ghosn, 2002, Saving the business without losing the company, Harvard Business Review, 80 (1): 37–45; (4) E. Thornton, 1999, Remaking Nissan, Business Week, November 15: 70–76.

Why did Renault and DaimlerChrysler choose to broaden their *geographic* scope by acquiring car companies in Japan? Why didn't they, for example, broaden their *product* scope by acquiring firms in other industries (such as aerospace, weapons, and power systems, as Daimler-Benz had done before)? Why did one acquisition succeed and another fail? What can firms do to improve their odds for successfully diversifying, acquiring, and restructuring? These are some of the strategic questions we will address in this chapter.

Beginning with this chapter, Part III (Chapters 9–12) focuses on **corporate-level strategy** (or, in short, **corporate strategy**), which is how a firm creates value through the configuration and coordination of its multimarket activities.[1] In comparison, Part II (Chapters 5–8) dealt with **business-level strategy,** defined as the way to build competitive advantage in a discrete and identifiable market. While business-level strategy is evidently very important, for larger, multimarket firms, corporate-level strategy is equally or perhaps more important.[2] In other words, an understanding of corporate-level strategy helps us see the "forest," whereas business-level strategy focuses on the "trees."

This chapter concentrates on a key aspect of corporate strategy, **diversification,** which is adding new businesses to the firm that are distinct from its existing operations. Diversification is probably the single most researched, discussed, and debated topic in strategy. Firms can diversify in two ways: (1) **product diversification**—through entries into different product markets and industries, and (2) **geographic diversification**—through entries into different geographic areas such as new regions and countries. Although market entries can entail strategic alliances and green-field investments (see Chapter 6), our focus here is on **mergers and acquisitions (M&As)** and **restructuring.**

We will first introduce product diversification and geographic diversification, followed by a typology of how they intersect. We then develop a comprehensive model drawing on the industry-, resource-, and institution-based perspectives. Acquisitions and restructuring are examined next. As before, debates and extensions follow.

PRODUCT DIVERSIFICATION

Most firms start as small businesses focusing on a single product or service (or a few of them) with little diversification—known as a **single business strategy.** Over time, the firm may embark upon a product diversification strategy with two broad categories discussed in this section.

Product-Related Diversification

Product-related diversification refers to entries into new product markets and/or business activities that are related to a firm's existing markets and/or activities. The emphasis is on **operational synergy** (also known as **scale economies** or **economies of scale**), which is defined as increases in competitiveness beyond what can be achieved by engaging in two product markets and/or business activities separately. In other words, firms benefit from declining unit costs by leveraging product relatedness—that is, $2 + 2 = 5$. The sources of operational synergy can be (1) technologies (such as common platforms), (2) marketing (such as common brands), and (3) manufacturing (such as common logistics).[3] For instance, Northrop Grumman, a defense firm best known for the B-2 stealth bomber, has pursued such a strategy. Although Northrop only entered shipbuilding by acquiring Litton in 2001, it has now become the largest shipbuilder for the US Navy. On its own, Litton did not have the capability to integrate all the high-tech components the Navy wanted on a new class of destroyers, DD(X)—in other words, the unit costs to develop the DD(X) from scratch would be prohibitive. However, as part of Northrop, Litton had access to software, avionics, and the stealth technology from B-2 at much lower costs. Such synergy helped Litton, now a division of Northrop, to secure a lucrative, $3 billion contract to build the DD(X).[4] At present, most product-diversified companies around the world focus on "core competences" that can be leveraged across related industries and markets.

Product-Unrelated Diversification

Product-unrelated diversification refers to entries into industries that have no obvious product-related connections to the firm's current lines of business. For example, General Electric (GE) competes in appliances, lighting fixture, aircraft engines, broadcasting, and financial services. Product-unrelated diversifiers, such as GE, are called **conglomerates,** and their strategy is known as **conglomeration.** Instead of operational synergy, conglomerates focus on **financial synergy** (also known as **scope economies** or **economies of scope**), which is the increase in competitiveness for each individual unit that is financially controlled by the corporate headquarters beyond what can be achieved by each unit competing independently as stand-alone firms.

The motto is the same, $2 + 2 = 5$, but the mechanism to obtain financial synergy is different from operational synergy. Corporate headquarters' key role is to identify and fund profitable investment opportunities. In other words, a conglomerate serves as an **internal capital market** that channels financial resources to high-potential, high-growth areas.[5] Given that active external capital markets try to do the same, a key issue is whether the conglomerate's units in various industries (such as GE's aircraft engine division) outperform their stand-alone, independent competitors in respective industries (such as SNECMA). Stated differently, at issue is whether corporate headquarters can do a *better* job identifying and taking advantage of profitable opportunities than external capital markets can. If conglomerate units beat stand-alone rivals (which is something most GE units consistently do), then there is a **diversification premium** (or **conglomerate advantage**)—in other words, unrelated-product diversification adds value.[6] Otherwise, there can be a **diversification discount** (or **conglomerate disadvantage**) when conglomerate units are better off competing as stand-alone entities (see Closing Case). Shown in Strategy in Action 9.1 on page 363, the sum of the value of the units affiliated with Beatrice, when sold individually, was *larger* than the value of the conglomerate as a whole, a clear indication that in this case, conglomeration destroyed value.

Product Diversification and Firm Performance

The relationship between product diversification and firm performance has received significant attention. Hundreds of studies, mostly conducted in the West, suggest that on average (but not always), performance increases as firms shift from single-business strategies to product-related diversification, but performance decreases as firms change from product-related to product-unrelated diversification—in other words, the linkage seems to be inverted-U shaped (Figure 9.1 on page 364).[7] Essentially "putting all one's eggs in a single basket," single-business strategies can be potentially risky and vulnerable. "Putting one's eggs in different baskets," product-unrelated diversification may reduce risk, but most firms lack the strong capabilities necessary to successfully execute this strategy (discussed later). Consequently, product-related diversification, essentially "putting one's eggs in *similar* baskets," has emerged as a balanced way to both reduce risk and leverage synergy. This finding—first reported by Richard Rumelt in the 1970s—has provided the intellectual

STRATEGY IN ACTION 9.1. *Beatrice: The Rise and Fall of a US Conglomerate*

Founded in rural Nebraska in a town called Beatrice, the firm began as a small dairy producer in 1891. In the next several decades, Beatrice became a leading dairy firm through acquisitions. In 1956, however, the Federal Trade Commission (FTC) charged Beatrice with possessing "excessive" market power, forcing it to divest dairy plants and preventing it from acquiring other dairy firms.

The FTC action forced Beatrice to embark on product-unrelated diversification. By 1975, only 21 percent of its earnings were in dairy. Beatrice established a presence in cold storage, confectionery, bakeries, beverages, home and garden, chemicals, graphic arts, and printing. All targets were private, family-run businesses whose owners (now division managers) were largely left alone as long as financial results were satisfactory. Corporate headquarters did *not* try to integrate the new units and the word "synergy" was *never* used in annual reports from 1952 to 1976. Sales grew from $235 million in 1952 to $5.6 billion in 1976. The return to shareholders averaged more than 14 percent per year and the capital market reacted favorably. By 1976, as a "far-flung conglomerate" (see Figure 9.3 on page 367), Beatrice operated in twenty-seven countries.

Since 1976, with two new CEOs (one from 1976 to 1979 and another from 1979 to 1985), Beatrice moved toward more centralization by organizing the firm into six groups in search of "synergies." The firm unleashed an expensive, corporate-wide "We're Beatrice" marketing campaign. Headquarters staff increased from 161 in 1976 to 750 in 1985. The second CEO also had a tendency to get involved in operational details. In addition,

the acquisition strategy also changed toward making high-profile, expensive acquisitions of publicly traded firms such as Tropicana (1978) and Esmark (1984). Unfortunately, the capital market started to heavily discount Beatrice's stock. Between 1976 and 1985, every acquisition was met with a *reduction* in market value, and a total of $2 billion in market value was destroyed. In 1985, the CEO was forced to resign. Later that year, Beatrice was taken over by a management team advised by a leading corporate raider firm, Kohlberg, Kravis, and Robert (KKR, *http://www.kkr.com*), in the then-largest leveraged buyout (LBO) in history with $1 billion in premium to shareholders. Starting in 1986, Beatrice began to sell off divisions such as Avis and Tropicana. In 1990, the remaining Beatrice sold itself to ConAgra (*http://www.conagrafoods.com*) for $1.3 billion. In all, proceeds from asset sales reached $11.1 billion, which was 19 percent *more* than Beatrice's equity at the time of the LBO ($9.3 billion).

The story of Beatrice (1891–1990) is a fascinating history of the evolution of corporate diversification strategies in the United States in the twentieth century. Beatrice made more than 400 acquisitions and 90 divestitures. The pre-1976 Beatrice created value by acquisitions, the 1976–1985 Beatrice destroyed value by acquisitions, and the post-1986 Beatrice created value by divestitures.

Sources: Based on (1) G. Baker, 1992, Beatrice: A study in the creation and destruction of value, Journal of Finance, 47: 1081–1119; (2) T. Stuart & D. Collis, 1991, Beatrice Companies—1985, Harvard Business School case study.

underpinning for the corporate restructuring movement throughout the West since the 1980s.[8]

However, there are some important caveats concerning product-related diversification. Not all product-related diversifiers outperform product-unrelated diversifiers. In an age of "core competence," the continuous existence and prosperity of conglomerates such as GE, Siemens, and Virgin Group suggest that for a small group of highly capable firms, conglomeration may still add value in developed economies. Moreover, in emerging economies, a conglomeration strategy seems to be persisting, with some units (such as those affiliated with South Korea's Samsung Group, India's

FIGURE 9.1   **Product Diversification and Firm Performance**

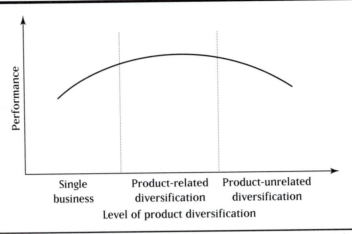

Source: Adapted from *Competing for Advantage, 1st edition* by R. E. Hoskisson, M. A. Hitt, & R. D. Ireland, p. 228. Copyright © 2004. Reprinted with permission of South-Western, a division of Thomson Learning: www.thomsonrights. com <http://www.thomsonrights.com>. Fax (800) 730-2215.

Tata Group, and Turkey's Koc Group) outperforming stand-alone competitors.[9] The reason many conglomerates fail is not because this strategy is inherently unsound, but because firms fail to implement it. Conglomeration calls for corporate managers to impose a strict financial discipline on constituent units and hold unit managers accountable—discipline of the sort GE's former chairman and CEO, Jack Welch, imposed on all divisions: "Either become the world's top one or two in your industry, or expect your unit to be sold." However, most corporate managers are not so "ruthless," and they may tolerate poor performance of some units, which can be subsidized by better units. By robbing the better units to aid the poor ones, corporate managers in essence practice "socialism." Over time, better units may lose their incentive to do well. Eventually, *corporate* performance suffers.

GEOGRAPHIC DIVERSIFICATION

Although geographic diversification can occur within one country (expanding from one city or state to another), in this chapter, we focus on **international diversification,** namely, the number and diversity of countries in which a firm competes (see also Chapter 6).

Limited Versus Extensive International Scope

Geographic diversification has two broad categories. The first is **limited international scope,** such as US firms focusing on NAFTA markets and Spanish firms concentrating on Latin America. The emphasis is on geographically and culturally adjacent countries. Relative to distant countries, entering geographically neighboring and/or historically close countries helps reduce the liability of foreignness (see Chapters 4 and 6 for details).

The second category is **extensive international scope,** maintaining a substantial presence beyond geographically and culturally neighboring countries. For example, the largest market for Honda is North America, with 54 percent of its sales (twice as large as 27 percent of its sales in its home region of Asia). Singapore's Flextronics (see Closing Case in Chapter 1) sells most of its output to North America (38 percent of sales), whereas Asia (home region) only absorbs 22 percent of its sales.[10]

While neighboring countries are not necessarily "easy" markets, success in distant countries obviously calls for a stronger set of competitive advantages to overcome the liability of foreignness there (see Chapter 6). Not surprisingly, most firms—if they internationalize at all—only have a limited degree of internationalization, and only a smaller set are active in a wide range of countries.

Geographic Diversification and Firm Performance

In this age of globalization, the calls for greater geographic diversification are frequent: All firms need to go "global," non-international firms need to start venturing abroad, and firms with a little international presence should widen their geographic scope. Presumably, firms that fail to heed such calls will experience grave ramifications. However, the evidence does *not* fully support this popular view. Based on hundreds of studies, two findings emerge (Figure 9.2).[11] First, at a low level of internationalization, a U-shaped relationship exists between geographic scope and firm performance, which suggests an initially negative effect of international expansion on performance before the positive returns are realized. This stems from the well-known hazard of liability of foreignness (see Chapter 6). Second, at moderate to high levels of internationalization, an inverted-U shape exists that implies a positive relationship between geographic scope and firm performance—but only to a certain extent, beyond which further expansion is again detrimental. In other words, the conventional wisdom suggesting that "the more global, the better" is actually misleading.

FIGURE 9.2   **Geographic Diversification and Firm Performance**

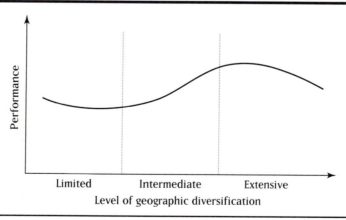

Source: Adapted from F. Contractor, S. K. Kundu, & C.-C. Hsu, 2003, A three stage theory of international expansion: The link between multinationality and performance in the service sector (p. 7), Journal of International Business Studies, 34: 5–18.

Not all firms have been sufficiently involved overseas to experience the ups and downs shown in Figure 9.2. Many studies report a U-shaped relationship because they only sample firms in the early to intermediate stages of internationalization.[12] Small, inexperienced firms are often vulnerable during the initial phase of overseas expansion.[13] On the other hand, many other studies document an inverted-U shape because their samples are biased for larger firms with moderate to high levels of diversification.[14] Many large multinational enterprises (MNEs) have a "flag planting" mentality, bragging about in how many countries they have a presence. However, their performance often suffers, thus necessitating some withdrawals. In 1995, Occidental Petroleum (Oxy) operated in sixteen countries with per-barrel profits a scant $1.20. By 2003, it had operations in only nine countries with per-barrel profits at $6.90, the best in the industry.[15]

Given the complexity, it is hardly surprising that a great debate has emerged on geographic diversification.[16] Shown in Figure 9.2, an intermediate range exists within which firm performance increases with geographic scope, leading some studies that sample firms in this range to conclude that "there is value in internationalization itself because geographic scope is found to be related to higher firm profitability."[17] However, other studies, which sample firms with a high level of geographic scope (such as Oxy), caution that "multinational diversification is apparently less valuable in practice than in theory."[18] Consequently, the recent consensus from the debate is to not only acknowledge the validity of both perspectives, but also to specify conditions under which each perspective (geographic diversification *helps* or *hurts* firm performance) is likely to hold (see Figure 9.2).[19]

COMBINING PRODUCT AND GEOGRAPHIC DIVERSIFICATION

Although most studies focus on a single dimension of diversification (product or geographic), which is already very complex, in practice, most firms (except single-business firms with no desire to internationalize) have to entertain both dimensions of diversification *simultaneously*.[20] Figure 9.3 on next page illustrates the four possible combinations. Firms in Cell 3 are **anchored replicators** because they focus on product-related diversification and a limited geographic scope. Anchored replicators seek to replicate a set of activities in related industries in a small number of countries anchored by the home country. For example, Cardinal Health, the leading US pharmaceutical distributor (seventeenth on the 2003 *Fortune* 500 list), pursues such a strategy (see Integrative Case 3.1).

Firms in Cell 1 are **multinational replicators,** because they engage in product-related diversification on the one hand and far-flung multinational expansion on the other hand. For instance, all the car companies mentioned in the Opening Case, Renault, Nissan, Daimler-Chrysler, and Mitsubishi, have pursued this combination.

Firms in Cell 2 are **far-flung conglomerates,** because they pursue both product-unrelated diversification and extensive geographic diversification. MNEs such as Bombardier, GE, Mitsui, Samsung, Siemens, and Vivendi Universal serve as examples.

Finally, in Cell 4 we find **classic conglomerates,** which engage in product-unrelated diversification within a small set of countries centered on the home

FIGURE 9.3   Combining Product and Geographic Diversification

Product Scope

	Related	Unrelated
Extensive	(Cell 1) *Multinational replicator*	(Cell 2) *Far-flung conglomerate*
Limited	(Cell 3) *Anchored replicator*	(Cell 4) *Classic conglomerate*

Geographic Scope

country. Current examples include India's Tata Group, Turkey's Koc Group, and China's Hope Group.

Overall, firms can strategically migrate from one cell to another, although it is difficult. For instance, most of the current multinational replicators (Cell 1) can trace their roots as anchored replicators (Cell 3). One interesting migratory pattern in the last two decades is that many classic conglomerates in developed economies, such as Denmark's GN Great Northern (see Integrative Case 1.1) and Sweden's Electrolux, which formerly dominated their home countries, have reduced their product scope, but significantly expanded their geographic scope—in other words, migrating from Cell 4 to Cell 1.[21] Further, asserting that firms in a particular cell will outperform those in other cells is naïve if not foolhardy. The fact is that in *every* cell, we can find both highly successful and highly unsuccessful firms. Next, we explore why this is the case.

A COMPREHENSIVE MODEL OF DIVERSIFICATION

Why do firms diversify? How can they increase the odds for success? The three leading perspectives—industry-, resource-, and institution-based views—address these questions individually and in combination, leading to a comprehensive model of diversification (Figure 9.4 on page 368).

Industry-Based Considerations

A straightforward motivation for diversification is the growth opportunities in an industry. If an industry has substantial growth opportunities (such as biotechnology), most incumbent firms have an incentive to engage in product-related diversification and/or international diversification. However, in a "sunset" industry (such as typewriters) in which most incumbents have a poor performance, some

FIGURE 9.4   A Comprehensive Model of Diversification

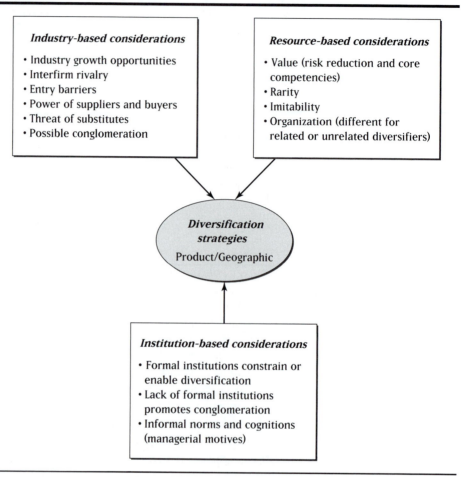

(or even most) incumbents may exit and pursue opportunities elsewhere through product-unrelated diversification.[22] Instead of exiting, some incumbents may engage in international diversification, by extending the life cycle of certain products in other countries. For example, while Kodak has been phasing out chemical-based photo films in developed economies, it is still aggressively marketing these films in low-income countries.

In addition to growth opportunities, the structural attractiveness of an industry, captured by the Porter five forces, also has a significant bearing on diversification. Recall that the first force, interfirm rivalry, is primarily manifested through two competitive strategies: cost leadership and differentiation. Pursuing each strategy may motivate firms to diversify. A cost leadership strategy may encourage firms to seek opportunities for product-related diversification. For example, PepsiCo, a cost leader, recently diversified into sports drinks. When demand for carbonated beverages, such as Pepsi and Mountain Dew, flattened out (at least in the United States),

PepsiCo's considerable distribution capabilities could find some synergy by adding the newly acquired Gatorade products. A differentiation strategy can also lead to product-related diversification. For instance, most of us saw the one-and-only (differentiated) Disney movie *Lion King*. Little did we know that Disney unleashed a total of 150 (!) related products based on *Lion King* (such as children's books, toys, mugs, and theme park attractions) and made $3 billion.

Second, the height of entry barriers does not always deter new entrants. For entrants determined to diversify their portfolio by entering the focal industry or country, high entry barriers often result in acquisitions as opposed to green-field entries. Acquiring an existing incumbent to gain immediate market access is usually the most efficient way to overcome entry barriers. For example, in 1980, foreign tire makers such as France's Michelin, Germany's Continental, and Japan's Bridgestone had less than 5 percent of the US market share, all through exports. By 1990, they controlled 60 percent of the US market through acquisitions.[23]

Bargaining power of suppliers and buyers, the third and fourth of the Porter five forces, respectively, may prompt firms to broaden their scope by acquiring suppliers upstream and/or buyers downstream. Such moves, as part of product-related diversification (some of which may be undertaken internationally), are motivated by the quest for market power. For example, Sony, diversifying downstream, has now become a leading player in movies and music.

The threat of substitute products, the last of the Porter forces, also has a bearing on diversification. An industry whose products can be easily substituted faces more threats from other firms currently not in the same industry. Kodak and Fuji have been directly threatened by electronics firms such as Sony, Samsung, and HP, which have all diversified into digital cameras. Until recently, Kodak and Fuji did not regard any of these electronics firms as competitors.

The industry-based view, by definition, has largely focused on product-related diversification with an industry focus (often in combination with geographic diversification). However, one important point, beyond the industry focus, is that all industries have the potential to be involved in product-*unrelated* diversification. Even for some of the structurally unattractive industries (such as airlines) where some incumbents are exiting by selling their assets, bear in mind that the fact that these assets find outside buyers shows that there are firms willing to enter these "unattractive" industries. For instance, a British conglomerate, Virgin Group, planned to launch a new discount airline, Virgin America, in the crowded US airline industry in 2005.[24]

Resource-Based Considerations

Shown in Figure 9.4, the resource-based view—outlined by the VRIO framework—has a set of complementary considerations underpinning diversification strategies.

Value

Does diversification, in its various forms and shapes, create value? The answer is "Yes," but only under certain conditions.[25] Compared with nondiversified, single-business firms, diversified firms are able to spread risk over several (product and country) markets. Even for overdiversified firms that have to restructure, no one is returning to a pure, single business with no diversification. The optimal point has always been some moderate level of diversification.

Beyond reducing risk, diversification can create value by leveraging certain core competencies, resources, and capabilities.[26] Honda, for instance, is renowned for its product-related diversification by leveraging its core competence in internal combustion engines. It not only competes in automobiles and motorcycles, but also in boat engines and lawn mowers. More recently, Honda has attempted to enter the small jet aircraft market. In another example, Denmark's International Service System (ISS) leveraged capabilities in cleaning and sterilizing slaughterhouses to enter the hospital services industry.[27]

Rarity

For diversification (in whatever form) to add value, firms must have unique skills to execute such a strategy. While many firms undertake acquisitions, a much smaller number of firms have mastered the art of post-acquisition integration. Consequently, firms that excel at integration, such as Ispat (see Closing Case in Chapter 3), possess *rarer* capabilities. For example, at Northrop (discussed earlier in this chapter), integrating acquired businesses is down to a "science." Each must conform to a carefully orchestrated plan of integration listing nearly 400 items, from how press releases should be issued to which accounting software to use. Unlike its bigger defense rivals such as Boeing and Raytheon, Northrop thus far has not stumbled with any of its acquisitions.

Imitability

Even when capabilities are valuable and rare, if rivals are able to imitate certain skills, then such skills cannot be a basis for competitive advantage. For this reason, Cardinal Health, a leader in manufacturing generic medicine and medical supplies (such as syringes), is now manufacturing pre-filled syringes (see Integrative Case 3.1). Both steps, making medicine and making syringes, are complex. Combining the two to make pre-filled syringes—a form of product-related diversification—raises the bar for rivals. Therefore, to make the pre-filled syringes safe and profitable becomes a hard-to-imitate capability.[28] In another example, Siderar, a recently privatized integrated steel producer in Argentina, outsourced "non-core" activities such as operating the port, oxygen plant, and thermoelectric facility, which could be easily imitated by rivals. By reducing its product scope, Siderar focused on harder-to-imitate activities (such as slab casting) and significantly improved its financial performance.[29]

Organization

Fundamentally, whether diversification adds value boils down to how firms are organized to take advantage of the benefits while minimizing the costs. Since Chapter 10 is devoted to organizational issues in international diversification, here we focus on product diversification. Given the recent popularity of product-related diversification, many people believe that product-unrelated diversification is an inherently value-destroying strategy. However, this is not true. With proper organization, product-unrelated diversification can add value.

TABLE 9.1   **Product-Related and Product-Unrelated Diversification**

	PRODUCT-RELATED DIVERSIFICATION	PRODUCT-UNRELATED DIVERSIFICATION
Synergy	Operational synergy	Financial synergy
Economies	Economies of scale	Economies of scope
Control emphasis	Strategic (behavior) control	Financial (output) control
Organizational structure	Centralization	Decentralization
Organizational culture	Cooperative	Competitive
Information processing	Intensive, rich communication	Less intensive communication

Shown in Table 9.1, product-related diversifiers need to foster a centralized organizational structure with a cooperative culture.[30] The key is to explore the operational links among various units, necessitating some units to be pulled back to coordinate with other units. For example, in order to maximize corporate profits when producing the movie *Lion King*, Disney's animation division had to wait before launching the movie until its merchandise divisions were ready to hawk related merchandise simultaneously. If the animation managers' bonuses were linked to the annual box-office receipts of the movie, they would obviously be eager to release the movie. But if bonuses were linked with overall corporate profits, then animation managers would be happy to assist and coordinate with their merchandise colleagues and would not mind waiting. Consequently, corporate headquarters should not evaluate division performance solely based on strict financial targets (such as sales). The principal control mechanism is **strategic control** (or **behavior control**), based on largely subjective criteria to monitor and evaluate the units' contributions with rich communication between corporate and divisional managers.

However, the best way to organize conglomerates is exactly the *opposite*. The emphasis is on **financial control** (or **output control**), based on largely objective criteria (such as return on investment) to monitor and evaluate the units' performance. Because most corporate managers have experience in only one industry (or a few) and none realistically can be an expert in the wide variety of unrelated industries represented in a conglomerate, corporate headquarters is forced to focus on financial control, which does not require a lot of rich, industry-specific knowledge. Otherwise, corporate managers will experience a tremendous **information overload** (too much information to process). Consequently, the appropriate organizational structure is decentralization with substantial divisional autonomy. To keep divisional managers focused on financial performance, their compensation should be directly linked with quantifiable unit performance. Thus, the relationship among various divisions is competitive, each trying to attract a larger share of the corporate investments. Such competition within an internal capital market is similar to stand-alone firms competing for more funds from the external capital market. The Virgin Group, for example, considers itself "a branded venture-capital firm" whose portfolio includes airlines, railways, beverages, and music stores. The corporate headquarters supplies a common brand (Virgin) and leaves divisional managers "alone" as long as they deliver sound performance.

Overall, the key to adding value through either product-related or product-unrelated diversification is the appropriate match between diversification strategy and organizational structure and control.[31] Conglomerates often fail when corporate managers impose a more centralized structure undermining lower-level autonomy (see Strategy in Action 9.1).

Institution-Based Considerations

Given that a combination of formal and informal institutions drive firm strategies such as diversification, we examine each set of institutions in turn in the following sections.

Formal Institutions

Formal institutions affect both product and geographic diversification. Formal institutional constraints designed to curtail product-related diversification inadvertently promoted the rise of conglomerates in the 1950s and 1960s in developed economies. In the United States, the post-1950 antitrust authorities viewed product-related diversification (especially through mergers) that was designed to enhance firms' market power within a broad industry as "anticompetitive" and challenged these firms (see Strategy in Action 9.1). Consequently, firms seeking growth (such as Beatrice) were forced to look beyond their primary industry, thus triggering a great wave of conglomeration. Interestingly, by the 1980s, the US government changed its mind and no longer critically scrutinized related mergers within the same industry. It is not a coincidence that the movement to dismantle conglomerates and focus on core competencies has taken off since the 1980s.

Similarly, the popularity of conglomeration in emerging economies is often underpinned by their governments' protectionist policies. Conglomerates (often called **business groups** in emerging economies) can leverage their connections with governments by obtaining licenses, arranging financial packages (often from state-owned or -controlled banks), securing technology, hiring and training labor forces, and establishing supply and distribution channels. As long as protectionist policies prevent significant foreign entries, these conglomerates can dominate domestic economies. However, when governments start to dismantle protectionist policies, competitive pressures from foreign multinationals (as well as domestic nondiversified rivals) may intensify. With markets opening, poorly performing conglomerates (or their units) may be acquired by foreign MNEs (see Chapter 11). These changes may force conglomerates to improve performance by reducing their scope (see Closing Case).[32]

Likewise, the significant rise of geographic diversification undertaken by numerous firms can be attributed, at least in part, to the gradual opening of many economies initiated by formal, market-supporting and market-opening policy changes (see Chapters 1, 4, and 6 for details).

Informal Institutions

Informal institutions can be found along normative and cognitive dimensions. Normatively, managers often try to behave in ways that will not be noticed as different and consequently singled out for criticism by shareholders, board directors, and the media. Therefore, when the norm is to engage in conglomeration, more and more managers may simply follow such a norm. Poorly performing firms are especially under such normative pressures. While early movers in conglomeration (such as GE) may indeed have special skills and insights to make such a complex strategy work, many late movers probably do not have these capabilities and simply jump on the "bandwagon" with poor performance.[33] Over time, this explains—at least partially—the massive disappointment with conglomeration in developed economies. Likewise, the rush to certain "hot" countries and regions, such as Latin America in the 1980s, Southeast Asia in the 1990s (prior to 1997), Mexico in the 1990s, and China in the 2000s, seems to be largely driven by an interest in following the norm (or the "fad"). Not surprisingly, many firms are not prepared to deal with these challenges and are burned.

Another informal driver for conglomeration is the cognitive dimension, namely, the internalized beliefs that guide managerial behavior.[34] Managers may have motives to advance their personal interests, which are not necessarily aligned with the interests of the firm and its shareholders. These are called **managerial motives** for diversification, such as (1) reducing managers' employment risk and (2) pursuing power, prestige, and income. Because single-business firms are often subject to the economy-wide ups and downs (such as recessions), managers' jobs and careers may be vulnerable. Therefore, managers often want to diversify their firms to reduce their own employment risk. In addition, because managerial power, prestige, and income are typically associated with a larger firm size, some managers may have self-interested incentives to overdiversify their firms, resulting in value destruction. Excessive diversification is often called **empire building.** Because formal **corporate governance** mechanisms (see Chapter 11) cannot completely regulate the numerous managerial actions that are largely guided by informal managerial cognitions, there is always some potential for empire building.[35]

In summary, the institution-based view suggests that formal and informal institutional conditions directly shape diversification strategy.[36] Taken together, the industry-, resource-, and institution-based views collectively explain how the scope of the firm evolves around the world, as introduced next.

The Evolution of the Scope of the Firm[37]

At its core, diversification as a strategic choice is essentially driven by economic benefits and bureaucratic costs. **Economic benefits** are the various forms of synergy (operational or financial) discussed earlier. **Bureaucratic costs** are the additional costs associated with a larger, more diversified organization, such as more employees and more expensive information systems. Overall, it is the difference between the benefits and costs that leads to certain diversification strategies. Since the economic benefits of the last unit of growth (such as the last acquisition) can be defined as **marginal economic benefits** (MEB) and the additional bureaucratic costs incurred as **marginal bureaucratic costs** (MBC), the scope of the firm is thus determined by a comparison between MEB and MBC.[38] Shown in Figure 9.5 on next page, the

FIGURE 9.5   What Determines the Scope of the Firm?

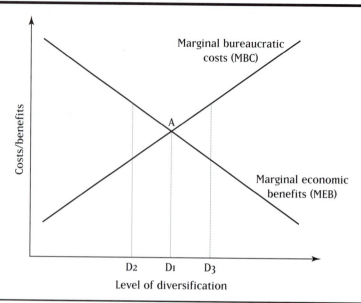

Source: Adapted from G. Jones & C. Hill, 1988, Transaction cost analysis of strategy-structure choices (p. 166), Strategic Management Journal, 9: 159–172. Reprinted by permission of John Wiley & Sons Limited.

optimal scope is at point A, where the appropriate level of diversification should be D_1. If the level of diversification is D_2, there are some economic benefits to gain by moving up to D_1. Conversely, if a firm overdiversifies to D_3, reducing the scope to D_1 becomes necessary. As a result, by focusing on MEB and MBC we can analyze how the scope of the firm in various countries evolves over time.

In the United States (Figure 9.6) between the 1950s and 1970s, if we assume MBC to be constant (an assumption relaxed later), the MEB curve shifted upward, resulting in an expanded scope of the firm on average (moving from D_1 to D_2). This is because (1) formal institutions such as antitrust policies blocked growth opportunities within the same industry through product-related diversification (especially for large firms), (2) organizational capabilities emerged to derive financial synergy from conglomeration, and (3) these actions diffused through imitation, which led to an informal, but visible, norm among managers that such growth was legitimate. During that time, external capital markets, which were less sophisticated compared with what they are now, were supportive, believing that conglomerates had an advantage in allocating capital (see Strategy in Action 9.1).

However, by the early 1980s, significant transitions occurred along industry, resource, and institutional dimensions. First, the government no longer critically scrutinized M&As within the same industry. Second, a resource-based analysis suggested that given the VRIO hurdles, it would be extremely challenging—although not impossible—to derive competitive advantage from conglomeration (discussed earlier). In other words, with the firm's expanded scope, MBC also increased, often outpacing the increase in MEB (Figure 9.6). Many firms (such as Beatrice)

FIGURE 9.6   **The Evolution of the Scope of the Firm in the United States: 1950–1970 and 1970–1990**

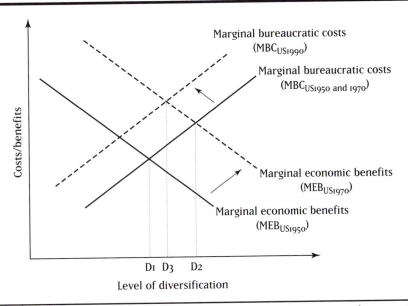

Source: M. W. Peng, S.-H. Lee, & D. Wang, "What determines the scope of the firm over time? A focus on institutional relatedness" from Academy of Management Review. Copyright © 2005. Reprinted by permission of Academy of Management Review via Copyright Clearance Center.

over-diversified and destroyed value. Consequently, there was a dramatic reversal in US investor sentiment toward conglomeration: Positive in the 1960s, neutral in the 1970s, and negative in the 1980s (Strategy in Action 9.1).[39] Parallel to these developments, external capital markets became better developed, with more analysts, more accessible databases, and more transparent and real-time reporting, all of which allowed financial resources to be channeled more efficiently to high-potential firms. As a result, the conglomerate advantage of serving as an internal capital market became less attractive. Finally, informal norms and cognitions changed, as managers increasingly became more disciplined and focused on shareholder value maximization and believed that reducing the scope of the firm was the "right" thing to do. All these factors combined to push the appropriate scope of the firm from D_2 to D_3 in Figure 9.6 by the 1990s.

Globally, an interesting extension to this discussion is the puzzle of why conglomeration, which has been recently discredited in developed economies, is not only in vogue, but also in some (although not all) cases adds value in emerging economies at present. Figure 9.7 (p. 376) shows how conglomerates in emerging economies may add value at a higher level of diversification, whereby firms in developed economies are not able to do so. This analysis relies on two critical and reasonable assumptions. The first is that at a given level of diversification, $MEB_{EmergingEcon} > MEB_{DevelopedEcon}$. This is primarily because of underdeveloped external capital markets in emerging economies, which make conglomerates more attractive as internal capital markets.[40]

FIGURE 9.7   **The Optimal Scope of the Firm: Developed versus Emerging Economies at the Same Time**

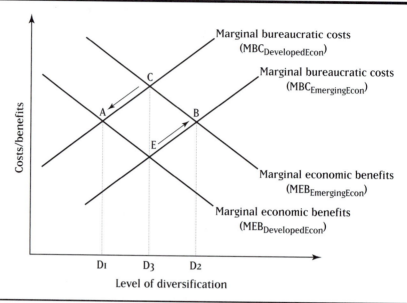

Source: M. W. Peng, S.-H. Lee, & D. Wang, 2005, "What determines the scope of the firm over time? A focus on institutional relatedness" from Academy of Management Review. Copyright © 2005. Reprinted by permission of Academy of Management Review via Copyright Clearance Center.

A second assumption is that at a given level of diversification, $\text{MBC}_{\text{EmergingEcon}} <$ $\text{MBC}_{\text{DevelopedEcon}}$. Because of the weaknesses of formal market-supporting institutions in emerging economies, informal constraints play a *larger* role in regulating economic exchanges (see Chapter 4). Most conglomerates in these countries are family firms, whose managers rely more on informal personal (and often family) relationships to get things done. Relative to firms in developed economies, firms in emerging economies typically are less bureaucratic, less formal, and less professional, which may result in lower bureaucratic costs.

Consequently, for any scope between D_1 and D_2 (such as D_3) in Figure 9.7, while firms in developed economies at point C need to be downscoped toward point A (D_1), firms in emerging economies can still gain room at point E, which can move up to point B (D_2). However, bear in mind that conglomerates in emerging economies confront the same problem that plagues those in developed economies: The wider the scope, the harder it is for corporate headquarters to coordinate, control, and invest properly in different units. Evidently, for conglomerates in emerging economies, there is also a point beyond which further diversification may backfire. The conglomerate advantage is especially likely to be eroded when external capital markets in emerging economies become better developed.[41] The Closing Case, on South Korean *chaebols*, provides some details about the perils of overdiversification.

Overall, industry dynamics, resource repertoires, and institutional conditions are not static, nor are diversification strategies. The next two sections describe two primary means for expanding and contracting firm scope—through acquisitions and restructuring, respectively.

ACQUISITIONS

A major means of diversification, along both product and geographic dimensions, is acquisitions. Therefore, this section first sets straight the terms used and then introduces motives for M&As. This is followed by a discussion on M&A performance and some suggestions for improving the odds for success.

Setting the Terms Straight

Although the term **mergers and acquisitions (M&As)** is often used, in reality, acquisitions dominate the scene. An **acquisition** is the transfer of control of assets, operations, and management from one firm (target) to another (acquirer), the former becoming a unit of the latter. For example, Compaq is now a unit of HP (see Video Case 3.1). A **merger** is the combination of assets, operations, and management of two firms to establish a new legal entity. For instance, the merger between South African Brewery and Miller Beer resulted in SABMiller. Internationally, only approximately 3 percent of cross-border M&As are mergers. Even many so-called "mergers of equals" turn out to be one firm taking over another (such as Daimler-Chrysler). A recent *World Investment Report* published by the United Nations opines that "the number of 'real' mergers is so low that, for practical purposes, 'M&As' basically mean 'acquisitions'."[42] Consequently, we will use the two terms, "M&As" and "acquisitions," interchangeably.

Specifically, we focus on **cross-border (international) M&As,** whose various types are illustrated in Figure 9.8 (p. 378). This is not only because of our global focus in this book, but also because of (1) the high percentage of international deals among all M&As and (2) the high percentage of M&As among foreign direct investment (FDI) flows.[43] Globally, cross-border activities represent approximately 30 percent of all M&As and in some countries (such as Australia) they exceed domestic M&As.[44] M&As represent the largest proportion of FDI flows, reaching 80 percent of global FDI by the late 1990s (down to 60 percent more recently due to recessions).

The three primary categories of M&As are (1) horizontal, (2) vertical, and (3) conglomerate. First, **horizontal M&As** refer to deals involving competing firms in the same industry (such as BP/Amoco).[45] Approximately 70 percent of the cross-border M&As are horizontal. Second, **vertical M&As,** another form of product-related diversification, are deals that allow the focal firms to acquire suppliers (upstream) and/or buyers (downstream) (such as Sony/Columbia Pictures). Approximately 10 percent of cross-border M&As are vertical. Finally, **conglomerate M&As** are transactions involving firms in product-unrelated industries (such as Vivendi/Universal). Approximately 20 percent of cross-border M&As are conglomerate deals.

The terms of M&As can be friendly or hostile. In **friendly M&As,** the board and management of a target firm agree to the transaction (although they may initially resist). **Hostile M&As**—also known as **hostile takeovers**—are undertaken against the wishes of the target firm's board and management, who reject M&A offers. Domestically, especially in the United States, hostile M&As are more frequent, reaching

FIGURE 9.8   **Types of Cross-Border Mergers and Acquisitions**

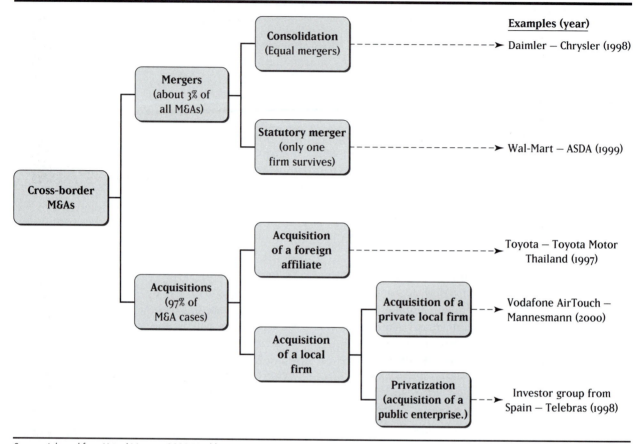

Source: Adapted from United Nations, 2000, World Investment Report 2000 *(p. 100), New York: UN*

14 percent of all deals in the 1980s (although the number went down to 4 percent in the 1990s). Internationally, hostile M&As are very rare, accounting for less than 0.2 percent of all deals and less than 5 percent of total value. In Germany and Japan, for example, hostile takeovers until recently had been considered taboo. Not surprisingly, despite their rarity, hostile takeovers, such as Vodafone AirTouch's takeover of Mannesman in 2000 (see Strategy in Action 9.2 on next page and Video Case 3.2), tend to be emotional and high profile, provoking significant debates.

Motives for Mergers and Acquisitions

At the most fundamental level, we can identify three drivers for M&As: (1) synergistic, (2) hubris, and (3) managerial motives, which can be illustrated by the industry-, resource-, and institution-based perspectives (Table 9.2 on next page). In terms of synergistic motives, the most frequently mentioned industry-based rationale for M&As is to enhance and consolidate market power.[46] For example, after a series of M&As in three years (such as Daimler/Chrysler, Renault/Nissan, and

STRATEGY IN ACTION 9.2. *Vodafone AirTouch Takes Over Mannesman*

In November 1999, the world's largest mobile phone group, Britain's Vodafone AirTouch (*http://www. vodafone.co.uk*), announced a $130 billion takeover bid for its German alliance partner and rival, Mannesmann (*http://www.mannesmann.com*). Vodafone AirTouch itself was the result of a $66 billion merger between Vodafone and AirTouch of the United States (*http://www.airtouch.com*) completed only in January 1999. Vodafone and Mannesman had a series of joint ventures in Europe and a gentlemen's agreement not to compete in each other's home market. However, in October 1999, Mannesman broke this understanding by acquiring Orange (*http://www.orange.co.uk*), Vodafone's rival in Britain. Seeing the Orange acquisition as a kick in its teeth, Vodafone decided to act.

No foreign firm had previously succeeded in a hostile takeover in Germany. The response in Germany was predictable. Worker unions were outraged. Media sensationalized the perils of such "global business cannibalism." German Chancellor Gerard Shroeder accused hostile takeovers of being "always negative." The British response was equally one-sided. British Prime Minister Tony Blair rejected Shroeder's claim as "exaggerated" and inconsistent with the principles of European market integration. In the final analysis, Mannesman was

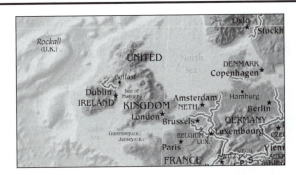

not really "German"—non-German shareholders held two-thirds of its shares. In February 2000, citing that "the shareholders have decided," Mannesmann's managers conceded—but also successfully raised the transaction value to $203 billion, which represented 6 percent of the *combined* GDP of Great Britain and Germany.

Sources: Based on (1) R. Monks & N. Minow, 2001, Corporate Governance, 2nd ed. (pp. 285–286), Oxford, UK: Blackwell; (2) J. F. Weston, M. Mitchell, & J. H. Mulherin, 2003, Takeovers, Restructuring, and Corporate Governance, 4th ed. (pp. 480–482), Upper Saddle River, NJ: Pearson Prentice Hall.

TABLE 9.2   Motives Behind Mergers and Acquisitions

	INDUSTRY-BASED ISSUES	RESOURCE-BASED ISSUES	INSTITUTION-BASED ISSUES
Synergistic motives	▪ Enhance and consolidate market power ▪ Overcome entry barriers ▪ Reduce risk ▪ Scope economies	▪ Leverage superior managerial capabilities ▪ Access to complementary resources ▪ Learning and developing new skills	▪ Respond to formal institutional constraints and transitions ▪ Take advantage of market opening and globalization
Hubris motives		▪ Managers' over-confidence in their capabilities	▪ Herd behavior—following norms and chasing fads of M&As
Managerial motives			▪ Self-interested actions such as empire-building guided by informal norms and cognitions

STRATEGY IN ACTION 9.3. *L'Oreal Acquires Mininurse*

L'Oreal (*http://www.loreal.com*) is the global leader in the cosmetics industry with $17 billion in sales in 2002. It has been operating in China since 1997. Although sales in China amounted to less than 1 percent of global sales ($140 million in 2002), the country is one of the fastest growing markets, with a 66 percent growth in 2003. In China, L'Oreal has dominated high- and medium-end markets. However, the toughest nut to crack seems to be the vast mass market. Consequently, in 2003 L'Oreal acquired Mininurse, a local entrepreneurial firm launched in 1992 ($49 million sales in 2003). Mininurse was one of the top three skincare brands in China with a 5 percent market share and 280,000 distribution outlets. In comparison, L'Oreal only had 12,000 such outlets in China. This acquisition would not only enable L'Oreal to possess a successful mass market brand, but also access more distribution outlets to push its other brands in second- and third-tier Chinese cities.

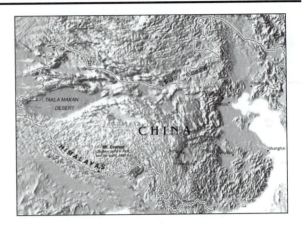

Sources: Based on (1) L. Kressmann, 2003, China: Acquisition of Mininurse brand, http://www.loreal.com, December 11 (accessed May 25, 2004); (2) P. Morris, 2004, Watch out China, the Avon Lady may come calling, Asia Times, February 20 (http://www.atimes.com, accessed May 25, 2004).

Ford/Jaguar), the top ten automakers increased their global market share from 69 percent in 1996 to 80 percent in 1999.[47] The 2004 merger between Air France and KLM Royal Dutch Airlines created the world's largest airline group. These horizontal acquisitions not only eliminate rivals, but also reduce redundant assets and excess capacity.

From a resource-based perspective, the most important synergistic rationale is to leverage superior organizational resources.[48] Another M&A driver is to access complementary resources that can facilitate organizational learning.[49] For instance, because L'Oreal, which dominates the high- and medium-end cosmetics markets in China, does not know how to tackle the vast mass market there, it recently acquired a local mass-market leader, Mininurse (see Strategy in Action 9.3).

From an institution-based perspective, M&As are often a response to formal institutional constraints and transitions.[50] As noted earlier, both the rise of conglomeration in the 1950s and its fall in the 1980s correspond to the tightening and loosening of US antitrust policies governing horizontal M&As, respectively. In addition, acquisitions are often embarked upon to take advantage of opportunities associated with market opening (such as privatization).[51] For instance, by making some twenty acquisitions (mostly privatizations), two leading Spanish banks with little prior international experience, Santander and Bilbao Vizcaya, became the largest foreign banks in Latin America in less than a decade (the 1990s) (see Integrative Case 3.2). Acquisitions in developed countries and acquisitions in emerging economies are markedly different. In developed economies, three-fourths of FDI inflows are typically through acquisitions, whereas in emerging economies, about one-third of such inflows are based on acquisitions. This difference largely stems from (1) the fewer worthy target firms to acquire in emerging economies and (2) the relatively underdeveloped nature of the market for corporate control there.

While all the synergistic motives add value (in theory at least), hubris and managerial motives, unfortunately, may reduce value. **Hubris** refers to managers' over-confidence in their capabilities.[52] Managers of acquiring firms make two very strong statements.[53] The first is that "We can manage *your* assets better than you [the target firm managers] can!" The second statement is even bolder. Given that acquirers of publicly listed firms always have to pay an **acquisition premium** (the difference between the acquisition price and the market value of target firms), this essentially says: "We are smarter than the market!" To the extent that the external capital market is (relatively) efficient and that the market price of target firms is a true reflection of their intrinsic value, there is simply no hope to profit from such acquisitions. Even when we assume the capital market to be inefficient, it is still apparent that when the premium is too high, acquiring firms must have overpaid.[54] Especially when multiple firms are bidding for the same target, the winning acquirer may suffer from "the winner's curse" of auctions; that is, the winner has a tendency to overpay. From an institution-based perspective, many managers are motivated to join the acquisition "bandwagon" when some first-mover firms start doing some deals in an industry.[55] The fact that M&As come in "waves" speaks volumes about such a "herd behavior." During each "wave," early movers in M&As may have spent a lot of time and resources in performing due diligence.[56] Late movers, eager to catch up, may be prompted by a "Wow! Get it!" mentality, sometimes putting together a major deal in as little as a week.[57] Not surprisingly, many such deals turn out to be busts.

While the hubris motives suggest that managers may *unknowingly* overpay for targets, **managerial motives** posit that for self-interested reasons, some managers may have *knowingly* overpaid acquisition premiums for target firms. Driven by self-interested norms and cognitions to reduce employment risk and build "empires" (discussed earlier), some managers may have deliberately overdiversified their firms through M&As in their quest for more power, prestige, and money—these are known as **agency problems** (see Chapter 11 for details).[58]

Overall, synergistic motives add value, and hubris and managerial motives destroy value. Both these positive and negative motives may *simultaneously* coexist.[59] Next, we discuss how they impact performance.

Performance

Despite the popularity of M&As, their performance record is rather sobering. As many as 70 percent of M&As reportedly fail. On average, the acquiring firms' performance does not improve after acquisitions and is often negatively affected.[60] Target firms, after being acquired and becoming internal units, often perform worse than when they were independent, stand-alone firms.[61] The only identifiable winners are the shareholders of target firms, who may experience on average a

TABLE 9.3   **Symptoms of Merger and Acquisition Failures**

	PROBLEMS FOR ALL M&As	PARTICULAR PROBLEMS FOR CROSS-BORDER M&As
Pre-acquisition: Overpayment for targets	▪ Managers overestimate their ability to create value ▪ Inadequate pre-acquisition screening ▪ Poor strategic fit	▪ Lack of familiarity with foreign cultures, institutions, and business systems ▪ Inadequate number of worthy targets ▪ Nationalistic concerns against foreign takeovers (political and media levels)
Post-acquisition: Failure in integration	▪ Poor organizational fit ▪ Failure to address multiple stakeholder groups' concerns	▪ Clashes of organizational cultures compounded by clashes of national cultures ▪ Nationalistic concerns against foreign takeovers (firm and employee levels)

24 percent increase in their stock value during the period of the transaction (thanks to the acquisition premium).[62] Shareholders of acquiring firms experience a 4 percent loss of their stock value during the same period. The combined wealth of shareholders of both acquiring and target firms is marginally positive, less than 2 percent.[63] While these findings are mostly from three decades of M&A data in the United States (where half of the global M&As take place and most of the M&A research is done), they probably also apply to cross-border acquisitions.[64]

Why do many acquisitions fail? Problems can be identified in both pre- and post-acquisition phases (Table 9.3). During the pre-acquisition phase, because of executive hubris and/or managerial motives, acquiring firms may overpay for targets—in other words, they fall into a "synergy trap."[65] For example, in 1998, when Chrysler was profitable, Daimler-Benz paid $40 billion, a 40 percent premium over market value, to acquire Chrysler. Given that Chrysler's expected performance was already built into its existing share price at a *zero* premium, Daimler-Benz's willingness to pay such a high premium was indicative of (1) strong managerial capabilities to derive synergy, (2) high levels of hubris, or (3) significant managerial self-interests—or all of the above. As it turned out, the US (and the global) economy entered a recession, and Chrysler suffered from severe sales drops. Whatever synergy there was, it fell far short of the required performance improvements priced into the 40 percent acquisition premium (see Opening Case in Chapter 11).

Another primary pre-acquisition problem is inadequate screening and failure to achieve **strategic fit,** which is about the effective matching of complementary strategic capabilities. In the rush to preempt or follow competitors, many firms fail to achieve strategic fit. For example, the 1999 acquisition (claimed as a "merger") of Sweden's Astra by Britain's Zeneca—both in the pharmaceutical industry—might lack strategic fit. While the combined firm had greater scale economies, both had a large number of soon-to-expire patents that would no longer serve as entry barriers to deter generic drug manufacturers in the early twenty-first century.[66]

Because of greater institutional and cultural distances internationally, pre-acquisition problems can be even worse. Also, in oligopolistic industries (such as automobiles and pharmaceuticals) with fewer worthy targets, other firms may feel an urgency to "rush in" without adequately considering crucial strategic fit issues once rivals start to "cherry pick" targets. In addition, nationalistic concerns against foreign acquisitions may erupt. This is not only confined to the less developed economies. For example, when Japanese firms acquired Rockefeller Center and Hollywood studios in the 1980s and 1990s, the US media reacted with indignation—remember the movie, *The Rising Sun*?

During the post-acquisition phase, numerous integration problems may pop up. Even when the acquiring firms have paid attention to strategic fit, it is important to also consider **organizational fit,** which is the similarity in cultures, systems, and structures.[67] One study reported that a striking 80 percent of acquiring firms do *not* analyze organizational fit with targets.[68] For instance, on paper, Daimler-Benz and Chrysler were a good strategic fit both in terms of complementary product lines and geographic scope, but there seemed to be inadequate organizational fit. American managers resented the dominance of German managers, who promised the deal would be a "merger of equals." German top executives disliked being paid two-thirds less than their Chrysler colleagues (see Opening Case in Chapter 11). These cultural clashes led to a mass exodus of American managers leaving Chrysler—a common phenomenon in acquired firms.[69]

Another issue is the failure to address multiple stakeholders' concerns during integration, which involves job losses, restructured responsibilities, diminished power, and much else that is stressful. Shown in Figure 9.9, a variety of stakeholders, such as investors and customers as well as employees at all levels, have substantial concerns during M&As. Most companies focus on task issues (such as standardizing

FIGURE 9.9   Stakeholders' Concerns During Mergers and Acquisitions

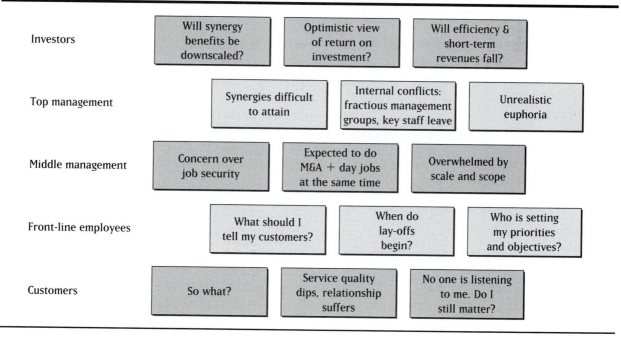

financial reporting) first, and pay inadequate attention to people issues, resulting in low morale and high turnover, especially among their best talents.[70]

In cross-border M&As, integration difficulties may be much worse because organizational culture clashes are compounded by national culture clashes.[71] When Four Seasons acquired a hotel in Paris, the simple "American" request that employees smile at customers was resisted by French employees and laughed at by the local media as "la culture Mickey Mouse."[72] After Clifford Chance, a London law firm, acquired New York's Rogers & Wells in 1999, nineteen of the top American partners left. The reason? Rogers & Wells, like most American law firms, used an "eat-what-you-kill" system to divide profits among partners, whereas Clifford Chance followed the British norm to pay partners based on seniority. American star performers understandably disliked the British system.[73] In another example, Ghosn's radical approaches at Nissan (see Opening Case) initially provoked not only criticisms from Japanese politicians and the media, but also hate mail from employees slated to lose their jobs.

Overall, although acquisitions are often the largest capital expenditures most firms ever make, they are frequently the worst planned and executed business activities of all.[74] Unfortunately, when merging firms try to sort out the mess, competitors are likely to launch aggressive attacks to take advantage of the chaos (see Chapter 8). For instance, while Boeing struggled in near total chaos with its acquisition of McDonnell Douglas (including a complete production halt) in 1996, Airbus quickly increased its share from one-third to one-half of the global market. Likewise, when HP was distracted by its highly controversial acquisition of Compaq from 2002 to 2003, Dell invaded HP's stronghold in printers and unleashed a price war in PCs and servers. Adding all of these factors together, it is hardly surprising that most M&As fail.

Improving the Odds for Acquisition Success

At the very minimum, managers need to make sure (1) that they do not pay too much for targets, avoid a bidding war, and be willing to walk out when premiums are too high; (2) that they engage in adequate due diligence concerning both strategic fit and organizational fit to avoid nasty surprises after the acquisition; and (3) that they adequately address the concerns of multiple stakeholders, try to keep the best talents, and are prepared to deal with roadblocks thrown out by people whose jobs and power may be jeopardized.[75] On top of these minimum points, leading-edge practitioners such as GE further suggest that integration management is a full-time job and needs to be recognized as a distinct business function, just like operations and marketing.[76]

RESTRUCTURING

Restructuring is often undertaken in connection with diversification and acquisitions. This section sets straight the terms used, introduces the motives for restructuring, and then discusses how to improve the odds for restructuring success.

Setting the Terms Straight

Although the term **restructuring** normally refers to adjusting firm size and scope through either diversification (expansion or entry), divestiture (contraction or exit), or both,[77] the most common definition for restructuring is the *reduction* of firm size and scope. Here we will adopt this more frequently used definition.[78] There is a historical reason behind this one-sided use of the word "restructuring." By the 1980s and 1990s when this word surfaced in our vocabulary, many firms suffered from overdiversification and became interested in reducing size and scope. Using this definition, there are two primary ways of restructuring: (1) **downsizing** (reducing the number of employees through lay-offs, early retirements, and outsourcing)[79] and (2) **downscoping** (reducing the scope of the firm through divestitures and spin-offs).[80] The flipside of downscoping is **refocusing,** namely, narrowing the scope of the firm to focus on a few areas.[81]

Motives for Restructuring

We can draw on industry-, resource-, and institution-based views to understand the motives for restructuring.[82] From an industry-based perspective, a rising level of competition within an industry (such as telecommunications) often triggers restructuring.[83] Ericsson, for example, was forced to downsize from 110,000 employees in 2001 to 60,000 in 2003, exit three aging businesses, and close 75 percent of R&D labs.[84] Given that a primary motivation for M&As is to eliminate redundant assets, industries experiencing many M&As (such as automobiles) often unleash major restructuring efforts.[85]

The resource-based perspective suggests that while restructuring may bring some benefits, there are also significant costs (such as organizational chaos, anxiety, frustration, and low morale). When most competitors restructure, these restructuring activities may not generate sustainable value, are not rare, are imitable, and cause organizational problems. In other words, firms cannot "'save' or 'shrink' their way to prosperity."[86]

From an institution-based perspective, by the 1980s and 1990s, firms in developed economies increasingly felt institutional pressures from capital markets to restructure.[87] More and more managers accepted restructuring as a part of legitimate business undertaking.[88] However, there are also strong institutional pressures *against* restructuring. In the United States, restructuring, job loss, and outsourcing (recently labeled "off-shoring") have been controversial issues in every presidential election since the 1990s (see Opening Case in Chapter 1). By law in Germany, all "redundancies" must be negotiated by workers' councils, whose members (understandably) are not keen to vote themselves out of jobs. In Central and Eastern Europe, where some restructuring is often urgently needed, many managers are reluctant to do so.[89] In Asia, even after the rude awakening of the 1997 financial crisis, restructuring has still been "sporadic and glacially slow."[90] Overall, corporate restructuring is not widely embraced around the world.[91]

Increasing the Odds for Restructuring Success

Given the high risks and high stakes involved, firms will do better if they (1) use restructuring as a last—not first—resort and (2) manage survivors more effectively (such as treating departing employees fairly and decently). How to restructure knowledge-intensive firms, whose organizational memory and capabilities are largely embedded in employees, is especially tricky.[92] For example, when management consulting firm Accenture had to cut 600 positions, it used partially paid "sabbaticals," by paying 20 percent of salary for six to twelve months and allowing employees to keep a work phone number, laptop, and e-mail address. Toyota, when facing cost pressures in 2001, sent hundreds of skilled blue-collar workers from Japan to its US subsidiary in Kentucky as half-paid "advisors." Although these non-English-speaking Japanese workers could hardly "advise" the American labor force (which was the most productive in Toyota and did not need much advice anyway), the message the company sent to both Japanese and American work forces that it would try as much as possible to keep them served as a tremendous morale booster.

DEBATES AND EXTENSIONS

The complexity of diversifying, acquiring, and restructuring has led to numerous debates, some of which have been discussed earlier. Here, we outline three leading debates: (1) product relatedness versus other forms of relatedness, (2) global versus regional geographic diversification, and (3) acquisitions versus alliances.

Product Relatedness versus Other Forms of Relatedness

This debate centers on what exactly relatedness is. Product relatedness is seemingly straightforward and widely used; however, it has attracted at least three significant points of contention. First, how to actually measure product relatedness remains debatable. A "product-related" firm based on one particular measure may be considered "unrelated" if a different measure is used.[93] For example, General Motors (GM), when measured by history, investments, and lines of business, is uncontroversially known as a product-related diversifier. However, if we use a different measure, the actual contributions of different lines of business to corporate profits, General Motors Acceptance Corporation (GMAC), which is GM's financial subsidiary, looms large. In 2003, GMAC made *ten* times the profits of GM's auto divisions. Half of GMAC's profits came from selling mortgages (including the new Ditech.com unit), which are *unrelated* to GM's core automobile products and related car loans. In other words, GM, which could mean "General Mortgages," "looks a lot more like a financial institution that happens to sell cars and trucks than an automaker."[94]

Second, beyond measurement issues, an important school of thought—known as the **dominant logic** school—argues that product relatedness does not only refer to the visible product linkages. Rather, relatedness can be a common underlying dominant logic that connects various businesses in a diversified firm.[95] Consider Britain's easyGroup, which operates easyJet (airline), easyCar (rental), easyInternetcafe, and easyCinema, among others. A dominant logic can be identified underneath its conglomerate skin. This logic actively manages supply and demand. Early and/or nonpeak-hour customers get cheap deals (such as 20 cents a movie), and late and/or peak-hour customers pay a lot more. For example, charges at the Internet cafes rise as the seats fill up. While many firms (such as airlines) practice such "yield management," none has been so aggressive as the easyGroup.[96] Therefore, instead of treating the easyGroup as an "unrelated conglomerate," perhaps we may label it a "related yield management firm."

Finally, from an institution-based view, some product-unrelated conglomerates may be linked by **institutional relatedness,** defined as "a firm's informal linkages with dominant institutions in the environment which confer resources and legitimacy."[97] For example, sound informal relationships with government agencies in countries (usually emerging economies) where such agencies control crucial resources such as licensing, financing, and labor pools would encourage firms to leverage such relationships by entering multiple industries. In emerging economies, solid connections with banks—a crucial financial institution—may help raise financing to enter multiple industries, whereas stand-alone entrepreneurial start-ups without such connections often have a hard time securing financing. This idea helps explain why new start-ups (such as Amazon and eBay) dominate e-commerce in developed economies, whereas new units of old-line conglomerates (such as Hong Kong's Wharf and Singapore's Sembcorp) dominate e-commerce in emerging economies. Despite the Western advice to downscope, some conglomerates in emerging economies have recently *expanded* their scope by entering new industries such as e-commerce. In other words, a firm that is classified as a "product-unrelated" conglomerate may actually enjoy a great deal of institutional relatedness.

Global Geographic Diversification versus Regional Geographic Diversification

In this age of globalization, the optimal geographic scope for MNEs is hotly debated. Despite the often heard observation (and criticism from antiglobalization activists) that MNEs are expanding "globally" to take over the world, Alan Rugman and Alain Verbeke report that, surprisingly, even among the largest *Fortune* Global 500 MNEs, few are truly "global."[98] Using some reasonable criteria (at least 20 percent of sales in *each* of the three regions of the Triad consisting of Asia, Europe, and North America, but less than 50 percent in any one region), they find a total of only nine MNEs to be global (Column 1 of Table 9.4 on next page). Since Africa, Latin America, and the Middle East are completely ignored, if we require that a global MNE must have 10 percent of sales in *each* continent, the number of such true global MNEs will shrink even further. Next to global MNEs, twenty-five firms are bi-regional MNEs, which have at least 20 percent of sales in each of two regions of

TABLE 9.4   **Geographic Diversification of the Largest Multinational Enterprises (MNEs) by Sales**

	"GLOBAL" MNEs[1]		"BI-REGIONAL" MNEs[2]		"HOST REGION-BASED" MNEs[3]		"MOST INTERNATIONALIZED" MNEs[4]
1	IBM	1	BP Amoco	1	DaimlerChrysler	1	ExxonMobil
2	Sony	2	Toyota	2	ING Group	2	General Motors
3	Philips	3	Nissan	3	Royal Ahold	3	BP Amoco
4	Nokia	4	Unilever	4	Honda	4	Ford
5	Intel	5	Motorola	5	Santander	5	Royal Dutch/Shell
6	Canon	6	GlaxoSmithKline	6	Delhaize 'Le Lion'	6	General Electric
7	Coca-Cola	7	EADS	7	AstraZeneca	7	Toyota
8	Flextronics	8	Bayer	8	News Corporation	8	ChevronTexaco
9	LVMH	9	Ericsson	9	Sodexho Alliance	9	TotalFinaElf
		10	Alstom	10	Manpower	10	IBM
		11	Aventis	11	Wolseley	11	Volkswagen
		12	Diageo			12	E.On
		13	Sun Microsystems			13	RWE Group
		14	Bridgestone			14	Honda
		15	Roche			15	Fiat
		16	3M			16	Vivendi Universal
		17	Skanska			17	Nestle
		18	McDonald's			18	Unilever
		19	Michelin			19	Deutsche Telekom
		20	Kodak			20	Suez
		21	Eletrolux			21	Vadafone
		22	BAE			22	Telefonica
		23	Alcan			23	ABB
		24	L'Oreal			24	News Corporation
		25	Lafarge			25	Hutchison Whampoa

1. "Global" MNEs have at least 20 percent of sales in each of the three regions of the Triad (Asia, Europe, and North America), but less than 50 percent in any one region.

2. "Bi-regional MNEs" have at least 20 percent of sales in each of two regions of the Triad, but less than 50 percent in any one region.

3. "Host-region based" MNEs have more than 50 percent of sales in one of the Triad regions other than their home region.

4. "Most internationalized" MNEs have the highest "transnationality index," calculated by the United Nations as the average of (1) foreign/total sales, (2) foreign/total assets, and (3) foreign/total employment.

Sources: All data are from 2001. The first three columns are adapted from A. Rugman & A. Verbeke, 2004, A perspective on regional and global strategies of multinational enterprises (pp. 8–10), Journal of International Business Studies, 35: 3–18. The last column is adapted from United Nations, 2003, World Investment Report 2003 (p. 5), New York and Geneva: United Nations.

the Triad but less than 50 percent in any one (Column 2 of Table 9.4). Interestingly, eleven MNEs are "host-region based," with at least 50 percent of sales in one of the Triad regions other than their home region (Column 3 of Table 9.4). The majority of the remaining *Fortune* Global 500 (over 400) are "home-region oriented" MNEs—in other words, they are regional, but *not* global, firms.

These findings are supported by United Nations data on the top twenty-five "most internationalized" MNEs (Column 4 of Table 9.4).[99] These MNEs have the highest "transnationality index," calculated as the average of (1) foreign/total sales, (2) foreign/total assets, and (3) foreign/total employment. Yet, only five of these twenty-five firms—BP Amoco, Toyota, IBM, Honda, and News Corporation—can be found in any of the three other columns in Table 9.4. The majority of these "most internationalized" MNEs seem to only focus on their home region.

Can or should most MNEs further "globalize" their geographic scope? There are two answers to this question. First, most MNEs know what they are doing and their current geographic scope is the maximum they can manage. Some of them may have already overdiversified and will need to downscope internationally. Second, these data only capture a snapshot in time (2001) and some MNEs may become more "globalized" over time While the debate goes on, at the very least, it has taught us one important lesson: Be careful when using the word "global." The *majority* of the largest MNEs are not necessarily very "global" in their geographic scope.

Acquisitions versus Alliances

Despite the proliferation of acquisitions, their lackluster performance has led to a debate regarding whether they have been overused. Strategic alliances are an alternative to acquisitions (see Chapter 7). However, many firms seem to have plunged straight into "merger mania." Even when many firms pursue both M&As and alliances, these activities are often undertaken in isolation.[100] While many large MNEs have an M&A function and some have set up an alliance function, virtually no firm has established a combined "mergers, acquisitions, *and* alliances" function.[101] In practice, firms should explicitly compare and contrast acquisitions and alliances.[102]

Compared with acquisitions, strategic alliances—despite their own problems—cost less and allow firms to learn from working with each other before engaging in full-blown acquisitions.[103] Many poor acquisitions (such as DaimlerChrysler) would probably have been better off had firms pursued alliances first. At present, however, it is inconclusive whether alliances are actually better than acquisitions.[104] Nevertheless, it is imperative that firms seriously and thoroughly investigate alliances as an alternative to acquisitions (see Chapter 7 for details).

IMPLICATIONS FOR STRATEGISTS

At the corporate strategy level, diversification has daunting challenges, enormous complexity, and difficult implementation through acquisitions and/or restructuring. Yet, numerous firms undertake these strategies. Overall, an interesting historical parallel exists between the US M&A wave around the end of the nineteenth century and the global M&A wave around the end of the twentieth century. The US M&A wave was fueled by technological innovations (such as the railway and telegraph) allowing for more consolidation, developments in financial markets, and institutional constraints banning interfirm collaboration (labeled "anticompetitive"—see Chapter 8). The end result was the emergence of *nationwide* industries, markets, and competitors (such as US Steel).[105] Advancing technologies (such as the Internet) also fueled the more recent global M&A wave. Financial developments and institutional transitions (such as privatization) have further accelerated the emergence of *worldwide* industries and markets and necessitated numerous cross-border M&As.

In terms of the four most fundamental questions in strategy, this chapter directly answers Question 3: What determines the scope of the firm? Industry conditions, firm capabilities, and institutional constraints and opportunities in both developed and emerging economies all help shape corporate scope. In addition, why firms differ (Question 1) and how firms behave (Question 2) boils down to why they choose different diversification strategies and how they carry out these strategies, respectively. Finally, what determines the international success and failure of firms (the first half of Question 4) can be answered by whether appropriate *product* diversification strategies are in place. It is important to caution against a simplistic view, typical in developed economies at present, that product-related diversification is the best. Such a strategy only adds value when supported by a centralized and cooperative organizational architecture (Table 9.1) and more efficient external capital markets. While in this chapter we have touched on the second half of Question 4, centered on *geographic* diversification, a more complete answer will be developed in Chapter 10, which is entirely devoted to how to organize better internationally.

Chapter Summary

1. Corporate diversification has two dimensions: (1) product and (2) geographic diversification.

2. Product-related diversification focuses on operational synergy and scale economies. Product-unrelated diversification (conglomeration) stresses financial synergy and scope economies. At present, product-related diversification is favored in developed economies, whereas product-unrelated diversification is widely used in emerging economies.

3. Geographically diversified firms can have a limited or extensive international scope. At a low level of internationalization, a U-shaped relationship exists between geographic scope and firm performance. At moderate to high levels of internationalization, an inverted U-shape exists.

4. Most firms pursue product and geographic diversification simultaneously, with four possible strategic postures: (1) anchored replicators, (2) multinational replicators, (3) far-flung conglomerates, and (4) classic conglomerates.

5. A comprehensive model of diversification is driven by industry-, resource-, and institution-based considerations.

6. Most M&As are acquisitions, which take place along (1) horizontal, (2) vertical, and (3) conglomerate dimensions. The terms of the transaction can be friendly or hostile.

7. M&As are driven by (1) synergistic, (2) hubris, and/or (3) managerial motivations. Approximately 70 percent of M&As reportedly fail. To improve the odds for success, acquiring firms are advised (1) not to overpay, (2) to focus on both strategic and organizational fit, and (3) to address the concerns of multiple stakeholders.

8. Restructuring involves downsizing, downscoping, and refocusing.

9. Three leading debates are (1) product relatedness versus other forms of relatedness, (2) global versus regional geographic diversification, and (3) acquisitions versus alliances.

Key Terms

acquisition	cross-border (international) M&A	hostile M&A
acquisition premium	diversification	hostile takeover
agency problems	diversification discount	hubris
anchored replicators	diversification premium	information overload
bureaucratic costs	dominant logic	institutional relatedness
business group	downscoping	internal capital market
business-level strategy	downsizing	international diversification
classic conglomerate	economic benefits	managerial motives
conglomerate advantage	empire building	marginal bureaucratic costs
conglomerate disadvantage	far-flung conglomerate	marginal economic benefits
conglomerate M&A	financial control	merger
conglomerate	financial synergy	merger and acquisition (M&A)
conglomeration	friendly M&As	multinational replicator
corporate governance	geographic diversification	operational synergy
corporate strategy	horizontal M&A	
corporate-level strategy		

organizational fit	refocusing	single business strategy
product diversification	restructuring	strategic control
product-related diversification	scale economies	strategic fit
product-unrelated diversification	scope economies	vertical M&A

Critical Discussion Questions

1. Some argue that shareholders can diversify their stockholdings and that there is no need for firms to use corporate diversification to reduce risk for shareholders. The upshot is that instead of excess earnings (known as "free cash flows") being used by the corporation to diversify (such as acquiring other firms and entering new countries), they should be returned to shareholders as dividends and firms should pursue single-business or focused strategies. Do you agree or disagree with this statement? Why?

2. Product-unrelated diversification (conglomeration) is now widely discredited in developed economies. However, in some cases it still seems to add value in emerging economies. Is this interest in conglomeration likely to hold or decrease in emerging economies over time? Why?

3. Concerning the costs and benefits of geographic diversification, one school of thought advises firms to "be bold" by entering as many countries as possible (the ideal being the traditional "global strategy"). Another school suggests "not too bold"—that is, firms should venture to culturally and institutionally neighboring countries, but not to too distant countries. How would you participate in this debate?

4. **ON ETHICS:** Mass lay-offs associated with restructuring, although widely used, are often viewed as unethical (and even labeled as "corporate cannibalism" by some critics). When facing market downturns, an alternative is for the whole firm to have an across-the-board pay cut while preserving all current jobs. What are the ethical dilemmas in these two alternatives?

5. **ON ETHICS:** As a CEO, you are trying to decide whether to acquire a foreign firm. The size of your firm will double after this acquisition and will become the largest in your industry. On the one hand, you are excited about the opportunities to be a leading captain of industry and the associated power, prestige, and income (you expect your salary, bonus, and stock option to double next year). On the other hand, you have just read this chapter and are troubled by (1) the fact that 70 percent of M&As reportedly fail and (2) the uncertain strategic and organizational fit between the two firms (despite some superficial fit on the surface). How would you proceed?

Closing Case: From Diversification Premium to Diversification Discount in South Korea

Large conglomerates (business groups), such as Hyundai (http://www.hmc.co.kr), Samsung (http://www.samsung.co.kr), LG (http://www.lg.co.kr), and Daewoo (http://www.daewoo.com), are called chaebols in South Korea (hereafter Korea). They dominate the economy, contributing approximately 40 percent of Korea's GDP as of 1996. In 1996, Samsung had eighty subsidiaries, Hyundai fifty-seven, LG forty-nine, and Daewoo thirty—scattered in different industries such as automobiles, chemicals, construction, electronics, financial services, semiconductors, shipbuilding, steel, and telecommunications. Why and how did chaebols, all from humble roots in focused industries, grow to become such sprawling conglomerates? In 1985, the chairman of LG shared an intriguing story:

My father and I started a cosmetic cream factory in the late 1940s. At that time, no company could supply us with plastic caps of adequate quality for cream jars, so we had to start a plastic business. Plastic caps alone were not sufficient to run the plastic molding plant, so we added combs, toothbrushes, and soap boxes. This plastics business also led us to manufacture electric fan blades and telephone cases, which in turn led us to manufacture electrical and electronic products and telecommunications equipment. The plastics business also took us into oil refining, which needed a tanker shipping company. The oil refining company alone was paying an insurance premium amounting to more than half the total revenue of the then largest insurance company in Korea. Thus, an insurance company was started.

Similar versions of the story are shared by virtually all chaebols. What the story does not reveal is the visible hand of the Korean government, which channeled finan-cial resources to fund chaebols' growth. In the meantime, the government protected domestic markets from foreign competition.

However, the cozy, protected environment did not last forever. Because Korea's eagerness to join the OECD prior to its accession in 1996 resulted in external pressures to open the economy, the government gradually removed import restrictions. In addition, capital markets became more open and vibrant. Between 1984 and 1996, the stock capitalization/GDP ratio experienced a whopping 782 percent increase (from 3 percent in 1984 to 29 percent in 1996). At the same time, labor costs rose as Korean workers in the new democratic era (since the late 1980s) became more assertive. Internationally, chaebol products were often stuck in the middle between high-end Japanese offerings and low-end Chinese merchandise.

Confronting such rising environmental turbulence by the 1990s, chaebols increased their scope. The average number of affiliates of the top thirty chaebols grew from seventeen per group in 1987 to twenty-two in 1996, a 30 percent increase. In the process, they took on a high level of debt based on extensive cross-guarantees among group member firms. Banks were happy to provide loans, believing that chaebols were "too big to fail." The debt/equity ratio ended up being on average 617 percent for the top thirty chaebols. In some extreme cases, New Core's debt/equity ratio was 1,225 percent, Halla's was 2,066 percent, and Jinro's was 3,765 percent.

Unfortunately, by the time the Asian economic crisis of 1997 struck, chaebols took an enormous beating. Their excessive borrowing and reckless growth were sharply criticized. Of the thirty top chaebols in 1996, close to half of them, including New Core, Halla (http://www.halla.com), and Jinro (http://www.jinro.co.kr), have gone through bankruptcy proceedings or bank-sponsored restructuring programs. Daewoo, ranked number four in 1996, has literally been broken up (see Opening Case in Chapter 7). All surviving chaebols have sold businesses and substantially reduced their scope.

In retrospect, signs of chaebols' troubles had been like "writings on the wall" before the crisis. At one time, chaebols carried a diversification premium, with affiliates outcompeting comparable independent firms (about 10 percent higher sales between 1984 and 1987). However, rising environmental turbulence coupled with growing firm size and complexity proved to be a lethal combination. Between 1994 and 1996, there was a diversification discount, with sales of chaebol member firms at least 5 percent less than comparable independent firms. The obviously unsustainable debt loads were another sign. Finally, the better developed external capital markets further eroded the chaebols' internal capital market advantage.

In hindsight, it is amazing to see chaebols having been applauded as the champions of Korean economic development and a worthy organizational model for other developing economies to emulate prior to 1997. Since 1997, chaebols often have been painted with a negative brush, and even blamed for the country's economic crisis. Both positions seem extreme. Chaebols probably were neither "paragons" nor "parasites." Their roles simply changed. Chaebols as conglomerates added value during earlier days, but past some point of inflection (probably the early 1990s), their drawbacks started to outweigh benefits.

Case Discussion Questions

1. Drawing on industry-, resource-, and institution-based views, explain why conglomeration (product-unrelated diversification) became a dominant corporate strategy in postwar Korea.

2. What kind of synergy did chaebols try to derive? How could chaebols add value?

3. What turned chaebols' diversification premium into a diversification discount?

4. Is product-related diversification always better than conglomeration?

5. Some argue that chaebols as an organizational species will die. What lies ahead for chaebols in Korea, and for conglomerates in emerging economies in general?

Sources: Based on (1) J. Chang, T. Khanna, & K. Palepu, 1998, Korea Stock Exchange 1998, Harvard Business School case 9-199-033; (2) S. J. Chang & J. Hong, 2002, How much does the business group matter in Korea? Strategic Management Journal, 23: 265–274; (3) M. Guillen, 2001, The Limits of Convergence, Princeton, NJ: Princeton University Press; (4) H. Kim, R. Hoskisson, L. Tihanyi, & J. Hong, 2004, The evolution and restructuring of diversified business groups in emerging markets: The lessons from chaebols in Korea, Asia Pacific Journal of Management, 21: 25–48; (5) K. B. Lee, M. W. Peng, & K. Lee, 2004, From diversification premium to diversification discount during institutional transitions, Working paper, Fisher College of Business, The Ohio State University.

Notes

Abbreviation list

AME – *Academy of Management Executive*

AMJ – *Academy of Management Journal*

AMR – *Academy of Management Review*

APJM – *Asia Pacific Journal of Management*

ASQ – *Administrative Science Quarterly*

BW – *Business Week*

EMJ – *European Management Journal*

JB – *Journal of Business*

JBR – *Journal of Business Research*

JEP – *Journal of Economic Perspectives*

JF – *Journal of Finance*

JIBS – *Journal of International Business Studies*

JIM – *Journal of International Management*

JM – *Journal of Management*

JMS – *Journal of Management Studies*

JWB – *Journal of World Business*

LRP – *Long Range Planning*

MIR – *Management International Review*

OSc – *Organization Science*

SMJ – *Strategic Management Journal*

1. D. Collis & C. Montgomery, 1997, *Corporate Strategy* (p. 5), Chicago: Irwin.

2. R. Adner & C. Helfat, 2003, Corporate effects and dynamic managerial capabilities, *SMJ,* 24: 1011–1025; E. Bowman & C. Helfat, 2001, Does corporate strategy matter? *SMJ,* 22: 1–23; T. Brush & P. Bromiley, 1997, What does a small corporate effect mean? *SMJ,* 18: 825–835.

3. T. Brush, 1996, Predicted change in operational synergy and post-acquisition performance of acquired businesses, *SMJ,* 17: 1–24; L. Cote, A. Langley, & J. Pasquero, 1999, Acquisition strategy and dominant logic in an engineering firm, *JMS,* 36: 919–952; P. Davis, R. Robinson, J. Pearce, & S. Park, 1992, Business unit relatedness and performance, *SMJ,* 13: 349–361; M. Goold & A. Campbell, 2000, Taking stock of synergy, *LRP,* 33: 72–96; M. Farjoun, 1998, The

independent and joint effects of the skill and physical bases of relatedness in diversification, *SMJ,* 19: 611–630; D. Kim & B. Kogut, 1996, Technological platforms and diversification, *OSc,* 7: 283–301; C. St. John & J. Harrison, 1999, Manufacturing-based relatedness, synergy, and coordination, *SMJ,* 20: 129–145; J. Steenkamp, R. Batra, & D. Alden, 2003, How perceived brand globalness creates brand value, *JIBS,* 34: 53–65; I. Stern & A. Henderson, 2004, Within-business diversification in technology-intensive industries, *SMJ,* 25: 487–505.

4. C. Palmeri, 2004, Northrop's heavy artillery, *BW,* March 8: 52–54.

5. J. Liebeskind, 2000, Internal capital markets: Benefits, costs, and organizational arrangements, *OSc,* 11: 58–76.

6. K. B. Lee, M. W. Peng, & K. Lee, 2004, From diversification premium to diversification discount during institutional transitions, Working paper, Fisher College of Business, The Ohio State University.

7. R. Bettis, 1981, Performance differences in related and unrelated diversified firms, *SMJ,* 2: 379–394; K. Palepu, 1985, Diversification strategy, profit performance, and the entropy measure, *SMJ,* 6: 239–255; M. Lubatkin & P. Lane, 1996, Psst . . . The merger mavens still have it wrong! *AME,* 10: 21–37; C. Montgomery, 1982, The measurement of firm diversification, *AMJ,* 25: 299–307; L. Palich, L. Cardinal, and C. C. Miller, 2000, Curvilinearity in the diversification-performance linkage, *SMJ,* 21: 155–174; G. Szeless, M. Wiersema, & G. Muller-Stewens, 2003, Portfolio interrelationships and financial performance in the context of European firms, *EMJ,* 21: 146–163;

8. R. Rumelt, 1974, *Strategy, Structure, and Economic Performance,* Boston: Harvard Business School Press.

9. W. Chu, 2001, Contingency organizations and shared values, *APJM,* 18: 83–99; T. Khanna & K. Palepu, 2000, Is group affiliation profitable in emerging markets? *JF,* 55: 867–891; L. Keister, 2000, *Chinese Business Groups,* Oxford, UK: Oxford University Press; T. Khanna & J. Rivkin, 2001, Estimating the performance effects of business groups in emerging markets, *SMJ,* 22: 45–74; M. Li & Y. Wong, 2003, Diversification and economic performance, *APJM,* 20: 243–265;

L. Nachum, 1999, Diversification strategies of developing country firms, *JIM,* 5: 115–140.

10. A. Rugman & A. Verbeke, 2004, A perspective on regional and global strategies of multinational enterprises (pp. 8–10), *JIBS,* 35: 3–18.

11. F. Contractor, S. Kundu, & C. Hsu, 2003, A three-stage theory of international expansion, *JIBS,* 34: 5–18.

12. N. Capar & M. Kotabe, 2003, The relationship between international diversification and performance in service firms, *JIBS,* 34: 345–355; G. Qian, 1997, Assessing product-market diversification of US firms, *MIR,* 37: 127–149.

13. M. Lyles, T. Saxton, & K. Watson, 2004, Venture survival in a transition economy, *JM,* 30: 351–375.

14. C. Baden-Fuller & J. Stopford, 1991, Globalization frustrated, *SMJ,* 12: 493–507; J. M. Geringer, P. Beamish, & R. da Costa, 1989, Diversification strategy and internationalization, *SMJ,* 10: 109–119; L. Gomes & K. Ramaswamy, 1999, An empirical examination of the form of the relationship between multinationality and performance, *JIBS,* 30: 173–188; D. Sullivan, 1994, The "threshold of internationalization," *MIR,* 34: 165–186.

15. C. Palmeri, 2003, Occidental: From excess to success, *BW,* April 7: 65–66.

16. J. Collins, 1990, A market performance comparison of US firms active in domestic, developed, and developing countries, *JIBS,* 22: 271–287; J. Doukas & L. Lang, 2003, Foreign direct investment, diversification, and firm performance, *JIBS,* 34: 153–172; R. Grant, A. Jammine, & H. Thomas, 1988, Diversity, diversification, and profitability among British manufacturing companies, *AMJ,* 31: 771–801; W. Kim & E. Lyn, 1987, Foreign direct investment theories, entry barriers, and reverse investments in US manufacturing industries, *JIBS,* 18: 53–67; M. Kotabe, S. Srinivasan, & P. Aulakh, 2002, Multinationality and firm performance, *JIBS,* 33: 79–97; A. Michel & I. Shaked, 1986, Multinational corporations vs. domestic corporations, *JIBS,* 17: 89–101; J. Reuer & M. Leiblein, 2000, Downside risk implications of multinationality and international joint ventures, *AMJ,* 43: 203–214.

17. A. Delios & P. Beamish, 1999, Geographic scope, product diversification, and the corporate performance of Japanese firms (p. 724), *SMJ,* 20: 711–727.

18. J. M. Geringer, S. Tallman, & D. Olsen, 2000, Product and international diversification among Japanese multinational firms (p. 76), *SMJ,* 21: 51–80.

19. A. Goerzen & P. Beamish, 2003, Geographic scope and multinational enterprise performance *SMJ,* 24: 1289–1306.

20. M. Hitt, R. Hoskisson, & H. Kim, 1997, International diversification, *AMJ,* 40: 767–798; D. Hoopes, 1999, Measuring geographic diversification and product diversification, *MIR,* 39: 277–292; W. C. Kim, P. Hwang, & W. Burgers, 1989, Global diversification strategy and corporate profit performance, *SMJ,* 10: 45–57; L. Nachum, 2004, Geographic and industrial diversification of developing country firms, *JMS,* 41: 273–294; L. Palich, G. Carini, & S. Seaman, 2000, The impact of internationalization on the diversification-performance relationship, *JBR,* 48: 43–54; M. Sambharya, 1995, The combined effect of international diversification and product diversification strategies on the performance of US-based multinational corporations, *MIR,* 35: 197–218; S. Tallman & J. Li, 1996, Effects of international diversity and product diversity on the performance of multinational firms, *AMJ,* 39: 179–196; S. Vachani, 1991, Distinguishing between related and unrelated international geographic diversification, *JIBS,* 22: 307–322; C. Wan, 1998, International diversification, industrial diversification, & firm performance of Hong Kong MNCs, *APJM,* 15: 205–217.

21. L. Bengtsson, 2000, Corporate strategy in a small open economy, *EMJ,* 18: 444–453; K. Meyer, 2003, Global focusing: From domestic conglomerate to global specialist, Working paper, Copenhagen Business School.

22. C. Park, 2003, Prior performance characteristics of related and unrelated acquirers, *SMJ,* 24: 471–480; K. Ramaswamy, 1997, The performance impact of strategic similarity in horizontal mergers, *AMJ,* 40: 697–715.

23. R. Rajan, P. Volpin, & L. Zingales, 2000, The eclipse of the US tire industry, in S. Kaplan (ed.), *Mergers and*

Productivity (pp. 51–86), Chicago: University of Chicago Press.

24. K. Capell, 2004, Richard Branson's next big adventure, *BW,* March 8: 44–45.

25. G. Bruton & B. Oviatt, 1994, Performance of acquisitions of distressed firms, *AMJ,* 37: 972–989; A. Seth, 1990, Sources of value creation in acquisitions, *SMJ,* 11: 431–447.

26. J. Pennings & H. Barkema, 1994, Organizational learning and diversification, *AMJ,* 37: 608–614.

27. J. Galbraith, 2000, *Designing the Global Corporation,* San Francisco: Jossey-Bass; D. Miller, 2003, An asymmetry-based view of advantage, *SMJ,* 24: 961–976.

28. J. Cullivan, 2004, A strategy perspective from Cardinal Health, Presentation, Fisher College of Business, The Ohio State University, May 12.

29. O. Toulan, 2002, The impact of market liberalization on vertical scope: The case of Argentina, *SMJ,* 23: 551–560.

30. N. Argyres, 1996, Capabilities, technological diversification, and divisionalization, *SMJ,* 17: 395–410.

31. C. Hill, M. Hitt, & R. Hoskisson, 1992. Cooperative versus competitive structures in related and unrelated diversified firms, *OSc,* 3: 501–521.

32. M. Guillen, 2000, Business groups in emerging economies, *AMJ,* 43: 362–380; T. Khanna & K. Palepu, 2000, The future of business groups in emerging markets, *AMJ,* 43: 268–285; R. Hoskisson, A. Cannella, L. Tihanyi, & R. Faraci, 2004, Asset restructuring and business group affiliation in French civil law countries, *SMJ,* 25: 525–539.

33. K. Carow, R. Heron, & T. Saxton, 2004, Do early birds get the returns? *SMJ,* 25: 563–585.

34. R. Calori, G. Johnson, & P. Sarnin, 1994, CEOs' cognitive maps and the scope of the organization, *SMJ,* 15: 437–457; P. Thornton, 2001, Personal versus market logics of control, *OSc,* 12: 294–311.

35. M. Kroll, P. Wright, L. Toombs, & H. Leavell, 1997, Forms of control, *SMJ,* 18: 85–96; P. Wright, M. Kroll, & D. Elenkov, 2002, Acquisition returns, increase in firm size, and CEO compensation, *AMJ,* 45: 599–608; P. Wright, M. Kroll, A. Lado, & B. Van Ness, 2002, The

structure of ownership and corporate acquisition strategies, *SMJ,* 23: 41–54.

36. S. Olin, 1998, Why are there islands of conscious power found in the ocean of ownership? *JMS,* 35: 719–746; B. Kogut, G. Walker, & J. Anand, 2002, Agency and institutions, *OSc,* 13: 162–178; M. Mayer & R. Whittington, 2003, Diversification in context, *SMJ,* 24: 773–781; W. Wan, 2005, Country resource environments, firm capabilities, and corporate diversification strategies, *JMS* (in press); W. Wan & R. Hoskisson, 2003, Home country environments, corporation diversification strategies, and firm performance, *AMJ,* 46: 27–45.

37. This section draws heavily from M. W. Peng, S. Lee, & D. Wang, 2005, What determines the scope of the firm over time? A focus on institutional relatedness, *AMR* (in press).

38. G. Jones & C. Hill, 1988, Transaction cost analysis of strategy-structure choice, *SMJ,* 9: 159–172.

39. S. Chatterjee, 1986, Types of synergy and economic value, *SMJ,* 7: 119–139; M. Lubatkin, 1987, Merger strategies and stockholder value, *SMJ,* 8: 39–54; M. Lubatkin & H. O'Neill, 1987, Merger strategies and capital market risk, *AMJ,* 30: 665–684; A. Shleifer & R. Vishny, 1991, Takeovers in the 60s and the 80s, *SMJ,* 12: 51–59.

40. J. Jorgensen, T. Hafsi, & M. Kiggundu, 1986, Towards a market imperfections theory of organizational structure in developing countries, *JMS,* 23: 417–442.

41. D. Ahlstrom & G. Bruton, 2004, Turnaround in Asia, *APJM,* 21: 5–24; H. Kim, R. Hoskisson, L. Tihanyi, & J. Hong, 2004, The evolution and restructuring of diversified business groups in emerging markets, *APJM,* 21: 25–28.

42. United Nations, 2000, *World Investment Report 2000* (p. 99), New York: United Nations.

43. H. Barkema & F. Vermeulen, 1998, International expansion through start-up or acquisition, *AMJ,* 41: 7–27; K. Brouthers & L. Brouthers, 2000, Acquisition or green-field start-up? *SMJ,* 21: 89–98.

44. A. Arikan, 2004, Cross-border mergers and acquisitions (p. 239), in B. Punnett & O. Shenkar (eds.), *Handbook*

for International Management Research (pp. 239–264), Ann Arbor: University of Michigan Press.

45. M. Lubatkin, W. Schulze, A. Mainkar, & R. Cotterill, 2001, Ecological investigation of firm effects on horizontal mergers, *SMJ,* 22: 335–358.

46. H. Singh & C. Montgomery, 1987, Corporate acquisition strategies and economic performance, *SMJ,* 8: 377–386; R. Krishnan, S. Joshi, & H. Krishnan, 2004, The influence of mergers on firms' product-mix strategies, *SMJ,* 25: 587–611.

47. United Nations, 2000, *World Investment Report 2000* (p. 128).

48. G. Ahuja & R. Katila, 2001, Technological acquisitions and the innovation performance of acquiring firms, *SMJ,* 22: 197–220; J. Anand & A. Delios, 2002, Absolute and relative resources as determinants of international acquisitions, *SMJ,* 23: 119–134; J. Harrison, M. Hitt, R. Hoskisson, & R. D. Ireland, 2001, Resource complementarity in business combinations, *JM,* 27: 679–690; H. Harzing, 2002, Acquisitions versus green-field investments, *SMJ,* 23: 211–227; S. Karim & W. Mitchell, 2000, Path-dependent and path-breaking change, *SMJ,* 21: 1061–1081; D. Loree, C. Chen, & S. Guisinger, 2000, International acquisitions, *JWB,* 35: 300–315; M. Lubatkin, W. Schulze, A. Mainkar, & R. Cotteril, 2001, Ecological investigation of firm effects in horizontal mergers, *SMJ,* 22: 335–357; T. Saxton & M. Dollinger, 2004, Target reputation and appropriability, *JM,* 30: 123–147; A. Seth, 1990, Sources of value creation in acquisitions, *SMJ,* 11: 431–446; D. Schweiger & P. Very, 2001, International mergers and acquisitions special issue, *JWB,* 36: 1–2.

49. A. Ranft & M. Lord, 2002, Acquiring new technologies and capabilities, *OSc,* 13: 420–441.

50. M. Lubatkin, R. Calori, P. Very, & J. Veiga, 1998, Managing mergers across borders, *OSc,* 9: 670–684.

51. J. Doh, 2000, Entrepreneurial privatization strategies, *AMR,* 25: 551–571; K. Meyer & S. Estrin, 2001, Brownfield entry in emerging markets, *JIBS,* 32: 574–584; K. Uhlenbruck & J. De Castro, 2000, Foreign acquisitions in Central and Eastern Europe, *AMJ,* 43: 381–402.

52. R. Roll, 1986, The hubris hypothesis of corporate takeovers, *JB,* 59: 197–216.

53. P. Buckley & P. Ghauri, 2002, *International Mergers and Acquisitions* (p. 2), London: Thomson.

54. K. Fowler & D. Schmidt, 1989, Determinants of tender offer post-acquisition performance, *SMJ,* 10: 339–350; P. Haunschild, A. Davis-Blake, & M. Fichman, 1994, Managerial overcommitment in corporate acquisition processes, *OSc,* 5: 528–540.

55. T. Amburgey & A. Miner, 1992, Strategic momentum, *SMJ,* 13: 335–348.

56. D. Angwin, 2001, Mergers and acquisitions across European borders, *JWB,* 36: 32–57.

57. M. Hitt, J. Harrison, & D. Ireland, 2001, *Mergers and Acquisitions* (p. 18), New York: Oxford University Press.

58. M. Hayward, 2003, Professional influence, *SMJ,* 24: 783–801; I. Kesner, D. Shapiro, & A. Sharma, 1994, Brokering mergers, *AMJ,* 37: 703–721; G. Walker & J. Barney, 1990, Management objectives in mergers and acquisitions, *SMJ,* 11: 79–85.

59. K. Brouthers, P. van Hastenburg, & J. van den Ven, 1998, If most mergers fail why are they so popular? *LRP,* 31: 347–353; A. Seth, K. Song, & R. Pettit, 2000, Synergy, managerialism, or hubris? *JIBS,* 31: 387–405.

60. D. King, D. Dalton, C. Daily, & J. Covin, 2004, Meta-analyses of post-acquisition performance, *SMJ,* 25: 187–200

61. D. Ravenscraft & F. Scherer, 1987, *Mergers, Sell-Offs, and Economic Efficiency,* Washington: Brookings.

62. D. Datta, G. Pinches, & V. Narayanan, 1992, Factors influencing wealth creation from M&As, *SMJ,* 13: 67–84.

63. G. Andrade, M. Mitchell, & E. Stafford, 2001, New evidence and perspectives on mergers, *JEP,* 15: 103–120.

64. P. Ghemawat & F. Ghadar, 2000, The dubious logic of global mega-mergers, *HBR,* July-August: 65–72.

65. M. Sirower, 1997, *The Synergy Trap,* New York: Free Press. See also M. Hayward & D. Hambrick, 1997, Explaining the premiums paid for large acquisitions, *ASQ,* 42: 103–127.

66. Hitt, Harrison, & Ireland, 2001, *Mergers and Acquisitions* (p. 89).

67. D. Datta, 1991, Organizational fit and acquisition performance, *SMJ,* 12: 281–298; D. Jemison & S. Sitkin, 1986, Corporate acquisitions: A process perspective, *AMR,* 11: 145–163.

68. T. Grubb & R. Lamb, 2000, *Capitalize on Merger Chaos* (p. 14), New York: Free Press.

69. A. Buchholtz, B. Ribbens, & I. Houle, 2003, The role of human capital in postacquisition CEO departure, *AMJ,* 46: 506–514; A. Cannella & D. Hambrick, 1993, Effects of executive departures on the performance of acquired firms, *SMJ,* 14: 137–152; R. Davis & A. Nair, 2003, A note on top management turnover in international acquisitions, *MIR,* 43: 171–183; J. Krug & W. H. Hegarty, 2001, Predicting who stays and leaves after an acquisition, *SMJ,* 22: 185–196; J. Walsh, 1989, Doing a deal, *SMJ,* 10: 307–322.

70. J. Birkinshaw, H. Bresman, & L. Hakanson, 2000, Managing the post-acquisition integration process, *JMS,* 37: 395–425; A. Pablo, 1994, Determinants of acquisition integration level, *AMJ,* 37: 803–837; A. Risberg, 2001, Employee experiences of acquisition processes, *JWB,* 36: 58–84; E. Vaara, 2003, Postacquisition integration as sensemaking, *JMS,* 40: 859–894.

71. S. Chatterjee, M. Lubatkin, D. Schweiger, & Y. Weber, 1992, Cultural differences and shareholder value in related mergers, *SMJ,* 13: 319–334; J. Child, D. Faulkner, & R. Pitkethly, 2001, *The Management of International Acquisitions,* Oxford, UK: Oxford University Press; D. Datta & G. Puia, 1995, Cross-border acquisitions, *MIR,* 35: 337–359; M. Lubatkin, R. Calori, P. Very, & J. Veiga, 1998, Managing mergers across borders, *OSc,* 9: 670–684; K. Meyer & E. Lieb-Doczy, 2003, Post-acquisition restructuring as evolutionary process, *JMS,* 40: 459–482; P. Morosini, S. Shane, & H. Singh, 1998, National cultural distance and cross-border acquisition performance, *JIBS,* 29: 137–158; A. Nahavandi & A. Malekzadeh, 1988, Acculturation in mergers and acquisitions, *AMR,* 13: 79–90; R. Olie, 1994, Shades of culture and institutions in international mergers, *OSt,* 15: 381–405; K. Uhlenbruck, 2004, Developing acquired foreign subsidiaries, *JIBS,* 35: 109–123; P. Very, M. Lubatkin, R. Calori, & J. Veiga, 1997, Relative standing and the performance of recently acquired European firms, *SMJ,* 18: 593–614; R. Weber & C. Camerer, 2003, Cultural conflict and merger failure, *MS,* 49: 400–415; Y. Weber, O. Shenkar, & A. Raveh, 1996, National and corporate cultural fit in mergers/acquisitions, *MS,* 42: 1215–1227.

72. R. Hallowell, D. Bowen, & C. Knoop, 2002, Four Seasons goes to Paris (p. 19), *AME,* 16: 7–24.

73. *Economist,* 2004, Trying to get the right balance, February: 65–67.

74. Grubb & Lamb, 2000, *Capitalize on Merger Chaos.*

75. J. Baum, S. Li, & J. Usher, 2000, Making the next move, *ASQ,* 45: 766–801; H. Bresman, J. Birkinshaw, & R. Nobel, 1999, Knowledge transfer in international acquisitions, *JIBS,* 30: 439–469; L. Capron & N. Pistre, 2002, When do acquirers earn abnormal returns? *SMJ,* 23: 781–795; J. Haleblian & S. Finkelstein, 1999, The influence of organizational acquisition experience on acquisition performance, *ASQ,* 44: 29–56; M. Hayward, 2002, When do firms learn from their acquisition experience? *SMJ,* 23: 21–40; R. Larsson & S. Finkelstein, 1999, Integrating strategic, organizational, and human resource perspectives on mergers and acquisitions, *OSc,* 10: 1–26; J. Reuer, O. Shenkar, & R. Ragozzino, 2004, Mitigating risk in international mergers and acquisitions, *JIBS,* 35: 19–32; F. Vermulen & H. Barkema, 2001, Learning through acquisitions, *AMJ,* 44: 457–477.

76. R. Ashkenas, L. DeMonaco, & S. Francis, 1998, Making the deal real, *HBR,* January-February: 165–178.

77. H. Bowman & H. Singh, 1993, Corporate restructuring, *SMJ,* 14: 5–14; L. Capron, P. Dussauge, & W. Mitchell, 1998, Resource redeployment following horizontal acquisitions in Europe and North America, *SMJ,* 19: 631–661; S. Chang, 1996, An evolutionary perspective on diversification and corporate restructuring, *SMJ,* 17: 587–611.

78. R. Hoskisson & R. Johnson, 1992, Corporate restructuring and strategic change, *SMJ,* 13: 625–634; C. Markides, 1995, Diversification, restructuring, and economic performance, *SMJ,* 16: 101–118.

79. A. Budros, 1999, A conceptual framework for analyzing why organizations downsize, *OSc,* 10: 69–82;

R. Hamilton & Y. Chow, 1993, Why managers divest, *SMJ*, 14: 479–484.

80. R. Hoskisson & M. Hitt, 1994, *Downscoping*, New York: Oxford University Press.

81. R. Johnson, 1995, Antecedents and outcomes of corporate refocusing, *JM*, 22: 439–483.

82. G. Bruton, D. Ahlstrom, & J. Wan, 2003, Turnaround in East Asian firms, *SMJ*, 24: 519–540; R. DeWitt, 1998, Firm, industry, and strategy influences on choice of downsizing approach, *SMJ*, 19: 59–79; V. Gupta & J. Wang, 2004, From corporate crisis to turnaround in East Asia, *APJM*, 21: 213–233; S. Maheshwari & D. Ahlstrom, 2004, Turning around a state-owned enterprise, *APJM*, 21: 75–101.

83. J. Bethel & J. Liebeskind, 1993, The effects of ownership structure on corporate restructuring, *SMJ*, 14: 15–32; P. Gibbs, 1993, Determinants of corporate restructuring, *SMJ*, 14: 51–68; D. Hatfield, J. Liebeskind, & T. Opler, 1996, The effects of corporate restructuring on aggregate industry specialization, *SMJ*, 17: 55–72.

84. S. Reed, 2002, Saving Ericsson, *BW*, November 11: 64–68.

85. D. Bergh & M. Lawless, 1998, Portfolio restructuring and limits to hierarchical governance, *OSc*, 9: 87–102; L. Capron, W. Mitchell, & A. Swaminathan, 2001, Asset divestiture following horizontal acquisitions, *SMJ*, 22: 817–844; G. Fisher, J. Lee, & L. Jones, 2004, An exploratory study of company turnaround in Australia and Singapore following the Asia crisis, *APJM*, 21: 149–170; D. Hurry, 1993, Restructuring in the global industry, *SMJ*, 14: 69–82; K. O'Shaughnessy & D. Flanagan, 1998, Determinants of layoff announcements following M&As, *SMJ*, 19: 989–999; J. Robins, 1993, Organization as strategy, *SMJ*, 14: 103–118; E. Zajac & M. Kraatz, 1993, A diametric forces model of strategic change, *SMJ*, 14: 83–102.

86. W. Cascio, 2002, Strategies for responsible restructuring (p. 81), *AME*, 16: 80–91; W. Cascio, C. Young, & J. Morris, 1997, Financial consequences of employment change decisions in major US corporations, *AMJ*, 40: 1175–1189.

87. E. Zuckerman, 2000, Focusing the corporate product, *ASQ*, 45: 591–619.

88. P. Barr, J. Stimpert, & A. Huff, 1992, Cognitive change, strategic action, and organizational renewal, *SMJ*, 13: 15–36.

89. I. Filatotchev, T. Buck, & V. Zhukov, 2000, Downsizing in privatized firms in Russia, Ukraine, and Belarus, *AMJ*, 43: 286–304.

90. M. Carney, 2004, The institutions of industrial restructuring in Southeast Asia (p. 174), *APJM*, 21: 171–188; S. White, 2004, Stakeholders, structure, and the failure of corporate governance reform initiatives in post-crisis Thailand, *APJM*, 21: 103–122.

91. M. Makhija, 2004, The value of restructuring in emerging economies, *SMJ*, 25: 243–267; K. Meyer, 2004, Stakeholder influence and radical change, *APJM*, 21: 235–253.

92. S. Fisher & M. White, 2000, Downsizing in a learning organization, *AMR*, 25: 244–251; P. Shah, 2000, Network destruction, *AMJ*, 43: 101–112.

93. J. Simpert & I. Duhaime, 1997, In the eyes of the beholder, *SMJ*, 18: 111–126; J. Robins & M. Wiersema, 2003, The measurement of corporate portfolio strategy, *SMJ*, 2003: 39–59.

94. D. Welch, 2003, For GM, mortgages are the motor, *BW*, August 4: 36.

95. G. Hamel & C. K. Prahalad, 1994, *Competing for the Future*, Boston: Harvard Business School Press; A. Ilinitch & C. Zeithaml, 1995, Operationalizing and testing Galbraith's center of gravity theory, *SMJ*, 16: 401–410; Markides & P. Williamson, 1996, Corporate diversification and organizational structure, *AMJ*, 39: 340–367; C. K. Prahalad & R. Bettis, 1986, The dominant logic, *SMJ*, 7: 485–501.

96. *Economist*, 2003, The big easy, May 31: 57.

97. Peng, Lee, & Wang, 2005, What determines the scope of the firm over time?

98. Rugman & Verbeke, 2004, A perspective on regional and global strategies of multinational enterprises.

99. United Nations, 2003, *World Investment Report 2003* (p. 5).

100. J. Hagedoorn & B. Sadowski, 1999, The transition from strategic alliances to mergers and acquisitions, *JMS*, 36: 87–107.

101. J. Dyer, P. Kale, & H. Singh, 2003, Do you know when to ally or acquire? Working paper, Brigham Young University.

102. J. Hennart & S. Reddy, 1997, The choice between mergers/acquisitions and joint ventures, *SMJ*, 18: 1–12; D. Yiu & S. Makino, 2002, The choice between joint venture and wholly owned subsidiary, *OSc*, 13: 667–683.

103. P. Porrini, 2004, Can a previous alliance between an acquirer and a target affect acquisition performance?,

JM, 30: 545–562; M. Zollo & J. Reuer, 2003, Experience spillovers across corporate development activities, Working paper, INSEAD.

104. A. McGahan & B. Villalonga, 2002, Does governance form matter? Working paper, Harvard Business School.

105. A. Chandler, 1990, *Scale and Scope*, Cambridge, MA: Harvard University Press.

chapter

10

STRUCTURING, LEARNING, AND INNOVATING MULTINATIONALLY

Outline

- The strategy–structure relationship
- Multinational strategies and structures
- A comprehensive model of multinational structure, learning, and innovation
- Worldwide learning, innovation, and knowledge management
- Debates and extensions
- Implications for strategists

Opening Case: PolyGram/Universal Music Group Makes Local Stars Shine Globally

Universal Music Group (UMG, http://www.new.umusic.com) is the new name for PolyGram, after it was acquired by Seagram (http://www.seagram.com) and then by Vivendi Universal (http://www.vivendiuniversal.com). At present, UMG is the world's largest music company with a network of subsidiaries in seventy-one countries. UMG is also the worldwide market leader with a 24 percent market share. In North America, UMG's artists include Bon Jovi, Mariah Carey, Shania Twain, and Sting. In Europe, they include Ms. Dynamite, Snow Patrol, and U2. In Asia, stars such as Jacky Cheung, Hacken Lee, Kou Shibasashi, and Alan Tam are enlisted.

Originally established as a small recording arm for Siemens (http://www.siemens.com) and Philips (http://www.philips.com), PolyGram outperformed better-known rivals such as EMI (http://www.emigroup.com) and Sony Music (http://www.sonymusic.com) to attain global leadership in its industry. How did PolyGram (now UMG) do it? While there are many intriguing answers, one key area of distinction seems to be PolyGram's unique structure, which allowed it to turn selected local artists into international stars. Originally with a decentralized, country-based structure, PolyGram intended to be a leading player in each country in which it competed. Its talent spotters made nightly forays to local bars, clubs, and concert halls, searching for the raw material with star potential. If they found a promising young artist in Hong Kong, for example, the Hong Kong subsidiary would produce a record for the local market.

While successful, this country-based structure missed out on the profit potential to make national stars into regional or even global stars. Some, although not all, star performers in Hong Kong, for example, might also succeed in China, Taiwan, Southeast Asia, and perhaps elsewhere. If the company could identify and leverage these talents with international potential, it could earn very attractive returns. This was because most competitors, such as EMI and Sony, sourced the majority of their talents from just two "mainstream" countries: Great Britain and the United States. Intense competition for talents inflated the cost of signing new artists in these two countries. Consequently, it became much more profitable to unlock the international potential of an artist or group popular in a nonmainstream market, for example, Björk from Iceland, who sang at the opening ceremony of the 2004 Athens Olympics. As a result, a record company can sign artists who are local stars in

Iceland, Hong Kong, or Venezuela at a fraction of the cost for a similar star in Great Britain or the United States.

The challenge, of course, lies in how to identify such local talents with international potential. Searching for a new star, even locally, is always like looking for the proverbial needle in the haystack. Each new song is an inherently risky innovation and very few local artists have international appeal. Moreover, because PolyGram's staff in key countries such as Great Britain and the United States lacked the detailed, implicit knowledge about what made each local act successful, it was difficult for them to judge which local acts could be "reformulated" internationally. PolyGram thus confronted the challenge of combining very complex, tacit, and hard-to-describe knowledge, namely, linking its understanding of what made a local artist successful with its knowledge of whether this distinctiveness would sell records in other countries. Although such knowledge has no written rules, it is not entirely based on "gut feelings" or "hunches" either. PolyGram would have to call on the combined knowledge of talent spotters, producers, and promotional specialists dispersed in far-flung places around the globe.

Having decided to embark on this more international strategy, PolyGram found its country-based structure inadequate. It thus formed a new structure, featuring a network of International Repertoire Centers (IRCs). This network consisted of seventy-five professionals, located in twenty-one sourcing centers—seven centers in Great Britain, five in the United States, and one each in Australia, Canada, France, Germany, Hong Kong, Italy, Japan, The Netherlands, and Switzerland. IRC professionals had a single mandate: To analyze repertoire sourced by their local colleagues and then identify and exploit those with international potential. They were evaluated and rewarded on the basis of their success in generating international sales from local acts. Experts suggest that what has propelled PolyGram (now UMG) to the top of the global music industry is this deeply embedded, knowledge-based capability to identify, source, and leverage local repertoire internationally through its network of IRCs.

Sources: Based on (1) Y. Doz, J. Santos, & P. Williamson, 2001, From Global to Metanational (pp. 17–18), Boston: Harvard Business School Press; (2) http://www.new.umusic.com (accessed June 19, 2004).

How can multinational enterprises (MNEs) such as PolyGram/UMG be appropriately structured so they can be successful both locally and internationally? How can they learn country tastes, global trends, and market transitions that call for structural changes? How can they increase the odds for success when generating inherently risky and uncertain innovative products and services? These are some of the strategic questions we will address in this chapter. The focus here is on relatively large MNEs with significant international diversification (see Chapter 9). Importantly, this is the topic traditional "global strategy" textbooks emphasize. Because this book broadens the scope of "global strategy" to be "strategy around the globe" (see Chapter 1), we have already covered a wider set of topics including strategic issues confronting smaller, entrepreneurial firms (Chapter 5). Nevertheless, this chapter covers some very important material that underlies the success and failure of larger MNEs.

We start by discussing the crucial relationship between strategy and structure. Next, we highlight a comprehensive model of multinational structure, learning, and innovation. We then discuss learning, innovation, and knowledge management. Debates and extensions follow as usual.

THE STRATEGY–STRUCTURE RELATIONSHIP

Organizational structure (also known as **organizational design** or **organizational architecture**) refers to a firm's formal reporting relationships, procedures, and controls.[1] What drives organizational structure? Not surprisingly, it is usually firm strategy that drives organizational structure. This intuitive idea was first proposed by Alfred Chandler in the 1960s.[2] When PolyGram's strategy was to become a market leader in each of the countries in which it competed, a decentralized, country-based structure made sense (Opening Case). However, when the firm's new strategy called for global leadership in its industry, the original, country-based structure became inadequate. Consequently, a number of IRCs were formed to create a better fit with the new strategy of leveraging some local stars' global potential. For MNEs such as PolyGram, making such structural changes is costly and may introduce some chaos (at least initially). Understandably, there is often substantial **inertia** (forces resistant to changes) in favor of the status quo. Therefore, firms only embark on structural changes when there is a substantial misfit with their strategies and/or when there are grave performance problems—as shown in the case of Nestlé (see Strategy in Action 10.1 on next page).

Moreover, the strategy–structure relationship is not a "one-way street." As much as strategy drives structure, structure also drives strategy.[3] In MNEs such as PolyGram, a decentralized structure treating each country unit as a stand-alone entity facilitates a strategy that maximizes local responsiveness (called a **multidomestic** strategy—discussed later). However, this structure is not conducive for a new strategy that calls for worldwide coordination that taps into local talents for international stardom (called a **transnational** strategy—discussed later). In short, structure can both *enable* and *constrain* strategy. Consequently, PolyGram could carry out its new strategy only by implementing new structural solutions such as the IRCs.

Overall, a *reciprocal* relationship exists between strategy and structure.[4] An appropriate fit between strategy and structure may become a source of competitive advantage. An inappropriate fit may cause performance problems and call for strategic changes, structural changes, or both.[5] This perspective will be more fully developed in the next section.

MULTINATIONAL STRATEGIES AND STRUCTURES

This section first introduces the integration–responsiveness framework centered on the pressures for cost reductions and local responsiveness. We then outline the four strategic choices and the four corresponding organizational structures. Finally,

STRATEGY IN ACTION 10.1. *Nestlé Phases Out Its Multidomestic Strategy*

In 2003, Nestlé (*http://www.nestle.com*) had annual sales of $74 billion, 253,000 employees, 511 factories in 86 countries, and 8,000 (!) brands that were sold in virtually every country in the world. As the world's biggest food company, Nestlé had for many years adopted a multidomestic strategy supported by a decentralized, geographic area structure, in which country managers were given wide leeway on everything from purchasing to packaging. By being locally responsive, this structure helped Nestlé tremendously on the marketing side.

However, the operating margins at Nestlé trailed those at rivals such as Unilever (*http://www.unilever. com*), Danone (*http://www.danonegroup.com*), and Kraft Foods (*http://www.kraftfoods.com*) by as much as 50 percent recently. Peter Brabeck, Nestlé's CEO since 1997, identified gaining control of the decentralized structure as the key challenge. He argued that the highly decentralized structure, which, for example, had five different e-mail systems, had been a disaster for Nestlé from an efficiency standpoint. For example, the headquarters in Switzerland had no idea about the costs of raw materials its subsidiaries bought, in total, from around the world. This prohibited Nestlé from negotiating better

contracts with suppliers and centralizing production. In one extreme case, each of Nestlé's more than forty US factories purchased raw materials independently. Thus, they ended up paying more than twenty different prices for vanilla to the *same* supplier.

Brabeck's aim was to turn this far-flung collection of autonomous businesses into an effective, single global company. One of his main projects was called GLOBE—"global business excellence"—involving 2,000 people worldwide working to standardize everything Nestlé did. In addition, $200 million were spent in a deal with SAP (*http://www.sap.com*), a leading enterprise-level software integrator firm, to integrate Nestlé's reporting systems. Overall, Nestlé cut costs by $2.8 billion. Margins jumped and market capitalization tripled to close to $100 billion in 2003.

Sources: This case was written by David H. Zhu (University of Michigan). It is based on (1) Business Week, 2003, Nestle is starting to slim down at last, October 27: 56–58; (2) Economist, 2004, Daring, defying, to grow, August 7: 55–57; (3) Nestlé Group 2003, http://www.nestle.com (accessed June 28, 2004); (4) The Players, 2003, Online profiles of Peter Brabeck, January 8, http://www.oracle.com (accessed May 1, 2004). Reprinted by permission of the author.

within an MNE context, this section revisits the reciprocal relationship between strategies and structures.

Pressures for Cost Reductions and Local Responsiveness

MNEs primarily confront two sets of pressures: those for cost reductions and those for local responsiveness. The framework of how to simultaneously deal with these two sets of pressures is called the **integration–responsiveness framework,** because cost pressures often call for global integration and local responsiveness usually urges MNEs to adapt locally.[6] In both domestic and international competition, **pressures for cost reductions** are almost universal, especially for firms competing on cost leadership. For example, MNEs' aggressive outsourcing of call center functions to India and Ireland is indicative of how companies respond to pressures for cost reductions. Because Chapter 2 has detailed discussions on the crucial issues associated with cost reductions, we will not repeat them here (consult Chapter 2 if necessary).

Unique to international competition are the **pressures for local responsiveness,** which are reflected in different (1) consumer preferences, (2) distribution channels, and (3) host country demands. Consumer preferences vary tremendously around the world. For example, beef-based hamburgers brought by the likes of McDonald's obviously would find no customers in India, a land where cows are sacred. Large package boxes containing Nestlé baby formula with a beautiful baby face printed on the box surface (its standard package) were once boycotted by some angry African consumers who erroneously thought that the boxes contained babies (!). Distribution channels also vary internationally. Supermarkets dominate countries such as Germany and the United States, requiring suppliers to deliver products in larger packages and less frequently. Smaller shops still dominate in Japan and Mexico, necessitating more frequent and hence more costly deliveries of products in smaller packages. Finally, host country demands and expectations add to the pressures for local responsiveness. The Chinese government insisted on an increasing percentage of locally made components for foreign-branded cars made in China.[7] Canadian-based Bombardier manufactures an "Austrian version" of railcars in Austria, a "German version" in Germany, a "Belgian version" in Belgium, and so on. Although not required by European governments, Bomdardier believes that such local responsiveness is essential for making sales in Europe.[8]

Taken together, while being locally responsive certainly makes local customers and governments happy, these actions unfortunately increase costs. Given the universal interest in lowering costs, a natural tendency is to downplay (or ignore) the different needs and wants of various local markets and to market a "global" version of products and services—ranging from the "global car" to the "global song." The intellectual underpinning of the movement to "globalize" offerings can be traced to a 1983 article written by Theodore Levitt, with a self-explanatory title: "The Globalization of Markets."[9] Levitt argued that advancing modern communication and transportation technologies have led to a convergence of consumer tastes from different countries. As evidence, Levitt pointed out standardized consumer products such as Coke Classic, Levi Strauss jeans, and Sony color TV, which are successful on a worldwide basis. Levitt predicted that such convergence would characterize most product markets of the world in the future.

Levitt's article has often been used as an intellectual underpinning that propels many MNEs to integrate their products globally while minimizing local adaptation. In the automobile industry, Ford, GM, and Mitsubishi experimented with "world car" designs. MTV pushed ahead with the belief that viewers would flock to "global" (essentially American) programming. Unfortunately, most of these experiments have not been successful. Automakers found wide-ranging differences among consumer tastes around the globe. The Toyota Camry, for instance, is the best-selling car in the United States, but a poor seller in Japan. MTV has eventually realized that there is no "global song." In a nutshell, in the name of minimizing costs and capturing converging consumer tastes, the movement to standardize products on a worldwide basis has often backfired (see Chapter 1). In short, one size does not fit all. The upshot is that MNEs cannot afford to focus on one dimension (integration) at the expense of another (responsiveness).[10] Next, we discuss how firms can pay attention to *both* dimensions.

Four Strategic Choices

Based on the integration–responsiveness framework, Figure 10.1 uses the two dimensions of the pressures for cost reductions and local responsiveness to plot the four possible strategic choices for MNEs: (1) home replication, (2) multidomestic, (3) global, and (4) transnational.[11] Each strategy has a set of pros and cons outlined in Table 10.1 (their corresponding structures shown in Figure 10.1 are discussed in the next section).

Home replication strategy, by definition, emphasizes the international replication of home country–based competencies such as production scales, distribution efficiencies, and brand power.[12] In manufacturing, this is usually manifested in an export strategy. In services, this can often be done through licensing and franchising

FIGURE 10.1   **Multinational Strategies and Structures: The Integration–Responsiveness Framework**

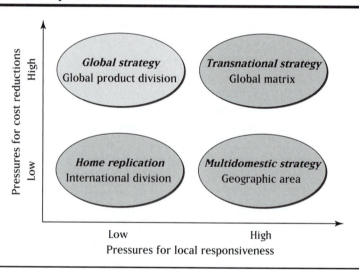

TABLE 10.1   **Four Strategic Choices for Multinational Enterprises**

	ADVANTAGES	DISADVANTAGES
Home replication	▪ Leverages home country–based advantages ▪ Relatively easy to implement	▪ Lack of local responsiveness ▪ May result in foreign customer alienation
Multidomestic	▪ Maximizes local responsiveness	▪ High costs due to duplication of efforts in multiple countries ▪ Too much local autonomy
Global	▪ Leverages low-cost advantages	▪ Lack of local responsiveness ▪ Too much centralized control
Transnational	▪ Cost efficient while being locally responsive ▪ Engages in global learning and diffusion of innovations	▪ Organizationally complex ▪ Difficult to implement

(see Chapter 6). This strategy is relatively easy to implement and usually the first one adopted when firms venture abroad.

On the disadvantage side, this strategy suffers from a lack of local responsiveness. By default, the home replication strategy focuses on the home country, which makes sense when the majority of a firm's customers are domestic. However, when the firm aspires to broaden its international scope to reach more foreign customers, failing to be mindful of foreign customers' needs and wants may result in their alienation. For instance, Wal-Mart, when entering Brazil, set up an exact copy of its stores in the United States, with a large number of American footballs. Unfortunately for Wal-Mart, in Brazil—the land of soccer and winner of five World Cups—no one (other than a few American expatriates in their spare time) plays American football.

Multidomestic strategy is an extension of the home replication strategy. The multidomestic strategy focuses on a number of foreign countries/regions, each of which is regarded as a stand-alone "domestic" market worthy of significant attention and adaptation. This strategy, which sacrifices global efficiencies, is effective when there are clear differences among national and regional markets and low pressures for cost reductions. As noted earlier, MTV, which started with a home replication strategy (literally, broadcasting American programming) when first venturing overseas to Western Europe, has switched to a multidomestic strategy. It currently has eight channels—each in a different language—for Western Europe alone.

In terms of disadvantages, the multidomestic strategy has to shoulder high costs because firms duplicate their efforts in multiple countries. The costs of producing such a variety of programming at MTV are obviously greater than the costs of producing one set of programming. As a result, this strategy is only appropriate in industries when the pressures for cost reductions are not significant. Another drawback is potentially too much local autonomy. Each subsidiary regards its country to be so unique that it is difficult to introduce corporate-wide changes. For example, Unilever had seventeen country subsidiaries in Europe in the 1980s and it took as long as four years to "persuade" all seventeen subsidiaries to introduce a single new detergent across Europe.

Global strategy is the opposite of the multidomestic strategy. Its hallmark is developing and distributing standardized products and services worldwide to reap the maximum benefits from low-cost advantages. While both the home replication and global strategies minimize local responsiveness, a crucial difference is that an MNE pursuing a global strategy is not limited to basing its major operations at home. In a number of countries, the MNE may designate **centers of excellence,** which are defined as subsidiaries explicitly recognized as a source of important capabilities, with the intention that these capabilities be leveraged by and/or disseminated to other subsidiaries.[13] For example, Merck Frosst Canada, the Canadian subsidiary of Merck, is a center of excellence in R&D. Hewlett Packard's (HP) Singapore subsidiary is a center of excellence in manufacturing. Centers of excellence are often given a **worldwide mandate,** namely, the charter to be responsible for one MNE function throughout the world. HP's Singapore subsidiary, for instance, has a worldwide mandate to develop, produce, and market all of HP's handheld products.

In general, MNEs pursuing a global strategy prefer to minimize product customization because customization raises costs. If customization is necessary, MNEs often minimize it. For example, airlines buying Boeing or Airbus jets can only choose different engines (all standardized, similar to tires for cars) and seating configurations. In terms of disadvantages, such a strategy obviously sacrifices local responsiveness. This strategy makes great sense in industries where cost reduction pressures are paramount and local responsiveness pressures are relatively insignificant, such as many commodity industries (oil, semiconductors, and tires). However, as noted earlier, in numerous industries, ranging from automobiles to consumer products, a "one-size-fits-all" global strategy may be inappropriate. Consequently, arguments that all industries are becoming global and all firms need to pursue a global strategy are potentially misleading.

Transnational strategy aims to capture "the best of both worlds" by endeavoring to be both cost efficient and locally responsive.[14] Nestlé, for instance, has endeavored to phase out its multidomestic strategy to increase cost competitiveness while not significantly sacrificing local responsiveness (Strategy in Action 10.1). In addition to cost efficiency and local responsiveness, a third hallmark of this strategy is global learning and diffusing innovations.[15] Traditionally, the diffusion of technological and organizational innovations in MNEs is a one-way flow, from the home country to various host countries—the label "home replication" says it all! This one-way flow is based on the assumption that the home country is the best location for generating innovations, an assumption which is increasingly challenged by critics, who make two points. First, as MNEs increasingly match with each other in production efficiency and geographical reach, the next competitive frontier lies in innovations. Given that innovations are inherently risky and uncertain, there is no guarantee that the home country will generate the highest quality innovations.[16] Second, for many large MNEs, their subsidiaries have acquired various capabilities that are conducive for local innovations, some of which may have potential for wider applications elsewhere.[17] GM, for example, has ownership stakes in Daewoo, Fiat, Opel, Saab, Subaru, and Suzuki. Historically, GM employed a multidomestic strategy and each subsidiary could decide what cars to produce. Consequently, some of these subsidiaries developed locally formidable, but globally underutilized, innovation capabilities. It makes sense for GM to tap into some of these local capabilities for wider applications.

Taking these two points together, MNEs that engage in a transnational strategy promote global learning and innovation diffusion in multiple ways. Innovations not only flow from the home country to host countries (which is the traditional flow), but also flow from host countries to the home country and flow among subsidiaries in multiple host countries.[18] Connecting these geographically dispersed operations creates a flow of knowledge about market conditions and internal capabilities (discussed later). PolyGram's combination of knowledge about local talents and global appeal serves as a case in point (see Opening Case).

On the disadvantage side, a transnational strategy is organizationally complex and difficult to implement. The increased knowledge sharing and coordination

FIGURE 10.2   International Division Structure at Cardinal Health

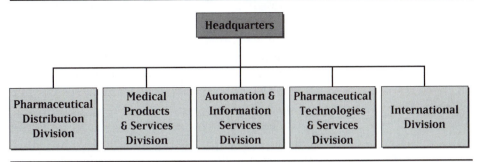

Source: Based on author's interview and www.cardinal.com (accessed August 10, 2004). Cardinal Health is headquartered in Dublin, Ohio. Also see Integrative Case 3.1.

may slow down decision-making speed. Simultaneously trying to achieve cost efficiencies, local responsiveness, and global learning places contradictory demands on MNEs (discussed in the next section).

Overall, MNEs essentially have four strategic choices when competing internationally. Given the various pros and cons, however, no optimal strategy emerges. The popular idea that "a global strategy is the best" can be misleading. Advocates of a transnational strategy need to recognize the significant organizational challenges associated with it. This point leads to our next topic.

Four Organizational Structures

Also shown in Figure 10.1, four organizational structures are appropriate for the four strategic choices outlined previously: (1) international division structure, (2) geographical area structure, (3) global product division structure, and (4) global matrix structure.

International division structure is typically set up when firms initially expand abroad, often engaging in a home replication strategy. For example, Figure 10.2 shows Cardinal Health's new international division, in addition to its four product divisions, which focus on the US health care markets (see also Integrative Case 3.1). Although this structure is intuitively appealing, it often leads to two problems. First, foreign subsidiary managers, whose input is channeled through the international division, are not given sufficient voice relative to the heads of domestic divisions.[19] Second, by design, the international division serves as a "silo" whose activities are not coordinated with the rest of the firm, because the rest of the firm focuses on domestic activities. Consequently, many firms phase out this structure after the initial stage of overseas expansion.

Geographic area structure, which organizes the MNE according to different countries and regions, is the most appropriate structure for a multidomestic strategy. Figure 10.3 on next page illustrates such a structure for Ispat, a leading steelmaker (see Closing Case in Chapter 3). A **geographic area** can be a country or a region that is led by a **country manager** or **regional manager**. Each area largely stands

FIGURE 10.3   Geographic Area Structure at Ispat

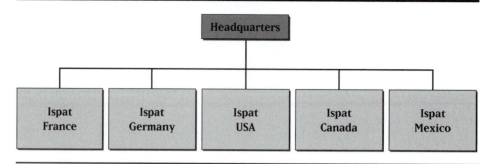

Source: Adapted from www.ispat.com (accessed June 30, 2004). Ispat is headquartered in London, United Kingdom. Also see Chapter 3 Closing Case.

alone, containing its own set of value creation activities (such as R&D, production, and marketing). In contrast to the foreign subsidiary managers' limited voice in the international division structure, country and regional managers who care about being locally responsive carry a great deal of weight in a geographic area structure. Interestingly and paradoxically, *both* the strengths and weaknesses of this structure lie in its capability to facilitate local responsiveness. While being locally responsive can be a virtue, it may also cause the MNE to fragment into highly autonomous, hard-to-control "fiefdoms."

Global product division structure, which is the opposite of the geographic area structure, supports the global strategy. Figure 10.4 shows such an example from EADS, a leading aerospace firm whose most famous product is the Airbus. This structure treats each product division as a stand-alone entity with full worldwide—as opposed to domestic—responsibilities for its activities. This structure helps firms focus on pressures for cost efficiencies, because it allows for consolidation on a worldwide (or at least regional) basis and reduces inefficient duplication in multiple countries. For example, Unilever reduced the number of its soap-producing factories in Europe from ten to two after adopting this structure. Recently, more firms are

FIGURE 10.4   Global Product Division Structure at European Aeronautic Defense and Space Company (EADS)

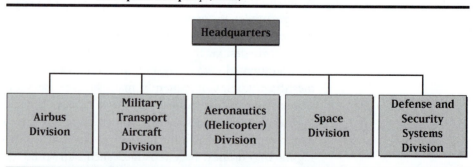

Source: Adapted from www.eads.com (accessed June 30, 2004). EADS is headquartered in Munich, Germany and Paris, France.

FIGURE 10.5   A Hypothetical Global Matrix Structure

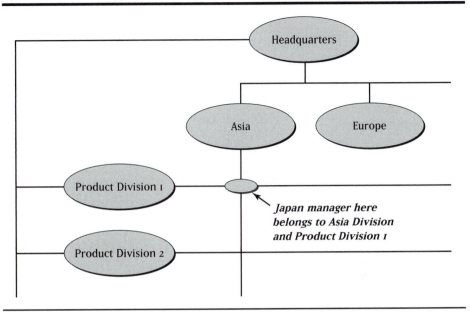

using the global product division structure because of the popularity of global strategy (noted earlier). Many MNEs (such as Ford) have phased out the geographical area structure in favor of the global product division structure, although its noticeable drawback is that local responsiveness suffers.

Global matrix structure is often used to alleviate the disadvantages associated with both geographic area and global product division structures, especially for MNEs adopting a transnational strategy. Shown in Figure 10.5, its hallmark is sharing and coordinating responsibilities between product divisions and geographic areas to be both cost efficient and locally responsive. In this hypothetical example, the manager in charge of Japan reports to Product Division 1 and Asia (area) Division, both of which have equal decision-making power.

In theory, the global matrix structure supports the goals of the transnational strategy. However, in practice, this structure often has difficulty delivering. The reason is simple: While managers (such as the Japan manager) usually find enough headaches dealing with one boss, they do not appreciate having to deal with two bosses, who are often in conflict (!). For example, Product Division 1 may decide that Japan is too tough a nut to crack and that there are more promising markets elsewhere, thus ordering the Japan manager to *curtail* her investment and channel resources elsewhere. This makes sense because Product Division 1 cares about its global market position and is not wedded to any particular country. However, Asia Division, which is evaluated by how well it does in Asia, may beg to differ. It argues that to be a leading player in Asia, it cannot afford to be a laggard in Japan. Therefore, Asia Division demands that the Japan manager *increase* her investment in the country. Facing these conflicting demands, the Japan manager, who prefers to be "politically correct," does not want to make any move before consulting corporate headquarters. Eventually, headquarters may provide a resolution. However, in the process, crucial time may be lost and important windows of opportunity for competitive actions may be missed.

Taken together, the matrix structure, despite its merits on paper,[20] may add layers of management, slow down decision speed, and increase costs while not showing significant performance improvement. No conclusive evidence supports the superiority of the matrix structure.[21] Having experimented with the matrix structure, a number of MNEs, such as the highly visible Swiss-Swedish conglomerate ABB, have now moved back to the simpler and easier-to-manage global product structure. Even when the matrix structure is still in place, global product divisions are often given more power than geographic area divisions. The following quote from the then CEO of Dow Chemical (an early adopter of the matrix structure) is sobering:

> We were an organization that was matrixed and depended on teamwork, but there was no one in charge. When things went well, we didn't know whom to reward; and when things went poorly, we didn't know whom to blame. So we created a global [product] divisional structure, and cut out layers of management. There used to be 11 layers of management between me and the lowest level employees, now there are five.[22]

Although the matrix structure may be too formal and too bureaucratic, this idea is not without merit. Consequently, many MNEs have tried to build a "flexible" matrix structure largely based on corporate-wide *informal* networks, contacts, and shared visions and norms. How they accomplish this is discussed later when we deal with learning and innovation.

Overall, the positioning of the four structures in Figure 10.1 is not random. They evolve from the relatively simple international division through either geographic area or global product division structures and may finally reach the more complex global matrix stage. These paths represent the possible evolutionary trajectories of MNEs, which may grow from having a limited international presence to being sophisticated global players. While not every MNE experiences all these structural stages and the evolution is not necessarily in one direction (consider, for example, ABB's withdrawal from the matrix structure), the model presented in Figure 10.1, first proposed by John Stopford and Lou Wells in the 1970s and known as the **Stopford and Wells model,** does represent the cornerstone of most experiments and discussions on MNE structures.[23]

The Reciprocal Relationship Between Multinational Strategies and Structures

The reciprocal relationship between strategies and structures, discussed earlier, can be vividly portrayed within MNEs. Three key ideas stand out. First, the fit between strategies and structures, as exemplified by the pairs in each of the four cells in Figure 10.1, is crucial.[24] A misfit, such as combining a global strategy with a geographic area structure, may have grave performance consequences. Second, the relationship is two-way. To the extent that certain strategies facilitate certain structures, a given structure also supports a particular strategy. Finally, strategies and structures are not static. The constant changes in industry conditions, firm capabilities, and institutional environments often require strategies, structures, or both to change.[25] For example, in Europe, many MNEs traditionally pursued a multidomestic strategy that was supported by the geographic area structure with a subsidiary for each country (such as the seventeen subsidiaries for Unilever). However, significant integration within the European Union recently made this once value-adding strategy/structure match obsolete. Consequently, many MNEs have now moved toward a pan-European strategy (a mini version of the global strategy) with a regionwide structure. Unilever, for instance, created a Lever Europe group to oversee the seventeen subsidiaries and consolidated a number of operations to save costs.

A COMPREHENSIVE MODEL OF MULTINATIONAL STRUCTURE, LEARNING, AND INNOVATION

Now that we have outlined the basic strategy/structure configurations, it is time to introduce a comprehensive model of multinational structure, learning, and innovation, which, as before, draws on the three leading perspectives on strategy (see Figure 10.6 on next page).

Industry-Based Considerations

Why are MNEs structured differently? Why do they emphasize different forms of learning and innovation? For example, industrial-products firms (such as semiconductor makers) tend to adopt global product divisions, whereas consumer-goods companies (such as cosmetics producers) often rely on geographic area divisions. Industrial-products firms typically emphasize technological innovations, while consumer-goods companies place premiums on learning consumer trends and generating repackaged and recombined products as marketing innovations (such as Heinz's marketing of *green* ketchup to appeal to children). The different nature of industries provides a clue to why MNEs are structured differently and emphasize different innovations.[26] Industrial-products firms value technological and engineering knowledge, which is not location-specific (such as how to most efficiently make semiconductor chips). Consumer-goods industries, on the other hand, must develop intimate knowledge about consumer tastes, which are location-specific (such as what kinds of potato chips consumers *in Hungary* would prefer).[27]

In addition, the Porter five forces again help explain the issue at hand. Within a given industry, as competitors increasingly match each other in cost efficiencies and local responsiveness, their rivalry naturally focuses on learning and innovation.[28] This is especially true in oligopolistic industries (such as automobiles, chemicals, and cosmetics), whose number of competitors has shrunk recently because of mergers and acquisitions (see Chapter 9).

The height of entry barriers also shapes MNE structure, learning, and innovation. Why do many MNEs phase out the multidomestic strategy and geographic

FIGURE 10.6   A Comprehensive Model of Multinational Structure, Learning, and Innovation

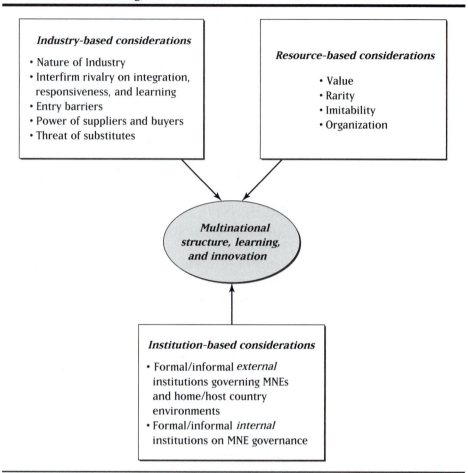

area division structure by consolidating production in a small number of world-scale facilities? One underlying motivation is that smaller, suboptimal-scale production facilities scattered in a variety of countries do not effectively deter potential entrants. Massive, world-scale facilities in strategic locations can serve as more formidable deterrents.[29] Honda, for example, built a world-scale factory for the Accord in Ohio.

Bargaining power of suppliers and buyers also has a bearing on MNE structure, learning, and innovation. When buyer firms move internationally, they increasingly demand that suppliers provide integrated offerings—that is, buyer firms want to purchase the same supplies at the same price and quality in every country in which they operate. Components suppliers are thus often forced—or at least encouraged (!)—to internationalize. Otherwise, these suppliers run the risk of losing a substantial chunk of business. Not surprisingly, as Toyota invested in southern China recently, *all* of its top thirty suppliers set up factories in adjacent areas.

The threat of substitute products has a relatively small impact on MNE structure, but has a direct bearing on learning and innovation. R&D often generates innovative substitutes. 3M's "Post-It" notes, for example, can partially substitute for glue and tapes, and PCs have rendered typewriters obsolete.

Resource-Based Considerations

Shown in Figure 10.2, the resource-based view—exemplified by the VRIO framework—adds a number of insights to the issue at hand.[30] First, the question of value must be confronted.[31] When making structural changes, determining whether the new structures add concrete value is crucial. As noted earlier, the global matrix structure's often-questionable net value-added has disillusioned even some of its most energetic practitioners (such as ABB and Dow Chemical).

Another consideration is the value of innovation. Despite firms' "almost slavish worship of innovation," the truth is that the vast majority of innovations simply fail to reach the market and that five to nine out of ten new products which do reach the market end up being financial failures.[32] In other words, cool ideas and hot products, unfortunately, do not guarantee market success.[33] In another influential article, "Creativity is Not Enough" (published in 1963), Theodore Levitt wrote that "the fact that you can put a dozen inexperienced people in a room and conduct a brainstorming session that produces exciting new ideas shows how little relative importance ideas themselves actually have."[34] There is a crucial difference between an innovator and a *profitable* innovator. The latter not only has plenty of good ideas, but also a lot of **complementary assets** (such as appropriate organizational structures and marketing muscles) to add value to innovation (see Chapter 3). Philips, for example, is a great innovator, having invented such technologies as rotary shavers, videocassettes, and compact discs (CDs). However, its capabilities to profit from these innovations lag behind those of Sony and Matsushita, which had much stronger complementary assets.

A second question is rarity. When all competitors are moving toward a global strategy, this strategy, in itself, cannot be a source of differentiation. In an effort to improve global coordination, many MNEs spend millions of dollars to equip themselves with enterprise resource planning (ERP) packages provided by SAP and Oracle. Because any MNE can buy these packages from the same ERP vendors, these packages are not rare and thus do not qualify as firm-specific capabilities for the adopting firm (such as Nestlé—see Strategy in Action 10.1).

Even when capabilities are valuable and rare, they have to pass a third hurdle, namely, imitability. Formal structures are easier to observe and imitate than informal structures. This is one of the reasons why the informal, flexible matrix is in vogue now. What exactly is an elusive informal, flexible matrix? Christopher Bartlett and Sumantra Ghoshal, two leading advocates of the transnational strategy, suggest that the informal, flexible matrix "is less a structural classification than a broad organizational concept or philosophy, manifested in organizational capability and management mentality."[35] It is obviously a lot harder—if not impossible—to imitate an intangible philosophy or mentality than to imitate a tangible structure.

The last hurdle is organization, namely, how MNEs are organized, both formally and informally, around the world. As discussed previously, if MNEs are able to derive the organizational benefits of the matrix structure without being burdened by a formal matrix structure (that is, building an informal, flexible, invisible matrix), they are likely to outperform rivals.

Institution-Based Considerations

MNEs face two sets of the rules of the game: formal and informal institutions governing (1) *external* relationships and (2) *internal* relationships, as discussed next.

Formal and Informal External *Institutions*

Externally, MNEs are subject to the formal institutional frameworks erected by various home- and host-country governments.[36] For instance, to protect domestic employment, home-country governments may manipulate tax rules to encourage MNEs to invest at home. The British government taxes British MNEs' foreign earnings at a higher rate than their domestic earnings. In another example, home-country governments may, for political reasons, discourage or ban MNEs from structuring certain operations in "sensitive" countries. Now that the Cold War is over, US defense firms such as Boeing and Lockheed Martin are eager to set up R&D subsidiaries in Russia, whose rocket scientists are some of the best (and certainly cheapest!) in the world. These firms have been warned by the US government not to perform any mission-critical R&D there.

Host-country governments, on the other hand, often attract, encourage, or coerce MNEs into undertaking activities that they may otherwise abdicate. For example, basic manufacturing generates low-paying jobs, does not provide sufficient **technology spillovers** (foreign technology being diffused domestically), and carries little prestige. Advanced manufacturing, on the other hand, moves up the value chain, generates better jobs, provides more technology spillovers, and leads to better reputations.[37] Therefore, host-country governments (such as those in China, Hungary, and Singapore) often use a combination of "carrots" (such as tax incentives, matching grants, and free infrastructure upgrades) and "sticks" (such as threats to block market access domestically) to attract MNE investments in advanced manufacturing. Other prized MNE investments include world-scale factories with global mandates, advanced R&D labs, and regional headquarters, all of which generate higher-paying jobs and higher-quality spillovers.

In addition to formal institutions, MNEs also confront a series of informal institutions governing their relationships with home- and host-country environments.[38] In the United States, despite heated presidential election debates, few laws ban MNEs from aggressively setting up overseas structures. However, strategists contemplating such moves have to weigh the informal, but vocal, backlash against such activities, which often result in domestic job losses. Numerous elements of informal institutions are also important when dealing with host countries. For instance, Airbus has more than 1,500 suppliers from more than thirty countries. It spends 40 percent of its procurement budget with US suppliers in more than forty states. While Airbus is not formally required to "farm out" supply contracts, its sourcing decisions are guided by the informal norm of reciprocity: If one country's suppliers are involved with Airbus, airlines based in that country, many of which are state-owned and -influenced, are more likely to buy Airbus aircraft. There are both normative and cognitive dimensions behind such expanded geographic reach. Normatively, if Boeing has major supply relationships in Japan, Airbus would feel compelled to do the same. Cognitively, Airbus may increasingly feel that such subcontracting is the right thing to do—not only politically, but also economically. All the suppliers have demonstrated that they can meet Airbus's quality and cost demands. Thus, Airbus may become more proactive in seeking high quality, innovative suppliers around the world.

Formal and Informal Internal Institutions

The internal rules of the game determine how MNEs are governed. Formally, the organizational charts shown in Figures 10.2 through 10.5 specify the primary scope of responsibilities of various parties. For example, heads in product divisions or geographic area divisions can be held accountable. Most MNEs have evaluation, reward, and punishment systems in place based on these formal rules.

However, the formal organizational charts do not reveal the informal rules of the game, such as organizational norms, values, and networks.[39] The nationality of the head of foreign subsidiaries is such an example. Without formal regulations, MNEs essentially have three choices: (1) a home-country national as the head of a subsidiary (such as an American for a subsidiary of a US-headquartered MNE in India), (2) a host-country national (such as an Indian for the same subsidiary), or (3) a third-country national (such as an Australian for the same subsidiary). MNEs from different countries have different norms when making these appointments. Most Japanese MNEs seem to follow an informal rule: Heads of foreign subsidiaries, at least initially, need to be Japanese nationals.[40] In comparison, European MNEs are more likely to appoint host- and third-country nationals to lead subsidiaries. As a group, US MNEs' practices seem to be between the Japanese and European practices. These staffing approaches may reflect strategic differences.[41] Home-country nationals, especially those long-time employees of the same MNE at home, are more likely to have developed a better understanding of the informal workings of the firm and to be better socialized into its dominant norms and values. Consequently, the Japanese propensity to appoint home-country nationals is conducive for their preferred, global strategy, which values globally coordinated and controlled actions.[42] Conversely, the European comfort in appointing host- and third-country nationals is indicative of European MNEs' (traditional) preference for a multidomestic strategy.

Beyond the nationality of subsidiary heads, the nationality of top executives at the highest level (such as chairman, CEO, and board members) seems to follow another informal rule: They are (almost always) home-country nationals. To the extent that top executives are ambassadors of the firm and that the MNE headquarters' country of origin is a source of differentiation (for example, a German MNE is often perceived to be different from an Italian MNE), home-country nationals would seem to be the most natural candidates for top positions. However, in the eyes of stakeholders, such as employees and governments around the world, a top echelon consisting of largely one nationality does not bode well for an MNE aspiring to "globalize" everything it does. Some critics even argue that this reflects "corporate imperialism."[43] Consequently, some leading MNEs have appointed non–home-country nationals to top posts. The Coca-Cola Company, for instance, appointed Neville Isdell, a native of Ireland, to be its chairman and CEO in 2004. Such non–home-country nationals bring substantial diversity to the organization, which may be a plus. However, such diversity puts an enormous burden on these nonnative top executives to clearly articulate the values and behaviors expected of an MNE's senior managers.[44] Proctor & Gamble (P&G), for example, appointed Durk Jager, a native of the Netherlands, to be its chairman and CEO in 1999. Unfortunately, Jager's numerous change initiatives almost brought the venerable company to a grinding halt and he was quickly forced to resign in 2000. Since then, the old rule is back: an American executive now leads P&G.[45]

Overall, while formal internal rules on how the MNE is governed may reflect conscientious strategic choices, informal internal rules are often taken for granted and deeply embedded in administrative heritages, thus making them difficult to change. This is especially true when dealing with learning, innovation, and knowledge management, as discussed next.

WORLDWIDE LEARNING, INNOVATION, AND KNOWLEDGE MANAGEMENT

This section first sets the key terms straight, and then introduces knowledge management in four types of MNEs. Next, we outline the globalization of R&D, followed by a discussion of the pathologies and solutions in knowledge management.

Setting the Terms Straight

Underpinning the recent emphasis on worldwide learning and innovation is the emerging interest in knowledge management. Before defining "knowledge management," we need to understand what "knowledge" is. Knowledge is broader, deeper, and richer than data or information.[46] **Data** present "discrete, objective facts about events in our world," and **information** is "organized around a body of data."[47] Consequently, **knowledge** can be conceptualized as a fluid mix of skills, experiences, and insights that provides a framework for evaluating and incorporating information.[48] Thus, **knowledge management** can be defined as the structures, processes, and systems that actively develop, leverage, and transfer knowledge. Some scholars argue that knowledge management is *the* defining feature of MNEs.[49]

However, many individuals and companies regard knowledge management as simply information management. Taken to an extreme, "such a perspective can result in a profoundly mistaken belief that the installation of sophisticated information technology (IT) infrastructure is the be-all and end-all of knowledge management."[50] Knowledge management not only depends on IT, but also more broadly on informal social relationships within the MNE. This is because knowledge has two categories: (1) explicit knowledge and (2) tacit knowledge. **Explicit knowledge** is codifiable (that is, it can be written down and transferred without losing much of its richness). Virtually all the knowledge captured, stored, and transmitted by IT is explicit. **Tacit knowledge,** on the other hand, is noncodifiable and its acquisition and transfer require hands-on practice.[51] For instance, a driving manual represents a body of explicit knowledge. However, mastering this manual without any road practice does not make you a good driver. Tacit knowledge is evidently more important and harder to transfer and learn—it can only be acquired through learning by doing (driving in this case). Consequently, from a resource-based perspective, explicit knowledge captured by IT may represent strategically *less* important knowledge. The capabilities to manage the hard-to-codify and -transfer tacit knowledge are more important.

Knowledge Management in Four Types of MNEs

The differences in knowledge management among four types of MNEs (refer to Figure 10.1) fundamentally stem from the interdependence (1) between the headquarters and foreign subsidiaries and (2) among various subsidiaries (Table 10.2).[52] In MNEs pursuing a home replication strategy, such interdependence is moderate and the role of subsidiaries is largely to adapt and leverage parent company competencies. Thus, knowledge of new products, processes, and technologies is mostly developed at the center and flown to subsidiaries, representing the traditional "one-way" flow. Starbucks, for instance, insists on replicating around the world its US coffee shop concept, down to the elusive "atmosphere" (see Opening Case in Chapter 6).

TABLE 10.2   Knowledge Management in Four Types of Multinational Enterprises

STRATEGY	HOME REPLICATION	MULTIDOMESTIC	GLOBAL	TRANSNATIONAL
Interdependence	Moderate	Low	Moderate	High
Role of foreign subsidiaries	Adapting and leveraging parent company competencies	Sensing and exploiting local opportunities	Implementing parent company initiatives	Differentiated contributions by subsidiaries to integrate worldwide operations
Development and diffusion of knowledge	Knowledge developed at the center and transferred to subsidiaries	Knowledge developed and retained within each subsidiary	Knowledge mostly developed and retained at the center and key locations	Knowledge developed jointly and shared worldwide
Flow of knowledge	Extensive flow of knowledge and people from headquarters to subsidiaries	Limited flow of knowledge and people in both directions (to and from the center)	Extensive flow of knowledge and people from the center and key locations to other subsidiaries	Extensive flow of knowledge and people in multiple directions

Sources: Adapted from (1) C. Bartlett & S. Ghoshal, 1989, Managing Across Borders: The Transnational Solution (p. 65), Boston: Harvard Business School Press; (2) T. Kostova & K. Roth, 2003, Social capital in multinational corporations and a micro-macro model of its formation (p. 299), Academy of Management Review, 28 (2): 297–317.

In multidomestic MNEs, the interdependence is low. Knowledge management centers on developing knowledge that can best tackle local markets. For example, PolyGram used to focus only on generating local hits for each of the countries in which it competed (Opening Case). Consequently, there is only a limited flow of knowledge and people from and toward headquarters.

In MNEs pursuing a global strategy, the interdependence is increased. Knowledge is developed and retained at the center and a few "centers of excellence." Consequently, the knowledge and people flow extensively from headquarters and these centers to other subsidiaries. Subsidiaries are supposed to faithfully carry out central commands. For example, the Texas Instruments subsidiary in Japan dutifully carried out the order from headquarters to drop prices and *lose* money, based on the knowledge provided by the center that Japanese rivals' cost structure could not sustain a price war in their home country (see Chapter 8).

High interdependence and extensive bi-directional flows of knowledge are hallmarks of transnational MNEs.[53] For example, Yokogawa Hewlett-Packard (HP), HP's subsidiary in Japan, won a coveted Japanese Deming Award for quality in 1982. The subsidiary was then charged with transferring such knowledge to the rest of the HP family, which resulted in a ten-fold improvement in *corporate*-wide quality by 1992.[54] In another example, extending a popular ice cream developed in Argentina based on the locally popular caramelized milk dessert, Haagen-Dazs introduced this Dulce De Leche flavor throughout the United States and Europe. Within one year, it became the second most popular Haagen-Dazs ice cream flavor (second only to vanilla).[55] Particularly fundamental to transnational MNEs are knowledge flows among dispersed subsidiaries. Instead of a top-down hierarchy, the MNE can be conceptualized as an **integrated network of subsidiaries** (sometimes called an **N-form**), each not only developing locally relevant knowledge, but also aspiring to contribute globally beneficial knowledge that enhances the MNE's *corporate*-wide competitiveness as a whole.[56] Again, PolyGram subsidiaries' combination of local and global knowledge serves as a case in point (see Opening Case).

Globalizing Research and Development

While virtually all MNE functions need to better manage and extend their knowledge, R&D represents an especially crucial arena for knowledge management. Relative to production and marketing, only more recently has R&D emerged as an important function to be internationalized—often known as **innovation-seeking investment** (see Chapter 6).[57] For instance, many IT firms such as Samsung and ST Microelectronics have R&D subsidiaries in Silicon Valley and India. Airbus has a significant R&D presence in Wichita, Kansas, home of major aerospace R&D in the United States. France's telecommunications giant Alcatel has a major R&D unit in China commanding 15 percent of its global R&D budget (see Closing Case in Chapter 7).

From an industry-based standpoint, the intensification of competition for innovation drives R&D's globalization. Global R&D provides a vehicle for gaining

STRATEGY IN ACTION 10.2. *Shiseido Smells at Innovations in France*

France is the undisputed global innovation leader in perfumes. Blending ancient art with modern R&D, the knowledge of how to make attractive perfumes is tacit and hard to codify. Non-French firms, such as Japan's Shiseido (*http://www.shiseido.co.jp*), face the significant challenge of how to access (or "plug in to") and manage such knowledge efficiently. In 1984, Shiseido established its Europe TechnoCentre in France (led by Japanese expatriates) to gather and transfer intelligence for the head office in Japan, which would then process and digest such knowledge. However, Shiseido perfumes developed in Japan initially failed in France.

In 1990, Shiseido realized that to plug in to the fragrance knowledge in France, it had to have some of its people work side by side with the French masters of the trade. Consequently, Shiseido established a new subsidiary, Beauté Prestige International (BPI), aiming at the top end of the French market. In a very unusual step for a Japanese MNE, Shiseido hired a reputable French female CEO, who leveraged her social capital to recruit a staff of top-notch French perfume developers. Despite some cultural conflicts, the Japanese let the French "run the show" in R&D, planning, and marketing, whereas Japanese expatriates learned by close observation, interaction, and simply "smelling." Shiseido then opened its own plant in Gien in the heart of the French perfume

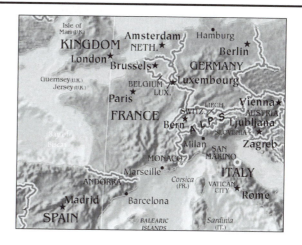

"cluster." In 1992, Shiseido successfully launched two "designer brand" perfumes in France: Eau d'Issey and Jean Paul Gaultier. Since then, Shiseido has transferred such knowledge to Japan and elsewhere. At present, Shiseido is the world's fourth largest cosmetics firm.

Sources: Based on (1) Y. Doz, J. Santos, & P. Williamson, 2001, *From Global to Metanational* (pp. 66–67), Boston: Harvard Business School Press; (2) http://www.www.shiseido-europe.com (accessed June 28, 2004).

access to, or extracting benefits from, a foreign country's local talents and expertise.[58] Recall our earlier discussions in Chapters 4 and 6 on the importance of creating an agglomeration of high caliber, innovative firms within a country or region—called a "cluster" by Michael Porter (refer to Figure 4.3 in Chapter 4).[59] For foreign firms, a most effective way to access such a cluster is to be there through FDI—as Shiseido did in France (see Strategy in Action 10.2). For instance, in the biotechnology industry, Israel has twice as many scientists on a per capita basis as the United States, which makes Israel a very attractive site for R&D investments.[60] In the computer peripherals industry, Taiwan produces 60 percent of scanners, keyboards, and mice in the world. Although the core technologies may originate from Silicon Valley, new knowledge about their design and manufacturing is most likely to come from Taiwan, which attracts R&D investments in that industry.

From a resource-based standpoint, a fundamental basis for competitive advantage is innovation-based firm heterogeneity (that is, being different).[61] Decentralized

TABLE 10.3 Pathologies in Knowledge Management

ELEMENTS OF KNOWLEDGE MANAGEMENT PROCESSES	COMMON PATHOLOGIES
Knowledge acquisition	Failure to share and integrate external knowledge
Knowledge retention	Employee turnover and knowledge leakage
Knowledge outflow	"How does it help me?" syndrome
Knowledge transmission	Inappropriate channels
Knowledge inflow	"Not invented here" syndrome and absorptive capacity

Source: Adapted from A. Gupta & V. Govindarajan, 2004, Global Strategy and Organization (p. 109), New York: Wiley.

R&D work performed by different locations and teams around the world virtually guarantees persistent heterogeneity in the solutions the teams generate. On the other hand, highly centralized R&D may reduce heterogeneity.[62] GSK (formerly Glaxo-SmithKline), for example, has aggressively spun off R&D units as it becomes clear that simply adding more researchers in centralized R&D units does not necessarily increase global learning and innovation.

Pathologies and Solutions in Knowledge Management[63]

Institutionally, how MNEs employ formal and informal rules of the game has a significant bearing on the success or failure of global R&D. Shown in Table 10.3, a number of informal "rules" can be regarded as pathologies of knowledge management. In knowledge acquisition, many MNEs prefer to invent everything internally. Consequently, they often limit knowledge sharing, both among various units and also with the external research community (such as banning the publication of results). However, for large firms, there are actually *diminishing* returns for R&D.[64] Consequently, a new model, called "open innovation," is emerging.[65] This model relies on more collaborative research, among various internal units, with external firms (through R&D contracts, alliances, and outsourcing—see Chapters 6 and 7), and with university labs. Evidence shows that firms that skillfully share research (including publishing results in the public domain) outperform those that fail to do so.[66] For instance, despite having an R&D staff of 7,500, P&G has been unable to keep up with the pace of innovation. In the past fifteen years, it had developed only *one* successful new brand, the Swiffer dust mop. Consequently, P&G attempted to source innovations externally. P&G's goal was to increase the number of externally sourced innovations from 20 percent in 2003 to 50 percent by 2006.[67]

In knowledge retention, the usual problems of employee turnover are compounded when the employees are key R&D personnel, whose departure will lead to knowledge leakage.[68] In knowledge outflow, the "How does it help me?" syndrome emerges. Specifically, managers of the source subsidiary may view outbound knowledge sharing with other subsidiaries as diverting scarce time, energy, and resources. Further, some managers may believe that "knowledge is power"—monopolizing certain useful knowledge may be viewed as the currency to acquire and retain power within the MNE.

Even when certain subsidiaries are willing to share knowledge, inappropriate transmission channels may still torpedo effective knowledge sharing.[69] Given the advancement in IT, it is tempting to establish **global virtual teams,** which do not meet face to face, to transfer knowledge. Unfortunately, such teams often have to confront tremendous communication and relationship barriers, ranging from language and cultural differences to less-than-perfect communication technology (videoconferences, for example, can hardly show body language).[70] In general, the more deeply members of global virtual teams know each other (often through direct interaction over extended periods of time), the greater the teams' likelihood of success.

Finally, recipient subsidiaries may present two pathologies that block successful knowledge inflows. First, the "not invented here" syndrome causes some managers to resist accepting ideas from other units. Second, recipient subsidiaries' **absorptive capacity**—namely, their "ability to recognize the value of new information, assimilate it, and apply it"—may be limited.[71] For instance, R&D subsidiaries in Hungary in the early 1990s were largely staffed by locals who only had a vague idea of how a market economy worked. Yet, the government often demanded that MNEs perform the most advanced R&D there, ignoring the limited absorptive capacity of the recipient subsidiaries. The results were often less than satisfactory.[72]

As solutions to combat these pathologies, corporate headquarters can manipulate the formal rules of the game, such as (1) tying bonuses with measurable knowledge outflows and inflows, (2) using high-powered, corporate- or business-unit-based incentives (as opposed to individual- and single-subsidiary-based incentives), and (3) investing in codifying tacit knowledge.[73] However, these formal policies fundamentally boil down to the very challenging (if not impossible) task of how to accurately measure inflows and outflows of tacit knowledge. The nature of tacit knowledge simply resists such formal bureaucratic practices. Consequently, MNEs often must rely on a great deal of informal integrating mechanisms, such as (1) facilitating management and R&D personnel networks among various subsidiaries through joint teamwork, training, and conferences and (2) promoting strong organizational (that is, MNE-specific) cultures and shared values and norms for cooperation among subsidiaries.[74]

The key idea is that instead of using traditional, formal command-and-control structures, which may be ineffective, knowledge management is best facilitated by informal **social capital,** which refers to the informal benefits individuals and organizations derive from their social structures and networks.[75] Because of social capital, individuals are more likely to go out of their way to help friends and acquaintances. Consequently, managers of the China subsidiary are more likely to provide managers of the Chile subsidiary with needed knowledge if they know each other and have some social relationship. Otherwise, managers of the China subsidiary may not be as enthusiastic to provide such help if the call for help comes from managers of the Cameroon subsidiary, with whom there is no social relationship. Overall, the micro, informal interpersonal relationships among managers of various units may greatly facilitate macro, intersubsidiary cooperation among various units—in short, a **micro-macro link.**[76]

DEBATES AND EXTENSIONS

Deciding how to manage complex MNEs has led to numerous debates, some of which have been discussed earlier (such as the debate on the matrix structure). Here we outline two of the leading debates not previously discussed: (1) corporate controls versus subsidiary initiatives and (2) customer-focused dimensions versus integration, responsiveness, and learning.

Corporate Controls versus Subsidiary Initiatives

One of the leading debates on how to manage large firms is centralization versus decentralization (see Closing Case). Arguments in favor of centralization include (1) capability to facilitate corporate-wide coordination, (2) consistency in decision-making, and (3) sufficient power for corporate-level managers to initiate necessary changes. However, counterarguments suggest that decentralization (1) reduces corporate-level managers' overload of responsibilities and improves decision quality, (2) better motivates subsidiary-level managers and employees through empowerment, and (3) permits greater speed, flexibility, and innovation. In an MNE setting, the debate boils down to central controls versus subsidiary initiatives. A starting point is that subsidiaries are not necessarily at the receiving end of commands from headquarters. For example, when headquarters requires that certain practices (such as quality circles) be adopted, some subsidiaries may be in full compliance, others may engage in "ceremonial adoption" (paying lip service), and still others may refuse to adopt.[77]

In addition to reacting to headquarters' demands differently, some subsidiaries may actively pursue their own, *subsidiary*-level strategies and agendas.[78] These activities are known as **subsidiary initiatives,** defined as the proactive and deliberate pursuit of new business opportunities by a subsidiary to expand its scope of responsibility.[79] Consider, for example, NCR's subsidiary in Dundee, Scotland, which produced automatic teller machines (ATM) and was on the verge of closure because of quality problems in 1980. The subsidiary general manager, while working to improve product quality, developed a vision for Dundee as NCR's key subsidiary for ATMs. Although the ATM group located in the headquarters in Dayton, Ohio actively resisted this idea, the subsidiary manager persisted, privately sponsoring Dundee's R&D program using subsidiary resources. Dundee's global market share reached 20 percent in 1984. In 1985, responsibility for the global ATM business was officially transferred to Dundee.

Such subsidiary initiatives are increasingly common (see Strategy in Action 10.3 on next page for another example). Most recent writers are in favor of such entrepreneurial behavior—as long as subsidiary managers act in good faith. These authors argue that subsidiary capabilities grow (and decline) at varying paces and that a corporate charter (such as being in charge of the ATM business) is not permanent.[80] Such entrepreneurial units may inject a much-needed spirit of entrepreneurship throughout the larger, more bureaucratic corporation.[81]

STRATEGY IN ACTION 10.3. *A Subsidiary Initiative at Honeywell Canada*

Honeywell Limited (*http://www.honeywell.ca*) is a wholly-owned Canadian subsidiary—hereafter "Honeywell Canada"—of the Minneapolis-based Honeywell, Inc. (*http://www.honeywell.com*). Until the mid-1980s, Honeywell Canada was a traditional branch plant for the Canadian market, which produced approximately one-tenth the volume of the main manufacturing operations in Minneapolis. By the late 1980s, the winds of change unleashed by the US-Canadian Free Trade Agreement (later to become NAFTA) threatened the very survival of Honeywell Canada, whose inefficient (suboptimal scale) operations could face closure when the high tariffs came down and Made-in-USA products could enter Canada duty-free. Canadian managers in the subsidiary entrepreneurially proposed to the headquarters that their plant be upgraded and given the mandate to produce for all of North America. In exchange, they agreed to shut down some inefficient lines and let the Minneapolis operations handle their production. Although the US manufacturing managers were understandably negative, the head of the homes division was open-minded. Negotiations followed and

the Canadian proposal was eventually adopted. Consequently, Honeywell Canada was designated as a Honeywell "Center of Excellence" for valves and actuators. At present, Honeywell Canada is Canada's leading controls company.

Sources: Based on (1) J. Birkinshaw, 2000, Entrepreneurship in the Global Firm (p. 26), London: Sage; (2) http://www.honeywell.ca (accessed June 28, 2004); (3) http://www.honeywell.com (accessed June 28, 2004)

However, counterarguments can be made that from the corporate headquarters' perspective, it is hard to distinguish between subsidiary initiative and empire-building. For instance, a lot is at stake when MNEs determine which subsidiaries will become "centers of excellence" with worldwide mandates.[82] Subsidiaries that fail to attain this status may see their roles marginalized and, in the worst case, their facilities closed. Subsidiary managers are often host-country nationals (such as Canadian managers at Honeywell Canada in Strategy in Action 10.3), who would naturally prefer to strengthen their subsidiary—if only to protect local (and their own) employment and not necessarily to be "patriotic." However, these tendencies, although natural and legitimate, are not necessarily consistent with the MNE's *corporate*-wide goals. These tendencies, if not checked and controlled, can lead to chaos.[83]

In theory, the ideal relationship between headquarters and subsidiaries and among subsidiaries themselves would follow the "Swiss Confederation" model that leverages business and cultural diversity—the jargon is the "integrated network" model or the "N-form" (discussed earlier in this chapter). In practice, however, in addition to a few notable well-managed "Swiss Confederations," there seem to be many "Afghanistans torn by conflicts among the divisional warlords and their tribes."[84] For example, until the recent changes (unleashed in 2004 by a new CEO), Motorola's own employees frequently referred to its various subsidiaries and units as "warring tribes."[85] Consequently, solving the contradictions between corporate controls and subsidiary initiatives remains a challenge (see Closing Case).

Customer-Focused Dimensions versus Integration, Responsiveness, and Learning[86]

As our previous discussion indicates, juggling the three dimensions of integration, responsiveness, and learning has often made the global matrix structure so complex that it is unworkable. However, instead of simplifying, many MNEs have added new dimensions that make their structure *more* complex. Often, new, customer-focused dimensions of structure are placed on top of an existing structure, resulting in a four- or five-dimension matrix.

There are three primary customer-focused dimensions. The first is a **global account structure** to supply customers (often other MNEs) in a coordinated and consistent way across various countries. The emphasis is to give large customers dedicated support teams that report exclusively to a global account executive. Most **original equipment manufacturers** (**OEM**s)—namely, contract manufacturers that produce goods that do *not* carrying their own brands (such as the makers of Nike shoes and Microsoft's Xbox)—use this structure. For example, Singapore's Flextronics, the world's largest electronics OEM, has dedicated global accounts for its largest customers, such as Dell, Palm, and SonyEricsson (see Closing Case in Chapter 1). Second, an **industry sector structure** is commonly seen in professional service firms. Accenture (formerly Andersen Consulting), for instance, has focused on four industries and eight service functions (such as supply chain management). Third, a **solutions-based structure** is often used. As a "customer solution" provider, IBM would sell whatever combination of hardware, software, and services that customers prefer, whether that means selling IBM products or selling rivals' offerings. MNEs such as IBM and HP have recently (re)organized themselves along "front-end" and "back-end" dimensions, with the more diverse "front-end" units dealing with customers directly and more integrated "back-end" units focusing on production and support functions.

While focusing on customers is a great way to add value,[87] the challenge is how to best structure the organization to meet this goal. The typical starting point is to put in place informal or temporary solutions rather than create entirely new layers or units. To handle a global customer, the first stage usually entails appointing a global account manager who informally coordinates all the different subsidiaries that sell to the customer. Next the firm would assemble a temporary, cross-division and cross-subsidiary team. However, this ad hoc approach can quickly run out of control, resulting in subsidiary managers' additional duties to report to three or four informal bosses in addition to doing their "day jobs." Eventually, new formal structures may be called for, resulting in inevitable bureaucracy.

In many ways, the new customer-focused dimensions cut across all three existing "mainstream" dimensions, namely, integrating on a global basis, responding to customers in single and multiple markets, and learning how to best meet customers' needs and wants. The fact that many MNEs, despite being under a great deal of cost pressures, have added these new dimensions indicates that the existing three dimensions may not be enough. So what is the solution when confronted with the value-added potential of adding customer-focused dimensions and their associated complexity, bureaucracy, and cost? One recommendation is to *simplify* both product and geographic scope (see Chapter 9).[88] For instance, in 2003, ABB, when facing grave performance problems, significantly downsized and downscoped, transforming its sprawling matrix structure (labeled "Byzantine" by critics) to a mere two global product divisions, power technology and automation.[89]

IMPLICATIONS FOR STRATEGISTS

MNEs represent the ultimate large, complex, and geographically dispersed business organizations. The challenges associated with multinational structure, learning, and innovation are daunting, the complexity is enormous, and the implementation is difficult. Consider multinational structure in terms of the four most fundamental questions in strategy. First, why do firms such as MNEs differ in their structure, learning, and innovation? A short answer is that their different strategies fundamentally drive these activities. Second, how do MNEs behave? Given the reciprocal relationship between strategies and structures, the structural arrangements that MNEs put in place both help them accomplish certain strategies and constrain them from pursuing other strategies—unless they unleash strategic changes, structural changes, or both. Third, what determines the scope of the firm? Because Chapter 9 has focused on product scope, we have emphasized international scope here. The particular strategies the MNEs choose significantly determine the international scope. For example, a home replication strategy results in a relatively smaller international scope, whereas a multidomestic strategy leads to a wider geographic scope worldwide. Global and transnational strategies most likely call for an intermediate scope, because these MNEs are more interested in focusing their work (such as R&D) on the few most advantageous locations. Finally, what determines the international success and failure of firms? This chapter suggests a number of answers, such as (1) an appropriate match between strategies and structures, (2) a value-adding fit between strategies and structures on one hand and marketplace demands and customer preferences on the other hand, and (3) a strong capability in knowledge management centered on global learning and innovation, often involving worldwide R&D. In short, a winning formula seems to be "think global, act local."

Chapter Summary

1. A reciprocal relationship exists between strategy and structure: Strategy drives structure, which, in turn, drives strategy. A misfit would call for strategic changes, structural changes, or both.

2. Governing multinational strategy and structure is an integration–responsiveness framework that focuses on how to deal with pressures for cost reductions and pressures for local responsiveness.

3. The four strategy/structure pairs are (1) home replication strategy/international division structure, (2) multidomestic strategy/geographic area structure, (3) global strategy/global product division structure, and (4) transnational strategy/global matrix structure.

4. The global matrix structure, despite its merits, often becomes too complex. Consequently, many MNEs have sought to develop a flexible, "informal" matrix.

5. Some argue that knowledge management centered on global learning and innovation is *the* defining feature of MNEs. Knowledge management primarily focuses on tacit knowledge.

6. Globalization of R&D calls for capabilities to combat a number of pathologies associated with knowledge creation, retention, outflow, transmission, and inflow. Formal structures and controls are less likely to be effective, and informal social capital is often more useful.

7. The two leading debates highlighted are (1) corporate controls versus subsidiary initiatives and (2) customer-focused dimensions versus integration, responsiveness, and learning.

Key Terms

absorptive capacity

centers of excellence

complementary assets

country manager

data

explicit knowledge

geographic area structure

global account structure

global matrix

global product division

global strategy

global virtual teams

home replication strategy

industry sector structure

inertia

information

integrated network of subsidiaries

integration-responsiveness framework

international division

knowledge

knowledge management

micro-macro link

multidomestic strategy

N-form

organizational design

organizational structure	regional manager	tacit knowledge
original equipment manufacturers (OEMs)	social capital	technology spillovers
pressures for cost reductions	solutions-based structure	transnational strategy
pressures for local responsiveness	Stopford and Wells model	worldwide mandate
	subsidiary initiatives	

Critical Discussion Questions

1. Some say that strategy drives structure, others suggest that structure drives strategy, and still others argue that a reciprocal relationship exists between strategy and structure. What do you think? Why? Can you find any concrete examples to support *each* of these three positions?

2. In this age of globalization, some gurus argue that all industries are becoming global and that all firms need to adopt a global strategy. Do you agree with this statement? Why or why not?

3. Some suggest that the global matrix structure is the final frontier for MNE structure. Yet, the matrix's drawbacks often seem to outweigh its benefits and many MNEs have withdrawn from it. In the absence of the matrix, what are the likely structural arrangements for modern MNEs that strive to take care of integration, responsiveness, and learning simultaneously?

4. ***ON ETHICS:*** You are the general manager of the best-performing subsidiary in an MNE. Because bonuses are tied to subsidiary performance, your bonus is the highest among general managers of all subsidiaries. Now corporate headquarters is organizing managers from other subsidiaries to visit and learn from your subsidiary. You would like to share your "tricks," but you also worry that if your subsidiary is no longer the star unit when other subsidiaries' performance catches up, your bonus will go down (given the limited pool of bonus funds). What are you going to do?

5. ***ON ETHICS:*** You are a corporate R&D manager at Boeing and are thinking about transferring some R&D work to China, India, and Russia, where local talents are superb and labors costs are reasonable (the work performed by a $70,000 US engineer reportedly can be done by an engineer in one of these countries for less than $7,000). However, US engineers at Boeing have staged protests against such moves. US politicians are similarly vocal against such job losses. Finally, the US government has warned Boeing not to perform any classified, sensitive, and defense-related R&D in any of these countries. What are you going to recommend to your CEO?

Closing Case: Centralized and Decentralized Strategic Planning at the Oil Majors

According to some critics, strategic planning may be in crisis. Historically top-down, bureaucratic, and formalized strategic planning is argued to be unable to keep up with the turbulent world of modern competition. Since the 1990s, many corporate planning departments have been downsized, and critics predict the demise of strategic planning. However, at the world's major oil companies now known as the Oil Majors (some of which were known as the Seven Sisters a century ago), such as BP Amoco (http://www.bpamoco.com), ChevronTexaco (http://www.chevrontexaco.com), Elf (http://www.total.com), ENI (http://www.eni.it), ExxonMobil (http://www.exxonmobil.com), Shell (http://www.shell.com), and Texaco (http://www.texaco.com), such a demise seems unlikely as strategic planning continues to play an important, although transformed, role.

Usually ranked among the world's largest enterprises, the Oil Majors have complex operations spanning the globe. The uncertainty of their markets and the large capital requirements call for careful planning. Coordinating multinational value chains (extraction in one country, and refining, distribution, and consumption in other countries) leads to challenging problems. As a result, the Oil Majors were among the first group of firms to pioneer the creation of corporate planning departments in the 1960s, and have been leading-edge practitioners of centralized strategic planning.

Since the 1970s, the competitive environment has experienced a great deal of turmoil, because of the Oil Shocks, international wars and tensions in the Middle East, and civil wars and chaos in major oil-producing countries such as Nigeria, Russia, and Venezuela. As the accuracy of market forecasts—especially of crude oil prices—declines sig-

nificantly, the danger of relying on these forecasts becomes apparent. BP, for example, came to the brink of catastrophe in 1992 by relying on an oil price of $20 a barrel, whereas the price experienced a significant drop since 1986.

In response to the heightened uncertainty, strategic planning at the Oil Majors has been transformed in three significant ways. First, forecasting is reduced, whereas scenario planning, based on multiple scenarios with numerous "reference prices," is increasingly used, especially at Shell. Most planning horizons are shortened from ten to fifteen years to five years or less. Second, planning becomes less formal with less emphasis on written documentation and more on open discussions. At ExxonMobil, the annual planning meetings between divisional and corporate management have been cut from three to four days to a half-day.

Third and perhaps most significantly, all Oil Majors have decentralized their decision-making. The combination of a more turbulent environment and a new focus on improving shareholder returns characterized by active mergers, acquisitions, and consolidations (see Chapters 9 and 11) has pushed decision-making increasingly down to the subsidiary and divisional level. This lower-level decision-making allows for better, speedier response to fast-changing circumstances in many different countries. Capital expenditure limits above which subsidiary and divisional managers need corporate approval have all risen—for instance, to $50 million at ExxonMobil and $150 million at BP. On the other hand, subsidiary and divisional managers are increasingly held accountable for performance targets. An inevitable corollary of these changes is that subsidiary and divisional managers must be free to select strategies capable of delivering the required performance. As a result, since the 1990s, strategy formulation has taken place, for the most part, outside of the corporate strategic planning systems. Strategic decisions are now typically "bottom up," proposed and made by subsidiary and divisional managers, and are subsequently incorporated into corporate strategic plans.

Overall, the corporate planning staff has indeed been reduced since the 1990s. For example, at Shell, the staff has been reduced from 48 to 17. However, the prediction that the planning staff may become an endangered species is premature, because now almost all major subsidiaries and divisions have planning units. The subsidiary and divisional planning staff routinely outnumbers the corporate planning staff—for instance, 416 versus 72 at ENI. Overall, at the Oil Majors, strategic planning has become more decentralized, less corporate-staff driven, and more informal, while plans themselves become shorter term, more goal focused, and less specific.

Case Discussion Questions

1. What are the advantages and disadvantages of centralized strategic planning at the Oil Majors? What about those of decentralized strategic planning?

2. What are the industry-, resource-, and institution-based factors making the Oil Majors believe that the benefits of decentralized planning outweigh its drawbacks recently?

3. What are the potential problems if all divisions and subsidiaries pursue their own initiatives and merely "inform" the corporate headquarters of their actions?

4. What aspects of knowledge management discussed in this chapter might be particularly relevant for enhancing the effectiveness of decentralized planning?

Sources: Based on (1) R. Grant, 2003, Strategic planning in a turbulent environment, Strategic Management Journal, 24: 491–517; (2) T. Herbert, 1999, Multinational strategic planning, Long Range Planning, 32: 81–87; (3) L. Heracleous, 1998, Strategic thinking or strategic planning, Long Range Planning, 31: 481–487; (4) H. Mintzberg, 1994, The Rise and Fall of Strategic Planning, New York: Free Press; (5) D. Simpson, 1998, Why most strategic planning is a waste of time and what you can do about it, Long Range Planning, 31: 476–480.

Notes

Abbreviation list

AME – Academy of Management Executive

AMJ – Academy of Management Journal

AMR – Academy of Management Review

APJM – Asia Pacific Journal of Management

ASQ – Administrative Science Quarterly

BW – Business Week

IBR – International Business Review

JEBO – Journal of Economic Behavior and Organization

JIBS – Journal of International Business Studies

JIM – Journal of International Management

JM – Journal of Management

JMS – Journal of Management Studies

JR – Journal of Retailing

JWB – Journal of World Business

LRP – Long Range Planning

MIR – Management International Review

MS – Management Science

OSc – Organization Science

SBE – Small Business Economics

SMJ – Strategic Management Journal

1. J. Galbraith, 1995, *Designing Organizations*, San Francisco: Jossey-Bass; M. Harris & A. Raviv, 2002, Organization design, *MS*, 48: 852–865.

2. A. Chandler, 1962, *Strategy and Structure*, Cambridge, MA: MIT Press.

3. J. Fredrickson, 1986, The strategic decision process and organizational structure, *AMJ*, 11: 280–297.

4. W. Acar, R. Keatings, K. Aupperle, W. Hall, & R. Engdahl, 2003, Peering at the past century's corporate strategy through the looking glass of time-series analysis, *JMS*, 40:1225–1254; T. Amburgey & T. Dacin, 1994, As the left foot follows the right? The dynamics of strategic and structural change, *AMJ*, 6: 1427–1452; C. Hill & R. Hoskisson, 1987, Strategy and structure in the multiproduct firm, *AMR*, 12: 331–341; G. Jones &

C. Hill, 1988, Transaction cost analysis of strategy-structure choice, *SMJ*, 9: 159–172; R. Kazanjian & R. Drazin, 1987, Implementing internal diversification, *AMR*, 12: 342–354.

5. L. Donaldson, 1987, Strategy and structural adjustment to regain fit and performance, *JMS*, 24: 1–24; I. Harris & T. Ruefli, 2000, The strategy/structure debate, *JMS*, 37: 587–603; D. Jennings & S. Seaman, 1994, High and low levels of organizational adaptation, *SMJ*, 15: 459–475; D. Ketchen, J. Combs, C. Russell, C. Shook, M. Dean, J. Runge, F. Lohrke, S. Naumann, D. Haptonstahl, R. Baker, B. Beckstein, C. Handler, H. Honig, & S. Lamoureux, 1997, Organizational configurations and performance, *AMJ*, 40: 223–240.

6. C. K. Prahalad & Y. Doz, 1987, *The Multinational Mission*, New York: Free Press.

7. M. W. Peng, 2000, Controlling the foreign agent: How governments deal with multinationals in a transition economy, *MIR*, 40 (2): 141–165.

8. C. Hill, 2005, *International Business*, 5th ed. (p. 427), Burr Ridge, IL: McGraw-Hill Irwin.

9. T. Levitt, 1983, The globalization of markets, *HBR*, May-June: 92–102.

10. C. Baden-Fuller & J. Stopford, 1991, Globalization frustrated, *SMJ*, 12: 493–507; M. de Mooij & G. Hofstede, 2002, Convergence and divergence in consumer behavior, *JR*, 78: 61–69; A. Rugman, 2001, *The End of Globalization*, New York: AMACOM.

11. J. Birkinshaw, A. Morrison, & J. Hulland, 1995, Structural and competitive determinants of a global integration strategy, *SMJ*, 16: 637–655; A. Harzing, 2000, An empirical analysis and extension of the Bartlett and Ghoshal typology of multinational companies, *JIBS*, 31: 101–120; A. Harzing, 2002, Acquisitions versus green-field investments, *SMJ*, 23: 211–227; K. Roth & D. Ricks, 1992, Goal configuration in a global industry context, *SMJ*, 15: 103–120.

12. R. Griffin & M. Pustay, 2005, *International Business*, 4th ed. (p. 317), Upper Saddle River, NJ: Prentice Hall.

13. T. Frost, J. Birkinshaw, & P. Ensign, 2002, Centers of excellence in multinational corporations (p. 997), *SMJ*, 23: 997–1018. See also U. Anderson & M. Forsgren, 2000, In search of centers of excellence, *MIR*, 40: 329–350; G. Reger, 2004, Coordinating globally dispersed research centers of excellence, *JIM*, 10: 51–76.

14. C. Bartlett & S. Ghoshal, 1989, *Managing Across Borders: The Transnational Solution*, Boston: Harvard Business School Press.

15. K. Cool, I. Dierickx, & G. Szulanski, 1997, Diffusion of innovations within organizations, *OSc*, 8: 543–559; J. Pennings & F. Harianto, 1992, The diffusion of technological innovations, *SMJ*, 13: 29–46.

16. S. Brown & K. Eisenhardt, 1995, Product development, *AMR*, 20: 343–378; J. Cantwell, J. Dunning, & O. Janne, 2004, Towards a technology-seeking explanation of US direct investment in the United Kingdom, *JIM*, 10: 5–20; C. Christensen & M. Raynor, 2003, *The Innovator's Solution*, Boston: Harvard Business School Press; T. Murtha, S. Lenway, & J. Hart, 2001, *Managing New Industry Creation*, Stanford, CA: Stanford University Press; M. Schulz, 2001, The uncertain relevance of newness, *AMJ*, 44: 661–681.

17. J. Birkinshaw & N. Hood, 1998, Multinational subsidiary evolution, *AMR*, 23: 773–796; A. Rugman & A. Verbeke, 2001, Subsidiary-specific advantages in multinational enterprises, *SMJ*, 22: 237–250.

18. J. Jarillo & J. Martinez, 1990, Different roles for subsidiaries, *SMJ*, 11: 501–512.

19. B. Lamont, V. Sambamurthy, K. Ellis, & P. Simmonds, 2000, The influence of organizational structure on the information received by corporate strategies of multinational enterprises, *MIR*, 40: 231–252.

20. S. Davis & P. Lawrence, 1977, *Matrix*, Reading, MA: Addison-Wesley.

21. L. Burns & D. Wholey, 1993, Adoption and abandonment of matrix management programs, *AMJ*, 36: 106–139; T. Devinney, D. Midgley, & S. Venaik, 2000, The optimal performance of the global firm, *OSc*, 11: 674–695; J. Johnson, 1995, An empirical analysis of the integration-responsiveness framework, *JIBS*, 26: 621–635; K. Roth & A. Morrison, 1990, An empirical analysis of the integration-responsiveness framework in global industries, *JIBS*, 21: 541–64.

22. R. Hodgetts, 1999, Dow Chemical CEO William Stavropoulos on structure (p. 30), *AME*, 13: 29–35.

23. J. Stopford & L. Wells, 1972, *Managing the Multinational Enterprise*, New York: Basic Books. See also J. Birkinshaw, S. Ghoshal, C. Markides, J. Stopford, & G. Yip (eds.), 2003, *The Future of the Multinational Company*, London: Wiley.

24. J. Daniels, P. Pitts, & M. Tetter, 1985, Strategy and structure of US multinationals, *AMJ,* 27: 292–307; W. Davidson & P. Haspeslagh, 1982, Shaping a global product organization, *HBR,* 60 (4): 125–132; W. Egelhoff, 1988, Strategy and structure in multinational corporations, *SMJ,* 9: 1–14; M. Habib & B. Victor, 1991, Strategy, structure, and performance of US manufacturing and service MNCs, *SMJ,* 12: 589–606; J. Wolf & W. Egelhoff, 2002, A reexamination and extension of international strategy-structure theory, *SMJ,* 23: 181–189.

25. G. Benito, B. Grogaard, & R. Narula, 2003, Environmental influences on MNE subsidiary roles, *JIBS,* 34: 443–456; C. Carpano, J. Chrisman, & K. Roth, 1994, International strategy and environment, *JIBS,* 25: 639–656; A. Jaeger & B. Baliga, 1985, Control systems and strategic adaptation, *SMJ,* 6: 115–134; T. Malnight, 2001, Emerging structural patterns within multinational corporations, *AMJ,* 44: 1187–1210; T. Murtha, S. Lenway, & R. Bagozzi, 1998, Global mind-sets and cognitive shift in a complex multinational corporation, *SMJ,* 19: 97–114; M. Ruef, 1997, Assessing organizational fitness on a dynamic landscape, *SMJ,* 18: 837–853; R. Whitley, G. Morgan, W. Kelley, & D. Sharpe, 2003, The changing Japanese multinational, *JMS,* 40: 643–672.

26. M. Makhija, K. Kim, & S. Williamson, 1997, Measuring globalization of industries using a national industry approach, *JIBS,* 28: 679–710.

27. T. Chi, P. Nystrom, & P. Kircher, 2004, Knowledge-based resources as determinants of MNC structure, *JIM,* 10: 219–38.

28. K. Atuahene-Gima, 2003, The effects of centrifugal and centripetal forces on product development speed and quality, *AMJ,* 46: 359–373; D. Dougherty & C. Hardy, 1996, Sustained product innovation in large, mature organizations, *AMJ,* 39: 1120–1153; L. Franko, 1989, Global corporate competition, *SMJ,* 10: 449–474; M. Lawless & P. Anderson, 1996, Generational technological change, *AMJ,* 39: 1185–1217; S. Zahra & A. Nielsen, 2002, Sources of capabilities, integration, and technology commercialization, *SMJ,* 23: 377–398.

29. S. Kobrin, 1991, An empirical analysis of the determinants of global integration, *SMJ,* 12: 17–31.

30. R. Burgelman & Y. Doz, 2001, The power of strategic integration, *SMR,* 42 (3): 28–38; D. Collis, 1991, A resource-based analysis of global competition, *SMJ,* 12: 49–68; P. Cloninger, 2004, The effect of service intangibility on revenue from foreign markets, *JIM,* 10: 125–146; A. Delios & P. Beamish, 2001, Survival and profitability, *AMJ,* 44: 1028–1039; A. Delios & W. Henisz, 2000, Japanese firms' investment strategies in emerging economies, *AMJ,* 43: 305–324; E. Danneels, 2002, The dynamics of product innovation and firm competencies, *SMJ,* 23: 1095–1022; J. Song, 2002, Firm capabilities and technology ladders, *SMJ,* 23: 191–211; S. Tallman, 1991, Strategic management models and resource-based strategies among MNEs in a host country, *SMJ,* 12: 69–82.

31. K. Ojah & L. Monplaisir, 2003, Investors' valuation of global product R&D, *JIBS,* 34: 457–472.

32. J. Andrew & H. Sirkin, 2003, Innovating for cash (p. 77), *HBR,* September: 76–83.

33. M. Gittelman & B. Kogut, 2003, Does good science lead to valuable knowledge? *MS,* 49: 366–382.

34. Cited in Andrew & Sirkin, 2003, Innovating for cash (p. 77).

35. Bartlett & Ghoshal, 1989, *Managing Across Borders* (p. 209).

36. T. Murtha & S. Lenway, 1994, Country capabilities and the strategic state, *SMJ,* 15: 113–130.

37. Y. Akbar & J. McBride, 2004, Multinational enterprise strategy, foreign direct investment, and economic development, *JWB,* 39: 89–105; S. Bhaumik, S. Estrin, & K. Meyer, 2004, Determinants of employment growth at MNEs, Working Paper 707, William Davidson Institute, University of Michigan; N. Driffield & M. Munday, 2000, Industrial performance, agglomeration, and foreign manufacturing investment in the UK, *JIBS,* 31: 21–37; L. Eden, E. Levitas, & R. Martinez, 1997, The production, transfer, and spillover of technology, *SBE,* 9: 53–66; S. Feinberg & S. Majumdar, 2001, Technology spillovers from FDI, *JIBS,* 32: 421–437; W. Hejazi & A. E. Safarian, 1999, Trade, foreign direct investment, and R&D spillovers, *JIBS,* 30: 491–511; X. Liu, P. Siler, C. Wang, & Y. Wei, 2000, Productivity spillovers from foreign direct investment, *JIBS,* 31: 407–425; K. Meyer, 2004, Perspectives on multinational enterprises in emerging economies, *JIBS,* 35: 259–276; M. Wright, I. Filatotchev, T. Buck, & K. Bishop, 2002, Foreign partners in the former Soviet Union, *JWB,* 37: 165–179.

38. T. Blumentritt & D. Nigh, 2002, The integration of subsidiary political activities in multinational corporations, *JIBS*, 33: 57–77; J. Laurila & M. Ropponen, 2003, Institutional conditioning of foreign expansion, *JMS*, 40: 725–751; T. Kostova & S. Zaheer, 1999, Organizational legitimacy under conditions of complexity, *AMR*, 24: 64–81; R. Ramamurti, 2004, Developing countries and MNEs, *JIBS*, 35: 277–283; P. Rosenzweig & H. Singh, 1991, Organizational environments and the multinational enterprise, *AMR*, 16: 340–361.

39. A. Ferner, 2000, The underpinnings of "bureaucratic" control systems, *JMS*, 37: 521–539; D. Marginson, 2002, Management control systems and their effects on strategy formation at middle-management levels, *SMJ*, 23: 1019–1031; N. Nohria & S. Ghoshal, 1994, Differentiated fit and shared values, *SMJ*, 15: 491–502; N. Nooderhaven & A. Harzing, 2003, The "country-of-origin effect" in multinational corporations, *MIR*, 43: 47–66.

40. P. Beamish & A. Inkpen, 1998, Japanese firms and the decline of the Japanese expatriate, *JWB*, 33: 35–50.

41. N. Boyacigiller, 1990, The role of expatriates in the management of interdependence, complexity, and risk in multinational corporations, *JIBS*, 21: 357–381; Y. Gong, 2003, Subsidiary staffing in multinational enterprises, *AMJ*, 46: 728–739; Y. Paik & J. Sohn, 2004, Expatriate managers and MNCs' ability to control international subsidiaries, *JWB*, 39: 61–71; R. Peterson, J. Sargent, N. Napier, & W. Shim, 1996, Corporate expatriate HRM policies, internationalization, and performance in the world's largest MNCs, *MIR*, 36: 215–230.

42. J. Johansson & G. Yip, 1994, Exploiting globalization potential, *SMJ*, 15: 579–601; J. Sohn, 1994, Social knowledge as a control system, *JIBS*, 25: 295–325; R. Tung, 1982, Selection and training procedures of US, European, and Japanese multinational firms, *CMR*, 25: 57–71.

43. C. K. Prahalad & K. Lieberthal, 1998, The end of corporate imperialism, *HBR*, 76 (4): 68–79.

44. L. Palich & L. Gomez-Mejia, 1999, A theory of global strategy and firm efficiency, *JM*, 25: 587–606; P. Pitcher & A. Smith, 2001, Top management team heterogeneity, *OSc*, 12: 1–18; O. Richard, T. Barnett, S. Dwyer, & K. Chadwick, 2004, Cultural diversity in management, firm performance, and the moderating role of entrepreneurial orientation, *AMJ*, 47: 227–240; L. Yaconi, 2001, Cross-cultural role expectations in nine European country-units of a multinational enterprise, *JMS*, 38: 1187–1215.

45. R. Berner, 2003, P&G: New and improved, *BW*, July 7: 52–63.

46. T. Davenport, J. Harris, D. DeLong, & A. Jacobson, 2001, Data to knowledge to results, *CMR*, 43: 117–137; H. Tsoukas & E. Vladimirou, 2001, What is organizational knowledge?, *JMS*, 38: 573–593.

47. R. Bhagat, B. Kedia, P. Harveston, & H. Triandis, 2002, Cultural variations in the cross-border transfer of organizational knowledge (p. 205), *AMR*, 27: 204–221.

48. T. Davenport & L. Prusak, 1998, *Working Knowledge*, Boston: Harvard Business School Press; I. Nonaka & H. Takeuchi, 1997, *The Knowledge-Creating Company*, Oxford, UK: Oxford University Press.

49. L. Argote, B. McEvily, & R. Reagans, 2003, Managing knowledge in organizations, *MS*, 49: 571–582; R. Bettis & C. K. Prahalad, 1995, The dominant logic, *SMJ*, 16: 5–14; H. Bresman, J. Birkinshaw, & R. Nobel, 1999, Knowledge transfer in international acquisitions, *JIBS*, 30: 439–462; J. Child & R. McGrath, 2001, Organizations unfettered, *AMJ*, 44: 1135–1148; Y. Chuang & J. Baum, 2003, It's all in the name, *ASQ*, 48: 33–59; K. Conner & C. K. Prahalad, 1996, A resource-based theory of the firm, *OSc*, 7:472–501; M. Crossan & I. Berdrow, 2003, Organizational learning and strategic renewal, *SMJ*, 24: 1087–1105; M. Crossan, H. Lane, & R. White, 1999, An organizational learning framework, *AMR*, 24: 522–537; R. Grant, 1996, Toward a knowledge-based theory of the firm, *SMJ*, 17: 109–122; G. Huber, 1991, Organizational learning, *OSc*, 2: 88–115; B. Kogut & U. Zander, 1993, Knowledge of the firm and the evolutionary theory of the multinational corporation, *JIBS*, 24: 625–645; R. Langlois, 2002, Modularity in technology and organization, *JEBO*, 49: 19–37; J. March, 1991, Exploration and exploitation in organizational learning, *OSc*, 2: 71–87; S. Matusik & C. Hill, 1998, The utilization of contingent work, knowledge creation, and competitive advantage, *AMR*, 23: 680–697; O. Sorenson, 2003, Interdependence and adaptability, *MS*, 49: 446–463; J. Thomas, S. Sussman, & J. Henderson, 2001, Understanding strategic learning, *OSc*, 12: 331–345; D. Vera & M. Crossan, 2004, Strategic leadership and organizational learning, *AMR*, 29: 222–240.

50. A. Gupta & V. Govindarajan, 2004, *Global Strategy and Organization* (p. 104), New York: Wiley.

51. X. Martin & R. Salomon, 2003, Knowledge transfer capacity and its implications for the theory of the multinational enterprise, *JIBS,* 34: 356–373; U. Schultze & C. Stabell, 2004, Knowing what you don't know? *JMS,* 41: 549–573; G. Szulanski, 1996, Exploring internal stickiness, *SMJ,* 17: 27–43.

52. K. Hewett, M. Roth, & K. Roth, 2003, Conditions influencing headquarters and foreign subsidiary roles in marketing activities and their effects on performance, *JIBS,* 34: 567–585; K. Ito & E. Rose, 1994, The genealogical structure of Japanese firms, *SMJ,* 15: 35–51; S. Kumar & A. Seth, 1998, The design of coordination and control mechanisms for managing JV-parent relationships, *SMJ,* 19: 579–599; Y. Luo & H. Zhao, 2004, Corporate link and competitive strategy in multinational enterprises, *JIM,* 10: 77–105.

53. J. Anand & A. Delios, 1997, Location specificity and the transferability of downstream assets to foreign subsidiaries, *JIBS,* 28: 579–604; M. Lord & A. Raft, 2000, Organizational learning about new international markets, *JIBS,* 31: 573–589; Y. Luo & M. W. Peng, 1999, Learning to compete in a transition economy: Experience, environment, and performance, *JIBS,* 30: 269–296; J. M. Shaver, W. Mitchell, & B. Yeung, 1997, The effect of own-firm and other-firm experience on foreign direct investment survival in the United States, *SMJ,* 18: 811–824.

54. M. Porter, H. Takeuchi, & M. Sakakibara, 2000, *Can Japan Compete?* (p. 80), Cambridge, MA: Perseus.

55. Y. Doz, J. Santos, & P. Williamson, 2001, *From Global to Metanational,* Boston: Harvard Business School Press.

56. G. Hedlund, 1994, A model of knowledge management and the N-form corporation, *SMJ,* 15: 73–90.

57. P. Almeida, 1996, Knowledge sourcing by foreign multinationals, *SMJ,* 17: 155–166; K. Asakawa & M. Lehrer, 2003, Managing local knowledge assets globally, *JWB,* 38: 31–42; R. Belderbos, 2003, Entry mode, organizational learning, and R&D in foreign affiliates, *SMJ,* 24: 235–255; J. Birkinshaw & N. Hood, 2000, Characteristics of foreign subsidiaries in industry clusters, *JIBS,* 31: 141–154; J. Cheng & D. Bolon, 1993, The management of multinational R&D, *JIBS,* 24: 1–18; T. Frost, 2001, The geographic sources of foreign subsidiaries' innovations, *SMJ,* 22: 101–123; W. Kuemmerle, 1999, The drivers of foreign direct investment into research and development, *JIBS,* 30: 1–24; M. Lehrer & K. Asakawa, 2002, Offshore knowledge incubation, *JWB,* 37: 297–306; J. Penner-Hahn, 1998, Firm and environmental influences on the mode and sequence of foreign R&D activities, *SMJ,* 19: 149–168; M. Zedtwitz, O. Gassman, & R. Boutellier, 2004, Organizing global R&D, *JIM,* 10: 21–49.

58. M. W. Peng & D. Wang, 2000, Innovation capability and foreign direct investment, *MIR,* 40: 79–83.

59. M. Porter, 1990, *The Competitive Advantage of Nations,* New York: Free Press.

60. O. Shenkar & Y. Luo, 2004, *International Business* (p. 339), New York: Wiley.

61. L. Cardinal, 2001, Technological innovation in the pharmaceutical industry, *OSc,* 12: 19–36; R. Henderson & I. Cockburn, 1994, Measuring competence? *SMJ,* 15: 63–84; R. Katila & G. Ahuja, 2002, Something old, something new, *AMJ,* 45: 1183–1194; A. Knott, 2003, Persistent heterogeneity and sustainable innovation, *SMJ,* 24: 687–705; M. Mone, W. McKinley, & V. Barker, 1998, Organizational decline and innovation, *AMR,* 23: 115–132; W. Robinson & J. Chiang, 2002, Product development strategies for established market pioneers, early followers, and late entrants, *SMJ,* 23: 855–866; M. Sakakibara, 1997, Heterogeneity of firm capabilities and cooperative R&D, *SMJ,* 18: 143–164; G. Verona, 1999, A resource-based view of product development, *AMR,* 24: 132–142.

62. N. Argyres & B. Silverman, 2004, R&D, organization structure, and the development of corporate technological knowledge, *SMJ,* 25: 929–958; S. Roden & C. Gulanic, 2004, More than network structure, *SMJ,* 25: 541–562.

63. This section draws heavily from Gupta & Govindarajan, 2004, *Global Strategy and Organization.*

64. S. Graves & N. Langowitz, 1993, Innovative productivity and returns to scale in the pharmaceutical industry, *SMJ,* 14: 593–605; H. Greve, 2003, A behavioral theory of R&D expenditures and innovations, *AMJ,* 46: 685–702.

65. G. Ahuja & R. Katila, 2001, Technological acquisitions and the innovation performance of acquiring firms, *SMJ,* 22: 197–220; U. Andersson, M. Forsgren, & U. Holm, 2002, The strategic impact of external networks, *SMJ,* 23: 979–996; D. Gerwin & J. Ferris, 2004, Organizing new product development projects in strategic alliances, *OSc,* 15: 22–37; J. Hagedoorn & G. Duysters, 2002, External sources of innovative capabilities, *JMS,* 39: 167–188; A. Lam, 2003, Organizational learning in

multinationals, *JMS*, 40: 673–703; J. S. Lee, J. Lee, & H. Lee, 2003, Exploration and exploitation in the presence of network externalities, *MS*, 49: 553–570; W. McCutchen, P. Swamidas, & B. Teng, 2004, R&D risktaking in strategic alliances, *MIR*, 44: 53–67; T. Menon & J. Pfeffer, 2003, Valuing internal vs. external knowledge, *MS*, 49: 497–513; M. Mol, P. Pauwels, P. Matthyssens, & L. Quintens, 2004, A technological contingency perspective on the depth and scope of international outsourcing, *JIM*, 10: 287–305; R. Narula & G. Duysters, 2004, Globalization and trends in international R&D alliances, *JIM*, 10: 199–218; R. Reagans & B. McEvily, 2003, Network structure and knowledge transfer, *ASQ*, 48: 240–267; F. Rothaermel & D. Deeds, 2004, Exploration and exploitation alliances in biotechnology, *SMJ*, 25: 201–221; W. Sheremata, 2004, Competing through innovation in network markets, *AMR*, 29: 359–377.

66. H. Greve & A. Taylor, 2000, Innovations as catalysts for organizational change, *ASQ*, 45: 54–80; D. Hoopes & S. Postrel, 1999, Shared knowledge, "glitches," and product development performance, *SMJ*, 20: 837–865; J. Spencer, 2003, Firms' knowledge-sharing strategies in the global innovation system, *SMJ*, 24: 217–233; J. Sorensen & T. Stuart, 2000, Aging, obsolescence, and organizational innovation, *ASQ*, 45: 81–112; M. Yamin & J. Otto, 2004, Patterns of knowledge flows and MNE innovative performance, *JIM*, 10: 239–258.

67. Berner, 2003, P&G; J. Greene, 2003, Reinventing corporate R&D, *BW*, September 22: 74–76

68. J. Song, P. Almeida, & G. Wu, 2003, Learning-by-hiring, *MS*, 49: 351–365.

69. R. Daft & R. Lengel, 1986, Organization information requirements, media richness, and structural design, *MS*, 32: 554–571; S. Ghoshal, H. Korine, & G. Szulanski, 1994, Interunit communication in multinational corporations, *MS*, 40: 96–110; R. Nobel & J. Birkinshaw, 1998, Innovation in multinational corporations, *SMJ*, 19: 479–496.

70. B. Ambos & B. Schlegelmilch, 2004, The use of international R&D teams, *JWB*, 39: 37–48; T. Atamer & D. Schweiger, 2003, Transnational horizontal project teams, *JWB*, 38: 81–83; S. Chevrier, 2003, Crosscultural management in multinational project groups, *JWB*, 38: 141–149; P. C. Earley & E. Mosakowski, 2000, Creating hybrid team cultures, *AMJ*, 43: 26–49; K. Goodall & J. Roberts, 2003, Only connect:

Teamwork in the multinational, *JWB*, 38: 150–160; B. Kirkman, B. Rosen, P. Tesluk, & C. Gibson, 2004, The impact of team empowerment on virtual team performance, *AMJ*, 47: 175–192; K. Lagerstrom & M. Andersson, 2003, Creating and sharing knowledge within a transnational team, *JWB*, 38: 84–95; R. Lunnan & T. Barth, 2003, Managing the exploration vs. exploitation dilemma in transnational "bridging teams," *JWB*, 38: 110–126; M. Maznevski & K. Chudoba, 2000, Building space over time, *OSc*, 11: 473–492; A. Mendez, 2003, The coordination of globalized R&D activities through project teams organization, *JWB*, 38: 96–109; M. Montoya-Weiss, A. Massey, & M. Song, 2001, Getting it together, *AMJ*, 44: 1251–1262; J. Salk & M. Brannen, 2000, National culture, networks, and individual performance in a multinational management team, *AMJ*, 43: 191–202; D. Schweiger, T. Atamer, & R. Calori, 2003, Transnational project teams and networks, *JWB*, 38: 127–140; M. Zellmer-Bruhn, 2003, Interruptive events and team knowledge acquisition, *MS*, 49: 514–528.

71. W. Cohen & D. Levinthal, 1990, Absorptive capacity, *ASQ*, 35: 128–152; P. Lane, J. Salk, & M. Lyles, 2001, Absorptive capacity, learning, and performance in international joint ventures, *SMJ*, 22: 1139–1162; M. Lenox & A. King, 2004, Prospects for developing absorptive capacity through internal information provision, *SMJ*, 25: 331–345; M. Schulz, 2003, Pathways of relevance, *OSc*, 14: 440–459; W. Tsai, 1999, Knowledge transfer in intraorganizational networks, *AMJ*, 44: 996–1005; A. Van Den Bosch, H. Volberda, & M. Boer, 1999, Coevolution of firm absorptive capacity and knowledge environment, *OSc*, 10: 551–568; S. Zahra & G. George, 2002, Absorptive capacity: A review, reconceptualization, and extension, *AMR*, 27: 185–203.

72. M. Lyles & J. Salk, 1996, Knowledge acquisition from foreign parents in IJVs, *JIBS*, 27: 877–903.

73. W. C. Kim & R. Mauborgne, 1998, Procedural justice, strategic decision making, and the knowledge economy, *SMJ*, 19: 328–338; R. Muralidharan & R. Hamilton, 1999, Aligning multinational control systems, *LRP*, 32: 352–361; K. Roth & S. O'Donnell, 1996, Foreign subsidiary compensation strategy, *AMJ*, 39: 678–703; T. Zenger & W. Hesterly, 1997, The disaggregation of corporations, *OSc*, 8: 209–222.

74. P. Ensign, 2002, Reputation and technological knowledge sharing among R&D scientists in the

multidivisional, multinational firm, PhD dissertation, University of Montreal; H. Kim, J. Park, & J. Prescott, 2003, The global integration of business functions, *JIBS*, 34: 327–344; M. Hansen, 1999, The search-transfer problem, *ASQ*, 44: 82–111; I. Manev & W. Stevenson, 2001, Nationality, cultural distance, and expatriate status, *JIBS*, 32: 285–304; S. O'Donnell, 2000, Managing foreign subsidiaries, *SMJ*, 21: 525–548; W. Ouchi, 1980, Markets, bureaucracies, and clans, *ASQ*, 25: 129–141; R. Reagans & E. Zuckerman, 2001, Networks, diversity, and productivity, *OSc*, 12: 502–517; M. Subramaniam, S. Rosenthal, & K. Hatten, 1998, Global new product development processes, *JMS*, 35: 773–796; M. Subramaniam & N. Venkatraman, 2001, Determinants of transnational new product development capability, *SMJ*, 22: 359–378; M. Thomas-Hunt, T. Odgen, & M. Neale, 2003, Who's really sharing? *MS*, 49: 464–477; E. Tsang, 2002, Acquiring knowledge by foreign partners from international joint ventures in a transition economy, *SMJ*, 23: 835–854; P. Wang, T. Tong, & C. Koh, 2004, An integrated model of knowledge transfer from MNC parent to China subsidiary, *JWB*, 39: 168–182.

75. T. Kostova & K. Roth, 2003, Social capital in multinational corporations and a micro-macro model of its formation, *AMR*, 28: 297–317. See also P. Adler & S. Kwon, 2002, Social capital, *AMR*, 27: 17–40; K. Turner & M. Makhija, 2005, The role of organizational controls in managing knowledge, *AMR* (in press).

76. M. W. Peng & Y. Luo, 2000, Managerial ties and firm performance in a transition economy: The nature of a micro-macro link, *AMJ*, 43: 486–501; W. Tsai & S. Ghoshal, 1998, Social capital and value creation, *AMJ*, 41: 464–476; A. Zaheer, B. McEvily, & V. Perrone, 1998, Does trust matter?, *OSc*, 9: 1–20.

77. S. Beechler & J. Zhang, 1994, The transfer of Japanese-style management to American subsidiaries, *JIBS*, 25:467–491; R. Durand, 2003, Predicting a firm's forecasting ability, *SMJ*, 24: 821–838; R. Edwards, A. Ahmad, & S. Moss, 2002, Subsidiary autonomy, *JIBS*, 33: 183–192; T. Kostova & K. Roth, 2002, Adoption of an organizational practice by subsidiaries of multinational corporations, *AMJ*, 45: 215–233.

78. B. Allred & K. S. Swan, 2004, Contextual influences on international subsidiaries' product technology strategy, *JIM*, 10: 259–286; S. Floyd & P. Lane, 2000, Strategizing throughout the organization, *AMR*, 25: 154–177; M. Geppert, K. Williams, & D. Matten, 2003, The social construction of contextual rationalities in MNCs, *JMS*, 40: 617–641; M. Kriger, 1988, The increasing role of subsidiary boards in MNCs, *SMJ*, 9: 347–360; J. Medcof, 2001, Resource-based strategy and managerial power in networks of internationally dispersed technology units, *SMJ*, 22: 999–1012; K. Moore, 2001, A strategy for subsidiaries, *MIR*, 41: 275–290; W. Newburry, 2001, MNC interdependence and local embeddedness influences on perception of career benefits from global integration, *JIBS*, 32: 497–507; J. Taggart, 1998, Strategy shifts in MNC subsidiaries, *SMJ*, 19: 663–81.

79. J. Birkinshaw, 2000, *Entrepreneurship in the Global Firm* (p. 8), London: Sage Publishing, Inc.

80. C. Galunic & K. Eisenhardt, 2001, Architectural innovation and modular corporate forms, *AMJ*, 44: 1229–1249; L. Poppo, 2003, The visible hands of hierarchy within the M-form, *JMS*, 40: 403–430.

81. J. Birkinshaw, N. Hood, & S. Jonsson, 1998, Building firm-specific advantages in multinational corporations, *SMJ*, 19: 221–241; R. Burgelman, 1983, A process model of internal corporate venturing in the diversified firm, *ASQ*, 28: 223–244; J. Stopford & C. Baden-Fuller, 1994, Creating corporate entrepreneurship, *SMJ*, 15: 521–536.

82. S. Feinberg, 2000, Do world product mandates really matter? *JIBS*, 31: 155–167.

83. Y. Cheng & A. Van de Ven, 1996, Learning the innovation journey, *OSc*, 7: 593–614; K. Koput, 1997, A chaotic model of innovative search, *OSc*, 8: 528–542; D. Polley, 1997, Turbulence in organizations, *OSc*, 8: 445–457.

84. L. Franko, 2003, Designing multinational organizations (p. 104), in Birkinshaw et al. (eds.), 2003, *The Future of the Multinational Company* (pp. 100–114).

85. R. Crockett, 2004, Reinventing Motorola, *BW*, August 2: 82–83.

86. This section draws heavily from J. Birkinshaw & S. Terjesen, 2003, The customer-focused multinational, in Birkinshaw et al. (eds.), *The Future of the Multinational Company* (pp. 115–127).

87. T. Hult & D. Ketchen, 2001, Does market orientation matter? *SMJ*, 22: 899–907.

88. *Economist*, 2004, Simplifying Philips, June 12: 66.

89. S. Reed, 2003, Work your magic, Herr Dormann, *BW*, Feb 10: 46.

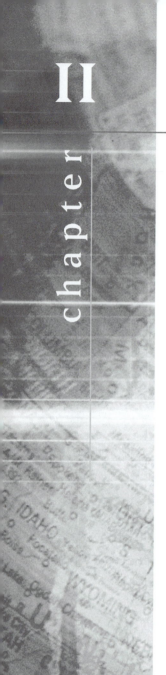

GOVERNING THE CORPORATION AROUND THE WORLD

Outline

- Defining corporate governance
- Owners
- Managers
- Board of directors
- Governance mechanisms as a package
- A global perspective
- Industry-, resource-, and institution-based views on corporate governance
- Debates and extensions
- Implications for strategists

Opening Case: DaimlerChrysler

Since Daimler-Benz (http://www.daimler-benz.com) and Chrysler (http://www.chrysler.com) *merged in 1998, their differences in corporate governance, such as (1) board composition, (2) board functions, and (3) executive compensation, have attracted significant attention. In terms of board composition, US firms use a single board of directors consisting of both inside (executive) and outside (nonexecutive) directors—75 percent of the directors on Chrysler's board were outsiders. German firms use a two-tier board system: an upper, supervisory board (consisting of nonexecutives) and a lower, management board (consisting of executives). By law, half of the members of the supervisory board have to come from employees—a unique practice called "codetermination." Shareholders (usually banks) typically control the other half of the supervisory board.*

The boards also function differently. A typical US board meets relatively frequently—Chrysler's met almost once every month. Daimler-Benz's supervisory board met only six times a year, a high number by German standards. In general, it seems obvious that a board that seldom met would be less informed and less able to monitor management than one that met frequently. This contrast is dramatic between Chrysler's and Daimler-Benz's boards. The Chrysler board was informed of the impending merger in February 1998, three months ahead of its announcement. Jurgen Schrempp, Daimler-Benz's CEO and chairman of the management board, kept both boards in the dark. He informed the management board only in April and the supervisory board in May, only one day (!) before the merger was announced.

Another key difference is executive pay. US executives are often granted lucrative stock options. German law does not even recognize stock options. German executive pay is modest compared with US levels. In 1997, the ten members of Daimler-Benz's management board earned a total of $11 million, of which about $1.5–2 million went to Schrempp. In that year, Robert Eaton, chairman and CEO of Chrysler, received salary and bonus of $4.6 million and cashed in stock options for another $5 million. Overall, the top five Chrysler executives took home more than three times what their ten Daimler-Benz colleagues made.

DaimlerChrysler (http://www.daimlerchrysler.com) was initially proclaimed as a "merger of equals," with two co-chairmen, Schrempp and Eaton. However, it soon became clear who was in charge: DaimlerChrysler would be incorporated under German law. On the thorny issue of executive pay, both sides agreed that pay levels would remain unchanged for two years. The first post-merger annual report caused substantial concerns among US shareholders, because its disclosure (although legal in Germany) was significantly less than expected. For example, it had no details on executive pay, director stock ownership, or largest owners. With this German takeover in all but name, morale was low among US executives and many left. Germans, on the other hand, resented that American managers made two or three times more. In 2001, Eaton stepped down as a co-chairman earlier than planned and was replaced by a German executive.

With intense competition in the post-9/11 recession, the promised $3 billion of "synergy" from this merger, for which Daimler-Benz paid $40 billion, remained as elusive as ever. By the end of 2003, DaimlerChrysler shares lost 56 percent of their value. Worse yet, in an interview published in 2000, Schrempp confirmed that he had never intended to treat Chrysler as equal; instead it would become a division of DaimlerChrysler. When asked why he had not stated his true intention during merger talks, he suggested it was because Chrysler shareholders would not have agreed. These remarks quickly triggered a revolt among former Chrysler shareholders, who believed that they had been misled and denied takeover premium. In 2003, DaimlerChrysler paid $300 million to settle a class

action case, and Schrempp himself was dragged into a US court in a case filed by Kirk Kerkorian, formerly the largest Chrysler shareholder who controlled 14 percent of its shares. With 4 percent of DaimlerChrysler shares, Kerkorian was its third largest shareholder.

In 2004, Schrempp was nominated by Business Week as one of the worst managers of the year. In the shareholder meeting in April, he endured hours of criticism (including calls for his ouster), for having destroyed more than $40 billion in shareholder value since the Chrysler merger. Thanks to the norm in Germany that CEOs deserve multiple chances, Schrempp ultimately won key votes. Nevertheless, the 87 percent of the votes he got was widely seen as a sharp reprimand in a passive shareholder culture where 99 percent approval is routine.

Sources: Based on (1) Business Week, 2004, Worst managers: Jurgen Schrempp, January 12: 72–73; (2) Economist, 2003, The way we govern now, January 11: 59–61; (3) G. Edmondson, 2004, Daimler's fumbles are firing up Europe's shareholders, Business Week, April 19: 52; (4) R. Grover, 2003, What a difference a phrase makes, Business Week, November 24: 110–111; (5) R. Monks & N. Minow, 2001, Corporate Governance, Oxford, UK: Blackwell.

Why do we see differences in corporate governance practices at large corporations such as Daimler-Benz, Chrysler, and now DaimlerChrysler? How can we ensure that professional managers such as Schrempp and Eaton, who hold a relatively small (or no) amount of equity, advocate shareholder value? What can be done if they don't? These are some of the key questions we will address in this chapter, which focuses on how to govern the corporation around the world. Corporate governance has caught worldwide attention recently, propelled by governance scandals in Western firms such as Enron, Royal Ahold, and Parmalat and governance failures in emerging economies such as the Asian financial crisis (1997) and the Russian default (1998) (see Video Cases 3.3–3.6).[1] Understanding corporate governance is not only important for firms operating domestically, but also crucial for cross-border operations.

This chapter first defines what corporate governance is, followed by a discussion of its "tripod" (owners, managers, and board of directors). Next, we introduce internal and external governance mechanisms from a global perspective. Then, industry-, resource-, and institution-based views on corporate governance are outlined. As before, debates and extensions follow.

DEFINING CORPORATE GOVERNANCE

Corporate governance is defined as "the relationship among various participants in determining the direction and performance of corporations."[2] The primary participants are (1) owners, (2) managers, and (3) board of directors—collectively known as the "tripod" underpinning corporate governance (Figure 11.1). Other participants include stakeholders, such as employees, customers, suppliers, creditors, and the community. Because owners such as shareholders are a major (and some view as the most important) group of stakeholders, for composition simplicity, we refer to *nonshareholder stakeholders* when using the term "stakeholders" (see also Chapter 12). Next, we discuss each of the three legs of the tripod.

OWNERS

Owners provide capital, bear risks, and own the firm—in other words, they are capitalists. Their status in the global economy is so foundational that they give rise to the term *capitalism.* Although ownership patterns vary around the world, the three broad patterns are (1) concentrated versus diffused ownership, (2) family ownership, and (3) state ownership.

Concentrated versus Diffused Ownership

Private ownership is the hallmark of capitalism. Founders usually start up firms and completely own and control these enterprises on an individual or family basis. This is referred to as **concentrated ownership and control.** However, the amount of capital a family group—however rich it may be—can raise is limited (see Chapter 5). At some point, if the firm aspires to grow, the owners' desire to keep the firm in family hands will have to accommodate the arrival of other shareholders.[3]

FIGURE 11.1   The Tripod of Corporate Governance

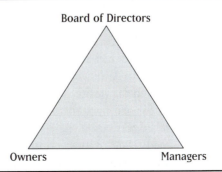

Source: Adapted from R. A. G. Monks & N. Minow, 2001, Corporate Governance *(cover), Oxford, UK: Blackwell.*

Most large, publicly traded US and UK corporations are now characterized by **diffused ownership,** with numerous small shareholders, but none with a dominant level of control. In such firms, there is a separation of **ownership and control,** in that ownership is dispersed among many small shareholders and control is largely concentrated in the hands of salaried, professional managers who own little (or no) equity.[4]

If majority or dominant owners (such as founders) do not personally run the firm, they are naturally interested in keeping a close eye on how the firm is run. However, dispersed owners, each with a small stake, have neither the incentive nor resources to do so. Most small shareholders, for example, do not show up at annual shareholder meetings. They simply prefer to free ride and hope that other shareholders will properly monitor and discipline the management. If the small shareholders are not happy, they sell the stock and invest elsewhere. However, if all shareholders behaved in this manner, managers would end up acquiring significant *de facto* control power.

However, the rise of large institutional investors, such as professionally managed mutual funds and pension pools, has significantly changed this picture.[5] From 1980 to 1996, large institutional investors nearly doubled their share of ownership of US corporations from under 30 percent to over 50 percent.[6] Similar patterns can be found in UK firms. Therefore, ownership of US and UK firms has gradually become more concentrated recently—largely in the hands of institutional investors. Institutional investors have both the incentive and resources to closely monitor and control managerial actions. The increased size of institutional holdings limits the institutional investor's ability to dump the stock, because when an investor's stake is large enough, selling out depresses the share price and harms the seller. Therefore, actively exercising shareholder rights, as opposed to selling the stock, becomes more appealing for institutional investors (see Video Case 3.6).

While the image of widely held corporations is a reasonably accurate description of modern large US and UK firms, it is *not* the case in other parts of the world. Outside the Anglo-American world, there is relatively little separation of ownership and control. Most large firms are typically owned and controlled by families or the state, which participate in management.[7] Next, we turn our attention to these firms that are owned by family or the state.

Family Ownership

Although most small firms in the world are owned and controlled by families, interestingly, the vast majority of *large* corporations throughout continental Europe, Asia, Latin America, and Africa still feature concentrated family ownership and control.[8] On the positive side, family ownership and control may provide better incentives for the firm to focus on long-run performance and may also minimize the conflict between owners and professional managers typically encountered in widely owned firms.[9] However, on the negative side, family ownership and control may lead to the selection of less qualified managers (who happen to be the sons, daughters, and relatives of owners), the destruction of value because of dysfunctional family conflicts, and the expropriation of minority shareholders (discussed in a later section on "Principal-Principal Conflicts").[10] At present, no conclusive evidence exists on the positive or negative role of family ownership and control on the performance of large corporations.[11] What is undisputed is that from a global perspective, concentrated family ownership and control of large corporations is the norm outside the Anglo-American world.

State Ownership

Other than families, the state is a major owner of firms in many parts of the world. Until the late 1980s, state ownership was extensive throughout communist countries—commanding 95 percent and 78 percent of GDP in the former Soviet Union and China, respectively, at the beginning of their reforms. Outside the communist bloc, in Africa, Asia, and Latin America, state ownership was similarly extensive. In many developed economies, state ownership was also high—commanding 17 percent, 14 percent, and 11 percent of GDP in France, Italy, and Great Britain, respectively, during the early 1980s.

Since the 1980s, state ownership has been largely discredited, as one country after another—ranging from Britain to Brazil to Belarus—realized that their state-owned enterprises (SOEs) often perform poorly. In brief, SOEs suffer from an incentive problem. Although in theory all citizens, including employees, are owners, in practice, they have neither rights to claim the residual income generated from SOEs (as capitalist shareholders would), nor rights to control SOEs, much less power to transfer or sell "their" property. SOEs are *de facto* owned and controlled by government agencies far removed from ordinary citizens and employees. As a result, SOE managers and employees are not motivated to improve performance, which they can hardly benefit from personally. In a most cynical fashion, SOE employees in the former Soviet Union summed it up well: "They pretend to pay us and we pretend to work."

Since the 1980s, a wave of privatization has hit the world involving more than one hundred countries. The SOE share of the global GDP has declined from more than 10 percent in 1979 to approximately 5 percent today.[12] Nevertheless, privatization is far from finished in most countries. The state continues to play an important—albeit somewhat reduced—role in many firms (such as retaining a "golden share" with veto power in nearly one third of *privatized* Russian firms).

In summary, owners can be capitalist shareholders, families, or governments. While the most typical form of ownership in US and UK firms is diffused ownership, concentrated family and state ownership dominate the corporate landscape in much of the world.

MANAGERS

Managers, especially executives on the **top management team** (**TMT**) led by the **chief executive officer** (**CEO**), represent another crucial leg of the corporate governance tripod. This section discusses how to govern professional, SOE, and family managers.

Principal-Agent Conflicts

The relationship between shareholders and professional managers can be characterized as a relationship between principals and agents—or an **agency relationship** in short. **Principals** are persons (such as owners) delegating authority, and **agents** are persons (such as managers) to whom authority is delegated. **Agency theory** suggests a simple, yet profound, proposition: Because the interests of principals and agents do not completely overlap, inherently there will be **principal-agent conflicts.** These conflicts result in **agency costs,** which include (1) principals' costs of monitoring and controlling agents, (2) agents' costs of bonding, and (3) the residual loss because the interests of the principals and the agents do not align.[13] In a corporate setting, when shareholders (principals) are interested in maximizing the long-term value of their stock, managers (agents) may be more interested in maximizing their own power, income, and perks (see Chapter 9).

Manifestations of agency problems include excessive on-the-job consumption (such as corporate jets), low-risk, short-term investments (such as maximizing current earnings while cutting long-term R&D), and empire-building (such as value-destroying acquisitions). In general, the larger the firm, the higher the executive compensation. In 1980, the average US CEO earned approximately 42 times what the average blue-collar worker earned. Today, the ratio is more than 400 times.[14] Despite some performance improvement, it seems difficult to argue that the average firm improved its performance by ten times since 1980, which probably would have justified such tenfold increase of executive compensation.[15] While the costs of empire-building and compensation that shareholders have to shoulder are direct evidence of agency costs, some indirect evidence is perhaps as compelling.[16] For example, one of the most macabre academic studies finds that some sudden executive deaths—in plane crashes or from heart attacks—are accompanied by an *increase* in share prices of the firms these executives managed.[17] This evidently suggests that these executives, when they were alive, destroyed corporate value and that the capital market, sadly (and some may even say cruelly), was pleased with such tragedies.

Likewise, agency problems are extensive in SOEs. Because governments often have conflicting goals, such as developing the economy, creating wealth, and maintaining full employment, they usually have inadequate resources to monitor what is going on in thousands of SOEs. Managers as agents thus acquire significant control power, typically bargaining for a performance target as low as possible and hoarding as much slack as possible.[18] Not surprisingly, numerous SOEs have been run "to the ground," thus triggering reforms.

The primary reason agency problems persist is because of **information asymmetries** between principals and agents—in other words, agents almost always know more about the property they manage than principals do. As a leading agent, the CEO knows far more about the firm than shareholders or government officials. While it is possible to reduce information asymmetries, it probably is not realistic to completely eliminate agency problems.

Principal-Principal Conflicts

Since concentrated—not diffused—ownership and control by families is the norm in many parts of the world, different kinds of conflicts are at play. One of the leading indicators of concentrated family ownership and control is the practice of appointing family members as board chairman, CEO, and other TMT members. In East Asia (excluding China), approximately 57 percent of the corporations have board chairmen and CEOs from the controlling families.[19] In continental Europe, the number is 68 percent.[20] The families are able to do so, because they are controlling (although not necessarily majority) shareholders. For example, in 2003, thirty-year-old James Murdoch was appointed CEO of British Sky Broadcasting (BSkyB), Europe's biggest satellite broadcaster, in the face of loud minority shareholder resistance. The reason? James' father is Rupert Murdoch, who controlled 35 percent of BSkyB and chaired the board.

The BSkyB case is a classic example of the conflicts in family-owned and family-controlled firms. Instead of conflicts between principals (shareholders) and agents (professional managers), the primary conflicts are between two classes of principals: controlling shareholders and minority shareholders—in other words, **principal-principal conflicts**[21] (see Figure 11.2 and Table 11.1 on next page). Family managers such as Rupert and James Murdoch, who represent (or are) controlling shareholders, often advance family interests at the expense of minority shareholders. Although as owners, family managers have incentives to maintain firm value, their dominant position as *both* principals and agents (managers) may allow them to override traditional governance mechanisms designed to curtail principal-agent conflicts. For example, the board of directors, a mechanism designed to supervise the CEO, will be hardly effective when the CEO being evaluated is the son of the board chairman.

The result is that family managers, who represent (or are) controlling shareholders, may engage in **expropriation** of minority shareholders, defined as activities which enrich the controlling shareholders at the expense of minority shareholders.[22] For example, managers from the controlling family may simply divert resources from the firm for personal or family use. First coined in the Czech Republic, this activity is vividly nicknamed **tunneling**—digging a tunnel to sneak out.[23] For example, at Italy's Parmalat, billions of dollars were tunneled out by family managers (see Strategy in Action 11.1 on page 449). While tunneling is illegal, expropriation can be legally done through **related transactions,** where controlling owners sell firm assets to another firm they own at below-market prices or spin off the most profitable part of a public firm and merge it with another of their private firms (see Closing Case).[24] Family managers often establish private firms, with the express purpose of carrying out such related transactions. Despite the multinational presence of Rupert Murdoch's media empire (News Corporation, Fox Network, and *The Times* of London, in addition to BSkyB), probably few would have heard of his 100 percent privately owned firm, Cruden Investments, which sits on top of the entire "pyramid" of his companies.[25]

Overall, while corporate governance practice and research traditionally focuses on how to control professional managers because of the separation of ownership and

FIGURE 11.2   Principal-Agent Conflicts and Principal-Principal Conflicts

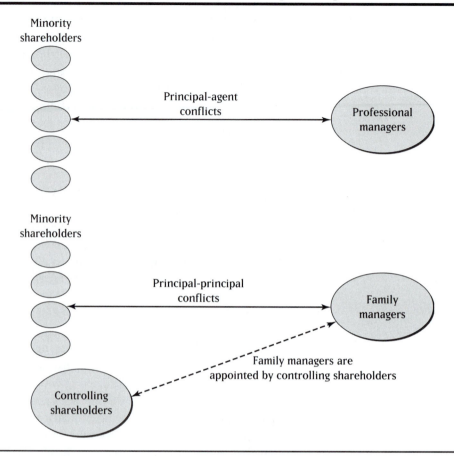

TABLE 11.1   Principal-Agent Conflicts versus Principal-Principal Conflicts

	PRINCIPAL-AGENT CONFLICTS	PRINCIPAL-PRINCIPAL CONFLICTS
Ownership pattern	Dispersed—shareholders holding 5 percent of equity are regarded as "blockholders."	Dominant—often greater than 50 percent of equity is controlled by the largest shareholders.
Manifestations	Strategies that benefit entrenched managers at the expense of shareholders (such as shirking, excessive compensation, and empire-building).	Strategies that benefit controlling shareholders at the expense of minority shareholders (such as minority shareholder expropriation and cronyism).
Institutional protection of minority shareholders	Formal constraints (such as courts) are more protective of shareholder rights. Informal norms adhere to shareholder wealth maximization.	Formal institutional protection is often lacking. Informal norms are typically in favor of controlling shareholders.
Market for corporate control	Active, at least in principle as the "governance mechanism of last resort."	Inactive even in principle. Concentrated ownership thwarts notions of takeover.

Source: Adapted from M. Young, M. W. Peng, D. Ahlstrom, & G. Bruton, 2002, Governing the corporation in emerging economies: A principal-principal perspective, Academy of Management Best Papers Proceedings, Denver.

STRATEGY IN ACTION 11.1. *Italy's Parmalat Turns Sour*

On December 15, 2003, something troubling happened at Parmalat (*http://www.parmalat.com*), one of the world's largest dairy firms with headquarters in Italy and operations in Argentina, Brazil, Chile, China, France, Germany, Hungary, Mexico, Paraguay, Russia, Spain, United States, and Uruguay. On that day, Calisto Tanzi, founder, chairman, and CEO, resigned. Italian prosecutors discovered that managers simply invented assets to offset as much as $16.2 billion in liabilities and falsified accounts over a fifteen-year period, forcing the $9.2 billion company into bankruptcy on December 27. Parmalat thus justified its nomination as "Europe's Enron." As with Enron (see Video Cases 3.4 and 3.5), Parmalat's problems may have been ignored for longer than necessary because people were taken in by the firm's constant self-promotion. No one knows for certain whether missing funds were used to plug operating losses, pay creditors, or illegally enrich top managers, who come from the founding family. The fake balance sheet figures allowed Parmalat to continue borrowing. Tanzi also confessed to misappropriating some $620 million to cover losses in other family-owned companies.

Prior to the outbreak of the scandal, Parmalat had already acquired a reputation for lack of transparency. From a corporate governance standpoint, Parmalat's big investors had utterly failed to use their leverage to alter the behavior of Tanzi and his lieutenants. Indeed, it is not yet clear whether investors made any real effort to demand better disclosure and an end to "funny financing." Respected global banks, including Citigroup

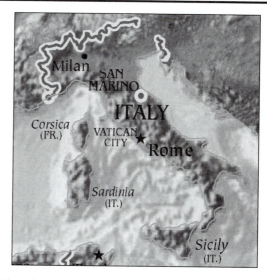

(*http://www.citigroup.com*), J.P. Morgan (*http://www.jpmorgan.com*), and Deutsche Bank (*http://www.deutsche-bank.de*), were too willing to construct the derivatives deals by which Parmalat transferred funds offshore. Parmalat failed to disclose a lot of information to Standard & Poor's (S&P, *http://www.standardandpoors.com*), yet the agency happily issued investment-grade ratings on its bonds. Only when the firm entered crisis mode did it become clear how wrong S&P had been.

Sources: This case was written by Yi Jiang (Fisher College of Business, The Oho State University). It is based on (1) Economist, 2003, Déjà vu all over again? December 20: 95-96; (2) Economist, 2004, Turning sour, January 3: 8-9; (3) G. Edmondson, 2004, How Parmalat went sour, Business Week, January 12: 46–48. Reprinted by permission of the author.

control in most US and UK corporations, how to govern SOE managers and family managers in firms with concentrated ownership and control is of equal or probably higher importance in other parts of the world.

BOARD OF DIRECTORS

As an intermediary between owners and managers, the board of directors oversees and ratifies strategic decisions and evaluates, rewards, and, if necessary, penalizes top managers.

Key Features of the Board

Key features of the board include (1) size, (2) composition, (3) ownership, (4) leadership, and (5) interlocks. Each is an important dimension of board functions.

Board Size

The average size of the board varies around the world. At present, US boards typically have ten to eleven members. A board without a critical mass of capable directors is not able to fulfill its multidimensional functions.[26] However, an excessively large board, such as a typical Japanese board (until recently) with several dozen directors, can severely delay decision speed. Not surprisingly, leading Japanese firms have radically downsized their boards since the 1990s (such as going from forty-two directors to thirteen at Nissan, from thirty-seven to seventeen at NEC, and from thirty-nine to ten at Sony).[27] One way to make a large board more manageable is to establish committees, such as audit, compensation, and nomination committees, each charged with a specialized mission.

Board Composition

Otherwise known as the insider/outsider mix, board composition has attracted significant attention. The trend around the world is to introduce more **outside directors,** who are defined as nonmanagement members of the board. Outside directors presumably are more independent from management and can better safeguard shareholder interests.[28] In the United States, less than a half century ago, most boards were made up entirely or largely of **inside directors,** who were top executives. In the recent, post-Enron era, many US firms are rapidly heading in the opposite direction—favoring a board that is entirely independent, with the exception of the CEO and perhaps the chief financial officer (CFO). In comparison, Japanese boards, for example, only introduce outside directors, who are typically from banks, when the firm is in financial difficulties.[29]

Although there is a widely held belief in favor of a higher proportion of outside directors, academic research has *failed* to empirically establish a link between the outsider/insider ratio and firm performance.[30] Recent scandals indicate that even "stellar" companies with a majority of outside directors on the board (on average 74 percent of outside directors at Enron, Global Crossing, Qwest, and Tyco in the year before their scandals erupted) can still be plagued by significant governance problems.[31] Some of these outside directors, although not firm employees, may have family and/or professional relationships with the firm or firm management.

Board Ownership

Outside directors are busy people often holding other full-time jobs elsewhere. Given the competition for their time and attention, how can they be motivated to do a better job? Offering an ownership stake to directors is usually regarded as a good incentive.[32] On average, 91 percent of the board directors in US Standard & Poor's (S&P) 500 firms own stock, and 56 percent of the S&P 500 boards are comprised entirely of directors with shareholdings.

Board Leadership

Board leadership—whether the board is led by a separate chairman or the CEO who doubles as a chairman, a situation known as **CEO duality**—is also an important feature. From an agency theory standpoint, if the board is to supervise agents such as the CEO, it seems imperative that the board be chaired by a separate individual.[33] Otherwise, how can the CEO be evaluated by the body that he or she chairs?[34] However, a corporation led by two top leaders—a board chairman and a CEO—may lack a unity of command and experience a top-level conflict. Not surprisingly, there is significant divergence across countries. For instance, while a majority of the large UK firms separate the two top jobs, most large US firms combine them. A practical difficulty often cited by US boards is that it is very hard to recruit a capable CEO without the board chairman title.

In other countries, both practices can be found. In countries such as Germany and Austria with two-tier boards, the chairman of the supervisory board is always a nonexecutive, whereas the management board is chaired by the CEO (see Opening Case). In East Asia and Latin America where most firms have concentrated family ownership and control, there is extensive CEO duality. The jury is still out regarding the effectiveness of these two practices, since academic research does *not* support the view that firms led by a separate board chairman necessarily outperform those with CEO duality.[35] However, firms around the world are being pressured to split the two top jobs to at least show that they are serious about controlling the CEO. In US firms with CEO duality, the trend now is to appoint a **lead independent director,** who chairs the board's **executive sessions** (a very confusing term, which refers to sessions held by outside directors that do *not* involve company executives).

Board Interlocks

Who the directors are and where they come from are also important factors. Directors tend to be economic and social elites who share a sense of camaraderie and reciprocity. When one person affiliated with one firm sits on the board of another firm, an **interlocking directorate** has been created. Firms often establish relationships through such board appointments. For instance, outside directors from financial institutions often facilitate financing.[36] Outside directors experienced in joint ventures and acquisitions may help the focal firms engage in these practices.[37]

Among all directors, only a small percentage (usually less than 20 percent) are multiple directors serving on more than one board (usually two). In the United States, Frank Carlucci, a former Secretary of Defense and chairman of the Carlyle Group himself, served on twenty boards (!) in 1992. In Hong Kong, the most heavily connected director, David Li, chairman of the Bank of East Asia, sat on nine boards in 1996.[38] Critics argue that "no one, however talented, can hope to sit on the boards of that many companies and effectively monitor the management of each."[39] In fact, one of the boards David Li served on was Enron's. In the post-Enron environment, such unusual practices are increasingly rare. However, the importance of interlocking directorates is likely to increase, because most firms are seeking to add more outside directors.

What Do Boards Do?

In a nutshell, boards of directors perform (1) control, (2) service, and (3) resource acquisition functions.[40] Corporate law in most countries dictates that boards must exercise discipline and control over managers. According to agency theory, managers—if left to their own devices—may pursue actions that benefit themselves at the expense of shareholders. Boards' effectiveness in serving the control function stems from their (1) independence, (2) deterrence, and (3) norms.

First, the ability to effectively control managers fundamentally boils down to how independent directors are. While inside directors (executives) who report to the CEO are not likely to properly monitor and control their boss, outside directors who are personally friendly to and loyal to the CEO are unlikely to challenge managerial decisions either. Exactly for this reason, CEOs often nominate family members, personal friends, and other seemingly independent directors with a known reputation for being passive on other boards.[41]

Second, there is a lack of deterrence on the part of directors should they fail to protect shareholder interests. Courts usually will not second-guess board decisions in the absence of bad faith or insider dealing. Directors are thus often protected from the consequences of bad decisions.

Third and finally, there is often a lack of norms for directors to challenge management. Most existing norms are to uncritically support the CEO. Most of the information about the firm that directors receive is through the CEO, who is understandably interested in painting a "rosy picture." Moreover, in the face of increased board independence, CEOs often enhance their ingratiation and persuasion toward directors.[42] In addition, directors who "stick their necks out" by confronting the CEO in meetings tend to be frozen out of board deliberations.[43] When they raise a point, nobody picks it up. When informal meetings are called, they are not invited. These norms significantly discourage independently minded directors.

In addition to monitoring and control, another important function of the board is service—primarily advising the CEO.[44] While some directors are passive, directors who are actively involved in strategy formulation tend to have a positive impact on firm performance.[45] It is very time-consuming for directors to be so actively involved. For example, the average number of hours US directors devoted to board duties increased from approximately thirteen hours a month in 2001 to close to twenty in 2003 (a 54 percent increase). British directors reportedly spent on average twenty-five hours a month in 2003.[46]

Finally, another crucial board function is resource acquisition for the focal firm, often through interlocking directorates.[47] For example, in Germany and Japan, bankers serving on the board help line up financing. In Thailand, military officers on corporate boards add to the legitimacy of ethnic Chinese firms that are politically vulnerable.[48] In China, outside directors from buyers, suppliers, and alliance partners bring in more resources resulting in higher sales growth.[49]

Overall, until recently, many boards of directors have been closed, elite-based clubs that "rubber stamp" (approve without scrutiny) managerial actions. Prior to the 1997 economic crisis, many South Korean boards, for example, did not even bother to hold meetings and board decisions would be literally "rubber stamped"—not even by directors themselves; corporate secretaries would stamp all the rubber seals of directors that were kept in the corporate office. However, change is in the air throughout the world for boards to increase their activism. In South Korea, board meetings are now regularly held and seals personally stamped by directors.

Directing Strategically

To function effectively, directors have to be "nose in, but hands off," which is one of the most demanding tasks. Given the comprehensive functions of control, service, and resource acquisition and the limited time and resources directors have, directors have to prioritize strategically. How directors prioritize strategically differs significantly around the world. In US and UK firms, the traditional focus, which stems from their separation of ownership and control, is on the boards' control function. While the service function is still important, the resource acquisition role, although important in practice, tends to be criticized by policymakers, activists, and the media, who often regard activities such as interlocking directorates as "collusive." Consequently, recent US regulations—in particular the Sarbanes-Oxley Act of 2002—emphasize the control function almost to the exclusion of the resource acquisition function. Some scholars have voiced concerns that such a lack of balance may lead to unhealthy board functioning in the future.[50]

Because outside directors are not likely to have enough first-hand knowledge about the firm, they are forced to focus on financial performance targets and numbers—known as **financial control** (see Table 11.2). Financial control may encourage the CEO to focus on the short run at the expense of long-run shareholder interests (such as maximizing current earnings by reducing R&D). Therefore, inside directors, who are executives, can bring first-hand knowledge to board deliberations, allowing for a more sophisticated understanding of some managerial actions (such as investing in the future while not maximizing current earnings). A board informed by such inside views is able to exercise **strategic control,** basing its judgment beyond a mere examination of financial numbers (also see Chapter 9). It seems that a healthy board requires both kinds of control, thus calling for a balanced composition of insiders and outsiders.[51]

In the rest of the world, many boards are established and modeled after Anglo-American boards. However, the similarities between them are often more in

TABLE 11.2   Outside Directors versus Inside Directors

	Pros	Cons
Outside directors	▪ Presumably more independent from management (especially the CEO) ▪ More capable of monitoring and controlling managers ▪ Good at financial control	▪ Independence may be illusory ▪ "Affiliated" outside directors may have family or professional relationships with the firm or management ▪ Not good at strategic control
Inside directors	▪ Firsthand knowledge about the firm ▪ Good at strategic control	▪ Non-CEO inside directors (executives) may not be able to control and challenge the CEO

form than in substance. In practice, a great deal of emphasis is on resource acquisition—through interlocking directorates and cross shareholdings. The service role is less pronounced, and the control function is often hardly detectable.[52] Overall, while boards in theory should perform the three roles of control, service, and resource acquisition, in practice, the relative emphasis differs significantly across countries.

GOVERNANCE MECHANISMS AS A PACKAGE

Governance mechanisms can be broadly classified as internal and external ones—otherwise known as voice-based and exit-based mechanisms, respectively. **Voice-based mechanisms** refer to shareholders' willingness to work with managers, usually through the board of directors, by "voicing" their concerns. **Exit-based mechanisms,** in contrast, indicate that shareholders no longer have patience and are willing to "exit" by selling their shares. This section outlines each of these mechanisms and emphasizes the point that it is the combination of voice- and exit-based mechanisms that come together as a *package* that determines governance effectiveness.[53]

Internal (Voice-Based) Governance Mechanisms

The two internal governance mechanisms typically employed by boards can be characterized as (1) "carrots" and (2) "sticks." In order to better motivate managers, stock options used as carrots that transform managers from agents to principals have become increasingly popular. This helps explain the rise of executive compensation in recent decades. Many believe that increasing management ownership is likely to encourage managers to take risk and innovate, instead of engaging in risk-averse and even shirking activities.[54]

The underlying idea is pay for performance, which seeks to link executive compensation—of not only the CEO, but also other managers and directors—with firm performance.[55] While in theory this idea is sound, in practice it has a number of drawbacks. If accounting-based measures (such as return on sales) are used, managers are often able to manipulate numbers to make them look better than they actually are. If market-based measures (such as stock prices) are adopted, managers often argue that stock prices are subject to too many forces beyond their control. Consequently, the pay-for-performance link in executive compensation is usually not very strong.[56] However, it is important not to dismiss this idea completely. Pay-for-performance relationships are much stronger in firms with concentrated—as opposed to diffused—ownership profiles, probably because large shareholders are able to assert more control over executive compensation.[57]

In general, boards are likely to use carrots before considering sticks.[58] However, when facing continued performance failures, boards may have to dismiss the CEO and other top managers. Recently, top management turnover has become increasingly frequent. Among the 2,500 largest publicly traded companies around the world, a striking 40 percent of all CEO changes during 2002 were firings for underachievement.[59] There was a sharp increase compared with previous years. From 1995 to 2002, the frequency of CEO turnover in Europe rose a whopping

192 percent, compared with just a 2 percent increase in North America, where company bosses have traditionally enjoyed less job security.[60] In brief, boards seem to be more "trigger-happy" and increasingly unwilling to give CEOs the benefit of the doubt. Because top managers have to shoulder substantial firm-specific employment risk (a fired CEO is extremely unlikely to run another publicly traded company), they naturally demand more generous compensation—a premium on the order of 30 percent or more—before taking on new CEO jobs. This in part explains the rapidly rising levels of executive compensation.[61]

In the face of managers determined to pursue their self-interests, neither carrots nor sticks will be successful. In terms of providing more carrots, no direct linear relationship exists between management ownership and firm performance. One study reports that firm performance rises as management ownership is increased up to 5 percent (managers are better motivated) and then again above 25 percent (managers become dominant owners who care more). However, firm performance *suffers* when management ownership is in the 5–25 percent range, because in this (mid)range, managers enjoy sufficient power to act in a self-serving manner with relative impunity.[62] In other words, **management entrenchment**—managers put their self-interests ahead of shareholders' interests—is especially likely in such a midrange of management ownership. This seems to be happening in numerous large privatized firms in Russia and other post-Soviet republics where managers have controlled a midrange of equity and deeply entrenched themselves.

Likewise, firing current managers in itself does not improve firm performance. It boils down to whether the new managers are any better. While usually inside CEO candidates are promoted in a more routine succession, boards often look for outside candidates when firms are in a mess.[63] However, because new CEOs brought in from the outside have to rapidly deliver turnaround results in an unfamiliar environment, it is not surprising that new CEOs from the outside often fail.

External (Exit-Based) Governance Mechanisms

The three external governance mechanisms are (1) market for product competition, (2) market for corporate control, and (3) market for leveraged buyouts. Product market competition is a powerful force compelling managers to maximize profits and, in turn, shareholder value. However, from a corporate governance perspective, product market competition *complements* the market for corporate control and the market for leveraged buyouts, each of which is outlined next.

The Market for Corporate Control

This is the main external governance mechanism, otherwise known as the takeover market or the mergers and acquisitions (M&A) market (see Chapter 9). It is essentially an arena where different management teams contest for the control rights of corporate assets. As an external, hostile governance mechanism, the market for corporate control serves as a disciplining mechanism of last resort when internal governance mechanisms fail. The underlying logic is spelled out by agency theory, which suggests that when managers engage in self-interested actions and internal governance mechanisms fail, firm stock will be undervalued by investors. Under these circumstances, other management teams, which recognize an opportunity to reorganize or redeploy the firm's assets and hence to create new value, bid for the rights to manage the firm. The market for corporate control was relatively inactive prior to the 1980s. However, the 1980s ushered in a large wave of M&As and restructuring. While on average the value of US takeover activities stayed at 2–3 percent of the GDP during the one hundred years before the 1980s (including three previous M&A waves), M&As accounted for approximately 6 percent of the GDP by the late 1980s.[64]

Nearly half of all major US corporations received a hostile takeover offer in the 1980s. Even firms with a very large size (long regarded by empire-building managers as a safety device that would prevent takeovers) were no longer immune. This is because rival management teams, some of which were known as **raiders,** were often able to take on extensive leverage by raising significant debts to finance their acquisitions. The most extreme case was the use of **junk bonds**—bonds that are rated below investment grade by the top bond-rating agencies.

How effective is the market for corporate control? Three findings emerge: (1) On average, shareholders of target firms earn sizable acquisition premiums. (2) Shareholders of acquiring firms experience slight, but insignificant, losses.[65] (3) A substantially higher level of top management turnover occurs following M&As.[66] Evidently, some "deadwood" managers are driven out.

However, managers are not passive. They have actively lobbied for political and legislative support such as the enactment of antitakeover laws. In addition, the sophistication and variety of antitakeover defensive mechanisms have increased since the 1980s. For example, *all* listed firms in the Netherlands have adopted multiple antitakeover mechanisms.[67] In Russia, "antitakeover mechanisms" in some cases literally mean *armed* fortification of factories and offices, manned by corporate security forces and cooperative local law enforcement officers, who defend against "corporate raiders"—real *armed* raiders sponsored by some oligarchs who (often illegally) exercise their "shareholder rights" (see Integrative Case 3.4).[68]

Each of these antitakeover mechanisms is designed to make the costs of takeovers prohibitive. Examples include (1) "greenmail," (2) "poison pill," and (3) "golden parachutes." **Greenmail** refers to repurchasing large blocks of shares from potential acquirers, in essence protecting managers' jobs at shareholders' expense.[69] **Poison pill** refers to the rights to either purchase additional shares or sell shares to the bidder at prices substantially higher than market value.[70] **Golden parachutes** are large compensation packages to incumbent managers should their firms be taken over. While stock markets, not surprisingly, view greenmails and poison pills negatively,[71] golden parachutes are often viewed *positively*.[72] This is because golden parachutes, interestingly, serve to align the interests of shareholders and managers. In corporate control contests, financially secured managers supported by golden parachutes are not likely to resist as much as those who are not financially secured.

In summary, while internal mechanisms aim at "fine-tuning," the market for corporate control enables the "wholesale" removal of entrenched managers. As a radical approach, the market for corporate control has its own limitations. It is very costly to wage such financial battles. In addition, a large number of M&As seem to be driven by sheer hubris or empire-building, and the long-run profitability of post-merger firms is not particularly impressive (see Chapter 9). Nevertheless, the net impact, at least in the short run, seems to be positive, because the threat of takeovers does limit managers from diverging from the goal of maximizing shareholder wealth.

The Market for Leveraged Buyouts (LBOs)

Instead of being taken over, a large number of firms have been bought out by incumbent managers, often in alliance with friendly outside investor groups. In an LBO, managers and investors issue bonds and use the cash raised to buy the firm's stock—in essence replacing shareholders with bondholders and transforming the firm from a public to a private entity. As another external governance mechanism, LBOs utilize the bond market, as opposed to stock market, to discipline managers. LBOs are associated with three major changes in corporate governance. First, LBOs change managers' incentives by providing them with substantial equity stakes. Second, the high amount of debt imposes strong financial discipline. Finally, LBO sponsors closely monitor the firms they have invested in. Overall, evidence suggests that LBOs improve efficiency, at least in the short run.[73] However, the picture is less clear for the long run, because LBOs might have forced managers to reduce investments in long-run R&D.[74]

Internal Mechanisms + External Mechanisms = Governance Package

Taken together, the internal and external mechanisms can be considered a "package." These various mechanisms operate interdependently and as potential substitutes or complements.[75] Although the pressure for better corporate governance has been on the rise throughout the world since the 1980s, most countries, including some of the most developed ones such as Japan and Germany, do not have an active market for corporate control. As a result, the US experience, featuring the world's most active market for corporate control, shows what could happen if both internal and external governance mechanisms are available and interacting.

If the 1980s, with the rise of hostile takeovers, can be regarded as "the decade of confrontation," the 1990s can be characterized as "the decade of friendly M&As" (see also Chapter 9). While 14 percent of the US M&As in the 1980s—a record high number—involved a hostile bid (7 percent of which were successful), only 4 percent of the M&As in the 1990s entailed such hostility (only 3 percent of which were successful).[76] By the late 1990s the volume of M&As scaled new heights, reaching a striking 15 percent of US GDP. What led to this interesting combination of very active M&As and relatively friendly relationships between acquiring and target firms in the 1990s? In a nutshell, the answer lies in improved corporate governance in *both* internal and external governance mechanisms.

Michael Jensen, a leading agency theorist, argues that failures of internal governance mechanisms in the 1970s finally activated the market for corporate control in the 1980s.[77] Managers initially resisted. However, over time, many firms that were not takeover targets or that successfully defended themselves against such attempts ended up restructuring and downsizing—doing exactly what raiders would have done had these firms been taken over. For example, boards at takeover target firms' *competitors* often "preemptively" dismissed their own "deadwood" managers.[78] In other words, the strengthened external mechanisms force firms to improve their internal mechanisms. Recall that an important part of the internal mechanisms is more generous executive compensation, especially stock options. As a result, managers could share in the market returns from the voluntarily restructured companies they manage. As the interests of shareholders and of managers become more closely aligned, shareholder value thus becomes more of an ally rather than an enemy. The upshot is that with stronger internal governance mechanisms, the need for crude and costly external mechanisms such as hostile takeover battles was reduced by the 1990s.

Overall, since the 1980s, American managers have become much more focused on stock prices, resulting in a new term, **shareholder capitalism,** that has been spreading around the world.[79] In Europe, executive stock options have become popular and M&As more frequent.[80] In Asia and Latin America, the importance of board oversight has been increasingly discussed. In Russia, after the 1998 collapse, there are now some traces of modern corporate governance.[81]

A GLOBAL PERSPECTIVE

Having introduced various components of corporate governance mechanisms, we are now in a position to discuss how these different mechanisms are combined in different parts of the world, with an emphasis on (1) the Anglo-American and continental European-Japanese systems and (2) the corporate governance underpinning of the privatization movement around the globe.

Internal and External Governance Mechanisms Around the World

Illustrated in Figure 11.3, different corporate ownership and control patterns around the world naturally lead to a different mix of internal and external mechanisms. The most familiar type is shown in Cell 4, exemplified by most large US and UK corporations. While the external governance mechanisms such as the market for corporate control are relatively active and well-developed, internal governance mechanisms are relatively weak because of the separation of ownership and control, which gives managers significant *de facto* control power.

The opposite can be found in Cell 1, namely, firms in continental Europe and Japan where the market for corporate control is relatively inactive. In France, as recent as the late 1990s, M&As were condemned by some government officials as "a social massacre with massive layoffs."[82] The German chancellor, Gerhard Schroder, remarked in 1999 that "hostile takeovers are always negative" (see Strategy in Action 9.2 in Chapter 9). Consequently, the primary governance mechanisms remain concentrated ownership and control.[83] The controlling shareholders are often families and banks, which have a vested interest in making sure there are decent returns on their investment.

FIGURE 11.3   Internal and External Governance Mechanisms: A Global Perspective

External governance mechanisms

		Weak	Strong
	Strong	(Cell 1) Germany Japan	(Cell 2) Canada
Internal governance mechanisms			
	Weak	(Cell 3) State-owned enterprises	(Cell 4) United States United Kingdom

Source: Cells 1, 2, and 4 adapted from E. R. Gedajlovic & D. M. Shapiro, 1998, Management and ownership effects: Evidence from five countries (p. 539), Strategic Management Journal, 19: 533–553. The label of Cell 3 is suggested by the present author.

Overall, the **Anglo-American** and **continental European–Japanese** (otherwise known as **German-Japanese**) systems represent the two primary corporate governance families in the world, with a variety of labels (see Table 11.3). Given that both the United States and United Kingdom as a group and continental Europe and Japan as another group are highly developed, successful economies, it is difficult and probably not meaningful to argue whether the Anglo-American or German-Japanese system is better.[84] Evidently, each has different strengths and weaknesses.

However, other corporate governance systems do not easily fit into such a simple dichotomous world. Placed in Cell 2, Canada has *both* a relatively active market for corporate control and a large number of firms with concentrated ownership and control—more than 380 of the 400 largest Canadian firms are controlled by a single shareholder.[85] Canadian managers thus face powerful internal and external constraints.

Finally, some firms, mostly SOEs (of all nationalities), are in the unfortunate position of having both weak external and internal governance mechanisms (Cell 3). Pre-reform SOEs in the former Soviet bloc and China serve as examples. Externally, product market competition was minimal due to a shortage economy. The external

TABLE 11.3   Two Primary Families of Corporate Governance Systems

CORPORATIONS IN THE UNITED STATES AND UNITED KINGDOM	CORPORATIONS IN CONTINENTAL EUROPE AND JAPAN
Anglo-American corporate governance models	German-Japanese corporate governance models
Market-oriented, high-tension systems	Bank-oriented, network-based systems
Rely mostly on exit-based, external mechanisms	Rely mostly on voice-based, internal mechanisms
Shareholder capitalism	Stakeholder capitalism

market for corporate control simply did not exist (and is still virtually absent). Internally, SOE managers were supervised by government agencies that acted as *de facto* "owners." However, government officials, who were agents themselves, had little motivation to strictly police SOEs. Instead, SOE managers knew that they operated with a **soft budget constraint** in that they could usually ask for more handouts and bailouts from the government if necessary. Not surprisingly, this almost total lack of internal and external governance mechanisms led to grave SOE performance problems.

Overall, firms around the world are governed by a combination of internal and external governance mechanisms. For firms in Cells 1, 2, and 4, internal and external mechanisms can partially substitute for one another (for example, weak boards may be partially substituted by a strong market for corporate control). However, it is not viable to be stuck in Cell 3 with both weak internal and external mechanisms in the long run. The next section develops this perspective further.

Strengthening Governance Mechanisms through Privatization

From a corporate governance standpoint, the global privatization wave can be considered a movement to migrate out of the unfortunate Cell 3 in Figure 11.3. An important question, of course, is which direction to go. For SOEs in developed economies, they, upon privatization, would naturally migrate from Cell 3 to the respective cells for the private-firm counterparts in their own countries (such as Cell 1 for German firms and Cell 4 for UK firms).

The privatization directions for SOEs in countries such as Poland and Russia are fascinating because they, historically, do not belong to any of the other three cells. When Central and Eastern European (CEE) countries started their privatization reforms in the early 1990s, foreign advisors (who were often American and British nationals) usually recommended the Anglo-American governance model featuring dispersed shareholders and a strong market for corporate control. However, most policymakers and practitioners in CEE argued that in the absence of functioning capital markets, it would not be realistic to move from Cell 3 to Cell 4 directly. Instead, these countries typically adopted a two-phase model of privatization (see Figure 11.4), first through buyouts by managers and employees (to secure their support) and then via the introduction of outside investors and new managers (to facilitate restructuring). Overall, privatization in CEE often moved SOEs first from Cell 3 to Cell 1 and then attempted to move toward Cell 4.

FIGURE 11.4   A Two-Phase Model of Privatization and Restructuring of State-Owned Enterprises in Central and Eastern Europe

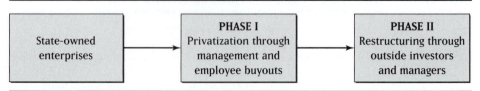

Source: M. W. Peng, 2000, Business Strategies in Transition Economies (p. 115), Thousand Oaks, CA: Sage Publishing, Inc.

STRATEGY IN ACTION 11.2. *Poland's Elektrim Grows and Shrinks Its Scope*

Elektrim (*http://www.elektrim.pl*) until 1989 was a monopoly foreign trader of electrical equipment and turnkey power systems produced by Polish enterprises. In the early 1990s, it was privatized with inside managers and employees being the largest shareholders. In 1992, Elektrim was the first to be listed on the newly opened Warsaw Stock Exchange, and its shares were mostly purchased by domestic institutional investors and individuals. Emboldened by the additional cash that was raised, managers, who became the new owners, embarked upon a conglomeration strategy. By the end of 1993, Elektrim had a stake in eighty-seven companies in five industries, which not only included the electrical equipment industry, but also food processing, cement, construction, and banking.

Such empire-building was unsustainable and began to change in the late 1990s. The change was driven by the lack of transparency in the business group, inefficient allocation of capital among different businesses, and lack of expertise in newly acquired businesses. More significantly, however, change was triggered by the new controlling shareholders at that time, foreign institutional investors, who demanded streamlining and focusing. In 1999, with a new CEO, Elektrim divested

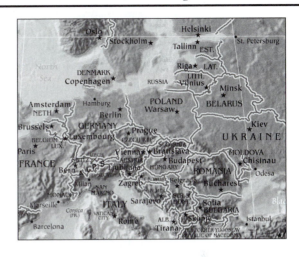

more than seventy noncore subsidiaries and focused on three related core businesses: telecommunications, power-generating equipment, and cables.

Source: Based on (1) I. Filatotchev, M. Wright, K. Uhlenbruck, L. Tihanyi, & R. E. Hoskisson, 2003, Governance, organizational capabilities, and restructuring in transition economies (p. 338), Journal of World Business, 38: 331–347 and (2) http://www.elektrim.pl (accessed August 10, 2004).

Nearly two decades of privatization in CEE (and other parts of the world) suggests three lessons.[86] First, privatization to insiders helps improve the performance of *small* firms, because such ownership and control is an efficient way to better motivate managers and employees. Second, in *large* corporations, similar privatization to insiders, without external governance pressures, is hardly conducive for needed restructuring. Throughout CEE, managers are often deeply entrenched because of their high ownership positions.[87] Third, outside ownership and control, preferably by blockholders, funds, foreigners, and/or banks, are more likely to facilitate restructuring.[88] Such outside ownership and control do not happen frequently, because incumbent managers do not necessarily welcome such outside "intrusion." However, when outsiders such as institutional investors do come in, they may actively assert their power.[89] For example, in Russia, approximately 10 percent of the CEOs were fired at the *first* shareholder meeting by coalitions of institutional investors and employees.[90] In Poland, the very quick rise of a new conglomerate, Elektrim (because of new inside manager-owners' empire-building), and its equally quick demise (because of foreign institutional investors' pressures) are indicative of these dynamics (see Strategy in Action 11.2).

Overall, there is evidence that privatization may work because improved governance and better motivation, while far from perfect, tend to lead to better firm performance.[91] Because it takes a combination of well-developed internal and external mechanisms as a package to properly govern the firm, it is not surprising that the privatization journey is far from over in many parts of the world.

INDUSTRY-, RESOURCE-, AND INSTITUTION-BASED VIEWS ON CORPORATE GOVERNANCE

As before, we draw on the three leading perspectives in strategy to better understand corporate governance. Unlike previous chapters, we do not call this a "comprehensive" model because the primary perspective driving corporate governance is not any of these three theories; rather, as discussed earlier, it is agency theory. But still, the three leading theories have a lot to add to the discussion.

Industry-Based Considerations

The nature of industry sometimes questions widely accepted conventional wisdom regarding (1) outside directors, (2) insider ownership, and (3) CEO duality.[92] Having more outside directors on the board is often regarded as a performance-boosting practice. However, in industries characterized by rapid innovation requiring significant R&D investments (such as information technology), outside directors may have a *negative* impact on firm performance[93] This is because directors need to have intimate knowledge and solid experience and firms need to embark on more complex, novel strategies in such industries, which may require more strategic control. In contrast, outside directors tend to focus on financial control, which may be inappropriate in these types of industries.

Another example is the widely noted link between inside management ownership and firm performance. Research finds that for firms in low-growth, stable industries, *no* relationship exists between the two.[94] Only in relatively high-growth, turbulent industries has this relationship been found. While increased insider ownership is designed to encourage managers to take more risks, opportunities to profitably take such risks probably are more likely to appear in high-growth, turbulent industries.[95]

A third example is the often-criticized practice of CEO duality. In industries experiencing great turbulence, the presence of a single leader may allow a faster and more unified response to changing events.[96] These benefits may outweigh the potential agency costs created by such duality.

Overall, governance practices need to fit with the nature of the industry in which firms are competing. This cautions against prescribing universal "best" practices.

Resource-Based Considerations

From a corporate governance standpoint, some of the most valuable, unique, and hard-to-imitate firm-specific resources (the first three in the VRIO framework) are the skills and abilities of top managers and directors—often regarded as **managerial human capital.**[97] Some of these capabilities are unique, such as international experience. Executives without such first-hand experience are often handicapped when their firms try to expand overseas. In addition, the social networks of these executives, often through board interlocks, are unique and likely to add value.[98] Also, top managerial talents are hard to imitate—unless they are hired away by competitor firms.

The last crucial component in the VRIO framework is O: organizational. It is within an organizational setting—typically in TMTs and boards—that top managers and directors function.[99] An often-debated topic is diversity. Some argue that TMT and board diversity boosts firm performance,[100] while others suggest that diversity lengthens debates, slows decision speed, and (in the worst case) results in conflicts.[101] Other studies find such diversity to add value, but only under certain circumstances.[102] For example, firms embarking on more complex strategies, in particular international expansion, may benefit more from TMT and board diversity.[103]

Managerial resources may have a different impact on firm performance during the tenure of managers, which can be broadly divided into (1) learning, (2) harvest, and (3) decline stages.[104] The first few years are often characterized by learning. The next, harvest phase, is likely to produce the best firm performance because managers capitalize on prior learning. However, if executives have been in office for a very long time (such as fifteen years), they may become complacent, unwilling to learn, and defensive when questioned. This is the phase during which managers are particularly likely to entrench themselves and become "deadwood." The evolution of Michael Eisener, CEO and chairman of Walt Disney since 1984—from being a great value contributor to a much resented leader by shareholders recently—is a case in point. The upshot is that boards have to be particularly vigilant when dealing with "old-timer" CEOs.[105]

Overall, the few people at the top of an organization can make a world of difference. Corporate governance mechanisms need to properly motivate and discipline these top talents to make sure that they make a positive impact.

Institution-Based Considerations

Formal Institutional Frameworks

Formal and informal institutions profoundly affect how corporations are governed. A fundamental difference in corporate governance exists between the separation of ownership and control in Anglo-American corporations and the concentration of ownership and control in the rest of the world. While there are many explanations behind such a key difference, a leading explanation is an institutional one. In brief, better formal legal protection of investor rights, especially those held by *minority* shareholders, in the United States and United Kingdom encourages founding families and their heirs to dilute their equity to attract minority shareholders and delegate day-to-day management to professional managers. Given reasonable investor protection, founding families themselves (such as the Rockefellers) may over time feel comfortable becoming minority shareholders of the firms they founded. On the other hand, when formal legal and regulatory institutions are dysfunctional, founding families *must* run their firms directly. In the absence of investor protection, bestowing management rights to outside, professional managers may invite abuse and theft. Therefore, founding families as controlling shareholders are not willing to hire outside managers—unless they allow these managers to marry into the family.[106] In addition, prospective minority shareholders may be less willing to invest without sufficient protection, thus forcing concentrated ownership to become the default mode.

Strong evidence supports the view that if the formal legal and regulatory institutions protecting shareholders are weak, then ownership and control rights become more concentrated—in other words, there is some substitution between the two. Common-law countries (the United States, United Kingdom, and former British colonies) generally have the strongest legal protection of investors and lowest concentration of corporate ownership.[107] Within common-law countries, such ownership concentration is higher for firms in emerging economies (such as Hong Kong, India, Israel, and South Africa) than developed economies (such as Australia, Canada, Ireland, and New Zealand). One study finds that the top three shareholders held an average of 51 percent equity in a sample of twenty-eight emerging economies (including both common-law and non–common-law countries), as opposed to 41 percent in twenty-one developed economies.[108] These large shareholders—often called **blockholders** because of the large blocks of shares they hold—in emerging economies usually need to have a significantly higher percentage (such as above 50 percent) of shares to ensure control, whereas blockholders are typically defined in the United States as any shareholders with a mere 5 percent holding (or above) of the firm. In short, concentrated ownership and control is an answer to possibly rampant principal-agent conflicts when shareholder rights are not sufficiently protected by the legal system.

However, what is good for controlling shareholders is not necessarily good for an economy. As noted earlier, minimizing principal-agent conflicts through the concentration of ownership and control, unfortunately, introduces more principal-principal conflicts. Consequently, minority shareholders, if they are informed enough to be aware of these possibilities and still decide to invest (many may refuse to invest), are likely to discount the shares floated by family owners, resulting in lower corporate valuations, fewer publicly traded firms, inactive and smaller capital markets, and, in turn, lower levels of economic development in general.

Given that almost every country desires vibrant capital markets and economic development, it seems puzzling that the Anglo-American-style of investor protection is not universally embraced. It is important to note that at its core, corporate governance ultimately is a choice about *political* governance. For largely historical reasons, most countries have made hard-to-reverse political choices. For example, the German practice of "codetermination"—employees control 50 percent of the votes on supervisory boards—is an outcome of political decisions made by postwar German governments (see Opening Case). Although the practice reduces labor flexibility and results in high labor (and overall) costs, it is difficult to change. Owners have to counterbalance such labor power by controlling the other half of votes on supervisory boards, and the only way to do this is to maintain concentrated (as opposed to diffused) ownership. Otherwise, if German firms were to have US/UK-style dispersed ownership and still allow employees to control 50 percent of the votes on supervisory boards, these firms would end up becoming *employee-* dominated firms.

Changing political choices, although not impossible, will encounter significant resistance, especially from incumbents (such as German labor unions or Asian families) who benefit from the present system.[109] In the nine countries of East Asia (excluding China), the top fifteen families on average control approximately 53 percent of the listed assets and 39 percent of the GDP.[110] Some of the leading business families not only have great connections with the government, sometimes, they *are* the government. For example, the current (2004) prime ministers of Italy and Thailand—Silvio Berlusconi and Thaksin Shinawatra, respectively—come from leading business families in these countries.[111]

Only when extraordinary events erupt would some politicians muster sufficient political will to initiate major corporate governance reforms. The grand failure of socialism, especially SOEs, around the world and the privatization movement as a result speaks volumes about how this journey—despite its tremendous difficulties— would be embarked upon. The spectacular corporate scandals in the United States (such as Enron) are another example prompting more serious political reforms.

However, merely changing formal institutions, which can be done through the stroke of a pen given sufficient political will, may not be enough. For example, formal efforts to introduce dispersed ownership in Japan by the US occupation forces in the late 1940s failed because of the lack of informal institutions that could legitimize such new practices. Therefore, it is also important to understand informal institutional frameworks which underpin corporate governance practices.

Informal Institutional Frameworks

In the last two decades around the world, why and how have informal norms and values concerning corporate governance changed to such a great extent? In the United States and United Kingdom, the idea of shareholder capitalism has graduated from minority view to orthodoxy.[112] In the rest of the world, this idea is rapidly spreading. At least three sources of these changes can be identified: (1) the rise of capitalism, (2) the impact of globalization, and (3) the global diffusion of best practices. The recent changes in corporate governance around the world are part of the greater political, economic, and social movement that embraces capitalism. The triumph of capitalism naturally boils down to the triumph of *capitalists*—otherwise known as shareholders. However, "free markets" are not necessarily free. Even some of the most developed countries have experienced significant governance failures, calling for a sharper focus on shareholder values. Collectively, these changes have pushed for better corporate governance globally.

While most changes take place on a country-by-country basis, at least three aspects of recent globalization have a bearing on corporate governance. First, as foreign direct investment (FDI) increases, firms with different governance systems and norms come into contact, naturally exposing their differences (see Opening Case).

Being aware of the alternatives, shareholders as well as managers and policymakers are no longer easily persuaded that "our way" is the most natural and most efficient way of corporate governance.[113] Second, **foreign portfolio investment** (**FPI**)—foreigners purchasing stocks and bonds, but not directly managing operations (which would be FDI)—has scaled new heights. For example, in Japan, foreign institutional investors' shares tripled from 6 percent to 18 percent of the total listed equity over one decade (1993 to 2003).[114] These investors naturally demand better shareholder protection before committing their funds. Finally, the global thirst for capital has prompted many firms to pay attention to corporate governance. Many foreign firms, for example, have listed their stock on New York and London Stock Exchanges. In exchange for such privileges, they have to comply with US and UK listing requirements (discussed later in the section on "Global Convergence versus Divergence").

In addition, the changing norms and values are also directly promoted by the global diffusion of codes of best practices. Led by Britain's *Cadbury Report* in 1992, the global proliferation of such codes is striking (see Table 11.4). A lot of these codes are advisory and not legally binding. Therefore, they are largely informal. However, firms feel explicit pressures to "voluntarily" adopt these codes. For example, in Russia, although adopting the 2002 Code of Corporate Conduct is in theory voluntary, large firms that opt not to adopt have to publicly explain why, essentially naming and shaming themselves that they are laggards in corporate governance.

While different countries engage in country-specific efforts, international organizations such as the Organization for Economic Cooperation and Development (OECD)—which includes all developed economies and such emerging economies as the Czech Republic, Hungary, Mexico, Poland, South Korea, and the Slovak Republic—have spearheaded the efforts to globally diffuse some of the best practices. In 1999, the OECD published the *OECD Principles of Corporate Governance*, suggesting that the overriding objective of the corporation should be to optimize shareholder returns over time.[115] The *Principles* are nonbinding even for the thirty OECD member countries, and nonmember countries have no obligation to adopt them. Nevertheless, the global norms seem to be moving toward the *Principles*. For example, China and Taiwan, both nonmembers of OECD, have recently taken a page from the *Principles* and allowed shareholders to bring class action lawsuits.[116]

Slowly but surely, change is in the air in almost every country. Although some companies and countries may adopt such changes for "window dressing" purposes,

TABLE 11.4   Selected Corporate Governance (CG) Codes Around the World Since the 1990s

DEVELOPED ECONOMIES	EMERGING ECONOMIES
Cadbury Report (United Kingdom, 1992)	King Report (South Africa, 1994)
Dey Report (Canada, 1994)	Confederation of Indian Industry Code of CG (India, 1998)
Bosch Report (Australia, 1995)	Korean Stock Exchange Code of Best Practice (Korea, 1999)
CG Forum of Japan Code (Japan, 1998)	Mexican Code of CG (Mexico, 1999)
German Panel on CG Code (Germany, 2000)	Code of CG for Listed Companies (China, 2001)
Sarbanes-Oxley Act (United States, 2002)	Code of Corporate Conduct (Russia, 2002)

over time, some of the new shapes and forms of corporate governance may indeed change these firms' and their managers' deeply held cognitive beliefs.

DEBATES AND EXTENSIONS

There is no question that recent changes in corporate governance are driven by debates, some of which have already been alluded to. This section discusses three other major debates: (1) opportunistic agents versus managerial stewards, (2) efficient versus inefficient capital markets, and (3) global convergence versus divergence.

Opportunistic Agents versus Managerial Stewards

Agency theory assumes managers to be agents who may engage in self-serving, opportunistic activities if left to their own devices. However, critics contend that most managers are likely to be honest and trustworthy. Managerial mistakes may be due to a lack of competence, information, or luck, but not necessarily due to self-interest. Thus, it may not be fair to characterize all managers as opportunistic agents. Although very influential, agency theory therefore has been criticized as an "anti-management theory of management."[117] Recently, a "pro-management" theory, **stewardship theory,** has emerged that suggests that by and large, managers can be viewed as stewards of owners' interests.[118] It argues that most managers desire achievement, affiliation, and self-actualization. Safeguarding shareholders' interests and advancing organizational goals—as opposed to managers' own self-serving agenda—will maximize (most) managers' own utility functions.

Stewardship theorists agree that agency theory is useful when describing a certain portion of managers and under certain circumstances (such as when managers are under siege during takeover battles).[119] However, if all principals view all managers as self-serving agents with a number of control mechanisms to put managers on a "tight leash," some managers, who view themselves as stewards, may be so frustrated that they end up engaging in the very self-serving behavior agency theory seeks to minimize. In other words, as a self-fulfilling prophecy, an excessive focus on tight control of managers may actually *induce* opportunistic behavior.[120]

Efficient versus Inefficient Capital Markets

One criticism leveled against shareholder capitalism is to question the belief that shareholders—or, in the aggregate, capital markets—are always right. Originating from Adam Smith's idea of the "invisible hand," an **efficient market hypothesis** suggests that shareholders base their valuation of a firm's share price on a rational assessment of *all* publicly available information.[121] In other words, capital markets, consisting of numerous players, are efficient in rewarding high-potential, well-governed firms and punishing low-potential, poorly run firms.

However, critics contend that such market efficiency is *assumed*, but not proven. They make three points. First, in many emerging economies, capital market efficiency is questionable. In fact, the paucity of good firm-specific information in emerging economies has led global investors—rightly or wrongly—to lump all emerging economies together.[122] Consequently, when a few large firms in a major emerging economy experience major problems, they may reduce investor confidence *throughout* emerging economies, creating a domino effect (as evidenced by the 1997–98 crises in Asia and Russia, which negatively impacted Latin America). Second, shareholders rely on firm-specific information provided by the firm. The likes of Enron and Parmalat have taught us that shareholders—and in turn capital markets—in some of the most developed countries can be misled and fooled, at least temporarily.

Finally, in the absence of fraud, market mistakes are still possible, collectively made by investors due to "irrational" exuberance (or pessimism). *Overvalued* equity, according to Michael Jensen, can be regarded as "managerial heroin," which feels good at the beginning, but causes massive pain in the end.[123] This is because managers may use overvalued equity to finance acquisitions to satisfy the unreasonably high capital market growth expectations and destroy value in the end. For instance, Nortel, a leading Canadian telecommunications equipment maker, launched a striking nineteen acquisitions in four years (1997 to 2001). In a vicious cycle, Nortel used acquisitions to meet market analysts' expectations, which then rose as a result. The rising expectations, in turn, could only be met by even more acquisitions. Eventually, Nortel's stock, which rose from $13 in 1997 to $86 in 2000, crashed to less than $2 in 2003. Overall, while empire-building traditionally may lead to undervalued equity (consistent with the efficient market hypothesis), some empire building may lead to overvalued equity caused by market *inefficiency*.

In summary, while capital markets are not necessarily a "random walk," sufficient sources of inefficiency exist in both developed and emerging economies to question the validity of the market efficiency hypothesis. The upshot seems to be that shareholders may not always be right.

Global Convergence versus Divergence

Another leading debate is whether corporate governance is converging or diverging globally. Convergence advocates argue that globalization will unleash a "survival-of-the-fittest" process by which firms will be forced to adopt globally the best practices exemplified by Anglo-American practices.[124] They note that global investors are willing to pay a premium for stock in firms with Anglo-American-style transparent governance, prompting other firms to follow such norms. VTech in Hong Kong serves as a case in point (Strategy in Action 11.3). Most of the recent corporate governance codes (Table 11.4) largely draw from core Anglo-American concepts, such as an explicit focus on shareholder wealth and an emphasis on transparency. International organizations such as the OECD have been rapidly promoting these Anglo-American principles as the global standard. Emboldened by these principles, shareholder activism, an unheard-of phenomenon in many parts of the world, is now becoming more visible (see Closing Case).

One interesting phenomenon often cited by convergence advocates is **cross-listing,** namely, firms increasingly list their shares on foreign stock exchanges.[125] By the late 1990s, 14 percent and 22 percent of the firms listed on the New York and

Strategy in Action 11.3. *Hong Kong's VTech Strives for Excellence in Governance*

During the 1997–98 Asian economic crisis, stock prices of most Hong Kong listed firms plummeted. Yet, VTech (*http://www.vtech.com*), Hong Kong's largest electronics manufacturer, saw its stock price more than double (from US$1.87 on June 30, 1997 to US$4.33 on December 31, 1998). At least two reasons contributed to this stellar performance. First, VTech dominated two niche markets, electronic learning aids for kids and cordless telephones. It had more than 60 percent of the electronic educational toy market in the United States and Europe. Its cordless phones had 50 percent of the US market. Only less than 5 percent of its sales were in Asia. Second and perhaps equally important, in a departure from the traditional family businesses that dominated the Hong Kong corporate landscape (see Closing Case), VTech has been built differently with a particular attention to corporate governance. Allan Wong, the founder who established VTech in 1976, professed that his aim was to increase shareholder value. VTech disclosed more information than was required by law. During interviews, Allan Wong took pains to emphasize that VTech was not a family firm because no family member sat on the top management team or the board. Although headquartered in Hong Kong, VTech is really an international outfit. Five of its nine board members were foreigners. All its manufacturing was done in China, where it employed more than 20,000 workers. R&D was largely carried out in the US and Europe.

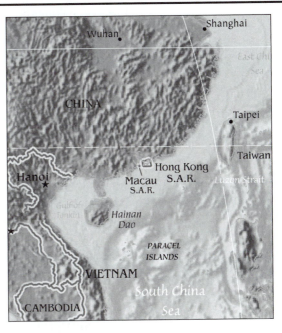

Sources: This case was written by David Ahlstrom (Chinese University of Hong Kong), Michael N. Young (Chinese University of Hong Kong), and Garry Bruton (Texas Christian University). It is based on (1) M. N. Young, D. Ahlstrom, & G. Bruton, 2004, Globalization and corporate governance in East Asia: The transnational solution, Management International Review, 44 (2): 31–50; (2) A. Tanzer, 1998, The VTech phenomenon, Forbes, October 19: 162–171; and (3) VTech investors relations department communication with the authors, April 2004. Reprinted by permission of the authors.

London Stock Exchanges, respectively, were foreign firms. Such cross-listing is primarily driven by the desire to tap into larger pools of capital. Foreign firms thus have to comply with US and UK securities laws and may adopt Anglo-American corporate governance norms. There is evidence, for instance, that Japanese firms listed in New York and London, compared with those listed at home, are relatively more concerned about shareholder value.[126] A US or UK listing can be viewed as a signal of the firm's commitment to shareholder value, thus resulting in higher valuations.[127] For instance, of the sixty firms traded on the Russian Trading System (as of 2003), fifty-seven listed their shares on the NYSE.[128] Overall, cross-listed firms are often viewed as carriers of Anglo-American corporate governance norms and values around the world.

However, critics contend that governance practices will continue to diverge throughout the world.[129] Marching toward "shareholder capitalism" in the absence of the underlying institutional foundations (such as investor protection) is not likely to succeed. For example, promoting more concentrated ownership and control is often recommended as a solution to combat principal-agent conflicts in US and UK firms. However, making the same recommendation to reform firms in continental Europe, Asia, and Latin America may be counterproductive, because often the main problem there is that controlling shareholders typically already have too much ownership and control. So the solution may lie in how to *reduce* the concentration of ownership and control. While exporting US/UK-style regulations to other countries is possible (by the stroke of a pen), it is difficult, if not impossible, to transplant the norms, values, and traditions around the world without changing the underlying structure of concentrated ownership and control (see Closing Case).[130] Finally, some fundamental differences also exist between US and UK practices. For example, in addition to the split on CEO duality (the UK against, the US for) discussed earlier, none of the US antitakeover defenses (such as poison pills) is legal in the United Kingdom.

In the case of cross-listed firms, divergence advocates make three points. First, compared to US firms, these foreign firms have significantly larger boards, more inside directors, lower institutional ownership, and more concentrated ownership.[131] In other words, cross-listed foreign firms do not necessarily adopt US governance practices before or after listing. Second, despite the popular belief that US and UK securities laws would apply to cross-listed foreign firms, in practice, these laws have rarely been effectively enforced against foreign firms' "tunneling" practices.[132] Finally, recent changes in US regulations have promoted more divergence. Since the enactment of the Sarbanes-Oxley Act in 2002, Porsche, Fuji Film, and EADS (parent company of Airbus) have all cancelled plans for US listings, and LVMH delisted its NASDAQ-traded shares, citing an inability or unwillingness to comply.[133]

Overall, in a global economy, complete divergence in corporate governance is probably unrealistic, especially for large firms in search of capital from global investors. On the other hand, complete convergence also seems unlikely. What is more likely is some sort of "cross-vergence" balancing the expectations of global investors and those of local stakeholders.[134] For example, this is evidenced by the fact that (1) US and UK firms have recently increased their ownership concentration (in the hands of institutional investors) and that (2) board structure in Germany and Japan is moving toward the Anglo-American model with a meaningful number of outsiders.

Finally, in addition to these three debates, another unexplored big debate is stakeholder capitalism versus shareholder capitalism. Chapter 12 is entirely devoted to this debate.

IMPLICATIONS FOR STRATEGISTS

As an English term, "corporate governance" had not been coined prior to the late 1970s. In many parts of the world, debates have erupted on how to properly translate this strange and foreign term into local languages.[135] Yet, corporate governance has now entered the highest levels of corporate and political discussions throughout the world. No strategic manager can afford to ignore it.

A better understanding of corporate governance can help answer the four fundamental questions in strategy. First, why do firms differ? Firm differ in corporate governance because of the different nature of industries, different abilities to motivate and discipline managers, and different institutional frameworks. Second, how do firms behave? Given that most corporations throughout the world have similar basic components of corporate governance (owners, managers, and boards), the primary sources of differences stem from how these components relate and interact with each other to set the direction of the corporate ship. Third, what determines the scope of the firm? From a corporate governance standpoint, a wide scope may be indicative of managers' empire-building and risk reduction. Finally, what determines the international success and failure of firms? Although research is still inconclusive,[136] there is reason to believe—in the aggregate and in the long run—that better governed firms will be rewarded with a lower cost of capital and consequently better firm performance. In other words, as firms increasingly match each other on products, services, and technologies, corporate governance may become one of the last frontiers of competitive differentiation, thus urging firms to "race to the top."

Chapter Summary

1. Corporate governance is the relationship among various participants in determining the direction and performance of corporations. Its "tripod" includes (1) owners, (2) managers, and (3) boards.

2. In the United States and United Kingdom, firms with a separation of ownership and control dominate the corporate landscape. In most other parts of the world, firms with concentrated ownership and control in the hands of families or governments are predominant.

3. In firms that separate ownership and control, the primary conflicts are principal-agent conflicts, namely, between owners and professional managers. In firms with concentrated ownership, principal-principal conflicts between controlling shareholders and minority shareholders are more important.

4. Boards of directors perform (1) control, (2) service, and (3) resource acquisition functions. Around the world, boards differ in (1) size, (2) composition, (3) ownership, (4) leadership, and (5) interlocks.

5. Internal, voice-based mechanisms and external, exit-based mechanisms combine as a package to determine corporate governance effectiveness. The market for corporate control and the market for leveraged buyouts are two primary means of external mechanisms.

6. Different combinations of internal and external governance mechanisms lead to four main groups: (1) Anglo-American group, (2) continental European–Japanese group, (3) Canadian group, and (4) SOE group (of all nationalities). Viewed in this perspective, the privatization movement around the world can be considered as efforts to strengthen corporate governance effectiveness.

7. Industry-, resource-, and institution-based views shed considerable light on governance issues.

8. Three leading debates discussed are (1) opportunistic agents versus managerial stewards, (2) efficient versus inefficient capital markets, and (3) global convergence versus divergence.

Key Terms

agency relationship

agency theory

agents

Anglo-American corporate governance system

blockholders

CEO duality

concentrated ownership and control

continental European– Japanese corporate governance system

corporate governance

cross-listing

diffused ownership

efficient market hypothesis

executive sessions

exit-based mechanisms

expropriation

foreign portfolio investment (FPI)

German-Japanese corporate governance system

golden parachutes

greenmail

information asymmetries

inside directors

interlocking directorate

junk bonds

lead independent director

management entrenchment

managerial human capital

market for corporate control

market for leveraged buy outs

outside directors

poison pill

principal-agent conflicts

principal-principal conflicts

principals

raiders

related transactions

shareholder capitalism

soft budget constraint

stewardship theory

top management team (TMT)

tunneling

voice-based mechanisms

Critical Discussion Questions

1. Some argue that the Anglo-American style of separating ownership and control is an inevitable outcome for large corporations. Others contend that this is one variant (among several) of how large corporations can be governed and that it is not necessarily the most efficient or most desirable ownership and control pattern for large firms elsewhere in the world. What do you think?

2. Experiences from many regions suggest that privatization by merely transferring ownership from public to private hands is hardly enough to improve corporate governance and performance for large corporations. Why is this the case?

3. Recent corporate governance reforms in various countries urge (and often require) firms to add more outside directors to their boards and separate the jobs of board chairman and CEO. Yet, academic research has not been able to conclusively confirm the merits of these practices. Why?

4. ***ON ETHICS:*** The rise of shareholder capitalism forces managers to focus on maximizing shareholder returns as *the* single driving objective of the firm. Yet, managers and firms are often called on to serve the needs of other stakeholders such as employees and local communities, whose demands are often in conflict with shareholder return maximization. As managers, what are the ethical dilemmas when choosing strategic courses of action for the corporation? (You may want to read Chapter 12 in preparation for this question)

5. ***ON ETHICS:*** As a chairman/CEO, you are trying to choose between two candidates for one outside independent director position on your board. One is another CEO, a longtime friend in a different industry whose board you have served on for many years. The other is a known corporate governance guru whose tag line is "No need to make fat cats fatter." You are confident that placing him on the board will earn you kudos among analysts and journalists for inviting a leading critic to scrutinize your work. But you worry that he will try to prove his widely publicized theory that CEOs are overpaid—in other words, your compensation can be on the line. Who would you choose?

Closing Case: David Webb: A Shareholder Activist in Hong Kong

Although Hong Kong may have a reputation of housing one of the world's most sophisticated financial markets, minority shareholders have a tradition of being abused by controlling shareholders. For example, in 2002, the controlling shareholders of Boto (http://www.boto.com.hk), a plastic Christmas tree maker, sold almost all of its profitable assets to a private group of investors led by Boto's chairman at a knockdown price, despite opposition by three-quarters of minority shareholders. Although Hong Kong regulations were largely cut and pasted from British statutes, the nature of Hong Kong's listed corporations means that the laws leave gaping loopholes that are

exploited by controlling shareholders. Because most listed British firms do not have controlling shareholders, the board is apt to fairly reflect the interests of all shareholders. However, in Hong Kong, thirty-two of the thirty-three "blue chips" in the Hang Seng Index, except HSBC (http://www.hsbc.com), have controlling shareholders— a single person or group of persons, typically from a family, who have the ability to control the board.

Crusading against such an Establishment, David Webb, who was one of the fifty "Stars of Asia" featured by Business Week *in 2000, is a unique character in the emerging shareholder activism movement in Hong Kong.*

According to Business Week, he "has almost single-handedly changed the terms of the corporate governance debate in Hong Kong." Webb, a native of England and an Oxford University graduate, moved to Hong Kong in 1991. He worked in investment banking and corporate finance until 1998 when he retired to become a full-time investor. His website (http://www.webb-site.com) now boasts 8,500 subscribers. He is an outspoken critic at many shareholder meetings and an advocate for minority shareholders. "He gets up people's noses," says a leading fund manager in Hong Kong. Fat cats hate him; investors love him. In April 2003, he was elected to the board of Hong Kong Exchanges & Clearing Ltd., the publicly listed company that runs the Stock Exchange of Hong Kong. Now that he has a seat at the table, Webb suggested that "management might have to listen a little more carefully."

As it stands now, the families that control most Hong Kong companies simply appoint directors and railroad their elections through at shareholder meetings. To force real votes, Webb has launched what he calls Project Poll, which is to have every motion at shareholder meetings determined by a poll on a "one share one vote" basis rather than a show of hands. He believes that this is a more transparent process and it stops companies from filling meetings with insiders who put up their hands in support of every motion. After buying ten shares in each of the thirty-three companies that make up the Hang Seng Index, he has been regularly attending shareholder meetings and demanding formal votes on all proposals. That does not win him many friends among the tycoon set accustomed to doing cozy deals without outside scrutiny. Webb recognizes that the primary problems in corporate governance in Hong Kong—and also across Asia—arise from the concentrated ownership and control of companies.

With holdings totaling at least HK$143 million (US$18 million), Webb has been using his web site to help increase awareness of the problem. In 2001, Webb took his

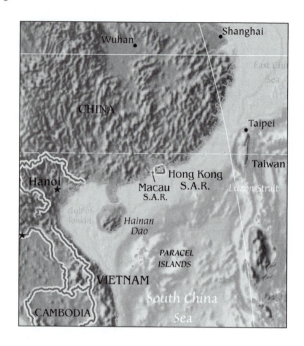

campaign one step further by formulating a proposal to establish the Hong Kong Association of Minority Shareholders. The idea was to give minority shareholders a bigger public voice by pushing the government to be more vigilant about enforcing existing rules. However, in April 2002, the Hong Kong government rejected the proposal.

Nevertheless, policymakers are not entirely hostile. Webb has been invited to serve on a number of corporate governance reform committees. Webb opined: "Critics might say it's an effort to make it look like they're doing something for shareholders. But I take the position that it's better to lobby from the inside rather than the outside . . . You can't rock the boat if you are swimming around outside it."

Case Discussion Questions

1. What is the primary type of conflict in corporate governance in Hong Kong? Why do transplanted British laws and regulations seem to be ineffective?

2. What are David Webb's motivations? Why are there not many minority shareholders in Hong Kong who actively participate in corporate governance like Webb?

3. *How effective are Webb's "in your face" challenges of the current practices? Will these challenges change the prevailing norms, values, and regulations on corporate governance in Hong Kong?*

4. *If you were Webb, what would be your recommendations to reform corporate governance in Hong Kong, Asia, and emerging economies more broadly?*

Sources: This case was written by Yi Jiang (Fisher College of Business, The Ohio State University). It is based on (1) M. Clifford, 2003, A crusader in Hong Kong, Business Week International Edition, May 19 (online); (2) B. Einhorn, 2002, The foxes guarding Hong Kong's hens, Business Week, August 26 (online); (3) J. Parry, 2001, Campaigning in Hong Kong to stop abuses by controlling shareholders, International Herald Tribune, December 8 (online); (4) http://www.webb-site.com, 2002, Government rejects HAMS proposal. Reprinted by permission of the author.

Notes

Abbreviation list

AER – *American Economic Review*

AJS – *American Journal of Sociology*

AME – *Academy of Management Executive*

AMJ – *Academy of Management Journal*

AMR – *Academy of Management Review*

APJM – *Asia Pacific Journal of Management*

ASQ – *Administrative Science Quarterly*

BW – *Business Week*

CMR – *California Management Review*

EJ – *Economic Journal*

JAE – *Journal of Accounting and Economics*

JBV – *Journal of Business Venturing*

JEL – *Journal of Economic Literature*

JEP – *Journal of Economic Perspectives*

JF – *Journal of Finance*

JFE – *Journal of Financial Economics*

JIBS – *Journal of International Business Studies*

JLE – *Journal of Law and Economics*

JM – *Journal of Management*

JMS – *Journal of Management Studies*

JPE – *Journal of Political Economy*

JWB – *Journal of World Business*

MIR – *Management International Review*

OSc – *Organization Science*

SAM – *SAM Advanced Management Journal*

SMJ – *Strategic Management Journal*

1. C. Daily, D. Dalton, & A. Cannella, 2003, Corporate governance, *AMR,* 28: 371–382; C. Daily, D. Dalton, & N. Rajagopalan, 2003, Governance through ownership, *AMJ,* 46: 151–159; P. Phan, 2001, Corporate governance in the newly emerging economies, *APJM,* 18: 131–136; M. Serapio & O. Shenkar, 1999, Reflections on the Asian crisis, *MIR,* 39: 3–12.

2. R. Monks & N. Minow, 2001, *Corporate Governance* (p. 1), Oxford, UK: Blackwell.

3. W. Boeker & R. Karichalil, 2002, Entrepreneurial transitions, *AMJ,* 45: 818-826; T. Nelson, 2003, The persistence of founder influence, *SMJ,* 24: 707–724.

4. A. Berle & G. Means, 1932, *The Modern Corporation and Private Property,* New York: MacMillan.

5. L. Tihanyi, R. Johnson, R. Hoskisson, & M. Hitt, 2003, Institutional ownership differences and international diversification, *AMJ,* 46: 195–211.

6. B. Holmstrom & S. Kaplan, 2001, Corporate governance and merger activity in the United States (p. 131), *JEP,* 15: 121–44.

7. R. La Porta, F. Lopez-de-Silanes, & A. Shleifer, 1999, Corporate ownership around the world, *JF,* 54: 471–517.

8. M. Carney & E. Gedajlovic, 2002, The coupling of ownership and control and the allocation of financial resources, *JMS,* 39: 123–146; S. Claessens, S. Djankov, & L. Lang, 2000, The separation of ownership and control in East Asian corporations, *JFE,* 58: 81–112; S. Thomson & T. Pederson, 2000, Ownership structure and economic performance in the largest European companies, *SMJ,* 21: 689–705.

9. R. Anderson & D. Reeb, 2003, Founding-family ownership and firm performance, *JF,* 58: 1301–1328;

E. Fama & M. Jensen, 1983, Separation of ownership and control, *JLE,* 26: 301–325; T. Habbershon, M. Williams, & I. MacMillan, 2003, A unified systems perspective of family firm performance, *JBV,* 18: 451–465.

10. S. Chang, 2003, Ownership structure, expropriation, and performance of group-affiliated companies in Korea, *AMJ,* 46: 238–254; L. Gomez-Mejia, M. Nunez-Nickel, & I. Gutierrez, 2001, The role of family ties in agency contracts, *AMJ,* 44: 81-95; D. Miller, L. Steier, & I. Breton-Miller, 2003, Lost in time, *JBV,* 18: 513–531; W. Schulze, M. Lubatkin, R. Dino, & A. Buchholtz, 2001, Agency relationships in family firms, *OSc,* 12: 99–116.

11. M. W. Peng & Y. Jiang, 2004, Family ownership and control in large corporations: The good, the bad, the irrelevant, Working paper, Fisher College of Business, The Ohio State University.

12. J. De Castro & K. Uhlenbruck, 1997, Characteristics of privatization, *JIBS,* 28: 123–143; W. Megginson & J. Netter, 2001, From state to market, *JEL,* 39: 321–389; M. W. Peng, 2000, *Business Strategies in Transition Economies,* Thousand Oaks, CA: Sage Publishing; R. Ramamurti, 1992, Why are developing countries privatizing? *JIBS,* 23: 225–249.

13. K. Eisenhardt, 1989, Agency theory, *AMR,* 14: 57–74; M. Jensen & W. Meckling, 1976, Theory of the firm: Managerial behavior, agency cost, and ownership structure, *JFE,* 3: 305–360.

14. J. Bryne, 2002, How to fix corporate governance, *BW,* May 6: 69–78.

15. J. Combs & M. Skill, 2003, Managerialist and human capital explanations for key executive pay premiums, *AMJ,* 46: 63–77.

16. M. Hayward, V. Rindova, & T. Pollock, 2004, Believing one's own press, *SMJ,* 25: 637–653.

17. W. Johnson, R. Magee, N. Nagarajan, & H. Newman, 1985, An analysis of the stock price reaction to sudden executive deaths, *JAE,* 7: 151–174.

18. J. Tan & M. W. Peng, 2003, Organizational slack and firm performance during economic transitions: Two studies from an emerging economy, *SMJ,* 24 (13): 1249–1263.

19. Claessens, Djankov, & Lang, 2000, The separation of ownership and control in East Asian corporations.

20. M. Faccio & L. Lang, 2002, The ultimate ownership of Western European corporations, *JFE,* 65: 365–395.

21. M. Young, M. W. Peng, D. Ahlstrom, & G. Bruton, 2002, Governing the corporation in emerging economies: A principal-principal perspective, *Academy of Management Best Papers Proceedings.*

22. R. Dharwadkar, G. George, & P. Brandes, 2000, Privatization in emerging economies, *AMR,* 25: 650–669.

23. S. Johnson, R. La Porta, F. Lopez-de-Silanes, & A. Shleifer, 2000, Tunneling, *AER,* 90: 22–27.

24. S. Chang & J. Hong, 2000, Economic performance of group-affiliated companies in Korea, *AMJ,* 43: 429–448.

25. R. Grover & T. Lowry, 2004, Rupert's world (p. 60), *BW,* January 19: 52–60.

26. D. Dalton, C. Daily, J. Johnson, & A. Ellstrand, 1999, Number of directors and financial performance, *AMJ,* 42: 674–684; J. Goodstein, K. Gautam, & W. Boeker, 1994, The effects of board size and diversity on strategic change, *SMJ,* 15: 241–250.

27. T. Yoshikawa & P. Phan, 2001, Alternative corporate governance systems in Japanese firms, *APJM,* 18: 183–205.

28. A. Ellstrand, L. Tihanyi, & J. Johnson, 2002, Board structure and international political risk, *AMJ,* 45: 769–777; S. T. Certo, 2003, Influencing initial public offering investors with prestige, *AMR,* 28: 432–446.

29. E. Gedajlovic & D. Shapiro, 2002, Ownership structure and firm profitability in Japan, *AMJ,* 45: 565–575; S. Kaplan & B. Minton, 1994, Appointments of outsiders to Japanese boards, *JFE,* 36: 225–258.

30. D. Dalton, C. Daily, A. Ellstrands, & J. Johnson, 1998, Meta-analytic reviews of board composition, leadership structure, and financial performance, *SMJ,* 19: 269–290; M. W. Peng, 2004, Outside directors and firm performance during institutional transitions, *SMJ,* 25 (5): 453–471.

31. S. Finkelstein & A. Mooney, 2003, Not the usual suspects, *AME,* 17: 101–113.

32. D. Hambrick & E. Jackson, 2000, Outside directors with a stake, *CMR,* 42: 108–117.

33. D. Worrell, C. Nemec, & W. Davidson, 1997, One hat too many? *SMJ,* 18: 499–507.

34. I. Kesner & R. Johnson, 1990, An investigation between board composition and stockholder suits, *SMJ,* 11: 317–326.

35. B. R. Baliga, R. C. Moyer, & R. Rao, 1996, CEO duality and firm performance. *SMJ,* 17: 41–53; D. Harris &

C. Helfat, 1998, CEO duality, succession, capabilities, and agency theory, *SMJ*, 19: 901–904; J. Tian & C. Lau, 2001, Board composition, leadership structure, and performance in Chinese shareholding companies, *APJM*, 18: 245–263.

36. M. Mizruchi & L. Stearns, 1994, A longitudinal study of borrowing by large American firms, *ASQ*, 39: 118–140.

37. G. Davis & H. Greve, 1997, Corporate elite networks and governance changes in the 1980s, *AJS*, 103: 1–37; R. Gulati & J. Westphal, 1999, Cooperative or controlling? *ASQ*, 44: 473–506; P. Haunschild & C. Beckman, 1998, When do interlocks matter? *ASQ*, 43: 815–44; L. Heracleous & J. Murray, 2001, Networks, interlocking directors, and strategy, *APJM*, 18: 137–160.

38. K. Au, M. W. Peng, & D. Wang, 2000, Interlocking directorates, firm strategies, and performance in Hong Kong: Towards a research agenda (p. 32), *APJM*, 17: 29–47.

39. Monks & Minow, 2001, *Corporate Governance* (p. 188); M. Young, A. Buchholtz, & D. Ahlstrom, 2004, How can board members be empowered if they are "spread too thin"? *SAM* (in press).

40. A. Hillman & T. Dalziel, 2003, Board of directors and firm performance, *AMR*, 28: 383–396; J. Johnson, C. Daily, & A. Ellstrand, 1996, Boards of directors, *JM*, 22: 409–438; S. Zahra & J. Pearce, 1989, Boards of directors and corporate financial performance, *JM*, 15: 291–334.

41. T. Pollock, H. Fischer, & J. Wade, 2002, The role of power and politics in the repricing of executive options, *AMJ*, 45: 1172–1183; J. Westphal & E. Zajac, 1995, Who shall govern? *ASQ*, 40: 60–83; E. Zajac & J. Westphal, 1996, Director reputation, CEO-board power, and the dynamics of board interlocks, *ASQ*, 41: 507–529.

42. J. Westphal, 1998, Board games: How CEOs adapt to increases in board independence, *ASQ*, 43: 511–537.

43. J. Westphal & P. Khanna, 2004, Keeping directors in line, *ASQ*, 48: 361–399.

44. N. Athanassiou & D. Nigh, 1999, The impact of US company internationalization on top management team advice networks, *SMJ*, 20: 93–92.

45. M. Carpenter & J. Westphal, 2001, The strategic context of external network ties, *AMJ*, 44: 639–660; B. Golden & E. Zajac, 2001, When will boards influence strategy? *SMJ*, 22: 1087–1111; R. Johnson, R. Hoskisson, & M. Hitt, 1993, Board of director involvement in restructuring, *SMJ*, 14: 33–50; W. Judge & C. Zeithaml, 1992, Institutional and strategic choice perspectives on board involvement in the strategic decision process, *AMJ*, 35: 766–794; P. Stiles, 2001, The impact of the board on strategy, *JMS*, 38: 627–650; J. Westphal & J. Fredrickson, 2001, Who directs strategic change? *SMJ*, 22: 1113–1137.

46. *Economist*, 2004, Where's all the fun gone? (p. 75). March 20: 75–77.

47. B. Boyd, 1990, Corporate linkages and organizational environment, *SMJ*, 11: 419–430; A. Hillman, A. Cannella, & R. Paetzold, 2000, The resource dependence role of corporate directors, *JMS*, 37: 213–255.

48. M. W. Peng, K. Au, & D. Wang, 2001, Interlocking directorates as corporate governance in Third World multinationals: Theory and evidence from Thailand, *APJM*, 18: 161–181.

49. M. W. Peng, 2004, Outside directors and firm performance during institutional transitions, *SMJ*, 25 (5): 453–471.

50. A. Hillman & K. Haynes, 2004, Institutional environment, board functions, and firm performance, Working paper, Arizona State University.

51. B. Baysinger & R. Hoskisson, 1990, The composition of boards of directors and strategic control, *AMR*, 15: 72–87; R. Hoskisson & M. Hitt, 1988, Strategic control and relative R&D investment in large multi-product firms, *SMJ*, 16: 605–621; R. Hoskisson & T. Turk, 1990, Corporate restructuring, *AMR*, 15: 459–477.

52. M. Young, D. Ahlstrom, G. Bruton, & E. Chan, 2001, The resource dependence, service, and control functions of boards of directors in Hong Kong and Taiwanese firms, *APJM*, 18: 223–244.

53. J. Coles, V. McWilliams, & N. Sen, 2001, An examination of the relationship of governance mechanisms to performance, *JM*, 27: 23–50.

54. T. Eisenmann, 2002, The effects of CEO equity ownership and firm diversification on risk taking, *SMJ*, 23: 513–534; J. McGuire & E. Matta, 2003, CEO stock options, *AMJ*, 46: 255–265; H. Tosi, J. Katz, & L. Gomez-Mejia, 1997, Disaggregating the agency contract, *AMJ*, 40: 584–602; S. Zahra, 1996, Governance, ownership, and corporate entrepreneurship, *AMJ*, 39: 1713–1735.

55. H. Barkema & L. Gomez-Mejia, 1998, Managerial compensation and firm performance, *AMJ*, 41: 135–145; M. Carpenter & W. G. Sanders, 2002, Top management team compensation, *SMJ*, 23: 367–375; M. Conyon & S. Peck, 1998, Board control, remuneration committees, and top management compensation, *AMJ*, 41: 146–157; B. Main, A. Bruce, & T. Buck, 1996, Total board remuneration and company performance, *EJ*, 106: 1627–1644.

56. P. David, R. Kochhar, & E. Levitas, 1998, The effect of institutional investors on the level and mix of CEO compensation, *AMJ*, 41: 200–208; S. Finkelstein & B. Boyd, 1998, How much does the CEO matter? *AMJ*, 41: 179–199; L. Gomez-Mejia & R. Wiseman, 1997, Reframing executive compensation, *JM*, 23: 291–374; M. Jensen & K. Murphy, 1990, Performance pay and top management incentives, *JPE*, 98: 225–263; H. Tosi & L. Gomez-Mejia, 1989, The decoupling of CEO pay and performance, *ASQ*, 34: 169–189; J. Westphal & E. Zajac, 1994, Substance and symbolism in CEOs' long-term incentive plans, *ASQ*, 39: 367–390.

57. L. Gomez-Mejia, M. Larraza-Kintana, & M. Makri, 2003, The determinants of executive compensation in family-controlled public corporations, *AMJ*, 46: 226–237; W. Schulze, M. Lubatkin, & R. Dino, 2003, Toward a theory of agency and altruism in family firms, *JBV*, 18: 473–490.

58. J. Walsh & J. Seward, 1990, On the efficiency of internal and external corporate control mechanisms, *AMR*, 15: 421–458.

59. *Economist*, 2003, Coming and going, October 25: 12–14.

60. P. Gumbel, 2004, Spring cleaning, *Time*, June (bonus section): A8–A14.

61. M. Ezzamel & R. Watson, 1998, Market comparison earning and the bidding up of executive cash compensation, *AMJ*, 41: 221–232.

62. R. Morck, A. Shleifer, & R. Vishny, 1988, Management ownership and market valuation, *JFE*, 20: 293–315. See also P. Wright, M. Kroll, A. Lado, & B. Van Ness, 2002, The structure of ownership and corporate acquisition strategies, *SMJ*, 23: 41–53.

63. E. Biggs, 2004, CEO succession planning, *AME*, 18: 105–107; W. Boeker & J. Goodstein, 1993, Performance and successor choice, *AMJ*, 36: 172–186;

A. Cannella & M. Lubatkin, 1993, Succession as a sociopolitical process, *AMJ*, 36: 763–793; W. Ocasio & H. Kim, 1999, The circulation of corporate control, *ASQ*, 44: 532–562; W. Shen & A. Cannella, 2002, Power dynamics with top management and their impacts on CEO dismissal, *AMJ*, 45: 1195–1206; E. Zajac & J. Westphal, 1996, Who shall succeed? *AMJ*, 39: 64–90.

64. Holmstrom & Kaplan, 2001, Corporate governance and merger activity in the United States (p. 123).

65. G. Jarrell, J. Brickley, & J. Netter, 1988, The market for corporate control: The empirical evidence since 1980, *JEP*, 2: 49–68; M. Jensen & R. Ruback, 1983, The market for corporate control, *JFE*, 2: 5–50.

66. J. Krug & W. Hegarty, 1997, Postacquisition turnover among US top management teams, *SMJ*, 18: 667–675; J. Walsh, 1988, Top management turnover following mergers and acquisitions, *SMJ*, 9: 173–183.

67. R. Kabir, D. Cantrijn, & A. Jeunink, 1997, Takeover defenses, ownership structure, and stock returns in the Netherlands, *SMJ*, 18: 97–109.

68. D. McCarthy, S. Puffer, & S. Shekshnia (eds.), 2004, *Corporate Governance in Russia*, Cheltenham, UK: Edward Elgar.

69. R. Kosnik, 1987, Greenmail: A study of board performance in corporate governance, *ASQ*, 32: 163–185.

70. G. Davis, 1991, Agents without principles, *ASQ*, 36: 583–613.

71. C. Sundaramurthy, J. M. Mahoney, & J. T. Mahoney, 1997, Board structure, antitakeover provisions, and stockholder wealth, *SMJ*, 18: 231–245.

72. H. Singh & F. Harianto, 1989, Management-board relationships, takeover risk, and the adoption of golden parachutes, *AMJ*, 32: 7–24; J. Wade & C. O'Reilly, 1990, Golden parachutes, *ASQ*, 35: 587–604.

73. I. Fox & A. Marcus, 1992, The causes and consequences of leveraged management buyouts, *AMR*, 17: 62–85; P. Phan & C. Hill, 1995, Organizational restructuring and economic performance in leveraged buyouts, *AMJ*, 38: 704–739; A. Seth & J. Esterwood, 1993, Strategic redirection in large management buyouts, *SMJ*, 14: 251–273; S. Thompson & M. Wright, 1995, Corporate governance, *EJ*, 105: 690–703; M. Wiersema & J. Liebeskind, 1995, The effects of leveraged buyouts on

corporate growth and diversification in large firms, *SMJ*, 16: 447–460; M. Wright, S. Thompson, & K. Robbie, 1992, Venture capital and management-led leveraged buy-outs, *JBV*, 7: 47–71.

74. W. Long & D. Ravenscraft, 1993, LBOs, debt, and R&D intensity, *SMJ*, 14: 119-136; S. Zahra & M. Fescina, 1991, Will leveraged buyouts kill US corporate research and development? *AME*, 5: 7–21.

75. K. Rediker & A. Seth, 1995, Boards of directors and substitution effects of governance mechanisms, *SMJ*, 16: 85–99.

76. G. Andrade, M. Mitchell, & E. Stafford, 2001, New evidence and perspectives on mergers, *JEP*, 15: 103–120.

77. Jensen, 1993, The modern industrial revolution, exit, and failure of internal control systems, *JF*, 48: 831–880.

78. S. Chatterjee, J. Harrison, & D. Bergh, 2003, Failed takeover attempts, corporate governance, and refocusing, *SMJ*, 24: 87–96; P. Gibbs, 1993, Determinants of corporate restructuring, *SMJ*, 14: 51–68; J. Walsh & R. Kosnik, 1993, Corporate raiders and their disciplinary role in the market for corporate control, *AMJ*, 36: 671–700.

79. M. Useem, 1996, *Investor Capitalism,* New York: Basic Books.

80. A. Tuschke & W. G. Sanders, 2003, Antecedents and consequences of corporate governance reform, *SMJ*, 24: 631–49.

81. T. Buck, 2003, Modern Russian corporate governance, *JWB*, 38: 299–313.

82. M. Roe, 2003, *Political Determinants of Corporate Governance* (p. 67), New York: Oxford University Press.

83. T. Pederson & S. Thomsen, 1997, European patterns of corporate ownership, *JIBS,* 28: 759–778.

84. A. Shleifer & R. Vishny, 1997, A survey of corporate governance (p. 774), *JF,* 52: 737–783. See also J. Henderson & K. Cool, 2003, Corporate governance, investment bandwagons, and overcapacity, *SMJ,* 24: 349–373.

85. E. Gedajlovic & D. Shapiro, 1998, Management and ownership effects (p. 536), *SMJ,* 19: 533–553.

86. A. Cuervo, 2000, Explaining the variation in the performance effects of privatization, *AMR,* 25: 581–591; R. Ramamurti, 2000, A multilevel model of privatization in emerging economies, *AMR,* 25: 525–551.

87. T. Buck, I. Filatotchev, & M. Wright, 1998, Agents, stakeholders, and corporate governance in Russian firms, *JMS*, 35: 81–104; I. Filatotchev, T. Buck, & V. Zhukov, 2000, Downsizing privatized firms in Russia, Ukraine, and Belarus, *AMJ,* 43: 286–304.

88. K. Meyer & S. Estrin, 2001, Brownfield entry in emerging markets, *JIBS,* 32: 575–584; S. Ramaswamy, 2001, Organizational ownership, competitive intensity, and firm performance, *SMJ,* 22: 989–998; K. Uhlenbruck & J. De Castro, 2000, Foreign acquisitions in Central and Eastern Europe, *AMJ,* 43: 381–402.

89. B. Belev, 2003, Institutional investors in Bulgarian corporate governance reform, *JWB,* 38: 361–374; K. Ramaswamy & M. Li, 2001, Foreign investors, foreign directors, and corporate diversification, *APJM,* 18: 207–22.

90. M. W. Peng, T. Buck, & I. Filatotchev, 2003, Do outside directors and new managers help improve firm performance? An exploratory study in Russian privatization, *JWB,* 38 (4): 348–360.

91. P. Mar & M. Young, 2001, Corporate governance in transition economies, *JWB,* 36: 280–302.

92. Y. Zhang & N. Rajagopalan, 2003, Explaining new CEO origin, *AMJ,* 46: 327–338.

93. C. Hill & S. Snell, 1998, External control, corporate strategy, and firm performance in research intensive industries, *SMJ,* 9: 577–590; E. Zajac & J. Westphal, 1994, The costs and benefits of managerial incentives and monitoring in large US corporations, *SMJ,* 15: 121–142.

94. I. Kesner, 1987, Directors' stock ownership and organizational performance, *JM,* 13: 499–508; M. Li & R. Simerly, 1998, The moderating effect of environmental dynamism on the ownership-performance relationship, *SMJ,* 19: 169–79.

95. R. Beatty & E. Zajac, 1994, Managerial incentives, monitoring, and risk bearing, *ASQ,* 39: 313–335; M. Carpenter, T. Pollock, & M. Leary, 2003, Testing a model of reasoned risk-taking, *SMJ,* 24: 803–820.

96. B. Boyd, 1995, CEO duality and firm performance, *SMJ,* 16: 301–312; S. Finkelstein & R. D'Aveni, 1994, CEO duality as a double-edged sword, *AMJ,* 37: 1079–1108; W. Judge, I. Naoumova, & N. Koutzevol, 2003, Corporate governance and firm performance in Russia, *JWB,* 38: 385–396.

97. R. Castanias & C. Helfat, 2001, The managerial rents model, *JM*, 27: 661–678; A. Cannella & M. Monroe, 1997, Contrasting perspectives on strategic leaders, *JM*, 23: 213–237; J. Conger, E. Lawler, & D. Finegold, 2001, *Corporate Boards*, San Francisco: Jossey-Bass; D. Harris & C. Helfat, 1997, Specificity of CEO human capital and compensation, *SMJ*, 18: 895–920; K. Roth, 1995, Managing international interdependence, *AMJ*, 38: 200–232; N. Rajagopalan & D. Datta, 1996, CEO characteristics, *AMJ*, 39: 197–215.

98. C. Collins & K. Clark, 2003, Strategic human resource practices, top management team social networks, and firm performance, *AMJ*, 46: 740–751; M. Geletkanycz, B. Boyd, & S. Finkelstein, 2001, The strategic value of CEO external directorate networks, *SMJ*, 22: 889–898; M. W. Peng & Y. Luo, 2000, Managerial ties and firm performance in a transition economy: The nature of a micro-macro link, *AMJ*, 43 (3): 486–501.

99. K. Eisenhardt & M. Zbaracki, 1992, Strategic decision-making, *SMJ*, 13: 17–37; D. Forbes & F. Milliken, 1999, Cognition and corporate governance, *AMR*, 24: 489–505; J. Fredrickson, 1984, The comprehensiveness of strategic decision processes, *AMJ*, 27: 445–466; D. Hambrick & P. Mason, 1984, Upper echelons, *AMR*, 9: 193–206; V. Papadakis, S. Lioukas, & D. Chambers, 1998, Strategic decision-making processes, *SMJ*, 19: 115–147; R. Priem & D. Harrison, 1994, Exploring strategic judgment, *SMJ*, 15: 311–324.

100. I. Filatotchev & S. Toms, 2003, Corporate governance, strategy, and survival in a declining industry, *JMS*, 40: 895–920; D. Hambrick, T. Cho, & M. Chen, 1996, The influence of top management team heterogeneity on firms' competitive moves, *ASQ*, 41: 659–684; C. Homburg, H. Krohmer, & J. Workman, 1999, Strategic consensus and performance, *SMJ*, 20: 339–357; H. Krishnan, A. Miller, & W. Judge, 1997, Diversification and top management team complementarity, *SMJ*, 18: 361–374; O. Richard, 2000, racial diversity, business strategy, and firm performance, *AMJ*, 43: 164–177; J. Westphal & L. Milton, 2000, How experience and network ties affect the influence of demographic minorities on corporate boards, *ASQ*, 45: 366–398.

101. D. Knight, C. Pearce, K. G. Smith, J. Olian, H. Sims, K. A. Smith, & P. Flood, 1999, Top management team

diversity, group process, and strategic consensus, *SMJ*, 20: 445–465; C. H. Miller, L. Burke, & W. Glick, 1998, Cognitive diversity among upper-echelon executives, *SMJ*, 19: 39–58; R. Priem, D. Lyon, & G. Dess, 1999, Inherent limitations of demographic proxies in top management team heterogeneity research, *JM*, 25: 935-953; C. West & C. Schwenk, 1996, Top management team strategic consensus, demographic homogeneity, and firm performance, *SMJ*, 17: 571–576; T. Zenger & B. Lawrence, 1989, Organizational demography, *AMJ*, 32: 353–376.

102. M. Jensen & E. Zajac, 2004, Corporate elites and corporate strategy, *SMJ*, 25: 507–524; T. Simons, L. Pelled, & K. Smith, 1999, Making use of difference, *AMJ*, 42: 662–673.

103. M. Carpenter, 2002, The implications of strategy and social context for the relationship between top management team heterogeneity and firm performance, *SMJ*, 23: 275–284; L. Tihanyi, A. Ellstrand, C. Daily, & D. Dalton, 2000, Composition of the top management team and firm international diversification, *JM*, 26: 1157–1177; W. G. Sanders & M. Carpenter, 1998, Internationalization and firm governance, *AMJ*, 41: 158–178.

104. D. Hambrick & G. Fukutomi, 1991, The seasons of a CEO's tenure, *AMR*, 16: 719–742; D. Miller & J. Shamsie, 2001, Learning across the life cycle, *SMJ*, 22: 725–745.

105. C. Hill & P. Phan, 1991, CEO tenure as a determinant of CEO pay, *AMJ*, 34: 707–717; M. Lynall, B. Golden, & A. Hillman, 2003, Board composition from adolescence to maturity, *AMR*, 28: 416–431; W. Shen, 2003, The dynamics of the CEO-board relationship, *AMR*, 28: 466–478.

106. M. Burkart, F. Panunzi, & A. Shleifer, 2003, Family firms, *JF*, 58: 2167–2201.

107. R. La Porta, F. Lopez-de-Silanes, A. Shleifer, & R. Vishny, 1998, Law and finance, *JPE*, 106: 1113–1155.

108. Young, Peng, Ahlstrom, & Bruton, 2002, Governing the corporation in emerging economies.

109. R. Rajan & L. Zingales, 2003, The great reversals, *JFE*, 69: 5–50.

110. Claessens, Djankov, & Lang, 2000, The separation of ownership and control in East Asian corporations (p. 108).

111. S. White, 2004, Stakeholders, structure, and the failure of corporate governance reform initiatives in post-crisis Thailand, *APJM,* 21: 103–122.

112. G. Davis & T. Thomspon, 1994, A social movement perspective on corporate control, *ASQ,* 39: 141–173.

113. A. Hassel, M. Hopner, A. Kurdelbusch, B. Rehder, & R. Zugehor, 2003, Two dimensions of the internationalization of firms, *JMS,* 40: 705–723.

114. *Economist,* 2003, Japanese stock markets: Plus ca change, November 8: 75.

115. OECD, 1999, *OECD Principles of Corporate Governance,* Paris: OECD.

116. OECD, 2003, *Experiences from the Regional Corporate Governance Roundtables* (p. 23), Paris: OECD.

117. L. Donaldson, 1995, *American Anti-management Theories of Management,* Cambridge, UK: Cambridge University Press.

118. J. Davis, F. D. Schoorman, & L. Donaldson, 1997, Toward a stewardship theory of management, *AMR,* 22: 20–47; P. Lee & H. O'Neill, 2003, Ownership structure and R&D investments of US and Japanese firms, *AMJ,* 46: 212–225.

119. P. Lane, A. Cannella, & M. Lubatkin, 1998, Agency problems as antecedents to unrelated mergers and diversification, *SMJ,* 19: 555–578.

120. S. Ghoshal & P. Moran, 1996, Bad for practice: A critique of the transaction cost theory, *AMR,* 21: 31–47; C. Sundaramurthy & M. Lewis, 2003, Control and collaboration, *AMR,* 28: 397–415.

121. G. Hansen & C. Hill, 1991, Are institutional investors myopic? *SMJ,* 12: 1–16.

122. R. Morck, B. Yeung, & W. Yu, 2000, The information content of stock markets, *JFE,* 58: 215–260.

123. M. Jensen, 2003, The agency costs of overvalued equity, Working paper, Harvard Business School.

124. M. Rubach & T. Sebora, 1998, Comparative corporate governance, *JWB,* 33: 167–184.

125. M. W. Peng, K. Au, & D. Wang, 2004, Board interlocks and corporate performance among firms listed abroad, Working paper, Fisher College of Business, The Ohio State University.

126. T. Yoshikawa & E. Gedajlovic, 2002, The impact of global capital market exposure and stable ownership on investor relations practices and performance of Japanese firms, *APJM,* 19: 525–540.

127. C. Doidge, K. A. Karolyi, & R. Stulz, 2003, Why are foreign firms listed in the US worth more? *JFE,* 71: 205–238.

128. D. McCarthy & S. Puffer, 2003, Corporate governance in Russia (p. 401), *JWB,* 38: 397–415.

129. R. Aguilera & G. Jackson, 2003, The cross-national diversity of corporate governance, *AMR,* 28: 447–465; J. Charkham, 1994, *Keeping Good Company,* Oxford, UK: Oxford University Press; M. Guillen, 2001, *The Limits of Convergence,* Princeton, NJ: Princeton University Press.

130. G. Bruton, D. Ahlstrom, & J. Wan, 2003, Turnaround in East Asian firms, *SMJ,* 24: 519–540; M. Carney & E. Gedajlovic, 2001, Corporate governance and firm capabilities, *APJM,* 18: 335–354.

131. G. Davis & C. Marquis, 2003, The globalization of stock markets and convergence in corporate governance, in R. Swedberg (eds.), *Economic Sociology of Capitalist Institutions,* Cambridge, UK: Cambridge University Press.

132. J. Siegel, 2003, Can foreign firms bond themselves effectively by renting US securities laws? Working paper, Harvard Business School.

133. *BW,* 2004, Who needs US markets? February 16: 13.

134. M. Young, D. Ahlstrom, & G. Bruton, 2004, Globalization and corporate governance in East Asia, *MIR,* 44: 31–50.

135. M. W. Peng, 2000, Book review of O. K. Tam (1999), *The Development of Corporate Governance in China,* *AME,* 14 (1): 155–156.

136. J. Sonnenfeld, 2004, Good governance and the misleading myths of bad metrics, *AME,* 18 (1): 108–113.

STRATEGIZING WITH CORPORATE SOCIAL RESPONSIBILITY

Outline

- A stakeholder view of the firm
- A comprehensive model of corporate social responsibility
- Debates and extensions
- Implications for strategists

Opening Case: Salmon, Salmon, Everywhere

You may have noticed the proliferation of salmon in grocery stores and restaurants in North America, Europe, and Asia recently. The explosion of global salmon supply is not due to an increase of wild salmon catch, which has been in steady decline for decades. In fact, the industrial revolution, along with dams, pollution, and increasingly powerful fishing fleets, nearly pushed the wild Atlantic salmon to extinction (Pacific salmon are still relatively safe). Since the 1960s, various governments have worked with nongovernmental organizations (NGOs) such as the North Atlantic Salmon Conservation Organization (http://www.nasco.int) and the Atlantic Salmon Federation (http://www.asf.ca) to buy out fishermen. For example, in the largest such program, the Canadian government spent $72 million (Canadian) to buy out 7,000 fishermen in the Maritime Provinces during the 1980s and 1990s.

As the wild salmon disappear, salmon farming (or aquaculture) has been on the rise. Starting in Norway as a cottage industry in the late 1960s, salmon farming quickly spread to Canada, Great Britain, Iceland, and Ireland in the 1970s, the United States in the 1980s, and Chile in the 1990s. Farm-raised salmon live in sea cages. They are fed pellets to speed their growth (from fertilized eggs to nine-pound fish in 2.5 years—twice as fast as in the wild), pigments to mimic the pink hue of wild salmon flesh, and pesticides to kill the lice that go hand-in-hand with an industrial feedlot. Atlantic salmon farming, still dominated

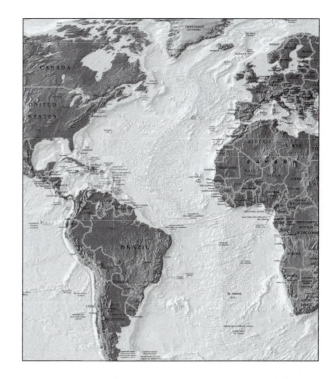

by Norwegian firms and followed by Chilean companies, has exploded into a $2 billion a year global business that produced approximately 660,000 tons of fish in 2000. In comparison, wild salmon catch in the Atlantic, only allowed by Great Britain and Ireland, was only 3,000 tons in the same year. In essence, it is Atlantic salmon farming companies that have provided all the delicious and nutritious salmon, which has been transformed from a rare, expensive seasonal delicacy to a common "chicken of the sea" to be enjoyed by everyone year-round. In addition, Atlantic salmon farming has brought undeniable benefits, such as taking commercial fishing pressure off wild salmon stocks and providing employment to depressed maritime regions. For example, in western Scotland, salmon aquaculture employs approximately 6,400 workers.

However, here is the catch: farm-raised salmon (1) foul the nearby sea, (2) spread diseases and sea lice, and (3) allow escaped fish to interbreed with wild salmon. Each of these problems has become a growing controversy. First, heavy concentration of fish in a tiny area—up to 800,000 in one floating cage—leads to food and fecal waste that promotes toxic algae blooms, which, in turn, have led to the closure of shell fishing in nearby waters. Second, sea lice outbreaks at fish farms in Ireland, Norway, and Scotland have devastating effects on wild salmon and other fish. In Cobscook Bay, the aquaculture center of Maine, 2.1 million tainted fish recently had to be slaughtered. The third and probably most serious problem lies in escaped salmon. Many salmon have escaped whenever seals chewed through pens, storms demolished cages, or fish were spilled during handling. In Scotland, for example, nearly 300,000 farmed fish escaped in 2002. Research has found that escaped salmon interbreed with wild salmon. In Norwegian rivers, which are salmon spawning grounds, 10 to 35 percent of the "wild" fish are actually escaped salmon.

Wild salmon are an amazing species, genetically programmed to be able to find their spawning grounds in rivers after years of wandering in the sea. Although at present, only one egg out of every 4,000 is likely to complete such an epic journey, the salmon has been a magical fish in the legends of Iceland, Ireland, Norway, and Scotland. These legends are threatened by the escaped, farm-raised salmon and the hybrid they produce with wild salmon, because genetically homogenous salmon (descended from aquaculture fish) are ill suited to find these rivers and less able to cope with threats such as disease and climate change. In short, the biodiversity of the wild salmon stocks, already at dangerously low levels, is threatened. In response, the Norwegian government has recently banned a number of wild-salmon fjords and rivers from aquaculture. Defenders of fish farming, however, argue that all farming alters, and sometimes damages, the environment. If modern agricultural pesticides, fertilizers, and growth hormones were invented today, they probably would be banned. Defenders thus argue that there is no reason that the emerging aquaculture industry needs to be held by higher standards.

Sources: Based on (1) Economist, 2003, A new way to feed the world, August 9: 9; (2) Economist, 2003, The promise of a blue revolution, August 9: 19–21; (3) F. Montaigne, 2003, Everybody loves Atlantic Salmon: Here's the catch, National Geographic, 204 (1): 100–123.

Do these salmon aquaculture companies have a responsibility to help restore the *wild* salmon stocks? Should they consider reducing output? Reducing the fish density of sea cages? Laying off some workers? Shutting down operations? Or doing business as usual? Obviously these questions have no easy answers. This chapter helps you answer some of these and other strategic questions concerning corporate social responsibility. **Corporate social responsibility** (CSR) refers to "consideration of, and response to, issues beyond the narrow economic, technical, and legal requirements of the firm to accomplish social benefits along with the traditional

FIGURE 12.1   A Stakeholder View of the Firm

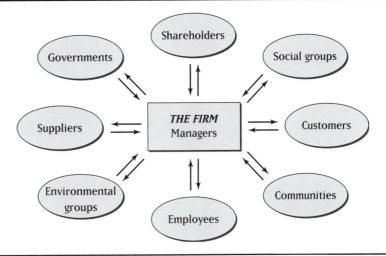

Source: Adapted from T. Donaldson & L. Preston, 1995, The stakeholder theory of the corporation: Concepts, evidence, and implications (p. 69), Academy of Management Review, 20: 65–91. Copyright © 1995. Reprinted by permission of Academy of Management Review via Copyright Clearance Center.

economic gains which the firm seeks."[1] Although, historically, CSR issues have been on the "back burner" of strategy discussions, these issues are increasingly brought to the forefront of corporate agendas.[2] While this chapter is the last in this book, by no means do we suggest that CSR is the least important topic. Instead, we believe that this chapter is one of the best ways to *integrate* all three leading perspectives on strategy, namely, industry-, resource-, and institution-based views.[3] Specifically, this chapter continues and expands our earlier discussion on ethics in Chapter 4.

At the heart of CSR is the concept of **stakeholder,** which is "any group or individual who can affect or is affected by the achievement of the organization's objectives."[4] Shown in Figure 12.1, while shareholders certainly are an important group of stakeholders, other stakeholders include managers, nonmanagerial employees (hereafter "employees"), suppliers, customers, communities, governments, and social and environmental groups. Because Chapter 11 has already dealt with shareholder interests at length, this chapter focuses on other *nonshareholder stakeholders,* which we term "stakeholders" in this chapter for composition simplicity. A leading debate on CSR is whether managers' efforts to promote the interests of these stakeholders are at odds with their fiduciary duty to safeguard shareholder interests. To the extent that firms are *not* social agencies and that their primary function is to serve as economic enterprises, firms should not—and are unable to—take on all the social problems of the world. Yet, on the other hand, failing to heed certain CSR imperatives may be self-defeating in the long run. Therefore, the key is how to strategize with CSR.

The remainder of this chapter first introduces a stakeholder view of the firm and then discusses a comprehensive model of CSR based on the three leading perspectives on strategy. As before, debates and extensions follow.

A STAKEHOLDER VIEW OF THE FIRM

This section introduces the quest for global sustainability as a big picture perspective, identifies primary and secondary stakeholder groups, reviews a fundamental debate concerning the role of CSR for firms, and highlights the role of managers as a unique group of stakeholders. The focus is on the emergence of a stakeholder view of the firm.

A Big Picture Perspective

Strategy is about the "big picture." A stakeholder view of the firm, with a quest for global sustainability, probably represents the *biggest* picture associated with the firm. A key goal for CSR is **global sustainability,** which is defined as the ability "to meet the needs of the present without compromising the ability of future generations to meet their needs."[5] It not only refers to a sustainable social and natural environment, but also sustainable capitalism.[6] Globally, at least three sets of drivers are related to the urgency of global sustainability in the twenty-first century.[7] First, rising levels of population, poverty, and inequity associated with globalization are calling for new solutions. The repeated protests staged around the world since the Seattle protests in 1999 are just visible tips of an iceberg brewing antiglobalization sentiments. Second, compared with the relatively eroded power of national governments in the wake of globalization, NGOs and other civil society stakeholders—often emboldened by new technology such as the Internet—have increasingly assumed the role of monitor and in some cases enforcer of social and environmental standards.[8] Finally, industrialization has created some irreversible effects on the global environment. Global warming, ozone depletion, air and water pollution, soil erosion, and deforestation are global problems demanding solutions.[9]

The complex, multidimensional drivers that support global sustainability have substantially expanded the radar screen of strategic analysis by including many direct and indirect players who participate in and/or are affected by the game that firms play. For large firms such as multinational enterprises (MNEs) with operations spanning the globe, their CSR areas, shown in Table 12.1, seem mind-boggling. This bewilderingly complex "big picture" forces managers to *prioritize*. To prioritize, a disparate, yet systematically comprehensible, set of primary and secondary stakeholders must be identified.[10]

Primary and Secondary Stakeholder Groups

Primary stakeholder groups are defined as constituents on which the firm relies for its continuous survival and prosperity.[11] Shareholders, managers, employees, suppliers, and customers—together with governments and communities whose laws and regulations must be obeyed and to whom taxes and other obligations may be due—are typically considered as primary stakeholders. Firm performance can be seriously undermined if any primary stakeholder group becomes dissatisfied and withdraws efforts.[12] This can happen when managers pursue self-interests, employees have high absenteeism, suppliers reduce quality, customers boycott the firm's products, and governments impose predatory taxes.

TABLE 12.1   **Corporate Social Responsibilities for Multinational Enterprises (MNEs) as Recommended by International Organizations**

MNEs and Host Governments:	MNEs and Environmental Protection:
▪ Should not interfere in the internal political affairs of the host country (OECD, UN)	▪ Should respect the host country laws and regulations concerning environmental protection (OECD, UN)
▪ Should consult governmental authorities and national employers' and workers' organizations to ensure that their investments conform to the economic and social development policies of the host country (ICC, ILO, OECD, UN)	▪ Should cooperate with host governments and international organizations in the development of national and international environmental protection standards (ICC, UN)
▪ Should provide host governments the information necessary for correctly assessing tax obligations (ICC, OECD)	▪ Should supply to host governments information concerning the environmental impact of MNE activities (ICC, UN)
▪ Should give preference to local sources for components and raw materials if prices and quality are competitive (ICC, ILO)	**MNEs and Consumer Protection:**
▪ Should reinvest some profits in the host country (ICC)	▪ Should preserve the safety and health of consumers by disclosing appropriate information, labeling correctly, and advertising accurately (UN)
MNEs and Laws, Regulations, and Politics:	**MNEs and Employment Practices:**
▪ Should respect the right of every country to exercise control over its natural resources (UN)	▪ Should cooperate with host governments to create jobs in certain locations (ICC)
▪ Should refrain from improper or illegal involvement in local politics (OECD)	▪ Should try to increase employment opportunities and standards in host countries (ILO)
▪ Should not pay bribes or render improper benefits to public servants (OECD, UN)	▪ Should give advance notice of plant closures and mitigate the adverse effects (ICC, OECD)
MNEs and Technology Transfer:	▪ Should establish nondiscriminatory employment policies (ILO, OECD)
▪ Should cooperate with host governments in assessing the impact of transfers of technology to developing countries and should enhance their technological capacities (OECD, UN)	▪ Should respect the rights of employees to engage in collective bargaining (ILO, OECD)
▪ Should develop and adapt technologies to the needs of host countries (ICC, ILO, OECD)	**MNEs and Human Rights:**
▪ Should conduct research and development activities in developing countries, using local resources and talents to the greatest extent possible (ICC, UN)	▪ Should respect human rights and fundamental freedoms in host countries (UN)
▪ Should provide reasonable terms and conditions when granting licenses for industrial property rights (ICC, OECD)	▪ Should respect the social and cultural objectives, values, and traditions of host countries (UN)

Sources: Based on (1) ICC: The International Chamber of Commerce Guidelines for International Investment (http://www.iccwbo.org); (2) ILO: The International Labor Office Tripartite Declarations of Principles Concerning Multinational Enterprises and Social Policy (http://www.ilo.org); (3) OECD: The Organization for Economic Cooperation and Development Guidelines for Multinational Enterprises (http://www.oecd.org); (4) UN: The United Nations Code of Conduct on Transnational Corporations (http://www.un.org).

Secondary stakeholder groups are defined as "those who influence or affect, or are influenced or affected by, the corporation, but they are not engaged in transactions with the corporation and are not essential for its survival."[13] Examples include the media and a wide range of social and environmental groups. For example, environmental groups (such as Greenpeace) often take it upon themselves to promote pollution-reduction technologies. Fair labor practice groups (such as the Fair Labor

Association) frequently challenge firms that allegedly fail to provide decent labor conditions for employees at home and abroad. Anticorruption groups (such as Transparency International) usually champion corruption-free practices (see Table 4.4 in Chapter 4). While the firm does not depend on secondary stakeholder groups for its survival, such groups may have the potential to cause significant embarrassment and damage to a firm.

The stakeholder view asserts that instead of only pursuing the economic bottom line, such as profits and shareholder returns, firms should pursue a more balanced **triple bottom line,** consisting of *economic, social,* and *environmental* performance, by simultaneously satisfying the demands of all stakeholder groups.[14] Because some competing demands obviously exist, the CSR proposition represents a dilemma. In fact, it has provoked a fundamental debate, which is introduced next.

A Fundamental Debate: What Social Responsibility?

The CSR debate centers on the nature of the firm in society. Why does the firm exist?[15] Most people would intuitively answer: "To make money"—or as Milton Friedman, a University of Chicago economist and Nobel laureate, eloquently suggested: "The business of business is business."[16] The idea that the firm is an economic enterprise seems to be uncontroversial. At issue is whether the firm is *only* an economic enterprise.

One side of the debate argues that "the social responsibility of business is to increase its profits," which is the title of Friedman's influential article published in 1970. This free market school of thought draws upon Adam Smith's idea that pursuit of economic self-interest (within legal and ethical bounds) leads to efficient markets. Free market advocates believe that the first and foremost stakeholder group is shareholders, whose interests managers have a fiduciary duty (required by law) to look after. To the extent that the hallmark of our economic system remains capitalism, the providers of capital—namely, capitalists or shareholders—deserve a commanding height in managerial attention. In fact, since the 1980s, a term that explicitly places shareholders as the single most important stakeholder group, namely, *shareholder capitalism,* has been coined. Originated in the United States, such a model of shareholder-centered capitalism has become increasingly influential in other parts of the world (see Chapter 11).

Advocates of shareholder capitalism argue that if firms attempt to attain social goals, such as providing employment and social welfare, managers will lose their focus on profit maximization (and its derivative, shareholder value maximization).[17] Consequently, firms may lose their character as capitalistic enterprises and become *socialist* organizations. This perception of socialist organization is not a pure argumentative point, but an accurate characterization of numerous state-owned enterprises (SOEs) throughout the pre-reform Soviet Union, Central and Eastern Europe, and China, as well as other developing countries in Africa, Asia, and Latin America. SOEs in general have poor economic performance. As a result, a major global movement in the last two decades has been privatization, in essence, to remove the social function of these firms and restore their economic focus through private ownership (see Chapter 11). Overall, the free market school is not only dominant throughout developed economies, but also increasingly influential in emerging economies that embrace free market principles. It has also provided much of the intellectual basis for globalization that is spearheaded by MNEs.

It is against such a formidable and influential school of thought that the CSR movement has emerged. Few, if any, CSR advocates argue for a revival of socialism in the world. So the whole debate takes place within the constraints of capitalism (many CSR advocates are professors in business schools, which are, by design, capitalistic institutions). The goal of the CSR movement is a more humane capitalism, in which justice and fairness can be addressed. Advocates argue that a free market system that takes the pursuit of self-interest and profit as its guiding light—although in theory constrained by rules, contracts, and property rights—may in practice fail to constrain itself, thus often breeding greed, excesses, and abuses.[18] Firms and managers, if left to their own devices, would almost always choose self-interest over public interest. While not denying that shareholders are important stakeholders, CSR advocates argue that all stakeholders have an *equal* right to bargain for a "fair deal."[19] Given stakeholders' often conflicting demands, the very purpose of the firm, instead of being a profit-maximizing entity, is argued to serve as a vehicle for coordinating stakeholders' interests. Therefore, success in addressing the concerns of multiple stakeholder interests, rather than in meeting conventional economic criteria, would constitute the ultimate test of firm performance.[20]

Starting in the 1970s as a peripheral voice in an ocean of free market believers, the CSR school of thought has slowly but surely made progress to become a more central part of strategy discussions. The movement has two driving forces. First, even as free markets march around the world, the gap between the haves and have-nots has *widened*. Although many emerging economies have been growing by leaps and bounds, the per capita income gap between developed economies and much of Africa, Asia (except the Four Tigers), and Latin America has widened. While 2 percent of the world's children living in America enjoy 50 percent of the world's toys (see Strategy in Action 2.3 in Chapter 2), one-quarter of the children in Bangladesh and Nigeria are in their countries' workforce.[21] Even within developed economies such as the United States, the income gap between the upper and lower echelons of society has widened. In 1980, the average American CEO was paid 40 times more than the average worker. The ratio is now above 400. Although American society accepts a greater income inequality than many other societies do, aggregate data of such widening inequality often stimulate calls for reforming the "leaner and meaner" capitalism. However, the response from free market advocates is that as long as there is competition, there will always be *both* winners and losers. What CSR critics describe as "greed" is often translated as "incentives" in the vocabulary of free market advocates.

A second reason behind the rise of the CSR movement seems to be the waves of disasters and scandals. For example, in 1984, Union Carbide's Bhopal, India plant accidentally released toxic chemicals that killed more than 3,000 people and injured another 300,000. In 1989, the oil tanker *Exxon Valdez* spilled a tanker-load of oil in the pristine waters of Alaska. In 1992, the Russian government unleashed a mass privatization program, which has been nicknamed "grabbization" as inside managers and officials grabbed state assets at the expense of the public. In 2001 and 2002, corporate scandals of the likes of Enron, WorldCom, and Parmalat rocked the world

STRATEGY IN ACTION 12.1. *Why Corporate Social Responsibility in Russia Now?*

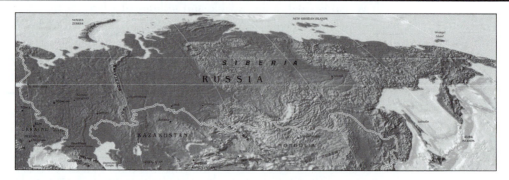

CSR is clearly in the air in Russia. The Putin administration recently unleashed a rash of legislation, including a Code of Corporate Conduct. Many Russian companies and executives, including some previously notorious oligarchs who plundered state assets during privatization in the 1990s, are now talking about sustainable development. The World Bank has sponsored CSR conferences and training workshops in Russia. An interesting question is: Why CSR now?

The banking industry in Russia serves as a case in point to answer this question. After the overnight ruble devaluation in the early 1990s, when most of the general public lost the savings they had held in the state-owned, Soviet-era Sberbank (*http://www.sberf.ru.eng*), the only bank at the time, trust in the state-owned bank diminished in a direct proportion to the ruble's value. This explains why Russians put virtually all the money they had left in the newly emerged private banks in the mid-1990s.

Unfortunately, most founders of the private banks acted opportunistically. After the 1998 economic crash, most private banks either went bankrupt or simply closed their offices without any explanation. The social uproar was very similar to the recent corporate scandals in the United States, although on a larger scale. As a result, Russians in general do not trust any financial organizations, and prefer to keep their savings at home (mostly under the mattresses) in the form of dollars or euros. The next form of financial organization that people might trust is probably foreign banks that will be able to eventually enter following Russia's accession to the WTO in the next few years.

Facing such a bleak outlook, how do the Russian banks cope? In an effort to project a more trustworthy image and combat the opportunistic tendency on the part of some firms and managers, emphasizing CSR might be a reasonable answer. While this is an uphill battle, CSR can become a potential source of differentiation. That is why leveraging CSR as a coping strategy has been brought to the forefront of strategy discussions in many Russian banks and other firms recently.

Source: Adapted from M. W. Peng & Y. Ruban, 2005, Institutional transitions and strategic choices: Implications for corporate social responsibility in Russia, in The World Bank (ed.), Corporate Responsibility and Sustainable Competitiveness in Russia, *Washington: The World Bank (in press).*

(see Strategy in Action 11.1 in Chapter 11 and Video Case 3.4). Not surprisingly, new disasters and scandals often propel CSR to the forefront of public policy and strategy discussions. For example, the recent rise of the CSR movement in Russia can be directly attributed to the excesses in the 1990s (see Strategy in Action 12.1).[22]

A Unique Group of Stakeholders

In this debate, both the free market and CSR camps have two important agreements. First, both agree not to rock the capitalistic boat. Second, both agree on the unique and central role of managers. Whatever the magnitude of its stake, each stakeholder group is a part of the nexus of exchange relationships (some direct and others indirect) with the firm (see Figure 12.1). However, managers as a stakeholder group are unique in that they are the only group positioned at the center of all these relationships.[23] Further, they make decisions on behalf of the firm that affect all other stakeholders. Therefore, it is important to understand how managers make decisions concerning CSR, as illustrated next by the three leading perspectives on strategy.

A COMPREHENSIVE MODEL OF CORPORATE SOCIAL RESPONSIBILITY

While some people do not view CSR as an integral part of strategy, a comprehensive model of CSR (see Figure 12.2) shows that the three traditional leading perspectives on strategy can help explain CSR with relatively little adaptation and extension. This section articulates this case.

FIGURE 12.2   **A Comprehensive Model of Corporate Social Responsibility**

Industry-based considerations
- Rivalry among competitors
- Threat of potential entry
- Bargaining power of suppliers
- Bargaining power of buyers
- Threat of substitutes

Resource-based considerations
- Value
- Rarity
- Imitability
- Organizational capabilities

Scale and scope of corporate social responsibility activities

Institution-based considerations
- Reactive strategy
- Defensive strategy
- Accommodative strategy
- Proactive strategy

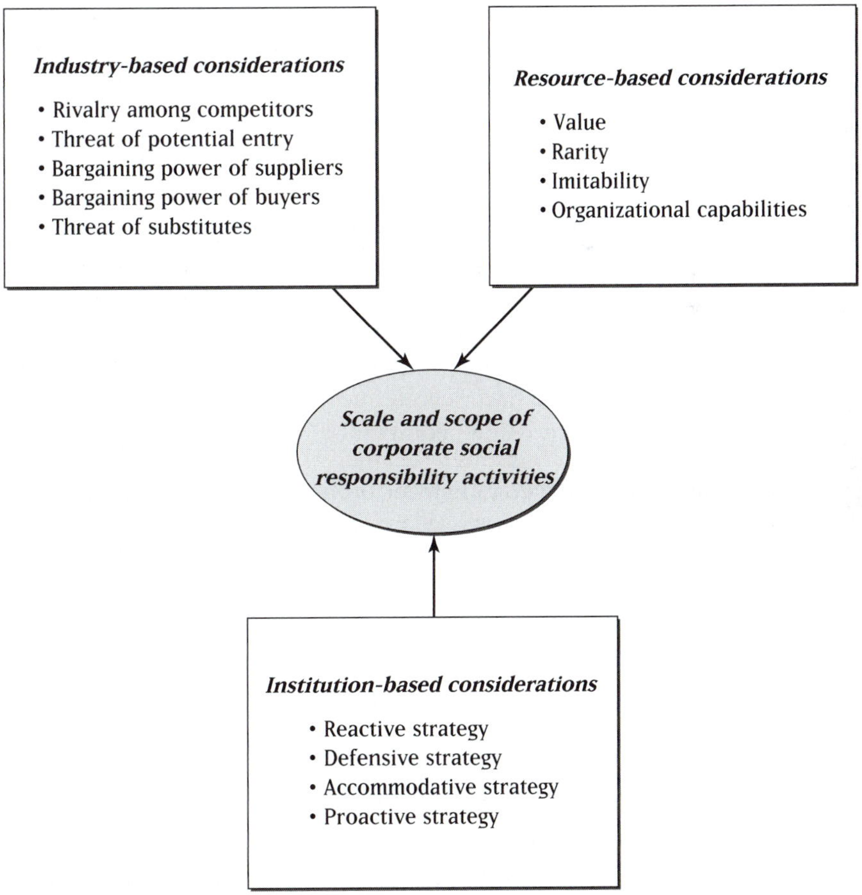

Industry-Based Considerations

The industry-based view, exemplified by the five forces framework, can be extended to help understand the emerging competition on CSR.

Rivalry among Competitors

The more concentrated an industry is, the more likely that competitors will recognize their mutual interdependence based on old ways of doing business that are not up to the higher CSR standards (see Chapter 8). Under these circumstances, it is easier for incumbents to resist CSR pressures. For example, when facing mounting pressures to reduce car emission levels, the Big Three carmakers in the United States—together with their allies in the oil industry—lobbied politicians, challenged the science of global climatic change, and pointed to the high costs of reducing emissions.[24] This strategy worked initially, when in 2001 the Bush administration (which has strong ties to the oil industry) pulled out of the Kyoto Protocol, a treaty committed to lower emission levels that the United States signed in 1997.

A corollary, however, is that when the number of rivals increases, it becomes difficult or even impossible to sustain a united front against CSR pressures—in other words, collusion (which in this case is not even very tacit) can collapse (see Chapter 8). In the global automobile industry, while it is relatively easier to coordinate the actions of US-based firms, it is simply not possible to enlist the support from European and Japanese automakers aiming to *outcompete* US rivals. In 2002, Honda and Toyota unleashed the world's first commercially available fuel cell cars, which do not burn gasoline and are powered by electricity converted by hydrogen. The Big Three eventually realized that they could potentially face extinction if they did business "as usual" in an increasingly environmentally conscious world. For example, in June 2003 when Ford celebrated its one hundredth birthday, Sierra Club, a major environmental NGO, took out full-page advertisements in leading magazines designed to crash Ford's party, with data indicating that Ford's vehicles had *worse* mileage in 2003 than they had nearly a century ago (see Figure 12.3). The combination of these relentless competitive and CSR pressures forced the Big Three to change their minds and became more interested in environmentally friendly vehicles.[25]

Threat of Potential Entry

How can incumbents raise entry barriers to deter potential entrants? Some evidence suggests that experience accumulated from being first movers in pollution-control technologies can create entry barriers that favor incumbents.[26] There are differences between the two major types of pollution-control technologies. The first is more proactive: *pollution prevention*. Like defects, pollution typically reveals flaws in product design or production. Pollution-prevention technologies reduce or eliminate pollutants by using cleaner alternatives, often resulting in superior products (such as fuel cells for cars). The second pollution-control area is more reactive, "end-of-pipe" *pollution reduction,* often added as a final step to capture pollutants prior to their discharge.[27] The effectiveness of the technologies is not equal. The technologies likely to give incumbents the most effective entry barrier are in the area of proactive,

FIGURE 12.3   **Sierra Club Challenges Ford Motor Company**

1903-2003
A CENTURY OF INNOVATION...

...EXCEPT AT FORD.

Model T: 25 mpg   **Explorer: 16 mpg**

Nearly a century ago, Ford's Model T got 25 miles to the gallon. Today, Ford's cars and trucks average 22.6 miles per gallon, and the Explorer gets just 16 miles per gallon. That's not progress.

In fact, Ford has fallen behind. Foreign automakers are leading the way by putting smarter transmissions, better engines, sleeker aerodynamics, and other innovative fuel saving technologies into their vehicles. Japanese automakers are driving the future with hybrid cars that average over 50 mpg. And five years after the introduction of the hybrids, Ford has failed to make and market one of its own.

So for Ford on its 100th birthday — we have a wish: Do better — use existing technology to make cleaner cars that go farther on a gallon of gas, save your customers money and time at the pump, clean up the environment and cut our country's need for oil. **Begin your second century with innovation truly worth celebrating.**

To find out more about fuel economy innovations available to Ford right now, go to: *www.sierraclub.org/freedom.*

Explore, enjoy and protect the planet
www.sierraclub.org

Source: Advertisement in Business Week (June 16, 2003, p. 103). Reprinted with permission from Sierra Magazine.

pollution prevention.[28] For instance, at Dow Chemical, the return on pollution-prevention projects in its Waste Reduction Always Pays (WRAP) program averaged better than 60 percent in the 1990s (see Closing Case). Chevron's Save Money and Reduce Toxics (SMART) and 3M's Pollution Prevention Pays (3P) programs are similar examples that not only deliver direct, triple-bottom line benefits, but also heighten entry barriers for potential entrants.[29] Overall, incumbents' early investments in certain CSR-related activities may allow them to ride down experience curves and deter potential entrants.

Bargaining Power of Suppliers

If socially and environmentally conscious suppliers provide unique, differentiated products with few or no substitutes, their bargaining power is likely to be substantial. For example, Coca-Cola is the sole provider of Coke syrup to its bottlers around the world, most of which are independently owned by franchisees. Coca-Cola is thus able to assert its bargaining power by requiring that all of its bottlers certify that their social and environmental practices are responsible. Coca-Cola also encourages its bottlers to support social programs, such as financing start-up kiosks for small businesses in South Africa and Vietnam, donating free drinks to flood victims in Austria and the Czech Republic, and promoting reading among school children in forty-two countries including the United States.

Bargaining Power of Buyers

By leveraging their bargaining power, individual and corporate buyers interested in CSR may extract substantial concessions from the focal firm. An example of the power of individual consumers is the controversy regarding Shell's 1995 decision to sink an oil platform in the North Sea. This decision led to strong protests organized by Greenpeace in Germany, which caused an 11 percent drop in Shell gas station sales in one month. Such pressures forced Shell to reverse its decision and dismantle the oil platform on shore at great cost.[30]

An example of how corporate buyers extract concessions is the recent efforts made by Nike, which acted in response to criticisms for its failure to eradicate "sweatshop" practices throughout its supply chain. Although Nike does not own its supplier factories, Nike is able to enact a worldwide monitoring program for all supplier factories, using both internal and third-party auditors. For "clean" contractors that have never engaged in "sweatshop" practices, this simply adds a ton of work such as documentation and hosting auditors as well as extra costs. For "sweatshop" operators, this requires some very fundamental and costly changes to the way they do business. Not surprisingly, both groups initially resisted Nike's efforts. Nevertheless, Nike has been able to "just do it," by throwing its weight around.

Finally, buyers can increase bargaining power when they are in great difficulties. Dying HIV/AIDS patients in Africa, Asia, and Latin America, backed by their governments and CSR groups, often demand that pharmaceutical firms headquartered in rich, developed economies (1) donate free drugs, (2) lower drug prices, and (3) release patents to allow for local manufacturing of cheaper, generic versions of the same drugs. While pharmaceutical firms have been resisting these attempts, they may eventually be forced to give in (see Opening Case in Chapter 4).

Threat of Substitutes

If substitutes are superior to existing products and costs are reasonable, they may attract more customers. For example, wind power, which is much more environmentally friendly than fossil-fuel sources of power (such as oil and coal) and safer than nuclear power, may have great potential. In this regard, General Electric's establishment of a Wind Energy group seems to be a proactive step in exploring this substitute technology. At present, wind power requires heavy government subsidies to become comercially viable. However, its future is likely to be promising, given the increasing depletion of fossil fuel and the growing awareness of the risks associated with conventional technologies (such as terrorism risks at nuclear power plants).[31] Overall, the possible threat of substitutes requires firms to vigilantly scan the larger environment, instead of narrowly focusing on the focal industry.

Turning Threats to Opportunities

Taken together, the five forces framework suggests two lessons. First, it reinforces the important point that not all industries are equal in terms of their exposure to CSR challenges. Energy- and materials-intensive industries (such as chemicals) are more vulnerable to environmental scrutiny. Labor-intensive industries (such as apparel) are more likely to be challenged on fair labor practice grounds. However, despite varying degrees of exposure, no industry may be completely immune from CSR. Table 12.2 (p. 496) shows the widening list of industries challenged by environmentalists, one of the core CSR groups.

Given the increasingly inescapable responsibility to be good corporate citizens, the second lesson is that industries and firms may want to selectively, but proactively, turn some of these threats into opportunities.[32] For example, instead of treating NGOs as threats, Home Depot, Lowe's, and Unilever have their sourcing policies certified by NGOs. Dow Chemical has established community advisory panels in most of its locations worldwide. Many managers traditionally treat CSR as a nuisance, because it creates regulations, added costs, and liabilities. Such an attitude may underestimate strategic business opportunities associated with CSR. The most proactive managers and the companies they lead are far-sighted to embrace CSR challenges through selective, but preemptive, investments and sustained engagement—in essence, making their CSR activities a source of *differentiation* as opposed to an additional item of cost.

Resource-Based Considerations

CSR-related resources and capabilities can include (1) *tangible* technologies, processes, and alliances, and (2) *intangible* skills, attitudes, and commitments.[33] The VRIO framework first introduced in Chapter 3 can be extended to cover CSR, as shown in the following paragraphs.

Value

Do a firm's CSR-related resources and capabilities add value? For many large firms, especially MNEs, their arsenal of financial, technological, and human resources can be applied toward a variety of CSR causes. For example, firms can choose to appease

TABLE 12.2   Industries Challenged by Environmentalists

1960s	1970s	1980s	1990s
Coal mining and pollution	Aerosols	Aerosols	Aerosols
Detergents	Airports	Agriculture	Agriculture
Mining	Asbestos	Airports	Air conditioning
Pesticides	Automobile fuel efficiency	Animal testing	Airlines and airports
Water (dams)	Biotechnology	Automobile exhaust	Animal testing
	Chemicals	Biotechnology	Armaments
	Coal mining and pollution	Chemicals	Automobile fuels and cars
	Deep sea fishing	Coal mining and pollution	Banking
	Detergents	Computers	Biotechnology
	Heavy trucks	Deep sea fishing	Catering
	Metals	Detergents	Chemicals
	Nuclear power	Fertilizers	Coal mining and pollution
	Oil tankers	Forestry	Computers
	Packaging	Incineration	Crematoria
	Passenger jets	Insurance	Detergents
	Pesticides	Landfill	Dry cleaning
	Pulp mills	Nuclear power	Electrical equipment
	Tobacco	Oil tankers	Electricity supply
	Toxic waste	Onshore oil and gas	Fashion
	Transport	Packaging	Fertilizers
	Water	Paints	Fish farming (Opening Case)
	Whaling	Pesticides	Fishing
		Plastics	Forestry
		Pulp and paper	Incineration
		Refrigeration	Insurance
		Supermarkets	Landfill
		Tobacco	Meat processing
		Toxic waste	Mining
		Tropical hardwoods	Motorways
		Tuna fishing	Nuclear power
		Water	Office supplies
		Whaling	Oil tankers
			Onshore oil and gas
			Packaging
			Paints
			Pesticides
			Plastics
			Property
			Pulp and paper
			Refrigeration
			Shipping
			Supermarkets
			Textiles
			Tires
			Tobacco
			Tourism
			Toxic waste
			Transport
			Tropical hardwoods
			Water

Sources: Adapted from J. Elkington, 1994, Towards the sustainable corporation: Win-win-win business strategies for sustainable development (p. 95), California Management Review, winter: 90–100.

antinuclear groups by refusing to purchase energy from nuclear power plants; to please anti-"sin"-industry groups by not dealing with tobacco, alcohol, and gambling industries; and to respond to human rights groups by not doing business in (or with) countries accused of human rights violations. These activities can be categorized as **social issue participation** not directly related to managing primary stakeholders. Research suggests that these activities may actually *reduce* shareholder value.[34] Overall, although social issue participation may create some remote social and environmental value, to the extent that one of the legs of the tripod of the triple bottom line is economic, these capabilities do not qualify as value-adding firm resources and capabilities.

In contrast, expertise, techniques, and processes associated with the direct management of primary stakeholder groups are likely to add value.[35] For example, US companies excelling in diversity programs may gain a leg up when dealing with two primary stakeholder groups: employees and customers. Between 2000 and 2020, the number of Hispanic, African, Asian, and Native Americans will reportedly grow by 42 million, whereas Caucasians will rise by a mere 10 million.[36] Many companies compete on diversity via internships, scholarships, ad campaigns, and aggressive recruitment of minority candidates. Firms most sought after by minority employees and customers must possess some very valuable resources and capabilities in the competition for the hearts, minds, and wallets of the future generation.[37]

Rarity

If competitors also possess certain valuable resources and capabilities, then the focal firm is not likely to gain a significant advantage by having them. For example, both Home Depot and Lowe's have their forest-products suppliers in Brazil, Indonesia, and Malaysia certify—via external verification by NGOs such as the Forest Stewardship Council—that their sources are from renewable forests. These complex processes require strong management capabilities, such as negotiating with local suppliers, undertaking internal verification, coordinating with NGOs for external verification, and disseminating such information to stakeholders. Since both firms, as well as a few other rivals, possess capabilities to manage these processes, they become valuable, but common (not rare), resources.

Unfortunately, valuable, but common, resources and capabilities only provide competitive *parity*. Only valuable and *rare* resources and capabilities can provide focal firms some advantage. For instance, the capabilities of BKK of Norway to obtain a sizable loan guarantee from the World Bank's Multilateral Investment Guarantee Agency to cover its acquisition of a power company in Nepal are both valuable and rare. These capabilities not only contribute to BKK's economic bottom line, but also count for social and environmental development of a large part of rural Nepal (see Strategy in Action 12.2 on next page). Only a small number of firms are able to simultaneously manage overseas acquisitions, work with international agencies, and contribute to the triple bottom line.

Imitability

Although valuable and rare resources and capabilities may provide some competitive advantage, such advantage is only temporary if competitors are able to imitate.[38]

STRATEGY IN ACTION 12.2. *Norway's BKK Acquires Nepal's HPL*

In 2001, Norway's Bergenshalvoens Kommunale Kraft-selskap (BKK, *http://www.bkk.com*) obtained a loan guarantee of $11 million from The World Bank's Multilateral Investment Guarantee Agency (MIGA, *http://www.miga.org*) to cover its $12.2 million acquisition of equity in Himal Power Limited (HPL, *http://www.hpl.com.np*) of Nepal. BKK required MIGA's coverage as a condition of acquisition. The coverage period is fifteen years, and is against the risk of transfer restriction, expropriation, and war and civil disturbance, all of which might take place in Nepal.

Not using any fossil fuel such as oil and coal, HPL is a sixty megawatt run-of-the-river clean-energy generator located about 100 kilometers east of Kathmandu. The project was the first foreign direct investment (FDI) in Nepal's energy sector and accounted for 22 percent of the country's installed capacity for electricity, significantly expanding low-cost electrification in rural Nepal. In addition, the project's community

outreach and development efforts have had a notable impact, especially in the areas of public health, education, and infrastructure (such as roads and bridges).

Source: Based on Multilateral Investment Guarantee Agency 2002 Annual Report (p. 31). Washington: The World Bank/MIGA.

Firms can only entertain some sustainable (not merely temporary) competitive advantage when resources and capabilities are not only valuable and rare but also hard to imitate. For example, pollution-*prevention* technologies may provide firms with a significant advantage, whereas pollution-*reduction* technologies offer no such advantage. This is because the relatively simple, "end-of-pipe" pollution-reduction technologies can be more easily imitated. On the other hand, pollution-prevention technologies are more complex and are more integrated with the entire chain of production. Rivals often have a harder time imitating such complex capabilities.

In addition, at some firms, CSR-related resources and capabilities are deeply embedded in very idiosyncratic managerial and employee skills, attitudes, and interpretations.[39] The socially complex way of channeling these people's energy and conviction toward CSR cannot be easily imitated over a short period of time. Haagen-Dazs, for example, finds it hard to imitate Ben & Jerry's Ice Cream, which is widely known for its dedication to CSR. Few top executives are as passionate about CSR as Anita Roddick, CEO of The Body Shop. The Body Shop's multidimensional engagement with a number of CSR issues around the world led by such a dedicated CEO makes it exceedingly difficult, if not impossible, for rivals to outcompete it on CSR.

Organization

Is the firm organized to exploit the full potential of its CSR resources and capabilities? Numerous components within a firm are relevant here, such as formal management control systems, codified production and engineering processes, and informal relationships between managers and employees. These components are often called **complementary assets,** because, by themselves, they have difficulty generating advantage. However, these complementary assets, when combined with valuable, rare, and hard-to-imitate capabilities, may enable a firm to fully utilize its CSR potential.

For example, assume Firm A is able to overcome the three hurdles—value, rarity, imitability—by achieving a comprehensive understanding of some competitors' "best practices" in pollution prevention. Although Firm A implements such "best practices," chances are that they will not work unless Firm A also possesses a number of complementary assets. This is because these process-focused best practices of pollution prevention are not done in isolation, so they are often difficult to separate from a firm's other activities. These best practices require a number of complementary assets, such as a continuous emphasis on process innovation, an uncompromising quest to reduce costs, and a dedicated workforce. These complementary assets are not developed as part of new environmental strategies; rather, these assets are grown from more general business strategies (such as differentiation). If such complementary assets are already in place, the firm can leverage them in the new pursuit of best environmental practices. Otherwise, single-minded imitation is not likely to be effective.[40]

Know Yourself, Know Your Opponents

The resource-based view suggests two important lessons, which can, again, be captured by Sun Tzu's timeless teaching on the importance of knowing "yourself" and "your opponents." First, while your opponents may engage in some high-profile CSR activities that give them a lot of bragging rights while contributing to their triple bottom line, blindly following these practices, while not knowing enough about "yourself" (you as a manager and the firm/unit you lead), may lead to disappointment. Instead of always chasing the newest best practices, firms are advised to select CSR practices that fit with their *existing* resources, capabilities, and especially complementary assets. It may be useful to view a CSR-intensive strategy as a special case of differentiation strategy.[41] Note that a differentiation strategy is not a winning formula for every firm, and it requires much more creativity and capability to make a differentiation strategy work (see Chapter 2). In a nutshell, managers must "pick their shots carefully."[42]

Second, the resource-based view helps solve a puzzle in the CSR debate since the 1970s. The puzzle—and a source of frustration to CSR advocates—is why there is no conclusive evidence of a direct, positive link between CSR and *economic* performance such as profits and shareholder returns.[43] Although some studies indeed report a *positive* relationship,[44] others find a *negative* relationship[45] or *no* relationship.[46] While there can be many answers to this intriguing mess, a resource-based answer suggests that because of capability constraints discussed earlier, many firms are not cut out for a CSR-intensive (differentiation) strategy. Because all studies have some sampling bias (no study is "perfect"), studies oversampling firms not ready for a high level of CSR activities are likely to report a negative relationship between CSR and economic performance; studies oversampling firms ready for CSR may find a positive relationship; and studies with more balanced samples may fail to find any statistically significant relationship.

Institution-Based Considerations

The institution-based view helps explain the gradual diffusion of the CSR movement and the strategic responses of firms.[47] Recall that at the most fundamental level, regulatory pressures underpin *formal* institutions, whereas normative and cognitive pressures support *informal* institutions. The strategic response framework consisting of (1) reactive, (2) defensive, (3) accommodative, and (4) proactive strategies, first introduced in Chapter 4, can be extended to explore how firms make CSR decisions (see Table 4.5).

Reactive Strategy

Reactive strategy is indicated by relatively little or no support of top management to CSR causes.[48] Firms do not feel compelled to act in the absence of some disasters and outcries. Even when some problems arise, denial is usually the first line of defense. Put another way, the need to accept some CSR is neither internalized through cognitive beliefs, nor becoming the norm in practice. That only leaves formal regulatory pressures to compel firms to comply. For example, many food and drug companies used to fight the food and drug safety standards that we take for granted today. The very basic idea that foods and drugs should be tested before they are sold to customers and patients was bitterly contested. Thousands of people ended up dying because of unsafe foods and drugs in America in most of the twentieth century before the Food and Drug Administration (FDA) was progressively granted more powers. This era is not necessarily over, as today, many dietary-supplement makers whose products are beyond the regulatory reach of the FDA continue to sell hundreds of untested "supplements" and deny responsibility for their products.[49] In another case, at present, in Italy, the price for the environmentally responsible disposal of industrial waste averages approximately $0.5 a pound. "Eco-mafia," which controls an estimated 30 percent of Italy's waste-management business, has often entered the bidding for as low as $0.05 per pound, and then dumped some of the toxic waste in pits, caves, lakes, and even farmland. Many cost-conscious manufacturers simply turn a blind eye with an "out of sight, out of mind" mentality.[50]

However, this blatant lack of responsiveness toward CSR has caused a huge backlash throughout the world. Against such a backdrop, some firms have undertaken a different strategy, which is introduced next.

Defensive Strategy

This strategy focuses on regulatory compliance. Top management may be somewhat involved in CSR activities, but the attitude generally views CSR as an added cost or nuisance. Firms admit responsibility, but often fight it. For example, after the establishment of the Environmental Protection Agency (EPA) in 1970, the US chemical industry resisted the intrusion of the EPA by arguing that greater levels of environmental controls added unbearable costs. The regulatory requirements were at significant odds with the norms and cognitive beliefs held by industry members at that time (see Table 12.3).[51]

In the absence of informal normative and cognitive beliefs, formal regulatory pressures are the only feasible way to push firms to change their strategic behavior. A key insight of the institution-based view is that individuals and organizations make *rational* choices given the right kind of incentives. For example, one efficient way to control pollution is to make polluters pay some "green" taxes. These can range from gasoline retail taxes to landfill charges on waste disposal. However, how demanding these regulatory pressures are remains controversial. For example, one side of the debate argues that tough environmental regulation may lead to higher costs and reduced competitiveness, especially when competing with foreign rivals that are not subject to such demanding regulations.[52] For example, some US polymer manufacturers complain that they are required to remove 80 percent of the pollutants in their production, whereas some of their foreign rivals only need to remove 50–60 percent of the pollutants. In other words, there is no "free environmental lunch."[53]

However, the CSR advocates, endorsed by former vice president Al Gore and strategy guru Michael Porter, argue that stringent environmental regulation may force firms to innovate, however reluctantly, thus benefiting the competitiveness of an industry and a country.[54] For instance, the 1970 Clean Air Act forced US firms to develop catalytic technologies to reduce automobile exhaust. Another example is a 1991 Japanese law, which set standards to make products easier to disassemble, thus making it easier to recycle parts of these products. In response, Hitachi, which initially resisted this law, redesigned products to simplify disassembly, by reducing parts in a washing machine by 16 percent and parts in a vacuum cleaner by 30 percent. The products become not only easier to disassemble, but also easier and cheaper to *assemble* in the first place, thus providing Hitachi with a significant cost

TABLE 12.3   **How the US Chemical Industry Responds to Environmental Pressures**

PHASE	PRIMARY STRATEGY	REPRESENTATIVE STATEMENTS FROM THE INDUSTRY'S TRADE JOURNAL, CHEMICAL WEEK
1. 1962–70	Reactive	Denied the severity of environmental problems and argued that these problems could be solved independently through the industry's technological prowess.
2. 1971–82	Defensive	"Congress seems determined to add one more regulation to the already 27 health and safety regulations we must answer to. This will make EPA [Environmental Protection Agency] a chemical czar. No agency in a democracy should have that authority" (1975).
3. 1983–88	Accommodative	"EPA has been criticized for going too slow ... Still, we think that it is doing a good job" (1982). "Critics expect overnight fix. EPA deserves credit for its pace and accomplishments" (1982).
4. 1989–present	Proactive	"Green line equals bottom line—The Clean Air Act equals efficiency. Everything you hear about the 'costs' of complying with CAA [Clean Air Act] is probably wrong ... Wiser competitors will rush to exploit the Green Revolution" (1990).

Sources: Adapted from A. Hoffman, 1999, Institutional evolution and change: Environmentalism and the U.S. chemical industry, Academy of Management Journal, 42: 351–371 for the phases and statements. Hoffman's last phase ended in 1993; the present author extended the phase to the present.

STRATEGY IN ACTION 12.3. *Codes of Conduct in the Sportswear Industry*

The global sportswear industry is dominated by six MNEs equally distributed over the Triad: Two from the United States (Nike, *http://www.nike.com* and Reebok, *http://www.reebok.com*), two from Germany (Adidas, *http://www.adidas.com* and Puma, *http://www.puma.com*), and two from Japan (Asics, *http://www.asics.com* and Mizuno, *http://www.mizuno.com*). While the alleged "sweatshop" practices of Nike's contractors in Indonesia and Vietnam, which are *not* owned or managed by Nike, have attracted significant public scrutiny and outcry since the 1990s, the entire industry has been under similar pressures. In response, Nike adopted a Code of Conduct with regard to contractor labor practices in 1992. During the 1990s, Nike revised its code twice, first to incorporate standards developed by the Apparel Industry Partnership in 1997 and subsequently to take into account Nike's new labor initiatives in 1998. Reebok, also criticized for its labor

practices in Indonesia in the early 1990s, drew up its Human Rights Protection Standards in 1992.

Following the two American market leaders, Puma adopted a code, Human Rights Undertaking to Observe Universal Standards, in 1995. Adidas followed in 1998. The leading Japanese producer, Mizuno, adopted a Code of Business Ethics more recently. However, Asics did not adopt a code of conduct by the late 1990s. When queried by researchers, Asics referred to its overall corporate philosophy, containing three sentences. One of these states: "We contribute to local prosperity by fulfilling our social responsibilities as a company."

Source: Based on (1) J. Burns & D. Spar, 2000, Hitting the wall: Nike and international labor practices, Harvard Business School case 700-047; (2) S. Frenkel & D. Scott, 2002, Compliance, collaboration, and codes of labor practice: The Adidas connection, California Management Review, 45 (1): 29–49; (3) R. Van Tulder & A. Kolk, 2001, Multinationality and corporate ethics: Codes of conduct in the sporting goods industry, Journal of International Business Studies, 32: 267–283.

advantage.[55] Despite such prominent examples, systematic evidence, however, is still ambiguous and mixed.[56]

Accommodative Strategy

This strategy has some support from top managers, who may increasingly view CSR as a worthwhile endeavor. Because formal regulations may be in place and informal social and environmental pressures on the rise, the CSR concern may be shared by a number of firms, thus leading to the emergence of some new industry norms. Further, some new managers passionate about or sympathetic toward CSR causes may have joined the organization, whereas some traditional managers may change their outlook, leading to increasingly strong cognitive beliefs that CSR is the right thing to do. In other words, from both normative and cognitive standpoints, it becomes a legitimate matter of social obligation to accept responsibility and do all that is required.[57] For example, in the US chemical industry, such transformation probably took place in the early 1980s (see Table 12.3).

One tangible action firms often take to indicate their willingness to accept CSR is to adopt **codes of conduct** (sometimes called **codes of ethics**). Firms under the most intense CSR criticisms, such as those in the sportswear industry, often actively engage in these activities (see Strategy in Action 12.3). However, adopting codes of conduct is not limited to certain industries. By the late 1980s, approximately 75 percent and 41 percent of the large US and European firms, respectively, adopted codes of conduct.[58] More than a decade later, the difference is no longer significant. This movement has also spread to other parts of the world. For example, in Hong Kong, only 20 out of 182 listed firms (11 percent) in 1994 had such codes.

However, by the end of 1996, over 1,600 large firms (listed and unlisted) and trade associations in Hong Kong (over 70 percent of the organizational population) adopted such codes, in part due to a government-led campaign to promote them.[59]

Interestingly (but not surprisingly), the content of these codes varies by individual firm, industry, and country.[60] US codes of conduct tend to pay less attention to immediate production concerns and more attention to secondary stakeholder issues, such as welfare of the community and environmental protection. Continental European codes concentrate more on production activities, such as quality management and limiting the environmental footprint of activities. British codes appear to be relatively closer to their US counterparts.[61] In Hong Kong, the codes focus narrowly on corruption prevention, but pay less attention to broader CSR issues.

There is an intense debate regarding the diffusion of codes of conduct. First, some argue that firms may not necessarily be sincere. This *negative* view suggests that given the rising interest in CSR, firms may be compelled to appear to be sensitive to CSR by impression management—in other words, "window dressing."[62] Many firms may chase fads by following what others are doing, while not having truly internalized the need to genuinely address CSR concerns. Second, an *instrumental* view suggests that CSR activities simply represent a useful instrument to help make good profits.[63] Firms are not necessarily becoming more "ethical." Finally, a *positive* view believes that firms may be self-motivated to "do it right" regardless of social pressures. Codes of conduct tangibly express values that organizational members view as central and enduring.[64]

The institution-based view suggests that all three perspectives are probably valid. This is to be expected given how institutional pressures work to instill value. Regardless of actual motive, the fact that firms are embarking on some tangible CSR journey is encouraging, and indicates that CSR's *legitimacy* is rising on the organizational agenda.[65] Even for firms adopting codes of conduct only for "window-dressing" purposes, publicizing a set of CSR criteria against which they can be judged opens doors for more scrutiny by concerned stakeholders. These pressures are likely to encourage internal transformations that make these firms more self-motivated, better corporate citizens. For example, Nike was forced to revise its code of conduct (first adopted in 1992) twice during the 1990s (see Strategy in Action 12.3). It probably is fair to say that Nike became a better corporate citizen in 2005 than it was in 1985.

Proactive Strategy

From a CSR perspective, the best firms proactively engage in CSR, constantly anticipating responsibility and endeavoring to do more than is required. Top management not only supports and champions CSR activities, but also views CSR as a source of differentiation. For example, in 1990, BMW anticipated its emerging responsibility associated with the German government's proposed "take-back" policy. It not only designed easier-to-disassemble cars, but also signed up the few high-quality dismantler firms as part of an exclusive recycling infrastructure. Further, BMW actively participated in public discussions and succeeded in establishing the BMW approach as the German national standard for automobile disassembly.

Other car companies were thus required to follow BMW's lead. However, they were left to fight over smaller, lower-quality dismantlers or develop in-house dismantling infrastructure from scratch, both of which cost more, whereas BMW scored points on the triple bottom line.[66] Now BMW has introduced advanced systems for automobile recycling into the United States.

Proactive firms often engage in three areas of activities. First, like BMW, they actively participate in regional, national, and international policy discussions. To the extent that policy discussions today may become regulations in the future, it seems better to get involved early and (hopefully) steer the course toward a favorable direction.[67] Otherwise, relatively passive firms are likely to have little input on the regulations imposed on them.[68] For instance, in 2002, the European Union Parliament passed a bill mandating that by 2006, all printer cartridges sold within the EU must be refillable and reusable. Customers typically spend twice as much on nonreusable printer cartridges and toner than on the actual printer over the life of a printer. Thus, the printer supply (*not* the printer itself) business for the market leader, Hewlett-Packard (HP), is extremely profitable. It carried 35 percent profit margins and generated $2.2 billion profits in 2002, contributing over 70 percent of the total profits of HP (after its merger with Compaq). The EU bill is a direct result of a cost and environmental outcry that could one day hurt HP.[69]

Second, proactive firms often build alliances with stakeholder groups. For example, many firms collaborate with NGOs. Because of the historical tension and distrust, these "sleeping with the enemy" alliances are not easy to handle. The key lies in identifying relatively short-term, manageable projects of mutual interest. Starbucks, for example, worked with Conservation International to create a line of biodiversity-friendly "shade-grown" coffee produced in Mexico. United Parcel Service collaborated with the Alliance for Environmental Innovation to help packaging material suppliers reduce air pollution by almost 50 percent and energy use by 12 percent.[70]

Third, proactive firms often engage in *voluntary* activities that go beyond what the regulations require.[71] Although examples of industry-specific self-regulation abound,[72] an area of intense global interest is the pursuit of the International Standards Organization (ISO) 14001 certification of environment management system (EMS). Headquartered in Switzerland, ISO is an influential NGO consisting of national standards bodies of 111 countries. Launched in 1996, the ISO 14001 EMS has become the gold standard for CSR-conscious firms.[73] Although not required by law, many MNEs, such as Ford, IBM, and Skanska, have adopted ISO 14001 standards in all their facilities worldwide, and firms such as GM, Toyota, and Siemens demand that all of their top-tier suppliers be ISO 14001 certified.

From an institutional perspective, these three areas of proactive activities indicate the managers' normative and cognitive beliefs about the importance of doing the "right thing." While doing the right thing probably includes a certain element of "window dressing" and a quest for better profits, it is hard to deny that these efforts provide some tangible social and environmental benefits. Perhaps the best example of how voluntary activities fill the voids left by formal regulations is the "pollution haven" debate. One side of the debate argues that because of heavier environmental regulation in developed economies, MNEs may have an incentive to shift pollution-intensive production to developing countries, whose environmental standards may be lower. To attract investment, developing countries may enter a "race to the bottom" by lowering (or at least not tightening) environmental standards and some may become "pollution havens."[74]

The other side argues that globalization does not necessarily have negative effects on the environment in developing countries to the extent suggested by the "pollution haven" hypothesis. This is largely because many MNEs' *voluntarily* adhere to environmental standards higher the requirements of host country authorities.[75] One study finds that US capital markets significantly reward these practices, thus refuting the perspective that being green constitutes a liability that depresses market value.[76] In general, most MNEs reportedly outperform local firms in environmental management.[77] According to another study in China, the underlying motivations behind MNEs' voluntary "green practices" can be attributed to (1) worldwide CSR pressures in general, (2) CSR demands made by customers in developed economies, and (3) MNE headquarters requirements for worldwide compliance with higher CSR standards (such as ISO 14001).[78] Although it is difficult to suggest that the "race to the bottom" does not exist, MNEs as a group do not necessarily add to the environmental burden in developing countries. Some MNEs may facilitate the diffusion of better environmental technologies and standards to these countries (see Closing Case). Overall, the "pollution haven" debate serves as an example of the power of informal normative and cognitive institutional pressures.

Making Strategic Choices

The typology of (1) reactive, (2) defensive, (3) accommodative, and (4) proactive strategies is an interesting menu provided for different firms to choose. At present, the number of proactive firms is still probably a minority. While many firms are compelled to do something, a lot of CSR activities probably are still "window dressing." Only sustained pressures along regulatory, normative, and cognitive dimensions may push and pull more firms to do more.[79]

DEBATES AND EXTENSIONS

Without exaggeration, the entire subject of this chapter is about debates. Some may even debate whether CSR materials belong in a global strategy text. Few of the other global (and mainstream) strategy books have a full chapter devoted to CSR (in addition to another full chapter, Chapter 4, on ethics, cultures, and institutions). Two of the more recent debates particularly relevant for international operations are featured here: (1) domestic versus overseas social responsibility and (2) active CSR engagement overseas versus nonintervention in local affairs.

Domestic versus Overseas Social Responsibility

For any firm operating internationally, balancing the often conflicting needs for domestic CSR vis-à-vis overseas CSR is challenging. Because corporate resources are limited, resources devoted to overseas CSR, unfortunately, often mean fewer resources devoted to domestic CSR. Take, for example, two *primary* stakeholder groups, domestic employees and communities. Expanding overseas, especially toward emerging economies, not only potentially increases corporate profits and shareholder returns, but also provides employment to host countries, increases standards of living there, and develops these economies, all of which have noble CSR dimensions (see Strategy in Action 1.1 in Chapter 1). However, often domestic employees and communities pay the price for this expansion. The devastation of job losses on such employees and communities is vividly portrayed in the movie *The Full Monty*, which is set in Sheffield, England, the former steel capital of Europe and the world. Laid-off steel mill workers ended up taking up an "alternative line of work" (male strip dancing). To prevent such a possible fate, for example, in 2004, DaimlerChrysler's German unions had to scrap a 3 percent pay raise and endure an 11 percent work hour increase (from 35 to 39 hours) with no extra pay in exchange for promises that 6,000 jobs would be kept in Germany for at least eight years—otherwise, their jobs would go to the Czech Republic, Poland, and South Africa. However, in all likelihood, such labor deals will only slow down, but not stop, the outgoing tide of jobs in developed economies. The wage differentials are just too great. "When we find a certain product can be made with a 50 percent decrease in salary costs in another country," argued a German executive who set up production in China, "we cannot avoid that if we want to stay competitive."[80]

From a CSR standpoint, are the MNEs doing the right or wrong things by moving (and threatening to move) jobs and work overseas and ignoring their responsibilities to primary stakeholder groups such as domestic employees and communities? Few laid off German employees would move to Poland (let alone China or South Africa) to seek work, so most of them will end up being social welfare recipients of Germany. Therefore, one may argue that MNEs' actions shirk their CSR by increasing the social burdens of their home countries. Unions, media, and politicians (such as the former US presidential candidate John Kerry, who coined the term "Benedict Arnold CEOs" after a traitor in the American Revolution) often attack the executives who make these decisions. However, from a corporate governance perspective—especially the "shareholder capitalism" variant on the rise recently in countries such as Germany—MNEs are doing nothing wrong by minimizing costs and maximizing shareholder returns (see Chapter 11).

Although framed in a domestic versus overseas context, the heart of this debate boils down to the foundational thorny point that frustrates CSR advocates:[81] In a capitalist society, the shareholders—otherwise known as *capitalists*—are the ones who matter at the end of the day (see Chapter 11). When companies have enough resources, it would be nice to take care of domestic employees and communities. However, when confronted with relentless pressures for cost cutting, downsizing, and restructuring (see Chapter 9), managers must prioritize.[82] Paradoxically, in this age of globalization with the CSR movement on the rise, the great migration of jobs away from developed economies—of both blue and white collar types (see Opening Case in Chapter 1)—is also accelerating. While people and countries at the bottom of the global economic pyramid (see Strategy in Action 1.1) welcome such migration (the Chinese, for example, call it the "inevitable transfer of the global economic center of gravity"), domestic employees and communities in developed economies as well as unions and politicians who represent their interests frankly hate it. The intensity of this politically explosive debate is likely to heat up in the years to come because there is no clear solution other than protectionism or phasing out capitalism to adopt socialism (which by definition focuses on *social* responsibilities).

Active CSR Engagement Overseas versus Nonintervention in Local Affairs[83]

In the international arena, MNEs are now expected to engage in active CSR overseas. Advocates argue that morally, this seems to be the "right" thing to do. MNEs that fail to engage in CSR are often sharply criticized by NGOs.[84] Shell, for example, was criticized for "not lifting a finger" when the then Nigerian military government brutally cracked down on rebels, including execution of the leader, Ken Saro-Wiwa, in the Ogoni region in which Shell operated. However, such well-intentioned calls for greater CSR engagement are in direct conflict with a long-standing principle governing the relationship between MNEs and host countries: nonintervention in local affairs, especially politically (see the *first* bullet point in Table 12.1).

The nonintervention principle originated from concerns that MNEs investing in developing economies might engage in political activities against the national interests of the host country. For example, in Chile in the 1970s the democratically elected, but socialist, government of President Salvador Allende threatened to expropriate the assets of ITT (a US-based MNE) and other MNEs. Allegedly in connection with the Central Intelligence Agency, ITT promoted the overthrow of President Allende, who was killed in a coup. Consequently, the idea that MNEs should not interfere in the domestic political affairs of the host countries has been enshrined in a number of codes of MNE conduct endorsed by leading international organizations such as the UN and OECD (see Table 12.1).

However, CSR advocates have been emboldened by some MNEs' actions during the apartheid era in South Africa, when local laws required racial segregation of the workforce. While many MNEs withdrew, those that remained were encouraged by the Sullivan Principles to challenge, breach, and seek to dismantle the apartheid system, undermining the government's power base. BP, for example, desegregated their employees. Emboldened by the successful removal of the apartheid regime in South Africa in 1994, CSR advocates unleashed a new campaign, stressing the necessity for MNEs to flex their muscles to engage in actions that often constitute political activity, in particular in the human rights area. Shell, for instance, after its widely criticized lack of action in Nigeria, abandoned noninterference and since 1996 explicitly endorsed the United Nations Declaration on Human Rights and committed itself to support such rights "within the legitimate role of business."

What exactly is the "legitimate role" of CSR initiatives in host countries? In almost every country, local laws and norms exist that some foreign MNEs may find objectionable. In India, a number of "untouchable" groups exist. In Malaysia, ethnic Chinese are discriminated against by law. In Japan, ethnic Koreans are singled out. In Estonia, Latvia, and Lithuania, ethnic Russian citizens are given a hard time (they have to pass local language tests to vote or have a passport). In many Arab countries, women do not have equal legal rights as men do. In the United States, a number of groups (ranging from American Indians to homosexuals) claim to be discriminated against. At the heart of this debate is whether foreign MNEs should spearhead efforts to remove some of these discriminatory practices or should remain politically neutral by conforming to current host country laws and norms. In the absence of agreed-upon "bright line" rules, MNEs must test the "gray boundaries" of permissible political involvements, while attempting not to upset host governments. This obviously is a nontrivial challenge.

IMPLICATIONS FOR STRATEGISTS

For current and would-be strategists, once again, this chapter has suggested that the three leading perspectives can help answer the four fundamental questions. First, why do firms differ in CSR activities? Firm differences can be found in (1) industry structures, (2) firm-specific capabilities, and (3) formal and informal institutional pressures. Second, how do firms behave in the CSR arena? Some are reactive and defensive, others are accommodative, and still others are proactive. Cutting-edge firms often undertake voluntary actions that go beyond formal, regulatory requirements. Third, what determines a firm's CSR scope? While industry structures, resource bases, and formal institutional pressures are likely to ensure some minimal involvement, firms with a broad range of CSR engagements are likely to be characterized by managers and employees who intrinsically feel the need to "do it right." In other words, the scope fundamentally boils down to differences in the informal, normative and cognitive beliefs held by managers and employees. Finally, what determines the international success and failure of firms? To the extent that the triple bottom line is increasingly becoming the performance criteria, the best performers are likely to be those firms that can integrate CSR activities into the core economic functions of the firm while addressing social and environmental concerns.

From its economics roots, strategy has expanded to become a multidisciplinary area of practice and research. Probably one of the most vivid aspects of such expansion is the recent incorporation of CSR into the strategy repertoire. This expansion is making many strategists in practice and in academia uncomfortable. The globally ambiguous and different CSR standards, norms, and expectations do not help either.[85] As a result, many strategists continue to relegate CSR to the "back burner" of strategy discussions.[86] However, this does not seem to be the attitude that current and would-be strategists should have. If some previously doubted the necessity for this expansion of strategic thinking, recent corporate scandals have removed such doubts.[87] Possibly, some readers of this book will someday assume CSR responsibilities, as CSR gradually becomes a career track (for positions such as corporate ethics officers).

It is important to note that we live in a dangerous period of global capitalism. In the *post-Seattle, post-9/11, post-Enron* world (see Chapter 1), managers (especially those at the top) as a unique group of stakeholders, have an important and challenging responsibility. If they are unable to build a more humane capitalism through CSR efforts, public resentment in the current economic downturn around the world may feed into a distrust of free markets that is more widespread than the current antiglobalization sentiments. In other words, free markets are not necessarily free. For various stakeholders around the world interested in strengthening global capitalism, the challenge is "how to fashion external control and oversight mechanisms that make corporations more responsive to changing societal expectations without robbing them unnecessarily of their flexibility to remain economically efficient and competitive instruments of wealth production and distribution."[88]

Chapter Summary

1. Corporate social responsibility (CSR) refers to consideration of, and response to, issues beyond the narrow economic, technical, and legal requirements of the firm to accomplish social benefits along with the traditional economic gains that the firm seeks.

2. A stakeholder is any individual or group who can affect or is affected by the achievement of a firm's objectives. A stakeholder view of the firm urges companies to pursue a more balanced triple bottom line, consisting of economic, social, and environmental performance.

3. Despite the fierce defense of the free market school, especially its shareholder capitalism variant, the CSR movement has now become a more central part of strategy discussions.

4. Industry-, resource-, and institution-based considerations form the backbone of a comprehensive model of CSR.

5. When confronting CSR pressures, the strategic response framework suggests that firms can employ (1) reactive, (2) defensive, (3) accommodative, and (4) proactive strategies.

6. While the CSR arena is full of debates in general, we highlight two leading debates that are especially relevant for MNEs: (1) domestic versus overseas social responsibility and (2) active CSR engagement overseas versus nonintervention in local affairs.

Key Terms

codes of conduct	global sustainability	social issue participation
codes of ethics	primary stakeholder groups	stakeholder
complementary assets	secondary stakeholder groups	triple bottom line
corporate social responsibility		

Critical Discussion Questions

1. In a landmark *Dodge v. Ford* case in 1919, the Michigan State Supreme Court determined whether Henry Ford could withhold dividends from the Dodge brothers (and other shareholders of the Ford Motor Company) to engage in what today would be called CSR initiatives. With a resounding "No," the court opined that "a business organization is organized and carried on primarily for the profits of the stockholders." If the court were to decide on this case this year (or in 2019), what do you think would be the likely outcome? How would you act if *you* were the judge?

2. Some believe that tough environmental regulations add costs, reduce firm competitiveness, and drive some firms to invest elsewhere. Others argue that tough environmental regulations force firms to innovate and thus to enhance firm competitiveness. What do you think?

3. **ON ETHICS:** Some argue that CSR is ultimately a profit-making initiative. Others suggest that CSR does not necessarily have to boost the financial bottom line. What do you think?

4. **ON ETHICS:** Some argue that investing in emerging economies greatly increases the economic development and standard of living of the bottom of the global economic pyramid (see Strategy in Action 1.1 in Chapter 1). Others contend that moving jobs to low-cost countries not only abandons CSR for domestic employees and communities in developed economies, but also exploits the poor in these countries and destroys the environment—hardly noble CSR activities. If you were (1) the CEO of an MNE headquartered in a developed economy moving production to a low-cost country, (2) the leader of a labor union in the home country of the MNE, which is losing a lot of jobs, and (3) the leader of an environmental NGO in the low-cost country in which the MNE invests, how would you participate in this debate?

5. **ON ETHICS:** Hypothetically, your MNE is the largest foreign investor in (1) Vietnam where religious leaders are reportedly being prosecuted, (2) China where human rights abuses are often being reported, or (3) Estonia where ethnic Russian citizens are being discriminated against by law. As the country manager there, you understand that the MNE is being pressured by NGOs of all stripes to help the oppressed groups in these countries. You also understand that the host government could be upset if your firm is found to engage in local political activities that are deemed inappropriate. These alleged activities, which you personally find distasteful, are not directly related to your operations. Among your options, what are the ethical dilemmas? How should you proceed?

Closing Case: Dow Chemical in America and China

Dow Chemical (http://www.dow.com) is a leading US-based MNE in the chemical industry. Its global competitors include America's DuPont (http://www.dupont.com), Great Britain's ICI (http://www.ici.com), and the German trio of BASF (http://www.basf.com), Hoechst (http://www.hoechst.com), and Bayer (http://www.bayer.com). Among these rivals, DuPont might be Dow's number one rival. In 2002, Dow's annual sales were $28 billion with operations in fifty-four countries. In comparison, DuPont's annual sales were $27 billion with operations in seventy countries.

Both Dow and DuPont paid considerable attention to their CSR. Dow's home page proudly notes: "Committed to the principles of sustainable development, Dow and its approximately 50,000 employees seek to balance economic, environmental, and social responsibilities." DuPont's home page also states: ". . . our core values have remained constant: commitment to safety, health, and the environment; integrity and high ethical standards; and treating people with fairness and respect." For over a decade, Dow has advocated "Responsible Care," a voluntary, industry-wide commitment to safely handle its chemicals. DuPont has also developed a project called "Reducing Safety and Health Incidents and Environmental Footprint" since 1987 to publicize its safety, health, and environmental progress.

Although the Montreal Protocol required that trichloroethane (TCA) solvent—a widely used industrial chemical that also depletes ozone—be phased out by the end of 1995, Dow decided, in 1990, to exit its lucrative 1,1,1-TCA solvent business. Because of its high life-cycle environmental costs, Dow exited this business well ahead of the US government-mandated phase-out date by

moving investment to research and development into more benign substitute materials. In less than three years, four new, nonchlorinated solvent products were on the market to substitute for TCA products. The introduction of new products not only reduced waste and emissions, but also significantly cut costs. A study completed in 1996 at a Dow facility showed that process changes would have eliminated 500,000 pounds (lb) of waste and allowed the company to shut down a hazardous waste incinerator, saving more than $1 million a year. DuPont also realized the need for exiting the 1,1,1-TCA solvent business due to environmental concerns. However, its plan in the late 1980s was to get out of the industry before 2000, a schedule that was unacceptable to the government. Although DuPont adjusted its schedule to meet the requirements of the Montreal Protocol, DuPont took a back seat to the commercialization of many TCA substitutes.

Dow not only exited the business in the United States, but also worldwide. This included a rapidly expanding TCA business in China. China, like most developing countries, was exempted from the Montreal Protocol until well into the twenty-first century. However, Dow recognized that rapid increases in the use of ozone-depleting substances in countries such as China could have disastrous worldwide environmental ramifications. It seems that the whole world is calling for new, less poisonous substitutes for TCA. How to obtain the leading position in the markets for the potential new products thus became a big concern. Therefore, Dow decided to voluntarily go beyond what was required by the Chinese regulations. Dow worked closely with Chinese business and government leaders to encourage the adoption of substitute materials over the next several years. By the late 1990s, Dow exited the TCA business in China well ahead of the mandated date. Accordingly, it became a market leader in TCA substitutes in China. During this process, Dow obviously enjoyed certain first mover advantages in its competition with other firms, including DuPont.

Case Discussion Questions

1. What benefits would Dow Chemical receive by exiting the lucrative TCA business in the United States ahead of the US government-mandated phase-out date?

2. The "pollution haven" hypothesis suggests that MNEs will take advantage of lower environmental standards in developing countries by moving production of TCA there and then marketing it locally

and exporting it to the rest of the world. This prediction did not hold in the case of Dow. Why?

3. Why did Dow decide to phase out TCA in China well ahead of local regulations?

4. Evaluate Dow's performance along the triple bottom line (economic, social, and environmental) in the United States, China, and worldwide.

Sources: This case was written by Mike W. Peng and David H. Zhu (University of Michigan). It is based on (1) L. Greer & C. Sels, 1997, When pollution prevention meets the bottom line, Environmental Science & Technology, September (http://www.pubs.acs.org); (2) C. Hill, 2003, Dow Chemical's matrix structure, in C. Hill, International Business, 4th ed. (p. 447), Chicago: McGraw-Hill Irwin; (3) S. Hart, 1995, A natural-resource-based view of the firm, Academy of Management Review, 20: 986–1014; (4) http://www.dow.com (accessed July 28, 2003); (5) http://www.dupont.com (accessed April 7, 2004). Reprinted by permission of the authors.

Notes

Abbreviation list

AME – Academy of Management Executive

AMJ – Academy of Management Journal

AMR – Academy of Management Review

APJM – Asia Pacific Journal of Management

ASQ – Administrative Science Quarterly

BAS – Business and Society

BEQ – Business Ethics Quarterly

BW – Business Week

CMR – California Management Review

EJ – Economic Journal

HBR – Harvard Business Review

JAPP – Journal of Accounting and Public Policy

JBE – Journal of Business Ethics

JEL – Journal of Economic Literature

JIBS – Journal of International Business Studies

JIM – Journal of International Management

JM – Journal of Management

JMS – Journal of Management Studies

JWB – Journal of World Business

MIR – Management International Review

MS – Management Science

NYTM – New York Times Magazine

OSc – Organization Science

SMJ – Strategic Management Journal

SMR – MIT Sloan Management Review

TC – Transnational Corporations

1. K. Davis, 1973, The case for and against business assumption of social responsibilities (p. 312), AMJ, 16: 312–322.

2. T. Donaldson, 2003, Taking ethics seriously—a mission now more possible, AMR, 28: 363–366.

3. J. Post, L. Preston, & S. Sachs, 2002, Managing the extended enterprise, CMR, 45: 6–28.

4. E. Freeman, 1984, Strategic Management: A Stakeholder Approach (p. 46), Boston: Pitman.

5. World Commission on Environment and Development, 1987, Our Common Future (p. 8), Oxford: Oxford University Press.

6. R. Rajan & L. Zingales, 2003, *Saving Capitalism from the Capitalists,* New York: Crown.

7. P. Bansal, 2002, The corporate challenge of sustainable development, *AME,* 16 (2): 122–131; T. Gladwin, J. Kennelly, & T. Krause, 1995, Shifting paradigms for sustainable development, *AMR,* 20: 874–907; S. Hart & M. Milstein, 2003, Creating sustainable value, *AME,* 17 (2): 56–67; P. Shrivastava, 1995, The role of corporations in achieving ecological sustainability, *AMR,* 20: 936–960; M. Starik & G. Rands, 1995, Weaving an integrated web, *AMR,* 20: 908–935.

8. J. Doh & H. Teegen (eds.), *Globalization and NGOs,* New York: Praeger.

9. J. Carey, 2004, Global warming, *BW,* August 16: 60–69.

10. R. Mitchell, B. Agle, & D. Wood, 1997, Toward a theory of stakeholder identification and salience, *AMR,* 22: 853–886; P. Nutt, 1998, Framing strategic decisions, *OSc,* 9: 195–216.

11. M. Clarkson, 1995, A stakeholder framework for analyzing and evaluating corporate social performance (p. 106), *AMR,* 20: 92–117; T. Kochan & S. Rubinstein, 2000, Toward a stakeholder theory of the firm, *OSc,* 11: 367–386; R. Wolfe & D. Putler, 2002, How tight are the ties that bind stakeholder groups? *OSc,* 13: 64–80.

12. R. Coff, 1999, When competitive advantage doesn't lead to performance, *OSc,* 10: 119–133.

13. Clarkson, 1995, A stakeholder framework (p. 107).

14. T. Donaldson & L. Preston, 1995, The stakeholder theory of the corporation, *AMR,* 20: 65–91; J. Elkington, 1997, *Cannibals with Forks: The Triple Bottom Line of 21st Century Business,* New York: Wiley; A. Ilinitch, N. Soderstrom, & T. Thomas, 1998, Measuring corporate environmental performance, *JAPP,* 17: 383–408.

15. There is a sizable transaction cost economics literature that explores this question. See R. Coase, 1937, The nature of the firm, *Economica,* 4: 386–405; O. Williamson, 1985, *The Economic Institutions of Capitalism,* New York: Free Press. However, its economic focus has prevented any serious discussion concerning CSR.

16. M. Friedman, 1970, The social responsibility of business is to increase its profits, *NYTM,* September 13: 32–33.

17. M. Jensen, 2002, Value maximization, stakeholder theory, and the corporate objective function, *BEQ,* 12: 235–256.

18. H. Mintzberg, R. Simons, & K. Basu, 2002, Beyond selfishness, *SMR,* Fall: 67–74; D. Quinn & T. Jones, 1995, An agent morality view of business policy, *AMR,* 20: 22–42; A. Wicks & T. Jones, 1998, Organization studies and the new paradigm, *OSc,* 9: 123–140.

19. R. Buchholz, 2004, The natural environment: Does it count? *AME,* 18 (2): 130–133; O. Ferrell, 2004, Business ethics and customer stakeholders, *AME,* 18 (2): 126–129; J. Post, L. Preston, & S. Sachs, 2002, *Redefining the Corporation,* Stanford, CA: Stanford University Press.

20. D. Wood, 1991, Corporate social performance revisited, *AMR,* 16: 691–718.

21. J. Margolis & J. Walsh, 2003, Misery loves companies: Rethinking social initiatives by business, *ASQ,* 48: 268–305.

22. M. W. Peng & Y. Ruban, 2005, Institutional transitions and strategic choices: Implications for corporate social responsibility in Russia, in The World Bank (ed.), *Corporate Responsibility and Sustainable Competitiveness in Russia,* Washington, DC: The World Bank.

23. C. Hill & T. Jones, 1992, Stakeholder-agency theory, *JMS,* 29: 131–154.

24. D. Levy & D. Egan, 2003, A neo-Gramscian approach to corporate political strategy, *JMS,* 40: 803–829.

25. C. Dawson, 2002, Fuel cells: Japan's carmakers are flooring it, *BW,* December 23: 50–51; *Economist,* 2003, Extinction of the car giants, June 14: 11.

26. T. Dean & R. Brown, 1995, Pollution regulation as a barrier to new firm entry, *AMJ,* 38: 288–303; C. Nehrt, 1996, Timing and intensity effects of environmental investments, *SMJ,* 17: 535–547.

27. J. A. Aragon-Correa, 1998, Strategic proactivity and firm approach to the natural environment, *AMJ,* 41: 556–567; K. Buysse & A. Verbeke, 2003, Proactive environmental strategies, *SMJ,* 24: 453–470; M. Russo & P. Fouts, 1997, A resource-based perspective on corporate environmental performance and profitability, *AMJ,* 40: 534–559.

28. R. Klassen & D. C. Whyback, 1999, The impact of environmental technologies on manufacturing performance, *AMJ,* 42: 599–615.

29. S. Hart, 1995, A natural-resource-based view (p. 993), *AMR,* 20: 986–1014.

30. P. Christmann & G. Taylor, 2002, Globalization and the environment: Strategies for international voluntary environmental initiatives (p. 123), *AME,* 16 (3): 121–135.

31. M. Russo, 2003, The emergence of sustainable industries, *SMJ,* 24: 317–331.

32. S. Sharma, 2000, Managerial interpretations and organizational context as predictors of corporate choice of environmental strategy, *AMJ,* 43: 681–697.

33. J. A. Aragon-Correa & S. Sharma, 2003, A contingent resource-based view of proactive corporate environmental strategy, *AMR,* 28: 71–88; C. Neht, 1998, Maintainability of first mover advantages when environmental regulations differ between countries, *AMR,* 23: 77–97.

34. A. Hillman & G. Keim, 2001, Shareholder value, stakeholder management, and social issues: What's the bottom line? *SMJ,* 22: 125–139; M. Meznar, D. Nigh, & C. Kwok, 1998, Announcements of withdrawal from South Africa revisited, *AMJ,* 41: 715–730; P. Wright & S. Ferris, 1997, Agency conflict and corporate strategy, *SMJ,* 18: 77–93.

35. W. Judge & T. Douglas, 1998, Performance implications of incorporating natural environmental issues into the strategic planning process, *JMS,* 35: 241–262; R. Klassen & C. McLaughlin, 1996, The impact of environmental management on firm performance, *MS,* 42: 1199–1214.

36. M. France & W. Symonds, 2003, Diversity is about to get more elusive, not less, *BW,* July 7: 30–31.

37. O. Richard, 2000, Racial diversity, business strategy, and firm performance, *AMJ,* 43: 164–177; D. Turban & D. Greening, 1996, Corporate social performance and organizational attractiveness to prospective employees, *AMJ,* 40: 658–672.

38. S. Sharma & H. Vredenburg, 1998, Proactive corporate environmental strategy and the development of competitively valuable organizational capabilities, *SMJ,* 19: 729–754.

39. L. Andersson & T. Bateman, 2000, Individual environmental initiative, *AMJ,* 43: 548–570; M. Cordano & I. Frieze, 2000, Pollution reduction preferences of US environmental managers, *AMJ,* 43: 627–641; C. Egri & S. Herman, 2000, Leadership in the North American environmental sector, *AMJ,* 43: 571–604; C. Ramus & U. Steger, 2000, The roles of supervisory support behaviors and environmental policy in employee "ecoinitiatives" at leading-edge European companies, *AMJ,* 43: 605–626.

40. P. Christmann, 2000, Effects of "best practices" of environmental management on cost advantage: The role of complementary assets, *AMJ,* 43: 663–680.

41. A. McWilliams & D. Siegel, 2001, Corporate social responsibility: A theory of the firm perspective, *AMR,* 26: 117–127; P. P. Shrivastava, 1995, Environmental technologies and competitive advantage, *SMJ,* 16: 183–200.

42. N. Walley & B. Whitehead, 1994, It's not easy being green (p. 50), *HBR,* May–June: 46–52.

43. J. Griffin & J. Mahon, 1997, The corporate social performance and corporate financial performance debate: Twenty-five years of incomparable research, *BAS,* 36: 5–31; J. Harrison & R. E. Freeman, 1999, Stakeholders, social responsibility, and performance, *AMJ,* 42: 479–487.

44. S. Berman, A. Wicks, S. Kotha, & T. Jones, 1999, Does stakeholder orientation matter? *AMJ,* 42: 488–506; M. M. Russo & P. Fouts, 1997, A resource-based perspective on corporate environmental performance and profitability, *AMJ,* 40: 534–559; S. Waddock & S. Graves, 1997, The corporate social performance-financial performance link, *SMJ,* 18: 303–319.

45. Hillman & Keim, 2001, Shareholder value; Meznar et al., 1999, Announcements; Wright & Ferris, 1997, Agency conflict.

46. B. Agle, R. Mitchell, & J. Sonnenfeld, 1999, What matters to CEOs? An investigation of stakeholder attributes and salience, corporate performance, and CEO values, *AMJ,* 42: 507–525; D. Levy, 1995, The environmental practices and performance of transnational corporations, *TC,* 4: 44–68; A. McWilliams & D. Siegel, 2000, Corporate social responsibility and financial performance, *SMJ,* 21: 603–609.

47. P. D. Jennings & P. Zandbergen, 1995, Ecologically sustainable organizations: An institutional approach, *AMR,* 20: 1015–1052.

48. I. Henriques & P. Sadorsky, 1999, The relationship between environmental commitment and managerial perceptions of stakeholder importance, *AMJ,* 42: 87–99.

49. P. Hilts, 2003, *Protecting America's Health,* New York: Knopf.

50. *BW,* 2003, Italy and the eco-mafia, January 27: 46–50.

51. A. Hoffman, 1999, Institutional evolution and change, *AMJ,* 42: 351–371.

52. T. Newton & G. Harte, 1996, Green business: Technicist kitsch, *JMS,* 34: 75–98; Walley & Whitehead, 1994, It's not easy being green.

53. L. Amine, 2003, An integrated micro- and macro-level discussion of global green issues: "It isn't easy being green," *JIM,* 9: 373–393.

54. A. Gore, 1992, *Earth in the Balance,* New York: Harper Row; M. Porter & C. van der Linde, 1995, Green and competitive, *HBR,* 73 (5): 120–134.

55. Porter & van der Linde, 1995, Green and competitive. For counterarguments and evidence, see A. King & J. M. Shaver, 2001, Are aliens green? *SMJ,* 22: 1069–1085; A. Rugman & A. Verbeke, 1998, Corporate strategies and environmental regulations, *SMJ,* 19: 363–375.

56. A. Jaffe, S. Peterson, P. Portney, & R. Satvins, 1995, Environmental regulation and the competitiveness of US manufacturing: What does the evidence tell us? *JEL,* 33: 132–163.

57. S. Banerjee, 2001, Managerial perceptions of corporate environmentalism, *JMS,* 38: 489–513.

58. C. Langlois & B. Schlegelmilch, 1990, Do corporate codes of ethics reflect national character? Evidence from Europe and the United States, *JIBS,* 21: 519–539.

59. R. Snell & N. Herndon, 2000, An evaluation of Hong Kong's corporate code of ethics initiative, *APJM,* 17: 493–518.

60. A. Kolk & R. Van Tulder, 2004, Ethics in international business, *JWB,* 39: 49–60; G. Weaver, 2001, Ethics programs in global businesses: Culture's role, *JBE,* 30: 3–15.

61. I. Maignan & D. Ralston, 2002, Corporate social responsibility in Europe and the US, *JIBS,* 33: 497–514.

62. P. Bansal & I. Clelland, 2004, Talking trash: Legitimacy, impression management, and unsystematic risk, *AMJ,* 47: 93–103; D. Swanson, 1995, Addressing a theoretical problem by reorienting the corporate social performance model, *AMR,* 20: 43–64.

63. R. E. Freeman, 1999, Divergent stakeholder theory, *AMR,* 24: 233–236; T. Jones, 1995, Instrumental stakeholder theory, *AMR,* 20: 404–437.

64. R. Hooghiemstra, 2000, Corporate communication and impression management, *JBE,* 27: 55–68; C. Robertson & W. Crittenden, 2003, Mapping moral philosophies, *SMJ,* 24: 385–392.

65. J. Howard-Grenville & A. Hoffman, 2003, The importance of cultural framing to the success of social initiatives in business, *AME,* 17 (2): 70–84.

66. Hart, 1995, A natural-resource-based view (p. 995).

67. G. Keim, 2001, Business and public policy, in M. Hitt, R. E. Freeman, & J. Harrison (eds.), *The Blackwell Handbook of Strategic Management* (pp. 583–601), Oxford: Blackwell.

68. D. Schuler, K. Rehbein, & R. Cramer, 2002, Pursuing strategic advantage through political means, *AMJ,* 45: 659–672.

69. B. Elgin, 2003, Can HP's printer biz keep printing money? *BW,* July 14: 68–70.

70. D. Rondinelli & T. London, 2003, How corporations and environmental groups cooperate, *AME,* 17 (1): 61–76.

71. P. Bansal & K. Roth, 2000, Why companies go green, *AMJ,* 43: 717–737; P. Christmann & G. Taylor, 2002, Globalization and the environment, *AME,* 16: 121–135.

72. A. King & M. Lenox, 2000, Industry self-regulation without sanctions, *AMJ,* 43: 698–716.

73. R. Jiang & P. Bansal, 2003, Seeing the need for ISO 14001, *JMS,* 40: 1047–1067; D. Rondinelli & G. Vastag, 1996, International environmental standards and corporate policies, *EJ,* 39: 106–122.

74. H. J. Leonard, 1988, *Pollution and the Struggle for a World Product,* Cambridge: Cambridge University Press.

75. A. Rugman & A. Verbeke, 1998, Corporate strategy and international environmental policy, *JIBS,* 29: 819–833.

76. G. Dowell, S. Hart, & B. Yeung, 2000, Do corporate global environmental standards create or destroy market value? *MS,* 46: 1059–1074.

77. J. Child & T. Tsai, 2005, The dynamic between MNC strategy and institutional constraints in emerging economies: Environmental issues in China and Taiwan, *JMS* (in press); M. Hansen, 2003, Managing the environment across borders, *TC,* 12: 27–52.

78. P. Christmann & G. Taylor, 2001, Globalization and the environment: Determinants of firm self-regulation in China, *JIBS*, 32: 439–458.

79. A. Carroll, 2004, Managing ethically with global stakeholders, *AME*, 18 (2): 114–120.

80. C. Matlack, 2004, European workers' losing battle (p. 41), *BW*, August 9: 41.

81. R. E. Freeman, A. Wicks, & B. Parmar, 2004, Stakeholder theory and "The Corporate Objective Revisited," *OSc*, 15: 364–369; B. Victor & C. Stephens, 1994, The dark side of the new organizational forms, *OSc*, 5: 479–482.

82. A. Sundaram & A. Inkpen, 2004, The corporate objective revisited, *OSc*, 15: 350–363.

83. This section draws heavily from J. Kline, 2003, Political activities by transnational corporations, *TC*, 12: 1–26.

84. H. Teegen, 2003, International NGOs as global institutions, *JIM*, 9: 271–285.

85. T. Jones & A. Wicks, 1999, Convergent stakeholder theory, *AMR*, 24: 206–221; C. Robertson, J. Hoffman, & P. Hermann, 1999, Environmental ethics across borders, *MIR*, 39: 55–69; D. Robertson, 2002, Business ethics across cultures, in M. Gannon & K. Newman (eds.), *The Blackwell Handbook of Cross-Cultural Management* (pp. 361–392), Oxford: Blackwell.

86. J. Walsh, K. Weber, & J. Margolis, 2003, Social issues and management, *JM*, 39: 859–881.

87. P. Buller & G. McEvoy, 1999, Creating and sustaining ethical capability in the multinational corporation, *JWB*, 34: 326–343; K. Schnatterly, 2003, Increasing firm value through prevention of white-collar crime, *SMJ*, 24: 587–614; T. Thomas, J. Schermerhorn, & J. Dienhart, 2004, Strategic leadership of ethical behavior in business, *AME*, 18 (2): 56–69; J. Veiga, T. Golden, & K. Dechant, 2004, Why do managers bend company rules? *AME*, 18 (2): 84–91.

88. P. Sethi, 1995, Societal expectations and corporate performance (p. 21), *AMR*, 20: 18–21.

Video Case 3.1 (2 minutes 27 seconds)
HP-COMPAQ MERGER'S IMPACT IN ASIA

This video documents how Asian partners, distributors, and customers view the HP-Compaq merger. It primarily relates to the discussion of diversification and mergers and acquisitions (M&As) in Chapter 9. A crucial point is the drive to obtain stronger market power, by merging two firms and offering a more complete product line. A Chinese commentator in the video indicated that the most crucial battles for computers in the world today are fought in China, whereas the growth in developed economies is limited. A focus on the battle in China, which has elements of both product and geographic diversification, thus provides an interesting, non-US perspective on the impact of this merger.

Video Case 3.2 (2 minutes 5 seconds)
VODAFONE'S ACQUISITION

Strategy in Action 9.2 documents Vodafone's highly controversial acquisition of Germany's Mannesmann. This video is a continuation of Vodafone's acquisition strategy, focusing on its more recent interest in gaining control of France's second largest telecommunications company, Cegetel. This video, therefore, mainly supports Chapter 9's discussion on diversification and acquisition. While Vodafone used this new acquisition to geographically diversify, the seller (the French conglomerate Vivendi, which controlled Cegetel) was interested in reducing its scope of product diversification. Thus, elements of both geographic and product diversification underpin this case. What the video does not show is that in the end, Vodafone's attempt did not succeed.

Video Case 3.3 (1 minute 50 seconds)
VAPOR PROFITS

This video opens with the Communications Workers of America (CWA) protesting during an annual IBM shareholder meeting. The heart of the debate is how pension fund profits should be reported. Financial Accounting Standard 87 allows firms to increase their operating profits by including investment gains from pension funds. While this practice is legal, critics such as the CWA argue that it might artificially inflate corporate profits, which, in turn, might lead to undeserved and excessive executive bonuses (bonuses are typically a function of the amount of profits). Worse yet, the CWA contended that this practice misled shareholders and robbed retirees of their benefits and that companies, such as IBM, are only interested in this practice because of "executive greed." As evidence, a CWA spokesperson noted that IBM's CEO took home $200 million in stock options while "business is slowing down." IBM, on the other hand, defended its practice as "properly designed to motivate the company's executives and to align their interests with the interests of shareholders." Overall, this video provides an excellent case study for a variety of corporate governance topics discussed in Chapter 11, such as principal-agent conflicts and the role of managers. Secondarily, it is also relevant for corporate social responsibility and stakeholder management as highlighted in Chapter 12 (employees and retirees are a major stakeholder group) and the idea of legal, but potentially unethical, practices outlined in Chapter 4.

Video Case 3.4 (2 minutes 30 seconds)
ENRON COLLAPSE

Video Case 3.5 (1 minute 53 seconds)
ENRON ENERGY TRADING

These two related videos illustrate some background of the Enron scandal (Enron is mentioned a couple of times throughout the book, but there is no detailed discussion, because most readers presumably have already had enough of it from other sources). Video Case 3.4, "Enron Collapse," focuses on the US Senate's investigation, which criticized Enron's board of directors for failing to perform control responsibilities. This point, therefore, is directly relevant for discussing the board of directors' role in Chapter 11.

Video Case 3.5, "Enron Energy Trading," attempts to link the brownouts and power shortages in California in 2001, which cost consumers billions of dollars, and Enron's collapse later that year. Enron made lucrative profits through its energy trading. Although not proven, a commentator in the video accused Enron of "classic racketeering." In addition to its relevance to Chapter 11, this video is also a good point of departure when discussing business ethics (Chapter 4) and corporate social responsibility (Chapter 12).

Video Case 3.6 (2 minutes 3 seconds)
POST-ENRON PROXY CHALLENGES

A proxy fight is a corporate governance battle when dissident shareholders and management disagree and compete to win shareholder votes. The video starts with a 2002 case study of the State of Wisconsin Investment Board (SWIB) blocking the proposed acquisition of the Rain Forest Café by Landry's Seafood. As an institutional investor, SWIB held 13 percent of the Rain Forest Café stock and argued that the offer was too low. The video also alludes to the Hewlett family's and the Packard family's resistance to the merger of HP and Compaq (see also Video Case 3.1). The video concludes that while proxy fights are difficult to win for dissident shareholders, the tide of shareholder activism is rising. Overall, this video vividly illustrates voice-based, internal governance mechanisms in the wake of the Enron scandal (Chapter 11). Secondarily, it also alludes to the fact that acquirers increasingly have to pay premiums, thus casting doubts on their capability to deliver satisfactory post-acquisition performance (Chapter 9).

Integrative Case 3.1

CORPORATE STRATEGY AT CARDINAL HEALTH[1]

Mike W. Peng

Fisher College of Business, The Ohio State University

While the scale and scope of the $2 trillion US health care industry, which commands approximately 15 percent of the US GDP, is often reported, probably few people would be able to successfully answer this quiz: Which company is the largest player, ranked by sales, in the US health care industry? The answer is . . . Cardinal Health![2] Named as a "stealth empire" in a *Fortune* magazine article, Cardinal Health (*http://www.cardinal.com*) was ranked No. 17 by sales on the 2004 *Fortune* 500 list (up from No. 19 on the 2003 list). Founded in 1971 and listed since 1983 (NYSE: CAH), Cardinal Health, headquartered in Dublin, Ohio (a suburb of Columbus), at present produces annual revenues of more than $50 billion, significantly more than the revenues of seemingly more visible health care companies on both the pharmaceutical side (such as Pfizer) and the retail side (such as Walgreen). The hallmark of its corporate strategy is product-related diversification. In 2004, Cardinal

[1] This case was written by Mike W. Peng (Fisher College of Business, The Ohio State University) and supported by a National Science Foundation CAREER grant (SES-0238820). It is based on media publications, SEC filings, company documents, as well as the author's interviews and communications with Mr. John Cullivan, Senior Vice President, Strategic Planning and Corporate Development, to whom the author is grateful. The views expressed are those of the author and not those of the NSF, the company, or Mr. Cullivan. All errors remain the author's.

[2] A related quiz is: What is the biggest company in Ohio? Procter & Gamble? Kroger? Goodyear? It is none of the above. It is still Cardinal Health. In Central Ohio, its revenues top the region's next three biggest companies—financial services leader Nationwide Insurance, electric utility American Electric Power, and retailer The Limited Brands—*combined*.

Health consisted of four main divisions, each of which is a market leader in its respective field:

- Pharmaceutical Distribution and Provider Services Division: Cardinal Health is one of the nation's largest drug and medical supply wholesalers and by far the most efficient and most profitable one (one of Cardinal Health's main rivals, AmeriSourceBergen [*http://www.amerisourcebergen.com*], is bigger in drug distribution revenues but only half as profitable). Every day, it ships more than 2.5 million products through 40,000 deliveries. A full one-third of all pharmaceutical, laboratory, and medical and surgical products used in the United States flows through one of its logistics facilities.

- Medical/Surgical Products and Services Division: It manufactures one-quarter of all consumable and nonconsumable medical products used in the United States, ranging from latex gloves to surgical knives. One of every two surgeries performed in the country uses its products.

- Pharmaceutical Technologies and Services Division: It serves as a contract developer and manufacturer for nine out of the top ten pharmaceutical companies (known as the Big Pharma—see Opening Case in Chapter 4) and most major biotechnology firms. Delivering 90 percent of the doses of radiopharmaceuticals, Cardinal Health also runs the largest US nuclear pharmacy services.

- Automation and Information Services Division: It develops, manufactures, and markets machines that are used in hospitals, nursing homes, and other health care centers to safely dispense drugs and medical supplies while automatically managing their inventories. For example, fifteen of the top seventeen hospitals named by *US News & World Report* use its automated supply-dispensing machines.

In addition to product-related diversification within the United States, Cardinal Health is also a large multinational enterprise (MNE) with more than 50,000 employees (42 percent outside the United States) in twenty-two countries (see IC-3.1). Because it has traditionally kept its sight on the US health care industry, at present, only approximately 7 percent ($3.5 billion) of its revenues come from international sales. It is not surprising that Cardinal Health believes that there are large and diverse opportunities in the still fragmented $4 trillion health care industry

IC-3.1.   Cardinal Health's International Presence (2004)

Divisions	Pharmaceutical Distribution and Provider Services	Medical/Surgical Products and Services	Pharmaceutical Technologies and Services	Automation and Information Services
Argentina			X	
Australia			X	
Belgium		X	X	
Brazil			X	
Canada		X	X	X
China		X		
Dominican Republic		X		
France		X	X	
Germany		X	X	
Italy		X	X	
Japan		X	X	
Malaysia		X		
Malta		X		
Mexico		X		
Netherlands		X		
Spain		X	X	
Switzerland		X	X	
Thailand		X		
United Kingdom			X	
United States	X	X	X	X

worldwide. Why and how Cardinal Health has formulated and implemented its corporate strategy, driven primarily by product-related diversification in the United States and now gradually by international diversification, is the main focus of this case.

From Cardinal Foods to Cardinal Health

In 1971, the company was founded by the 26-year-old Robert Walter, who earned an MBA from Harvard in the same year, as Cardinal Foods, which had nothing to do with health care. Walter's father had been a food broker, so Walter knew a little about the food distribution business. But after ten years or so peddling ketchup it occurred to Walter that Cardinal Foods would never be a big fish in the food business. Walter then put on his MBA hat and did a classic SWOT analysis. His findings? (1) The drug distribution industry had 354 small, independently owned distributors, but only three larger, publicly listed firms. In other words, time was ripe for consolidation. (2) The drug business was growing faster than the economy, thus presenting more growth opportunities. (3) The particular products, when prescribed by a doctor, cannot be substituted—unlike, say, one brand of butter. Thus, in 1980, Cardinal Foods entered drug distribution by becoming Cardinal Distribution (covering both foods and drugs). Finally, the firm, having already sold off its food wholesale business in 1988, renamed itself Cardinal Health in 1994.

In 1983, the firm offered shares to the public. For fifteen years, Cardinal Health remained a single-business firm, by doing nothing other than acquiring smaller drug distributors and moving drugs from point A to point B. It bought pharmaceuticals from drugmakers such as Pfizer (its biggest supplier) and sold them to the likes of CVS (its largest buyer). Its profit was the tiny take from trucking the drugs from the factory to its warehouse, sorting and repackaging them, and finally delivering them.

Although drug distribution is, according to *Fortune*, "not sexy," Cardinal Health has become the undisputed leader. While the average person may know little of Cardinal Health, Wall Street loved it during the past twenty years for a simple but admirable reason: Its shares climbed 7,200 percent since it went public in 1983 (share price was $1.04 in 1983 versus $76 during its peak in early 2004). By comparison, the S&P 500 Index posted a 591 percent gain during the same period. During this period, Cardinal Health delivered on average an annual growth of 20 percent, earning it the endearing nickname Big Red among analysts.

Product-Related Diversification

Until 1995, the single-business strategy with a drug distribution focus worked well for Cardinal Health. However, in 1995, a competitor, FoxMeyer, tried to grab market share by undercutting Cardinal Health. Fearing that drug prices might collapse, Walter started to look for ways to diversify. FoxMeyer went bankrupt in 1996, but by then Cardinal Health's diversification strategy was underway.

How to diversify? As an intermediary, Cardinal Health developed close relationships with drug companies and hospitals. These relationships led to a three-pronged product-related diversification strategy. First, years of buying from drugmakers gave Walter the opening to start making generic and low-margin drugs and ingredients that drugmakers did not care to make themselves. Cardinal Health, for instance, bought the company that puts Advil into soft gel caps. These businesses eventually led to the Pharmaceutical Technologies and Services Division. Second, since Cardinal Health sells to hospitals, it made sense to acquire companies that manufacture medical and surgical products—to be hawked by the same sales force dealing with hospital purchasing departments. As a result, the Medical/Surgical Products and Services Division was formed. Finally, realizing that safety and costs are the two biggest concerns among health care providers, Cardinal Health, through its Automation and Information Services Division, has developed automated medicine dispensing machines that check and verify the intended patients for certain medicines. The most recent development is the Pyxis PatientStation, which has a bedside touch screen for medical professionals to access patient information and for patients to entertain themselves via television, video games, and the Internet. This screen is integrated with a bedside medicine dispenser, which can automatically open a specific drawer to provide the right drug and dosage. Nurses, who do not have to run around to get patient information and drugs, love it; so do patients. Overall, Cardinal Health has sought to deepen its involvement in the "chain of care" by positioning itself in the middle between drugmakers and health care providers. Leveraging product relatedness, Cardinal Health, for example, can program its Pyxis PatientStation to be filled with and supported by Cardinal-developed, -produced, and/or -distributed products.

Cardinal Health, along with its two main rivals McKesson (*http://www.mckesson.com*) and AmeriSourceBergen, command 93 percent of the drug distribution market in the United States. However, unlike its rivals, Cardinal Health has successfully diversified into related lines of higher margin business. As a result, drug distribution accounts for less than half of its profits even though it makes up more than 80 percent of revenues. Its three other divisions contribute less than 20 percent of revenues, but 50 percent of profits. The most profitable one is the smallest division, Automation and Information Services, which generated a mere 1.3 percent of revenues, but a hefty 11 percent of profits (see IC-3.2). At present, drug distribution, a low margin business to start with, is being squeezed by drugmakers that face escalating costs and health care providers (and ultimately patients, insurance companies, and HMOs) that demand lower prices. Clearly, Cardinal Health's three other divisions have much better room for future growth and profits. Overall, Cardinal Health is more diverse and better balanced than its rivals. Its returns on sales and on assets typically double those of McKesson and AmeriSourceBergen. While McKesson has begun

IC-3.2.   Cardinal Health Revenues and Operating Earnings by Division (2003)

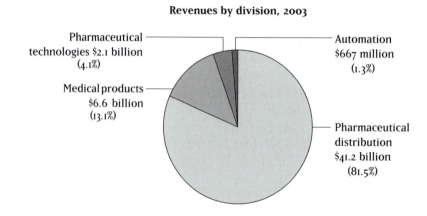

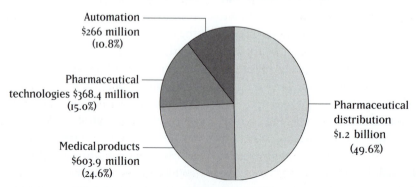

to imitate Cardinal Health's diversification strategy, AmeriSourceBergen has largely failed to do so thus far.

Acquisitions

How does Cardinal Health implement its diversification strategy? In one word, acquisitions. Between 1980 and 2004, Cardinal Health has acquired sixty companies. The buying spree peaked in the period of 1999 to 2001, during which an astounding total of thirty companies were acquired. Its largest acquisition, the $5.4 billion deal to acquire Allegiance, was undertaken during that period (in 1999). More recently, as Cardinal Health becomes much bigger, it is increasingly difficult to acquire any firm that will have a profound effect on the bottom line. Cardinal Health has now focused more on international acquisitions, as exemplified by the recent acquisitions of Intercare and ALARIS (to be discussed later).

Looking back, acquisitions are in the "blood" of this company. Its 1971 founding was through an acquisition of a food wholesaler. Its journey in drug distribution was embarked upon through its very first acquisition (after founding), Bailey Drug, in 1980. All three divisions were set up based on acquiring companies in these fields. In 1996, PCI Services was acquired to form the basis for the new Pharmaceutical Technologies and Services Division. Its Automation and Information Services Division was first established based on the 1996 acquisition of Pyxis. Its Medical-Surgical Products and Services Division was largely built on the foundation of Allegiance, acquired in 1999.

Interestingly, the well-founded fear that most acquisitions fail, substantiated by numerous studies and corporate "tragedies" (see Chapter 9), seem to stop at the gates of Cardinal Health. The secrets here? First, always focus on positive economic value-added by very carefully choosing only market leaders to acquire. Only a few of the earlier acquisitions, all of which involved acquiring regional drug distributors, would be characterized as "turnaround" types of acquisitions, namely, whipping underperforming businesses into better shape (see Chapter 11). All recent deals target leading companies in their niches. Second, look for both strategic fit and organizational fit (see Chapter 9). Third, retain top talents. Although post-acquisition executive turnovers tend to be high elsewhere, Cardinal Health has managed to retain most of the top talents at its acquired businesses. As leaders of market-leading firms in their niches, they presumably know what they are doing. Cardinal Health's reputation for trying to keep them reduces their fear and defensiveness during acquisition negotiations and also facilitates post-acquisition integration. Fourth and finally, Cardinal Health maintains a full-time merger integration team, consisting of a core cadre of four to five professionals experienced in the nuances associated with various aspects of acquisitions. When deployed, the team also includes a variety of ad hoc (one-time) members pulled from various corporate functions and related businesses.

The Intercare (2003) and Alaris (2004) Acquisitions

By 2003, although Cardinal Health had already had a fairly sizeable international presence, it mostly had been the result of inheritance, in particular, from the former Allegiance Corporation acquired in 1999, which had owned a number of manufacturing plants for medical and surgical products in Asia and Europe. The first significant international acquisition was the 2003 acquisition of Intercare. Listed on the London Stock Exchange as INT, Intercare (*http://www. intercareplc.co.uk*) was a leading British pharmaceutical products and services provider to the pharmaceutical and biotechnology industry in Europe. It operated throughout the United Kingdom and continental Europe, serving the global pharmaceutical market. It had 1,400 employees at nineteen sales, distribution, and manufacturing facilities throughout Europe. Its 2002 revenues were $468 million and the acquisition deal was worth $530 million.

There was a strong strategic fit between Cardinal Health and Intercare, as evidenced by Intercare's complementary product development, UK and continental European manufacturing and service capabilities, and a strong set of global customers, many of which were Cardinal Health customers. Intercare also brought valuable, unique, and hard-to-imitate capabilities in manufacturing pre-filled syringes. The making of syringes and of medicine inside them used to be two separate businesses, each of which was complex.

Intercare innovatively combined the two processes and made it harder for rivals to keep up. John Parker, the CEO of Intercare, and most of his lieutenants stayed with the new Cardinal Health subsidiary of Intercare. With the support of Cardinal Health's merger integration team, the integration, thus far (as of August 2004), has been progressing satisfactorily.

More recently, in mid-2004, Cardinal Health, through a $2 billion transaction, acquired ALARIS (*http://www.alarismed.com*), which was a leading global developer, marketer, and supplier of intravenous (IV) medication delivery and safety products including infusion pumps, monitoring instruments, and related disposables. Although US-based, ALARIS generated one-third of its 2003 revenues ($169 million out of a total of $534 million) from abroad, covering Europe, Asia, Australia, Africa, and Latin America. IV errors account for the largest percentage of fatal medication errors. ALARIS's products significantly reduce such errors and have great synergistic potential with Cardinal Health's Pyxis bedside systems.

The Strategic Problem

In July 2003, John Cullivan, an MIT Sloan School MBA graduate and formerly a senior consultant at Marakon Associates (*http://www.marakon.com*), was hired as Cardinal Health's Senior Vice President for Strategic Planning and Corporate Development. In this new position, Cullivan's mandate was to set up Cardinal Health's first-ever corporate strategy group, with three primary responsibilities: (1) help craft corporate strategy by advising senior leadership, (2) help develop business unit (divisional) strategy by working with business unit leadership, and (3) help improve the conditions and capabilities for consistently superior strategy development and delivery in each product group and country/region market.

In mid-August 2004, Cullivan was preparing a presentation to a forthcoming meeting of the board of directors. The focus of this discussion would be introducing the top strategic priorities for substantially growing Cardinal's market value. The company had a history of delivering top-tier shareholder value growth, but due to uncertainties and challenges associated with the health care industry and an SEC inquiry into its accounting practices, its market performance had stalled, falling back from a $28 billion market value in February 2004 to $19 billion in August 2004. Cardinal's challenge at this critical juncture therefore was determining the highest-value strategic opportunities for returning the company to its value-growth leadership position. Focusing more on the international side would clearly be a leading option to recommend. However, Cullivan realized that most of the current international activities, until the more recent Intercare and ALARIS acquisitions, had been low-cost manufacturing of products brought back and sold in the United States. For example, Cardinal Health was not even in the drug distribution business in Canada. To enter such distribution business, which Cardinal Health excels in the United States, would require substantial institutional knowledge about and relationships with health care players in various countries, which it currently lacks. In other words, Cardinal Health would try to become an "anchored replicator" with product-related diversification and limited international scope (see Figure 9.3 in Chapter 9). By staying within the broad global healthy care industry and deepening international involvement, it would eventually be possible to move the company toward being a "multinational replicator." The strategic question facing Cullivan and the board is: How?

Case Discussion Questions

1. What are the benefits and costs of Cardinal Health's product-related diversification strategy?

2. What has made Cardinal Health the biggest player in the US health care industry in general and the undisputed profitability leader in the drug distribution business in general?

3. To focus more on international activities, what are the main opportunities and obstacles?

4. Does Cardinal Health need to adjust its organizational structure (currently represented by the four US-focused product divisions) to create a better fit with its more internationally oriented strategy?

Sources: Based on media publications, SEC filings, company documents. The following sources were particularly helpful: (1) Cardinal Health Summary Annual Report 2003; (2) J. Cullivan, 2004, A strategy perspective from Cardinal Health, Presentation at the Fisher College of Business, The Ohio State University, May 12; (3) A. Lashinsky, 2003, Big man in the middle, Fortune, April 14; (4) B. Wolf, 2004, Cardinal can chirp now, Columbus Dispatch, March 21; (5) http://www.cardinal.com (accessed August 10, 2004).

Integrative Case 3.2

SPANISH BANKS IN LATIN AMERICA[1]

Mauro F. Guillén

The Wharton School, University of Pennsylvania

Adrian E. Tschoegl

The Wharton School, University of Pennsylvania

Two Spanish banks, with little prior international experience, became the largest foreign participants in commercial banking in Latin America through some twenty acquisitions in the 1990s.

During the 1990s, two Spanish banks with little prior foreign experience, Banco Santander (Santander) and Banco Bilbao Vizcaya (BBV), became the largest foreign participants in commercial banking in Latin America through some twenty acquisitions (see IC-3.1). Prior to the arrival of the Spanish banks, Citibank, BankBoston, Bank of Nova Scotia, and a few other European banks had been present in Latin America. Until the mid-1980s, Spanish banks had a very limited international presence. But during the 1980s and 1990s, Spain became the largest European investor in Latin America, due to its involvement in banking as well as telecommunications, air transportation, and utilities. Rarely have banks sought to dominate mass-market banking in foreign countries, let alone across so many different countries. The entrance of Spanish banks into Latin America thus

represents one of the boldest and most far-reaching initiatives in multinational retail banking to date.

This case focuses on the three most important banking markets in Latin America: Chile, Argentina, and Mexico. Three of the largest banks in Chile (Santander, BBV, and Banco Central Hispano [BCH]) are Spanish and have used acquisitions and

---

[1] This case is a condensed version of a longer case, "Spanish Banks in Latin America," by Mauro F. Guillén and Adrian E. Tschoegl, 2000, The New Conquistadors: Spanish Banks and the Liberalization of Latin American Financial Markets, The Wharton School, ECCH 300-133-1 and ECCH E300-133-1 (Spanish). Reprinted by permission of The Trustees of the University of Pennsylvania.

IC-3.1.   Acquisitions of Banks in Latin America by Spanish Banks

Country	Acquirer	Bank Acquired	% Stake	Acquisitions Date	Purchase Price (US$ million)
Argentina	Santander	Banco Rio de la Plata	35	1997–98	888
	BBV	Banco de Credito Argentino	72→100	1997	131
		Banco Frances del Rio de la Plata	35→52	1996	300
	OHCH[1]	Banco Tornquist	100	1996	75
Bolivia	OHCH	Banco Santa Cruz	100	1998	168
	BBV	Banco Industrial		1998[2]	
Brazil	Santander	Banco Noroeste	80	1997	500
		Banco Geral do Comercio	50.1	1997	202
	BBV	Banco Excel Economico	55	1998	450
Chile	Santander	Banco Osorno y La Union	51	1996	496
		Banco Espanol Chile	100	1982	50
	BBV	Banco Hipotecario de Fomento (BHIF)	55	1998	352
	OHCH	Banco Santiago	43	1995	252
Colombia	Santander	Banco Comercial Antioqueno	55	1997	146
	BBV	Banco Ganadero	44→59	1996	328
		Banco Nacional de Comercio		1998[2]	
Mexico	Santander	Grupo Financiero InverMexico	→61	1997	502
	BBV	Banco Oriente & Banco Cremi	100	1996	21
		Probursa	2→70	1991–96	480
	BCH	GFBital	8.3	1992	105
Paraguay	OHCH	Banco Asuncion			
Peru	Santander	Banco Interandino & Intervalores	100	1995	45
		Banco Mercantil	100	1995	44
	BBV	Banco Continental	60	1996	256
	OHCH	Banco del Sur	49.2	1995	108
Puerto Rico	Santander	Banco Central Hispano Puerto Rico	99.3	1996	289
		Caguas Central Federal Savings Bank	100	1990	51
		Bayamon Federal Savings	100	1989	n.a.
		Federal Savings Bank of Puerto Rico	100	1987	102
		Banco Credito y Ahorro Ponceno	100	1978	361
		First National Bank of Puerto Rico	100	1976	n.a.
Uruguay	Santander	Banco del Litoral Asociados	100	1982	n.a.
	BBV	Banco Pan de Azucar		1998[2]	
Venezuela	Santander	Banco de Venezuela	93.3	1996	351
	BBV	Banco Provincial	40	1996	300

Notes: 1. OHCH is a holding company jointly owned by Banco Central Hispano (BCH) and the Luksic family.
     2. Under negotiation at the time of case writing.

mergers to achieve their current positions. Chile was the first to liberalize its economy. Argentina has one of the highest per capita incomes in Latin America, as well as a large, growing economy, but remains highly under-banked (a significant portion of the adult population are not bank customers). Mexico nationalized its banking system in 1982 in response to a debt crisis but exempted Citibank, the only foreign bank. The commitments under NAFTA and OECD memberships and the *tequila* economic crisis in 1995 forced the Mexican government to allow foreign banks to acquire domestic banks. All three of these countries represent different situations, therefore creating an interesting comparison when studying the entrance of Spanish banks into Latin America.

Spain: The Home Setting

Since the 1970s, Spain transformed itself from being one of the most politically and economically inward-looking countries in Europe to one of the most open and dynamic. Spain went through the transformation to democracy in the late 1970s, economic growth following membership in the European Union in the late 1980s, and slowdown in the early 1990s. The Spanish banking system had been one of the most regulated and protected in the world. Restrictive rules made it difficult for banks to grow and foreign banks had been restricted from entering. However, in 1992, certain EU rules led to Spain allowing foreign banks to enter.

The most momentous changes between 1988–1994 in Spanish banking involved mergers among the largest banks. By 1994, the "Big Seven" had become the "Big Four": Santander, BBV, BCH, and Argentaria. BBV resulted from the merger between Bancos Bilbao and Vizcaya. Banco Central and Hispano-Americano merged to form BCH. Santander acquired Banesto. Lastly, the government reorganized the state-owned banks to create the mega-bank Argentaria. These mergers changed the competitive environment. Santander began a war among the large banks by creating its *Supercuenta*, which offered high interest rates on checking accounts, and by revolutionizing the mortgage loan market. BBV retaliated with its own *Supercuenta* and with *Libreton*,

an account offering lower interest rates as well as prizes.

By the mid-1990s, Santander and BBV were the largest banks in Spain, far ahead of other competitors. Santander had been founded in 1857. Over the years, Santander grew through acquisitions and through its creation of telephone banking in Spain. It started expansion abroad in the late 1980s with acquisitions in Portugal and the United States. In 1988, Santander set its sights on Latin America. By 1997, Latin American operations accounted for 50 percent of its foreign assets.

BBV was the result of the 1988 merger of Banco de Bilbao and Banco de Vizcaya. At that time, the newly merged bank was the largest bank in Spain. Bilbao had opened its first office abroad in 1902. Vizcaya started its first international venture in the late 1920s in Paris, but did not open other offices abroad until the 1970s. In 1997, 23 percent of BBV's consolidated assets were from foreign operations.

BCH and Argentaria both also had a presence in Latin America. BCH had been a latecomer to Latin America. Its strategy was to work through powerful local families and partnerships, while retaining management control. Argentaria reorganized investments in Chile, Argentina, and Uruguay that it inherited. It concentrated on corporate and foreign trade banking and also exploring pension banking.

Chile

Chile has enjoyed more economic growth than any other country in Latin America. Between 1990 and 1995, Chile averaged 7 percent annual GDP growth while lowering annual inflation from over 28 percent to 8 percent. The Mexican *tequila* effect that so badly crippled the Argentine economy in 1995 left Chile relatively unscathed. The private saving rates in Chile are amongst the highest in the world. Indisputably, Chile is the most competitive financial market in Latin America.

Merger activities in Chile's banking market were intense during the 1990s. Mergers helped Banco Santiago (50 percent foreign owned by BCH) into first place in size and Banco Santander Chile into second place. By the end of 1997, the banking industry consisted of fifteen private locally incorporated banks (four of these wholly or majority foreign owned and a few others with large foreign minority equity positions), plus the government-owned Banco del Estado de Chile. In addition, thirteen foreign banks operated as local branches of their parents. Overall, 20 percent of the banking system assets and loans were foreign.

Santander entered Chile in 1978 and acquired Banco Espanol Chile in 1982. In the 1990s, Santander targeted the lower middle to middle income consumers, due to strong growth in these areas and the strength of other foreign banks, especially Citibank and BankBoston, in the upper-income segments. By 1995, Santander was the sixth largest private commercial bank in the country. Then in 1996, it acquired Banco Osorno y La Union and became the second largest commercial bank in Chile. Santander succeeded in the Chilean market with its introduction of *superhipoteca,* a new mortgage product with aggressive pricing. This allowed Santander to gain approximately 20 percent of new mortgages.

BBV had only a single representative office in Chile for many years. But in 1998, BBV bought BHIF, which had a 4.5 percent market share and fifty-two branches in Chile, from the Siad family. BCH took a different route by creating a 50-50 holding company with a local partner and purchasing 43 percent of Banco Santiago from the central bank. *Euromoney* rated Banco Santiago as the best bank in Chile in 1997.

Argentina

At the beginning of the twentieth century, Argentina was one of the wealthiest countries in the world because of its success in exports. However, decades of instability followed. The country suffered hyperinflation, political volatility, and social unrest. In the early 1990s, Argentina's currency was pegged to the US dollar at parity to aid in decreasing inflation and a currency board was established. The reforms resulted in strong economic growth and huge foreign investment inflows. By the late 1990s, Argentina

was perhaps the richest country in Latin America with the best-educated population. However, much remained to be done on unemployment and export growth.

The biggest impediment to the development of the financial sector was instability and hyperinflation. Private banks were nationalized and privatized several times during the second half of the twentieth century, adding a lot of uncertainty to the financial sector. At one point total deposits fell to $2 billion (for a country of 33 million people) as people avoided bank accounts. As a result, Argentina was a very underbanked market. Even by the 1990s, it was estimated that roughly one-third of the adult population were still not bank customers. Most citizens settled all of their bills and even purchases of homes and cars in cash. To reach this untapped market, banks used nontraditional ideas. For example, Banco Rio de la Plata, owned by Santander, created automated service centers at gas stations. Banco de Galicia opened mini-branches at post offices throughout the country, and Citibank announced similar programs with Blockbuster and McDonald's. In addition, Argentina also had the lowest proportion of citizens with credit cards (17 percent) in Latin America (compared with 19 percent in Mexico and 21 percent in Chile), which was another area currently being explored by these large banks.

The *tequila* shock of 1994–95 resulted in a 20 percent fall in deposits as customers turned to cash or sent money abroad. By March 1995, roughly one in three Argentine banks was technically bankrupt. As a result, the number of commercial banks continued to fall. By 1997, there were 138, down from 469 in 1980 and 220 in 1990. Privatization reduced the number of state-owned banks from 35 in 1980 to 20 in 1997, and consolidation reduced the number of private banks from 179 to 118.

For many years Citibank and BankBoston had been among the most important foreign banks in Argentina. However, at the end of 1997 there were 34, including the Spanish banks. Santander entered by acquiring Banco Rio de la Plata, one of the most profitable banks in Argentina. BBV acquired

Banco Frances and Banco de Credito Argentino, upon entering. Banco Frances was well run and BBV had a hands-off approach. However, its second acquisition, Banco de Credito Argentino, caused many integration problems. Both Santander and BBV innovatively sold bank accounts that offered customers chances to win prizes, in order to outdo competitors. The central bank disapproved of this tactic, but found no legal reason to stop it.

Mexico

In 1994, Mexico joined NAFTA and became the first developing country to join the OECD, a prestigious organization whose members only included developed countries. However, during the same decade, poor financial leadership led to turmoil. The peso collapsed by 45 percent, forcing the United States to orchestrate an international bailout amounting to $52 billion. This turmoil was known as the *tequila* crisis. In the late 1990s, Mexico's banking system included fifty-two commercial and foreign banks. For a long time (1928–94), Citibank had been the only foreign bank operating in Mexico. When foreign banks were banned from entering the country in the 1930s, Citibank was allowed to stay. Between World War II and 1994, Mexico only allowed foreign banks to enter via representative offices.

Beginning in 1994, Mexico hesitantly opened to foreign banks. Under NAFTA, Mexico agreed to permit North American banks to establish locally owned subsidiaries and then extended the opening to all OECD member countries. Nevertheless, foreign control of local banks remained a sensitive subject in Mexico, and laws blocked foreigners from majority ownership in the country's three largest banks.

BBV was the first Spanish bank to enter Mexico. It entered through the invitation of Probursa, which became BBV Probursa. By the late 1990s, BBV Probursa had 335 branches in Mexico. The second Spanish entrant was BCH, which acquired Banco Atlantico from the government, as well as Bital. Third, Santander entered as a retail bank in 1997 when it acquired 61 percent of InverMexico, which included brokerage and insurance companies as well as Banco Mexicano.

Just as the Spanish banks did in Chile and Argentina, in Mexico they also introduced new ideas and competition. All three banks tried to build a strong depositor base, but pursued different strategies. In 1996, BBV introduced its *Libreton,* a move that Santander mimicked with its *Supercuenta.* Within a few months BBV could boast 460,000 new accounts and Santander 240,000. Now local banks also introduced these lottery-linked accounts, which qualified for deposit insurance. Bital, owned by BCH, did not introduce similar accounts but focused on service. It aggressively opened more branches. It also extended the traditional 9 am to 1 pm banking hours to 7 pm and introduced Saturday opening.

The Future

By the late 1990s, many analysts maintained that it was too early to tell whether entering retail banking in Latin America was a good idea, let alone which approach was best. What was clear was that the Spanish banks brought innovations and shook up what were cozy, stagnant markets. Longer-run, some observers worried about what would happen when margins in Latin America fell to more competitive levels, in a region fraught with instability. Experts ranked Santander and Citibank the two best banks in the region. However, it was not clear whether Citibank (and other foreign banks) would meet the Spaniards' challenge in the middle market segment or rather keep focusing on the upper income segment.

In 1999, Santander and BCH merged to form Banco Santander Central Hispano (BSCH) (*http://www.bsch.es*), which was the largest bank in the entire Euro zone in terms of market capitalization. BBV reacted by taking over Argentaria, the previously state-owned bank, to form BBVA (*http://www.bbva.es*). The most fundamental strategic question confronting executives at these Spanish banks was: Where and how to embark on the most profitable growth in Latin America and elsewhere as they entered the twenty-first century?

Case Discussion Questions

1. Drawing on industry-, resource-, and institution-based perspectives, explain why the Spanish banks were so keen to enter Latin American markets. Why weren't banks from other countries as aggressive as the Spanish banks?

2. What capabilities or know-how enabled the Spaniards to succeed in the region, at least thus far? Who were the Spanish banks competing against?

3. Which market—Argentina, Chile, Mexico—was most attractive from the point of view of a foreign bank? What entry modes did the Spanish banks—Santander, BBV, BCH—use? Did each bank choose the same entry mode for all markets? Why?

4. If you were an executive at a local bank or another foreign-owned bank (such as BankBoston), what would be your course of action in the face of the Spanish "invasion"?

Integrative Case 3.3
ELSCINT AND THE WORLDWIDE MEDICAL IMAGING INDUSTRY

Mona Makhija

Fisher College of Business, The Ohio State University

Uri Ben-Zion

Ben-Gurion University

Gdaliahu Harel

Technion Institute of Technology

An Israeli high-technology firm tried to carve out a niche in an industry where global scale and reach count.

Founded in 1969, Elscint was one of Israel's first high-technology companies, making a place for itself in the computer-based medical diagnostic imaging industry. This industry is concerned with the provision of medical diagnostic information to help replace invasive diagnostic procedures. The worldwide market for these imaging modalities has exhibited tremendous growth, going from approximately $1 billion in 1980 to $10.2 billion in 1998. Elscint's sales grew from $111 million in 1990 to $209 million in 1998. In addition, Elscint was responsible for a number of technological innovations associated with this industry. The Israeli government believed that high technology and globally oriented firms would serve as the engine of growth for its economy in the long run. Elscint therefore was an important example of the type of firm the Israeli government wanted to see more of in the Israeli economy.

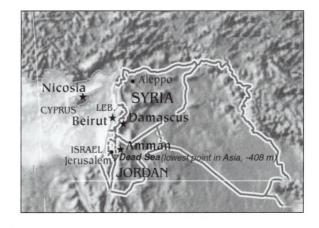

High-Technology Policies of the Israeli Government

Many in the Israeli government have long believed that high technology is an important driver of economic development, allowing firms to benefit from greater value-creating activities than other more traditional industries in agriculture or manufacturing. The greater value created from high technology comes from the intrinsic difficulty in developing such technology, therefore differentiating competitors. Technological capabilities result in important initial barriers to entry. Firms with the ability to develop and utilize higher levels of technology in their processes and products are therefore likely to gain global market share over competitors with lesser abilities in this regard. The higher returns earned can be reinvested in further technological developments, thereby continually enhancing barriers to entry and gaining market share. Technological developments also create "trickle-down" benefits to other parts of the economy.

Due to the high potential for economic growth from such activities, the Israeli government has had the goal of promoting a high-technology orientation in the economy since 1969. It was expected that the returns from this goal would be the creation of high-quality jobs, reduction of the trade deficit, as well as high productivity and growth. In particular, the government has supported small- and medium-sized firms' research and development activities that are associated with economic feasibility. To this end, low-cost loans have been provided to such firms for the development of new technologies through the Office of the Chief Scientist in the Ministry of Trade and Industry. These loans were returned only out of the proceeds of the R&D. If there were no proceeds, the loan became a grant. In the period 1987–94, the Office of the Chief Scientist paid out $1.4 billion in subsidies to 1,200 firms, supporting $3.5 billion in R&D.

Elscint has been a major beneficiary of these forms of government support, repeatedly receiving grants from the Office of the Chief Scientist. A particularly critical period in Elscint's history was 1985, when it almost went bankrupt due to a poor investment strategy. At that time, the government stepped in with additional funds, granted government guarantees to the banks for Elscint's loans, and pressed the banks to restructure and forgive part of Elscint's debt. This assistance was critical for Elscint's survival.

Israel appears to have benefited from its high-technology policies, particularly in terms of Israel's exports and employment. In general, agricultural and other low value-added exports have been declining as a proportion of total exports, while high-technology exports have been increasing. In 1997, Israeli exports totaled $30 billion, of which more than 60 percent were technology-based.[1] The Bank of Israel noted that exports from advanced sectors (those employing highly skilled personnel such as scientists and engineers) grew at 18.5 percent in the years 1997 and 1998, while those from more traditional sectors (with less skilled personnel) generally declined by 1.4 percent in the same period. The number of technological start-ups in Israel has been similarly dramatic.[2]

The success of Israel's high-technology policies can also be seen in terms of its contribution to the nation's industrial development. In the period 1987–94, the $3.5 billion dollars of supported R&D generated estimated sales of over $31 billion, creating 260,000 job-years. This constituted roughly 10 percent of industrial employment. In this same period, $1 of R&D was found to increase total factor productivity by an additional $0.45, annually contributing $0.30 of GDP on average, and earning a direct annual return of 13.4 percent for the economy. The impact of the subsidies also differed in terms of industrial sector. Electronics, communications, automation, and control equipment received roughly half the subsidies while generating nearly two thirds of the gains. While small firms received one-sixth of the subsidies, they contributed to over a quarter of the gains.

The Medical Imaging Industry

The medical diagnostics imaging industry has a number of important characteristics that influence the nature of

---

[1] Michael Eilan, "Less is More: Israel's Technology Policies," *National Institute for Research Advancement*, 1998. Reprinted by permission of the author.

[2] For an extensive discussion of such startups, see Yeheskel et al., "Cooperative Wealth Creation: Strategic Alliances in Israeli Medical Technology Ventures," *Academy of Management Executive*, 2001, pp. 16–25.

competition within the industry. First, it is an overwhelmingly global industry, with both customers and competitors located across a large number of countries. Sales are primarily to hospitals and clinics, which include teaching hospitals, community hospitals, private clinics, and hospital chains. These sales are made either directly or through unaffiliated leasing companies.

A second feature of this industry stems from the role of technological innovation. In this global arena, the maintenance of a long-term position in the market depends on the ongoing ability to introduce new technologically advanced products. Competition in the industry is primarily focused on providing advanced technological equipment with high-resolution imaging capability applicable to a wide variety of clinical procedures. Pricing, product reliability, and other performance indicators are also all important competitive features.

Given the global nature of the medical imaging market, the ability to market across national boundaries is a third important characteristic of this industry. In addition, customers expect a high level of service and after-sales support due to the complex nature of the machinery. The ability to provide service to customers is facilitated by a firm's global presence. Ongoing interaction with customers provides other important benefits, including information on medical developments that could provide the impetus for new products, adaptations required by hospitals due to infrastructural problems, and perspectives of the customers on competing products.

Finally, the changing structure of health care around the world has also affected the nature of competition in the medical imaging industry. In many countries, health care is nationalized, creating a downward pressure on the costs due to limited public funds. Even in the United States, health management organizations (HMOs) have sprung up to reduce costs of health care. These factors have reduced the potential for growth in the industry, in turn intensifying competition in the medical equipment market.

The worldwide medical diagnostic imaging market (including conventional X-ray and customer support services) has been led by five major industrial companies: General Electric Corporation (USA), Siemens (Germany), Toshiba (Japan), Philips (the Netherlands), and General Electric Company (UK). Other companies, including Elscint, Hitachi, Shimadzu, ADAC Laboratories, Sopha Medical of ATL, Hewlett-Packard, and Aloka, as well as many other smaller companies, share the remainder of the medical diagnostic imaging market. In general, the larger companies dominate the market, although there are clear differences in the market shares in different product segments and geographic regions. There is also evidence that market advantage is translated into some price differential.

Elscint's Global Strategy

The nature of worldwide competition in the medical imaging industry required that Elscint focus largely outside of Israel. Elscint marketed its products worldwide through sixteen wholly-owned marketing subsidiaries and various distributors, agents, and representatives in Western, Central, and Eastern Europe; North America; Commonwealth of Independent States; Latin America; the Middle East; the Pacific Rim (including China); South Africa; and Australia. Most of the company's revenues were generated by its own sales force, which consisted of about 260 people (plus nearly 600 in service). In addition, the majority of all of its revenues were generated outside of Israel (see IC-3.1). In each of its major targeted markets, the company had a dedicated sales force, with different persons focusing on one or more of its four principal imaging modalities.

In many respects, Elscint was a technology leader and pioneered several innovations, including the first integrated digital NM camera, intravaginal scanning, and interactive three-dimensional presentations. Each of the company's products included a substantial amount of proprietary software. Purchasers of the company's products had access to the company's broad and comprehensive library of software programs, developed and clinically tested over the past decade. The company had accumulated extensive experience both in the design of operating systems software and in the development of applications software.

IC-3.1.   Elscint's Revenues by Geographic Markets, 1992–1998 (in US $ million)

	1992	1993	1994	1995	1996	1997	1998
N. America	$ 64.952	$ 79.721	$ 67.051	$ 71.282	$ 77.820	$ 69.861	$ 61.351
Europe	105.197	103.998	100.817	122.888	140.797	118.342	92.840
S. America	20.878	21.687	25.644	27.985	38.649	50.597	31.630
Pacific Rim	13.280	17.646	22.495	35.567	29.502	30.608	27.813
Israel	9.010	8.654	11.496	14.417	18.206	25.046	41.324
Others	7.604	6.098	7.372	9.767	6.446	8.537	7.100
Total	**$220.891**	**$237.804**	**$234.875**	**$281.906**	**$311.420**	**$302.991**	**$262.058**

This enabled the company to provide its customers with new software versions, which enhanced and extended the capabilities of systems purchased by such customers. While Elscint's research and development activities focused on its core modalities and on those technologies upon which its products are dependent, the company also closely monitored the technological advances related to the critical components and subassemblies that it did not manufacture. Elscint worked with manufacturers of such components to keep abreast of changing technologies to provide its customers with improved products. Such components included, for example, X-ray tubes, high voltage power supplies, RF amplifiers, and photomultipliers. Elscint also closely monitored emerging technologies for their application to future products that may be developed by the company. In this regard, it had purchased the assets of several ongoing operations, which had significant research and development activities.

In the period of 1997–1998, Elscint employed approximately 280 R&D employees. Of these personnel, approximately 240 were located in Israel. Elscint's participation in four principal modalities is described below.

Computed Tomography

Computed tomography (CT) systems are based on a rotating X-ray assembly that irradiates the body in a transverse plane as it rotates around the patient. Data are collected from radiation detectors mounted on the opposite side of the assembly. These data are processed by a dedicated computer system to reconstruct a cross-sectional image of the body that is substantially more detailed than the simple projection image produced by conventional X-ray devices. Unlike conventional X-ray images, multiple CT images made along a longitudinal axis may then be combined to create a three-dimensional image of certain parts of the body without the interference of overlying tissue. This image can be manipulated by the physician to be viewed from any angle. The image can also be reconstructed to view any cross-section required. The three-dimensional and tissue differentiation capabilities of CT make it especially useful for diagnosis of the central nervous system (head and spine), tumors and cysts, and the effects of trauma. It is also effective for reconstructive surgery and surgical planning. CT has experienced substantial market acceptance since the mid-1970s.

In 1996, the competition in CT was led by GE Medical Systems (31 percent worldwide market share), Siemens Medical Systems (17 percent), and Picker International (16 percent). Elscint and three other firms shared 10 percent of the market. In 1994, the prices for the top-end systems of Elscint ranged from approximately $600,000 to $1,000,000, depending on system configuration and accessories. By 1996, these prices were from $500,000 to $900,000. For Elscint's low-end systems, prices in 1994 ranged from $300,000 to $600,000, depending on system configuration and accessories. By 1996, these prices ranged from $300,000 to $450,000, and in 1997, from $250,000 to approximately $400,000.

Nuclear Medicine Imaging

Nuclear medicine (NM) imaging is based upon the detection of gamma radiation emitted by radiopharmaceuticals that are administered to a patient, concentrating in the organs to be examined. Gamma cameras using large sodium iodide detectors and dedicated nuclear medicine workstations trace the gamma particles emitted by the radiopharmaceutical. A complex electro-optical system detects their location within the patient's body or the examined organ. A distribution map of these particles is computer generated and displayed, forming a representation of the radio pharmaceutical distribution in the patient's body. These data are either directly used for diagnosis or further processed by the nuclear medicine workstation. NM systems can provide detailed diagnostic information relating to the function of the organs. These capabilities are especially useful in diagnosing coronary artery disease, cancer, and neurological functions that manifest themselves in normal and abnormal brain metabolism. In recent years, single photon emission computerized tomography (SPECT), a technique which provides tomographic slices showing a three-dimensional distribution of radioisotope tracers, has become a standard capability in nuclear medicine imaging. Nuclear imaging began evolving as an important diagnostic imaging technology in the late 1960s.

Since 1993, Elscint offered positron emission tomography (PET) scanners to observe the consumption by cells of substances tagged with high-energy, short half-life radioisotopes generated by cyclotrons. PET provides images of higher spatial resolution than NM SPECT images.

With a total of twelve competitors, the market leaders in this modality included ADAC Laboratories (26 percent market share), Siemens Medical Systems (19 percent), GE Medical Systems (16 percent), and Picker (11 percent). Elscint's share of the market was 6 percent. In 1994, prices for Elscint's NM gamma

camera systems ranged from approximately $280,000 to $500,000. In 1996, the price range was from $150,000 to $500,000, and from $40,000 to $80,000 for a workstation.

Magnetic Resonance Imaging

Magnetic resonance imaging (MRI) technology utilizes strong and homogeneous magnetic fields and the magnetic properties of various nuclei in the body to produce signals that can be measured, analyzed, and manipulated by a dedicated computer system to produce tomographic images. MRI provides good image contrast without the ionizing radiation exposure that is the basis of the conventional X-ray, CT, and NM modalities. The MRI modality enables the user to view a wide variety of tissue cross-sections at different angles along various axes, enhancing the resolution of three-dimensional images and making it particularly useful for imaging the central nervous system and for cardiac and muscular-skeletal diagnosis. This modality also permits diagnosis of the body's vascular system through magnetic resonance angiography, through which blood vessels are imaged and diagnosed. It has the potential to precisely determine metabolic function and dysfunction through magnetic resonance spectroscopy, a technique with varied applications which to date have not been integrated into routine clinical use. MRI began to achieve commercial acceptance in the early 1980s.

There were a total of fifteen competitors in this modality in 1996. GE Medical Systems had 25 percent of the market, followed by Siemens Medical Systems (24 percent), Toshiba Medical Systems (15 percent), and Phillips Medical Systems (12 percent). Elscint's share of the market was 5 percent. Elscint's MRI systems ranged in price from $850,000 to $1,500,000 in 1994, from $650,000 to $1,500,000 in 1996, and from $650,000 to $1,400,000 in 1997.

Ultrasound Imaging

Ultrasound imaging (ULS) systems produce images by detecting and analyzing echoes of high-frequency sound waves focused on, and reflected back from, different organs within a patient's body. ULS has the ability to provide both static and dynamic images for analyzing an organ's function, as well as for tissue morphology. ULS also has the advantage of not using ionizing radiation, which makes it particularly suitable for the obstetrics/gynecology clinical segments. It is also widely used for cardiology and general radiology. ULS imaging was introduced as a practical imaging modality in the early 1970s.

The market leaders in this modality were Acuson (16 percent market share), ATL (14 percent), GE Medical Systems (13 percent), and Aloka (11 percent). Elscint had the sixth largest market share in this highly competitive segment, at 6 percent. Elscint faced more than thirty competitors in ultrasound imaging.

Other Products

In addition to the major modalities discussed above, Elscint had a small presence in several other medical imaging products as well, including mammography, connectivity solutions, and multi-imagers. Mammography is used for the screening and diagnosis of patients for breast cancer, using an X-ray system that is customized for this application. Since 1993, Elscint has had a computer-controlled, low-dose mammography system. In addition, Elscint has had a DICOM-compliant independent multi-modality diagnostic workstation, which provides enhanced viewing, processing analysis, manipulation, storage, and retrieval of images from different modalities. Virtual endoscopy provides noninvasive, computer-generated inner-body views similar to actual endoscopic procedures. In 1996 Elscint introduced advanced WAN (wide area network) solutions. These served to connect remote scanners to a central site for professional diagnostic services. Finally, multi-imagers involve a multiformat camera that is used as an output device for all of Elscint's imaging systems. It features the high spatial resolution and linearity necessary for high-quality hard-copy reproduction of computer-generated images. The multi-imager is an essential part of most medical imaging equipment. Elscint did not compete in the conventional X-ray market or in therapeutic equipment. In addition, it did not have a full line in other segments of the medical imaging field.

Elscint's sales are shown in IC-3.2. Overall, the breakdown of sales according to modalities shows that CT, the main modality of Elscint, accounted for half of sales as of 1998, with NM and MRI following second and third in importance.

The Road Ahead

By 1998, Elscint was a company at a crossroads. Although the worldwide industry for medical imaging modalities was driven by technological breakthroughs, by the 1990s cost considerations began to play a major role. As a relatively young firm that was also considerably smaller than others in its industry, it was clear that Elscint faced formidable threats from its competitors. The volume and complexity of its worldwide markets also made it difficult to compete. Although management understood that changes had to be made in their global strategy, it was unclear in which direction these should be made.

IC-3.2.   System Sales (Including Subassemblies) by Modality, 1993–1998 (in US $ million)*

	1993	1994	1995	1996	1997	1998
CT	66.3	74.1	100.9	109.4	92.4	100.4
MRI	32.6	22.8	22.6	49.5	49.1	22.9
NM	68.4	56.6	54.9	55.7	64.9	76.4
ULS	2.4	5.1	11.0	2.8	1.6	0.2
MAM	2.8	3.9	6.8	4.7	4.9	5.5
Others	1.6	1.6	5.1	4.7	3.2	3.9
Total	**174.1**	**164.1**	**201.3**	**226.8**	**216.0**	**209.3**

* Note that these figures do not reflect other sources of revenues such as fees from licensing, consulting, and after-sales services not included in initial sales.

Should Elscint divest some of its businesses? If so, which ones? How could it leverage its limited financial resources? Could Elscint rationally expect any more assistance from the Israeli government? These difficult questions faced the management of Elscint as they pondered the future.

Case Discussion Questions

1. Evaluate Elscint's global strategy. Has Elscint developed a competitive advantage in its industry? Is such a strategy appropriate for this particular industry?

2. Using Elscint as an example, do you believe that that the Israeli government's technology policies are appropriate? Why or why not?

3. Identify and discuss all the beneficiaries from the creation of Elscint. Are these the ones that the Israeli government originally intended?

4. In light of Elscint's performance, what, if anything, do you think the Israeli government should have done differently with respect to Elscint?

5. If you were a top executive at Elscint, how would you answer the strategic questions raised at the end of the case?

Integrative Case 3.4

ILIM PULP: CORPORATE GOVERNANCE BATTLES IN RUSSIA[1]

Daniel J. McCarthy

Northeastern University

Sheila M. Puffer

Northeastern University

Russia's leading forest products company defended itself against a high-profile hostile takeover.

In the spring of 2002, Ilim Pulp (*http://www.bestpaper.ru*), Russia's largest forest products company, became the target of a hostile takeover attempt by one of Russia's powerful oligarchs, Oleg Deripaska, and the saga continued well into 2004. The battle over Russia's forest products industry is understandable, given the country's still incomplete corporate governance structure, its nascent legal system, and the extraordinary attractiveness of the industry itself. Ilim, with 65 percent of its production going to export, is the most attractive takeover target in an industry that is one of the last to be consolidated. According to press reports, the battles are "also a sign that doing business in post-Soviet Russia—for Russian and Western investors—is still a tangled and complicated affair, with much of the battles taking place behind the scenes, in the media, and on the streets."

The Attractive Forest Products Industry

The forest products industry is clearly one of Russia's most attractive industries, a fact not lost on oligarchs like Oleg Deripaska, who is on record as wanting to consolidate the industry under his holding company, Continental Management. "The forest products sector ranks fifth in Russia's gross domestic product in terms of output volume," according to the media.

---

[1] This case "Ilim Pulp: Corporate Governance Battles in Russia" by Daniel J. McCarthy and Sheila M. Puffer, is based on Chapter 16 of D. J. McCarthy, S. M. Puffer, and S. V. Shekshnia (eds.), *Corporate Governance in Russia* (Cheltenham, UK and Northampton, MA: Edward Elgar Publishing, 2004), which contains complete references for the information cited in the case. Reprinted by permission of the authors.

"Most of the rest of Russia's natural resources sector has been taken over and the only industry in Russia that is not wholly consolidated is the pulp and paper industry." "Forestry is particularly attractive, as it has several of the features which made oil so tempting—a working industrial structure, large reserves, and an orientation to exports that earn hard currency," noted the *Economist*. "Forestry registered export sales of $4.2 billion last year, making Russia the world's fifth largest exporter of timber products." With its incredible reserves, the industry is poised for expansion on the world markets, except that plants are operating at close to their present capacity, and will require substantial investment to realize their growth potential.

Industry experts as well as potential investors agree that the industry has the potential to bring riches to some, and possibly contribute to the country's economic prosperity. The actual result will depend largely upon the way the ownership of the industry materializes. According to the Dow Jones News Service, "To many observers, pulp and paper is the next natural resource-based industry that will make fortunes for Russian tycoons and cause nightmares for Western European competitors. The natural resource is plentiful, the equipment is heavily depreciated, and energy, the only other major operating cost, is cheap. Under competent management, it adds up to a license to print money. Take ZAO Ilim Pulp Enterprises, the country's largest pulp and paper group. It is forecasting an operating profit of $282 million this year [2002] on sales of only $868 million despite a heavy capital expenditure program. Unfortunately for Ilim, such conspicuous success makes it an obvious target for corporate raiders."

The industry, and especially Ilim Pulp, has attracted the attention of Deripaska for many reasons, one of which is the extraordinary degree of concentration, with around ten plants producing nearly 90 percent of industry output. Ilim Pulp itself owns the largest mill, Kotlas, and the company produces over 60 percent of industry output in its four mills. The company has clearly shown that it will not easily give up such a valuable business. As one commentator noted: "The stakes are high—the Kotlas paper mill is one of the biggest in a country that boasts nearly a quarter of the world's forests. It is the centerpiece of Ilim Pulp Enterprise's forestry operations, which expects sales to top one billion dollars this year."

Improving Corporate Governance: A Two-Edged Sword

Founded in 1992 as a small trading company during the government's privatization program, Ilim Pulp became the largest forest products company in Russia. The company ranked among the world's top ten in terms of timber reserves and logging volumes, and among the top seventy in sales volume. Headquartered in St. Petersburg, it has operations throughout Russia, including three of the country's four largest pulp and paper mills as well as other mills, logging companies, a trading company, and a mill in the Czech Republic. The largest mill, the Kotlas plant in the far-northern Arkhangelsk region, was acquired in 1995, while the Bratsk mill was acquired in 1999 and the Ust-Ilimsk mill in 2000. The company's revenues were estimated to be approaching $900 million in 2002. Nearly two-thirds of the company's products are exported to more than ninety countries, particularly to Eastern Europe, China, and the Middle East. The company employed nearly 50,000 people in 2004.

Ilim is a privately held company controlled by four major shareholders with backgrounds in the forestry industry. Two were research analysts while two were engineers, and all had mill experience in Soviet times. The holding company is 100 percent owned by these four individuals, giving them control over 90 percent of Ilim's four major operations. One major subsidiary is 53 percent controlled by the four owners, while a German company, a strategic investor, owns 40 percent. "That's the structure right now [late 2002], and the job of combining everything under a unified share on our way to the capital markets is basically about consolidating the company so that it has a unified share structure owned by the holding company which would have some minority investors," explained then-senior managing director Mikhail Moshiashvili in a November 2002 interview with the authors.

Zakhar Smushkin, one of the founders, was appointed chairman of the board at the general shareholders' meeting on December 25, 2000, having been chief executive officer (CEO) since the company's start in 1992. He was succeeded as CEO by Sergey Kostylev, who had been chief financial officer (CFO) since 1993. These appointments were dictated by changes in the company's corporate governance requiring that major shareholders serve on the board of directors rather than on the executive board. Ilim's actions preceded the announcement in early 2002 of the Code of Corporate Conduct, which required the separation of CEO and chairman of the board. And in June 2001, the company announced that it had engaged PricewaterhouseCoopers (PWC) as its auditor, that its last three years would be restated, and that those and subsequent years would be reported according to IAS and GAAP standards. Its plans called for entering international financial markets in 2003, seeking listing on domestic and international stock exchanges.

Recognizing the progressive steps in Ilim's corporate strategy as well as the company's increasing value, an industry source reported: "A few years ago, IPE [Ilim Pulp Enterprises] adopted the corporate strategy of operating its mills on a Western standard. This meant the company had to present a transparent financial history in order to obtain financing from the international markets. . . . PWC valued the Kotlas unit at around $600 million. . . . Kotlas's value had risen to $1 billion one year later, following a series of investments."

Unfortunately, Ilim's efforts at improving corporate governance through transparency and proper organizational structures, in an attempt to attract international investors, also drew the unwelcome attention of a powerful corporate raider, Deripaska. Dow Jones News Service reported: "Ilim's current plight is a stark warning to all those Russian companies seeking to make a break with a sometimes murky past. In order to gain international respectability and attract foreign capital, they have become more transparent. But that merely advertises their attractiveness to the kind of financier whose grasp they are trying to escape." Derek

Bloom, a partner with a law firm, Coudert Brothers in St. Petersburg, added: "The company's attempts to address the concerns some people may have had about its structure prompted the attack by exposing the value of the company. The previous lack of transparency reflected what had been a common and prudent response to problems faced by many Russian companies."

The Initial Battle for Ilim Pulp

The attack by a powerful corporate raider was to play out over a couple of years in a drama involving big business, an aggressive oligarch, numerous court cases, and even President Putin himself. Ilim owned a number of mills, each of which was a separate stock company with its own shares, the great majority of which was owned by Ilim as a holding company. The initial battle occurred in December 2001 when oligarch Deripaska's private armed security force occupied Ilim Pulp's Bratsk pulp mill as the culmination of a Bratsk minority shareholder challenge. Deripaska also laid claim to Ilim's Ust-Ilimsk plant using the same technique. This approach had all the earmarks of Deripaska's many strong-arm takeovers during the 1990s that consolidated his control of over 70 percent of the country's aluminum industry in his company, Sibirsky Aluminium or Sibal, which was subsequently named Basovyi Element. "The two enterprises were ultimately recovered by Ilim," reported the *Economist,* "but only after its owners had secured financial backing from a rival magnate, oil baron Mikhail Khodorkovsky." Also in 2001, a group of former competitors filed charges in a US district court seeking damages of $3 billion against Deripaska's company for alleged murder, bribery, fraud, and money laundering. These charges were rejected by the company as untrue.

The Next Salvo

The next salvo was fired on April 25, 2002, five time zones away from Ilim's Kotlas mill located in the far northern Arkhangelsk region. A minority Kotlas shareholder who owned a mere twenty shares filed a suit at a local court in Siberia's Kemerovo region, alleging that Ilim had not complied with all the conditions of its 1994 privatization. Other charges alleged that the Kotlas mill had been unlawfully privatized, and also that investment obligations by the holding company, Ilim, had not been fulfilled. An earlier suit had alleged the same thing about Ilim's Bratsk mill. The judge declared in favor of this Kotlas minority "shareholder," awarding $113 million in damages against Ilim, and sequestering Ilim's Kotlas stock as collateral. These shares were then confiscated by the State Property Commission and resold to Deripaska and his partner for around $100 million. Ilim claimed that all this occurred before it was informed that anything was happening. "But what is certain," according to Dow Jones News Service, "is that the Property Fund took possession of Kotlas' shares and resold them before Ilim Pulp had any time to exercise any right of appeal and, it seems, without conducting even the most cursory check into the legality of the Kemerovo court's judgment."

In early August 2002, as Ilim was developing its legal defenses against the bizarre suit, Deripaska's private security forces prepared to take over the Kotlas mill. Ilim, however, had fortified the mill, which was defended by Ilim managers, the company's own security forces, and local law enforcement officers. The entrance to the plant was barricaded with buses, cars, and other such defenses. At this time, armed Sibal troops camped outside the Kotlas mill pushing for the chance for Sibal to install its own board of directors. Ilim's forces refused to turn the mill over to Deripaska's men, and Ilim filed countersuits in Russian courts. According to Ilim's chairman Zakhar Smushkin: "They've probably gone for our assets because they're the best in the sector."

An Oligarch's Ambitions

Deripaska's apparent plan was to combine the Kotlas mill with others owned by Sibal and its allies, and attempt to dominate the country's forest products industry. In July, Deripaska had announced plans to create a huge forest products company, and he and his partners had already acquired a 61 percent stake, disputed by Ilim, in the Kotlas mill. His company sought not only to take over the Kotlas Mill but also two other Ilim mills. It appeared that a new power grab at the Bratsk mill had begun in early August 2002. Ilim's chief operating officer (COO) Frank Graves, a Canadian, told the *Wall Street Journal*: "It's not that the bully wants to take our ball, but that the bully wants to take the whole bloody playground."

Ilim, which started as an export trading company, had acquired its shares legally with money that it had earned. However, illegitimate owners have used various pretexts to oust earlier owners. In the name of "shareholder rights," minority shareholders can do a lot with just one share. Ilim is hardly the first Russian forest products company in a decade to find itself in a battle to retain control. However, referring to the hostile takeover, Coudert Brothers LLP partner, Richard Dean, noted that in his many years in Russia he had never seen such a level of abuse of the judicial system: "Ilim's circumstances are pretty extraordinary. . . . This is a real case for the Russian government to prove it is serious about reform." And it was becoming ever clearer that Ilim's situation could become a landmark case in determining the future of Russian business and corporate governance, and seeing whether the legal system would support legitimate interests including private property.

Positive Signs

Some positive signs were developing. As an Ilim spokesman noted in 2002: "The dispute has dragged on since last fall in what could be a sign that Russia's rough and tumble days of carving up property are coming to an end. They could have swallowed us up two years ago and nobody would have noticed. . . . Now it's much harder for them to work, but they don't want to believe that times have changed." A 2002 Ilim release stated that "various decisions in four different courts all ruled in favor of Ilim in its quest to fend off the hostile takeover. The suits established the legitimacy of Ilim's ownership of the Kotlas mill, ruling against Sibal." And Russian law was changing in the direction of protecting ownership rights. Changes in the law that became effective in

August 2002 required shareholders involved in commercial disputes to bring proceedings to a court of arbitration in the region where the company was based. The changes meant "there'll be fewer opportunities for people in ski masks to seize control of a company," said the chairman of Russia's Supreme Court of Arbitration. Had the law been on the books earlier, the entire Ilim affair might not have occurred.

But progress would not develop without setbacks. Energoregistrator, the company that had become the new registrar of the Kotlas shares, had its license revoked by the Federal Commission for the Securities Market (FCSM) because the registrar violated shareholder rights. The legitimacy of a registrar is often the issue at the center of ownership battles in Russia, and thus the FCSM's decision appeared to be a major setback for Ilim. The commission's decision, however, was later overthrown by a court.

Two Russias

Even as the court battles continued, Ilim pressed on both with its case against Deripaska and with its attempts to become a legitimate member of the international business community. According to a 2002 Ilim press release: "We are committed to leading the way in Russia toward responsible business practices, including greater transparency and improved corporate governance. It is critical that we stay committed to Russian business reform as well as the growth and vitality of our company and industry." As noted in the same release, the president of the US-Russia Business Council, which Ilim had recently joined, recognized Ilim's progress: "We are pleased by Ilim Pulp's commitment to transparency, effective resource management, free market approach, and commitment to fair and legal resolution of property disputes."

Ilim's vice chairman, B. Zingarevich, summarized Ilim's situation when describing two Russias in a speech to the US-Russia Business Council in October 2002. One Russia he saw as a modern, civilized, dynamic country. The other was an isolated country where market principles are unknown, and which is plagued by pervasive corruption and illegal takeovers of independent enterprises. He summarized the

dilemma for many companies, stating: "You may go to bed in one Russia and wake up in the other. . . . To prevent the recurrence of these incidents we must build one Russia, where written and unwritten laws are the same and where property rights and universal principles of basic business ethics are respected." He added that, when Ilim executives realized that the laws did not seem to be protecting the company's rights, they went directly to President Putin and also publicized their situation in the Russian and international press. They thought that by going to the president, the company might benefit from Putin and the government's work toward improving the overall investment climate.

The Ilim Case in Context

The importance of the Ilim case for Russia's future and the country's corporate governance cannot be overstated. Derek Bloom, one of Ilim's American attorneys, commented in October 2002:

> *Numerous techniques and know-how have been developed to circumvent the requirements of applicable corporate law described above. Unfortunately, most of these techniques involve abusing the Russian courts and coopting government officials and making them serve as the tools and means for corporate raiders to acquire shares and assets from their true owners for a fraction of their value.... In this case, the would-be acquirer was facing a difficult problem—how could it acquire control of companies that have been 95 percent owned by Ilim Pulp since the time of their privatization eight years ago? The strategy that has been selected is to challenge the privatization itself. If the oligarch who had waged this battle were to be successful, it is questionable whether the concept of private property would ever take hold in the country.*

Ilim Prevails?

In November 2002, it appeared that Ilim would win its battle with Deripaska. Despite a number of delays before the case was reheard in Kemerovo, fortunately for Ilim, the court was changed to the regional commercial court from the original court of general jurisdiction. The change of venue was the result of a new Code of Commercial Court Procedure that had become effective in July. The commercial courts had a growing reputation for fairness and deeper knowledge of commercial law. The regional commercial court dismissed the allegations against Ilim, and Derek Bloom expressed confidence that the ruling would end the dispute, with a subsequent hearing, likely in Kemerovo.

On November 4, 2002, the Kemerovo court presidium overturned the $95 million decision against Ilim Pulp. At the same time, the presidium overturned a 5 billion ruble decision in a case brought by another superminority shareholder against a different Ilim subsidiary. An Ilim Pulp press release noted at the time that the lower courts had violated Russian law by neglecting to notify Ilim Pulp about the trial and lawsuits, and that they had failed to validate the plaintiffs' claims before ruling in Ilim's favor. The judge who had heard the original Kotlas lawsuit had been suspended for disciplinary reasons. The situation in late 2002 was put in perspective by Derek Bloom: "The story has broad importance. This really could cause chaos in that all major Russian companies could have questions raised about their privatization. The legal theory here would destabilize many leading Russian companies."

Little Victories

In spring 2003, Ilim achieved a key strategic objective by changing its organizational structure to a single or unified share structure with a central holding company. This required the approval of shareholders, as well as providing an opportunity for minority shareholders to cash out rather than continue as minority shareholders under the new structure. At the April 2003 annual shareholders' meeting, minority shareholders of Ilim's three companies, Kotlas, Pulp-Cardboard, and Bratskomplexholding, overwhelmingly approved such conversion of their shares to unified shares of the newly created open stock company, Ilim Forest Industries Enterprises.

On July 15, 2003, Ilim won another major court victory in its ongoing ownership battle. The High Arbitration Court of the Russian Federation sustained the rights of Ilim Pulp versus Sibirsky Aluminium (later renamed Basovyi Element) by upholding the legitimacy of both the Kotlas and Energoregistrator positions. In doing so, the Court denied the petition of Sibirsky's partners, one of which was the original registrar of the Kotlas shares from which Ilim switched when it engaged Energoregistrator as the registrar of its shares. This had been the trigger event for the FCSM to step in and declare that transfer invalid.

Despite this impressive court victory, it was clear that the dispute was still not settled. In January 2004, Ilim announced that it had made a proposal to Continental Management, Deripaska's forest products group, to resolve the dispute between the two parties. The proposal was reviewed by Continental's shareholders and subsequently lawyers for both parties began drafting a mutually acceptable agreement. The proposal called for settling the dispute amicably in a Russian court of arbitration.

Ilim Looks Ahead

In spite of the enormous distraction of the ownership dispute, Ilim continued to modernize its operations. The general director of the Kotlas mill stated in January 2004: "We have had smooth operations at the Kotlas mill for several years. We work evenly, consistently, and as an entire system. Last year we broke the Russian record by producing 912,000 tons of pulp. . . . This is due to investments in technological equipment made by Ilim Pulp. . . . We have everything to grow the business: infrastructure, energy resources, and people. I think that in April we will begin building a new Ilim Pulp wood processing plant." As further evidence of its commitment to the future, Ilim announced that it would invest more than 27 million euros in 2004 in the latest imported technology. This was part of a five-year (2003–2007) plan to invest 170 million euros in upgrading and improving Ilim's technology, plant, equipment, safety, and working conditions in order to compete effectively in world markets.

While Ilim continued to build a global business, the opposition reignited the controversy in the press.

In February 2004, in what was reported as a surprising and unclear prediction, Deripaska was quoted as saying: "Kotlas needs a good owner, and I think he will soon appear." As of this writing (August 2004), it seems clear again that the corporate governance battles are still not over.

Case Discussion Questions

1. Why should Russian corporations such as Ilim Pulp attempt to utilize good corporate governance?

2. Why is corporate governance a two-edged sword in transition economies such as Russia?

3. Familiar corporate governance terms such as "corporate raiders," "battles for corporate control," and "anti-takeover defenses" take on a new (and original!) meaning, sometimes involving armed raids, battles, and defenses as shown in this case. What is the role of the legal system in Russia? How about the role of the Russian government?

4. If you were a mutual fund manager in a Western country who specializes in investing in firms based in emerging economies such as Russia, would you consider buying Ilim Pulp's stock if it were listed? Why or why not?

Glossary

absorptive capacity. The ability to absorb new knowledge by recognizing the value of new information, assimilating it, and applying it.

acquisition. The transfer of control of assets, operations, and management from one firm (target) to another (acquirer); the former becoming a unit of the latter.

acquisition premium. The difference between the acquisition price and the market value of target firms.

agency costs. The costs associated with principal-agent relationships. They are the sum of (1) principals' costs of monitoring and controlling agents, (2) agents' costs of bonding, and (3) the residual loss because the interests of the principals and the agents do not align.

agency problems. Problems associated with agents making decisions in their best interest instead of in the best interest of principals. For example, some managers may deliberately overdiversify their firms in their quest for more power, prestige, and money.

agency relationship. The relationship between principals and agents.

agency theory. The theory about principal-agent relationships (or agency relationships in short). It focuses on principal-agent conflicts.

agents. Persons (such as managers) to whom authority is delegated.

agglomeration. Clustering economic activities in certain locations.

anchored replicators. Companies that seek to replicate a set of activities in related industries in a small number of countries anchored by the home country.

antitrust policy. Competition policy designed to combat monopolies, cartels, and trusts.

arm's-length transactions. Transactions in which parties keep a distance.

attack. An initial set of actions to gain competitive advantage.

backward integration. See backward vertical integration.

backward vertical integration. Acquiring and owning upstream assets.

bargaining power of suppliers. The ability of suppliers to raise prices and/or reduce quality of goods and services.

blockholders. Shareholders with large blocks of shares.

build-operate-transfer (BOT) agreements. A special kind of turnkey project in which contractors first build facilities, then operate them for a period of time, and then transfer back to clients. These BOT-type turnkey projects have a longer duration than traditional build-transfer type turnkey projects.

bureaucratic costs. The additional costs associated with a larger, more diversified organization, such as more employees and more expensive information systems.

business-level strategy. Strategy which builds competitive advantage in a discrete and identifiable market.

business process outsourcing (BPO). Turning over certain business processes (such as IT) to an outside supplier that performs on behalf of the focal firm.

capabilities. The tangible and intangible assets a firm uses to choose and implement its strategies.

capacity to punish. Having sufficient resources to deter and combat defection.

centers of excellence. MNE subsidiaries explicitly recognized as a source of important capabilities, with the intention that these capabilities be leveraged by and/or disseminated to other subsidiaries.

CEO duality. When the board is led by the CEO, who doubles as a chairman.

chief executive officer (CEO). The top executive in charge of the strategy and operations of a firm.

classic conglomerates. Companies that engage in product unrelated diversification within a small set of countries centered on the home country.

codes of conduct. Written policies and standards for corporate conduct.

cognitive pillar. The internalized, taken-for-granted values and beliefs that guide individual and firm behavior.

collectivism. The perspective that the identity of an individual is most fundamentally based on the identity of his or her collective group (such as family, village, or company).

collusive price setting. Monopolists or collusion parties setting prices at a level higher than the competitive level.

comarketing. Agreements among a number of firms to jointly market their products and services.

competition policy. Policy governing the rules of the game in competition, which determine the institutional mix of competition and cooperation that gives rise to the market system.

competitive dynamics. Actions and responses undertaken by competing firms.

complementary assets. Numerous noncore assets which complement and support the value-adding activities of core assets.

complementors. Firms selling products that add value to the products of a focal industry.

concentrated ownership and control. Ownership and control rights concentrated in the hands of owners.

concentration ratio. The percentage of total industry sales accounted for by the top four, eight, or twenty firms.

conglomerate advantage. The advantage of being associated with a product-unrelated firm (conglomerate).

conglomerate M&As. M&A transactions involving firms in product-unrelated industries.

conglomerates. Product-unrelated diversifiers.

constellations. Multipartner strategic alliances (also known as strategic networks).

contractual alliances. Alliances which are based on contracts and which do not involve the sharing of equity.

cooperative interfirm relationships. Cooperative relationships among firms.

core competencies. Core assets, resources, and capabilities for which firms are known.

corporate governance. The relationship among various participants in determining the direction and performance of corporations.

corporate-level strategy. Strategy about how a firm creates value through the configuration and coordination of its multimarket activities.

corporate social responsibility (CSR). The social responsibility of corporations. It pertains to consideration of, and response to, issues beyond the narrow economic, technical, and legal requirements of the firm to accomplish social benefits along with the traditional economic gains that the firm seeks.

corruption. The abuse of public power for private benefit usually in the form of bribery.

cost leadership. A competitive strategy which centers on competing on low cost and prices.

counterattack. A set of actions in response to attacks.

cross-border (international) M&As. Mergers and acquisitions which involve companies in multiple countries.

cross-listing. Firms list their shares on foreign stock exchanges.

cross-market retaliation. Retaliation in other markets when one market is attacked by rivals.

cross-shareholding. Both partners invest in each other to become cross-shareholders.

cultural distance. The difference between two cultures along some identifiable dimensions.

culture. The collective programming of the mind that distinguishes the members of one group or category of people from another.

data. Discrete, objective facts about events in our world.

defender. A strategy which leverages local assets that MNEs are either weak in or unaware of.

deterrence. Ability to scare away competitors before they cause any harm.

differentiation. A strategy which focuses on how to deliver products that customers perceive as valuable and different.

diffused ownership. An ownership pattern involving numerous small shareholders, none of which has a dominant level of control.

direct duplication. Competing firms match the focal firm's organizational components exactly—person-by-person, machine-by-machine, and brand-by-brand.

direct exports. Directly selling products made in the home country to customers in other countries.

dissemination risks. The risks associated with the unauthorized diffusion of firm-specific assets.

diversification. Adding new businesses to the firm that are distinct from its existing operations.

diversification discount. Reduced levels of performance because of association with a product-diversified firm (also known as conglomerate discount).

diversification premium. Increased levels of performance because of association with a product-diversified firm (also known as conglomerate advantage).

domestic demand. Demand for products and services within a domestic economy.

dominance. A situation whereby the market leader has a very large market share.

downscoping. Reducing the scope of the firm through divestitures and spin-offs.

downsizing. Reducing the number of employees through lay-offs, early retirements, and outsourcing.

downstream vertical alliances. Alliances with firms in distribution (downstream).

dumping. An exporter selling below cost abroad and planning to raise prices after eliminating local rivals.

duopoly. A special case of oligopoly which only has two players.

dynamic capabilities. Capabilities which are not static, are constantly changing, and are adapting to changing conditions.

economic benefits. Benefits brought by the various forms of synergy in the context of diversification.

economies of scale. Reductions in per unit costs by increasing the scale of production.

efficient market hypothesis. The hypothesis which suggests capital markets are efficient in the aggregate because shareholders base their valuation of a firm's share price on a rational assessment of all publicly available information.

emergent strategy. A strategy based on the outcome of a stream of smaller decisions from the "bottom up."

emerging economies. A label which describes fast-growing developing economies since the 1990s.

empire building. Excess diversification of the scope of the firm. This is often regarded as a symptom of agency problems on the part of managers.

enthusiastic internationalizers. Firms which internationalize eagerly and aggressively.

entrepreneurs. Individuals who identify and explore previously unexplored opportunities. They may be founders and owners of new businesses or managers of existing firms.

entrepreneurship. The identification and exploitation of previously unexplored opportunities.

entry barriers. The industry structures that increase the costs of entry.

equity-based alliances. Strategic alliances which involve the use of equity.

equity modes. Modes of foreign market entry which involve the use of equity.

ethical imperialism. The imperialistic thinking that one's own ethical standards should be applied universally around the world.

ethical relativism. The relative thinking that ethical standards vary significantly around the world and that there are no universally agreed upon ethical and unethical behaviors.

ethics. The norms, principles, and standards of conduct governing individual and firm behavior.

excess capacity. Additional production capacity currently underutilized or not utilized.

executive sessions. Sessions held by outside board directors that do not involve company executives.

exit-based mechanisms. Corporate governance mechanisms which focus on exit, indicating that shareholders no longer have patience and are willing to "exit" by selling their shares.

experience curves. The curves on which firms can drive down unit costs based on their experience with expanding scale.

explicit collusion. Firms directly and openly negotiate output and pricing and divide markets to reduce competition.

explicit knowledge. Knowledge that is codifiable (that is, it can be written down and transferred without losing much of its richness).

exploitation. Actions captured by terms such as refinement, choice, production, efficiency, selection, and execution.

exploration. Actions captured by terms such as search, variation, risk taking, experimentation, play, flexibility, discovery, and innovation.

export cartels. Alliances of firms that cooperate in exporting through quota- and price-fixing.

export intermediaries. Specialist firms that function as export departments of several manufacturers in noncompetitive lines.

expropriation. (1) of foreign assets: Confiscation of foreign assets invested in one country. (2) of minority shareholders: Activities which enrich the controlling shareholders at the expense of minority shareholders.

extender. A strategy that centers on leveraging homegrown competencies abroad by expanding into similar markets.

extensive international scope. Maintaining a substantial international presence beyond geographically and culturally neighboring countries.

extraterritoriality. The reach of one country's laws to other countries.

factor endowments. The endowments of production factors such as land, water, and people in one country.

familiarity. The extent to which tacit collusion is enhanced by a firm's awareness of the actions, intentions, and capabilities of rivals.

far-flung conglomerates. Conglomerate firms which pursue both extensive product-unrelated diversification and extensive geographic diversification.

feint. A firm's attack on a focal arena important to a competitor, but not the attacker's true target area.

financial control (or **output control**). Controlling subsidiary/unit operations strictly based on whether they meet financial/output criteria.

financial resources and capabilities. The depth of a firm's financial pockets.

financial synergy (also known as **scope economies** or **economies of scope**). The increase in competitiveness for each individual unit that is financially controlled by the corporate headquarters beyond what can be achieved by each unit competing independently as stand-alone firms.

firm strategy, structure, and rivalry. How industry structure and firm strategy interact to affect interfirm rivalry.

first mover advantages. The advantages that first movers enjoy and later movers do not.

five forces framework. A framework governing the competitiveness of an industry proposed by Michael Porter. The five forces are (1) the intensity of rivalry among competitors, (2) the threat of potential entry, (3) the bargaining power of suppliers, (4) the bargaining power of buyers, and (5) the threat of substitutes.

flexible manufacturing technology. Modern manufacturing technology which enables firms to produce differentiated products at low costs (usually on a smaller batch basis than the large batch typically produced by cost leaders).

follower internationalizers. Companies that follow their larger counterparts abroad as suppliers or service providers.

foreign direct investment (FDI). A firm's direct investment in production and/or service activities abroad.

foreign portfolio investment (FPI). Foreigners' purchase of stocks and bonds in one country. They do not directly manage operations.

formal institutions. Formal, written rules of the game, including laws, regulations, and rules (such as competition and regulation policy, intellectual property rights regime, contract law, and their enforcement).

formulation. The crafting and plotting of strategy.

forward integration. See forward vertical integration.

forward vertical integration. Acquiring and owning downstream assets.

franchising. Firm A's agreement to give firm B the rights to use A's proprietary technology and brands for a royalty fee paid to A by B. This term is usually used in service industries (essentially the same as licensing as used in manufacturing industries).

friendly M&As. Mergers and acquisitions in which the board and management of a target firm agree to the transaction (although they may initially resist).

gambit. A firm's withdrawal from a low-value market to attract rival firms to divert resources into the low-value market so that the original withdrawing firm can capture a high-value market.

game theory. A theory which focuses on competitive and cooperative interaction (such as in a prisoners' dilemma situation).

generic strategies. Strategies intended to strengthen the focal firm's position relative to the five competitive forces, including (1) cost leadership, (2) differentiation, and (3) focus.

geographic area structure. An organizational structure which organizes the MNE according to different countries and regions, and is the most appropriate structure for a multidomestic strategy.

global matrix. An organizational structure often used to alleviate the disadvantages associated with both geographic area and global product division structures, especially for MNEs adopting a transnational strategy.

global product division. An organizational structure which assigns global responsibilities to each product division.

global strategy. A particular form of international strategy, characterized by the production and distribution of standardized products and services on a worldwide basis.

global sustainability. The ability to meet the needs of the present without compromising the ability of future generations to meet their needs.

global virtual teams. Teams whose members are physically dispersed in multiple locations in the world. They cooperate on a virtual basis.

golden parachutes. Large compensation packages to incumbent managers should their firms be taken over.

governance. Formal mechanisms on how to control a firm.

green-field operations. Building factories and offices from scratch (on a proverbial piece of "green field" formerly used for agricultural purposes).

greenmail. Repurchasing large blocks of shares from potential acquirers, in essence, protecting managers' jobs at shareholders' expense.

hedging. Spreading out activities in a number of countries in different currency zones to offset the currency losses in certain regions through gains in other regions.

hierarchical model. A step-by-step model on foreign market entries.

home replication strategy. A strategy which emphasizes the international replication of home country–based competencies such as production scales, distribution efficiencies, and brand power.

horizontal alliances. Strategic alliances formed by competitors.

horizontal M&As. Merger and acquisition deals involving competing firms in the same industry.

hostile M&As (also known as **hostile takeovers**). Mergers and acquisitions undertaken against the wishes of the target firm's board and management, who reject M&A offers.

hubris. Managers' overconfidence in their capabilities.

human resources and capabilities. The knowledge, trust, and talents embedded within a firm that are not captured by its formal, tangible systems and structures.

hypercompetition. A way of competition centered on dynamic maneuvering intended to unleash a series of small, unpredictable but powerful, actions to erode the rival's competitive advantage.

 I

implementation. The ways strategy is carried out to reach its objectives.

incumbents. Current members of an industry that compete against each other.

indirect exports. Exporting indirectly through domestic-based export intermediaries.

individualism. The perspective that the identity of an individual is most fundamentally based on his or her own individual attributes (rather than the attributes of a group).

industrial organization (IO) economics. A branch of economics which seeks to better understand how firms in an industry compete and then how to regulate them.

industry-based view. A leading perspective on strategy which suggests that the strategic task is mainly to examine the five competitive forces affecting an industry (inter-firm rivalry, bargaining power of buyers, bargaining power of suppliers, threat of new entrants, and threat of substitutes) and that firm performance is most fundamentally determined by these industry attributes.

industry positioning. Ways to position a firm within an industry in order to minimize the threats presented by the five forces.

inertia. Forces that are resistant to changes.

informal institutions. Informal, unwritten rules of the game (including norms, cultures, and ethics).

informal, relationship-based, personalized exchange. A way of economic exchange based on informal relationships among transaction parties. Also known as relational contracting.

information. Organization of a body of data.

information asymmetries. Asymmetric distribution of information between two sides. For example, in principal-agent relationships, agents almost always know more about the property they manage than principals do.

information overload. Too much information to process.

initial public offering (IPO). The first round of public trading of company stock.

innovation resources and capabilities. A firm's assets and skills to (1) nurture and generate new ideas, (2) research and develop new products and services, and (3) innovate and change ways of organizing.

innovation-seeking. Firms that target countries and regions renowned for generating world-class innovations.

innovation-seeking investment. Investment made by innovation-seeking firms.

inside directors. Directors serving on corporate boards who are also full-time managers of these companies.

institutional distance. The extent of similarity or dissimilarity between the regulatory, normative, and cognitive institutions of two countries.

institutional framework. A framework of formal and informal institutions governing individual and firm behavior.

institutional relatedness. A firm's informal linkages with dominant institutions in the environment that confer resources and legitimacy.

institutional transitions. Fundamental and comprehensive changes introduced to the formal and informal rules of the game that affect organizations as players.

institution-based view. A leading perspective of strategy that argues that in addition to industry- and firm-level conditions, firms also need to take into account wider influences from sources such as the state and society when crafting strategy.

institutions. The humanly devised constraints that structure human interaction. Popularly known as the rules of the game.

intangible resources and capabilities. Hard-to-observe and difficult-to-codify resources and capabilities.

integrated network of subsidiaries (sometimes called an **N-form**). A network of MNE subsidiaries connected with multiple flows of knowledge, personnel, and technology.

integration-responsiveness framework. A framework of MNE management on how to simultaneously deal with two sets of pressures for global integration and local responsiveness.

intended strategy. A strategy that is deliberately planned for.

interlocking directorate. A situation whereby two or more firms share one director affiliated with one firm who serves on multiple boards.

internal capital market. A term used to describe the internal management mechanisms of a product-unrelated diversified firm (conglomerate) which operate as a capital market inside the firm.

internalization. The process of replacing a market relationship with a single multinational organization spanning both countries.

internalization advantage. The advantage associated with internalization, which is one of the three key advantages of being a multinational enterprise (the other two are ownership and location advantages).

international diversification. The number and diversity of countries in which a firm competes.

international division. A structure typically set up when firms initially expand abroad, often engaging in a home replication strategy.

international entrepreneurship. A combination of innovative, proactive, and risk-seeking behavior that crosses national borders and is intended to create wealth in organizations.

joint venture (JV). A "corporate child" that is a new entity given birth and jointly owned by two or more parent companies.

junk bonds. Bonds that are rated below investment grade by the top bond-rating agencies.

know-how. The intricate knowledge of how to make products and serve customers.

knowledge. A fluid mix of skills, experiences, and insights that provides a framework for evaluating and incorporating information.

knowledge management. The structures, processes, and systems that actively develop, leverage, and transfer knowledge.

late mover advantages. Advantages associated with being a later mover (also known as first mover disadvantages).

lead independent director. The designated independent director on the board who chairs the board's executive sessions (which refers to sessions held by outside directors that do *not* involve company executives).

learning race. A race in which alliance partners aim to outrun each other by learning the "tricks" from the other side as fast as possible.

learning by doing. A way of learning not by reading books but by engaging in hands-on activities.

liability of foreignness. The inherent disadvantage foreign firms experience in host countries because of their nonnative status.

liability of newness. The inherent disadvantage that entrepreneurial firms experience as new entrants.

licensing. Firm A's agreement to give Firm B the rights to use A's proprietary technology and trademark for a royalty fee paid to A by B. This term is usually used in manufacturing industries (essentially the same as franchising is used in service industries).

licensing/franchising agreements. Agreements according to which the licensor/franchiser sells the rights to intellectual property, such as patents and know-how, to the licensee/franchisee for a royalty fee.

limited international scope. Maintaining a limited international presence, primarily in geographically and culturally neighboring countries.

local content requirements. Government requirements that certain products be subject to higher import tariffs and taxes unless a given percentage of their value is produced domestically.

location specific advantage. Advantage associated with operating in a specific location, which is one of the three key advantages of being a multinational enterprise (the other two are ownership and internalization advantages).

long-term orientation. A perspective which emphasizes perseverance and savings for future betterment.

management entrenchment. Managers put their self-interests ahead of shareholders' interests.

managerial human capital. The skills and abilities acquired by top managers.

managerial motives. Managers may have motives to advance their personal interests, which are not necessarily aligned with the interests of the firm and its shareholders.

marginal bureaucratic costs (MBC). The bureaucratic costs of the last unit of organizational expansion (such as the last subsidiary established).

marginal economic benefits (MEB). The economic benefits of the last unit of growth (such as the last acquisition).

market commonality. The degree that two competitors' markets overlap.

market-seeking. Firms go after countries with the most lucrative markets that offer the highest price and strongest demand for their products and services.

mass customization. Mass produced but customized products.

merger. The combination of assets, operations, and management of two firms to establish a new legal entity. The transfer of control of assets, operations, and management from one firm (target) to another (acquirer); the former becoming a unit of the latter.

mergers and acquisitions (M&As). Firms either merging with or acquiring other firms.

micro-macro link. Micro, informal interpersonal relationships among managers of various units may greatly facilitate macro, interorganizational cooperation among various units.

monopoly. A situation whereby only one firm provides the goods and/or services for an industry.

multidomestic strategy. An extension of the home replication strategy that focuses on a number of foreign countries/regions as stand-alone domestic markets.

multimarket competition. Firms engage the same rivals in multiple markets.

multinational enterprises (MNEs). Firms that engage in foreign direct investment (FDI) by directly controlling and managing value-adding activities in other countries.

multinational replicators. Firms which engage in product-related diversification on one hand and far-flung multinational expansion on the other hand.

mutual forbearance. The reduction of competitive intensity among rivals which meet in multiple markets.

 N

nationalization. Turning privately owned assets over to the state.

network centrality. The extent to which a firm's position is pivotal with respect to others in the inter-firm network.

network externalities. The value a user derives from a product increases with the number (or the network) of other users of the same product.

non-equity modes. Modes of foreign market entries which do not involve the use of equity.

nongovernment organizations (NGOs). Organizations which take it upon themselves to fight for causes such as the environment, human rights, and consumer welfare without any government sponsorship or support.

non-scale-based low cost advantages. Low cost advantages which are not derived from the economies of scale.

nontariff barriers. Trade and investment barriers which do not entail tariffs.

normative pillar. How the values, beliefs, and norms of other relevant players influence the behavior of individuals and firms.

O

obsolescing bargain. The deals struck by MNEs and host governments, which change their requirements after the entry of MNEs.

occasional internationalizers. Firms which internationalize on an occasional (non-persistent) basis.

OLI advantages. Ownership, location, and internalization advantages which are typically associated with MNEs.

oligopoly. A situation whereby a few firms control an industry.

operational synergy. Synergy derived by having joint shared activities, personnel, and technologies.

opportunism. Self-interest seeking with guile.

option. An investment instrument that enables its holder, who has paid for a small fraction of an asset's value, the right (but not the obligation) to increase his/her investment to eventually acquire the asset.

organizational fit. The complementarity of partner firms' "soft" organizational traits, such as goals, experiences, and behaviors, that facilitate cooperation.

organizational learning. How an organization learns from its experience to carry out new tasks.

organizational resources and capabilities. A firm's formal planning, command, and control systems and structures.

organizational structure (also known as **organizational design** or **organizational architecture**). A firm's formal reporting relationships, procedures, and controls.

original equipment manufacturers (OEMs). Contract manufacturers that produce goods that do not carry their own brands.

outside directors. Non-management members of the board.

outsourcing. Turning over all or part of an activity to an outside supplier to improve the performance of the focal firm.

ownership advantage. Advantage associated with directly owning assets overseas, which is one of the three key advantages of being a multinational enterprise (the other two are location and internalization advantages).

 P

partner rarity. The difficulty to locate partners with certain desirable attributes.

path dependencies. Earlier events have significant effects on subsequent events.

perfect competition. A competitive situation in which price is set by the "market," all firms are price takers, and entries and exits are relatively easy.

physical resources and capabilities. A firm's plants, offices, equipment, geographic locations, and access to raw materials and distribution channels.

poison pill. The rights to either purchase additional shares or sell shares to the bidder at prices substantially higher than market value.

power distance. The degree of social inequality.

predatory pricing. (1) Setting prices below costs in the short run to destroy rivals and (2) intending to raise prices to cover losses in the long run after eliminating rivals.

pressures for cost reductions. Pressures for firms to reduce costs in order to stay competitive.

pressures for local responsiveness. Pressures for firms operating abroad to be responsive to the needs and wants of local customers.

price leader. A firm that has a dominant market share and sets "acceptable" prices and margins in the industry.

primary stakeholder groups. Constituents on which the firm relies for its continuous survival and prosperity.

principal-agent conflicts. Conflicts of interests between principals (such as shareholders) and agents (such as professional managers).

principal-principal conflicts. Conflicts of interests between two classes of principals: controlling shareholders and minority shareholders.

principals. Persons (such as owners) who delegate authority.

prisoners' dilemma. A famous "game" that propels game theory to prominence. In one scenario of this game, two prisoners suspected of a major crime (such as burglary) are separately interrogated and told that if either one confesses, the confessor will get a light sentence (such as one year) while the other will get a much harsher sentence (such as ten years). If neither confesses, both will be convicted for a lesser charge (such as trespassing) each for two years. If both confess, both will go to jail for ten years. Both prisoners thus face the dilemma of either cooperating with the authorities or not.

privatization. Turning state-owned enterprises and assets over to private firms.

product differentiation. The uniqueness of products that customers value.

product-related diversification. Entries into new product markets and/or business activities that are related to a firm's existing markets and/or activities.

product-unrelated diversification. Entries into industries that have no obvious product-related connections to the firm's current lines of business.

R

raiders. Individuals and firms which specialize in acquiring other firms, often in a hostile manner.

R&D contracts. Outsourcing agreements in R&D between firms (that is, firm A agrees to perform certain R&D work for firm B).

real option. An option investment in real operations as opposed to financial capital.

refocusing. Narrowing the scope of the firm to focus on a few areas.

regulatory pillar. How formal rules, laws, and regulations influence the behavior of individuals and firms.

related and supporting industries. Industries which are related to and/or support the focal industry.

related transactions. Controlling owners sell firm assets to another firm they own at below-market prices or spin off the most profitable part of a public firm and merge it with another of their private firms.

relational (or **collaborative**) **capabilities.** The capabilities to successfully manage interfirm relationships.

relational contracting. Contracting based on informal relationships (see also **informal, relationship-based, personalized exchange**).

replication. The repeated testing of theory under a variety of conditions.

reputational resources and capabilities. A firm's capabilities to develop and leverage its reputation as a solid provider of goods/services, an attractive employer, and/or a socially responsible corporate citizen.

resource-based view. A leading perspective of strategy which suggests that differences in firm performance are most fundamentally driven by differences in firm resources and capabilities.

resource heterogeneity. The assumption that firms, even those within the same industry, have different resources and capabilities.

resource immobility. The assumption that resources and capabilities that are unique to one firm cannot easily migrate to competing firms.

resources. The tangible and intangible assets a firm uses to choose and implement its strategies.

restrictions on entry modes. Certain modes of foreign entries (such as wholly owned subsidiaries) are restricted or banned by host country governments.

restructuring. (1) Adjusting firm size and scope through either diversification (expansion or entry), divestiture (contraction or exit), or both. (2) Reducing firm size and scope.

scale-based low cost advantages. Low cost advantages derived from economies of scale (the more a firm produces some products, the lower the unit costs become).

scale of entry. The amount of resources committed to foreign market entry.

secondary stakeholder groups. Stakeholders who influence or affect, or are influenced or affected by, the corporation, but they are not engaged in transactions with the corporation and are not essential for its survival.

seeking natural resources. Firms entering foreign markets in search of natural resources.

semiglobalization. A perspective on globalization which suggests that most measures of global integration (such as global trade, investment, and capital flows) have recently scaled new heights, but still fall far short of complete global integration.

serial entrepreneurs. People who start, grow, and sell several businesses throughout their careers.

shareholder capitalism. A view of capitalism which suggests that the most fundamental purpose for firms to exist is to serve the economic interests of shareholders (also known as capitalists).

single business strategy. A strategy which focuses on a single product or service with little diversification.

slow internationalizers. Firms which internationalize slowly.

small- and medium-sized enterprises (SMEs). Firms with less than 500 employees.

social capital. The informal benefits individuals and organizations derive from their social structures and networks.

social issue participation. Firms' participation in social causes not directly related to managing primary stakeholders.

soft budget constraint. The ability to ask for more handouts and bailouts from the government if the firm's expenditure exceeds its budget.

solutions-based structure. An MNE organization structure which caters to the needs of providing solutions for customers' problems.

speculation. Making bets on currency movements by committing to stable currencies.

sporadic (or **passive**) **exporting.** Occasional exporting not because of firms' proactive marketing abroad but because of unsolicited foreign inquiries and orders.

stage models. Models which suggest firms internationalize by going through predictable stages from simple steps to complex operations.

stakeholder. Any group or individual who can affect or is affected by the achievement of the organization's objectives.

stewardship theory. A theory which suggests that managers should be regarded as stewards of owners' interests.

Stopford and Wells model. A model of the evolution of MNE structures first proposed by John Stopford and Lou Wells in the 1970s.

strategic alliances. Voluntary agreements between firms involving exchanging, sharing, or codeveloping of products, technologies, or services.

strategic commitment. Large-scale commitment made to key country/product markets which is hard to reverse.

strategic control (or **behavior control**). Controlling subsidiary/unit operations based on whether they engage in desirable strategic behavior (such as cooperation).

strategic fit. The complementarity of partner firms' "hard" skills and resources, such as technology, capital, and distribution channels.

strategic groups. Groups of firms within a broad industry that compete against each other.

strategic investment. One partner invests in another as a strategic investor.

strategic management. A perspective of managing the firm from a strategic, "big picture" perspective.

strategic networks. Strategic alliances formed by multiple firms to compete against other such groups and against traditional single firms (also known as constellations).

strategy. A firm's theory about how to compete successfully.

strategy as action. A perspective which suggests that strategy is most fundamentally reflected by firms' pattern of actions.

strategy as integration. A perspective which suggests that strategy is neither solely about plan nor action and that strategy integrates elements of both schools of thought.

strategy as plan. A perspective which suggests that strategy is most fundamentally embodied in explicit, rigorous formal planning as in the military.

strong ties. More durable, reliable, and trustworthy relationships cultivated over a long period of time.

structure-conduct-performance (SCP) model. An industrial organization economics model which suggests that industry structure determines firm conduct (strategy), which in turn determines firm performance.

subsidiary initiatives. The proactive and deliberate pursuit of new business opportunities by an MNE's subsidiary to expand its scope of responsibility.

substitutes. Products of different industries that satisfy customer needs currently met by the focal industry.

substitution. The act of using substitute products to meet customer needs in the focal industry.

sunk costs. Irrevocable costs occurred and investments made.

Super 301. The popular name for Section 301 sanctions imposed by the 1974 Trade Act of the United States against foreign countries and companies which conspire to block US firms' access to foreign markets.

SWOT analysis. A strategic analysis of a firm's internal strengths (S) and weaknesses (W) and the opportunities (O) and threats (T) in the environment.

tacit collusion. Firms indirectly coordinate actions to reduce competition by signaling to others their intention to reduce output and maintain pricing above competitive levels.

tacit knowledge. Knowledge that is not codifiable (that is, hard to be written down and transmitted without losing much of its richness).

tangible resources and capabilities. Assets that are observable and more easily quantified.

tariff barriers. Taxes levied on imports.

technological resources and capabilities. Skills and assets that generate leading-edge products and services supported by patents, trademarks, copyrights, and trade secrets.

technology spillovers. Foreign technology being diffused domestically.

thrust. The classic frontal attack with brute force.

time compression diseconomies. A competitor's inability to successfully acquire in a short period of time the resources and capabilities that the focal firm has developed over a long period of time.

top management team (TMT). The team consisting of the highest level of executives of a firm led by the CEO.

transaction costs. Costs associated with economic transaction—or more broadly, costs of doing business.

transition economies. A subset of emerging economies consisting of former and weakened communist countries transitioning toward market capitalism.

transnational strategy. An MNE strategy which endeavors to be cost efficient, locally responsive, and learning driven simultaneously.

Triad. Three primary regions of developed economies: North America, Europe, and Japan.

triple bottom line. A performance yardstick consisting of economic, social, and environmental performance.

tunneling. Activities of managers from the controlling family of a corporation to divert resources from the firm for personal or family use.

turnkey projects. Projects in which clients pay contractors to design and construct new facilities and train personnel.

uncertainty avoidance. The extent to which members in different cultures accept ambiguous situations and tolerate uncertainty.

upstream vertical alliances. Alliances with firms on the supply side (upstream).

value chain. Goods and services produced through a chain of vertical activities that add value.

vertical M&As. Merger and acquisition deals involving suppliers (upstream) and/or buyers (downstream).

voice-based mechanisms. Corporate governance mechanisms which focus on shareholders' willingness to work with managers, usually through the board of directors, by "voicing" their concerns.

voluntary export restraint. An agreement in which the exporting country/company agrees not to aggressively export its products to another country.

weak ties. Relationships that are characterized by infrequent interaction and low intimacy.

wholly owned subsidiaries (WOS). Subsidiaries located in foreign countries which are entirely owned by the MNE.

worldwide mandate. The charter to be responsible for one MNE function throughout the world.

Index of Names

Index of Companies

Index of Topics